American Social Attitudes Data Sourcebook

1947-1978

Philip E. Converse

Jean D. Dotson

Wendy J. Hoag

William H. McGee III

Harvard University Press

Cambridge, Massachusetts, and

London, England

1980

Library of Congress Cataloging in Publication Data

Main entry under title:

American social attitudes data sourcebook, 1947-1978.

   Includes bibliographical references.
   1.  United States--Social conditions--1945-
--Public opinion.  2.  Public opinion--United
States.  I.  Converse, Philip E., 1928-
HN65.6819     303.3'8'0973    79-25398
ISBN 0-674-02880-5

# Contents

As both its name and its format imply, this volume is intended as a reference book. The reader curious about recent trends in the social and economic attitudes and situations of the American population will find it a fertile field for casual browsing. The more strenuous scholar interested in these trends will find it at least heuristic: a clue to little-known data sources, a compendium of intriguing empirical patterns, and a catalyst to serious research.

The inspiration for this enterprise came in no small measure from the social indicators movement, which began to flower in the latter half of the 1960s and emphasized the importance of developing portfolios of lengthening time-series measurements on a wider range of social phenomena than those captured by the Census Bureau or the system of national economic accounts.

To some degree this emphasis had been anticipated by a number of agencies involved in sample surveys of the national population, who had been repeatedly applying certain questionnaire items to the American population over a period of two decades or more. Within the Institute for Social Research at the University of Michigan, which has provided the data base for this volume, both the Political Behavior Program, with its sequence of election studies, and the Economic Behavior Program, with its studies of consumer attitudes and finances, had been self-consciously engaged in such repeated measurements back into the 1940s. Other investigators at the Institute's Survey Research Center, superintending more episodic national surveys, had borrowed intriguing items from earlier questionnaires to serve new purposes, thereby adding to the trove of measurements repeated across time. What was usually lacking, in the year-to-year flow of short-term grants and new research gambits, was a financial mechanism to support any retrospective assembly of these repeated measurements in more coherent time-series form.

A rare institutional grant awarded to the Institute for Social Research by the National Science Foundation (GI 29904) in 1971 provided the initial impetus for the work which underlies this volume. While the grant itself was addressed to an array of institutional developments, one clear emphasis was the role of the Institute in generating a more satisfying portfolio of long-term indicators of the nature and quality of American life. Much of this emphasis was forward-looking, and it has supported the development of new forms of measurement to provide benchmarks in the 1970s for continuing assessments in subsequent decades. At the same time, it seemed reasonable to devote a tithe of this grant to the retrospective task of assembling a catalogue of those items in the Institute's national survey archives which had been repeated at one time or another in the preceding quarter-century.

In a very real sense, this volume and its companion, the American National Election Studies Data Sourcebook: 1952-1978 represent the tip of the iceberg resulting from this endeavor. The first stage of retrieval involved a massive search of the institutional files for items that had been repeated in national surveys over the preceding twenty-five years. Under the able direction of Wendy Hoag, copies of nearly 200 questionnaires which had been applied to national samples in this period were relocated and laid side by side during the 1973-74 period. Given the fact that most of these questionnaires came from hour-long interviews involving upwards of 100 items each, the problem of finding repetitions was scarcely a trivial one. There seemed little alternative but to snip the questionnaires into strips and sort the strips into a large number of topical bins for subsequent examination and matching.

Once this was done, a pressing question arose as to when an actual repetition had occurred. For items worded identically, this was no problem. But for a very large number of items, there was obviously a common purpose but choice of wording varied in one degree or another. In general, we took a relatively conservative posture at this stage. While we would tolerate minor wording changes as representing "the same item," we set aside a considerable number of potential matches on grounds that however obvious the commonality of purpose, any substantial variation in actual question wording over time left the certification of constancy or change in response distributions moot. We also set aside at this stage a substantial number of repetitions of "face-sheet" or demographic items like race, education, or occupation, on grounds that the Census Bureau provided more accurate monitorings of the population in any event.

Despite the large number of items which were deleted as a result of these restrictions we were still faced with a massive mound of some 500 items which had been repeated at least twice over the course of the twenty-five-year period of national surveys. Excluded from this mound was the overall champion item, discovered by a zealous assistant, which had been repeated more frequently, and by some margin, than any other. It was the question "Why is that?"

At this point, a number of other considerations were brought to bear which served to winnow the pool of 500 items dramatically. For one thing, many of the repetitions had not produced rich and interesting time series. The most frequent number of repetitions was a mere two applications. Upon rare occasion, the two applications involved an item of high social interest posed to the population at times a decade or more apart. More often, the double application had occurred within the short span of a year or two, under the aegis of specific investigators who had pursued a topic for a period of a particular grant, and then turned their attention elsewhere. Some other question items, even those with a substantial history of repeated applications, seemed to have limited interest. Thus, for example, a rather handsome series involving plans about the purchase of refrigerators, while of conceivable interest to the industry itself, did not seem worth a major retrieval effort for a larger audience.

Another whole set of exclusions arose because not all questions, however exactly repeated they may have been, are coded in the same way. The problem is most apparent where questions are open-ended, giving successive investigators a wide latitude for code construction. But even closed questions can be tagged with variant response alternatives; where time comparability is concerned, such variation is as pre-emptive as a significant shift in the wording of the root question itself. Again, there were margins for judgment as to how "similar" a coding structure had to be for reasonable comparability, and faint variants in response categories can be seen even in this volume. Nonetheless, many repeated items were discarded from our initial pool once we had taken account of coding variation.

After all of this further winnowing had been carried out, we found ourselves still facing about 250 variables and a balance of funding from the original institutional grant which was beginning to run precariously low. At the outset, we had had two main goals. One was simply to produce a catalogue of question items on which there were at least incipient time series, so that subsequent investigators interested in a particular conceptual entity might know what forebear question wordings and code structures had been used to the same purpose, thus exact replication might produce data with a satisfying time perspective. As of 1975, this goal had been achieved. The second goal involved the production of a sourcebook which would not only identify the existence of repeated items, but would actually retrieve the distributions of responses in the American public to these items, so that time-series information might be disseminated to a broader community. Here the preservation of a pool as large as 250 items posed a dual problem: the problem of publishing such a large corpus of information, and the problem of costs of information retrieval, laid against dwindling resources.

The notion of differential information costs is a central one in several forms of abstract social science theory. Here we faced it in very concrete form. At one pole we had a large number of repeated items arising from the sequence of National Election Studies, which had long since been assembled and maintained on computer tapes for time-series use, thanks to the foresight of Warren Miller and his development in 1961 of the Inter-university Consortium for Political Research, which provided a funding mechanism for the care and nurture of past data bases. When we wanted to resurrect a response distribution for a particular Election Study, the tapes would be available for rapid mounting and the documentation concerning details such as code structure and sample design could be counted on to be impeccable. Many of the holdings of the Economic Behavior Program, particularly those data collected after 1960, could also be accessed at reasonable cost.

At the opposite pole, however, were the information costs associated with retrieval of results from the earlier applications of repeated items falling outside the ambit of these two Institute programs. A prototype of the dilemmas we encountered might involve a questionnaire item of high generic interest which had been applied in 1953, 1967, and 1971. The 1967 and 1971 observations, while on magnetic tape and reasonably accessible if only vaguely documented, would not by themselves constitute any very thrilling time series. But the data for the 1953 observation point, which would begin to make the whole series worthwhile, reside in a crumbling box of multiply-punched IBM cards, many of them warped, spindled, and mutilated, in stray warehouses in the environs of Ann Arbor, with the precise location at the initiation of search more or less unknown. The original investigator has long since disappeared, as has any anchoring lore about the actual number of respondents in the study or other revealing documentation. If the stakes seem high enough to retrieve a response distribution from such a 1953 study, we know that we can count on five or more person-weeks of effort and confusion, a figure which may reasonably be contrasted with the hour or so that might be required to extract a parallel response distribution from an Election Study of the early 1950s. These are differential information costs, where the differences are mounting into orders of magnitude.

Our concerns about how such a large corpus of information might be retrieved to be put into sourcebook form with the remaining resources were greatly relieved when Warren Miller secured a separate grant from the National Science Foundation on behalf of the Center for Political Studies to retrieve data and assemble a time-series sourcebook for the large number of political variables from the National Election Study series that numbered in our remaining pool of some 250 items. Indeed, while we continued to work with some few of the social and economic variables monitored regularly by the Election Study series, this division of labor served to split the pool of time-series items nearly in half. Thus the staff working on what had now become more narrowly a social and economic sourcebook was allowed to concentrate its retrieval and assembly efforts, as well as its remaining resources, on a pool of slightly fewer than 120 remaining items.

The preparation of this sourcebook has profited from the Center for Political Studies in two other distinct ways. Early in its own assembly efforts, the Center commissioned Edward Schneider to devise the necessary software to permit the base data, once retrieved, to be stored again on tape in a form such that final tabular material, including statistical calculations thereon, could be spun out as computer output in camera-ready and hence directly publishable form. This major effort had many advantages including great flexibility in formatting, the reduction of error due to repeated human intervention, and ease of updating time series with new observations. While the development of the Schneider system rendered a substantial amount of our own work investment obsolete, we gratefully adopted it. The Center for Political Studies also is to be thanked for providing sustaining funds for the completion of this sourcebook, after our original funds had been exhausted.

After the departure of Claire Macklin, who had designed the general structure of the originally projected sourcebook, Jean Dotson carried out the reorganization necessitated by the removal of the political variables into a separate sourcebook and generally supervised the final three years of work required to bring the project to completion. Bill McGee handled all of the later stages of the data retrieval, supervised the transfer of our work into the Schneider system, and wrote appendix B to this volume, providing details of sampling and study design for the national surveys contributing data to this volume.

Although we had nearly 120 social and economic variables with which to work after the partition, another two dozen or so of these were eliminated on technical grounds associated with the retrieval effort. Most of these deletions occurred for one of two reasons. In some instances closer work with the actual response distributions convinced us that, while question wordings and manifest coding structures were indeed similar enough to be reasonably comparable over time, the applications of those codes to the raw materials had almost certainly varied in erratic ways. This was particularly true where the definitions of non-content categories of "missing data" were concerned. The reader should be forewarned that such coding drift remains a possibility, even for the items which survived to this volume. But series in which such oddities were most blatant have been discarded. A number of other series fell by the wayside because retrieval of the earlier segments, on which the richness of the series depended, came to seem impractical. Once in a great while, the raw data could not be located, despite persistent efforts. In most instances, it could be seen in advance that while retrieval was possible, the costs would be prohibitive.

These further deletions left us with a body of some 95 variables upon which all assembly work was completed. Space limitations for this volume have occasioned the discarding at the eleventh hour of another dozen variables, chosen subjectively on grounds of lesser intrinsic interest.

If innumerable editorial decisions have underlain the final selection of variables, at least an equal number have been necessary to shape the form in which the data are presented here. From the outset, we felt that the most useful display for each variable would involve an initial presentation of the response distributions over time for the total sample, followed by repeats of the basic time series disaggregated by the most common demographic variables such as sex, race, age, and education, so that the reader could arrive at some first-approximation checks on hypotheses as to the sources of change visible in the total population. We also hoped to provide some graphic displays of the material, profiting from earlier investments made in this computer technology by Gregory Marks and Edward Schneider of the staff of the Center for Political Studies.

These general guidelines, which have in fact been followed in this volume, represented only a mere beginning on an endless chain of further decisions, many of which have of necessity been somewhat arbitrary and hence entirely subject to second guessing. Minor irregularities in the design or execution of specific studies contributing single time points to a given series were responsible for the largest number of special-case decisions. We have taken great pains to keep the reader alerted to these decisions with a system of footnotes.

Two more general editorial decisions were drawn from frustrations we have felt in examining other people's tabular displays based on percentaged response distributions. One of these involves the treatment of missing data. On the one hand, it is important to know, in assessing a series of percentage distributions, whether the bulk of missing data is large or small, and whether it shows noteworthy variation over time. On the other hand, once this cautionary information is in hand, it is usually preferable to delete the missing data in asking more probing questions concerning substantive changes in the distributions over time. Our practical solution has been to display missing data (beyond the typical handful of pure "not ascertained") in the initial table referring to the total population, but then to delete it in the subsequent disaggregated tables, save in a few rare instances where the missing data categories remain large (over 5 percent of the total, as a rule of thumb) and/or highly variable over time, and thus important for substantive diagnoses.

A second general practice may be more controversial. While some few of our items represent purely nominal categories, the vast majority are unequivocally ordered from "high" to "low." Now it is not entirely uncommon, in a time series involving five response categories, for instance, to note that percentages are increasing in the top category, suggesting an upward trend, but are increasing in the bottom category as well, suggesting a downward trend instead. Clearly what is needed, to sort the matter out rapidly, is a summary expression for the central tendency and dispersion of the total distribution, rather than some limited fraction of its range. Sensitive candidates for these expressions, such as the mean and standard deviation, are strictly speaking inappropriate to extract from mere ordinal ranks. Nevertheless, we have had the temerity to include such summary expressions for our ordinal variables. Anybody offended by this usage is invited to ignore them, since the full percentage distributions on which these summaries are based are everywhere presented in any event. They are included merely as an heuristic convenience, and we suspect that even those readers preferring to retreat to the safer percentages for finer work may nonetheless find them quite handy where initial reconnaissance is concerned.

It is obviously important, in longitudinal displays of the kind we are presenting, to keep the definitions of any partitioning or disaggregating variables like age or education as temporally comparable as possible. For most of our partitioning variables this poses no special problem. However, for a variable like income, both the meaning and the distribution in absolute dollars have changed mightily over the past thirty years. In a survey report of 1948 family income, for example, the highest category coded (of six) was "over $5,000," and barely more than 10 percent of the sample achieved such a figure. In a 1976 report coded in highly proliferated fashion, less than 20 percent of the population reported a family income as low as or lower than the $5,000 figure. Ideally, we might have tried to convert all of our income distributions into period-specific real incomes. Somewhat more simply, however, we decided to convert our income distributions at each time point into percentile ranges which could be taken as constant over time in at least a relative sense. Within the total sample in each study, five strata were created: at the low end of the income distribution a bottom sixth and a second sixth were distinguished, with a third of the population in the middle-income category; at the top end the most prosperous five percent of the distribution was isolated, and the next lower category covered the remainder of the population, from the sixty-eighth to the ninety-fifth percentile. In some few of the earlier studies, where family income was coded into quite coarse categories, such partitions could be only crudely approximated. After the mid-1950s, however, codes were much more proliferated, and approximations to these cutting points are quite close indeed.

As with income, the population distribution on education has shown a major upgrading since the 1940s. Given the sharp and stable intuitive meanings that attach to absolute divisions such as grade school, high school, and college, along with the fact that these distinctions are essentially fixed for life within cohorts by early adulthood, it seemed reasonable to leave the partitions absolute for the whole time span. "Grade school" here means eight years or less of formal schooling, even when the respondent may have had other non-academic training in addition. "College" means any college attendance. "High school" includes all of the intervening education groups.

The age divisions, which are otherwise self-explanatory, created occasional comparability problems, particularly for the coarsely coded earlier studies in the final elderly bracket, which was alternately defined as "over 65," "over 75," and the like. These variations are, however, explicitly flagged in the tabular materials.

A final round of editorial judgments has involved decisions about the inclusion of graphic presentations to supplement some of the tabular material. With one minor exception, all of the graphed data appear as well in conventional tabular form. While they are welcome additions, space would not permit us to provide graphs for more than a limited subset of our tables. Selection has proceeded along lines of presumed interest of particular variables and certain disaggregations thereof, coupled with judgments as to whether or not the graph helps to highlight intriguing changes. It may often be of theoretical importance that certain variables change as little as they do. Yet we have tended to select against such cases not because they are unimportant, but because a graph of horizontal lines is not very inspiring. A related problem arises when, with subgroup observations, there are clear trends across time and clear differences in subgroup values at any point in time, yet all of the lines are simply parallel. This is frequently the case with data of this sort, and what it says is that whatever generating mechanisms are forcing an upward or downward trend, they appear to be registering "across the board," or without differential effects among the subgroups which have been isolated. We show some graphs of this kind, particularly in cases where one's intuitive expectations about differential effects may be rather strong, given the specific variable and its relevance for subgroup differentiation. But since such parallel lines imply that the subgroups isolated are unrelated to the change effects, we refrain from showing anything like the proportion of such configurations that occur in nature in these data.

The world is a moving stage, and a part of this motion forms the substance of this volume. At the same time, the stage has moved while we have been at work, and this motion in itself has had vital implications for the scope of this volume.

We originally spread our net for repeated questionnaire items in the files of the Institute for Social Research as of the spring of 1973. Questions which became repeat items after that time naturally escaped our net. As work progressed and resources dwindled in 1976 and 1977, we began to ask ourselves about the necessity of updating our work even before its initial publication. After all, while we did not need to gauge the project against the deadline standards of the news media, it could be construed as odd that a compendium appearing in 1978 might contain no data collected after the first two or three months of 1973.

The question was especially discouraging, since it had been in the early 1970s, and for the same reasons that produced the notion of a sourcebook in the first place, that principal investigators at the Institute for Social Research had become increasingly conscious of the values of item replication. Programmatic research aimed at upgrading time series was beginning on a broader front, and researchers were paying closer attention to questions asked in earlier decades, by way of turning them overnight into long-span time series. Our cutoff date for the casting of our first net, pegged in early 1973, had caught little more than the first stirrings of such activity outside of the Election Study series and the Economic Behavior Program.

The array of new opportunities available by 1977 was impressive. Thus in 1965, for example, the Survey Research Center had conducted a major study of time use in the American population, and the study had been explicitly designed as a benchmark survey to be replicated in later periods. Such a replication was in fact carried out in 1974 and 1975, and it produced a substantial number of intriguing comparisons over the respectable period of a decade. These studies could have substantially increased the richness of our original 500 repeated items, but because of time definitions no items were represented in our net. This example could be multiplied in numerous substantive directions. The very embarrassment of new riches was sobering.

Two forms of updating were possible. A weak form involved the possibility of accepting our initial skein of variables located in 1973 as fixed, while merely returning to other studies conducted in the 1973-77 period for any further "readings" on those variables that had taken place in the interim. The radical form of updating would have required the recasting of the same broad net as in 1973, to find what was sure to be a very expanded haul of repetitions. Even if the radical form of updating had been fiscally possible, we knew that it would require many months of new ingestion and data assembly and create a major delay in publication plans. Therefore such an effort could not be countenanced, although we did decide to accept the modest delay in publication that would be associated with the weaker form of updating.

This decision, sure enough, raised the possibility of still further updates not merely to 1976, as before, but now through 1978, albeit in the weak version of such updating. Given our respect for the growing possibility of an infinite regress, we decided to match the American National Election Studies Data Sourcebook by including results from the 1978 Election Study, but holding the 1976 line elsewhere.

What all of this means is that while we feel that there are many fascinating data series in this volume as it stands, it would be regrettable if the reader were to conclude that this compilation exhausts the richness of time-series data in the files of the Institute for Social Research as they stand in 1978 or 1979. Because the stage has moved beneath us, it represents no more than a first glimpse.

In addition to the primary editors listed, this volume would not have been possible without the contributions of many other people. Horst Tiefenbach carried out the first stages of data retrieval, supplemented in a second stage by Michael MacKuen. Many months of painstaking labor in organizing the final tabular information, designing the computer graphics and converting the early work to the Schneider system were contributed by Christine Guzorek, Edith Behringer, and Judith Conner. Also involved in table and graph preparations for shorter stints were Sue Dotson, Michelle Hoyman, and Jack Thomas. Katherine Ward bore a major brunt of the earlier question assembly. Maureen

Kozumplik did a major share of the attendant typing.

Many other members of the Institute staff were extremely helpful in consultations with us. Tracing out documentation from earlier surveys were Irene Hess of the Survey Research Center and Evelyn Hansmire and Michael Nolte from the Economic Behavior Program. Janet Vavra, Elaine Wethington, and Verna Washington from the data archive of the Inter-university Consortium for Political and Social Research all made useful contributions, as did Barbara Thomas for the Omnibus surveys and Mary Senter for the Inter-Group Attitudes Survey. Other important computer consultation was provided by Sylvia Barge, Brian Cashman, and Susan Horvath.

We thank them all.

Philip E. Converse
Jean D. Dotson
Center for Political Studies                     Wendy J. Hoag
Ann Arbor                                        William H. McGee III

## Key to Study Identification

Each study contributing data to this volume is identified by the year in which it was conducted and a one-letter subscript designating the series of which it is a part. These subscripts are listed below. For further information on the studies, see appendix B.

| | |
|---|---|
| a | Surveys of Consumer Finances |
| b | Productive Americans Study |
| c | Winter Surveys of Consumer Attitudes and Behavior |
| d | Patterns of Family Change Study |
| e | Panel Study of Income Dynamics |
| f | Spring Surveys of Consumer Attitudes and Behavior |
| g | News Media Studies |
| h | Americans View Their Mental Health |
| i | Spring Omnibus Studies |
| j | Quality of American Life Study |
| k | Summer Surveys of Consumer Attitudes and Behavior |
| m | Fall Surveys of Consumer Attitudes and Behavior |
| n | American National Election Studies |
| p | Inter-Group Attitudes and Group Consciousness Study |
| q | Fall Omnibus Studies |

## Chapter 1. Attitudes toward Self And Others

Each of the nine chapters of this volume will begin with a brief introduction, of which this is the first. The purpose of these introductions should not be misunderstood. They scarcely pretend to constitute analyses of the ensuing data displays. Far from it. The purpose in the first instance is to indicate, if it is not already self-evident, both why the items were grouped as they were into a given chapter and what clustering or structure the flow of the presentations is meant to have. The second purpose is to provide a soupcon of the interesting morsels in each chapter, without for a moment pretending to digest or exhaust them. Part of the purpose of a volume of this sort is to invite the reader to some mental exercise of his own, and the introductions will leave a great deal of room for that.

Over the length of the volume, the subject matter stretches in a rough way from near to far. Most near is the self, and the self's image of others, so this is where we begin in this chapter. One cluster of series in our archives has to do with feelings about oneself: whether one feels happy and more or less in control of one's destiny. A second type of item involves one's location of oneself in the social order, an excuse for a time series on subjective social class location. We then turn to an examination of feelings about others, in two stages. In the first stage, "others" are undefined: we deal with mere trust in other people, whoever they may be. In the second stage, we move to feelings about specific social groupings, including some of which the respondent is a personal member.

We shall not, in general, take these introductions as an opportunity for pedagogy in the reading of tabular material. On the other hand, our first exhibit (table 1.1) poses a frequent problem in the reading of sample survey results extended over time. The item involved is a generic question as to the respondent's feelings of happiness, which is answerable at three levels: "Very happy," "Pretty happy," and "Not too happy." If one skims over the first row of this table, a span of data stretching for nearly twenty years, it is easy to conclude that "happiness is down", the largest proportion of the adult American population professing to be "very happy" occurred at the very first reading in 1957. The parallel proportion was markedly lower at the next readings in the early 1970s, and while the series appears to turn upward in the proportion labeling themselves "Very happy" as of 1976, the value is still below that of 1957. Hence, it would seem, happiness is indeed down.

But let us read on, and scan the bottom row of figures in the same table. There we find that the highest proportion of people choosing the least happy category also occurred in 1957. The differences in proportions from year to year here are smaller and, in fact, rarely exceed what we know to be a reasonable range of sampling error. Nonetheless, had we read this row first, avid for change, we would have concluded that "happiness is up," quite contrary to our first conclusion.

Both of these summary judgments cannot be true. One way of reconciling them is to recognize that any multiple-response distribution has some complexity which cannot be ignored. In the instance at hand, it may be more to the point to observe that happiness reports in 1957 showed greater dispersion, high and low, across the population than any of the responses measured since. This finding is a shade less satisfying if we insist on finding change in a more simplistic sense, but it is nonetheless food for thought.

The reader who feels that the divergent patterns of our first table must be rare specimens would do well to move on to the second table. Here the happiness responses are divided by the sex of the respondent. In this case, if we read the first row alone, we must conclude that women are happier than men, since in all six of the available comparisons women are more likely to say they are "Very happy" (although frequently by statistically insignificant margins!). Again, however, let us suspend judgment, for if we compare instead the bottom rows of these male-female tables, we find that almost always (five tries in six), women are more likely than men to select the least happy category offered, which must mean that they are in some general way less happy than men. Once again, however, these two generalizations cannot both be true at the same time. A generalization which does fit all of these data is that men are more likely than women to express their feelings of happiness in middling terms. Whether this inclusive generalization is more or less satisfying to the reader depends a great deal on what he or she brings to it, and this we cannot, quite appropriately, dictate.

Once beyond the happiness item, we encounter a set of items, starting with table 1.6, that are finally bound together in an Index of Personal Competence. These items were originally conceived to reflect facets of a common core. Interpreted with one end up, this common core involves deep-dyed feelings of competence as an individual, or what is sometimes called "ego strength," or feelings of control over one's destiny. Turned the other end up, one might speak of a measure of "fatalism," or resignation to a life which is largely beyond one's control. While the detailed components of the Index may vary in interesting ways, both by time and by population grouping, the summary Index itself seems to show a considerable stability, apart from a minor decline in such expressions in 1974, a year which cofeatured an alarming economic downturn under conditions which, while new, threatened to be permanent in terms of energy resources, and the first resignation in disgrace of an American president.

The next item, displayed in tables 1.21-1.26, involves reports of subjective location in the working class, the middle class, or some other entity. While there are fascinating internal variations in these data in terms of social groups and timing, the broadest message of this display is a rather simple one. As the occupation structure of the United States has drifted toward increasing fractions of the labor force in tertiary or "white-collar" service occupations since World War II, these subjective reports of class location have kept appropriate pace. The proportions of the American population who feel they are "middle class" and not "working class" has steadily increased throughout the period.

The next series, beginning with table 1.27, deals with feelings of trust in other people, generically defined, and is bound together once again at the end by a Trust in People Index. If the Personal Competence Index did not show much temporal variation, this Index of Trust shows more. What it seems to say is that interpersonal trust suffered something of a decline in the early 1970s, by comparison with its values in the 1960s. Whether 1976 has represented a significant rebound or not remains to be seen with subsequent updates of these series. The reader may find it profitable to lay these trends in interpersonal trust, tagged by specific dates of highs and lows, against a number of other series which appear later in the volume.

The final battery of material in the chapter stems from a series of items asking respondents to express on a "thermometer scale" their feelings, from warm to cool, about a variety of frequently delineated segments of the American population. These data once again have many buried facets of fascination, but for the last time in these introductions, we shall indulge in a moment of pedagogy. If one happens to cut into these data with a review of affective reactions to "the military" or "policemen," one finds a modest but general decline in the ratings. This change seems to make a certain amount of sense, since both groupings came under sharp attack in the late 1960s and early 1970s, the former for the Vietnam War, and the latter because of allegations of "police brutality." The problem

with this facile interpretation is that most of the other groups tested have also shown declining ratings in this span of time, including such groups as whites and Protestants. Affective ratings for labor unions have declined, as have those for big business. It is almost hard to find groups for which the ratings have remained constant, much less gone up. Candidates for reasonable constancy include such groups as blacks, a fact which in a relative sense may have major social significance in terms of campaigns for fundamental respect for blacks, aimed at both blacks and whites, and "groups" like Southerners, whose constancy of ratings is partly due to the fact that black feelings of negativism about "Southerners" has moderated remarkably since the beginnings of civil rights protest.

None of these subsidiary observations proves that the decline in ratings of the military and the police must be dissociated from familiar events and allegations of the late 1960s and early 1970s. Perhaps these are exactly the fountainheads of such decline. But the unsettling fact remains that the decline is scarcely unique to these groups and, indeed, involves other groups quite remote from the stigmata which these groups suffered. Hence a more cautious rethinking of these results seems in order. They may well be still further reflections of generic malaise and cynicism which invaded the American population in the 1960s, and which has also registered as a deteriorating level of confidence in national institutions, evident in our companion political sourcebook.

Attitudes toward Self And Others

Table 1.1
Present Happiness of Respondent
Total Population

QUESTION. Taking all things together, how would you say things are these
days--would you say that you're very happy, pretty happy, or not too
happy these days?

|  | | Year | | | | | |
|---|---|---|---|---|---|---|---|
|  | | 1957h | 1971j | 1972f | 1972n | 1976i | 1976h |
| Very happy | (5) | 34.7% | 28.8% | 26.7% | 21.8% | 29.7% | 32.1% |
| Pretty happy | (3) | 54.1 | 61.2 | 64.6 | 67.5 | 60.5 | 58.0 |
| Not too happy | (1) | 11.2 | 9.9 | 8.6 | 10.7 | 9.5 | 9.6 |
| Don't know | | 0.0 | 0.1 | ** | 0.1 | 0.4 | 0.3 |
| Total | | 100% | 100% | 100% | 100% | 100% | 100% |
| Weighted N | | 2452 | 9492 | 1287 | 1057 | 3005 | 4088 |
| Unweighted N | | 2452 | 2149 | 1287 | 1057 | 1389 | 2231 |
| Mean | | 3.47 | 3.38 | 3.36 | 3.22 | 3.40 | 3.45 |
| Standard Deviation | | 1.27 | 1.19 | 1.13 | 1.12 | 1.19 | 1.21 |

** Code distinction not made.

Figure 1.1
Present Happiness--Total Population

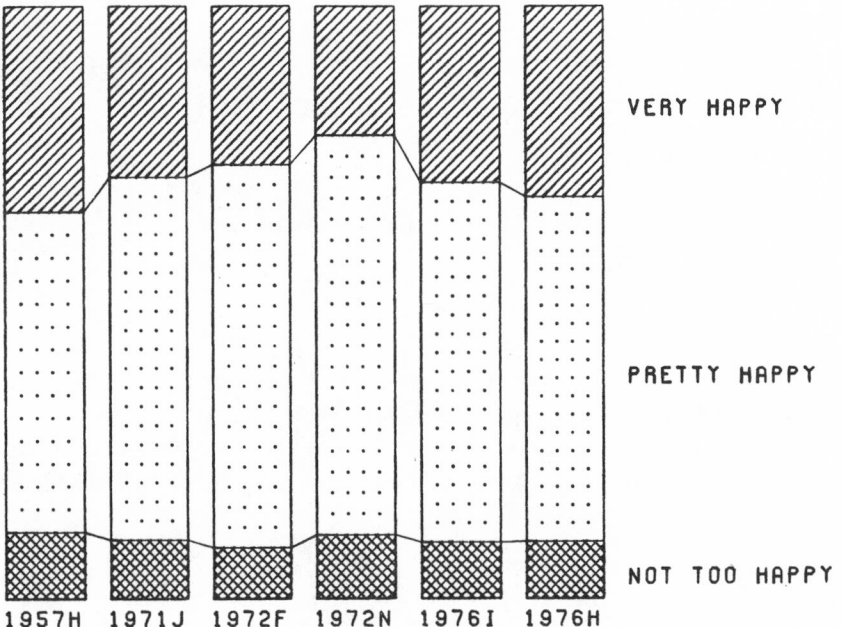

VERY HAPPY

PRETTY HAPPY

NOT TOO HAPPY

1957H  1971J  1972F  1972N  1976I  1976H

Attitudes toward Self And Others

Table 1.2
Present Happiness of Respondent
Sex of Respondent

|  |  |  | Year |  |  |  |  |
|---|---|---|---|---|---|---|---|
|  | 1957h | 1971j | 1972f | 1972n | 1976i | 1976h |  |
| Males Only | 32.9% | 28.6% | 24.7% | 21.6% | 28.7% | 31.0% | Very happy |
|  | 56.8 | 61.6 | 64.9 | 70.3 | 63.5 | 59.8 | Pretty happy |
|  | 10.3 | 9.8 | 10.4 | 8.1 | 7.8 | 9.2 | Not too happy |
|  | (1073) | (4480) | (539) | (458) | (1301) | (1806) | Weighted N |
|  |  |  |  |  |  |  |  |
| Females Only | 36.1 | 29.1 | 28.2 | 21.9 | 30.6 | 33.2 | Very happy |
|  | 52.0 | 60.9 | 64.4 | 65.4 | 58.6 | 56.9 | Pretty happy |
|  | 12.0 | 10.0 | 7.4 | 12.7 | 10.8 | 9.9 | Not too happy |
|  | (1378) | (5004) | (748) | (598) | (1693) | (2269) | Weighted N |

Table 1.3
Race of Respondent

|  | 1957h | 1971j | 1972f | 1972n | 1976i | 1976h |  |
|---|---|---|---|---|---|---|---|
| Whites Only | 36.0% | 30.2% | 27.7% | 23.5% | 31.3% | 34.2% | Very happy |
|  | 53.8 | 61.2 | 64.6 | 67.8 | 60.7 | 57.9 | Pretty happy |
|  | 10.2 | 8.6 | 7.7 | 8.7 | 8.1 | 8.0 | Not too happy |
|  | (2164) | (8239) | (1156) | (935) | (2557) | (3547) | Weighted N |
|  |  |  |  |  |  |  |  |
| Blacks Only | 22.3 | 19.5 | 17.5 | 6.7 | 22.1 | 19.4 | Very happy |
|  | 54.3 | 61.0 | 69.3 | 64.8 | 60.6 | 61.7 | Pretty happy |
|  | 23.4 | 19.4 | 13.2 | 28.6 | 17.4 | 18.9 | Not too happy |
|  | (188) | (973) | (114) | (105) | (317) | (407) | Weighted N |

Table 1.4
Present Happiness of Respondent
Education of Respondent

|  | Year | | | | | | |
|---|---|---|---|---|---|---|---|
|  | 1957h | 1971j | 1972f | 1972n | 1976i | 1976h | |
| Grade School Only | 23.5% | 23.2% | 20.6% | 16.6% | 27.3% | 23.9% | Very happy |
|  | 56.6 | 62.6 | 62.6 | 64.3 | 55.7 | 59.4 | Pretty happy |
|  | 19.9 | 14.2 | 16.9 | 19.1 | 17.0 | 16.7 | Not too happy |
|  | (797) | (2010) | (243) | (199) | (458) | (641) | Weighted N |
| High School Only | 39.0 | 29.9 | 28.2 | 22.4 | 28.5 | 30.8 | Very happy |
|  | 53.6 | 60.6 | 65.3 | 67.3 | 61.8 | 60.5 | Pretty happy |
|  | 7.4 | 9.5 | 6.5 | 10.3 | 9.7 | 8.7 | Not too happy |
|  | (1185) | (4830) | (660) | (535) | (1487) | (2028) | Weighted N |
| College Only | 43.0 | 31.0 | 28.3 | 23.9 | 33.1 | 38.3 | Very happy |
|  | 51.4 | 61.7 | 64.6 | 69.9 | 61.1 | 54.4 | Pretty happy |
|  | 5.5 | 7.4 | 7.1 | 6.2 | 5.8 | 7.4 | Not too happy |
|  | (453) | (2603) | (381) | (322) | (1030) | (1387) | Weighted N |

Table 1.5
Present Happiness of Respondent
Age of Respondent

|  | Year | | | | | | |
|---|---|---|---|---|---|---|---|
|  | 1957h | 1971j | 1972f | 1972n | 1976i | 1976h | |
| 18-24 Only | 42.3% | 29.7% | 26.2% | 17.6% | 24.1% | 29.8% | Very happy |
|  | 53.4 | 60.8 | 66.7 | 74.1 | 69.0 | 60.0 | Pretty happy |
|  | 4.3 | 9.5 | 7.1 | 8.2 | 6.9 | 10.2 | Not too happy |
|  | (163) | (1480) | (210) | (170) | (522) | (420) | Weighted N |
| 25-34 Only | 39.1 | 31.7 | 30.6 | 25.8 | 30.3 | 33.8 | Very happy |
|  | 55.2 | 60.6 | 61.5 | 65.2 | 60.9 | 57.9 | Pretty happy |
|  | 5.7 | 7.7 | 7.9 | 9.0 | 8.8 | 8.3 | Not too happy |
|  | (594) | (1926) | (278) | (233) | (637) | (1060) | Weighted N |
| 35-44 Only | 38.6 | 29.2 | 26.4 | 19.0 | 27.7 | 35.4 | Very happy |
|  | 51.9 | 61.2 | 70.0 | 69.8 | 65.4 | 56.4 | Pretty happy |
|  | 9.5 | 9.6 | 3.6 | 11.2 | 6.9 | 8.3 | Not too happy |
|  | (547) | (1619) | (220) | (179) | (477) | (690) | Weighted N |
| 45-54 Only | 34.0 | 25.9 | 22.6 | 21.7 | 30.4 | 33.1 | Very happy |
|  | 52.9 | 62.7 | 66.8 | 65.8 | 56.1 | 58.6 | Pretty happy |
|  | 13.2 | 11.3 | 10.5 | 12.5 | 13.4 | 8.3 | Not too happy |
|  | (456) | (1605) | (190) | (152) | (506) | (652) | Weighted N |
| 55-64 Only | 28.6 | 30.2 | 27.2 | 24.8 | 30.7 | 29.3 | Very happy |
|  | 55.9 | 59.7 | 62.7 | 67.5 | 58.5 | 60.4 | Pretty happy |
|  | 15.5 | 10.1 | 10.1 | 7.6 | 10.8 | 10.3 | Not too happy |
|  | (329) | (1285) | (169) | (157) | (417) | (639) | Weighted N |
| 65-74 Only | 24.9 | 28.5 | 27.6 | 20.4 | 36.7 | 30.8 | Very happy |
|  | 55.7 | 59.4 | 60.7 | 60.2 | 51.6 | 55.8 | Pretty happy |
|  | 19.4 | 12.1 | 11.7 | 19.4 | 11.8 | 13.5 | Not too happy |
|  | (350) | (1018) | (145) | (103) | (289) | (416) | Weighted N |
| 75 And Older Only | ** | 21.8 | 20.0 | 20.7 | 37.5 | 27.8 | Very happy |
|  | ** | 66.8 | 62.9 | 69.0 | 52.9 | 58.2 | Pretty happy |
|  | ** | 11.4 | 17.1 | 10.3 | 9.6 | 13.9 | Not too happy |
|  | ** | (542) | (70) | (58) | (136) | (194) | Weighted N |

** Code distinction not made.
Oldest age group coded as "65 And Older" in 1957h.

Table 1.6
Sure or Not Sure Life Would Work Out
Total Population

QUESTION: Have you usually felt pretty sure your life would work out the way you want it to,
or have there been times when you haven't been (very) sure?

|  | | Year | | | | | | | |
|---|---|---|---|---|---|---|---|---|---|
|  | | 1958n | 1960n | 1964n | 1968n | 1970n | 1971j | 1972n | 1974n | 1976n |
| Pretty sure | (5) | 46.3% | 47.0% | 46.6% | 38.3% | 37.7% | 40.0% | 35.9% | 35.7% | 36.7% |
| Depends | (3) | 0.2 | 0.6 | 0.5 | 0.4 | 0.3 | 0.4 | 0.1 | ** | ** |
| Sometimes not very sure | (1) | 52.8 | 51.9 | 52.4 | 58.5 | 59.9 | 59.6 | 62.2 | 62.7 | 61.2 |
| Don't know | | 0.7 | 0.5 | 0.5 | 2.7 | 2.0 | ** | 1.8 | 1.6 | 2.1 |
| Total | | 100% | 100% | 100% | 100% | 100% | 100% | 100% | 100% | 100% |
| Weighted Total | | 1777 | 1817 | 4273 | 2665 | 1870 | 9458 | 2697 | 2485 | 2396 |
| Unweighted Total | | 1415 | 1103 | 1677 | 1471 | 1689 | 2140 | 2697 | 1555 | 1903 |
| Mean | | 2.87 | 2.90 | 2.88 | 2.58 | 2.55 | 2.61 | 2.46 | 2.45 | 2.50 |
| Standard Deviation | | 1.99 | 1.99 | 1.99 | 1.95 | 1.94 | 1.96 | 1.93 | 1.92 | 1.94 |

** Code distinction not made.
1964n,1968n,and 1970n include Black supplement.

Figure 1.2
Sure/Not Sure Life Work Out by Race of R

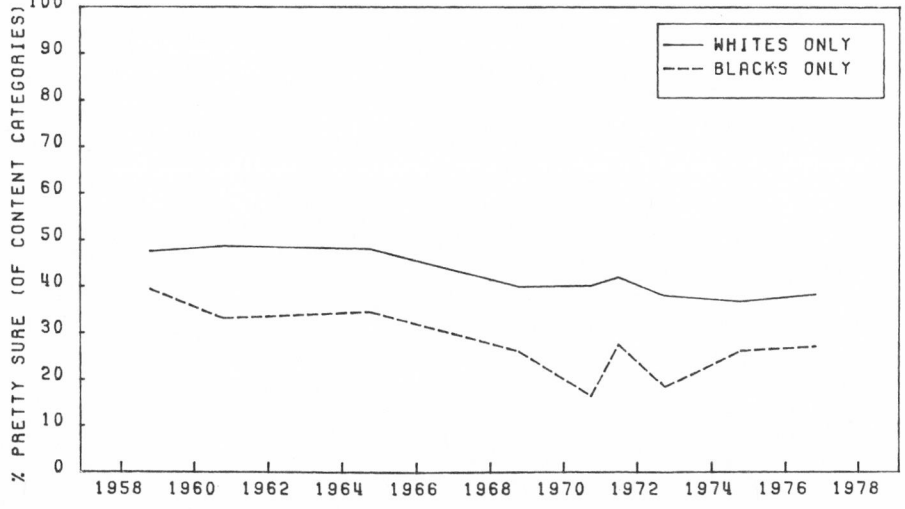

Figure 1.3
Sure/Not Sure Life Work Out by Education of R

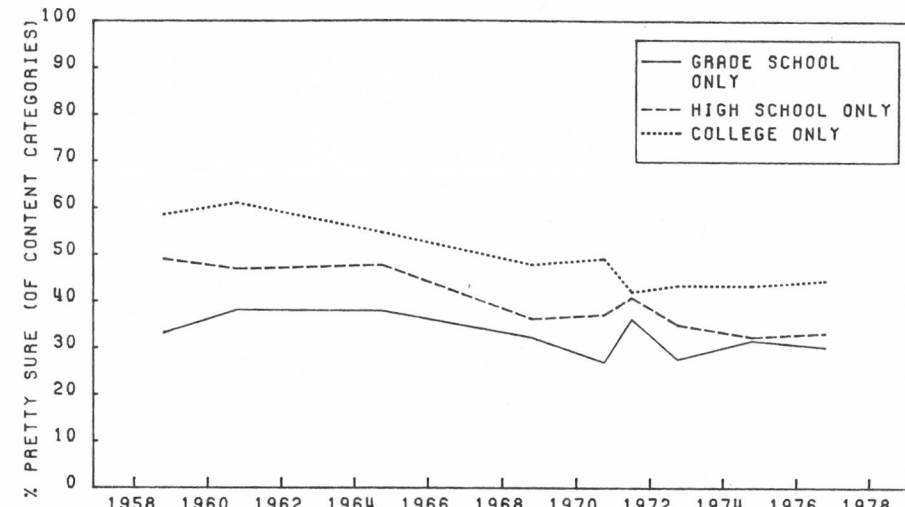

Table 1.7
Sure or Not Sure Life Would Work Out
Social Groups

| % Sure | 1958n | 1960n | 1964n | 1968n | Year 1970n | 1971j | 1972n | 1974n | 1976n | |
|---|---|---|---|---|---|---|---|---|---|---|
| Males Only | 48.3% | 48.5% | 48.7% | 41.5% | 42.1% | 40.2% | 40.1% | 36.9% | 42.4% | Sure |
| | (822) | (815) | (1898) | (1129) | (796) | (4460) | (1138) | (1029) | (961) | Weighted N |
| Females Only | 45.4 | 46.7 | 45.7 | 38.1 | 35.9 | 40.0 | 34.0 | 35.8 | 34.1 | Sure |
| | (939) | (982) | (2332) | (1453) | (1030) | (4956) | (1507) | (1417) | (1380) | Weighted N |
| Whites Only | 47.8 | 49.0 | 48.3 | 41.2 | 41.0 | 42.0 | 38.7 | 37.3 | 39.0 | Sure |
| | (1586) | (1631) | (3825) | (2310) | (1632) | (8171) | (2349) | (2180) | (2067) | Weighted N |
| Blacks Only | 39.4 | 33.1 | 34.9 | 26.3 | 16.7 | 27.6 | 18.8 | 26.7 | 27.9 | Sure |
| | (160) | (148) | (372) | (236) | (166) | (973) | (260) | (217) | (212) | Weighted N |
| Grade School Only | 33.9 | 38.7 | 38.1 | 33.3 | 27.9 | 36.2 | 28.6 | 32.1 | 31.8 | Sure |
| | (519) | (530) | (1032) | (576) | (419) | (2044) | (514) | (433) | (355) | Weighted N |
| High School Only | 49.1 | 46.9 | 48.0 | 37.2 | 37.7 | 40.8 | 35.4 | 32.9 | 33.7 | Sure |
| | (872) | (862) | (2183) | (1270) | (929) | (4790) | (1352) | (1233) | (1168) | Weighted N |
| College Only | 58.8 | 61.3 | 54.9 | 48.7 | 49.9 | 42.0 | 44.0 | 44.0 | 45.1 | Sure |
| | (354) | (400) | (990) | (733) | (473) | (2541) | (777) | (761) | (816) | Weighted N |
| 18-24 Only | 57.3 | 37.0 | 36.3 | 35.9 | 28.9 | 40.3 | 34.8 | 33.6 | 36.5 | Sure |
| | (89) | (54) | (306) | (206) | (251) | (1478) | (394) | (354) | (332) | Weighted N |
| 25-34 Only | 52.1 | 53.6 | 47.7 | 41.8 | 45.4 | 34.4 | 36.7 | 33.0 | 36.0 | Sure |
| | (399) | (390) | (886) | (519) | (361) | (1942) | (572) | (566) | (558) | Weighted N |
| 35-44 Only | 45.9 | 48.8 | 50.9 | 37.0 | 40.2 | 43.3 | 38.4 | 41.7 | 37.3 | Sure |
| | (458) | (455) | (943) | (549) | (320) | (1627) | (435) | (336) | (348) | Weighted N |
| 45-54 Only | 43.5 | 43.6 | 44.4 | 42.1 | 38.9 | 38.4 | 33.5 | 38.7 | 37.5 | Sure |
| | (340) | (349) | (849) | (516) | (311) | (1571) | (439) | (398) | (340) | Weighted N |
| 55-64 Only | 40.3 | 45.9 | 41.9 | 35.9 | 38.4 | 36.1 | 39.2 | 28.0 | 39.0 | Sure |
| | (248) | (279) | (618) | (365) | (284) | (1266) | (375) | (347) | (344) | Weighted N |
| 65-74 Only | 51.3 | 49.7 | 57.0 | 40.3 | 36.2 | 46.5 | 35.5 | 42.9 | 38.8 | Sure |
| | (152) | (199) | (421) | (290) | (185) | (995) | (265) | (275) | (259) | Weighted N |
| 75 And Older Only | 37.3 | 33.8 | 47.2 | 45.7 | 39.7 | 53.3 | 41.5 | 40.6 | 40.7 | Sure |
| | (75) | (71) | (197) | (129) | (104) | (520) | (147) | (143) | (150) | Weighted N |

Percentages based on content categories "Pretty Sure" and "Sometimes Not Very Sure".

Table 1.8
Sure or More Times Not Sure Life Would Work Out
Total Population

QUESTION: Have you usually felt pretty sure your life would work out the way you want it to, or have there been more times when you haven't been sure about it?

| | | Year | | | | | | | | |
|---|---|---|---|---|---|---|---|---|---|---|
| | | 1962k | 1963m | 1965b | 1968e | 1969e | 1970e | 1971e | 1972e | 1975e |
| Pretty sure | (5) | 60.8% | 60.1% | 57.7% | 56.5% | 61.0% | 60.2% | 63.2% | 61.8% | 65.7% |
| Pretty sure(qualified) | (4) | ** | ** | ** | 4.2 | 2.3 | 3.2 | 3.1 | 0.9 | 2.7 |
| Pro con | (3) | ** | ** | ** | 3.7 | 2.4 | 1.9 | 1.4 | 0.8 | 1.6 |
| More times not sure(qualified) | (2) | ** | ** | ** | 2.2 | 1.2 | 0.9 | 0.9 | 0.3 | 1.0 |
| More times not sure | (1) | 39.2 | 39.9 | 42.3 | 33.4 | 33.2 | 33.8 | 31.4 | 36.1 | 29.0 |
| Total | | 100% | 100% | 100% | 100% | 100% | 100% | 100% | 100% | 100% |
| Weighted Total | | 1294 | 1291 | 2138 | 99489 | 108674 | 118396 | 103244 | 113141 | 134026 |
| Unweighted Total | | 1294 | 1291 | 2138 | 3277 | 3624 | 4003 | 3615 | 4041 | 5175 |
| Mean | | 3.43 | 3.40 | 3.31 | 3.48 | 3.57 | 3.55 | 3.66 | 3.52 | 3.75 |
| Standard Deviation | | 1.95 | 1.96 | 1.98 | 1.85 | 1.87 | 1.87 | 1.84 | 1.91 | 1.81 |

** Code distinction not made.

Figure 1.4
Sure/More Times Not Sure by Sex of R

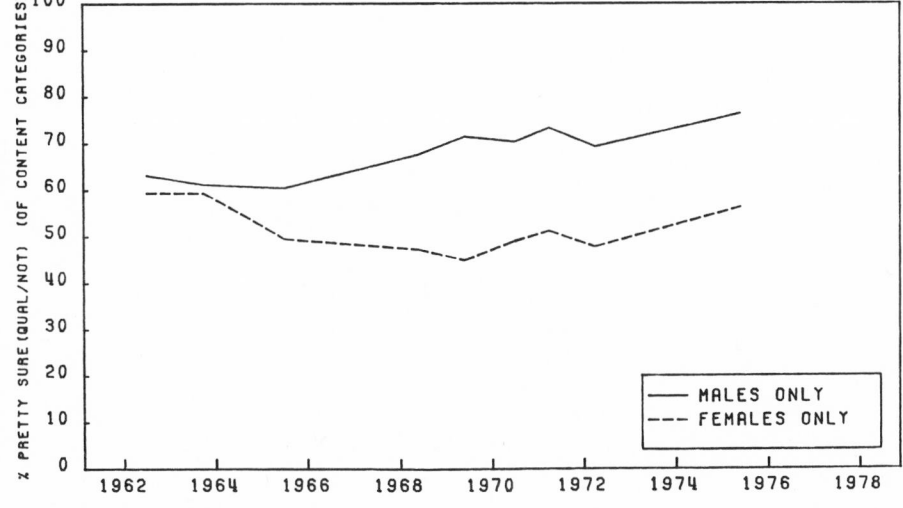

Figure 1.5
Sure/More Times Not Sure by Race of R

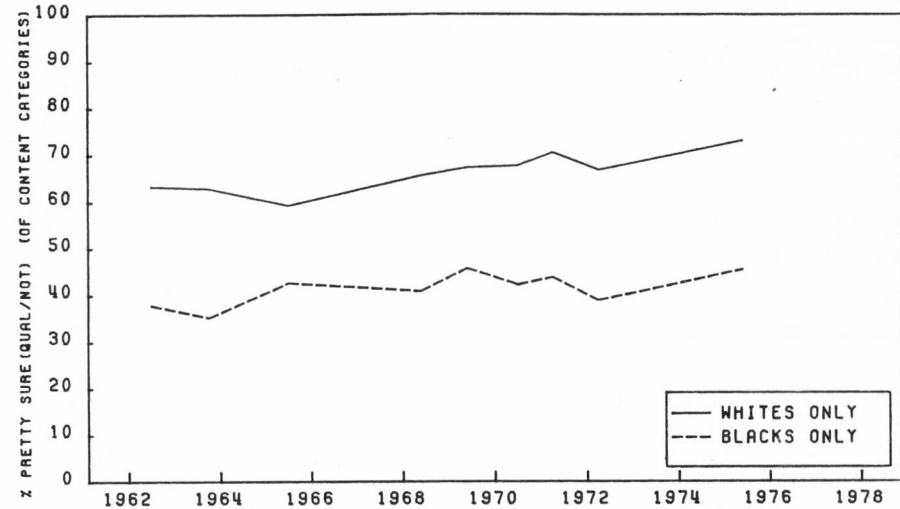

Table 1.9
Sure or More Times Not Sure Life Would Work Out
Social Groups

| % Sure | | | | | Year | | | | | |
|---|---|---|---|---|---|---|---|---|---|---|
| | 1962k | 1963m | 1965b | 1968e | 1969e | 1970e | 1971e | 1972e | 1975e | |
| Males Only | 63.2% | 61.2% | 60.5% | 67.7% | 71.5% | 70.4% | 73.3% | 69.3% | 76.3% | Sure(qual or not) |
| | (519) | (529) | (1584) | (73922) | (79054) | (84546) | (74082) | (80549) | (86950) | Weighted N |
| Females Only | 59.4 | 59.3 | 49.5 | 47.3 | 45.0 | 49.1 | 51.2 | 47.8 | 56.2 | Sure(qual or not) |
| | (773) | (762) | (554) | (21837) | (27051) | (31609) | (27699) | (31524) | (44387) | Weighted N |
| Whites Only | 63.3 | 62.9 | 59.3 | 65.6 | 67.3 | 67.7 | 70.5 | 66.8 | 73.0 | Sure(qual or not) |
| | (1165) | (1142) | (1905) | (84040) | (92453) | (100510) | (88080) | (96925) | (113063) | Weighted N |
| Blacks Only | 37.8 | 35.2 | 42.6 | 40.8 | 45.7 | 42.2 | 43.8 | 38.8 | 45.4 | Sure(qual or not) |
| | (111) | (125) | (204) | (10245) | (11583) | (12792) | (10963) | (12321) | (14970) | Weighted N |
| Grade School Only | 49.1 | 46.5 | 49.9 | 52.4 | 52.6 | 54.9 | 57.0 | 51.4 | 59.6 | Sure(qual or not) |
| | (369) | (361) | (625) | (24083) | (27507) | (27694) | (19478) | (21196) | (21690) | Weighted N |
| High School Only | 60.9 | 61.6 | 57.4 | 62.8 | 63.2 | 61.6 | 64.2 | 60.2 | 65.9 | Sure(qual or not) |
| | (634) | (656) | (990) | (43726) | (47732) | (54314) | (43814) | (53521) | (64798) | Weighted N |
| College Only | 75.7 | 74.9 | 67.1 | 73.6 | 78.4 | 78.7 | 82.0 | 77.5 | 81.4 | Sure(qual or not) |
| | (276) | (263) | (514) | (27516) | (30251) | (32589) | (29470) | (33936) | (42447) | Weighted N |
| 18-24 Only | 68.8 | 60.6 | 58.5 | 67.1 | 67.2 | 60.2 | 66.4 | 58.5 | 66.1 | Sure(qual or not) |
| | (77) | (99) | (130) | (7853) | (8543) | (11375) | (10124) | (11697) | (14814) | Weighted N |
| 25-34 Only | 64.9 | 60.9 | 59.7 | 63.0 | 69.2 | 69.2 | 71.5 | 70.9 | 70.0 | Sure(qual or not) |
| | (282) | (230) | (352) | (18441) | (20745) | (22778) | (20142) | (22568) | (29869) | Weighted N |
| 35-44 Only | 66.0 | 57.1 | 59.7 | 63.2 | 66.8 | 64.6 | 70.3 | 69.0 | 72.2 | Sure(qual or not) |
| | (265) | (268) | (432) | (21812) | (22965) | (23727) | (21589) | (22290) | (21341) | Weighted N |
| 45-54 Only | 48.5 | 59.4 | 51.9 | 60.4 | 64.0 | 65.3 | 62.8 | 61.2 | 70.3 | Sure(qual or not) |
| | (229) | (271) | (447) | (18526) | (20188) | (21808) | (18911) | (20964) | (24439) | Weighted N |
| 55-64 Only | 64.4 | 65.5 | 59.1 | 64.0 | 62.1 | 60.1 | 61.9 | 56.7 | 69.9 | Sure(qual or not) |
| | (191) | (194) | (379) | (15827) | (17915) | (18639) | (15827) | (17184) | (17617) | Weighted N |
| 65-74 Only | 55.0 | 61.2 | 59.0 | 64.3 | 58.0 | 64.6 | 69.4 | 59.0 | 67.3 | Sure(qual or not) |
| | (149) | (134) | (266) | (9547) | (11230) | (12498) | (11357) | (12332) | (14794) | Weighted N |
| 75 And Older Only | 63.4 | 56.6 | 56.5 | 61.1 | 62.8 | 67.3 | 68.7 | 56.3 | 67.7 | Sure(qual or not) |
| | (82) | (83) | (124) | (3561) | (4564) | (5266) | (3827) | (4953) | (8406) | Weighted N |

Sex coded for head of household and wife only in 1968e,1969e,1970e,1971e,1972e.
Race coded for head of household only in 1965b and for head and wife only in 1971e.
Education coded for head of household only in 1971e, and for head and wife only in all other studies.
Age coded for head of household only in 1962k,1965b,1968e,1969e,1970e,1971e,1972e, and 1975e.
Percentages based on content categories "Pretty Sure (qualified or not)" and "More Times Not Sure (qualified or not)".

Table 1.10
When R Plans Ahead, Do R's Plans Work Out as Expected?
Total Population

QUESTION: When you do make plans ahead, do you usually get to carry out things the way you expected, or do things usually come up to make you change your plans?

|  | | Year | | | | | | | | | |
|---|---|---|---|---|---|---|---|---|---|---|---|
|  | 1958n | 1960n | 1962k | 1964n | 1968n | 1970n | 1971j | 1972n | 1974n | 1976h | 1976n |
| Things work out as expected (5) | 54.0% | 59.3% | 57.3% | 59.4% | 46.4% | 40.6% | 50.5% | 46.9% | 42.7% | 60.9% | 46.3% |
| Depends/other (3) | 1.4 | 2.5 | ** | 4.5 | 3.3 | 2.8 | 2.8 | 1.9 | ** | 1.5 | ** |
| Have to change plans (1) | 44.0 | 37.9 | 42.7 | 35.9 | 47.5 | 54.5 | 46.6 | 49.1 | 55.5 | 36.0 | 50.6 |
| Don't know | 0.6 | 0.3 | ** | 0.1 | 2.8 | 2.1 | ** | 2.2 | 1.7 | 1.6 | 3.1 |
| Total | 100% | 100% | 100% | 100% | 100% | 100% | 100% | 100% | 100% | 100% | 100% |
| Weighted Total | 1755 | 1784 | 1262 | 1442 | 1344 | 1503 | 9432 | 2691 | 2468 | 4075 | 2389 |
| Unweighted Total | 1397 | 1078 | 1262 | 1442 | 1344 | 1503 | 2133 | 2691 | 1541 | 2225 | 1894 |
| Mean | 3.20 | 3.43 | 3.29 | 3.47 | 2.97 | 2.72 | 3.08 | 2.95 | 2.74 | 3.50 | 2.91 |
| Standard Deviation | 1.98 | 1.93 | 1.98 | 1.90 | 1.97 | 1.95 | 1.97 | 1.98 | 1.98 | 1.92 | 2.00 |

** Code distinction not made.

Figure 1.6
Plans Work Out by Race of R

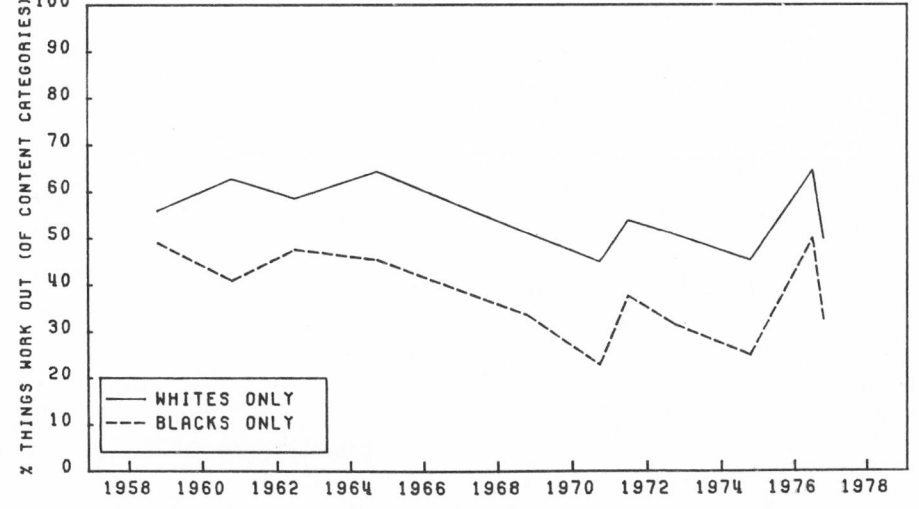

Figure 1.7
Plans Work Out by Education of R

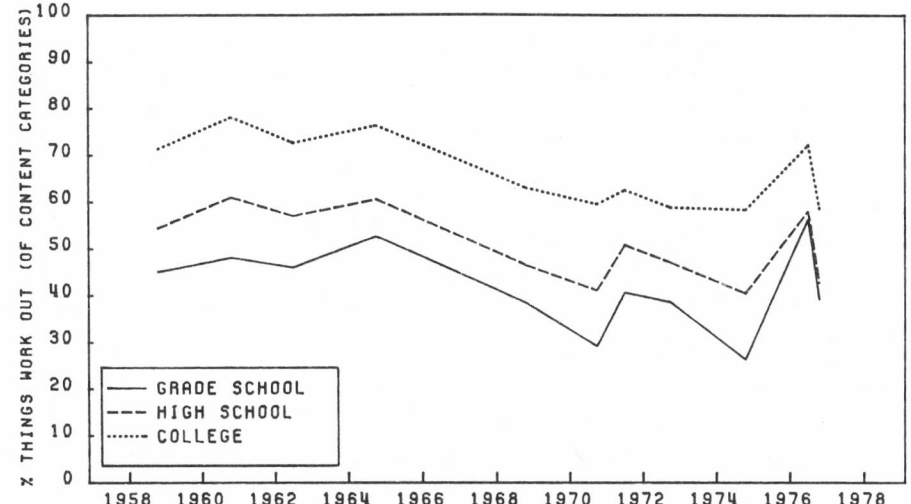

Table 1.11
When R Plans Ahead, Do R's Plans Work Out As Expected?
Social Groups

| % Work Out | | | | | | Year | | | | | | |
|---|---|---|---|---|---|---|---|---|---|---|---|---|
| | 1958n | 1960n | 1962k | 1964n | 1968n | 1970n | 1971j | 1972n | 1974n | 1976h | 1976n | |
| Males Only | 58.4% | 66.1% | 57.9% | 67.7% | 52.1% | 42.1% | 53.3% | 48.8% | 43.6% | 65.7% | 49.8% | Work out |
| | (812) | (790) | (506) | (606) | (553) | (618) | (4400) | (1109) | (1017) | (1745) | (953) | Weighted N |
| Females Only | 52.1 | 56.8 | 57.0 | 58.1 | 47.2 | 43.2 | 50.8 | 49.0 | 43.5 | 60.5 | 46.4 | Work out |
| | (907) | (944) | (754) | (769) | (709) | (811) | (4764) | (1468) | (1408) | (2203) | (1362) | Weighted N |
| Whites Only | 56.0 | 62.8 | 58.6 | 64.4 | 51.2 | 45.0 | 53.9 | 50.8 | 45.3 | 64.6 | 49.8 | Work out |
| | (1547) | (1572) | (1139) | (1224) | (1122) | (1270) | (7940) | (2292) | (2159) | (3427) | (2041) | Weighted N |
| Blacks Only | 49.0 | 41.0 | 47.6 | 45.4 | 33.6 | 22.9 | 37.7 | 31.5 | 25.0 | 50.0 | 32.5 | Work out |
| | (157) | (144) | (105) | (141) | (125) | (140) | (956) | (248) | (216) | (402) | (205) | Weighted N |
| Grade School Only | 45.1 | 48.1 | 46.0 | 52.7 | 38.4 | 29.2 | 40.7 | 38.6 | 26.4 | 56.5 | 39.2 | Work out |
| | (514) | (505) | (365) | (336) | (279) | (342) | (1954) | (503) | (444) | (612) | (354) | Weighted N |
| High School Only | 54.5 | 61.1 | 57.1 | 60.6 | 46.5 | 41.1 | 50.8 | 47.1 | 40.5 | 58.2 | 42.8 | Work out |
| | (846) | (839) | (616) | (711) | (624) | (733) | (4677) | (1314) | (1223) | (1958) | (1149) | Weighted N |
| College Only | 71.4 | 78.2 | 72.7 | 76.3 | 63.0 | 59.6 | 62.6 | 58.9 | 58.4 | 72.2 | 58.7 | Work out |
| | (346) | (385) | (267) | (321) | (359) | (349) | (2492) | (759) | (746) | (1362) | (807) | Weighted N |
| 18-24 Only | 54.0 | 46.2 | 66.7 | 56.1 | 45.9 | 36.6 | 45.6 | 43.9 | 43.8 | 52.1 | 47.0 | Work out |
| | (87) | (52) | (72) | (98) | (98) | (142) | (1435) | (392) | (352) | (413) | (328) | Weighted N |
| 25-34 Only | 58.5 | 67.1 | 56.2 | 60.9 | 52.9 | 47.2 | 56.0 | 51.7 | 44.9 | 59.7 | 45.7 | Work out |
| | (395) | (380) | (281) | (294) | (261) | (299) | (1887) | (553) | (568) | (1028) | (552) | Weighted N |
| 35-44 Only | 56.5 | 63.7 | 62.3 | 70.3 | 46.7 | 42.7 | 54.4 | 52.2 | 43.5 | 60.5 | 50.7 | Work out |
| | (448) | (444) | (260) | (303) | (272) | (246) | (1549) | (425) | (329) | (666) | (343) | Weighted N |
| 45-54 Only | 51.4 | 60.1 | 51.4 | 60.1 | 44.9 | 42.0 | 45.5 | 48.7 | 47.7 | 65.3 | 53.4 | Work out |
| | (333) | (343) | (216) | (278) | (254) | (264) | (1551) | (425) | (396) | (645) | (334) | Weighted N |
| 55-64 Only | 54.7 | 55.7 | 66.1 | 59.0 | 51.2 | 43.7 | 55.9 | 48.8 | 40.1 | 72.0 | 49.0 | Work out |
| | (243) | (255) | (186) | (205) | (172) | (231) | (1244) | (361) | (344) | (608) | (335) | Weighted N |
| 65-74 Only | 53.8 | 60.1 | 45.9 | 64.2 | 56.0 | 40.5 | 50.1 | 45.8 | 40.9 | 65.7 | 42.7 | Work out |
| | (143) | (193) | (148) | (134) | (141) | (158) | (970) | (264) | (274) | (399) | (258) | Weighted N |
| 75 And Older Only | 50.0 | 47.8 | 55.6 | 55.0 | 50.0 | 41.5 | 61.8 | 50.0 | 36.7 | 66.5 | 43.1 | Work out |
| | (70) | (67) | (81) | (60) | (60) | (82) | (519) | (142) | (139) | (185) | (152) | Weighted N |

Education and Age coded for head of household and wife only in 1962k.
Percentages based on content categories "Things Work Out" and "Have to Change Plans".

Table 1.12
Is It Better to Plan One's Life a Good Way Ahead?
Total Population

QUESTION: Do you think it is better to plan your life a good way ahead,
or would you say life is too much a matter of luck to plan ahead very far?

|  | | Year | | | | | |
|---|---|---|---|---|---|---|---|
|  | | 1968n | 1970n | 1971j | 1972n | 1974n | 1976n |
| Plan ahead | (5) | 61.2% | 64.3% | 54.8% | 66.3% | 56.6% | 61.2% |
| Depends | (3) | 1.0 | 1.3 | 2.1 | 1.0 | ** | ** |
| Too much luck to plan | (1) | 35.0 | 32.2 | 43.1 | 30.1 | 40.4 | 36.0 |
| Don't know | | 2.8 | 2.2 | ** | 2.5 | 3.0 | 2.8 |
| Total | | 100% | 100% | 100% | 100% | 100% | 100% |
| Weighted Total | | 1344 | 1499 | 9398 | 2690 | 2453 | 2386 |
| Unweighted Total | | 1344 | 1499 | 2128 | 2690 | 1531 | 1894 |
| Mean | | 3.54 | 3.66 | 3.23 | 3.74 | 3.33 | 3.52 |
| Standard Deviation | | 1.92 | 1.88 | 1.96 | 1.85 | 1.97 | 1.93 |

** Code distinction not made.

Attitudes toward Self And Others

Table 1.13
Is It Better to Plan One's Life a Good Way Ahead?
Social Groups

| % Plan | | | Year | | | | |
|---|---|---|---|---|---|---|---|
| | 1968n | 1970n | 1971j | 1972n | 1974n | 1976n | |
| Males Only | 70.1% | 71.7% | 60.2% | 73.3% | 63.8% | 69.4% | Plan |
| | (565) | (622) | (4360) | (1126) | (999) | (962) | Weighted N |
| Females Only | 58.5 | 62.8 | 52.1 | 65.3 | 54.4 | 58.3 | Plan |
| | (728) | (825) | (4840) | (1463) | (1380) | (1356) | Weighted N |
| Whites Only | 64.8 | 67.8 | 57.2 | 69.4 | 59.1 | 64.3 | Plan |
| | (1150) | (1286) | (7967) | (2300) | (2117) | (2045) | Weighted N |
| Blacks Only | 52.3 | 57.6 | 48.6 | 61.4 | 50.5 | 52.9 | Plan |
| | (128) | (139) | (965) | (251) | (218) | (205) | Weighted N |
| Grade School Only | 46.1 | 50.1 | 40.1 | 52.0 | 46.4 | 47.1 | Plan |
| | (293) | (349) | (1975) | (506) | (440) | (361) | Weighted N |
| High School Only | 61.2 | 66.4 | 55.7 | 66.3 | 54.2 | 58.9 | Plan |
| | (634) | (735) | (4704) | (1319) | (1210) | (1147) | Weighted N |
| College Only | 81.9 | 83.2 | 69.0 | 84.2 | 72.1 | 76.1 | Plan |
| | (365) | (358) | (2480) | (761) | (717) | (804) | Weighted N |
| 18-24 Only | 66.3 | 61.3 | 58.4 | 65.2 | 52.1 | 61.8 | Plan |
| | (98) | (142) | (1427) | (385) | (349) | (326) | Weighted N |
| 25-34 Only | 67.2 | 67.6 | 57.8 | 71.1 | 52.9 | 61.8 | Plan |
| | (256) | (306) | (1830) | (553) | (558) | (544) | Weighted N |
| 35-44 Only | 62.7 | 70.9 | 61.0 | 72.2 | 64.6 | 66.0 | Plan |
| | (279) | (254) | (1575) | (431) | (319) | (340) | Weighted N |
| 45-54 Only | 64.3 | 63.5 | 54.6 | 65.3 | 58.5 | 61.4 | Plan |
| | (258) | (263) | (1569) | (424) | (381) | (335) | Weighted N |
| 55-64 Only | 60.3 | 68.9 | 59.5 | 71.3 | 61.7 | 62.9 | Plan |
| | (184) | (235) | (1267) | (373) | (342) | (344) | Weighted N |
| 65-74 Only | 63.1 | 65.2 | 43.3 | 66.8 | 64.9 | 65.7 | Plan |
| | (149) | (158) | (984) | (262) | (262) | (260) | Weighted N |
| 75 And Older Only | 55.4 | 66.7 | 47.1 | 66.0 | 57.6 | 59.5 | Plan |
| | (65) | (81) | (543) | (147) | (144) | (158) | Weighted N |

Percentages based on content categories "Plan Ahead" and "Too Much Luck to Plan".

Table 1.14
Can R Run Own Life As Wanted?
Total Population

QUESTION: Some people feel they can run their own lives pretty much the way
they want to, others feel the problems of life are sometimes too big for them.
Which one are you most like?

| | | | Year | | | | |
|---|---|---|---|---|---|---|---|
| | 1968n | 1970n | 1971j | 1972n | 1974n | 1976h | 1976n |
| Can run own life (5) | 69.8% | 69.7% | 81.0% | 73.1% | 70.9% | 81.2% | 73.8% |
| Depends (3) | 2.2 | 1.4 | 1.2 | 0.8 | ** | 1.6 | ** |
| Problems of life too big (1) | 24.3 | 24.6 | 17.8 | 23.4 | 26.2 | 14.8 | 22.1 |
| Don't know | 3.8 | 4.3 | ** | 2.7 | 3.0 | 2.3 | 4.1 |
| Total | 100% | 100% | 100% | 100% | 100% | 100% | 100% |
| Weighted Total | 1343 | 1498 | 9476 | 2684 | 2450 | 4094 | 2392 |
| Unweighted Total | 1343 | 1498 | 2144 | 2684 | 1529 | 2237 | 1896 |
| Mean | 3.95 | 3.94 | 4.26 | 4.02 | 3.92 | 4.36 | 4.08 |
| Standard Deviation | 1.74 | 1.75 | 1.54 | 1.71 | 1.78 | 1.44 | 1.68 |

** Code distinction not made.

Table 1.15
Can R Run Own Life As Wanted?
Social Groups

% Run Own Life

| | 1968n | 1970n | 1971j | 1972n | 1974n | 1976h | 1976n | |
|---|---|---|---|---|---|---|---|---|
| | | | | Year | | | | |
| Males Only | 78.9% | 79.8% | 86.2% | 81.5% | 77.3% | 89.8% | 84.6% | Run own life |
| | (554) | (609) | (4455) | (1126) | (992) | (1773) | (951) | Weighted N |
| Females Only | 70.5 | 69.5 | 78.1 | 71.3 | 70.0 | 80.3 | 71.5 | Run own life |
| | (709) | (803) | (4908) | (1460) | (1385) | (2159) | (1343) | Weighted N |
| Whites Only | 77.3 | 77.6 | 83.6 | 78.3 | 75.4 | 86.4 | 79.6 | Run own life |
| | (1120) | (1259) | (8131) | (2306) | (2113) | (3434) | (2021) | Weighted N |
| Blacks Only | 48.0 | 40.2 | 68.0 | 51.0 | 51.4 | 72.1 | 51.6 | Run own life |
| | (127) | (132) | (969) | (245) | (214) | (387) | (204) | Weighted N |
| Grade School Only | 55.4 | 56.2 | 72.7 | 59.3 | 52.9 | 71.3 | 58.5 | Run own life |
| | (280) | (333) | (1990) | (501) | (444) | (613) | (349) | Weighted N |
| High School Only | 73.9 | 75.0 | 81.0 | 75.6 | 71.3 | 83.7 | 75.9 | Run own life |
| | (625) | (721) | (4799) | (1322) | (1204) | (1946) | (1145) | Weighted N |
| College Only | 89.6 | 88.7 | 90.9 | 87.0 | 88.1 | 91.7 | 86.9 | Run own life |
| | (357) | (355) | (2537) | (760) | (716) | (1354) | (793) | Weighted N |
| 18-24 Only | 86.7 | 73.9 | 85.5 | 76.5 | 82.2 | 90.0 | 79.7 | Run own life |
| | (98) | (142) | (1471) | (388) | (343) | (410) | (320) | Weighted N |
| 25-34 Only | 80.8 | 82.3 | 85.3 | 83.4 | 76.8 | 86.5 | 82.6 | Run own life |
| | (261) | (300) | (1881) | (559) | (556) | (1008) | (556) | Weighted N |
| 35-44 Only | 77.7 | 80.5 | 84.1 | 81.1 | 76.5 | 86.4 | 80.9 | Run own life |
| | (265) | (246) | (1608) | (429) | (323) | (668) | (336) | Weighted N |
| 45-54 Only | 77.1 | 72.1 | 80.2 | 73.9 | 72.0 | 80.9 | 80.6 | Run own life |
| | (253) | (262) | (1592) | (426) | (382) | (635) | (335) | Weighted N |
| 55-64 Only | 60.7 | 71.8 | 79.1 | 69.8 | 66.1 | 83.3 | 69.3 | Run own life |
| | (173) | (220) | (1268) | (361) | (345) | (615) | (334) | Weighted N |
| 65-74 Only | 64.6 | 61.8 | 75.3 | 63.8 | 66.5 | 82.9 | 70.3 | Run own life |
| | (147) | (157) | (986) | (260) | (254) | (410) | (255) | Weighted N |
| 75 And Older Only | 61.3 | 60.3 | 78.8 | 70.9 | 58.3 | 75.7 | 60.9 | Run own life |
| | (62) | (78) | (548) | (148) | (144) | (185) | (145) | Weighted N |

Percentages based on content categories "Can Run Own Life" and "Problems Too Big".

Table 1.16
Personal Competence Index
Total Population

|  | | Year | | | | | |
|---|---|---|---|---|---|---|---|
|  | | 1968n | 1970n | 1971j | 1972n | 1974n | 1976n |
| Least competent | (1) | 34.8% | 34.7% | 33.3% | 33.0% | 39.4% | 33.8% |
|  | (2) | 16.9 | 18.7 | 19.2 | 18.1 | 16.8 | 18.6 |
| Most competent | (3) | 48.3 | 46.6 | 47.6 | 48.9 | 43.8 | 47.6 |
| Total | | 100% | 100% | 100% | 100% | 100% | 100% |
| Weighted N | | 1291 | 1454 | 9344 | 2617 | 2428 | 2319 |
| Unweighted N | | 1291 | 1454 | 2113 | 2617 | 1520 | 1843 |
| Mean | | 2.14 | 2.12 | 2.14 | 2.16 | 2.04 | 2.14 |
| Standard Deviation | | 0.90 | 0.89 | 0.89 | 0.89 | 0.91 | 0.89 |

Index constructed from items displayed in Tables 1.6,1.10,1.12,and 1.14.

Figure 1.8
Personal Competence Index--Total Population

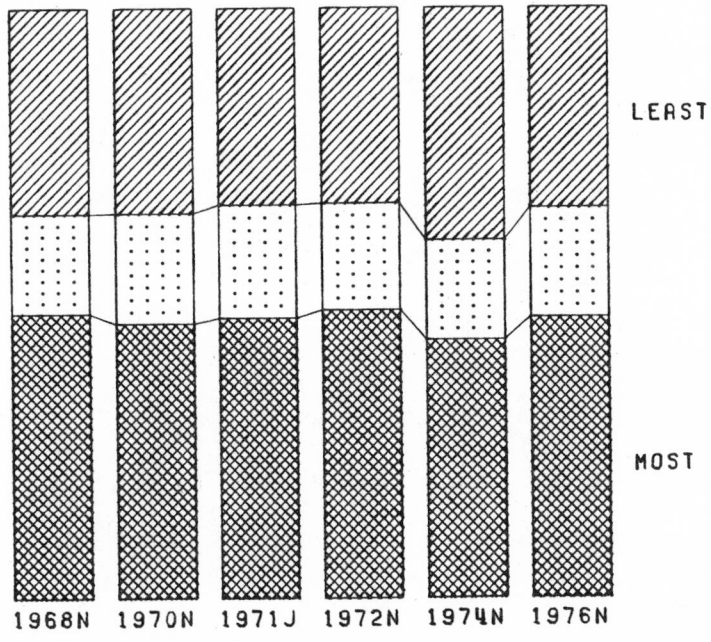

LEAST

MOST

1968N  1970N  1971J  1972N  1974N  1976N

Figure 1.9
Personal Competence Items  (from Tables 1.6,1.10,1.12,and 1.14)

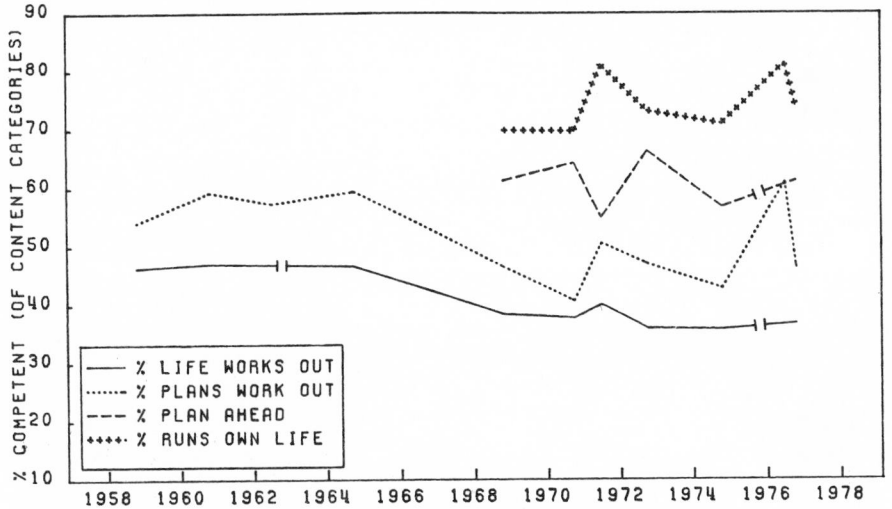

% COMPETENT (OF CONTENT CATEGORIES)

— % LIFE WORKS OUT
...... % PLANS WORK OUT
--- % PLAN AHEAD
++++ % RUNS OWN LIFE

Attitudes toward Self And Others

Table 1.17
Personal Competence Index
Sex of Respondent

|  | Year | | | | | | |
|---|---|---|---|---|---|---|---|
|  | 1968n | 1970n | 1971j | 1972n | 1974n | 1976n | |
| Males Only | 28.8% | 30.5% | 29.1% | 28.6% | 34.0% | 25.7% | Least competent |
|  | 18.5 | 19.9 | 21.3 | 20.3 | 19.3 | 20.9 | |
|  | 52.7 | 49.6 | 49.6 | 51.1 | 46.6 | 53.4 | Most competent |
|  | (562) | (627) | (4460) | (1135) | (1014) | (951) | Weighted N |
| Females Only | 39.4 | 38.0 | 37.0 | 36.3 | 43.3 | 39.4 | Least competent |
|  | 15.6 | 17.8 | 17.2 | 16.5 | 14.9 | 17.1 | |
|  | 45.0 | 44.3 | 45.8 | 47.2 | 41.8 | 43.6 | Most competent |
|  | (729) | (827) | (4884) | (1482) | (1414) | (1368) | Weighted N |

Table 1.18
Race of Respondent

|  | 1968n | 1970n | 1971j | 1972n | 1974n | 1976n | |
|---|---|---|---|---|---|---|---|
| Whites Only | 32.4% | 31.8% | 31.4% | 31.1% | 37.6% | 31.6% | Least competent |
|  | 17.1 | 18.9 | 19.2 | 17.8 | 17.1 | 18.5 | |
|  | 50.5 | 49.3 | 49.4 | 51.1 | 45.3 | 50.0 | Most competent |
|  | (1149) | (1296) | (8112) | (2326) | (2159) | (2048) | Weighted N |
| Blacks Only | 56.3 | 60.3 | 47.1 | 50.4 | 57.5 | 51.8 | Least competent |
|  | 13.5 | 16.9 | 19.7 | 20.5 | 13.2 | 17.7 | |
|  | 30.2 | 22.8 | 33.2 | 29.1 | 29.2 | 30.5 | Most competent |
|  | (126) | (136) | (960) | (254) | (219) | (204) | Weighted N |

Figure 1.10
Personal Competence by Sex of R

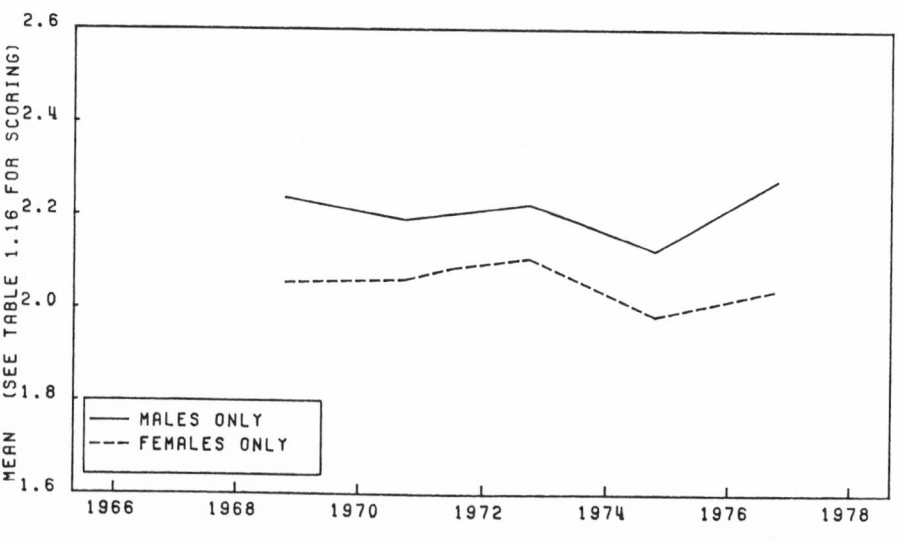

Figure 1.11
Personal Competence by Race of R

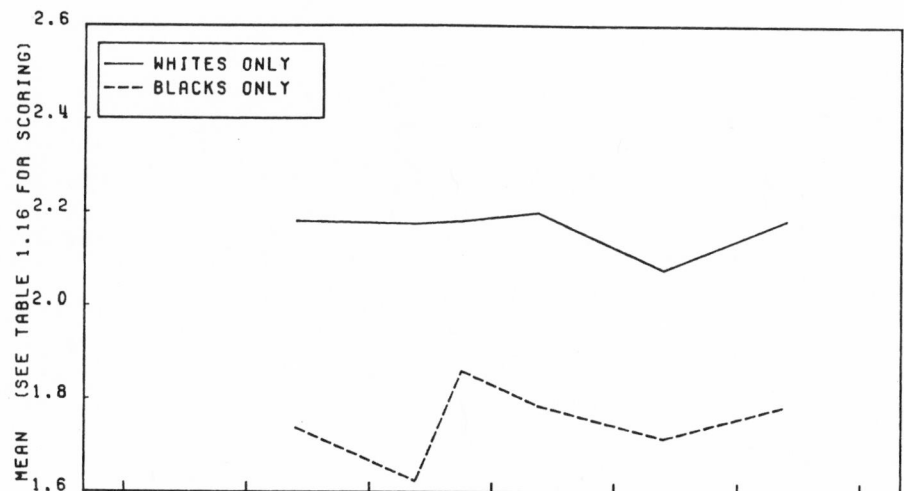

Attitudes toward Self And Others

Table 1.19
Personal Competence Index
Education of Respondent

|  | Year | | | | | | |
|---|---|---|---|---|---|---|---|
|  | 1968n | 1970n | 1971j | 1972n | 1974n | 1976n | |
| Grade School Only | 55.0% | 56.1% | 49.3% | 53.8% | 60.0% | 51.2% | Least competent |
|  | 12.0 | 15.1 | 16.3 | 11.0 | 13.5 | 14.0 | |
|  | 33.0 | 28.8 | 34.3 | 35.2 | 26.5 | 34.7 | Most competent |
|  | (291) | (344) | (1960) | (509) | (445) | (346) | Weighted N |
| High School Only | 38.2 | 33.8 | 33.4 | 34.1 | 42.5 | 38.6 | Least competent |
|  | 17.3 | 20.1 | 19.6 | 19.3 | 16.8 | 19.1 | |
|  | 44.5 | 46.1 | 47.0 | 46.6 | 40.7 | 42.3 | Most competent |
|  | (631) | (748) | (4760) | (1331) | (1232) | (1156) | Weighted N |
| College Only | 12.8 | 15.7 | 21.0 | 17.3 | 22.5 | 19.2 | Least competent |
|  | 20.1 | 19.3 | 20.8 | 20.6 | 18.5 | 20.0 | |
|  | 67.1 | 65.0 | 58.3 | 62.1 | 59.0 | 60.8 | Most competent |
|  | (368) | (357) | (2583) | (775) | (739) | (809) | Weighted N |

Figure 1.12
Personal Competence by Education of R

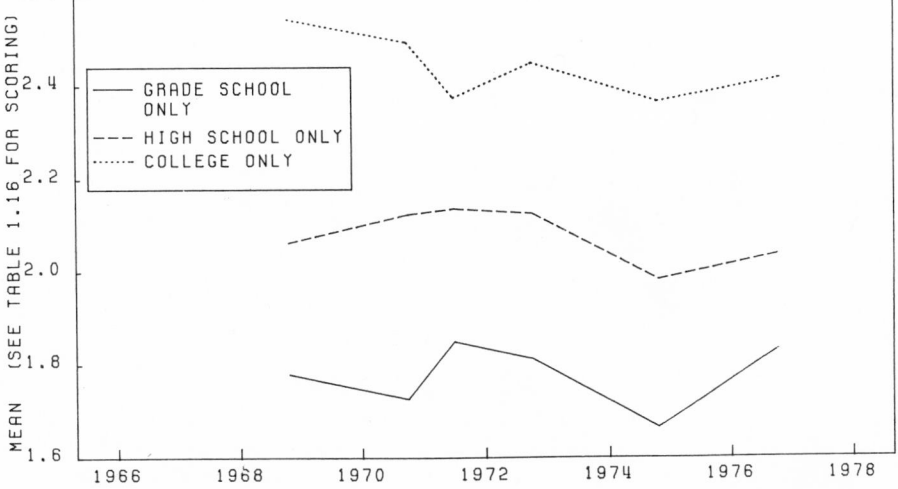

Figure 1.13
Personal Competence by Age of R

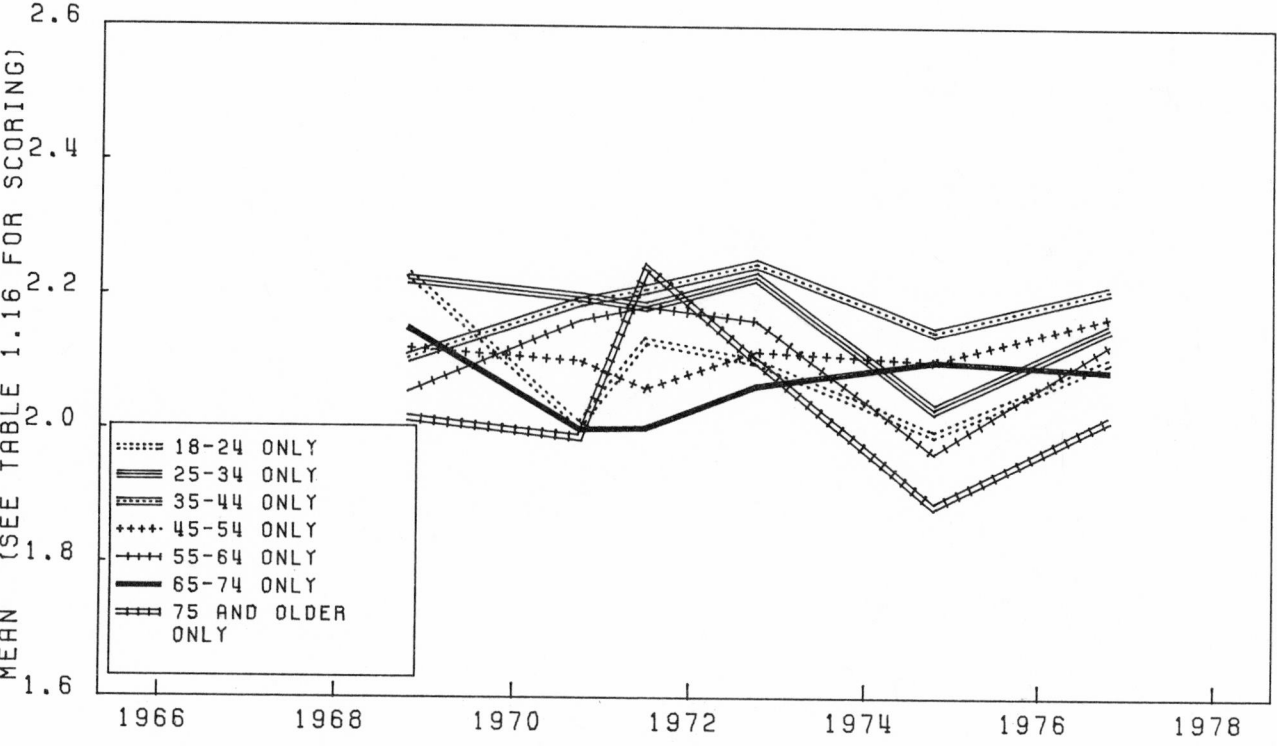

Attitudes toward Self And Others

Table 1.20
Personal Competence Index
Age of Respondent

|  | Year | | | | | | |
|---|---|---|---|---|---|---|---|
|  | 1968n | 1970n | 1971j | 1972n | 1974n | 1976n | |
| 18–24 Only | 30.0% | 37.0% | 33.3% | 36.1% | 39.1% | 34.3% | Least competent |
|  | 17.0 | 25.3 | 20.2 | 17.6 | 22.3 | 20.9 | |
|  | 53.0 | 37.7 | 46.5 | 46.3 | 38.5 | 44.8 | Most competent |
|  | (100) | (146) | (1462) | (391) | (358) | (331) | Weighted N |
| 25–34 Only | 28.4 | 30.7 | 30.2 | 28.2 | 40.1 | 32.8 | Least competent |
|  | 21.1 | 18.8 | 21.2 | 20.9 | 16.6 | 19.3 | |
|  | 50.6 | 50.5 | 48.6 | 50.9 | 43.3 | 48.0 | Most competent |
|  | (261) | (309) | (1901) | (564) | (573) | (548) | Weighted N |
| 35–44 Only | 36.1 | 28.2 | 30.2 | 28.4 | 35.0 | 30.5 | Least competent |
|  | 17.3 | 24.6 | 18.7 | 18.5 | 15.5 | 18.1 | |
|  | 46.6 | 47.2 | 51.1 | 53.1 | 49.5 | 51.4 | Most competent |
|  | (277) | (252) | (1612) | (437) | (329) | (340) | Weighted N |
| 45–54 Only | 35.7 | 37.0 | 36.7 | 34.5 | 37.7 | 31.8 | Least competent |
|  | 16.7 | 15.8 | 20.4 | 19.4 | 14.5 | 19.7 | |
|  | 47.7 | 47.2 | 42.8 | 46.1 | 47.8 | 48.5 | Most competent |
|  | (258) | (265) | (1592) | (432) | (393) | (340) | Weighted N |
| 55–64 Only | 40.3 | 34.6 | 30.6 | 34.2 | 42.5 | 35.1 | Least competent |
|  | 13.8 | 14.5 | 20.6 | 15.4 | 18.5 | 17.1 | |
|  | 45.9 | 50.9 | 48.8 | 50.4 | 39.0 | 47.8 | Most competent |
|  | (181) | (234) | (1269) | (371) | (346) | (343) | Weighted N |
| 65–74 Only | 34.7 | 42.8 | 43.3 | 38.9 | 36.6 | 36.7 | Least competent |
|  | 15.6 | 14.5 | 13.1 | 15.6 | 16.6 | 17.8 | |
|  | 49.7 | 42.8 | 43.5 | 45.4 | 46.8 | 45.5 | Most competent |
|  | (147) | (159) | (981) | (262) | (265) | (256) | Weighted N |
| 75 And Older Only | 43.8 | 41.5 | 30.8 | 37.7 | 50.0 | 42.0 | Least competent |
|  | 10.9 | 18.3 | 14.3 | 14.4 | 11.4 | 14.3 | |
|  | 45.3 | 40.2 | 54.9 | 47.9 | 38.6 | 43.7 | Most competent |
|  | (64) | (82) | (523) | (146) | (140) | (147) | Weighted N |

Table 1.21
Subjective Social Class
Total Population

QUESTION: There's been some talk these days about different social classes. Most people say they belong either to the middle class or to the working class.  Do you ever think of yourself as belonging in one of these classes? (IF YES) Which one? (IF NO OR DON'T KNOW) Well, if you had to make a choice, would you call yourself middle class or working class?

|  |  | 1952n | 1956n | 1958n | 1960n | 1964n | 1966n | 1968n | 1970n | 1972n | 1974n | 1976n | 1978n |
|---|---|---|---|---|---|---|---|---|---|---|---|---|---|
| Lower | (1) | 2.2% | 0.1% | 0.1% | ** | 0.1% | ** | 0.2% | 0.3% | 0.3% | 0.1% | 0.2% | 0.0% |
| Working | (2) | 59.0 | 61.0 | 60.0 | 65.3 | 55.8 | 58.1 | 53.6 | 52.8 | 54.2 | 54.0 | 51.8 | 52.3 |
| Middle | (3) | 35.5 | 35.9 | 38.4 | 32.1 | 40.0 | 39.7 | 43.5 | 46.2 | 44.5 | 44.8 | 45.5 | 46.9 |
| Upper | (4) | 1.7 | 0.2 | 0.1 | 0.1 | 0.6 | 0.4 | ** | 0.1 | 0.1 | ** | 0.1 | 0.1 |
| Other |  | 1.5 | 2.9 | 1.4 | 2.5 | 3.5 | 1.8 | 2.7 | 0.6 | 1.0 | 1.2 | 2.5 | 0.6 |
| Total |  | 100% | 100% | 100% | 100% | 100% | 100% | 100% | 100% | 100% | 100% | 100% | 100% |
| Weighted N |  | 1762 | 1748 | 1783 | 1910 | 4276 | 1275 | 3071 | 1825 | 2649 | 2414 | 2824 | 2222 |
| Unweighted N |  | 1762 | 1748 | 1421 | 1150 | 1679 | 1275 | 1656 | 1649 | 2649 | 1506 | 2212 | 2222 |
| Mean |  | 2.37 | 2.37 | 2.39 | 2.33 | 2.43 | 2.41 | 2.44 | 2.46 | 2.45 | 2.45 | 2.46 | 2.47 |
| Standard Deviation |  | 0.56 | 0.49 | 0.49 | 0.47 | 0.51 | 0.50 | 0.50 | 0.51 | 0.50 | 0.50 | 0.50 | 0.50 |

** Code distinction not made.
1964n,1968n,and 1970n include Black supplement.
"Other" includes "Don't know", "Refused, rejected idea of class" and "Other".
The 1952n question text offered "Lower" and "Upper" in addition to "Working" and "Middle".

Figure 1.14
Social Class--Total Population

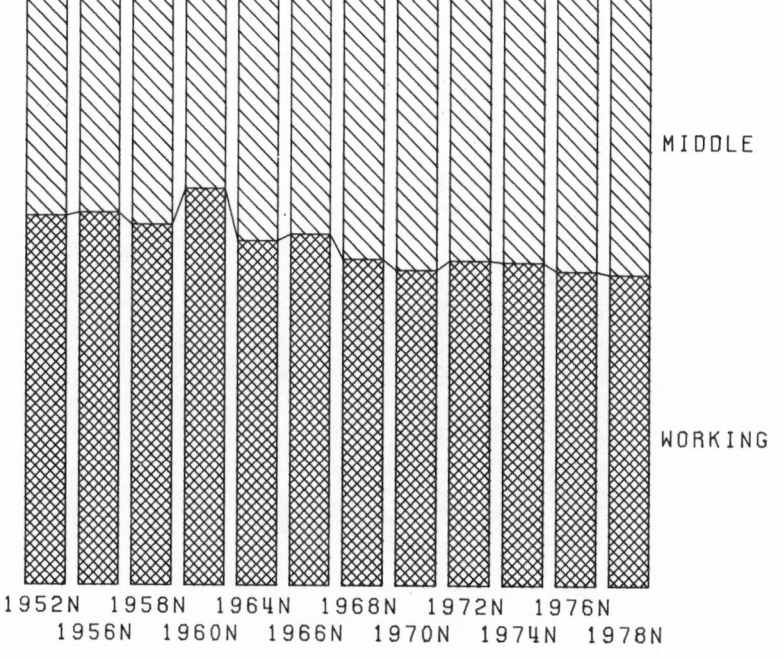

Figure 1.15
Social Class by Race of R

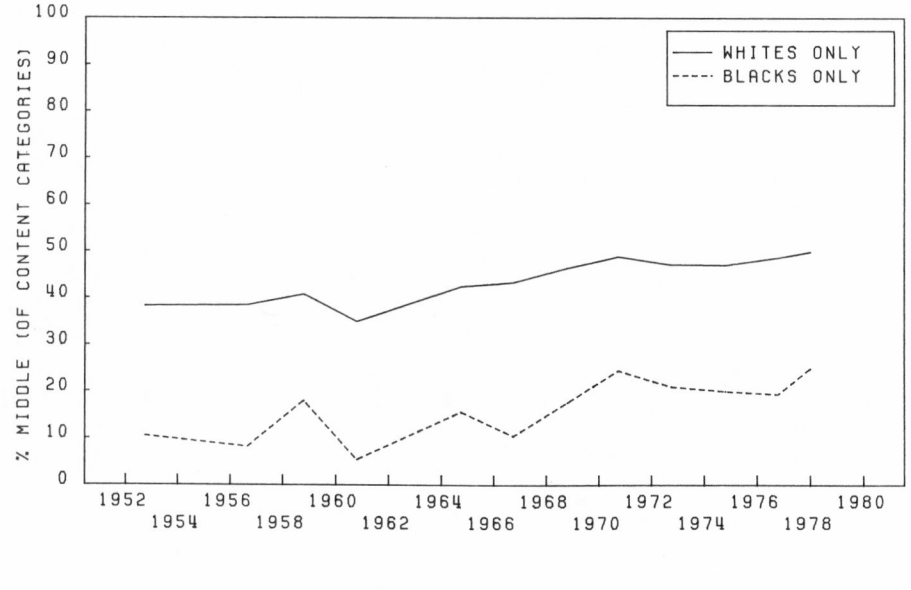

Table 1.22
Subjective Social Class
Sex of Respondent

|            |       |       |       |       |       | Year  |       |       |       |       |       |       |            |
|------------|-------|-------|-------|-------|-------|-------|-------|-------|-------|-------|-------|-------|------------|
|            | 1952n | 1956n | 1958n | 1960n | 1964n | 1966n | 1968n | 1970n | 1972n | 1974n | 1976n | 1978n |            |
| Males Only | 2.3%  | 0.0%  | 0.0%  | **    | 0.2%  | **    | 0.5%  | 0.4%  | 0.1%  | 0.0%  | 0.3%  | 0.1%  | Lower      |
|            | 62.6  | 62.6  | 63.3  | 69.8  | 58.7  | 61.3  | 58.3  | 57.0  | 56.8  | 57.4  | 56.7  | 55.8  | Working    |
|            | 33.5  | 37.4  | 36.6  | 30.2  | 40.6  | 38.4  | 41.2  | 42.5  | 43.1  | 42.6  | 43.0  | 44.1  | Middle     |
|            | 1.6   | 0.0   | 0.1   | 0.0   | 0.5   | 0.4   | **    | 0.2   | 0.0   | **    | 0.0   | 0.0   | Upper      |
|            | (797) | (759) | (826) | (858) | (1844)| (558) | (1305)| (796) | (1143)| (1017)| (1161)| (991) | Weighted N |
| Females Only | 2.2 | 0.1   | 0.1   | **    | 0.0   | **    | 0.0   | 0.3   | 0.4   | 0.1   | 0.2   | 0.0   | Lower      |
|            | 57.7  | 62.9  | 58.7  | 64.5  | 57.1  | 57.5  | 52.6  | 50.0  | 53.1  | 52.5  | 50.3  | 50.1  | Working    |
|            | 38.3  | 36.6  | 41.1  | 35.3  | 42.2  | 42.1  | 47.4  | 49.6  | 46.4  | 47.3  | 49.4  | 49.8  | Middle     |
|            | 1.8   | 0.3   | 0.1   | 0.2   | 0.7   | 0.4   | **    | 0.1   | 0.1   | **    | 0.1   | 0.2   | Upper      |
|            | (938) | (939) | (932) | (1005)| (2282)| (694) | (1683)| (1019)| (1480)| (1369)| (1587)| (1218)| W          |

Table 1.23
Race of Respondent

|             |       |       |       |       |       |       |       |       |       |       |       |       |            |
|-------------|-------|-------|-------|-------|-------|-------|-------|-------|-------|-------|-------|-------|------------|
|             | 1952n | 1956n | 1958n | 1960n | 1964n | 1966n | 1968n | 1970n | 1972n | 1974n | 1976n | 1978n |            |
| Whites Only | 1.5%  | 0.1%  | 0.1%  | **    | 0.1%  | **    | 0.1%  | 0.0%  | 0.1%  | 0.0%  | 0.2%  | 0.0%  | Lower      |
|             | 58.0  | 60.1  | 58.4  | 64.0  | 55.2  | 55.3  | 52.1  | 50.7  | 52.2  | 52.4  | 49.8  | 49.6  | Working    |
|             | 38.8  | 39.7  | 41.4  | 35.8  | 44.1  | 44.2  | 47.7  | 49.2  | 47.6  | 47.6  | 50.0  | 50.3  | Middle     |
|             | 1.7   | 0.2   | 0.1   | 0.1   | 0.6   | 0.5   | **    | 0.1   | 0.1   | **    | 0.1   | 0.1   | Upper      |
|             | (1561)| (1547)| (1583)| (1685)| (3726)| (1103)| (2682)| (1622)| (2328)| (2133)| (2399)| (1937)| Weighted N |
| Blacks Only | 9.6   | 0.0   | 0.0   | **    | 0.0   | **    | 0.8   | 3.6   | 1.2   | 0.5   | 0.4   | 0.5   | Lower      |
|             | 77.2  | 91.7  | 81.6  | 94.5  | 84.1  | 89.4  | 80.8  | 71.9  | 77.6  | 79.1  | 80.0  | 74.7  | Working    |
|             | 10.8  | 8.3   | 18.4  | 5.5   | 15.9  | 10.6  | 18.4  | 24.5  | 21.3  | 20.4  | 19.7  | 24.9  | Middle     |
|             | 2.4   | 0.0   | 0.0   | 0.0   | 0.0   | 0.0   | **    | 0.0   | 0.0   | **    | 0.0   | 0.0   | Upper      |
|             | (167) | (145) | (158) | (164) | (370) | (132) | (266) | (164) | (254) | (206) | (277) | (221) | Weighted N |

** Code distinction not made.

Attitudes toward Self And Others

Table 1.24
Subjective Social Class
Education of Respondent

|  | | | | | | | Year | | | | | | |
|---|---|---|---|---|---|---|---|---|---|---|---|---|---|
|  | 1952n | 1956n | 1958n | 1960n | 1964n | 1966n | 1968n | 1970n | 1972n | 1974n | 1976n | 1978n | |
| Grade School Only | 3.5% | 0.0% | 0.0% | ** | 0.0% | ** | 0.4% | 1.0% | 0.2% | 0.2% | 0.7% | 0.4% | Lower |
| | 71.6 | 83.1 | 80.0 | 85.4 | 82.1 | 81.2 | 76.5 | 76.0 | 76.8 | 79.7 | 74.9 | 73.3 | Working |
| | 23.7 | 16.9 | 20.0 | 14.6 | 17.6 | 18.5 | 23.1 | 23.0 | 23.0 | 20.1 | 24.4 | 26.4 | Middle |
| | 1.1 | 0.0 | 0.0 | 0.0 | 0.3 | 0.3 | ** | 0.0 | 0.0 | ** | 0.0 | 0.0 | Upper |
| | (708) | (520) | (521) | (567) | (1026) | (324) | (676) | (419) | (512) | (418) | (443) | (258) | Weighted N |
| High School Only | 1.7 | 0.1 | 0.1 | ** | 0.1 | ** | 0.1 | 0.2 | 0.4 | 0.0 | 0.1 | 0.0 | Lower |
| | 60.7 | 63.4 | 64.0 | 72.9 | 61.0 | 63.9 | 61.6 | 56.8 | 61.0 | 61.3 | 60.9 | 63.1 | Working |
| | 36.0 | 36.1 | 35.7 | 26.8 | 38.7 | 36.1 | 38.3 | 42.8 | 38.6 | 38.7 | 39.1 | 36.9 | Middle |
| | 1.6 | 0.4 | 0.1 | 0.2 | 0.1 | 0.0 | ** | 0.1 | 0.0 | ** | 0.0 | 0.0 | Upper |
| | (769) | (853) | (865) | (887) | (2122) | (632) | (1498) | (931) | (1347) | (1203) | (1385) | (1164) | Weighted N |
| College Only | 0.4 | 0.0 | 0.0 | ** | 0.0 | ** | 0.1 | 0.0 | 0.1 | 0.1 | 0.3 | 0.0 | Lower |
| | 25.3 | 28.3 | 25.8 | 28.2 | 24.0 | 25.0 | 25.3 | 24.4 | 28.9 | 29.2 | 30.6 | 30.2 | Working |
| | 70.8 | 71.7 | 73.9 | 71.8 | 74.1 | 73.6 | 74.6 | 75.4 | 70.7 | 70.7 | 68.9 | 69.5 | Middle |
| | 3.6 | 0.0 | 0.3 | 0.0 | 1.9 | 1.4 | ** | 0.3 | 0.3 | ** | 0.2 | 0.3 | Upper |
| | (253) | (318) | (357) | (408) | (954) | (296) | (811) | (460) | (762) | (744) | (919) | (784) | Weighted N |

** Code distinction not made.

Figure 1.16
Social Class by Education of R

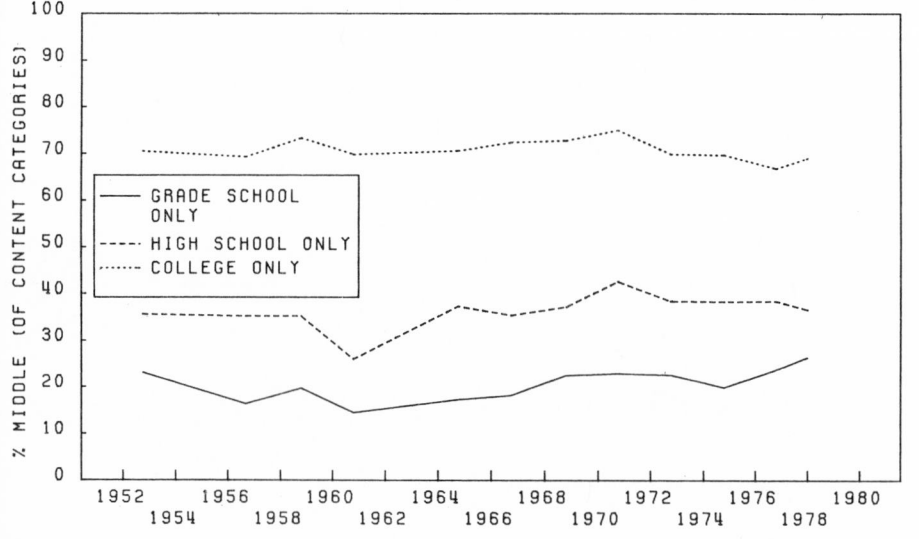

Figure 1.17
Social Class by Income of R

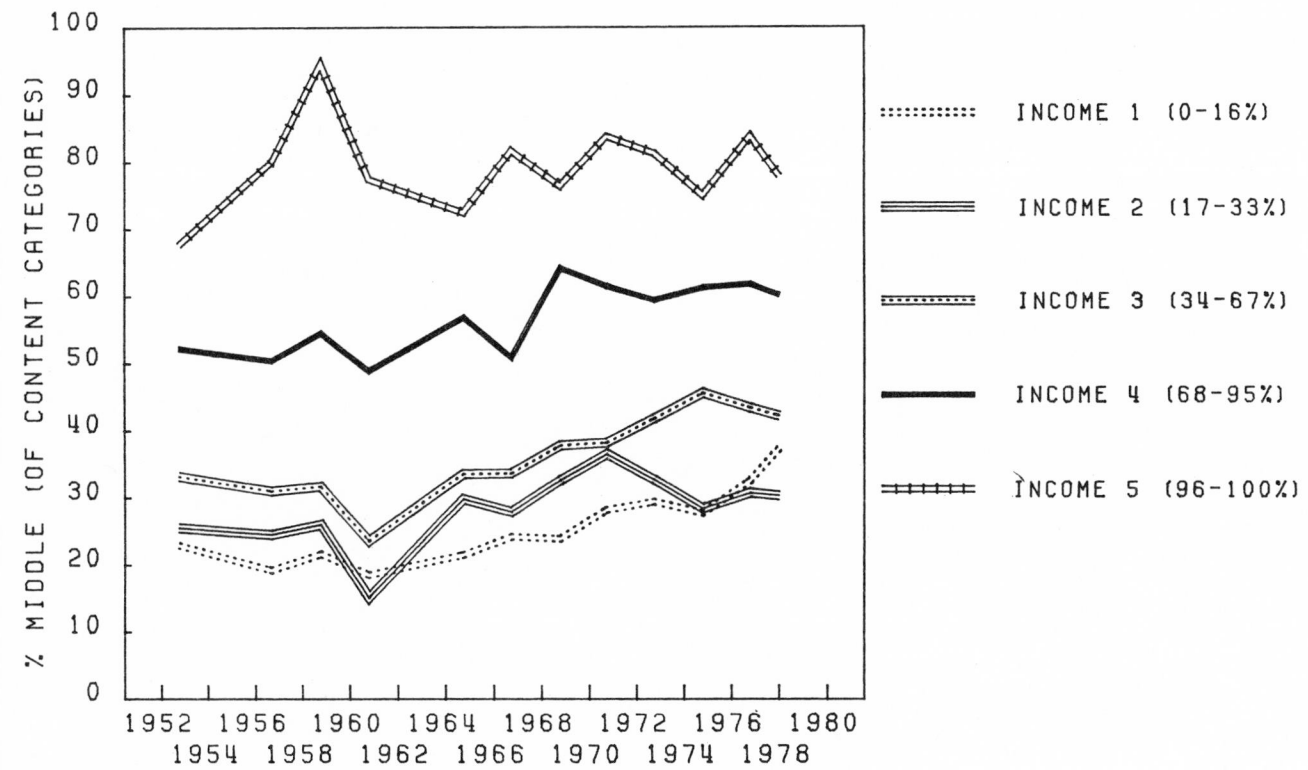

Table 1.25
Subjective Social Class
Age of Respondent

| | 1952n | 1956n | 1958n | 1960n | 1964n | 1966n | 1968n | 1970n | 1972n | 1974n | 1976n | 1978n | |
|---|---|---|---|---|---|---|---|---|---|---|---|---|---|
| | | | | | | | | | | | | Year | |
| 18-24 Only | 4.4% | 0.0% | 1.1% | ** | 0.0% | ** | 0.0% | 0.2% | 0.0% | 0.0% | 0.0% | 0.0% | Lower |
| | 67.5 | 68.9 | 67.8 | 62.1 | 63.3 | 51.3 | 43.3 | 47.6 | 54.0 | 54.4 | 56.5 | 51.6 | Working |
| | 28.1 | 31.1 | 31.0 | 37.9 | 36.7 | 48.7 | 56.7 | 52.2 | 46.0 | 45.6 | 43.5 | 48.4 | Middle |
| | 0.0 | 0.0 | 0.0 | 0.0 | 0.0 | 0.0 | ** | 0.0 | 0.0 | ** | 0.0 | 0.0 | Upper |
| | (114) | (106) | (87) | (58) | (294) | (117) | (224) | (247) | (385) | (355) | (377) | (347) | Weighted N |
| 25-34 Only | 2.2 | 0.0 | 0.0 | ** | 0.0 | ** | 0.3 | 1.7 | 0.4 | 0.0 | 0.4 | 0.0 | Lower |
| | 62.2 | 64.2 | 62.1 | 75.3 | 54.4 | 56.9 | 51.5 | 46.7 | 51.9 | 50.4 | 53.6 | 51.7 | Working |
| | 34.2 | 35.8 | 37.9 | 24.7 | 44.9 | 42.2 | 48.2 | 51.6 | 47.7 | 49.6 | 46.0 | 48.3 | Middle |
| | 1.4 | 0.0 | 0.0 | 0.0 | 0.7 | 0.9 | ** | 0.0 | 0.0 | ** | 0.0 | 0.0 | Upper |
| | (418) | (413) | (391) | (389) | (858) | (225) | (596) | (359) | (566) | (563) | (676) | (532) | Weighted N |
| 35-44 Only | 1.9 | 0.0 | 0.0 | ** | 0.3 | ** | 0.2 | 1.9 | 0.2 | 0.0 | 0.2 | 0.0 | Lower |
| | 68.0 | 61.0 | 60.6 | 60.3 | 53.2 | 54.6 | 52.0 | 53.6 | 49.9 | 51.9 | 50.5 | 55.2 | Working |
| | 29.2 | 38.7 | 39.4 | 39.7 | 46.2 | 45.4 | 47.8 | 44.6 | 49.4 | 48.1 | 49.3 | 44.8 | Middle |
| | 1.0 | 0.2 | 0.0 | 0.0 | 0.3 | 0.0 | ** | 0.0 | 0.5 | ** | 0.0 | 0.0 | Upper |
| | (415) | (431) | (459) | (468) | (935) | (273) | (621) | (320) | (429) | (322) | (414) | (391) | Weighted N |
| 45-54 Only | 0.7 | 0.0 | 0.0 | ** | 0.0 | ** | 0.2 | 1.9 | 0.7 | 0.5 | 0.0 | 0.3 | Lower |
| | 58.7 | 61.5 | 61.2 | 60.4 | 61.3 | 66.5 | 54.4 | 57.0 | 56.7 | 56.8 | 43.9 | 50.9 | Working |
| | 38.9 | 38.5 | 38.8 | 39.6 | 38.4 | 33.5 | 45.4 | 40.8 | 42.7 | 42.7 | 55.7 | 48.8 | Middle |
| | 1.7 | 0.0 | 0.0 | 0.0 | 0.4 | 0.0 | ** | 0.4 | 0.0 | ** | 0.4 | 0.0 | Upper |
| | (303) | (317) | (343) | (374) | (821) | (251) | (608) | (318) | (436) | (396) | (391) | (322) | Weighted N |
| 55-64 Only | 4.6 | 0.0 | 0.0 | ** | 0.0 | ** | 0.5 | 0.2 | 0.0 | 0.0 | 0.4 | 0.0 | Lower |
| | 50.6 | 61.5 | 64.6 | 73.1 | 63.0 | 60.0 | 61.5 | 56.5 | 59.4 | 56.5 | 56.1 | 55.6 | Working |
| | 43.6 | 38.0 | 35.0 | 26.9 | 35.6 | 39.4 | 38.1 | 43.3 | 40.6 | 43.5 | 43.5 | 44.1 | Middle |
| | 1.2 | 0.5 | 0.4 | 0.0 | 1.5 | 0.6 | ** | 0.0 | 0.0 | ** | 0.0 | 0.3 | Upper |
| | (241) | (221) | (246) | (290) | (616) | (170) | (444) | (290) | (374) | (331) | (393) | (295) | Weighted N |
| 65-74 Only | 1.9 | 0.0 | 0.0 | ** | 0.0 | ** | 0.0 | 0.6 | 0.0 | 0.0 | 0.5 | 0.0 | Lower |
| | 49.7 | 64.4 | 48.1 | 67.7 | 53.0 | 60.7 | 63.7 | 57.9 | 58.4 | 61.0 | 56.5 | 49.8 | Working |
| | 43.9 | 35.6 | 51.3 | 31.3 | 46.2 | 38.7 | 36.3 | 40.8 | 41.6 | 39.0 | 43.0 | 50.2 | Middle |
| | 4.5 | 0.0 | 0.6 | 1.0 | 0.7 | 0.7 | ** | 0.6 | 0.0 | ** | 0.0 | 0.0 | Upper |
| | (155) | (132) | (156) | (198) | (411) | (150) | (339) | (187) | (269) | (264) | (314) | (201) | Weighted N |
| 75 And Older Only | 1.5 | 0.0 | 0.0 | ** | 0.0 | ** | 0.0 | 1.2 | 0.0 | 0.0 | 0.0 | 0.0 | Lower |
| | 42.4 | 69.0 | 60.5 | 73.2 | 67.6 | 66.7 | 66.0 | 46.2 | 56.3 | 56.8 | 58.4 | 60.2 | Working |
| | 48.5 | 31.0 | 39.5 | 26.8 | 32.4 | 31.7 | 34.0 | 52.7 | 43.8 | 43.2 | 41.6 | 38.8 | Middle |
| | 7.6 | 0.0 | 0.0 | 0.0 | 0.0 | 1.7 | ** | 0.0 | 0.0 | ** | 0.0 | 1.0 | Upper |
| | (66) | (58) | (76) | (82) | (182) | (60) | (147) | (101) | (144) | (132) | (173) | (103) | Weighted N |

** Code distinction not made.

Attitudes toward Self And Others

Table 1.26
Subjective Social Class
Income of Respondent

|  | Year | | | | | | | | | | | | |
| --- | 1952n | 1956n | 1958n | 1960n | 1964n | 1966n | 1968n | 1970n | 1972n | 1974n | 1976n | 1978n | |
| Income 1 (0-16%) | 5.1% | 0.4% | 0.0% | ** | 0.4% | ** | 0.6% | 1.9% | 0.8% | 0.4% | 0.5% | 0.0% | Lower |
|  | 69.9 | 79.6 | 77.4 | 81.2 | 77.8 | 74.7 | 74.7 | 69.6 | 69.4 | 71.7 | 66.4 | 62.6 | Working |
|  | 23.5 | 20.0 | 22.2 | 18.8 | 21.9 | 24.7 | 24.6 | 28.5 | 29.8 | 27.9 | 33.1 | 37.4 | Middle |
|  | 1.5 | 0.0 | 0.4 | 0.0 | 0.0 | 0.6 | ** | 0.0 | 0.0 | ** | 0.0 | 0.0 | Upper |
|  | (336) | (260) | (261) | (271) | (787) | (154) | (463) | (247) | (480) | (495) | (478) | (318) | Weighted N |
| Income 2 (17-33%) | 4.5 | 0.0 | 0.3 | ** | 0.0 | ** | 0.0 | 0.2 | 0.4 | 0.0 | 0.5 | 0.0 | Lower |
|  | 69.0 | 74.9 | 73.2 | 84.4 | 69.4 | 71.9 | 66.8 | 63.3 | 66.4 | 71.3 | 68.3 | 69.7 | Working |
|  | 26.1 | 25.1 | 26.5 | 15.6 | 30.6 | 28.1 | 33.2 | 36.5 | 33.0 | 28.7 | 31.2 | 30.3 | Middle |
|  | 0.4 | 0.0 | 0.0 | 0.0 | 0.0 | 0.0 | ** | 0.0 | 0.2 | ** | 0.0 | 0.0 | Upper |
|  | (268) | (367) | (358) | (327) | (725) | (203) | (395) | (262) | (449) | (317) | (477) | (346) | Weighted N |
| Income 3 (34-67%) | 1.1 | 0.0 | 0.0 | ** | 0.0 | ** | 0.2 | 0.1 | 0.1 | 0.0 | 0.0 | 0.0 | Lower |
|  | 64.1 | 68.0 | 68.0 | 75.8 | 64.7 | 65.1 | 61.1 | 61.5 | 57.7 | 54.2 | 55.5 | 57.6 | Working |
|  | 33.5 | 32.0 | 32.0 | 24.2 | 35.1 | 34.4 | 38.7 | 38.4 | 42.2 | 45.8 | 44.5 | 42.3 | Middle |
|  | 1.2 | 0.0 | 0.0 | 0.0 | 0.3 | 0.5 | ** | 0.0 | 0.0 | ** | 0.0 | 0.2 | Upper |
|  | (644) | (510) | (484) | (524) | (1027) | (393) | (1141) | (577) | (803) | (799) | (851) | (608) | Weighted N |
| Income 4 (68-95%) | 0.8 | 0.0 | 0.0 | ** | 0.0 | ** | 0.0 | 0.0 | 0.0 | 0.0 | 0.0 | 0.0 | Lower |
|  | 44.6 | 48.5 | 44.9 | 49.4 | 40.3 | 47.7 | 33.8 | 37.9 | 40.5 | 37.9 | 36.3 | 39.4 | Working |
|  | 52.2 | 51.5 | 54.9 | 50.3 | 59.0 | 52.1 | 66.2 | 61.9 | 59.5 | 62.1 | 63.7 | 60.6 | Middle |
|  | 2.3 | 0.0 | 0.2 | 0.3 | 0.8 | 0.3 | ** | 0.2 | 0.0 | ** | 0.0 | 0.0 | Upper |
|  | (383) | (371) | (528) | (636) | (1175) | (390) | (761) | (598) | (687) | (557) | (618) | (523) | Weighted N |
| Income 5 (96-100%) | 0.0 | 0.0 | 0.0 | ** | 0.0 | ** | 0.6 | 0.0 | 0.0 | 0.0 | 0.0 | 0.0 | Lower |
|  | 20.6 | 16.9 | 5.4 | 21.7 | 19.4 | 18.3 | 21.9 | 14.4 | 16.7 | 25.0 | 15.2 | 20.3 | Working |
|  | 69.8 | 82.3 | 94.6 | 78.3 | 77.3 | 81.7 | 77.4 | 83.8 | 82.5 | 75.0 | 84.8 | 79.0 | Middle |
|  | 9.5 | 0.8 | 0.0 | 0.0 | 3.3 | 0.0 | ** | 1.8 | 0.8 | ** | 0.0 | 0.7 | Upper |
|  | (63) | (130) | (56) | (83) | (273) | (71) | (155) | (67) | (126) | (88) | (135) | (143) | Weighted N |

** Code distinction not made.

Table 1.27
Generally Speaking, Can Most People Be Trusted?
Total Population

QUESTION: Generally speaking, would you say that most people can be trusted, or that
you can't be too careful in dealing with people?

|  |  | 1964n | 1966n | 1968n | 1971j | 1972n | 1973i | 1974n | 1976n |
|---|---|---|---|---|---|---|---|---|---|
| Most can be trusted | (5) | 53.8% | 52.9% | 55.5% | 48.5% | 45.8% | 45.3% | 46.6% | 51.3% |
| Depends | (3) | 1.4 | 1.0 | 1.7 | 1.5 | ** | ** | ** | ** |
| Can't be too careful | (1) | 44.2 | 45.6 | 42.9 | 50.0 | 52.4 | 54.3 | 52.1 | 45.9 |
| Don't know |  | 0.5 | 0.5 | ** | ** | 1.8 | 0.4 | 1.3 | 2.8 |
| Total |  | 100% | 100% | 100% | 100% | 100% | 100% | 100% | 100% |
| Weighted Total |  | 4276 | 1284 | 2663 | 9547 | 2179 | 2777 | 2486 | 2400 |
| Unweighted Total |  | 1679 | 1284 | 1436 | 2161 | 2179 | 1421 | 1556 | 1907 |
| Mean |  | 3.19 | 3.15 | 3.25 | 2.97 | 2.87 | 2.82 | 2.89 | 3.11 |
| Standard Deviation |  | 1.98 | 1.98 | 1.97 | 1.98 | 2.00 | 1.99 | 2.00 | 2.00 |

** Code distinction not made.
1964n and 1968n include Black supplement.

Figure 1.18                                          Figure 1.19
Can People Be Trusted by Race of R                   Can People Be Trusted by Education of R

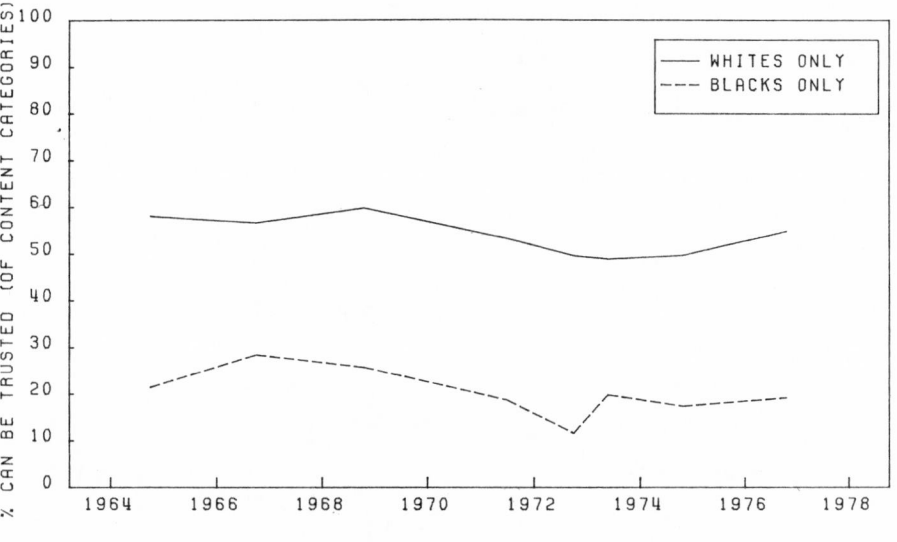

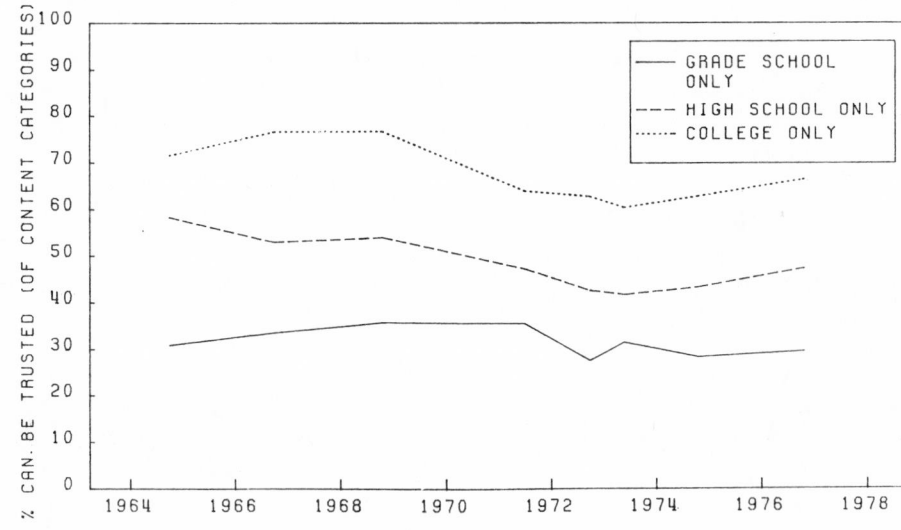

Attitudes toward Self And Others

Table 1.28
Generally Speaking, Can Most People Be Trusted?
Social Groups

% Can Trust

| | 1964n | 1966n | 1968n | 1971j | 1972n | 1973i | 1974n | 1976n | |
|---|---|---|---|---|---|---|---|---|---|
| Males Only | 56.1% | 57.3% | 56.2% | 48.5% | 49.5% | 46.8% | 49.4% | 56.4% | Can trust |
| | (1878) | (560) | (1138) | (4470) | (921) | (1226) | (1028) | (955) | Weighted N |
| Females Only | 53.9 | 50.8 | 56.5 | 49.8 | 44.5 | 44.5 | 45.7 | 50.2 | Can trust |
| | (2313) | (705) | (1481) | (4936) | (1218) | (1540) | (1425) | (1373) | Weighted N |
| | | | | | | | | | |
| Whites Only | 58.4 | 57.0 | 59.8 | 53.3 | 50.6 | 48.9 | 50.4 | 56.3 | Can trust |
| | (3789) | (1115) | (2346) | (8165) | (1899) | (2417) | (2181) | (2056) | Weighted N |
| Blacks Only | 21.5 | 28.6 | 25.7 | 18.7 | 11.8 | 19.8 | 17.4 | 19.9 | Can trust |
| | (372) | (133) | (237) | (973) | (212) | (232) | (224) | (212) | Weighted N |
| | | | | | | | | | |
| Grade School Only | 31.4 | 34.0 | 35.8 | 35.6 | 28.1 | 31.5 | 28.9 | 30.9 | Can trust |
| | (1019) | (329) | (589) | (2073) | (416) | (496) | (433) | (360) | Weighted N |
| High School Only | 58.3 | 53.2 | 54.1 | 47.3 | 43.1 | 41.7 | 43.8 | 48.4 | Can trust |
| | (2172) | (639) | (1291) | (4761) | (1081) | (1426) | (1243) | (1162) | Weighted N |
| College Only | 72.0 | 76.7 | 76.8 | 64.0 | 64.6 | 60.4 | 63.5 | 68.4 | Can trust |
| | (975) | (292) | (738) | (2531) | (641) | (839) | (759) | (806) | Weighted N |
| | | | | | | | | | |
| 18-24 Only | 43.2 | 56.0 | 62.1 | 43.5 | 38.3 | 33.0 | 52.1 | 48.0 | Can trust |
| | (310) | (116) | (206) | (1469) | (324) | (448) | (361) | (331) | Weighted N |
| 25-34 Only | 60.7 | 50.9 | 54.5 | 46.3 | 45.3 | 41.6 | 43.6 | 57.3 | Can trust |
| | (865) | (228) | (517) | (1931) | (455) | (599) | (573) | (548) | Weighted N |
| 35-44 Only | 60.9 | 61.5 | 60.2 | 59.0 | 55.5 | 47.5 | 49.4 | 55.8 | Can trust |
| | (939) | (273) | (565) | (1621) | (348) | (509) | (328) | (343) | Weighted N |
| 45-54 Only | 56.5 | 57.5 | 58.1 | 45.8 | 52.1 | 54.1 | 51.6 | 59.2 | Can trust |
| | (834) | (252) | (515) | (1549) | (355) | (488) | (395) | (340) | Weighted N |
| 55-64 Only | 55.8 | 47.7 | 54.9 | 52.2 | 48.8 | 52.5 | 46.4 | 55.0 | Can trust |
| | (622) | (172) | (379) | (1271) | (301) | (379) | (347) | (344) | Weighted N |
| 65-74 Only | 41.7 | 47.1 | 51.5 | 49.2 | 41.1 | 48.8 | 45.4 | 41.0 | Can trust |
| | (415) | (155) | (299) | (1015) | (214) | (242) | (273) | (264) | Weighted N |
| 75 And Older Only | 36.7 | 44.1 | 49.3 | 48.2 | 36.2 | 39.0 | 42.3 | 39.8 | Can trust |
| | (196) | (59) | (134) | (533) | (127) | (100) | (149) | (152) | Weighted N |

Percentages based on content categories "Most Can Be Trusted" and "Can't Be Too Careful".

Attitudes toward Self And Others

Table 1.29
If Given the Chance, Would People Try to Be Fair?
Total Population

QUESTION: Do you think most people would try to take advantage of you if they
got a chance, or would they try to be fair?

|  |  | Year | | | | | | |
|---|---|---|---|---|---|---|---|---|
|  |  | 1964n | 1968n | 1971j | 1972n | 1973i | 1974n | 1976n |
| Would take advantage | (1) | 29.2% | 29.7% | 31.5% | 36.8% | 35.4% | 39.5% | 35.5% |
| Depends | (3) | 3.0 | 2.6 | 2.6 | ** | ** | ** | ** |
| Would try to be fair | (5) | 66.8 | 67.1 | 65.9 | 58.9 | 62.4 | 57.6 | 59.9 |
| Don't know |  | 1.0 | 0.5 | ** | 4.3 | 2.2 | 2.8 | 4.6 |
| Total |  | 100% | 100% | 100% | 100% | 100% | 100% | 100% |
| Weighted Total |  | 4264 | 2660 | 9471 | 2179 | 2739 | 2473 | 2390 |
| Unweighted Total |  | 1674 | 1434 | 2143 | 2179 | 1401 | 1545 | 1899 |
| Mean |  | 3.76 | 3.75 | 3.69 | 3.46 | 3.55 | 3.37 | 3.51 |
| Standard Deviation |  | 1.82 | 1.82 | 1.85 | 1.95 | 1.92 | 1.97 | 1.93 |

** Code distinction not made.
1964n and 1968n include Black supplement.

Figure 1.20
People Try To Be Fair by Race of R

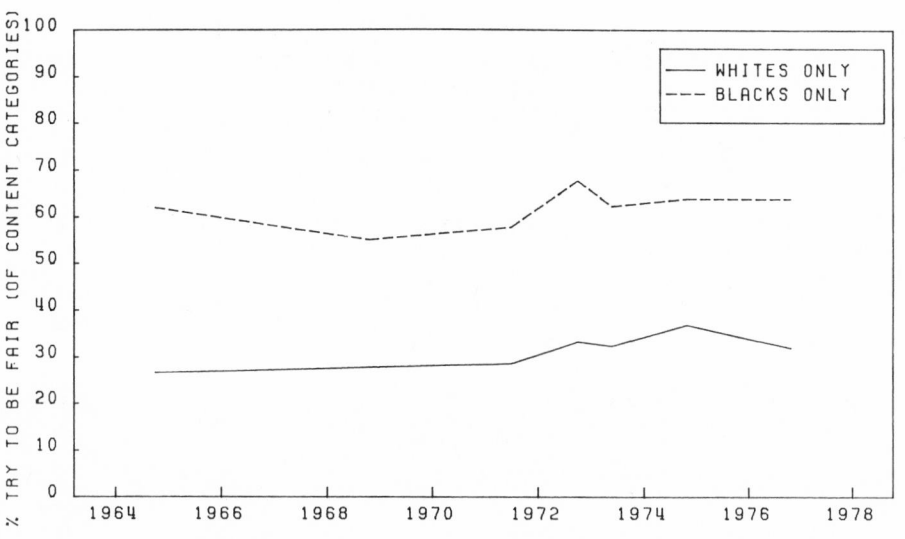

Figure 1 21
People Try To Be Fair by Education of R

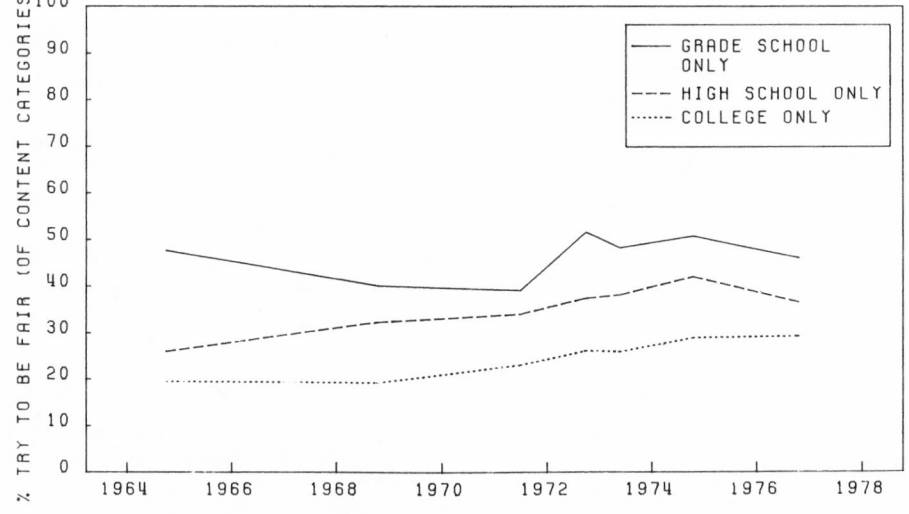

Attitudes toward Self And Others

Table 1.30
If Given the Chance, Would People Try To Be Fair?
Social Groups

| % Try To Be Fair | Year | | | | | | | |
|---|---|---|---|---|---|---|---|---|
| | 1964n | 1968n | 1971j | 1972n | 1973i | 1974n | 1976n | |
| Males Only | 69.0% | 65.4% | 65.0% | 60.7% | 59.7% | 57.0% | 61.0% | Try to be fair |
| | (1826) | (1112) | (4370) | (900) | (1195) | (1016) | (942) | Weighted N |
| Females Only | 70.1 | 72.3 | 70.1 | 62.2 | 67.0 | 61.0 | 64.2 | Try to be fair |
| | (2266) | (1465) | (4856) | (1186) | (1484) | (1387) | (1331) | Weighted N |
| | | | | | | | | |
| Whites Only | 73.1 | 72.0 | 71.4 | 65.4 | 67.6 | 62.0 | 66.5 | Try to be fair |
| | (3690) | (2314) | (8019) | (1861) | (2345) | (2143) | (2006) | Weighted N |
| Blacks Only | 37.1 | 45.0 | 42.2 | 27.1 | 37.7 | 34.0 | 31.5 | Try to be fair |
| | (369) | (231) | (944) | (199) | (223) | (212) | (203) | Weighted N |
| | | | | | | | | |
| Grade School Only | 51.4 | 59.4 | 60.8 | 45.8 | 51.7 | 46.9 | 51.1 | Try to be fair |
| | (1000) | (571) | (2012) | (402) | (472) | (420) | (353) | Weighted N |
| High School Only | 73.8 | 67.5 | 65.9 | 60.9 | 61.8 | 56.8 | 61.5 | Try to be fair |
| | (2129) | (1277) | (4715) | (1050) | (1374) | (1207) | (1127) | Weighted N |
| College Only | 80.3 | 80.6 | 76.9 | 72.7 | 74.0 | 70.4 | 69.6 | Try to be fair |
| | (938) | (726) | (2458) | (633) | (827) | (758) | (792) | Weighted N |
| | | | | | | | | |
| 18-24 Only | 57.1 | 72.1 | 57.3 | 51.9 | 51.6 | 52.0 | 52.3 | Try to be fair |
| | (296) | (204) | (1456) | (314) | (430) | (354) | (320) | Weighted N |
| 25-34 Only | 72.6 | 70.0 | 63.7 | 58.3 | 61.3 | 56.8 | 61.7 | Try to be fair |
| | (866) | (513) | (1897) | (446) | (576) | (555) | (536) | Weighted N |
| 35-44 Only | 74.9 | 67.9 | 72.0 | 67.0 | 63.8 | 59.7 | 64.3 | Try to be fair |
| | (921) | (557) | (1575) | (348) | (494) | (325) | (332) | Weighted N |
| 45-54 Only | 71.4 | 67.9 | 67.6 | 67.4 | 65.9 | 67.5 | 67.8 | Try to be fair |
| | (801) | (508) | (1544) | (341) | (472) | (394) | (337) | Weighted N |
| 55-64 Only | 67.6 | 67.0 | 70.9 | 63.0 | 72.1 | 58.1 | 64.1 | Try to be fair |
| | (615) | (364) | (1249) | (292) | (365) | (344) | (339) | Weighted N |
| 65-74 Only | 66.1 | 69.8 | 71.6 | 61.2 | 72.8 | 63.4 | 64.6 | Try to be fair |
| | (395) | (295) | (976) | (209) | (239) | (268) | (256) | Weighted N |
| 75 And Older Only | 56.4 | 79.2 | 82.6 | 63.6 | 68.6 | 59.9 | 68.9 | Try to be fair |
| | (188) | (130) | (512) | (121) | (102) | (137) | (147) | Weighted N |

Percentages based on content categories "Take Advantage" and "Try to Be Fair".

Attitudes toward Self And Others

Table 1.31
Do People Try to Be Helpful Most of the Time?
Total Population

QUESTION: Would you say that most of the time people try to be helpful, or that they are mostly
just looking out for themselves?

|  | | Year | | | | | | |
|---|---|---|---|---|---|---|---|---|
|  | 1964n | 1966n | 1968n | 1971j | 1972n | 1973i | 1974n | 1976n |
| Try to be helpful (5) | 54.3% | 51.9% | 58.2% | 54.8% | 46 9% | 52 6% | 50.7% | 51.9% |
| Depends/other (3) | 3.9 | 1.9 | 2.6 | 3.5 | ** | ** | ** | ** |
| Just look out for themselves (1) | 41.3 | 45.7 | 38.6 | 41.7 | 48.9 | 44.4 | 46.5 | 43.8 |
| Don't know | 0.5 | 0.5 | 0.6 | ** | 4.2 | 3.0 | 2.8 | 4.3 |
| Total | 100% | 100% | 100% | 100% | 100% | 100% | 100% | 100% |
| Weighted Total | 1445 | 1285 | 1344 | 9521 | 2174 | 2749 | 2450 | 2394 |
| Unweighted Total | 1445 | 1285 | 1344 | 2155 | 2174 | 1411 | 1529 | 1898 |
| Mean | 3.26 | 3.13 | 3.39 | 3.26 | 2.96 | 3.17 | 3.09 | 3.17 |
| Standard Deviation | 1.94 | 1.98 | 1.93 | 1.95 | 2.00 | 1.99 | 2.00 | 1.99 |

** Code distinction not made

Figure 1.22
People Helpful by Race of R

Figure 1.23
People Helpful by Education of R

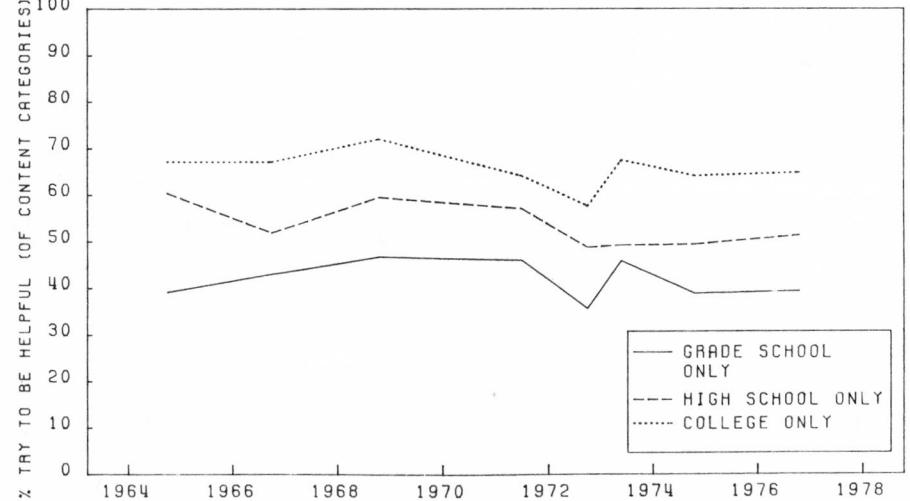

Table 1.32
Do People Try to be Helpful Most of the Time?
Social Groups

% Helpful

|  | 1964n | 1966n | 1968n | 1971j | 1972n | 1973i | 1974n | 1976n | |
|---|---|---|---|---|---|---|---|---|---|
| Males Only | 53.3% | 51.6% | 55.5% | 52.1% | 47.4% | 51.7% | 51.2% | 52.1% | Helpful |
|  | (615) | (554) | (568) | (4355) | (895) | (1178) | (1004) | (934) | Weighted N |
| Females Only | 59.6 | 54.4 | 63.7 | 61.0 | 50.0 | 56.3 | 52.9 | 55.6 | Helpful |
|  | (767) | (700) | (733) | (4836) | (1185) | (1489) | (1378) | (1356) | Weighted N |
| Whites Only | 58.3 | 54.4 | 62.1 | 60.2 | 52.2 | 57.7 | 54.8 | 57.0 | Helpful |
|  | (1227) | (1105) | (1156) | (7981) | (1845) | (2340) | (2114) | (2006) | Weighted N |
| Blacks Only | 45.8 | 43.2 | 40.6 | 33.3 | 19.7 | 29.8 | 30.7 | 30.3 | Helpful |
|  | (144) | (132) | (128) | (956) | (208) | (218) | (218) | (212) | Weighted N |
| Grade School Only | 39.2 | 43.1 | 46.8 | 46.1 | 35.7 | 45.9 | 38.9 | 39.4 | Helpful |
|  | (337) | (325) | (299) | (1952) | (409) | (471) | (434) | (350) | Weighted N |
| High School Only | 60.4 | 52.0 | 59.6 | 57.2 | 48.8 | 49.3 | 49.5 | 51.4 | Helpful |
|  | (718) | (631) | (639) | (4681) | (1046) | (1370) | (1196) | (1147) | Weighted N |
| College Only | 67.2 | 67.2 | 72.1 | 64.2 | 57.7 | 67.5 | 64.1 | 64.8 | Helpful |
|  | (320) | (293) | (362) | (2525) | (624) | (821) | (739) | (788) | Weighted N |
| 18-24 Only | 44.6 | 50.9 | 56.0 | 46.7 | 35.0 | 45.2 | 46.5 | 45.6 | Helpful |
|  | (101) | (116) | (100) | (1438) | (317) | (429) | (357) | (325) | Weighted N |
| 25-34 Only | 61.1 | 50.7 | 58.8 | 54.2 | 46.9 | 47.2 | 49.2 | 53.5 | Helpful |
|  | (288) | (225) | (255) | (1891) | (446) | (578) | (559) | (534) | Weighted N |
| 35-44 Only | 63.8 | 57.2 | 62.6 | 63.5 | 54.6 | 54.9 | 50.9 | 60.6 | Helpful |
|  | (307) | (271) | (278) | (1589) | (339) | (503) | (316) | (339) | Weighted N |
| 45-54 Only | 56.5 | 55.8 | 62.8 | 56.5 | 55.1 | 59.9 | 58.9 | 56.0 | Helpful |
|  | (278) | (249) | (261) | (1533) | (343) | (471) | (377) | (342) | Weighted N |
| 55-64 Only | 50.0 | 50.9 | 54.4 | 59.4 | 54.1 | 63.1 | 55.0 | 59.1 | Helpful |
|  | (204) | (175) | (182) | (1230) | (290) | (355) | (340) | (337) | Weighted N |
| 65-74 Only | 51.4 | 51.0 | 59.5 | 54.5 | 49.3 | 61.9 | 56.6 | 50.7 | Helpful |
|  | (138) | (151) | (153) | (977) | (209) | (231) | (265) | (257) | Weighted N |
| 75 And Older Only | 57.1 | 52.6 | 69.1 | 72.5 | 46.3 | 54.5 | 50.0 | 50.9 | Helpful |
|  | (63) | (57) | (68) | (524) | (123) | (99) | (138) | (146) | Weighted N |

Percentages based on content categories "Try to Be Helpful" and "Look Out for Themselves".

Attitudes toward Self And Others

Table 1.33
Trust in People Index
Total Population

|  |  | Year |  |  |  |  |  |
|---|---|---|---|---|---|---|---|
|  |  | 1964n | 1968n | 1971j | 1972n | 1974n | 1976n |
| Least trust in people | (1) | 27.2% | 24.8% | 28.7% | 35.3% | 36.1% | 31.9% |
|  | (2) | 10.3 | 10.4 | 11.5 | 12.3 | 10.0 | 9.4 |
|  | (3) | 12.7 | 12.0 | 14.6 | 10.8 | 11.3 | 11.0 |
| Most trust in people | (4) | 49.8 | 52.9 | 45.2 | 41.6 | 42.6 | 47.6 |
| Total |  | 100% | 100% | 100% | 100% | 100% | 100% |
| Weighted N |  | 1106 | 1042 | 7404 | 1679 | 1857 | 1770 |
| Unweighted N |  | 1106 | 1042 | 1689 | 1679 | 1181 | 1413 |
| Mean |  | 2.85 | 2.93 | 2.76 | 2.59 | 2.60 | 2.74 |
| Standard Deviation |  | 1.29 | 1.27 | 1.29 | 1.33 | 1.35 | 1.33 |

Index constructed from items displayed in Tables 1.27,1.29,and 1.31.

Figure 1.24
Trust in People--Total Population

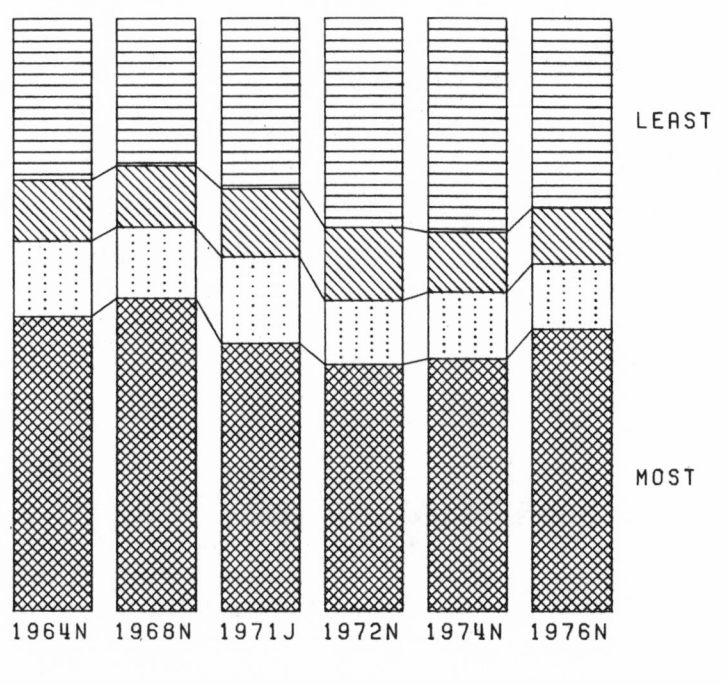

Figure 1.25
Trust in People Items (from Tables 1.27,1.29,and 1.31)

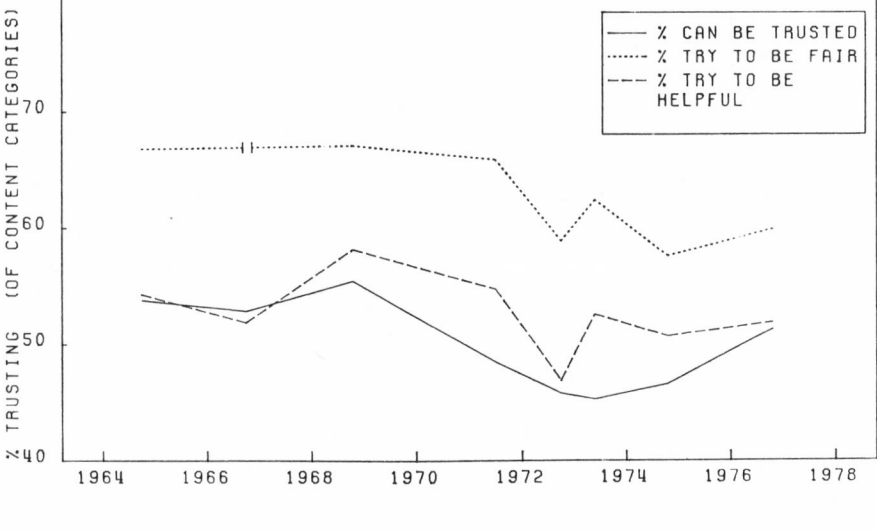

Table 1.34
Trust in People Index
Sex of Respondent

|              |        |        | Year   |        |        |        |                      |
| ------------ | ------ | ------ | ------ | ------ | ------ | ------ | -------------------- |
|              | 1964n  | 1968n  | 1971j  | 1972n  | 1974n  | 1976n  |                      |
| Males Only   | 28.8%  | 28.5%  | 31.5%  | 36.4%  | 38.0%  | 33.5%  | Least trust in people |
|              | 11.1   | 11.5   | 12.8   | 12.1   | 8.5    | 8.4    |                      |
|              | 11.1   | 8.0    | 13.2   | 8.9    | 11.4   | 9.7    |                      |
|              | 49.1   | 52.0   | 42.4   | 42.6   | 42.2   | 48.5   | Most trust in people |
|              | (479)  | (435)  | (3440) | (697)  | (766)  | (686)  | Weighted N           |
|              |        |        |        |        |        |        |                      |
| Females Only | 26.0   | 22.1   | 26.0   | 34.5   | 34.8   | 31.0   | Least trust in people |
|              | 9.7    | 9.6    | 10.2   | 12.5   | 11.1   | 10.1   |                      |
|              | 13.9   | 14.8   | 15.7   | 12.1   | 11.2   | 11.9   |                      |
|              | 50.4   | 53.5   | 48.2   | 40.8   | 42.9   | 47.1   | Most trust in people |
|              | (627)  | (607)  | (4004) | (982)  | (1091) | (1084) | Weighted N           |

Table 1.35
Race of Respondent

|              | 1964n  | 1968n  | 1971j  | 1972n  | 1974n  | 1976n  |                      |
| ------------ | ------ | ------ | ------ | ------ | ------ | ------ | -------------------- |
| Whites Only  | 24.4%  | 21.7%  | 24.6%  | 30.7%  | 32.8%  | 27.9%  | Least trust in people |
|              | 10.2   | 10.2   | 10.4   | 12.6   | 9.5    | 9.5    |                      |
|              | 12.0   | 11.6   | 14.9   | 10.7   | 11.9   | 11.0   |                      |
|              | 53.4   | 56.5   | 50.1   | 45.9   | 45.8   | 51.6   | Most trust in people |
|              | (973)  | (925)  | (6425) | (1480) | (1634) | (1558) | Weighted N           |
|              |        |        |        |        |        |        |                      |
| Blacks Only  | 47.6   | 50.0   | 54.1   | 72.8   | 64.5   | 66.9   | Least trust in people |
|              | 12.1   | 13.2   | 18.4   | 10.0   | 12.0   | 8.5    |                      |
|              | 16.9   | 14.2   | 12.9   | 11.7   | 8.2    | 8.5    |                      |
|              | 23.4   | 22.6   | 14.5   | 5.6    | 15.3   | 16.1   | Most trust in people |
|              | (124)  | (106)  | (820)  | (180)  | (183)  | (171)  | Weighted N           |

Attitudes toward Self And Others

Table 1.36
Trust in People Index
Education of Respondent

|  | Year | | | | | | |
|---|---|---|---|---|---|---|---|
|  | 1964n | 1968n | 1971j | 1972n | 1974n | 1976n | |
| Grade School Only | 44.6% | 37.1% | 37.1% | 52.5% | 51.5% | 45.7% | Least trust in people |
|  | 16.6 | 15.9 | 15.7 | 13.4 | 11.7 | 15.4 | |
|  | 12.9 | 15.1 | 16.2 | 12.2 | 10.3 | 12.7 | |
|  | 25.8 | 31.9 | 31.0 | 21.8 | 26.5 | 26.3 | Most trust in people |
|  | (271) | (251) | (1673) | (335) | (359) | (280) | Weighted N |
| High School Only | 23.9 | 25.7 | 30.1 | 35.3 | 38.3 | 34.2 | Least trust in people |
|  | 8.9 | 9.9 | 10.2 | 13.6 | 10.5 | 9.7 | |
|  | 14.4 | 12.8 | 15.9 | 11.4 | 12.4 | 12.8 | |
|  | 52.8 | 51.6 | 43.8 | 39.7 | 38.8 | 43.3 | Most trust in people |
|  | (585) | (514) | (3808) | (867) | (930) | (900) | Weighted N |
| College Only | 15.2 | 11.9 | 17.9 | 23.3 | 23.0 | 22.1 | Least trust in people |
|  | 7.0 | 6.1 | 10.1 | 9.2 | 7.5 | 6.2 | |
|  | 8.2 | 7.6 | 10.6 | 8.6 | 10.0 | 7.6 | |
|  | 69.7 | 74.4 | 61.3 | 58.8 | 59.5 | 64.1 | Most trust in people |
|  | (244) | (277) | (1930) | (476) | (560) | (586) | Weighted N |

Figure 1.26
Trust in People by Race of R

Figure 1.27
Trust in People by Education of R

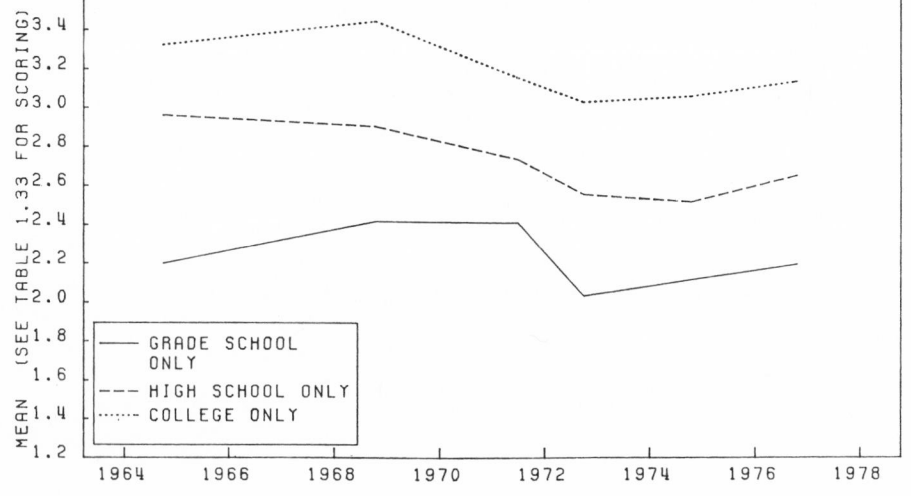

Table 1.37
Trust in People Index
Age of Respondent

|  | Year | | | | | | |
|---|---|---|---|---|---|---|---|
|  | 1964n | 1968n | 1971j | 1972n | 1974n | 1976n | |
| 18-24 Only | 39.5% | 24.3% | 38.8% | 46.2% | 42.3% | 44.3% | Least trust in people |
|  | 9.9 | 8.1 | 13.3 | 15.7 | 7.7 | 7.5 | |
|  | 16.0 | 10.8 | 13.4 | 11.4 | 7.7 | 9.0 | |
|  | 34.6 | 56.8 | 34.5 | 26.7 | 42.3 | 39.2 | Most trust in people |
|  | (81) | (74) | (1104) | (236) | (248) | (240) | Weighted N |
| 25-34 Only | 23.4 | 25.2 | 31.9 | 40.1 | 39.9 | 31.3 | Least trust in people |
|  | 9.5 | 10.2 | 12.1 | 10.8 | 10.3 | 9.9 | |
|  | 10.8 | 16.5 | 13.0 | 9.7 | 9.9 | 9.1 | |
|  | 56.3 | 48.1 | 43.0 | 39.5 | 39.9 | 49.8 | Most trust in people |
|  | (231) | (206) | (1490) | (372) | (456) | (403) | Weighted N |
| 35-44 Only | 20.9 | 24.1 | 23.0 | 29.7 | 37.8 | 27.6 | Least trust in people |
|  | 9.9 | 9.5 | 8.4 | 10.0 | 8.8 | 6.9 | |
|  | 12.3 | 8.2 | 13.1 | 7.5 | 8.0 | 11.1 | |
|  | 56.9 | 58.2 | 55.5 | 52.7 | 45.4 | 54.3 | Most trust in people |
|  | (253) | (220) | (1302) | (279) | (249) | (261) | Weighted N |
| 45-54 Only | 28.3 | 25.6 | 30.5 | 26.2 | 27.1 | 27.7 | Least trust in people |
|  | 8.2 | 8.5 | 10.3 | 15.6 | 12.7 | 11.0 | |
|  | 13.2 | 11.8 | 14.3 | 9.6 | 11.8 | 7.4 | |
|  | 50.2 | 54.0 | 44.8 | 48.6 | 48.4 | 53.9 | Most trust in people |
|  | (219) | (211) | (1318) | (282) | (306) | (269) | Weighted N |
| 55-64 Only | 28.8 | 27.4 | 24.3 | 34.2 | 35.4 | 30.9 | Least trust in people |
|  | 13.5 | 13.7 | 11.6 | 9.2 | 8.9 | 5.7 | |
|  | 10.3 | 6.8 | 16.0 | 10.8 | 16.0 | 12.5 | |
|  | 47.4 | 52.1 | 48.0 | 45.8 | 39.7 | 50.9 | Most trust in people |
|  | (156) | (146) | (998) | (240) | (257) | (264) | Weighted N |
| 65-74 Only | 31.5 | 25.4 | 27.1 | 34.8 | 30.2 | 34.3 | Least trust in people |
|  | 13.5 | 11.9 | 13.0 | 11.6 | 10.8 | 11.1 | |
|  | 15.3 | 12.7 | 15.0 | 18.3 | 15.6 | 16.9 | |
|  | 39.6 | 50.0 | 44.9 | 35.4 | 43.4 | 37.6 | Most trust in people |
|  | (111) | (126) | (775) | (164) | (212) | (216) | Weighted N |
| 75 And Older Only | 36.5 | 14.0 | 14.7 | 35.4 | 38.3 | 27.0 | Least trust in people |
|  | 9.6 | 10.5 | 11.6 | 17.7 | 10.3 | 19.8 | |
|  | 17.3 | 24.6 | 23.9 | 14.6 | 12.1 | 16.7 | |
|  | 36.5 | 50.9 | 49.8 | 32.3 | 39.3 | 36.5 | Most trust in people |
|  | (52) | (57) | (448) | (96) | (107) | (111) | Weighted N |

Attitudes toward Self And Others

Table 1.38
Feeling Thermometer for Big Business

QUESTION: I have here a card on which there is something that looks like a feeling
thermometer because it measures your feelings towards groups.  Here's how it works. If you don't know too much about a
group or don't feel particularly warm or cold towards them, then you should place them in the middle, at the fifty
degree mark.   If you have a warm feeling toward a group, or feel favorably toward it, you would give it a score
somewhere between fifty and one hundred degrees, depending on how warm your feeling is toward the group.   On the other
hand, if you don't feel very favorably toward some of these groups--if there are some you don't care for too much--then
you would place them somewhere between zero and fifty degrees.

|  | Year | | | | | | |
|---|---|---|---|---|---|---|---|
|  | 1964n | 1966n | 1968n | 1972n | 1974n | 1976n | |
| Total Population | 60.2 | 60.1 | 59.2 | 53.3 | 48.7 | 48.4 | Mean |
|  | 21.8 | 19.9 | 20.1 | 20.3 | 23.4 | 21.0 | Standard Deviation |
|  | (4551) | (1272) | (3006) | (1965) | (2352) | (2220) | Weighted N |
| Unweighted Total | 1791 | 1272 | 1623 | 1965 | 1969 | 1769 | |

1964n and 1968n include Black supplement.

Figure 1.28
FT--Big Business--Total Population

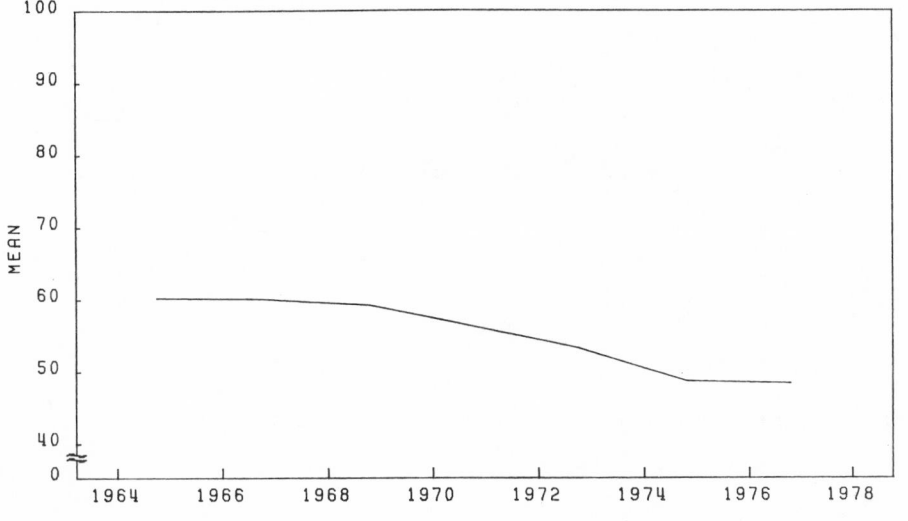

Table 1.39
Feeling Thermometer for Big Business by Social Groups

|  | Year | | | | | | |
|---|---|---|---|---|---|---|---|
|  | 1964n | 1966n | 1968n | 1972n | 1974n | 1976n | |
| Males Only | 60.4 | 61.8 | 60.3 | 53.2 | 48.0 | 49.4 | Mean |
|  | 23.5 | 21.2 | 21.1 | 20.6 | 24.3 | 21.7 | Standard Deviation |
|  | (2058) | (566) | (1330) | (881) | (1009) | (944) | Weighted N |
| Females Only | 60.0 | 58.7 | 58.4 | 53.5 | 49.2 | 47.6 | Mean |
|  | 20.2 | 18.7 | 19.3 | 20.2 | 22.6 | 20.5 | Standard Deviation |
|  | (2493) | (706) | (1676) | (1084) | (1343) | (1276) | Weighted N |
| Whites Only | 60.2 | 59.7 | 59.1 | 53.7 | 47.4 | 48.3 | Mean |
|  | 21.6 | 20.1 | 20.0 | 19.5 | 23.1 | 20.8 | Standard Deviation |
|  | (4110) | (1126) | (2700) | (1757) | (2103) | (1969) | Weighted N |
| Blacks Only | 60.0 | 63.5 | 61.0 | 51.1 | 60.3 | 47.6 | Mean |
|  | 23.4 | 18.8 | 21.1 | 26.3 | 23.6 | 23.8 | Standard Deviation |
|  | (411) | (130) | (276) | (185) | (203) | (192) | Weighted N |
| Grade School Only | 58.0 | 58.1 | 57.3 | 57.3 | 55.6 | 51.4 | Mean |
|  | 22.4 | 19.5 | 20.8 | 21.0 | 24.3 | 20.9 | Standard Deviation |
|  | (1106) | (324) | (648) | (328) | (365) | (288) | Weighted N |
| High School Only | 60.6 | 60.0 | 58.6 | 53.3 | 48.0 | 47.7 | Mean |
|  | 21.6 | 19.6 | 19.5 | 19.8 | 23.6 | 20.8 | Standard Deviation |
|  | (2338) | (643) | (1518) | (987) | (1190) | (1111) | Weighted N |
| College Only | 61.6 | 62.5 | 61.9 | 51.4 | 46.5 | 47.9 | Mean |
|  | 21.4 | 20.9 | 20.6 | 20.6 | 21.9 | 21.5 | Standard Deviation |
|  | (1075) | (301) | (835) | (650) | (770) | (823) | Weighted N |
| 18-24 Only | 56.8 | 63.0 | 56.9 | 47.2 | 44.2 | 43.3 | Mean |
|  | 19.4 | 18.3 | 19.2 | 19.5 | 22.3 | 20.4 | Standard Deviation |
|  | (356) | (118) | (231) | (324) | (358) | (326) | Weighted N |
| 25-34 Only | 59.4 | 59.1 | 57.8 | 48.6 | 44.5 | 41.7 | Mean |
|  | 20.6 | 17.7 | 19.8 | 18.6 | 22.6 | 20.2 | Standard Deviation |
|  | (940) | (230) | (602) | (431) | (559) | (547) | Weighted N |
| 35-44 Only | 60.4 | 60.5 | 59.9 | 53.6 | 48.3 | 46.2 | Mean |
|  | 21.8 | 20.4 | 19.5 | 19.4 | 23.9 | 19.9 | Standard Deviation |
|  | (1006) | (276) | (642) | (338) | (328) | (340) | Weighted N |
| 45-54 Only | 61.2 | 60.2 | 60.1 | 55.1 | 49.4 | 53.1 | Mean |
|  | 23.0 | 19.9 | 20.2 | 21.0 | 22.7 | 20.2 | Standard Deviation |
|  | (906) | (253) | (603) | (325) | (386) | (333) | Weighted N |
| 55-64 Only | 59.6 | 59.3 | 60.6 | 59.3 | 51.1 | 52.9 | Mean |
|  | 22.8 | 20.5 | 21.3 | 18.8 | 23.8 | 20.4 | Standard Deviation |
|  | (659) | (174) | (444) | (261) | (336) | (323) | Weighted N |
| 65-74 Only | 60.4 | 62.8 | 59.1 | 60.0 | 56.3 | 56.0 | Mean |
|  | 21.8 | 20.8 | 20.7 | 21.7 | 24.8 | 22.2 | Standard Deviation |
|  | (440) | (154) | (335) | (180) | (252) | (228) | Weighted N |
| 75 And Older Only | 64.1 | 51.9 | 58.7 | 60.5 | 58.8 | 56.5 | Mean |
|  | 21.7 | 22.6 | 20.5 | 21.0 | 20.1 | 20.2 | Standard Deviation |
|  | (228) | (58) | (141) | (92) | (111) | (110) | Weighted N |

Attitudes toward Self And Others

Table 1.40
Feeling Thermometer for Labor Unions

|  | Year | | | | | | |
|---|---|---|---|---|---|---|---|
|  | 1964n | 1966n | 1968n | 1972n | 1974n | 1976n | |
| Total Population | 57.7 | 58.4 | 56.4 | 55.5 | 54.0 | 46.8 | Mean |
|  | 25.8 | 25.9 | 23.9 | 21.9 | 24.0 | 21.8 | Standard Deviation |
|  | (4545) | (1273) | (2994) | (1977) | (2385) | (2219) | Weighted N |
| Unweighted Total | 1789 | 1273 | 1617 | 1977 | 1987 | 1769 | |

1964n and 1968n include Black supplement.

Figure 1.29                                   Figure 1.30
FT--Labor Unions--Total Population            FT--Labor Unions by Education of R

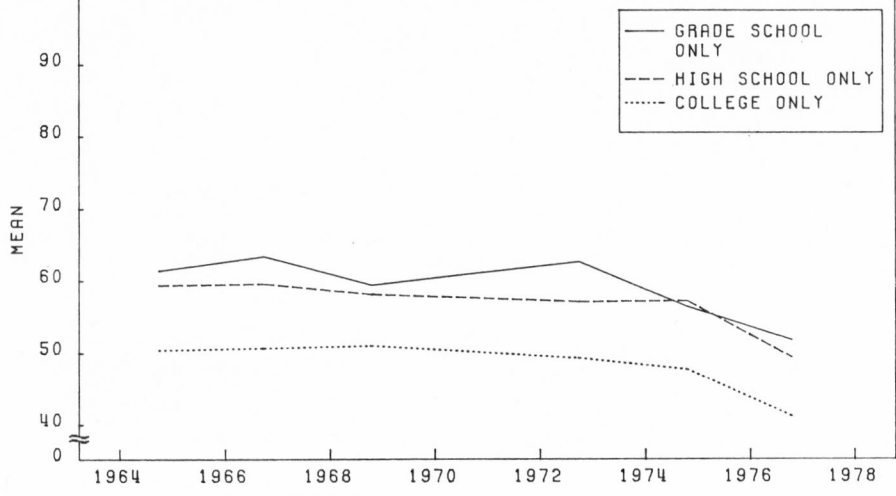

Table 1.41
Feeling Thermometer for Labor Unions by Social Groups

|  | Year | | | | | | |
|---|---|---|---|---|---|---|---|
|  | 1964n | 1966n | 1968n | 1972n | 1974n | 1976n | |
| Males Only | 59.6 | 59.9 | 57.3 | 54.7 | 52.2 | 46.0 | Mean |
|  | 26.8 | 27.4 | 24.4 | 22.8 | 24.8 | 22.3 | Standard Deviation |
|  | (2058) | (567) | (1320) | (890) | (1029) | (952) | Weighted N |
| Females Only | 56.2 | 57.1 | 55.7 | 56.2 | 55.4 | 47.3 | Mean |
|  | 24.9 | 24.5 | 23.4 | 21.1 | 23.3 | 21.4 | Standard Deviation |
|  | (2487) | (706) | (1674) | (1087) | (1356) | (1267) | Weighted N |
| Whites Only | 57.5 | 57.1 | 55.7 | 54.6 | 52.7 | 45.5 | Mean |
|  | 25.7 | 25.9 | 23.8 | 21.7 | 24.0 | 21.5 | Standard Deviation |
|  | (4104) | (1126) | (2690) | (1778) | (2137) | (1977) | Weighted N |
| Blacks Only | 59.8 | 67.4 | 62.5 | 64.9 | 65.8 | 59.4 | Mean |
|  | 27.3 | 23.4 | 23.7 | 21.7 | 20.8 | 22.1 | Standard Deviation |
|  | (411) | (131) | (276) | (174) | (202) | (185) | Weighted N |
| Grade School Only | 61.4 | 63.4 | 59.4 | 62.6 | 56.4 | 51.8 | Mean |
|  | 28.0 | 25.7 | 26.1 | 22.4 | 26.7 | 25.0 | Standard Deviation |
|  | (1109) | (323) | (640) | (325) | (369) | (303) | Weighted N |
| High School Only | 59.4 | 59.6 | 58.1 | 57.1 | 57.2 | 49.4 | Mean |
|  | 24.5 | 25.2 | 23.6 | 21.9 | 24.1 | 21.7 | Standard Deviation |
|  | (2332) | (645) | (1514) | (1012) | (1215) | (1101) | Weighted N |
| College Only | 50.4 | 50.7 | 51.0 | 49.3 | 47.7 | 41.2 | Mean |
|  | 25.0 | 25.5 | 21.5 | 20.0 | 21.3 | 19.6 | Standard Deviation |
|  | (1072) | (301) | (835) | (639) | (775) | (816) | Weighted N |
| 18-24 Only | 58.4 | 59.3 | 54.1 | 54.2 | 57.2 | 49.9 | Mean |
|  | 24.5 | 24.3 | 22.6 | 19.3 | 20.4 | 18.6 | Standard Deviation |
|  | (356) | (118) | (231) | (316) | (363) | (321) | Weighted N |
| 25-34 Only | 54.2 | 56.9 | 53.2 | 51.2 | 50.1 | 43.2 | Mean |
|  | 25.0 | 25.7 | 23.7 | 21.6 | 23.1 | 19.8 | Standard Deviation |
|  | (943) | (230) | (600) | (439) | (572) | (546) | Weighted N |
| 35-44 Only | 56.7 | 58.0 | 56.5 | 53.9 | 52.5 | 42.2 | Mean |
|  | 26.7 | 26.0 | 22.7 | 21.0 | 24.8 | 21.7 | Standard Deviation |
|  | (1006) | (276) | (642) | (344) | (327) | (336) | Weighted N |
| 45-54 Only | 59.5 | 59.6 | 58.7 | 57.8 | 57.2 | 49.6 | Mean |
|  | 25.8 | 25.3 | 24.3 | 21.7 | 24.5 | 21.3 | Standard Deviation |
|  | (903) | (255) | (605) | (329) | (386) | (330) | Weighted N |
| 55-64 Only | 61.5 | 59.6 | 59.1 | 59.3 | 55.5 | 50.7 | Mean |
|  | 26.5 | 28.0 | 25.3 | 21.9 | 24.4 | 23.8 | Standard Deviation |
|  | (659) | (174) | (440) | (273) | (345) | (341) | Weighted N |
| 65-74 Only | 60.9 | 59.0 | 57.0 | 59.5 | 55.3 | 47.1 | Mean |
|  | 22.7 | 26.6 | 24.0 | 25.3 | 25.9 | 24.5 | Standard Deviation |
|  | (437) | (153) | (331) | (175) | (255) | (226) | Weighted N |
| 75 And Older Only | 51.0 | 53.3 | 53.8 | 59.2 | 51.1 | 47.2 | Mean |
|  | 28.3 | 21.3 | 22.8 | 22.6 | 25.5 | 23.7 | Standard Deviation |
|  | (225) | (58) | (137) | (88) | (117) | (108) | Weighted N |

Table 1.42
Feeling Thermometer for the Military

|  | Year | | | | | |  |
|---|---|---|---|---|---|---|---|
|  | 1964n | 1968n | 1970n | 1972n | 1974n | 1976n |  |
| Total Population | 74.7 | 74.3 | 72.3 | 69.5 | 70.6 | 67.5 | Mean |
|  | 21.3 | 21.7 | 23.8 | 22.7 | 23.3 | 21.0 | Standard Deviation |
|  | (4548) | (2992) | (1803) | (2079) | (2413) | (2272) | Weighted N |
| Unweighted Total | 1790 | 1616 | 1629 | 2079 | 2018 | 1811 |  |

1964n,1968n,and 1970n include Black supplement.

Figure 1.31
FT--Military--Total Population

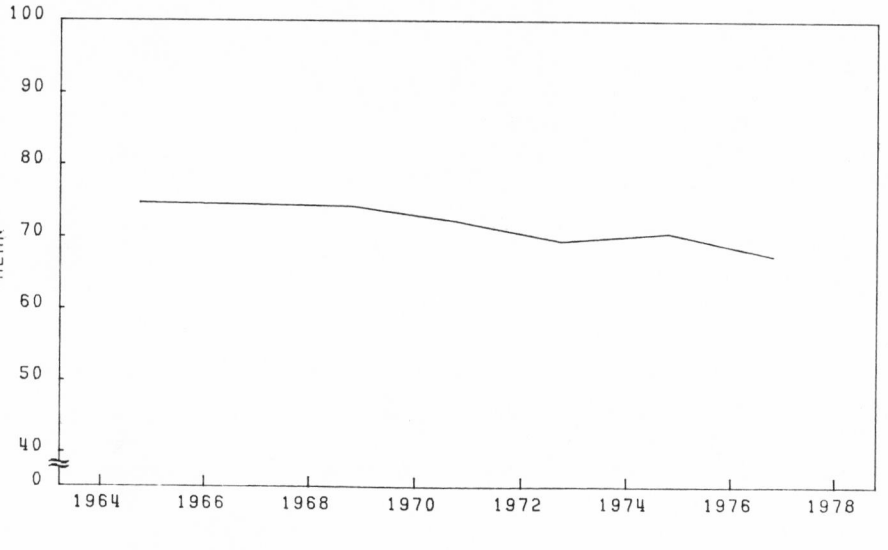

Figure 1.32
FT--Military by Education of R

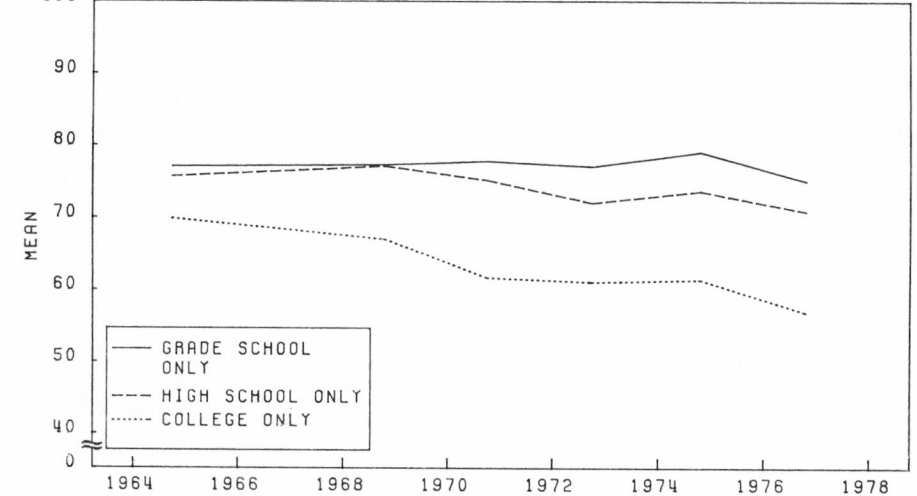

Attitudes toward Self And Others

Table 1.43
Feeling Thermometer for the Military by Social Groups

|  | Year | | | | | | |
|---|---|---|---|---|---|---|---|
|  | 1964n | 1968n | 1970n | 1972n | 1974n | 1976n | |
| Males Only | 74.2 | 73.4 | 70.8 | 67.1 | 68.7 | 65.7 | Mean |
|  | 22.4 | 21.6 | 24.9 | 23.7 | 23.4 | 21.7 | Standard Deviation |
|  | (2058) | (1320) | (789) | (911) | (1013) | (958) | Weighted N |
| Females Only | 75.1 | 75.1 | 73.4 | 71.4 | 72.0 | 68.9 | Mean |
|  | 20.4 | 21.9 | 22.8 | 21.8 | 23.1 | 20.4 | Standard Deviation |
|  | (2490) | (1672) | (1014) | (1168) | (1400) | (1314) | Weighted N |
| Whites Only | 74.8 | 74.2 | 72.8 | 69.9 | 70.2 | 67.1 | Mean |
|  | 21.3 | 21.7 | 23.6 | 22.2 | 23.3 | 21.0 | Standard Deviation |
|  | (4107) | (2688) | (1615) | (1855) | (2158) | (2023) | Weighted N |
| Blacks Only | 73.6 | 74.7 | 68.6 | 67.0 | 74.8 | 71.5 | Mean |
|  | 21.9 | 22.3 | 24.8 | 25.8 | 22.9 | 21.3 | Standard Deviation |
|  | (411) | (276) | (160) | (197) | (210) | (198) | Weighted N |
| Grade School Only | 77.1 | 77.3 | 77.8 | 77.1 | 79.1 | 75.1 | Mean |
|  | 21.2 | 19.3 | 21.4 | 19.2 | 20.2 | 19.5 | Standard Deviation |
|  | (1109) | (638) | (407) | (377) | (385) | (320) | Weighted N |
| High School Only | 75.7 | 77.1 | 75.2 | 72.1 | 73.7 | 70.9 | Mean |
|  | 20.8 | 20.6 | 21.6 | 21.5 | 21.4 | 19.3 | Standard Deviation |
|  | (2338) | (1514) | (917) | (1048) | (1228) | (1135) | Weighted N |
| College Only | 69.9 | 67.0 | 61.7 | 61.1 | 61.4 | 56.9 | Mean |
|  | 22.0 | 23.8 | 26.3 | 24.0 | 24.8 | 21.7 | Standard Deviation |
|  | (1069) | (835) | (473) | (653) | (772) | (818) | Weighted N |
| 18-24 Only | 71.1 | 65.7 | 65.9 | 56.9 | 58.2 | 58.7 | Mean |
|  | 22.0 | 28.0 | 27.3 | 26.4 | 27.8 | 22.2 | Standard Deviation |
|  | (356) | (231) | (254) | (330) | (366) | (332) | Weighted N |
| 25-34 Only | 72.5 | 73.7 | 71.1 | 65.2 | 68.0 | 60.9 | Mean |
|  | 23.0 | 21.9 | 25.3 | 22.8 | 23.0 | 22.0 | Standard Deviation |
|  | (943) | (600) | (360) | (453) | (573) | (551) | Weighted N |
| 35-44 Only | 73.5 | 76.4 | 72.5 | 70.3 | 71.9 | 65.2 | Mean |
|  | 21.6 | 20.3 | 22.3 | 21.6 | 18.9 | 18.6 | Standard Deviation |
|  | (1006) | (642) | (314) | (351) | (336) | (334) | Weighted N |
| 45-54 Only | 77.3 | 73.9 | 73.0 | 73.7 | 75.2 | 72.1 | Mean |
|  | 19.2 | 20.9 | 23.1 | 19.9 | 21.0 | 19.0 | Standard Deviation |
|  | (906) | (605) | (308) | (340) | (379) | (325) | Weighted N |
| 55-64 Only | 76.7 | 76.0 | 73.8 | 76.1 | 75.3 | 75.4 | Mean |
|  | 21.0 | 21.8 | 22.6 | 19.3 | 23.1 | 17.7 | Standard Deviation |
|  | (659) | (440) | (282) | (287) | (345) | (343) | Weighted N |
| 65-74 Only | 76.3 | 77.1 | 77.4 | 77.2 | 74.7 | 75.7 | Mean |
|  | 21.1 | 19.8 | 19.6 | 18.7 | 19.7 | 19.1 | Standard Deviation |
|  | (434) | (329) | (178) | (197) | (267) | (250) | Weighted N |
| 75 And Older Only | 75.1 | 73.4 | 76.3 | 78.7 | 80.9 | 74.9 | Mean |
|  | 19.8 | 18.7 | 21.6 | 16.7 | 16.6 | 19.2 | Standard Deviation |
|  | (228) | (137) | (96) | (108) | (126) | (129) | Weighted N |

Figure 1.33
FT--Military by Age of R

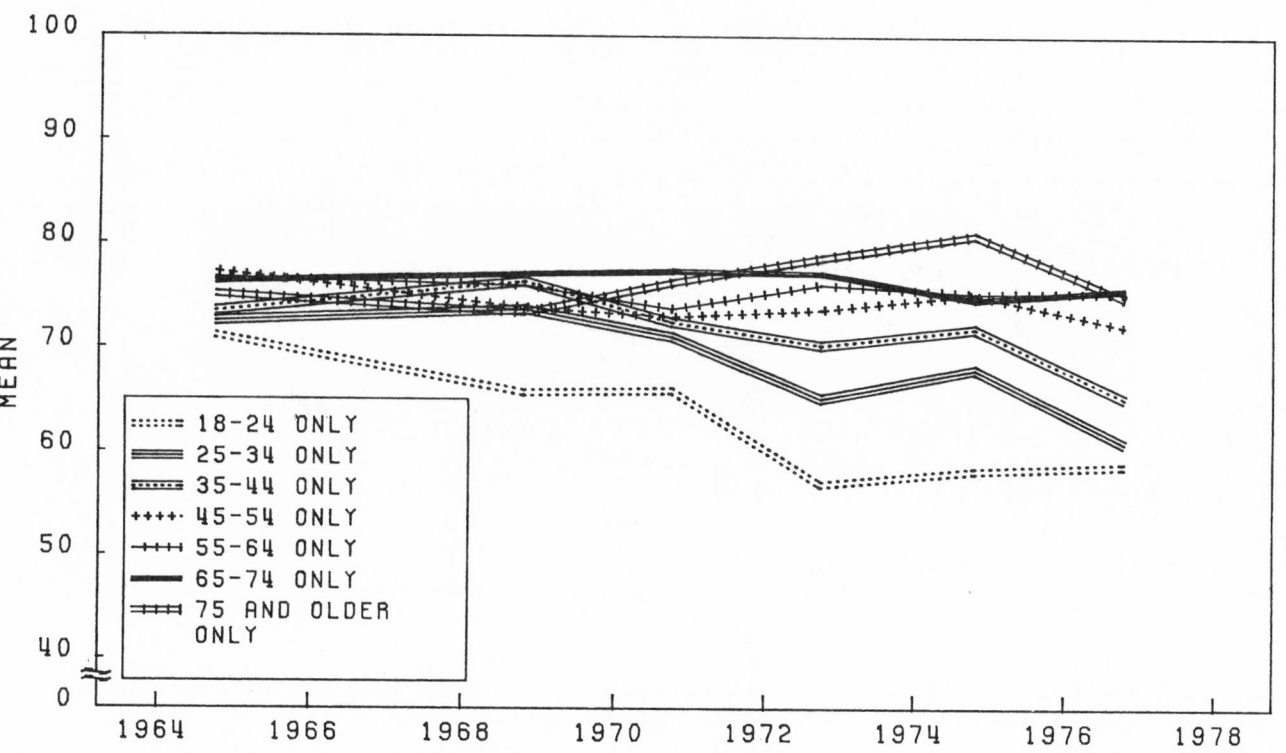

Attitudes toward Self And Others

Table 1.44
Feeling Thermometer for Policemen

|  | Year | | | | | |  |
|  | 1966n | 1968n | 1970n | 1972n | 1974n | 1976n |  |
| Total Population | 79.1 | 79.4 | 78.7 | 75.4 | 73.3 | 71.2 | Mean |
|  | 19.5 | 18.6 | 19.3 | 18.3 | 20.1 | 18.0 | Standard Deviation |
|  | (1273) | (2991) | (1840) | (2121) | (2460) | (2324) | Weighted N |
| Unweighted Total | 1273 | 1614 | 1664 | 2121 | 2050 | 1851 |  |

1964n and 1970n include Black supplement.

Figure 1.34
FT--Policemen--Total Population

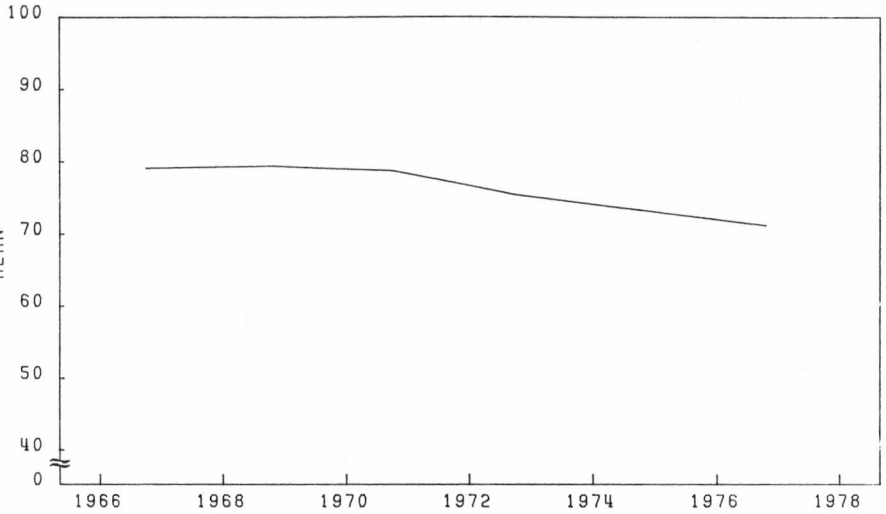

Figure 1.35
FT--Policemen by Race of R

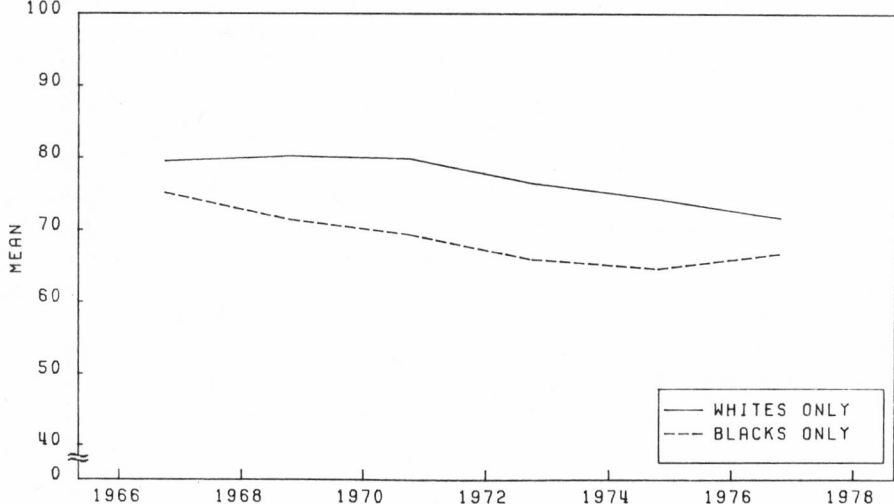

Attitudes toward Self And Others

Table 1.45
Feeling Thermometer for Policemen by Social Groups

| | Year | | | | | | |
|---|---|---|---|---|---|---|---|
| | 1966n | 1968n | 1970n | 1972n | 1974n | 1976n | |
| Males Only | 77.1 | 78.8 | 77.4 | 74.2 | 72.4 | 68.8 | Mean |
| | 21.4 | 18.6 | 20.3 | 18.9 | 20.5 | 18.7 | Standard Deviation |
| | (566) | (1318) | (796) | (920) | (1030) | (964) | Weighted N |
| Females Only | 80.6 | 79.8 | 79.7 | 76.2 | 74.0 | 72.9 | Mean |
| | 17.6 | 18.6 | 18.5 | 17.7 | 19.7 | 17.2 | Standard Deviation |
| | (707) | (1673) | (1043) | (1201) | (1430) | (1359) | Weighted N |
| | | | | | | | |
| Whites Only | 79.5 | 80.2 | 79.9 | 76.5 | 74.3 | 71.7 | Mean |
| | 19.2 | 18.1 | 18.6 | 17.3 | 19.2 | 17.7 | Standard Deviation |
| | (1125) | (2688) | (1643) | (1885) | (2194) | (2058) | Weighted N |
| Blacks Only | 75.1 | 71.4 | 69.4 | 65.9 | 64.6 | 66.7 | Mean |
| | 21.2 | 20.9 | 21.9 | 23.0 | 26.4 | 20.2 | Standard Deviation |
| | (132) | (273) | (167) | (209) | (216) | (204) | Weighted N |
| | | | | | | | |
| Grade School Only | 78.1 | 78.7 | 80.4 | 78.9 | 76.2 | 75.7 | Mean |
| | 20.7 | 18.7 | 20.9 | 18.4 | 20.2 | 17.6 | Standard Deviation |
| | (323) | (635) | (419) | (395) | (405) | (344) | Weighted N |
| High School Only | 79.9 | 80.6 | 79.7 | 76.5 | 73.9 | 72.3 | Mean |
| | 19.3 | 18.1 | 18.8 | 17.4 | 20.4 | 18.3 | Standard Deviation |
| | (646) | (1515) | (937) | (1068) | (1245) | (1155) | Weighted N |
| College Only | 78.1 | 77.8 | 75.3 | 71.4 | 71.1 | 67.6 | Mean |
| | 18.6 | 19.1 | 18.5 | 19.0 | 19.4 | 17.1 | Standard Deviation |
| | (300) | (836) | (479) | (657) | (781) | (824) | Weighted N |
| | | | | | | | |
| 18-24 Only | 76.2 | 76.4 | 72.1 | 66.7 | 64.3 | 66.7 | Mean |
| | 20.8 | 20.6 | 22.8 | 20.3 | 22.9 | 17.4 | Standard Deviation |
| | (118) | (231) | (256) | (333) | (367) | (335) | Weighted N |
| 25-34 Only | 78.6 | 75.9 | 78.6 | 73.3 | 72.7 | 67.2 | Mean |
| | 18.5 | 20.3 | 19.7 | 18.0 | 20.4 | 18.1 | Standard Deviation |
| | (229) | (602) | (361) | (457) | (573) | (558) | Weighted N |
| 35-44 Only | 78.7 | 81.2 | 78.5 | 75.8 | 74.2 | 68.5 | Mean |
| | 21.3 | 17.0 | 19.2 | 17.9 | 18.8 | 18.3 | Standard Deviation |
| | (276) | (638) | (319) | (352) | (341) | (343) | Weighted N |
| 45-54 Only | 80.2 | 79.0 | 78.7 | 77.4 | 74.4 | 72.1 | Mean |
| | 18.7 | 18.8 | 18.3 | 16.3 | 19.5 | 18.2 | Standard Deviation |
| | (256) | (604) | (316) | (351) | (393) | (340) | Weighted N |
| 55-64 Only | 80.1 | 82.5 | 81.0 | 80.5 | 75.5 | 76.7 | Mean |
| | 19.5 | 18.2 | 17.4 | 15.9 | 20.4 | 16.2 | Standard Deviation |
| | (175) | (438) | (292) | (293) | (350) | (346) | Weighted N |
| 65-74 Only | 80.1 | 81.3 | 81.4 | 80.1 | 77.8 | 77.8 | Mean |
| | 18.2 | 16.5 | 18.4 | 16.1 | 16.1 | 16.1 | Standard Deviation |
| | (153) | (333) | (184) | (207) | (274) | (257) | Weighted N |
| 75 And Older Only | 76.8 | 78.5 | 84.9 | 80.5 | 80.0 | 74.5 | Mean |
| | 18.6 | 16.2 | 14.1 | 17.2 | 12.5 | 17.7 | Standard Deviation |
| | (57) | (137) | (102) | (114) | (133) | (135) | Weighted N |

Table 1.46
Feeling Thermometer for Southerners

|                    | Year |  |  |  |  |
|                    | 1964n | 1968n | 1972n | 1976n |  |
|--------------------|-------|-------|-------|-------|--------------------|
| Total Population   | 63.4  | 61.2  | 65.5  | 62.0  | Mean               |
|                    | 23.6  | 23.3  | 18.9  | 17.7  | Standard Deviation |
|                    | (4550)| (2993)| (1978)| (2152)| Weighted N         |
| Unweighted Total   | 1790  | 1615  | 1978  | 1719  |                    |

1964n and 1968n include Black supplement.

Figure 1.36
FT--Southerners--Total Population

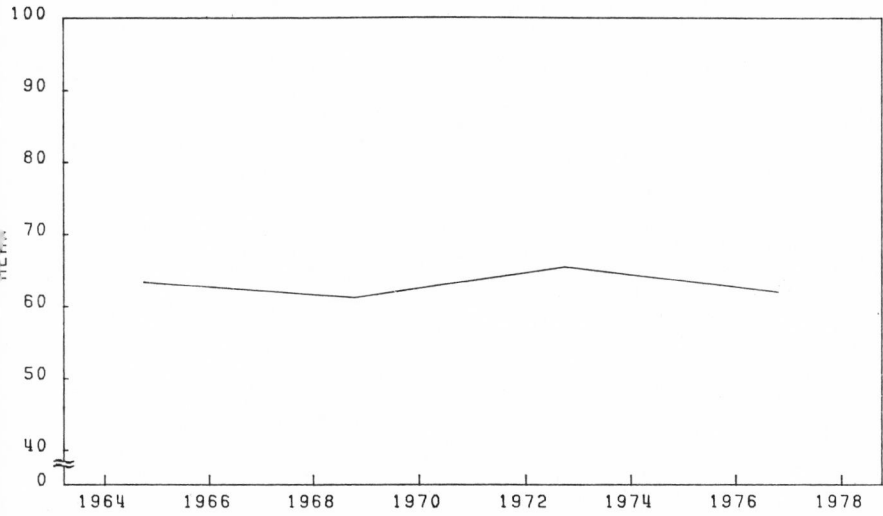

Figure 1.37
FT--Southerners by Race of R

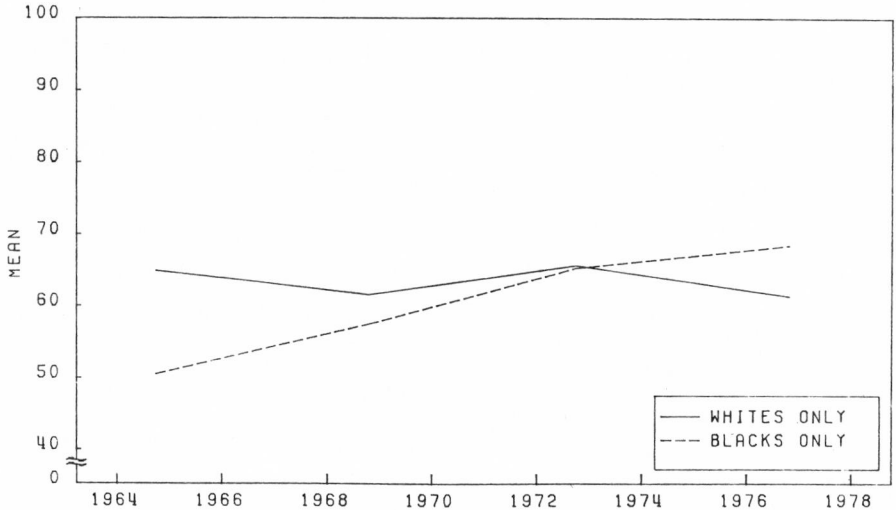

Attitudes toward Self And Others

Table 1.47
Feeling Thermometer for Southerners by Social Groups

|  | Year | | | | |
|---|---|---|---|---|---|
|  | 1964n | 1968n | 1972n | 1976n | |
| Males Only | 63.6 | 60.3 | 64.6 | 60.7 | Mean |
|  | 23.8 | 23.0 | 18.5 | 17.4 | Standard Deviation |
|  | (2063) | (1318) | (874) | (915) | Weighted N |
| Females Only | 63.2 | 61.8 | 66.3 | 62.9 | Mean |
|  | 23.3 | 23.6 | 19.2 | 17.8 | Standard Deviation |
|  | (2487) | (1675) | (1104) | (1237) | Weighted N |
|  |  |  |  |  |  |
| Whites Only | 64.9 | 61.6 | 65.7 | 61.4 | Mean |
|  | 22.6 | 22.9 | 18.7 | 17.5 | Standard Deviation |
|  | (4110) | (2692) | (1763) | (1907) | Weighted N |
| Blacks Only | 50.5 | 57.5 | 65.3 | 68.5 | Mean |
|  | 28.7 | 27.3 | 21.1 | 19.1 | Standard Deviation |
|  | (410) | (273) | (194) | (193) | Weighted N |
|  |  |  |  |  |  |
| Grade School Only | 64.6 | 63.8 | 68.1 | 68.6 | Mean |
|  | 24.1 | 22.9 | 20.2 | 20.2 | Standard Deviation |
|  | (1109) | (641) | (341) | (291) | Weighted N |
| High School Only | 63.2 | 60.3 | 66.3 | 62.1 | Mean |
|  | 23.0 | 23.2 | 18.4 | 17.3 | Standard Deviation |
|  | (2337) | (1514) | (1002) | (1053) | Weighted N |
| College Only | 62.4 | 60.6 | 63.0 | 59.3 | Mean |
|  | 24.2 | 23.9 | 18.8 | 16.5 | Standard Deviation |
|  | (1072) | (833) | (634) | (807) | Weighted N |
|  |  |  |  |  |  |
| 18-24 Only | 60.0 | 58.1 | 61.6 | 58.4 | Mean |
|  | 23.5 | 21.0 | 18.0 | 17.3 | Standard Deviation |
|  | (356) | (231) | (313) | (318) | Weighted N |
| 25-34 Only | 61.2 | 58.6 | 64.6 | 58.8 | Mean |
|  | 23.7 | 24.3 | 18.3 | 16.3 | Standard Deviation |
|  | (939) | (599) | (436) | (526) | Weighted N |
| 35-44 Only | 63.2 | 61.6 | 63.4 | 61.4 | Mean |
|  | 23.6 | 23.3 | 18.7 | 16.9 | Standard Deviation |
|  | (1004) | (640) | (331) | (325) | Weighted N |
| 45-54 Only | 64.9 | 59.7 | 67.1 | 63.8 | Mean |
|  | 22.9 | 22.5 | 18.7 | 17.7 | Standard Deviation |
|  | (906) | (602) | (328) | (326) | Weighted N |
| 55-64 Only | 63.9 | 64.4 | 68.9 | 65.6 | Mean |
|  | 24.3 | 22.9 | 19.3 | 18.2 | Standard Deviation |
|  | (658) | (437) | (273) | (319) | Weighted N |
| 65-74 Only | 66.6 | 64.0 | 69.3 | 65.7 | Mean |
|  | 22.4 | 23.2 | 20.5 | 19.0 | Standard Deviation |
|  | (443) | (335) | (190) | (208) | Weighted N |
| 75 And Older Only | 66.0 | 65.7 | 68.2 | 66.0 | Mean |
|  | 24.9 | 22.5 | 18.1 | 18.4 | Standard Deviation |
|  | (228) | (141) | (95) | (118) | Weighted N |

Table 1.48
Feeling Thermometer for Jews

|                     | Year |  |  |  |  |  |
|---------------------|--------|--------|--------|--------|--------|--------------------|
|                     | 1964n  | 1966n  | 1968n  | 1972n  | 1976n  |                    |
| Total Population    | 62.0   | 64.9   | 64.1   | 66.1   | 57.2   | Mean               |
|                     | 20.7   | 21.1   | 21.0   | 18.7   | 17.9   | Standard Deviation |
|                     | (4541) | (1266) | (2980) | (1966) | (2131) | Weighted N         |
| Unweighted Total    | 1787   | 1266   | 1610   | 1966   | 1695   |                    |

1964n and 1968n include Black supplement.

Figure 1.38
FT--Jews--Total Population

Figure 1.39
FT--Jews by Education of R

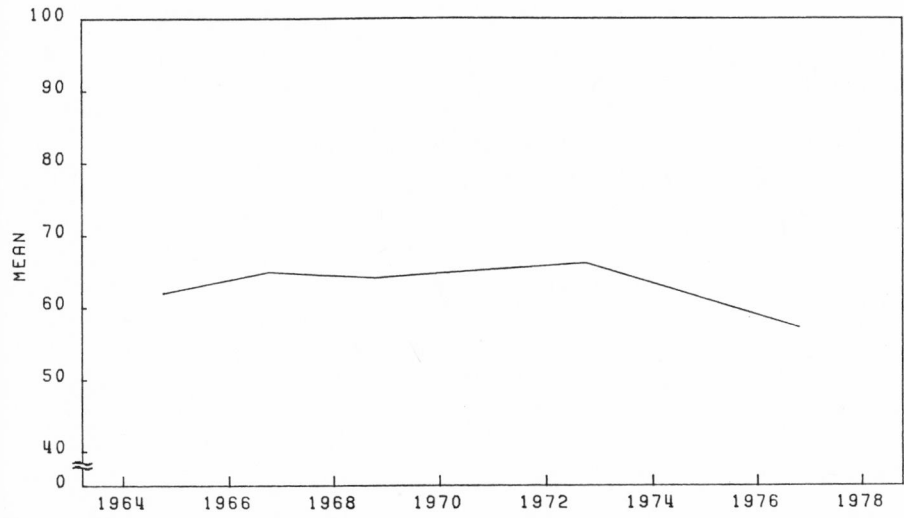

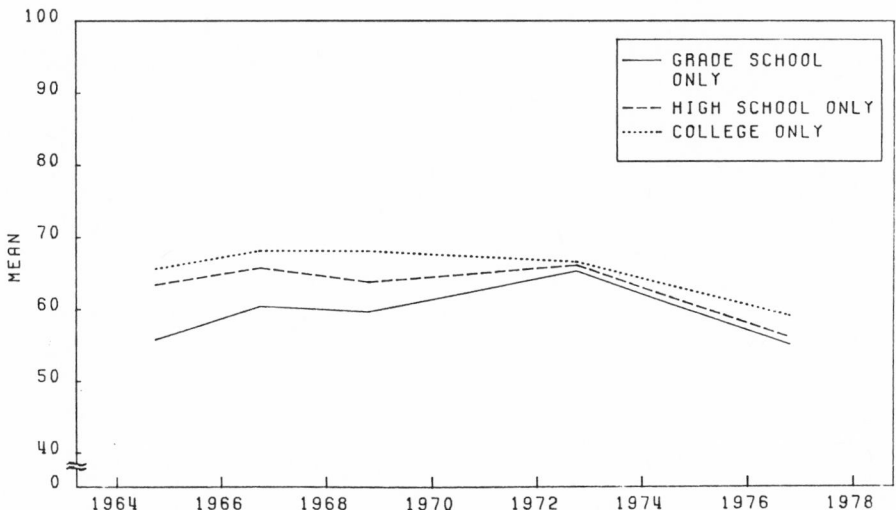

Attitudes toward Self And Others

Table 1.49
Feeling Thermometer for Jews by Social Groups

|  | 1964n | 1966n | 1968n | 1972n | 1976n |  |
|---|---|---|---|---|---|---|
| Males Only | 61.1 | 63.0 | 62.7 | 64.6 | 54.4 | Mean |
|  | 21.7 | 22.0 | 21.4 | 18.5 | 18.6 | Standard Deviation |
|  | (2058) | (564) | (1312) | (867) | (903) | Weighted N |
| Females Only | 62.7 | 66.3 | 65.2 | 67.3 | 59.2 | Mean |
|  | 19.8 | 20.2 | 20.7 | 18.8 | 17.1 | Standard Deviation |
|  | (2483) | (702) | (1668) | (1099) | (1228) | Weighted N |
| Whites Only | 62.3 | 64.7 | 64.1 | 66.5 | 57.2 | Mean |
|  | 20.5 | 21.0 | 20.9 | 18.4 | 17.8 | Standard Deviation |
|  | (4101) | (1119) | (2676) | (1761) | (1897) | Weighted N |
| Blacks Only | 59.1 | 66.5 | 62.6 | 63.2 | 57.7 | Mean |
|  | 22.7 | 22.3 | 22.0 | 20.9 | 18.6 | Standard Deviation |
|  | (410) | (131) | (276) | (179) | (176) | Weighted N |
| Grade School Only | 55.8 | 60.4 | 59.7 | 65.3 | 55.1 | Mean |
|  | 21.9 | 21.6 | 23.0 | 20.8 | 22.4 | Standard Deviation |
|  | (1109) | (322) | (636) | (337) | (263) | Weighted N |
| High School Only | 63.4 | 65.7 | 63.8 | 66.1 | 56.1 | Mean |
|  | 19.9 | 21.3 | 20.9 | 18.7 | 16.8 | Standard Deviation |
|  | (2331) | (640) | (1508) | (987) | (1061) | Weighted N |
| College Only | 65.6 | 68.1 | 68.1 | 66.6 | 59.1 | Mean |
|  | 19.9 | 19.4 | 18.9 | 17.6 | 17.4 | Standard Deviation |
|  | (1069) | (300) | (831) | (641) | (808) | Weighted N |
| 18-24 Only | 58.9 | 64.9 | 61.4 | 59.7 | 53.1 | Mean |
|  | 18.4 | 21.9 | 19.5 | 17.9 | 15.2 | Standard Deviation |
|  | (356) | (118) | (231) | (314) | (317) | Weighted N |
| 25-34 Only | 61.0 | 64.6 | 63.9 | 63.3 | 56.1 | Mean |
|  | 19.3 | 20.8 | 19.3 | 18.0 | 15.5 | Standard Deviation |
|  | (940) | (230) | (598) | (430) | (531) | Weighted N |
| 35-44 Only | 63.8 | 65.8 | 65.3 | 67.7 | 56.2 | Mean |
|  | 19.0 | 20.9 | 21.3 | 19.1 | 18.3 | Standard Deviation |
|  | (1003) | (272) | (642) | (333) | (325) | Weighted N |
| 45-54 Only | 63.2 | 64.3 | 63.6 | 69.1 | 60.3 | Mean |
|  | 22.2 | 21.4 | 22.3 | 16.5 | 18.7 | Standard Deviation |
|  | (903) | (256) | (597) | (324) | (320) | Weighted N |
| 55-64 Only | 60.8 | 64.9 | 67.7 | 69.8 | 60.3 | Mean |
|  | 22.4 | 20.2 | 21.7 | 19.2 | 19.1 | Standard Deviation |
|  | (658) | (171) | (440) | (271) | (317) | Weighted N |
| 65-74 Only | 62.6 | 65.2 | 62.8 | 70.0 | 59.0 | Mean |
|  | 21.8 | 22.5 | 21.6 | 19.7 | 19.8 | Standard Deviation |
|  | (440) | (153) | (327) | (187) | (209) | Weighted N |
| 75 And Older Only | 60.5 | 63.5 | 58.8 | 67.1 | 53.9 | Mean |
|  | 22.9 | 21.0 | 17.7 | 19.8 | 21.7 | Standard Deviation |
|  | (225) | (58) | (137) | (95) | (102) | Weighted N |

1964n and 1968n include Black supplement.

Table 1.50
Feeling Thermometer for Catholics

|  | Year | | | | | |
|---|---|---|---|---|---|---|
|  | 1964n | 1966n | 1968n | 1972n | 1976n | |
| Total Population | 66.1 | 65.0 | 64.8 | 67.7 | 62.9 | Mean |
|  | 22.6 | 24.5 | 22.9 | 19.6 | 17.7 | Standard Deviation |
|  | (1532) | (1269) | (1501) | (1991) | (2171) | Weighted N |
| Unweighted Total | 1532 | 1269 | 1501 | 1991 | 1728 | |

Figure 1.40
FT--Catholics--Total Population

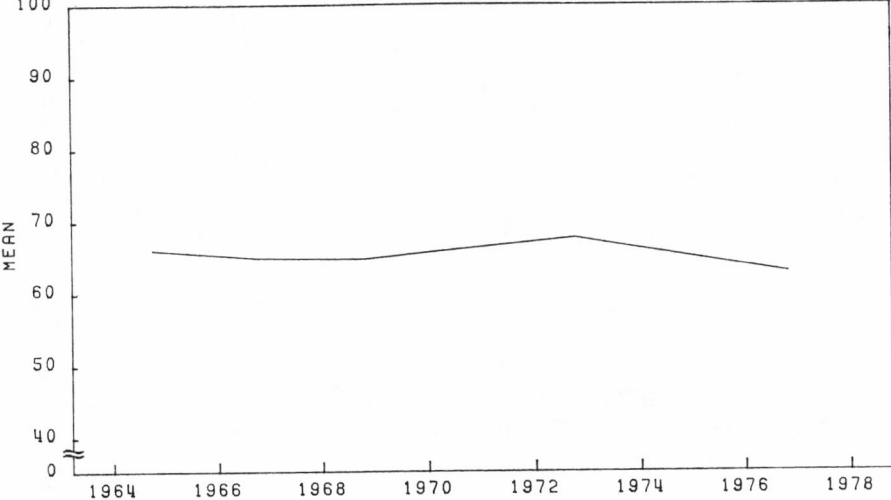

Attitudes toward Self And Others

Table 1.51
Feeling Thermometer for Catholics by Social Groups

|  | Year | | | | | |
|---|---|---|---|---|---|---|
|  | 1964n | 1966n | 1968n | 1972n | 1976n | |
| Males Only | 65.8 | 62.9 | 63.0 | 66.0 | 60.3 | Mean |
|  | 23.1 | 24.1 | 23.4 | 20.2 | 17.1 | Standard Deviation |
|  | (687) | (565) | (663) | (862) | (924) | Weighted N |
| Females Only | 66.3 | 66.8 | 66.2 | 69.0 | 64.8 | Mean |
|  | 22.2 | 24.7 | 22.5 | 19.0 | 17.9 | Standard Deviation |
|  | (845) | (704) | (838) | (1129) | (1247) | Weighted N |
| Whites Only | 66.3 | 64.4 | 64.9 | 67.6 | 62.6 | Mean |
|  | 22.9 | 24.7 | 22.8 | 19.6 | 17.6 | Standard Deviation |
|  | (1367) | (1121) | (1343) | (1791) | (1939) | Weighted N |
| Blacks Only | 63.8 | 68.2 | 61.5 | 69.5 | 63.3 | Mean |
|  | 19.6 | 22.3 | 23.6 | 19.0 | 18.4 | Standard Deviation |
|  | (155) | (132) | (144) | (173) | (164) | Weighted N |
| Grade School Only | 62.6 | 60.9 | 59.3 | 68.4 | 64.8 | Mean |
|  | 23.1 | 25.6 | 23.5 | 22.0 | 20.5 | Standard Deviation |
|  | (369) | (324) | (328) | (340) | (278) | Weighted N |
| High School Only | 67.7 | 66.3 | 66.1 | 68.3 | 63.2 | Mean |
|  | 22.5 | 24.7 | 23.6 | 18.8 | 18.1 | Standard Deviation |
|  | (794) | (640) | (751) | (1010) | (1077) | Weighted N |
| College Only | 66.5 | 66.9 | 67.0 | 66.6 | 61.7 | Mean |
|  | 22.1 | 22.4 | 20.7 | 19.5 | 16.1 | Standard Deviation |
|  | (360) | (301) | (420) | (640) | (810) | Weighted N |
| 18-24 Only | 64.7 | 69.3 | 65.4 | 64.2 | 60.0 | Mean |
|  | 21.2 | 21.3 | 24.1 | 19.1 | 16.5 | Standard Deviation |
|  | (120) | (118) | (112) | (320) | (322) | Weighted N |
| 25-34 Only | 68.5 | 67.1 | 66.1 | 64.3 | 60.3 | Mean |
|  | 22.5 | 23.6 | 22.2 | 19.8 | 17.0 | Standard Deviation |
|  | (323) | (230) | (302) | (434) | (540) | Weighted N |
| 35-44 Only | 65.5 | 65.3 | 67.4 | 67.9 | 59.0 | Mean |
|  | 22.8 | 24.6 | 22.9 | 19.9 | 17.3 | Standard Deviation |
|  | (334) | (272) | (323) | (339) | (324) | Weighted N |
| 45-54 Only | 66.8 | 65.1 | 65.1 | 69.9 | 66.1 | Mean |
|  | 22.4 | 24.9 | 22.2 | 18.3 | 17.5 | Standard Deviation |
|  | (305) | (255) | (301) | (324) | (324) | Weighted N |
| 55-64 Only | 64.1 | 62.0 | 64.9 | 71.7 | 66.9 | Mean |
|  | 23.1 | 25.0 | 23.4 | 18.9 | 17.1 | Standard Deviation |
|  | (221) | (173) | (218) | (276) | (313) | Weighted N |
| 65-74 Only | 64.7 | 63.6 | 60.5 | 71.6 | 67.3 | Mean |
|  | 22.5 | 25.5 | 23.6 | 19.5 | 19.1 | Standard Deviation |
|  | (149) | (154) | (168) | (186) | (215) | Weighted N |
| 75 And Older Only | 65.1 | 59.1 | 56.2 | 67.7 | 65.8 | Mean |
|  | 24.1 | 27.0 | 21.7 | 20.1 | 19.9 | Standard Deviation |
|  | (75) | (58) | (73) | (100) | (119) | Weighted N |

Attitudes toward Self And Others

Table 1.52
Feeling Thermometer for Protestants

|  | Year | | | | | |
|---|---|---|---|---|---|---|
|  | 1964n | 1966n | 1968n | 1972n | 1976n | |
| Total Population | 79.3 | 77.2 | 78.1 | 74.0 | 65.8 | Mean |
|  | 18.4 | 19.6 | 18.9 | 18.4 | 17.5 | Standard Deviation |
|  | (1529) | (1269) | (1498) | (2056) | (2234) | Weighted N |
| Unweighted Total | 1529 | 1269 | 1498 | 2056 | 1781 | |

Figure 1.41
FT--Protestants--Total Population

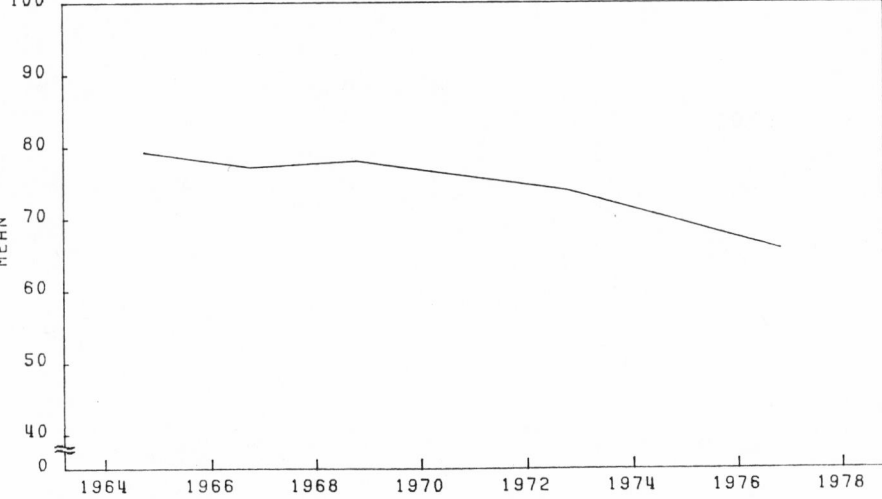

Table 1.53
Feeling Thermometer for Protestants by Social Groups

|  | Year | | | | | |
| --- | --- | --- | --- | --- | --- | --- |
|  | 1964n | 1966n | 1968n | 1972n | 1976n | |
| Males Only | 78.0 | 73.6 | 76.7 | 71.4 | 62.5 | Mean |
|  | 18.9 | 20.5 | 19.1 | 18.3 | 16.1 | Standard Deviation |
|  | (685) | (564) | (663) | (894) | (930) | Weighted N |
| Females Only | 80.4 | 80.1 | 79.2 | 75.7 | 68.1 | Mean |
|  | 17.9 | 18.4 | 18.7 | 18.2 | 18.0 | Standard Deviation |
|  | (844) | (705) | (835) | (1162) | (1304) | Weighted N |
| Whites Only | 79.2 | 77.3 | 77.5 | 73.8 | 65.6 | Mean |
|  | 18.2 | 19.8 | 18.9 | 18.3 | 17.3 | Standard Deviation |
|  | (1365) | (1120) | (1339) | (1838) | (1986) | Weighted N |
| Blacks Only | 81.8 | 77.2 | 82.9 | 75.2 | 70.6 | Mean |
|  | 19.0 | 18.0 | 18.5 | 18.8 | 18.5 | Standard Deviation |
|  | (154) | (133) | (145) | (190) | (186) | Weighted N |
| Grade School Only | 78.9 | 76.6 | 79.8 | 77.3 | 69.3 | Mean |
|  | 19.9 | 21.3 | 19.4 | 19.5 | 19.7 | Standard Deviation |
|  | (369) | (324) | (327) | (368) | (313) | Weighted N |
| High School Only | 79.9 | 78.1 | 78.5 | 74.6 | 65.8 | Mean |
|  | 17.8 | 18.9 | 19.1 | 17.9 | 17.8 | Standard Deviation |
|  | (790) | (641) | (750) | (1036) | (1099) | Weighted N |
| College Only | 79.0 | 75.9 | 76.1 | 70.5 | 64.3 | Mean |
|  | 17.6 | 19.2 | 18.0 | 18.0 | 15.8 | Standard Deviation |
|  | (361) | (300) | (419) | (651) | (817) | Weighted N |
| 18-24 Only | 74.2 | 75.0 | 73.7 | 66.2 | 59.5 | Mean |
|  | 18.9 | 19.4 | 20.1 | 17.8 | 15.2 | Standard Deviation |
|  | (120) | (118) | (112) | (325) | (322) | Weighted N |
| 25-34 Only | 76.7 | 75.1 | 74.6 | 69.4 | 60.1 | Mean |
|  | 18.8 | 18.7 | 19.2 | 18.8 | 15.2 | Standard Deviation |
|  | (321) | (229) | (302) | (442) | (541) | Weighted N |
| 35-44 Only | 79.6 | 78.1 | 79.2 | 74.4 | 63.5 | Mean |
|  | 17.8 | 19.8 | 18.2 | 18.3 | 16.5 | Standard Deviation |
|  | (333) | (274) | (322) | (344) | (331) | Weighted N |
| 45-54 Only | 81.6 | 76.7 | 77.6 | 75.1 | 70.5 | Mean |
|  | 17.1 | 19.9 | 19.2 | 16.5 | 17.9 | Standard Deviation |
|  | (307) | (255) | (302) | (338) | (329) | Weighted N |
| 55-64 Only | 78.0 | 77.5 | 80.5 | 80.1 | 71.3 | Mean |
|  | 19.6 | 19.6 | 18.3 | 16.4 | 17.6 | Standard Deviation |
|  | (221) | (173) | (217) | (285) | (332) | Weighted N |
| 65-74 Only | 83.0 | 80.9 | 81.9 | 78.9 | 72.5 | Mean |
|  | 18.1 | 19.7 | 18.4 | 18.2 | 18.1 | Standard Deviation |
|  | (148) | (153) | (168) | (198) | (235) | Weighted N |
| 75 And Older Only | 84.3 | 76.8 | 81.1 | 81.6 | 72.1 | Mean |
|  | 17.7 | 20.7 | 16.8 | 17.0 | 17.1 | Standard Deviation |
|  | (74) | (58) | (71) | (112) | (130) | Weighted N |

Table 1.54
Feeling Thermometer for Whites

|  | Year | | | | | | | |
|  | 1964n | 1966n | 1968n | 1970n | 1972n | 1974n | 1976n | |
| Total Population | 83.3 | 83.0 | 80.0 | 76.4 | 77.4 | 78.2 | 73.2 | Mean |
|  | 17.9 | 17.3 | 18.4 | 19.1 | 17.9 | 17.6 | 17.2 | Standard Deviation |
|  | (1532) | (1271) | (1500) | (1456) | (2112) | (2412) | (2332) | Weighted N |
| Unweighted Total | 1532 | 1271 | 1500 | 1456 | 2112 | 1512 | 1857 | |

Figure 1.42
FT--Whites--Total Population

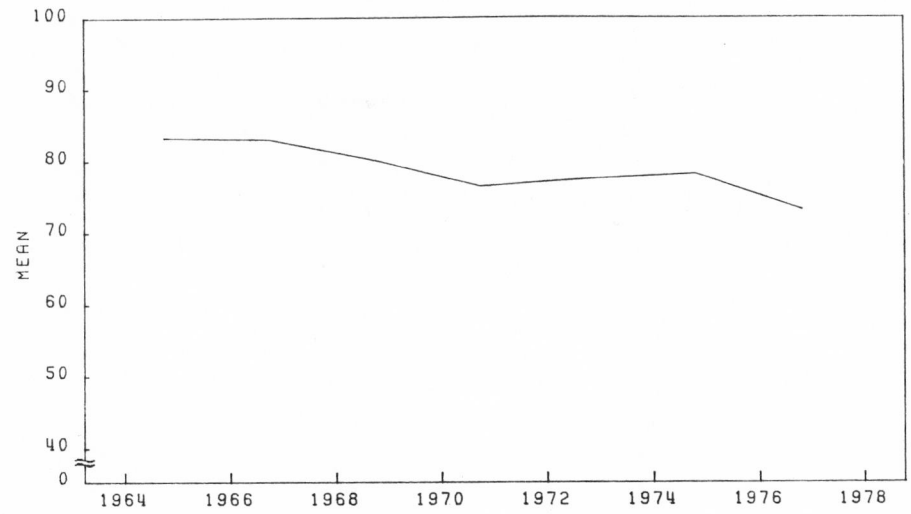

Figure 1.43
FT--Whites by Race of R

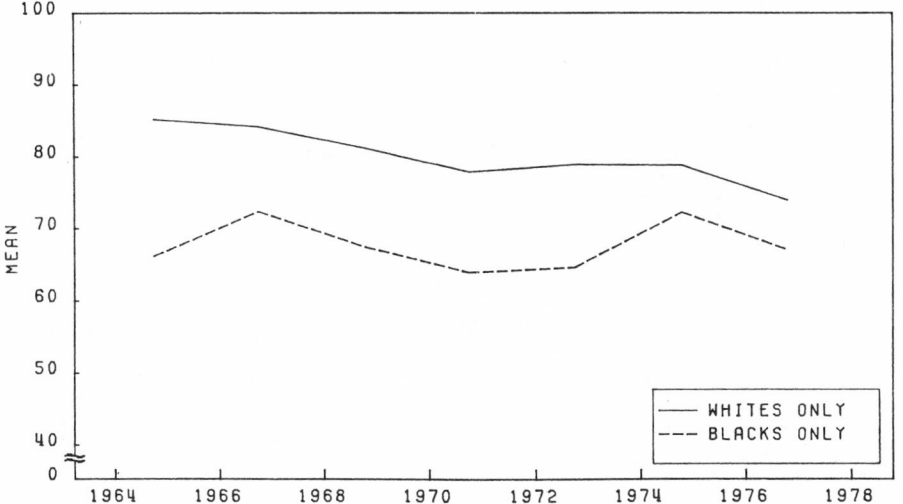

Attitudes toward Self And Others

Table 1.55
Feeling Thermometer for Whites by Social Groups

|  | Year | | | | | | | |
|---|---|---|---|---|---|---|---|---|
|  | 1964n | 1966n | 1968n | 1970n | 1972n | 1974n | 1976n | |
| Males Only | 83.3 | 80.7 | 79.2 | 75.6 | 75.9 | 76.4 | 69.8 | Mean |
|  | 18.1 | 18.1 | 18.4 | 19.6 | 17.9 | 18.0 | 16.7 | Standard Deviation |
|  | (687) | (565) | (662) | (627) | (916) | (1016) | (966) | Weighted N |
| Females Only | 83.3 | 84.8 | 80.6 | 77.0 | 78.6 | 79.6 | 75.5 | Mean |
|  | 17.8 | 16.4 | 18.3 | 18.6 | 17.8 | 17.1 | 17.2 | Standard Deviation |
|  | (845) | (706) | (838) | (829) | (1196) | (1398) | (1366) | Weighted N |
| Whites Only | 85.2 | 84.2 | 81.2 | 77.9 | 78.9 | 78.8 | 74.0 | Mean |
|  | 15.8 | 16.6 | 17.3 | 18.2 | 16.7 | 17.2 | 16.8 | Standard Deviation |
|  | (1367) | (1124) | (1343) | (1293) | (1880) | (2153) | (2060) | Weighted N |
| Blacks Only | 66.2 | 72.4 | 67.5 | 64.0 | 64.7 | 72.3 | 67.1 | Mean |
|  | 25.3 | 19.4 | 23.4 | 21.9 | 22.0 | 19.6 | 20.4 | Standard Deviation |
|  | (155) | (131) | (143) | (141) | (204) | (215) | (204) | Weighted N |
| Grade School Only | 84.5 | 85.4 | 82.3 | 79.4 | 81.2 | 83.4 | 78.3 | Mean |
|  | 18.3 | 16.6 | 18.0 | 17.8 | 18.4 | 16.8 | 17.6 | Standard Deviation |
|  | (369) | (324) | (328) | (349) | (395) | (433) | (349) | Weighted N |
| High School Only | 83.4 | 84.2 | 80.7 | 76.6 | 78.6 | 78.9 | 74.2 | Mean |
|  | 17.9 | 16.4 | 18.3 | 19.0 | 17.4 | 17.0 | 17.0 | Standard Deviation |
|  | (793) | (644) | (750) | (746) | (1062) | (1230) | (1150) | Weighted N |
| College Only | 82.0 | 77.7 | 76.8 | 73.1 | 73.2 | 74.2 | 69.5 | Mean |
|  | 17.3 | 18.7 | 18.5 | 19.4 | 17.4 | 18.1 | 16.6 | Standard Deviation |
|  | (361) | (299) | (420) | (355) | (654) | (742) | (826) | Weighted N |
| 18-24 Only | 81.2 | 80.6 | 78.6 | 72.2 | 71.5 | 72.2 | 68.3 | Mean |
|  | 19.1 | 17.6 | 18.1 | 20.8 | 19.0 | 18.3 | 16.9 | Standard Deviation |
|  | (120) | (118) | (112) | (144) | (334) | (354) | (335) | Weighted N |
| 25-34 Only | 79.7 | 81.8 | 75.4 | 75.2 | 74.0 | 77.1 | 68.8 | Mean |
|  | 20.4 | 17.0 | 19.6 | 20.0 | 18.8 | 17.5 | 16.4 | Standard Deviation |
|  | (323) | (229) | (303) | (301) | (455) | (573) | (558) | Weighted N |
| 35-44 Only | 82.6 | 82.1 | 80.0 | 74.6 | 75.5 | 76.5 | 70.4 | Mean |
|  | 17.5 | 17.5 | 18.6 | 18.8 | 18.5 | 18.5 | 17.2 | Standard Deviation |
|  | (334) | (276) | (321) | (259) | (354) | (327) | (340) | Weighted N |
| 45-54 Only | 84.0 | 81.1 | 80.9 | 75.5 | 79.6 | 78.8 | 74.9 | Mean |
|  | 18.0 | 19.4 | 17.5 | 19.7 | 16.1 | 16.8 | 17.6 | Standard Deviation |
|  | (307) | (256) | (302) | (269) | (348) | (387) | (344) | Weighted N |
| 55-64 Only | 86.0 | 85.1 | 82.1 | 79.7 | 82.6 | 83.8 | 77.5 | Mean |
|  | 15.3 | 15.3 | 18.3 | 16.7 | 15.3 | 15.6 | 15.7 | Standard Deviation |
|  | (221) | (174) | (217) | (239) | (289) | (344) | (345) | Weighted N |
| 65-74 Only | 86.9 | 87.9 | 83.9 | 80.2 | 83.2 | 81.0 | 80.0 | Mean |
|  | 14.8 | 14.4 | 16.2 | 16.2 | 15.5 | 15.3 | 16.1 | Standard Deviation |
|  | (148) | (153) | (170) | (151) | (207) | (272) | (258) | Weighted N |
| 75 And Older Only | 86.6 | 85.5 | 82.3 | 80.3 | 83.6 | 82.4 | 81.5 | Mean |
|  | 16.2 | 15.7 | 17.4 | 17.8 | 14.3 | 18.1 | 15.8 | Standard Deviation |
|  | (74) | (57) | (71) | (85) | (113) | (136) | (137) | Weighted N |

Attitudes toward Self And Others

Table 1.56
Feeling Thermometer for Blacks

|  | Year | | | | | | | |
|---|---|---|---|---|---|---|---|---|
|  | 1964n | 1966n | 1968n | 1970n | 1972n | 1974n | 1976n | |
| Total Population | 63.0 | 63.0 | 64.4 | 61.1 | 63.7 | 65.2 | 60.6 | Mean |
|  | 22.3 | 23.1 | 22.0 | 22.7 | 20.3 | 20.4 | 18.6 | Standard Deviation |
|  | (4537) | (1273) | (2979) | (1807) | (2099) | (2417) | (2288) | Weighted N |
| Unweighted Total | 1785 | 1273 | 1609 | 1636 | 2099 | 2018 | 1825 | |

1964n,1968n,and 1970n include Black supplement.

Figure 1.44
FT--Blacks--Total Population

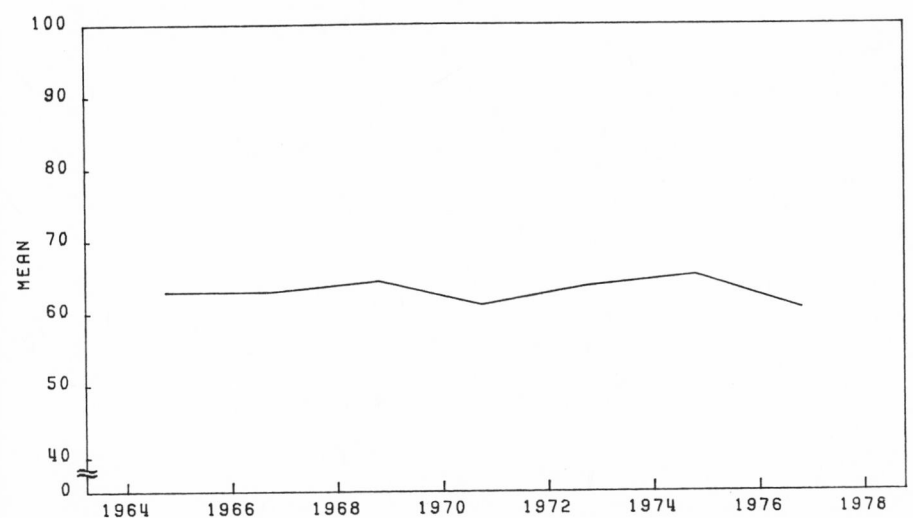

Figure 1.45
FT--Blacks by Race of R

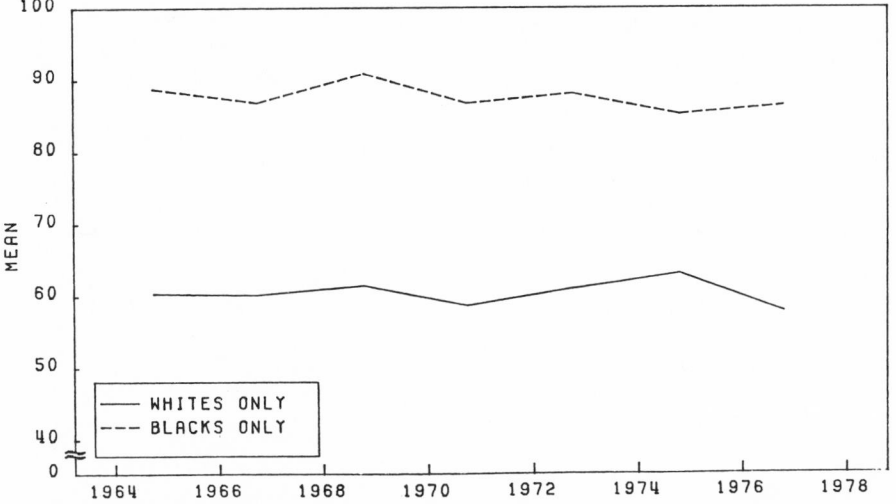

Table 1.57
Feeling Thermometer for Blacks by Social Groups

|  | Year | | | | | | | |
|---|---|---|---|---|---|---|---|---|
|  | 1964n | 1966n | 1968n | 1970n | 1972n | 1974n | 1976n | |
| Males Only | 61.4 | 61.6 | 62.3 | 59.0 | 61.5 | 62.2 | 57.6 | Mean |
|  | 22.9 | 23.1 | 22.6 | 23.5 | 20.8 | 20.9 | 18.6 | Standard Deviation |
|  | (2057) | (567) | (1317) | (791) | (912) | (1015) | (950) | Weighted N |
| Females Only | 64.3 | 64.1 | 66.0 | 62.8 | 65.4 | 67.3 | 62.7 | Mean |
|  | 21.8 | 23.1 | 21.4 | 22.0 | 19.7 | 19.8 | 18.4 | Standard Deviation |
|  | (2480) | (706) | (1662) | (1015) | (1187) | (1402) | (1338) | Weighted N |
| Whites Only | 60.4 | 60.2 | 61.5 | 58.7 | 61.0 | 63.1 | 57.8 | Mean |
|  | 21.3 | 22.2 | 21.0 | 21.7 | 19.1 | 19.6 | 16.9 | Standard Deviation |
|  | (4098) | (1126) | (2674) | (1611) | (1862) | (2151) | (2015) | Weighted N |
| Blacks Only | 88.8 | 86.9 | 90.9 | 86.8 | 88.1 | 85.2 | 86.4 | Mean |
|  | 14.5 | 14.9 | 11.8 | 17.1 | 11.7 | 16.7 | 15.3 | Standard Deviation |
|  | (409) | (131) | (275) | (166) | (210) | (217) | (212) | Weighted N |
| Grade School Only | 61.8 | 60.1 | 63.0 | 57.9 | 62.7 | 65.5 | 64.9 | Mean |
|  | 24.7 | 24.7 | 23.9 | 26.5 | 23.9 | 23.4 | 22.0 | Standard Deviation |
|  | (1109) | (325) | (636) | (412) | (383) | (395) | (336) | Weighted N |
| High School Only | 62.7 | 63.6 | 63.7 | 60.7 | 64.0 | 66.4 | 59.9 | Mean |
|  | 21.6 | 23.1 | 22.5 | 22.3 | 19.9 | 20.0 | 18.5 | Standard Deviation |
|  | (2328) | (644) | (1505) | (926) | (1062) | (1229) | (1132) | Weighted N |
| College Only | 65.0 | 64.8 | 66.9 | 64.8 | 63.8 | 63.4 | 59.6 | Mean |
|  | 21.1 | 20.3 | 19.3 | 19.2 | 18.4 | 19.1 | 17.0 | Standard Deviation |
|  | (1068) | (300) | (833) | (465) | (653) | (764) | (820) | Weighted N |
| 18-24 Only | 60.0 | 63.8 | 65.8 | 62.0 | 63.7 | 65.8 | 57.9 | Mean |
|  | 23.4 | 23.7 | 21.7 | 21.5 | 20.4 | 19.2 | 18.9 | Standard Deviation |
|  | (356) | (118) | (231) | (254) | (332) | (360) | (333) | Weighted N |
| 25-34 Only | 62.7 | 65.7 | 63.7 | 63.2 | 61.5 | 64.4 | 58.3 | Mean |
|  | 22.3 | 23.1 | 21.9 | 22.3 | 19.6 | 19.1 | 18.1 | Standard Deviation |
|  | (937) | (230) | (602) | (356) | (456) | (571) | (546) | Weighted N |
| 35-44 Only | 63.8 | 63.5 | 66.5 | 61.3 | 65.3 | 63.4 | 59.8 | Mean |
|  | 22.5 | 22.8 | 21.7 | 22.5 | 19.6 | 21.4 | 17.0 | Standard Deviation |
|  | (1002) | (276) | (641) | (312) | (351) | (337) | (337) | Weighted N |
| 45-54 Only | 63.2 | 64.7 | 62.5 | 58.7 | 64.7 | 67.4 | 63.4 | Mean |
|  | 22.6 | 23.1 | 22.8 | 25.1 | 20.1 | 19.4 | 16.9 | Standard Deviation |
|  | (903) | (256) | (601) | (312) | (346) | (388) | (338) | Weighted N |
| 55-64 Only | 61.1 | 60.2 | 65.7 | 61.1 | 64.2 | 65.1 | 62.8 | Mean |
|  | 21.3 | 22.4 | 22.2 | 22.2 | 21.4 | 22.2 | 19.4 | Standard Deviation |
|  | (658) | (174) | (440) | (286) | (289) | (341) | (343) | Weighted N |
| 65-74 Only | 65.8 | 60.6 | 64.0 | 60.6 | 63.5 | 65.1 | 62.7 | Mean |
|  | 20.8 | 22.8 | 22.9 | 21.7 | 20.7 | 21.4 | 20.7 | Standard Deviation |
|  | (440) | (154) | (321) | (178) | (201) | (266) | (247) | Weighted N |
| 75 And Older Only | 63.6 | 56.5 | 61.1 | 58.3 | 64.1 | 64.7 | 61.1 | Mean |
|  | 24.3 | 24.0 | 16.8 | 22.8 | 19.8 | 22.5 | 20.6 | Standard Deviation |
|  | (225) | (57) | (137) | (97) | (109) | (133) | (132) | Weighted N |

Chapter 2. Blacks And Whites

In the wake of civil rights ferment, the past two decades have witnessed major changes in racial attitudes in the United States. These changes are eloquently mirrored in our materials. This chapter thus provides a textbook case of the winds of social change.

Most of the attitudinal materials in the chapter show shifts since the early 1960s of 20 to 50 percentage points in the direction of increased liberalism in racial attitudes. At any given point in time during this period, we see that it has typically been the young and the well-educated who have expressed the most liberal views on racial matters, and it is not surprising that these segments of the population have led the way as change has occurred. But nearly parallel changes have taken place in all segments of the population. Indeed, in many instances it can be observed that people who are elderly or limited to grade-school educations have come by 1976 to show distributions of attitudes which now look remarkably like those displayed by the young or well-educated a dozen years before.

Here and there in the tables, however, there are hints that the thrust of change may not be continuing in a simple unidirectional way. For example, in the most general reactions to segregation or desegregation presented to open the chapter, it is evident that the proportion of the population favoring desegregation hit something of a high-water mark in the 1970-72 period and has been receding since. Making corresponding gains in popularity is the vaguer response of "Something in between" segregation and desegregation. Interestingly enough, this retreat to a more intermediate outcome is even more marked among blacks than among whites.

Beyond the numerous attitudinal items in this chapter, one set is made up of perceptions concerning the racial composition of one's neighborhood, friends, and local schools. Like the attitudinal items, these perceptions of actual racial segregation have shown lively change since 1964. The change is, of course, away from the perception that one's social surround is "All black" or "All white", toward at least somewhat greater racial integration.

These perceptual items are of greatest interest when we begin by grouping respondents by race, and then make comparisons as to relative change in advancing desegregation from one arena to another. The most limited changes are those reported for racial segregation in neighborhoods, a view that receives some confirmation from studies of objective residential segregation. White perceptions of pure racial segregation in their neighborhoods have in fact declined notably over this period, from an 80 percent "All white" report in 1964 to about 62 percent by 1976 (table 2.13). This is significant change, but it is considerably smaller than changes registering in the other perceptions. Moreover, while black case numbers are always few and hence sampling variability is very high over time, it is hard to see that blacks themselves have perceived much change in residential segregation since 1964.

Changes in segregation of schools register very clearly in these perceptual materials (tables 2.41-2.50). Reasonably enough, segregation is always sharper for grade schools than for high schools, which draw from wider areas. Nevertheless, the change in reports for both school levels are dramatic relative to the limited change in residential segregation. Most of the change in perceptions, especially among blacks, had run its course between 1964 and 1970 or 1972. Changes since that time have been minimal.

Among the backdrop formed by the preceding items, the reports of the racial composition of friends (tables 2.16-2.20), a socially significant datum for which no corresponding "objective" data are available are most striking. Among whites the likelihood that one's friends are "All white" has declined even more impressively than the corresponding reports for school segregation; and for blacks, the change in racial variety of friendships has at least matched, if not surpassed, the less optional changes in school segregation.

Table 2-1
Does R Favor Desegregation or Segregation?
Total Population

QUESTION. In general, are you in favor of desegregation, strict segregation, or something in between?

|  |  | Year | | | | | | |
|---|---|---|---|---|---|---|---|---|
|  |  | 1964n | 1968n | 1970n | 1972n | 1974q | 1976n | 1978n |
| Desegregation | (5) | 31.5% | 36.5% | 40.6% | 40.8% | 39.1% | 38.6% | 34.3% |
| Something in between | (3) | 44.1 | 46.7 | 42.9 | 44.6 | 49.5 | 49.2 | 54.3 |
| Strict segregation | (1) | 22.8 | 15.7 | 15.5 | 12.6 | 9.8 | 9.4 | 5.1 |
| Don't know |  | 1.5 | 1.1 | 1.0 | 2.0 | 1.7 | 2.9 | 6.3 |
| Total |  | 100% | 100% | 100% | 100% | 100% | 100% | 100% |
| Weighted N |  | 4598 | 2977 | 897 | 2674 | 2899 | 2804 | 2273 |
| Unweighted N |  | 1810 | 1607 | 946 | 2674 | 1474 | 2198 | 2273 |
| Mean |  | 3.18 | 3.42 | 3.51 | 3.58 | 3.60 | 3.60 | 3.62 |
| Standard Deviation |  | 1.47 | 1.39 | 1.42 | 1.36 | 1.28 | 1.27 | 1.14 |

1964n 1968n  and 1970n include Black supplement.

Figure 2-1
De/Segregation--Total Population

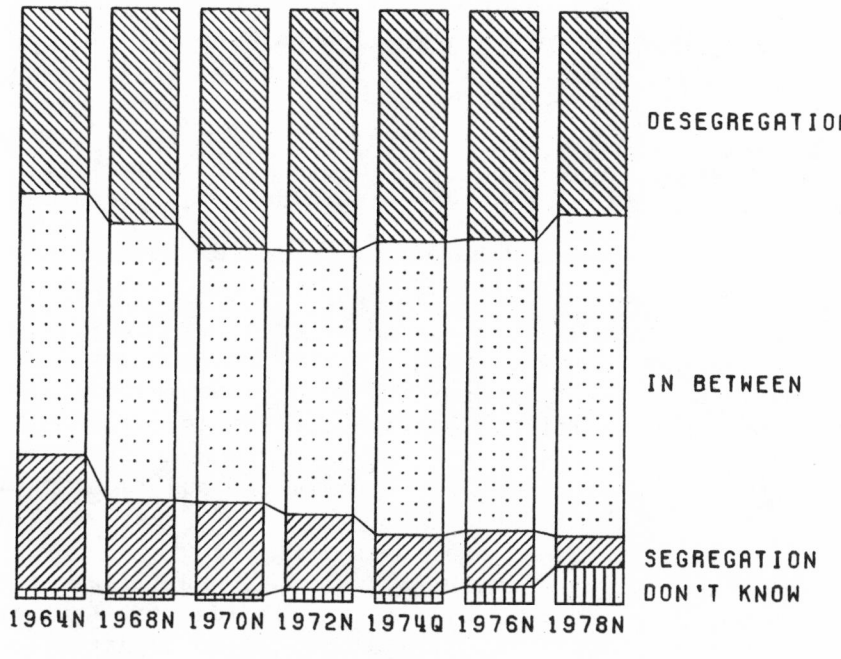

DESEGREGATION

IN BETWEEN

SEGREGATION
DON'T KNOW

1964N 1968N 1970N 1972N 1974Q 1976N 1978N

Blacks And Whites

Table 2.2
Does R Favor Desegregation or Segregation?
Sex of Respondent

|            | Year |  |  |  |  |  |  |  |
|------------|-------|-------|-------|-------|-------|-------|-------|---------------------|
|            | 1964n | 1968n | 1970n | 1972n | 1974q | 1976n | 1978n |                     |
| Males Only | 30.5% | 37.3% | 43.3% | 44.0% | 38.9% | 38.7% | 37.3% | Desegregation       |
|            | 45.5  | 48.3  | 39.6  | 43.0  | 51.1  | 52.7  | 58.9  | Something in between |
|            | 24.0  | 14.4  | 17.1  | 13.0  | 10.0  | 8.7   | 3.8   | Strict segregation  |
|            | (2044)| (1288)| (380) | (1134)| (1282)| (1148)| (948) | Weighted N          |
| Females Only | 33.2 | 36.6 | 39.3 | 39.8 | 40.4 | 40.5 | 36.0 | Desegregation       |
|            | 44.3  | 46.4  | 46.1  | 47.4  | 49.7  | 49.1  | 57.2  | Something in between |
|            | 22.5  | 17.0  | 14.5  | 12.7  | 9.9   | 10.4  | 6.8   | Strict segregation  |
|            | (2485)| (1657)| (508) | (1486)| (1568)| (1570)| (1181)| Weighted N          |

Table 2.3
Race of Respondent

|            | 1964n | 1968n | 1970n | 1972n | 1974q | 1976n | 1978n |                     |
|------------|-------|-------|-------|-------|-------|-------|-------|---------------------|
| Whites Only | 27.2% | 32.7% | 37.6% | 38.4% | 36.6% | 35.6% | 33.9% | Desegregation       |
|            | 47.7  | 50.2  | 45.5  | 47.4  | 53.2  | 53.9  | 60.7  | Something in between |
|            | 25.0  | 17.1  | 16.8  | 14.2  | 10.2  | 10.5  | 5.4   | Strict segregation  |
|            | (4086)| (2636)| (791) | (2316)| (2441)| (2381)| (1869)| Weighted N          |
| Blacks Only | 77.8 | 77.9 | 76.1 | 68.1 | 62.4 | 73.4 | 55.4 | Desegregation       |
|            | 16.6  | 18.8  | 19.9  | 30.0  | 31.7  | 25.1  | 38.0  | Something in between |
|            | 5.6   | 3.3   | 4.0   | 1.9   | 5.9   | 1.5   | 6.6   | Strict segregation  |
|            | (410) | (271) | (83)  | (263) | (290) | (271) | (213) | Weighted N          |

Figure 2.2
De/Segregation by Race of R

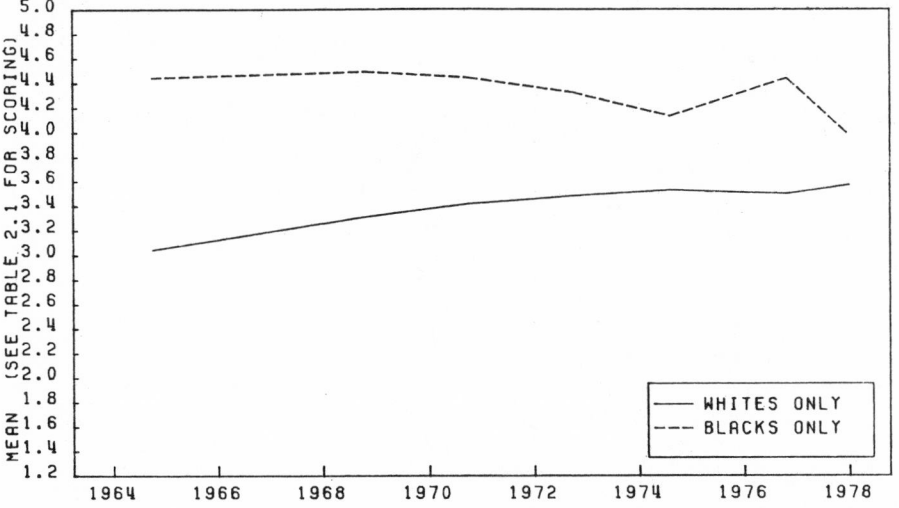

Blacks And Whites

Table 2.4
Does R Favor Desegregation or Segregation?
Education of Respondent

|  | Year | | | | | | | |
|---|---|---|---|---|---|---|---|---|
|  | 1964n | 1968n | 1970n | 1972n | 1974q | 1976n | 1978n |  |
| Grade School Only | 27.0% | 26.3% | 31.9% | 27.0% | 27.2% | 30.6% | 39.0% | Desegregation |
|  | 38.7 | 43.6 | 42.4 | 49.9 | 57.3 | 52.7 | 45.0 | Something in between |
|  | 34.3 | 30.0 | 25.7 | 23.1 | 15.5 | 16.7 | 16.0 | Strict segregation |
|  | (1115) | (653) | (224) | (503) | (452) | (428) | (231) | Weighted N |
| High School Only | 30.4 | 34.0 | 35.9 | 37.6 | 35.7 | 34.4 | 33.4 | Desegregation |
|  | 47.1 | 51.1 | 49.4 | 49.3 | 54.0 | 54.4 | 60.7 | Something in between |
|  | 22.6 | 14.9 | 14.7 | 13.1 | 10.3 | 11.3 | 5.9 | Strict segregation |
|  | (2312) | (1472) | (439) | (1341) | (1371) | (1352) | (1103) | Weighted N |
| College Only | 40.7 | 50.8 | 60.4 | 58.2 | 50.9 | 51.6 | 40.5 | Desegregation |
|  | 47.0 | 43.1 | 32.6 | 36.2 | 42.2 | 44.3 | 57.7 | Something in between |
|  | 12.3 | 6.2 | 7.0 | 5.6 | 6.9 | 4.0 | 1.8 | Strict segregation |
|  | (1072) | (813) | (223) | (773) | (1010) | (929) | (792) | Weighted N |

Figure 2.3
De/Segregation by Education of R

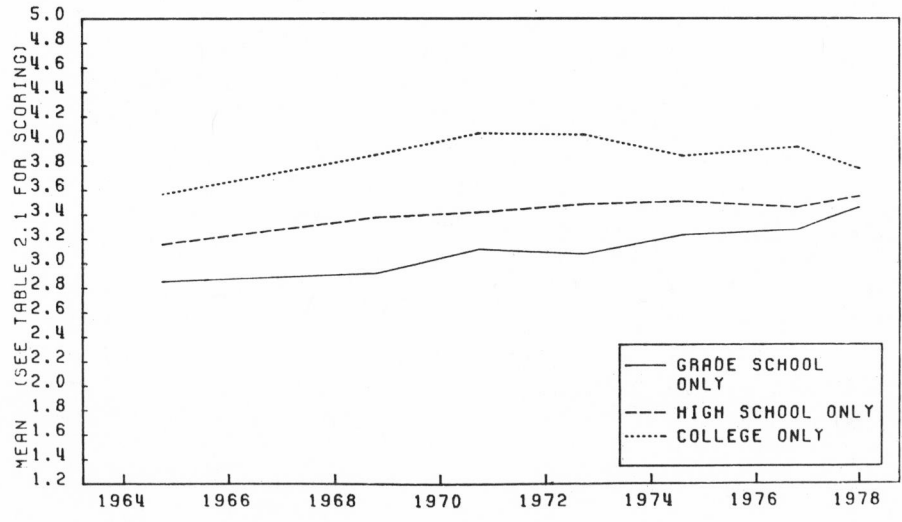

Blacks And Whites

Figure 2.4
De/Segregation by Age of R

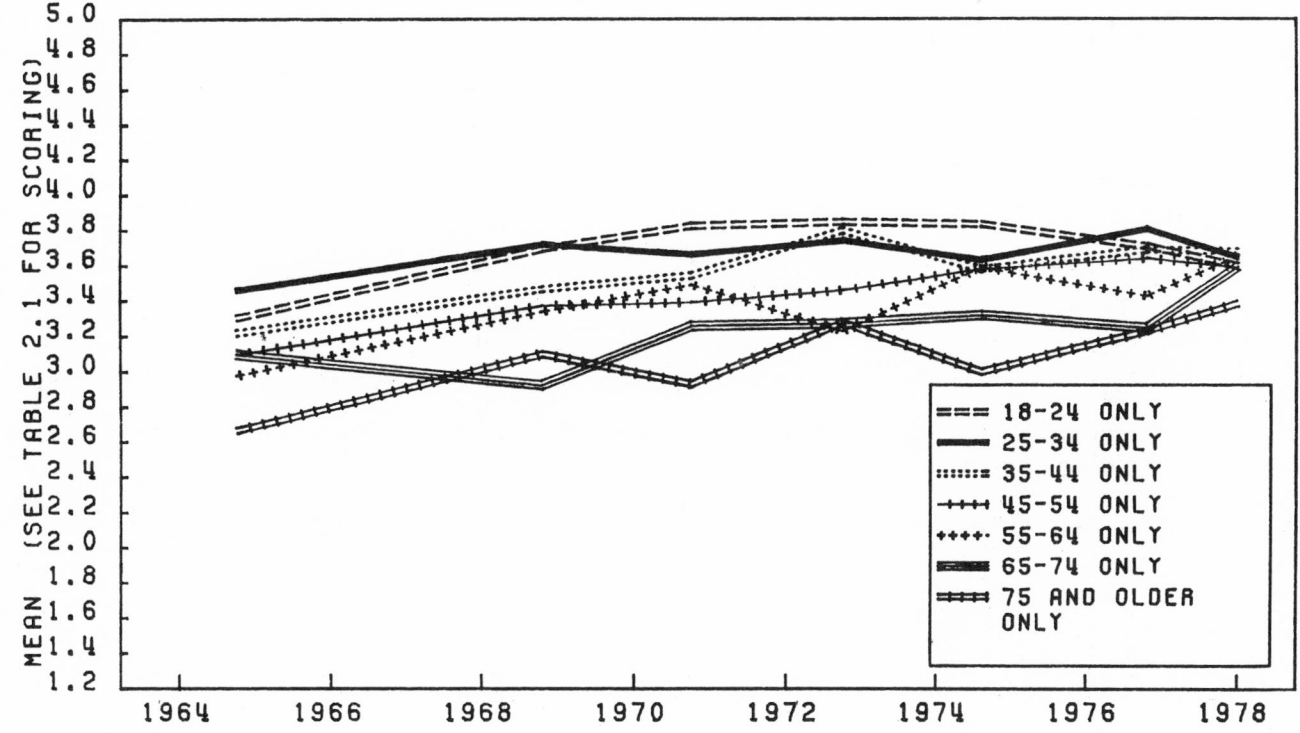

Blacks And Whites

Table 2.5
Does R Favor Desegregation or Segregation?
Age of Respondent

|  | Year | | | | | | | |
|---|---|---|---|---|---|---|---|---|
|  | 1964n | 1968n | 1970n | 1972n | 1974q | 1976n | 1978n | |
| 18-24 Only | 34.5% | 41.0% | 49.2% | 50.9% | 46.8% | 40.3% | 32.8% | Desegregation |
|  | 46.3 | 52.8 | 43.0 | 40.8 | 48.3 | 55.0 | 64.4 | Something in between |
|  | 19.3 | 6.1 | 7.8 | 8.4 | 4.9 | 4.7 | 2.8 | Strict segregation |
|  | (348) | (229) | (131) | (395) | (470) | (385) | (326) | Weighted N |
| 25-34 Only | 38.5 | 46.3 | 43.9 | 48.1 | 43.5 | 46.3 | 36.2 | Desegregation |
|  | 46.2 | 43.6 | 45.5 | 41.2 | 44.7 | 48.0 | 60.2 | Something in between |
|  | 15.3 | 10.1 | 10.6 | 10.7 | 11.7 | 5.7 | 3.6 | Strict segregation |
|  | (933) | (594) | (170) | (568) | (657) | (663) | (522) | Weighted N |
| 35-44 Only | 35.3 | 37.7 | 45.8 | 49.4 | 36.9 | 43.2 | 39.3 | Desegregation |
|  | 40.4 | 48.1 | 35.8 | 41.3 | 55.4 | 48.3 | 55.6 | Something in between |
|  | 24.3 | 14.2 | 18.4 | 9.3 | 7.7 | 8.5 | 5.1 | Strict segregation |
|  | (991) | (618) | (147) | (431) | (493) | (410) | (374) | Weighted N |
| 45-54 Only | 29.1 | 35.1 | 38.8 | 35.7 | 39.2 | 40.4 | 35.8 | Desegregation |
|  | 46.7 | 48.6 | 42.1 | 51.6 | 50.9 | 51.5 | 57.9 | Something in between |
|  | 24.2 | 16.3 | 19.1 | 12.6 | 9.9 | 8.2 | 6.2 | Strict segregation |
|  | (901) | (590) | (146) | (428) | (475) | (379) | (321) | Weighted N |
| 55-64 Only | 24.5 | 34.3 | 36.8 | 28.3 | 39.8 | 36.2 | 39.2 | Desegregation |
|  | 50.0 | 48.4 | 51.0 | 54.9 | 50.1 | 49.0 | 54.6 | Something in between |
|  | 25.5 | 17.3 | 12.1 | 16.8 | 10.1 | 14.8 | 6.2 | Strict segregation |
|  | (670) | (440) | (148) | (364) | (415) | (385) | (273) | Weighted N |
| 65-74 Only | 31.7 | 26.5 | 34.9 | 33.0 | 32.7 | 27.4 | 39.5 | Desegregation |
|  | 41.5 | 43.3 | 43.1 | 47.7 | 50.5 | 57.4 | 50.8 | Something in between |
|  | 26.8 | 30.2 | 22.0 | 19.3 | 16.8 | 15.1 | 9.7 | Strict segregation |
|  | (448) | (321) | (88) | (264) | (214) | (317) | (195) | Weighted N |
| 75 And Older Only | 22.2 | 27.5 | 27.5 | 35.1 | 16.8 | 32.1 | 31.2 | Desegregation |
|  | 38.9 | 50.0 | 41.5 | 43.7 | 66.4 | 47.3 | 56.9 | Something in between |
|  | 38.9 | 22.5 | 31.0 | 21.2 | 16.8 | 20.6 | 11.9 | Strict segregation |
|  | (221) | (142) | (51) | (151) | (113) | (165) | (109) | Weighted N |

Blacks And Whites

Table 2.6
Do Blacks Have a Right to Live Wherever They Want?
Total Population

QUESTION: Which of these statements would you agree with (more): 1) White people have a right to keep Black people/Negroes/Blacks out of their neighborhoods if they want to, or 2) Black people/Negroes/Blacks have a right to live wherever they can afford to (just like white people/anybody else).

|  | | Year | | | | | | |
|---|---|---|---|---|---|---|---|---|
|  | | 1964n | 1968n | 1970n | 1972n | 1974q | 1975p | 1976n |
| Whites can keep Blacks out | (1) | 26.5% | 22.2% | 19.1% | 15.7% | 9.5% | 12.5% | 8.2% |
| Blacks can live where they choose | (5) | 57.1 | 67.8 | 70.5 | 76.4 | 83.4 | 83.0 | 85.3 |
| Don't know | | 16.5 | 10.1 | 10.4 | 7.9 | 7.1 | 4.5 | 6.5 |
| Total | | 100% | 100% | 100% | 100% | 100% | 100% | 100% |
| Weighted N | | 4624 | 3087 | 915 | 2696 | 2956 | 1884 | 2851 |
| Unweighted N | | 1819 | 1666 | 964 | 2696 | 1505 | 1884 | 2234 |
| Mean | | 3.73 | 4.01 | 4.15 | 4.32 | 4.59 | 4.47 | 4.65 |
| Standard Deviation | | 1.86 | 1.72 | 1.64 | 1.50 | 1.21 | 1.35 | 1.13 |

1964n,1968n, and 1970n include Black supplement.

Figure 2.5
Can Blacks Live Anywhere?--Total Population

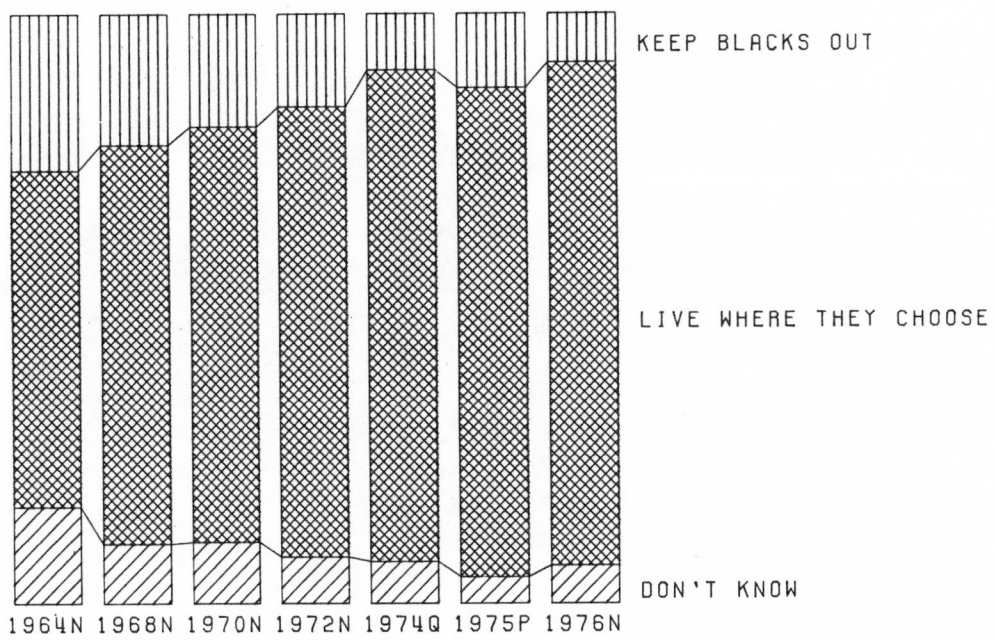

KEEP BLACKS OUT

LIVE WHERE THEY CHOOSE

DON'T KNOW

1964N 1968N 1970N 1972N 1974Q 1975P 1976N

Blacks And Whites

Table 2.7
Do Blacks Have a Right to Live Wherever They Want?
Sex of Respondent

|  | Year | | | | | | | |
|---|---|---|---|---|---|---|---|---|
|  | 1964n | 1968n | 1970n | 1972n | 1974q | 1975p | 1976n | |
| Males Only | 27.6% | 21.5% | 19.9% | 14.3% | 9.5% | 11.3% | 7.6% | Whites can keep Blacks out |
|  | 57.5 | 70.4 | 72.5 | 79.2 | 83.6 | 85.7 | 87.2 | Blacks can live where they choose |
|  | 14.9 | 8.1 | 7.6 | 6.5 | 6.9 | 2.9 | 5.3 | Don't know |
|  | (2095) | (1352) | (388) | (1160) | (1320) | (785) | (1197) | Weighted N |
| Females Only | 25.5 | 22.7 | 18.4 | 16.7 | 9.4 | 13.4 | 8.7 | Whites can keep Blacks out |
|  | 56.7 | 65.7 | 69.0 | 74.3 | 83.3 | 81.0 | 83.9 | Blacks can live where they choose |
|  | 17.7 | 11.6 | 12.5 | 8.9 | 7.3 | 5.6 | 7.4 | Don't know |
|  | (2529) | (1735) | (526) | (1536) | (1636) | (1099) | (1648) | Weighted N |

Table 2.8
Race of Respondent

|  | 1964n | 1968n | 1970n | 1972n | 1974q | 1975p | 1976n | |
|---|---|---|---|---|---|---|---|---|
| Whites Only | 29.2% | 24.4% | 20.9% | 17.5% | 10.3% | 14.1% | 9.2% | Whites can keep Blacks out |
|  | 53.3 | 64.9 | 67.8 | 73.8 | 82.2 | 81.2 | 83.6 | Blacks can live where they choose |
|  | 17.6 | 10.8 | 11.3 | 8.7 | 7.5 | 4.8 | 7.1 | Don't know |
|  | (4167) | (2766) | (816) | (2390) | (2539) | (1619) | (2482) | Weighted N |
| Blacks Only | 1.4 | 1.4 | 1.8 | 0.4 | 1.0 | 0.0 | 1.0 | Whites can keep Blacks out |
|  | 91.6 | 95.4 | 96.1 | 98.1 | 95.9 | 96.9 | 98.1 | Blacks can live where they choose |
|  | 6.9 | 3.2 | 2.1 | 1.5 | 3.1 | 3.1 | 0.9 | Don't know |
|  | (418) | (281) | (84) | (265) | (294) | (195) | (289) | Weighted N |

Figure 2.6
Can Blacks Live Anywhere? by Race of R

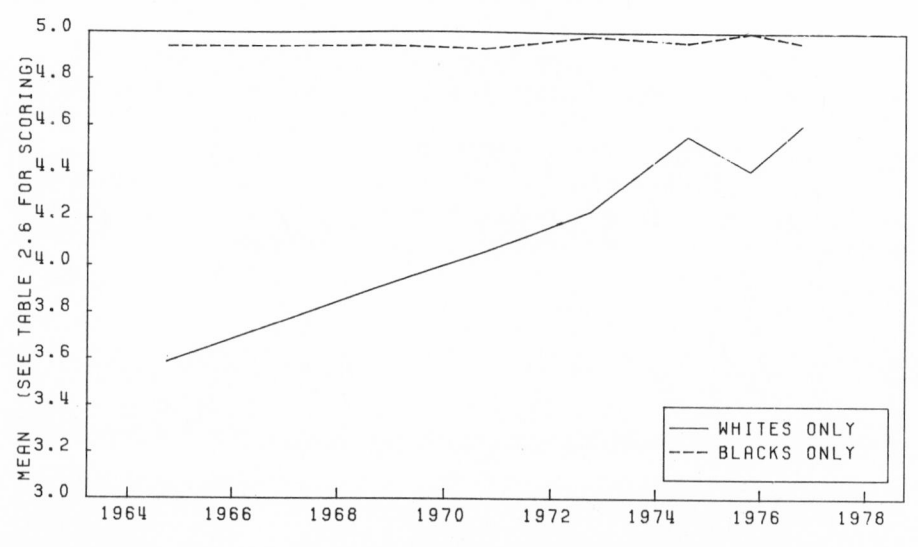

Blacks And Whites

Table 2.9
Do Blacks Have a Right to Live Wherever They Want?
Education of Respondent

| | | | | Year | | | | |
|---|---|---|---|---|---|---|---|---|
| | 1964n | 1968n | 1970n | 1972n | 1974q | 1975p | 1976n | |
| Grade School Only | 35.3% | 32.3% | 26.1% | 27.2% | 18.0% | 25.5% | 15.8% | Whites can keep Blacks out |
| | 46.0 | 54.6 | 58.4 | 60.9 | 70.2 | 64.8 | 72.8 | Blacks can live where they choose |
| | 18.7 | 13.0 | 15.5 | 11.9 | 11.8 | 9.7 | 11.4 | Don't know |
| | (1151) | (699) | (234) | (537) | (484) | (318) | (472) | Weighted N |
| High School Only | 25.6 | 20.1 | 21.3 | 16.0 | 9.6 | 12.1 | 9.0 | Whites can keep Blacks out |
| | 57.9 | 69.9 | 69.1 | 76.5 | 83.7 | 84.0 | 84.8 | Blacks can live where they choose |
| | 16.5 | 10.0 | 9.6 | 7.5 | 6.7 | 3.9 | 6.2 | Don't know |
| | (2344) | (1539) | (452) | (1368) | (1410) | (926) | (1418) | Weighted N |
| College Only | 19.1 | 17.5 | 7.4 | 7.2 | 5.5 | 6.7 | 3.3 | Whites can keep Blacks out |
| | 67.0 | 74.9 | 85.5 | 87.1 | 89.3 | 90.8 | 92.5 | Blacks can live where they choose |
| | 13.9 | 7.6 | 7.0 | 5.7 | 5.3 | 2.5 | 4.1 | Don't know |
| | (1099) | (842) | (226) | (788) | (1045) | (631) | (946) | Weighted N |

Figure 2.7
Can Blacks Live Anywhere? by Education of R

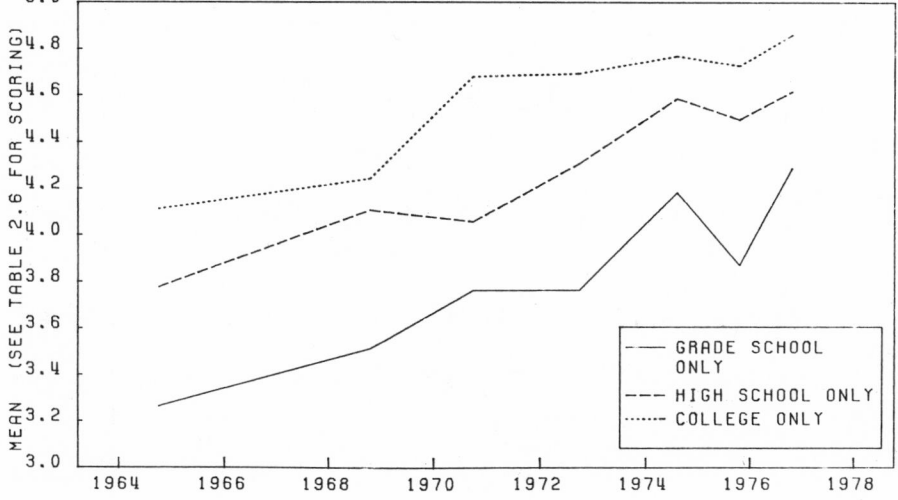

Blacks And Whites

Figure 2.8
Can Blacks Live Anywhere? by Age of R

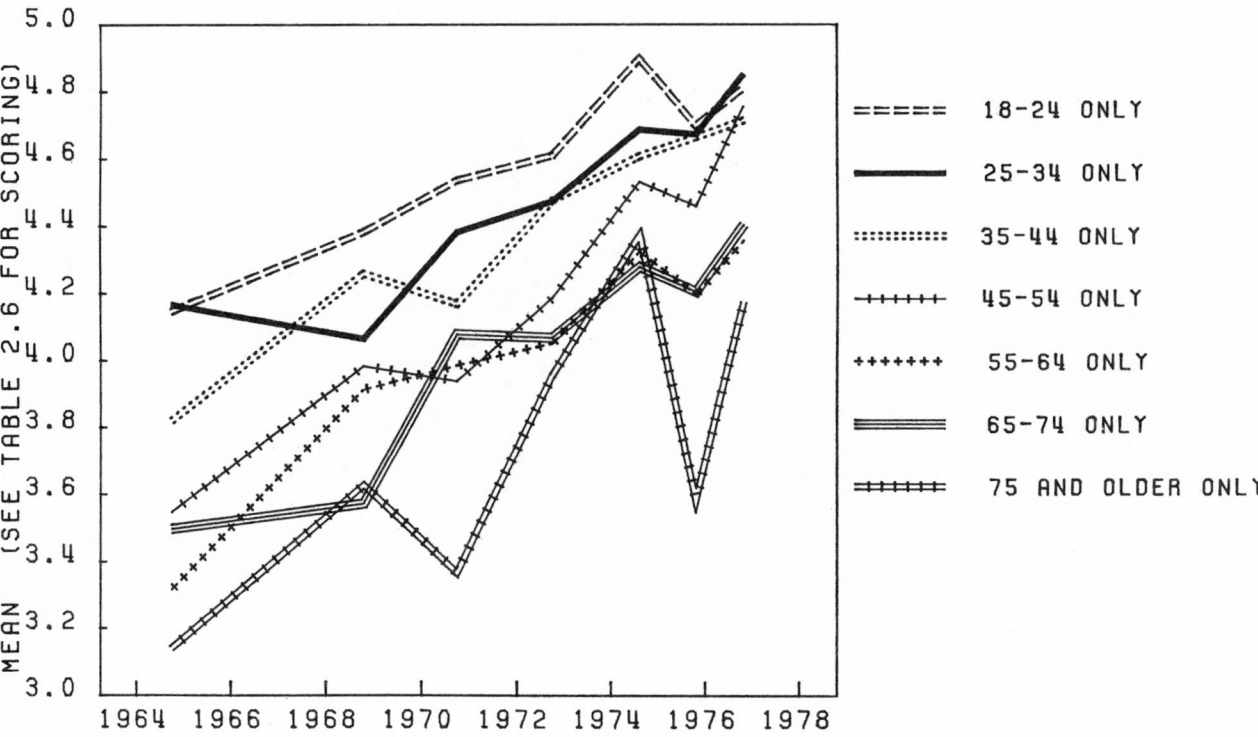

Blacks And Whites

Table 2.10
Do Blacks Have a Right to Live Wherever They Want?
Age of Respondent

|  | Year | | | | | | | |
|---|---|---|---|---|---|---|---|---|
|  | 1964n | 1968n | 1970n | 1972n | 1974q | 1975p | 1976n | |
| 18-24 Only | 18.5% | 14.7% | 11.2% | 9.5% | 2.5% | 7.3% | 4.6% | Whites can keep Blacks out |
|  | 68.1 | 80.2 | 85.0 | 88.4 | 94.5 | 89.7 | 92.2 | Blacks can live where they choose |
|  | 13.4 | 5.2 | 3.9 | 2.0 | 3.1 | 3.0 | 3.2 | Don't know |
|  | (357) | (232) | (132) | (398) | (487) | (301) | (392) | Weighted N |
| 25-34 Only | 17.7 | 21.7 | 13.9 | 12.5 | 7.6 | 8.0 | 3.6 | Whites can keep Blacks out |
|  | 67.2 | 71.1 | 76.0 | 82.9 | 89.0 | 90.4 | 92.6 | Blacks can live where they choose |
|  | 15.1 | 7.2 | 10.1 | 4.5 | 3.4 | 1.6 | 3.8 | Don't know |
|  | (948) | (608) | (173) | (574) | (674) | (448) | (692) | Weighted N |
| 35-44 Only | 26.2 | 16.7 | 19.5 | 12.2 | 9.1 | 8.2 | 6.9 | Whites can keep Blacks out |
|  | 62.5 | 73.3 | 74.3 | 80.8 | 83.5 | 89.7 | 89.0 | Blacks can live where they choose |
|  | 11.3 | 10.0 | 6.2 | 7.0 | 7.5 | 2.1 | 4.1 | Don't know |
|  | (1012) | (647) | (154) | (443) | (496) | (292) | (423) | Weighted N |
| 45-54 Only | 29.9 | 22.7 | 24.9 | 18.5 | 10.8 | 12.9 | 5.7 | Whites can keep Blacks out |
|  | 52.3 | 66.6 | 68.8 | 72.5 | 81.2 | 82.4 | 87.4 | Blacks can live where they choose |
|  | 17.8 | 10.7 | 6.4 | 9.0 | 8.0 | 4.8 | 6.9 | Don't know |
|  | (921) | (625) | (151) | (443) | (501) | (272) | (396) | Weighted N |
| 55-64 Only | 32.7 | 24.6 | 21.3 | 20.8 | 15.6 | 18.9 | 14.8 | Whites can keep Blacks out |
|  | 45.0 | 65.9 | 62.6 | 66.9 | 76.5 | 75.4 | 77.4 | Blacks can live where they choose |
|  | 22.3 | 9.5 | 16.1 | 12.2 | 7.9 | 5.7 | 7.7 | Don't know |
|  | (673) | (455) | (155) | (384) | (430) | (264) | (408) | Weighted N |
| 65-74 Only | 31.2 | 30.4 | 18.8 | 20.4 | 15.7 | 17.8 | 13.0 | Whites can keep Blacks out |
|  | 51.7 | 54.7 | 62.7 | 66.9 | 71.3 | 71.6 | 74.2 | Blacks can live where they choose |
|  | 17.1 | 14.9 | 18.5 | 12.7 | 13.0 | 10.7 | 12.7 | Don't know |
|  | (462) | (349) | (91) | (275) | (223) | (197) | (330) | Weighted N |
| 75 And Older Only | 34.2 | 28.8 | 33.5 | 22.3 | 12.2 | 30.9 | 17.8 | Whites can keep Blacks out |
|  | 39.3 | 55.0 | 48.6 | 63.1 | 65.6 | 56.4 | 68.4 | Blacks can live where they choose |
|  | 26.5 | 16.3 | 17.9 | 14.6 | 22.1 | 12.7 | 13.8 | Don't know |
|  | (234) | (160) | (54) | (157) | (131) | (110) | (188) | Weighted N |

Table 2 11
Racial Composition of Neighborhood
Total Population

QUESTION Is this neighborhood you live in  All White, Mostly White, About half and half, Mostly Negro/Black, All Negro/Black?

|  |  | Year | | | | | | | | |
|---|---|---|---|---|---|---|---|---|---|---|
|  |  | 1964n | 1968n | 1970n | 1971j | 1972f | 1972n | 1974q | 1975p | 1976n |
| All White | (1) | 72.3% | 68.1% | 66.9% | 61.8% | 64.0% | 58.5% | 55.4% | 57.8% | 54.7% |
| Mostly White | (2) | 15.2 | 18.7 | 20.8 | 23.3 | 23.3 | 27 3 | 32.9 | 28.9 | 30.2 |
| About half and half | (3) | 4.9 | 5.9 | 4.8 | 5.9 | 6.2 | 5.7 | 4.9 | 5.0 | 6.2 |
| Mostly Negro/Black | (4) | 4.3 | 4.7 | 5.1 | 6.7 | 4.5 | 4 6 | 4.9 | 4.9 | 5.2 |
| All Negro/Black | (5) | 3.0 | 2.1 | 2.0 | 2.2 | 1.6 | 3.4 | 1.6 | 3.1 | 2.9 |
| Don't know |  | 0.4 | 0.4 | 0.5 | 0.1 | 0.5 | 0.6 | 0.3 | 0.3 | 0.8 |
| Total |  | 100% | 100% | 100% | 100% | 100% | 100% | 100% | 100% | 100% |
| Weighted N |  | 4638 | 3086 | 907 | 9421 | 1290 | 2696 | 2950 | 1890 | 2856 |
| Unweighted N |  | 1831 | 1666 | 955 | 2131 | 1290 | 2696 | 1503 | 1890 | 2238 |
| Mean |  | 1.50 | 1.53 | 1.54 | 1.64 | 1.56 | 1.66 | 1.64 | 1.66 | 1.70 |
| Standard Deviation |  | 0.98 | 0.95 | 0.94 | 1.01 | 0.92 | 1.01 | 0.90 | 0.99 | 1.00 |

1964n,1968n, and 1970n include Black supplement.

Figure 2.9
Racial Composition of Neighborhood--Total Population

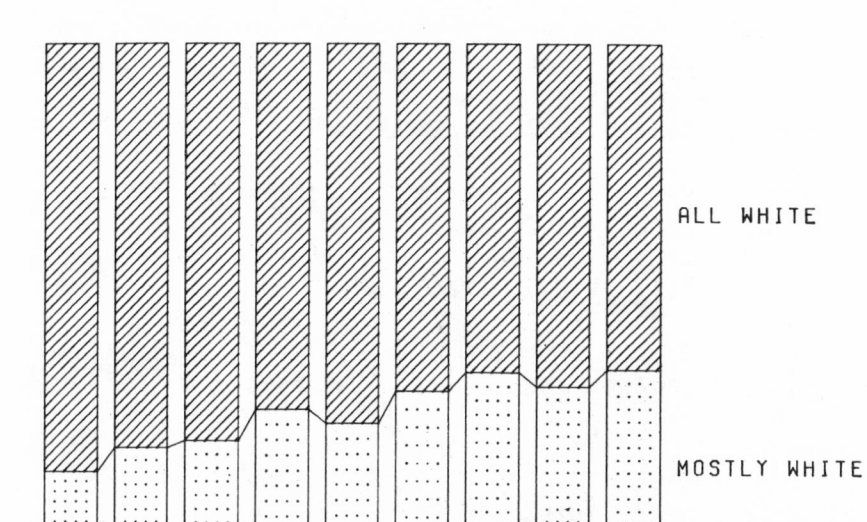

Table 2.12
Racial Composition of Neighborhood
Sex of Respondent

|  | Year | | | | | | | | |  |
|---|---|---|---|---|---|---|---|---|---|---|
|  | 1964n | 1968n | 1970n | 1971j | 1972f | 1972n | 1974q | 1975p | 1976n |  |
| Males Only | 73.1% | 69.1% | 65.7% | 61.8% | 63.0% | 58.1% | 52.3% | 58.5% | 54.5% | All White |
|  | 16.0 | 19.0 | 22.1 | 23.3 | 24.0 | 28.8 | 36.1 | 30.1 | 34.5 | Mostly White |
|  | 4.5 | 5.4 | 5.4 | 6.1 | 6.8 | 6.0 | 5.1 | 5.8 | 5.2 | Half and half |
|  | 3.9 | 5.1 | 4.7 | 6.4 | 5.0 | 4.5 | 5.2 | 4.2 | 4.1 | Mostly Black |
|  | 2.5 | 1.4 | 2.1 | 2.3 | 1.1 | 2.7 | 1.4 | 1.5 | 1.7 | All Black |
|  | (2098) | (1351) | (384) | (4485) | (543) | (1163) | (1311) | (792) | (1203) | Weighted N |
| Females Only | 72.0 | 67.9 | 68.3 | 61.8 | 65.1 | 59.4 | 58.2 | 57.5 | 55.6 | All White |
|  | 14.6 | 18.6 | 20.0 | 23.4 | 22.9 | 26.4 | 30.6 | 28.3 | 27.5 | Mostly White |
|  | 5.3 | 6.4 | 4.4 | 5.8 | 5.8 | 5.6 | 4.8 | 4.5 | 7.1 | Half and half |
|  | 4.7 | 4.3 | 5.3 | 7.1 | 4.2 | 4.7 | 4.7 | 5.5 | 6.0 | Mostly Black |
|  | 3.4 | 2.7 | 2.0 | 2.0 | 2.0 | 3.9 | 1.8 | 4.2 | 3.8 | All Black |
|  | (2540) | (1735) | (523) | (4936) | (747) | (1533) | (1639) | (1093) | (1647) | Weighted N |

Table 2.13
Race of Respondent

|  | 1964n | 1968n | 1970n | 1971j | 1972f | 1972n | 1974q | 1975p | 1976n |  |
|---|---|---|---|---|---|---|---|---|---|---|
| Whites Only | 80.0% | 75.9% | 74.4% | 70.2% | 71.4% | 65.9% | 62.6% | 65.3% | 62.0% | All White |
|  | 16.1 | 19.4 | 21.5 | 24.3 | 24.5 | 29.0 | 34.6 | 30.5 | 32.2 | Mostly White |
|  | 3.0 | 3.6 | 3.0 | 4.4 | 3.2 | 4.3 | 2.2 | 3.1 | 4.8 | Half and half |
|  | 0.9 | 1.1 | 1.0 | 1.1 | 0.9 | 0.7 | 0.6 | 1.0 | 1.0 | Mostly Black |
|  | 0.0 | 0.0 | 0.0 | 0.1 | 0.1 | 0.1 | 0.0 | 0.1 | 0.1 | All Black |
|  | (4182) | (2764) | (812) | (8206) | (1158) | (2389) | (2535) | (1626) | (2485) | Weighted N |
| Blacks Only | 1.7 | 1.1 | 0.7 | 0.4 | 0.0 | 0.8 | 0.0 | 1.0 | 0.0 | All White |
|  | 6.0 | 12.1 | 13.0 | 6.9 | 10.4 | 9.1 | 15.6 | 11.9 | 11.3 | Mostly White |
|  | 19.5 | 23.8 | 19.2 | 17.0 | 33.0 | 17.0 | 24.5 | 19.6 | 17.1 | Half and half |
|  | 39.3 | 39.9 | 45.3 | 56.2 | 39.1 | 39.4 | 43.9 | 39.2 | 42.8 | Mostly Black |
|  | 33.5 | 23.1 | 21.7 | 19.5 | 17.4 | 33.7 | 16.0 | 28.4 | 28.8 | All Black |
|  | (420) | (282) | (83) | (965) | (115) | (266) | (296) | (194) | (293) | Weighted N |

Table 2.14
Racial Composition of Neighborhood
Education of Respondent

| | | | | | Year | | | | | |
|---|---|---|---|---|---|---|---|---|---|---|
| | 1964n | 1968n | 1970n | 1971j | 1972f | 1972n | 1974q | 1975p | 1976n | |
| Grade School Only | 63.5% | 61.4% | 65.5% | 58.9% | 63.2% | 63.2% | 57.1% | 64.0% | 55.1% | All White |
| | 15.9 | 17.5 | 18.2 | 19.8 | 19.8 | 20.5 | 22.8 | 20.5 | 21.4 | Mostly White |
| | 7.8 | 9.7 | 6.5 | 7.2 | 8.3 | 6.8 | 8.5 | 3.8 | 7.5 | Half and half |
| | 7.0 | 8.0 | 6.7 | 10.3 | 5.4 | 4.9 | 7.9 | 6.0 | 8.3 | Mostly Black |
| | 5.7 | 3.5 | 3.0 | 3.9 | 3.3 | 4.7 | 3.7 | 5.7 | 7.7 | All Black |
| | (1155) | (695) | (229) | (2075) | (243) | (537) | (483) | (317) | (471) | Weighted N |
| | | | | | | | | | | |
| High School Only | 74.6 | 70.8 | 67.7 | 66.5 | 64.9 | 59.5 | 58.7 | 59.0 | 54.4 | All White |
| | 14.7 | 16.4 | 18.8 | 20.0 | 20.8 | 26.0 | 30.5 | 25.9 | 30.8 | Mostly White |
| | 4.7 | 6.2 | 5.4 | 5.4 | 7.3 | 6.1 | 4.3 | 5.5 | 7.4 | Half and half |
| | 3.5 | 4.3 | 5.9 | 6.0 | 5.8 | 4.7 | 4.8 | 6.1 | 4.9 | Mostly Black |
| | 2.6 | 2.3 | 2.2 | 2.0 | 1.2 | 3.7 | 1.6 | 3.5 | 2.5 | All Black |
| | (2357) | (1543) | (451) | (4744) | (661) | (1372) | (1410) | (935) | (1423) | Weighted N |
| | | | | | | | | | | |
| College Only | 77.7 | 69.8 | 68.1 | 55.6 | 64.2 | 54.6 | 50.8 | 53.1 | 56.4 | All White |
| | 15.9 | 24.5 | 27.9 | 32.3 | 29.7 | 34.7 | 41.1 | 38.0 | 34.2 | Mostly White |
| | 2.5 | 2.5 | 2.0 | 5.9 | 2.9 | 4.4 | 4.0 | 5.1 | 3.9 | Half and half |
| | 3.1 | 2.6 | 1.6 | 5.1 | 1.8 | 4.2 | 3.6 | 2.7 | 4.1 | Mostly Black |
| | 0.8 | 0.6 | 0.4 | 1.1 | 1.3 | 2.1 | 0.6 | 1.1 | 1.3 | All Black |
| | (1093) | (841) | (225) | (2556) | (382) | (784) | (1041) | (631) | (948) | Weighted N |

Table 2.15
Racial Composition of Neighborhood
Age of Respondent

| | Year | | | | | | | | | |
|---|---|---|---|---|---|---|---|---|---|---|
| | 1964n | 1968n | 1970n | 1971j | 1972f | 1972n | 1974q | 1975p | 1976n | |
| **18-24 Only** | 67.1% | 60.3% | 66.2% | 58.0% | 61.0% | 52.2% | 51.3% | 48.7% | 56.5% | All White |
| | 19.9 | 19.2 | 19.1 | 24.7 | 23.4 | 32.1 | 38.7 | 32.3 | 28.6 | Mostly White |
| | 5.1 | 12.7 | 5.7 | 7.2 | 7.3 | 6.6 | 3.9 | 11.3 | 6.5 | Half and half |
| | 4.2 | 5.7 | 6.7 | 6.7 | 4.4 | 5.3 | 4.8 | 3.7 | 4.9 | Mostly Black |
| | 3.7 | 2.2 | 2.3 | 3.3 | 3.9 | 3.8 | 1.2 | 4.0 | 3.6 | All Black |
| | (356) | (233) | (132) | (1484) | (209) | (397) | (488) | (300) | (394) | Weighted N |
| **25-34 Only** | 71.6 | 65.6 | 65.8 | 60.9 | 60.6 | 57.1 | 46.7 | 51.1 | 53.3 | All White |
| | 15.3 | 21.7 | 24.2 | 23.5 | 23.7 | 29.8 | 37.4 | 35.0 | 31.1 | Mostly White |
| | 5.9 | 6.3 | 3.5 | 7.9 | 7.9 | 6.5 | 8.5 | 4.7 | 7.5 | Half and half |
| | 3.8 | 4.1 | 4.9 | 6.5 | 6.5 | 4.0 | 6.4 | 6.3 | 6.6 | Mostly Black |
| | 3.4 | 2.3 | 1.6 | 1.2 | 1.4 | 2.6 | 0.9 | 2.9 | 1.5 | All Black |
| | (948) | (610) | (171) | (1913) | (279) | (576) | (670) | (448) | (692) | Weighted N |
| **35-44 Only** | 73.3 | 69.6 | 62.9 | 60.3 | 61.2 | 57.9 | 56.8 | 57.6 | 55.0 | All White |
| | 14.3 | 18.2 | 23.2 | 24.5 | 27.4 | 26.4 | 32.8 | 31.0 | 32.3 | Mostly White |
| | 4.5 | 4.6 | 6.3 | 5.6 | 5.5 | 6.2 | 4.3 | 4.1 | 7.1 | Half and half |
| | 4.8 | 5.7 | 6.2 | 7.7 | 4.1 | 6.6 | 4.9 | 5.5 | 4.0 | Mostly Black |
| | 3.0 | 1.8 | 1.4 | 1.9 | 1.8 | 3.0 | 1.2 | 1.7 | 1.7 | All Black |
| | (1018) | (649) | (151) | (1611) | (220) | (441) | (493) | (290) | (426) | Weighted N |
| **45-54 Only** | 71.9 | 67.2 | 72.2 | 62.9 | 66.7 | 61.6 | 64.5 | 64.3 | 56.2 | All White |
| | 15.7 | 21.8 | 17.6 | 21.1 | 24.3 | 24.8 | 27.2 | 24.3 | 31.6 | Mostly White |
| | 4.7 | 5.3 | 2.2 | 5.3 | 5.3 | 6.1 | 3.0 | 2.9 | 4.5 | Half and half |
| | 4.0 | 4.5 | 4.9 | 7.5 | 3.2 | 4.3 | 4.2 | 4.0 | 3.9 | Mostly Black |
| | 3.6 | 1.3 | 3.0 | 3.1 | 0.5 | 3.2 | 1.0 | 4.4 | 3.8 | All Black |
| | (918) | (625) | (149) | (1563) | (189) | (445) | (496) | (272) | (397) | Weighted N |
| **55-64 Only** | 75.0 | 69.4 | 70.2 | 65.1 | 66.3 | 62.7 | 57.1 | 63.5 | 51.5 | All White |
| | 16.1 | 16.4 | 16.4 | 23.5 | 23.8 | 26.9 | 31.9 | 24.4 | 32.3 | Mostly White |
| | 3.9 | 7.6 | 7.5 | 5.2 | 3.5 | 3.7 | 4.8 | 4.1 | 8.3 | Half and half |
| | 3.6 | 3.6 | 3.9 | 5.4 | 5.8 | 3.1 | 3.2 | 6.0 | 4.6 | Mostly Black |
| | 1.5 | 2.9 | 2.0 | 0.8 | 0.6 | 3.7 | 3.0 | 1.9 | 3.4 | All Black |
| | (679) | (449) | (153) | (1289) | (172) | (384) | (436) | (266) | (408) | Weighted N |
| **65-74 Only** | 71.0 | 72.6 | 65.1 | 64.6 | 70.3 | 61.5 | 58.5 | 64.5 | 58.1 | All White |
| | 14.8 | 15.3 | 24.8 | 22.3 | 17.9 | 24.9 | 29.5 | 25.0 | 27.2 | Mostly White |
| | 6.7 | 4.6 | 5.2 | 2.6 | 6.2 | 5.5 | 3.1 | 3.0 | 4.4 | Half and half |
| | 5.4 | 5.5 | 2.9 | 8.0 | 3.4 | 4.8 | 4.5 | 4.5 | 5.9 | Mostly Black |
| | 2.2 | 2.0 | 2.0 | 2.5 | 2.1 | 3.3 | 4.5 | 3.0 | 4.3 | All Black |
| | (465) | (349) | (92) | (1008) | (146) | (274) | (224) | (200) | (330) | Weighted N |
| **75 And Older Only** | 79.7 | 80.0 | 68.6 | 63.8 | 75.7 | 65.2 | 64.3 | 70.6 | 58.2 | All White |
| | 8.9 | 11.3 | 25.7 | 24.1 | 18.6 | 23.2 | 24.8 | 20.2 | 27.7 | Mostly White |
| | 3.0 | 1.9 | 1.1 | 6.3 | 4.3 | 4.5 | 3.1 | 2.8 | 2.7 | Half and half |
| | 5.1 | 3.8 | 3.4 | 3.2 | 1.4 | 1.3 | 7.0 | 1.8 | 6.4 | Mostly Black |
| | 3.4 | 3.1 | 1.1 | 2 6 | 0.0 | 5.8 | 0.8 | 4.6 | 5.1 | All Black |
| | (237) | (160) | (52) | (536) | (70) | (157) | (129) | (109) | (188) | Weighted N |

Blacks And Whites

Table 2.16
Racial Composition of Friends
Total Population

QUESTION: Are your friends: All White, Mostly White, About half and half, Mostly Negro/Black, All Negro/Black?

|  |  | Year |  |  |  |  |  |
|---|---|---|---|---|---|---|---|
|  |  | 1964n | 1968n | 1970n | 1972n | 1974q | 1976n |
| All White | (1) | 74.3% | 63.1% | 59.9% | 50.3% | 45.6% | 44.3% |
| Mostly White | (2) | 16.2 | 26.1 | 28.7 | 36.3 | 40.1 | 41.1 |
| About half and half | (3) | 2.8 | 3.5 | 4.6 | 6.9 | 8.7 | 8.3 |
| Mostly Negro/Black | (4) | 3.2 | 5.0 | 4.1 | 4.4 | 4.2 | 4.6 |
| All Negro/Black | (5) | 3.4 | 2.3 | 2.6 | 1.9 | 1.5 | 1.3 |
| Don't know |  | 0.1 | ** | 0.1 | 0.2 | 0.0 | 0.4 |
| Total |  | 100% | 100% | 100% | 100% | 100% | 100% |
| Weighted N |  | 4633 | 3080 | 909 | 2689 | 2959 | 2848 |
| Unweighted N |  | 1819 | 1661 | 957 | 2689 | 1507 | 2232 |
| Mean |  | 1.45 | 1.57 | 1.60 | 1.71 | 1.76 | 1.77 |
| Standard Deviation |  | 0.95 | 0.94 | 0.94 | 0.91 | 0.89 | 0.88 |

** Code distinction not made.
1964n, 1968n, and 1970n include Black supplement.

Figure 2.10
Racial Composition of Friends--Total Population

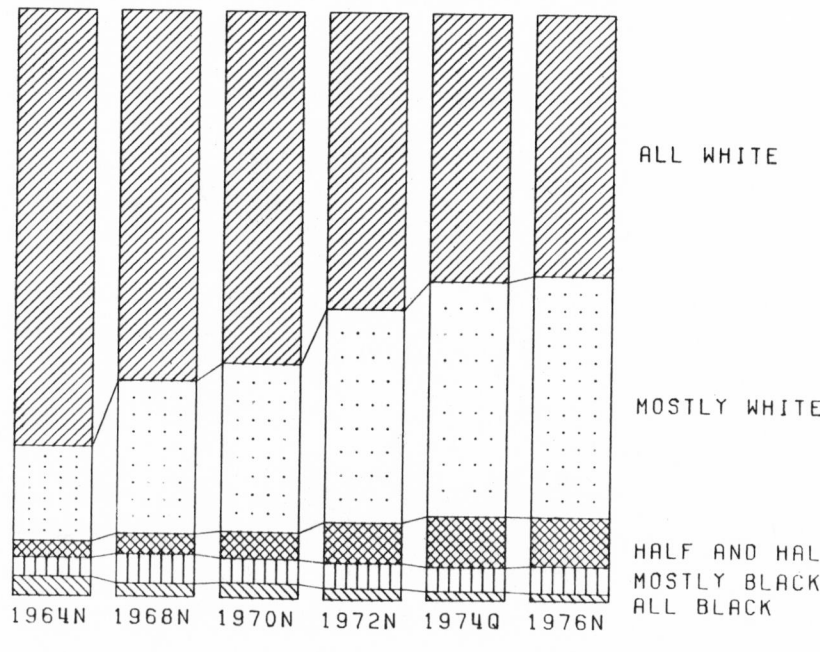

Blacks And Whites

Table 2.17
Racial Composition of Friends
Sex of Respondent

|  | Year | | | | | | |
|---|---|---|---|---|---|---|---|
|  | 1964n | 1968n | 1970n | 1972n | 1974q | 1976n | |
| Males Only | 71.4% | 57.7% | 56.2% | 44.3% | 39.6% | 38.4% | All White |
|  | 20.3 | 32.6 | 33.3 | 43.4 | 46.4 | 48.9 | Mostly White |
|  | 3.2 | 3.8 | 4.8 | 7.1 | 9.0 | 8.3 | Half and half |
|  | 3.1 | 4.5 | 3.8 | 3.8 | 4.0 | 3.6 | Mostly Black |
|  | 2.0 | 1.3 | 2.0 | 1.4 | 1.0 | 0.8 | All Black |
|  | (2098) | (1342) | (385) | (1162) | (1323) | (1198) | Weighted N |
|  |  |  |  |  |  |  |  |
| Females Only | 76.8 | 67.2 | 62.8 | 55.1 | 50.5 | 49.0 | All White |
|  | 12.8 | 21.1 | 25.4 | 31.1 | 35.0 | 35.9 | Mostly White |
|  | 2.5 | 3.3 | 4.4 | 6.7 | 8.4 | 8.2 | Half and half |
|  | 3.2 | 5.3 | 4.2 | 4.8 | 4.3 | 5.3 | Mostly Black |
|  | 4.6 | 3.1 | 3.1 | 2.3 | 1.9 | 1.7 | All Black |
|  | (2535) | (1738) | (524) | (1527) | (1636) | (1644) | Weighted N |

Table 2.18
Race of Respondent

|  | 1964n | 1968n | 1970n | 1972n | 1974q | 1976n | |
|---|---|---|---|---|---|---|---|
| Whites Only | 81.8% | 69.9% | 66.2% | 56.5% | 51.4% | 50.2% | All White |
|  | 17.5 | 28.3 | 31.6 | 39.8 | 43.9 | 45.4 | Mostly White |
|  | 0.8 | 1.7 | 2.2 | 3.6 | 4.5 | 4.3 | Half and half |
|  | 0.0 | 0.1 | 0.0 | 0.1 | 0.3 | 0.2 | Mostly Black |
|  | 0.0 | 0.0 | 0.0 | 0.0 | 0.0 | 0.0 | All Black |
|  | (4179) | (2762) | (814) | (2384) | (2550) | (2479) | Weighted N |
|  |  |  |  |  |  |  |  |
| Blacks Only | 0.0 | 0.4 | 0.4 | 0.0 | 0.0 | 0.5 | All White |
|  | 3.6 | 2.5 | 3.6 | 3.4 | 5.1 | 2.9 | Mostly White |
|  | 23.1 | 19.4 | 23.7 | 33.5 | 40.9 | 39.9 | Half and half |
|  | 35.2 | 52.2 | 44.1 | 43.7 | 39.2 | 43.5 | Mostly Black |
|  | 38.1 | 25.5 | 28.3 | 19.4 | 14.9 | 13.1 | All Black |
|  | (418) | (278) | (84) | (264) | (296) | (291) | Weighted N |

Blacks And Whites

Table 2.19
Racial Composition of Friends
Education of Respondent

|  | | Year | | | | | |
|---|---|---|---|---|---|---|---|
|  | 1964n | 1968n | 1970n | 1972n | 1974q | 1976n | |
| Grade School Only | 75.1% | 67.4% | 66.6% | 61.0% | 46.6% | 57.9% | All White |
|  | 8.3 | 15.2 | 19.1 | 22.3 | 30.9 | 20.9 | Mostly White |
|  | 6.0 | 6.0 | 5.6 | 9.2 | 13.6 | 9.2 | Half and half |
|  | 4.2 | 7.9 | 4.8 | 4.3 | 6.7 | 8.9 | Mostly Black |
|  | 6.4 | 3.4 | 3.8 | 3.2 | 2.3 | 3.1 | All Black |
|  | (1152) | (697) | (230) | (536) | (480) | (468) | Weighted N |
|  | | | | | | | |
| High School Only | 77.1 | 65.7 | 61.6 | 52.1 | 49.5 | 46.9 | All White |
|  | 15.2 | 23.5 | 26.0 | 34.2 | 36.4 | 38.7 | Mostly White |
|  | 1.7 | 3.3 | 4.3 | 6.9 | 8.5 | 8.9 | Half and half |
|  | 2.9 | 5.0 | 5.0 | 4.8 | 3.8 | 4.2 | Mostly Black |
|  | 3.1 | 2.5 | 3.1 | 1.9 | 1.8 | 1.3 | All Black |
|  | (2351) | (1537) | (452) | (1370) | (1418) | (1418) | Weighted N |
|  | | | | | | | |
| College Only | 68.0 | 54.5 | 50.1 | 40.2 | 40.1 | 34.3 | All White |
|  | 26.8 | 40.3 | 44.4 | 49.9 | 49.5 | 54.9 | Mostly White |
|  | 1.8 | 1.9 | 3.9 | 5.3 | 6.5 | 7.2 | Half and half |
|  | 2.7 | 2.5 | 1.3 | 3.6 | 3.4 | 3.0 | Mostly Black |
|  | 0.6 | 0.8 | 0.3 | 1.0 | 0.6 | 0.6 | All Black |
|  | (1098) | (839) | (225) | (781) | (1043) | (946) | Weighted N |

Table 2.20
Racial Composition of Friends
Age of Respondent

| | 1964n | 1968n | 1970n | 1972n | 1974q | 1976n | |
|---|---|---|---|---|---|---|---|
| 18-24 Only | 68.2% | 51.5% | 51.9% | 37.8% | 33.0% | 30.7% | All White |
| | 21.3 | 38.6 | 33.0 | 44.6 | 48.2 | 51.1 | Mostly White |
| | 2.6 | 3.4 | 6.4 | 9.3 | 12.5 | 11.7 | Half and half |
| | 4.8 | 3.9 | 5.2 | 5.8 | 4.3 | 4.3 | Mostly Black |
| | 3.1 | 2.6 | 3.4 | 2.5 | 2.0 | 2.0 | All Black |
| | (353) | (233) | (132) | (397) | (488) | (392) | Weighted N |
| 25-34 Only | 70.7 | 55.4 | 54.5 | 42.7 | 38.5 | 34.6 | All White |
| | 18.8 | 31.1 | 34.3 | 42.9 | 44.8 | 48.4 | Mostly White |
| | 2.2 | 4.4 | 5.1 | 6.8 | 8.2 | 10.1 | Half and half |
| | 3.8 | 6.3 | 3.5 | 5.7 | 6.3 | 6.4 | Mostly Black |
| | 4.4 | 2.8 | 2.6 | 1.9 | 2.2 | 0.4 | All Black |
| | (950) | (608) | (172) | (574) | (672) | (692) | Weighted N |
| 35-44 Only | 68.6 | 59.9 | 55.6 | 45.8 | 48.1 | 38.5 | All White |
| | 20.5 | 28.7 | 32.1 | 39.6 | 40.2 | 48.2 | Mostly White |
| | 3.5 | 3.6 | 4.8 | 7.1 | 6.5 | 8.9 | Half and half |
| | 3.4 | 4.7 | 4.4 | 4.8 | 4.0 | 3.7 | Mostly Black |
| | 3.9 | 3.1 | 3.2 | 2.7 | 1.2 | 0.7 | All Black |
| | (1020) | (644) | (151) | (440) | (495) | (424) | Weighted N |
| 45-54 Only | 76.1 | 67.0 | 59.9 | 54.1 | 48.6 | 47.6 | All White |
| | 14.9 | 23.1 | 29.8 | 34.2 | 39.8 | 41.2 | Mostly White |
| | 2.6 | 3.8 | 2.8 | 7.2 | 7.4 | 6.6 | Half and half |
| | 3.3 | 4.6 | 5.5 | 2.9 | 3.6 | 2.8 | Mostly Black |
| | 3.1 | 1.4 | 2.0 | 1.6 | 0.6 | 1.8 | All Black |
| | (918) | (624) | (149) | (443) | (500) | (395) | Weighted N |
| 55-64 Only | 80.5 | 64.2 | 63.5 | 60.3 | 49.8 | 48.6 | All White |
| | 12.1 | 24.4 | 25.0 | 31.9 | 37.0 | 38.0 | Mostly White |
| | 3.1 | 4.6 | 5.9 | 5.7 | 10.3 | 8.2 | Half and half |
| | 2.4 | 5.3 | 3.7 | 1.8 | 1.8 | 3.5 | Mostly Black |
| | 1.9 | 1.5 | 2.0 | 0.3 | 1.1 | 1.7 | All Black |
| | (679) | (455) | (154) | (386) | (438) | (407) | Weighted N |
| 65-74 Only | 78.4 | 73.0 | 71.7 | 61.9 | 60.6 | 67.0 | All White |
| | 13.7 | 18.0 | 22.1 | 27.1 | 25.3 | 21.7 | Mostly White |
| | 3.3 | 1.2 | 2.3 | 5.1 | 8.1 | 4.8 | Half and half |
| | 1.3 | 4.9 | 2.0 | 4.8 | 4.1 | 4.2 | Mostly Black |
| | 3.3 | 2.9 | 2.0 | 1.1 | 1.8 | 2.3 | All Black |
| | (462) | (345) | (92) | (274) | (222) | (327) | Weighted N |
| 75 And Older Only | 91.0 | 80.0 | 80.4 | 70.8 | 66.9 | 66.8 | All White |
| | 1.7 | 15.0 | 13.4 | 18.8 | 23.1 | 20.9 | Mostly White |
| | 2.1 | 0.6 | 1.7 | 3.2 | 6.2 | 4.3 | Half and half |
| | 2.6 | 3.8 | 1.7 | 3.9 | 3.8 | 6.7 | Mostly Black |
| | 2.6 | 0.6 | 2.8 | 3.2 | 0.0 | 1.3 | All Black |
| | (234) | (160) | (54) | (154) | (130) | (188) | Weighted N |

Blacks And Whites

Table 2.21
How Much Has the Position of Blacks Changed in the Past Few Years?
Total Population

QUESTION: In the past few years we have heard a lot about civil rights groups working to improve the position of the Negro/Black people in this country.  How much real change do you think there has been in the position of the Negro/Black people in the past few years, a lot, some, or not much at all?

|  |  | Year |  |  |  |  |  |  |
|---|---|---|---|---|---|---|---|---|
|  |  | 1964n | 1966n | 1968n | 1970n | 1972n | 1974q | 1976n |
| A lot | (5) | 40.6% | 39.4% | 49.6% | 52.4% | 55.1% | 55.8% | 59.0% |
| Some | (3) | 37.8 | 38.7 | 34.7 | 35.2 | 35.3 | 36.5 | 32.3 |
| Not much at all | (1) | 19.3 | 17.7 | 14.6 | 10.9 | 8.0 | 6.3 | 7.1 |
| Don't know |  | 2.3 | 4.2 | 1.1 | 1.6 | 1.5 | 1.4 | 1.6 |
| Total |  | 100% | 100% | 100% | 100% | 100% | 100% | 100% |
| Weighted N |  | 4628 | 1282 | 3090 | 912 | 2701 | 2975 | 2852 |
| Unweighted N |  | 1823 | 1282 | 1668 | 962 | 2701 | 1515 | 2235 |
| Mean |  | 3.43 | 3.45 | 3.71 | 3.84 | 3.96 | 4.00 | 4.05 |
| Standard Deviation |  | 1.50 | 1.48 | 1.45 | 1.36 | 1.28 | 1.23 | 1.25 |

1964n,1968n, and 1970n include Black supplement.

Figure 2.11
Has Position of Blacks Changed?--Total Population

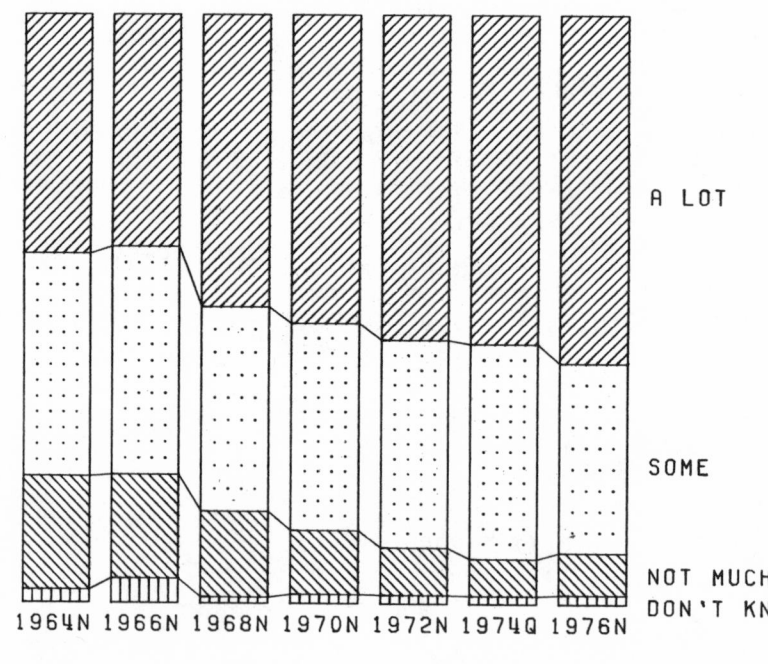

1964N 1966N 1968N 1970N 1972N 1974Q 1976N

A LOT

SOME

NOT MUCH
DON'T KNOW

Blacks And Whites

Table 2.22
How Much Has the Position of Blacks Changed in the Past Few Years?
Sex of Respondent

| | Year | | | | | | | |
|---|---|---|---|---|---|---|---|---|
| | 1964n | 1966n | 1968n | 1970n | 1972n | 1974q | 1976n | |
| Males Only | 42.6% | 41.6% | 51.1% | 56.4% | 57.5% | 54.6% | 59.7% | A lot |
| | 36.3 | 38.0 | 33.2 | 33.9 | 33.6 | 37.9 | 31.5 | Some |
| | 21.2 | 20.4 | 15.7 | 9.7 | 8.9 | 7.5 | 8.9 | Not much at all |
| | (2056) | (548) | (1343) | (384) | (1154) | (1320) | (1189) | Weighted N |
| Females Only | 40.7 | 40.7 | 49.4 | 50.9 | 54.8 | 58.2 | 60.3 | A lot |
| | 40.7 | 42.4 | 36.6 | 37.0 | 37.6 | 36.3 | 33.8 | Some |
| | 18.7 | 16.9 | 14.0 | 12.0 | 7.6 | 5.5 | 5.9 | Not much at all |
| | (2466) | (680) | (1714) | (514) | (1506) | (1614) | (1611) | Weighted N |

Table 2.23
Race of Respondent

| | 1964n | 1966n | 1968n | 1970n | 1972n | 1974q | 1976n | |
|---|---|---|---|---|---|---|---|---|
| Whites Only | 39.4% | 41.1% | 49.3% | 54.5% | 57.4% | 57.8% | 63.3% | A lot |
| | 39.6 | 39.8 | 35.5 | 34.7 | 34.6 | 36.1 | 30.7 | Some |
| | 21.0 | 19.2 | 15.3 | 10.8 | 8.0 | 6.1 | 5.9 | Not much at all |
| | (4074) | (1084) | (2736) | (799) | (2355) | (2524) | (2441) | Weighted N |
| Blacks Only | 60.0 | 41.1 | 59.4 | 39.1 | 43.8 | 44.2 | 32.1 | A lot |
| | 31.1 | 48.1 | 32.4 | 47.3 | 46.8 | 44.9 | 49.7 | Some |
| | 8.9 | 10.9 | 8.2 | 13.5 | 9.4 | 10.9 | 18.2 | Not much at all |
| | (415) | (129) | (281) | (84) | (265) | (294) | (289) | Weighted N |

Figure 2.12
Has Position of Blacks Changed? by Race of R

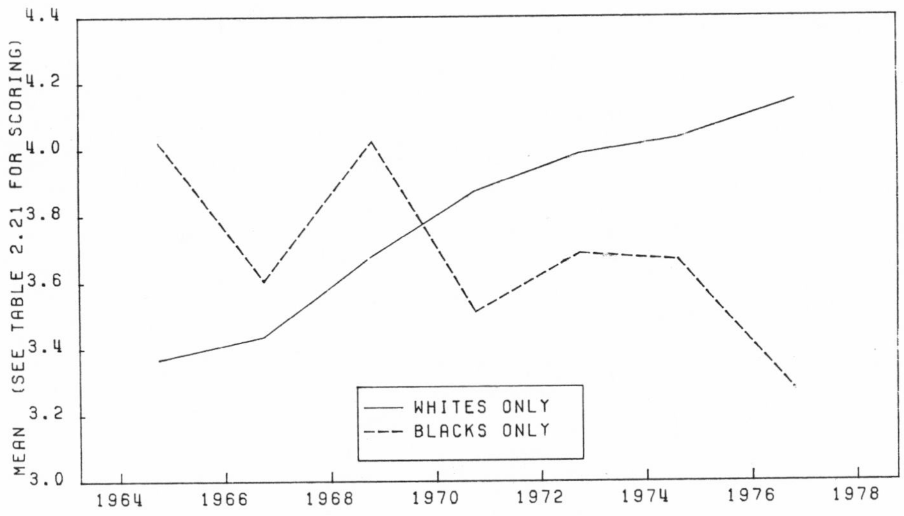

Table 2.24
How Much Has the Position of Blacks Changed in the Past Few Years?
Education of Respondent

|  | Year | | | | | | | |
|---|---|---|---|---|---|---|---|---|
|  | 1964n | 1966n | 1968n | 1970n | 1972n | 1974q | 1976n | |
| Grade School Only | 38.5% | 43.2% | 46.8% | 56.2% | 48.9% | 54.9% | 61.8% | A lot |
|  | 39.9 | 35.8 | 33.4 | 31.8 | 37.0 | 36.1 | 29.2 | Some |
|  | 21.6 | 21.0 | 19.8 | 12.0 | 14.0 | 9.0 | 9.0 | Not much at all |
|  | (1104) | (310) | (677) | (228) | (513) | (468) | (450) | Weighted N |
| High School Only | 41.1 | 42.5 | 50.7 | 53.3 | 56.3 | 57.2 | 61.8 | A lot |
|  | 38.9 | 37.7 | 35.4 | 35.6 | 36.1 | 37.0 | 31.6 | Some |
|  | 20.1 | 19.8 | 13.9 | 11.1 | 7.7 | 5.7 | 6.6 | Not much at all |
|  | (2293) | (621) | (1535) | (444) | (1359) | (1410) | (1395) | Weighted N |
| College Only | 44.3 | 36.0 | 51.8 | 49.7 | 59.9 | 56.8 | 56.2 | A lot |
|  | 37.8 | 51.7 | 36.1 | 40.2 | 34.9 | 37.3 | 36.4 | Some |
|  | 17.9 | 12.3 | 12.1 | 10.1 | 5.2 | 5.9 | 7.4 | Not much at all |
|  | (1092) | (292) | (840) | (224) | (785) | (1039) | (947) | Weighted N |

Table 2.25
How Much Has the Position of Blacks Changed in the Past Few Years?
Age of Respondent

|  | Year | | | | | | | |
|---|---|---|---|---|---|---|---|---|
|  | 1964n | 1966n | 1968n | 1970n | 1972n | 1974q | 1976n | |
| 18-24 Only | 44.2% | 40.7% | 51.1% | 46.0% | 52.0% | 46.7% | 49.2% | A lot |
|  | 32.7 | 43.4 | 33.9 | 40.7 | 38.8 | 49.0 | 43.4 | Some |
|  | 23.1 | 15.9 | 15.0 | 13.3 | 9.1 | 4.4 | 7.4 | Not much at all |
|  | (346) | (113) | (233) | (130) | (394) | (478) | (391) | Weighted N |
| 25-34 Only | 40.8 | 39.5 | 50.0 | 48.6 | 55.8 | 53.8 | 55.2 | A lot |
|  | 39.0 | 40.8 | 36.6 | 39.2 | 37.8 | 37.6 | 37.4 | Some |
|  | 20.2 | 19.7 | 13.4 | 12.2 | 6.5 | 8.6 | 7.4 | Not much at all |
|  | (936) | (223) | (610) | (169) | (572) | (665) | (687) | Weighted N |
| 35-44 Only | 42.2 | 41.9 | 49.5 | 56.3 | 59.5 | 57.5 | 57.4 | A lot |
|  | 38.5 | 40.8 | 35.6 | 33.3 | 32.0 | 35.3 | 33.2 | Some |
|  | 19.4 | 17.2 | 14.9 | 10.4 | 8.4 | 7.3 | 9.4 | Not much at all |
|  | (996) | (267) | (644) | (150) | (440) | (496) | (417) | Weighted N |
| 45-54 Only | 44.4 | 41.0 | 54.3 | 55.2 | 56.5 | 62.0 | 65.6 | A lot |
|  | 40.0 | 41.8 | 32.7 | 34.8 | 36.0 | 34.1 | 27.3 | Some |
|  | 15.6 | 17.2 | 13.0 | 10.0 | 7.5 | 3.8 | 7.2 | Not much at all |
|  | (900) | (244) | (615) | (147) | (439) | (498) | (391) | Weighted N |
| 55-64 Only | 36.0 | 46.7 | 51.9 | 57.0 | 56.5 | 64.0 | 66.9 | A lot |
|  | 43.0 | 34.1 | 33.6 | 35.4 | 35.6 | 30.0 | 28.0 | Some |
|  | 21.0 | 19.2 | 14.5 | 7.6 | 7.9 | 6.0 | 5.1 | Not much at all |
|  | (658) | (167) | (449) | (154) | (379) | (436) | (401) | Weighted N |
| 65-74 Only | 44.8 | 40.5 | 43.1 | 56.6 | 54.3 | 61.8 | 67.4 | A lot |
|  | 35.7 | 44.6 | 40.5 | 32.2 | 35.2 | 32.3 | 26.8 | Some |
|  | 19.5 | 14.9 | 16.4 | 11.2 | 10.5 | 5.9 | 5.8 | Not much at all |
|  | (442) | (148) | (341) | (88) | (267) | (220) | (320) | Weighted N |
| 75 And Older Only | 33.8 | 34.5 | 46.8 | 54.7 | 57.0 | 47.7 | 66.5 | A lot |
|  | 36.0 | 38.2 | 33.8 | 28.5 | 33.6 | 39.8 | 25.9 | Some |
|  | 30.3 | 27.3 | 19.5 | 16.8 | 9.4 | 12.5 | 7.6 | Not much at all |
|  | (228) | (55) | (154) | (54) | (149) | (128) | (178) | Weighted N |

Table 2.26
Are Civil Rights People Pushing Too Fast?
Total Population

QUESTION: Some say that the civil rights people have been trying to push too fast.  Others feel they haven't pushed fast enough.  How about you: Do you think that civil rights leaders are trying to push too fast, are going too slowly, or are moving about the right speed?

|  | | Year | | | | | | |
|---|---|---|---|---|---|---|---|---|
|  | | 1964n | 1966n | 1968n | 1970n | 1972n | 1974q | 1976n |
| Too fast | (5) | 63.9% | 64.0% | 63.0% | 52.2% | 45.8% | 36.0% | 39.3% |
| About right | (3) | 24.7 | 20.3 | 27.2 | 33.3 | 41.4 | 51.4 | 47.3 |
| Too slowly | (1) | 5.4 | 4.7 | 6.7 | 9.5 | 8.2 | 7.9 | 8.0 |
| Don't know | | 6.0 | 11.0 | 3.1 | 5.0 | 4.7 | 4.8 | 5.4 |
| Total | | 100% | 100% | 100% | 100% | 100% | 100% | 100% |
| Weighted N | | 4568 | 1279 | 3043 | 903 | 2677 | 2940 | 2826 |
| Unweighted N | | 1801 | 1279 | 1643 | 953 | 2677 | 1494 | 2214 |
| Mean | | 4.24 | 4.33 | 4.16 | 3.90 | 3.79 | 3.59 | 3.66 |
| Standard Deviation | | 1.18 | 1.15 | 1.23 | 1.34 | 1.28 | 1.22 | 1.25 |

1964n, 1968n, and 1970n include Black supplement.

Figure 2.13
Civil Rights Too Fast?--Total Population

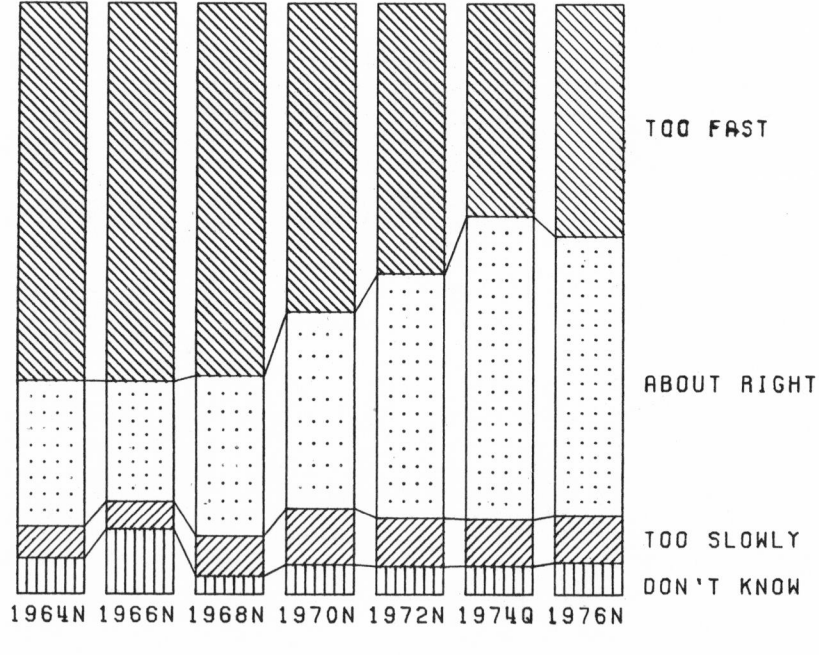

TOO FAST

ABOUT RIGHT

TOO SLOWLY

DON'T KNOW

1964N 1966N 1968N 1970N 1972N 1974Q 1976N

Blacks And Whites

Table 2.27
Are Civil Rights People Pushing Too Fast?
Sex of Respondent

|  | Year | | | | | | | |
|  | 1964n | 1966n | 1968n | 1970n | 1972n | 1974q | 1976n | |
| Males Only | 68.0% | 69.0% | 65.0% | 56.0% | 47.0% | 37.6% | 41.5% | Too fast |
|  | 22.6 | 18.4 | 25.3 | 32.0 | 40.4 | 51.1 | 46.6 | About right |
|  | 5.4 | 4.8 | 6.2 | 10.0 | 9.2 | 8.1 | 8.3 | Too slowly |
|  | 4.0 | 7.8 | 3.5 | 1.9 | 3.4 | 3.2 | 3.7 | Don't know |
|  | (2062) | (564) | (1324) | (385) | (1157) | (1316) | (1184) | Weighted N |
| Females Only | 60.5 | 60.0 | 61.4 | 49.3 | 44.8 | 34.6 | 37.7 | Too fast |
|  | 26.5 | 21.8 | 28.7 | 34.3 | 42.1 | 51.6 | 47.7 | About right |
|  | 5.3 | 4.6 | 7.0 | 9.1 | 7.4 | 7.6 | 7.9 | Too slowly |
|  | 7.7 | 13.6 | 2.8 | 7.3 | 5.7 | 6.2 | 6.7 | Don't know |
|  | (2506) | (715) | (1719) | (518) | (1520) | (1624) | (1635) | Weighted N |

Table 2.28
Race of Respondent

|  | 1964n | 1966n | 1968n | 1970n | 1972n | 1974q | 1976n | |
|  | --- | --- | --- | --- | --- | --- | --- | --- |
| Whites Only | 69.7% | 69.8% | 69.0% | 57.1% | 50.1% | 39.8% | 43.5% | Too fast |
|  | 20.9 | 16.4 | 23.5 | 31.1 | 39.3 | 50.6 | 46.5 | About right |
|  | 3.3 | 2.8 | 4.3 | 6.4 | 5.7 | 4.9 | 4.6 | Too slowly |
|  | 6.1 | 10.9 | 3.2 | 5.4 | 4.9 | 4.7 | 5.4 | Don't know |
|  | (4113) | (1126) | (2726) | (805) | (2371) | (2523) | (2457) | Weighted N |
| Blacks Only | 9.1 | 19.1 | 7.6 | 6.5 | 10.2 | 5.8 | 6.1 | Too fast |
|  | 62.3 | 50.0 | 62.5 | 52.9 | 57.0 | 55.5 | 53.2 | About right |
|  | 26.0 | 19.9 | 28.5 | 39.6 | 30.6 | 34.6 | 35.7 | Too slowly |
|  | 2.6 | 11.0 | 1.4 | 1.1 | 2.3 | 4.1 | 5.0 | Don't know |
|  | (416) | (136) | (277) | (83) | (265) | (292) | (288) | Weighted N |

Figure 2.14
Civil Rights Too Fast? by Race of R

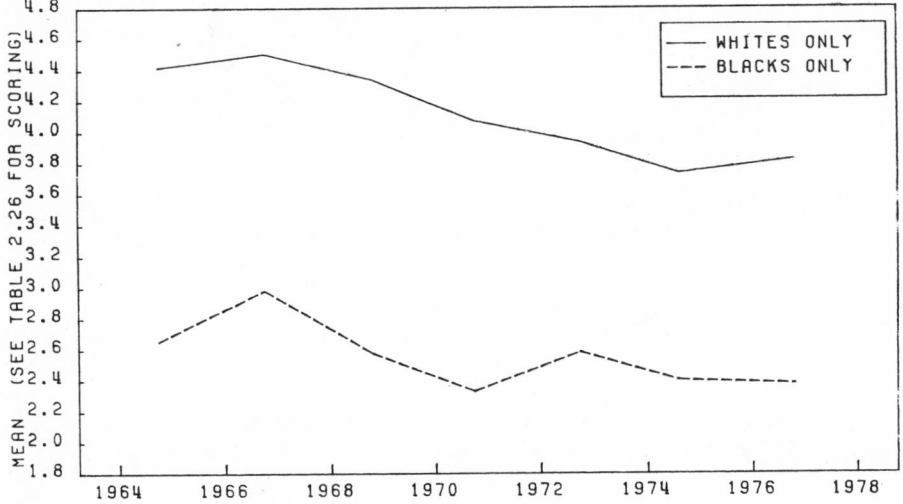

Blacks And Whites

Table 2.29
Are Civil Rights People Pushing Too Fast?
Education of Respondent

|  | Year | | | | | | |  |
|---|---|---|---|---|---|---|---|---|
|  | 1964n | 1966n | 1968n | 1970n | 1972n | 1974q | 1976n |  |
| Grade School Only | 56.9% | 62.7% | 59.9% | 54.9% | 49.2% | 33.2% | 40.0% | Too fast |
|  | 26.8 | 17.9 | 26.6 | 28.8 | 36.3 | 49.0 | 41.7 | About right |
|  | 5.3 | 3.3 | 7.5 | 6.9 | 5.6 | 7.9 | 8.0 | Too slowly |
|  | 11.0 | 16.1 | 6.0 | 9.4 | 8.8 | 10.0 | 10.2 | Don't know |
|  | (1142) | (335) | (695) | (232) | (532) | (482) | (470) | Weighted N |
| High School Only | 66.3 | 64.6 | 69.0 | 54.7 | 48.9 | 38.7 | 43.6 | Too fast |
|  | 23.2 | 19.6 | 23.4 | 34.1 | 40.6 | 50.9 | 43.7 | About right |
|  | 5.2 | 5.1 | 5.4 | 7.1 | 6.3 | 6.6 | 7.0 | Too slowly |
|  | 5.3 | 10.6 | 2.2 | 4.1 | 4.1 | 3.8 | 5.8 | Don't know |
|  | (2337) | (642) | (1524) | (450) | (1363) | (1403) | (1406) | Weighted N |
| College Only | 66.3 | 64.0 | 54.6 | 44.4 | 37.7 | 33.7 | 32.7 | Too fast |
|  | 25.6 | 24.9 | 35.0 | 36.8 | 46.2 | 52.9 | 55.2 | About right |
|  | 5.8 | 5.1 | 8.4 | 17.0 | 13.4 | 9.7 | 9.7 | Too slowly |
|  | 2.4 | 6.1 | 2.0 | 1.8 | 2.7 | 3.7 | 2.4 | Don't know |
|  | (1056) | (297) | (817) | (219) | (779) | (1038) | (935) | Weighted N |

Table 2.30
Are Civil Rights People Pushing Too Fast?
Age of Respondent

|  | Year | | | | | | | |
|---|---|---|---|---|---|---|---|---|
|  | 1964n | 1966n | 1968n | 1970n | 1972n | 1974q | 1976n | |
| 18-24 Only | 66.5% | 58.5% | 60.5% | 43.7% | 36.3% | 24.6% | 32.8% | Too fast |
|  | 22.7 | 31.4 | 25.8 | 38.2 | 47.1 | 57.9 | 53.5 | About right |
|  | 6.3 | 5.9 | 10.3 | 15.4 | 13.4 | 12.5 | 10.3 | Too slowly |
|  | 4.5 | 4.2 | 3.4 | 2.8 | 3.3 | 4.9 | 3.5 | Don't know |
|  | (352) | (118) | (233) | (130) | (397) | (487) | (389) | Weighted N |
| 25-34 Only | 62.8 | 64.6 | 57.3 | 53.7 | 43.6 | 32.6 | 35.5 | Too fast |
|  | 24.8 | 19.7 | 32.9 | 34.0 | 42.6 | 53.3 | 48.9 | About right |
|  | 7.6 | 6.1 | 8.4 | 10.9 | 10.8 | 9.7 | 11.3 | Too slowly |
|  | 4.8 | 9.6 | 1.3 | 1.4 | 3.0 | 4.5 | 4.2 | Don't know |
|  | (938) | (229) | (595) | (170) | (573) | (672) | (684) | Weighted N |
| 35-44 Only | 63.6 | 61.6 | 65.1 | 51.2 | 44.4 | 38.3 | 36.4 | Too fast |
|  | 25.4 | 23.6 | 27.6 | 29.5 | 41.9 | 54.1 | 49.3 | About right |
|  | 5.4 | 4.3 | 5.8 | 13.1 | 10.1 | 5.0 | 8.6 | Too slowly |
|  | 5.6 | 10.5 | 1.6 | 6.2 | 3.7 | 2.6 | 5.7 | Don't know |
|  | (1000) | (276) | (624) | (154) | (437) | (501) | (421) | Weighted N |
| 45-54 Only | 63.8 | 62.1 | 66.7 | 57.1 | 52.5 | 41.8 | 40.1 | Too fast |
|  | 26.1 | 22.3 | 25.4 | 32.6 | 38.0 | 49.8 | 46.6 | About right |
|  | 4.3 | 4.7 | 5.0 | 5.2 | 4.1 | 5.3 | 7.6 | Too slowly |
|  | 5.8 | 10.9 | 2.9 | 5.0 | 5.5 | 3.1 | 5.7 | Don't know |
|  | (901) | (256) | (615) | (149) | (440) | (488) | (395) | Weighted N |
| 55-64 Only | 67.5 | 70.9 | 68.9 | 53.6 | 52.2 | 40.2 | 50.3 | Too fast |
|  | 23.9 | 15.1 | 23.9 | 34.0 | 40.2 | 44.6 | 40.6 | About right |
|  | 3.6 | 3.5 | 5.5 | 6.8 | 4.2 | 8.4 | 4.2 | Too slowly |
|  | 5.1 | 10.5 | 1.8 | 5.6 | 3.4 | 6.8 | 4.8 | Don't know |
|  | (670) | (172) | (457) | (150) | (381) | (428) | (403) | Weighted N |
| 65-74 Only | 64.3 | 68.4 | 63.2 | 52.1 | 51.7 | 43.0 | 45.6 | Too fast |
|  | 21.3 | 13.5 | 24.5 | 35.6 | 35.8 | 46.6 | 43.1 | About right |
|  | 5.5 | 3.2 | 6.3 | 4.0 | 5.5 | 3.2 | 4.3 | Too slowly |
|  | 9.0 | 14.8 | 6.0 | 8.3 | 7.0 | 7.2 | 7.0 | Don't know |
|  | (456) | (155) | (351) | (91) | (271) | (221) | (328) | Weighted N |
| 75 And Older Only | 55.6 | 64.5 | 47.1 | 56.0 | 38.9 | 34.1 | 37.8 | Too fast |
|  | 26.9 | 11.3 | 30.6 | 28.6 | 43.3 | 46.5 | 44.8 | About right |
|  | 4.3 | 1.6 | 8.9 | 8.6 | 5.1 | 8.5 | 5.7 | Too slowly |
|  | 13.2 | 22.6 | 13.4 | 6.9 | 12.7 | 10.9 | 11.7 | Don't know |
|  | (234) | (62) | (157) | (52) | (157) | (129) | (184) | Weighted N |

Blacks And Whites

Table 2.31
Should Government Ensure Fairness for Blacks in Jobs?
Total Population

QUESTION: Some people feel that if Black people/Negroes/Colored people are not getting fair treatment in jobs the government in Washington ought to see to it that they do.  Others feel this is not the federal government's business.  Have you had enough interest in this question to favor one side over the other? (IF YES) How do you feel?  Should the government in Washington see to it that Blacks/Negroes/Colored people get fair treatment in jobs or leave these matters to the states and local communities/or stay out of this area?

|  |  | Year | | | | |
|  |  | 1964n | 1968n | 1972n | 1974q | 1975p |
|---|---|---|---|---|---|---|
| Government see to it | (1) | 38.6% | 38.3% | 41.7% | 38.4% | 39.4% |
| Depends | (3) | 7.3 | 6.4 | 6.0 | 7.5 | 7.6 |
| Leave it to states or local communities | (5) | 40.3 | 43.0 | 35.4 | 33.5 | 29.0 |
| No interest |  | 10.4 | 10.4 | 15.9 | 19.3 | 24.0 |
| Don't know |  | 3.4 | 2.0 | 1.1 | 1.1 | ** |
| Total |  | 100% | 100% | 100% | 100% | 100% |
| Weighted N |  | 4640 | 3082 | 2691 | 2942 | 1881 |
| Unweighted N |  | 1772 | 1632 | 2691 | 1497 | 1881 |
| Mean |  | 3.04 | 3.11 | 2.85 | 2.88 | 2.73 |
| Standard Deviation |  | 1.91 | 1.92 | 1.92 | 1.90 | 1.88 |

** Code distinction not made.
1964n and 1968n include Black supplement.

Figure 2.15
Fairness for Blacks in Jobs--Total Population

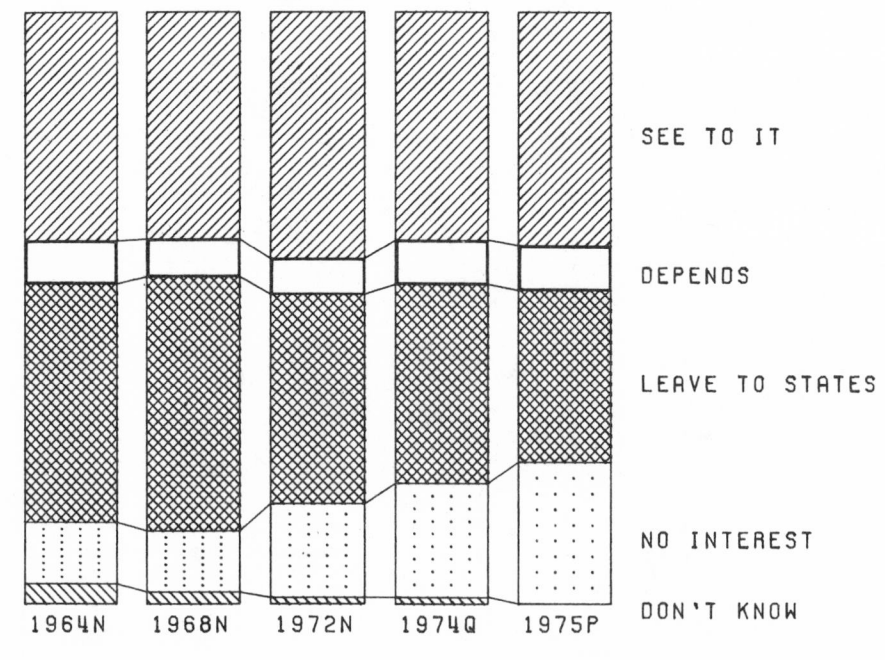

SEE TO IT

DEPENDS

LEAVE TO STATES

NO INTEREST

DON'T KNOW

1964N    1968N    1972N    1974Q    1975P

Blacks And Whites

Table 2.32
Should Government Ensure Fairness for Blacks in Jobs?
Sex of Respondent

|  | | Year | | | | |
|---|---|---|---|---|---|---|
|  | 1964n | 1968n | 1972n | 1974q | 1975p | |
| Males Only | 37.4% | 39.0% | 43.6% | 41.6% | 38.9% | Government see to it |
|  | 7.8 | 7.9 | 7.8 | 7.6 | 9.9 | Depends |
|  | 43.7 | 44.2 | 34.2 | 32.9 | 32.1 | Leave it to states or local communities |
|  | 8.6 | 7.6 | 13.5 | 17.4 | 19.1 | No interest |
|  | 2.4 | 1.4 | 0.9 | 0.5 | ** | Don't know |
|  | (2097) | (1349) | (1161) | (1308) | (789) | Weighted N |
| Females Only | 39.6 | 37.7 | 40.3 | 35.9 | 39.7 | Government see to it |
|  | 7.0 | 5.2 | 4.6 | 7.5 | 6.0 | Depends |
|  | 37.4 | 42.1 | 36.3 | 34.1 | 27.6 | Leave it to states or local communities |
|  | 11.8 | 12.6 | 17.6 | 20.9 | 26.7 | No interest |
|  | 4.2 | 2.4 | 1.2 | 1.7 | ** | Don't know |
|  | (2543) | (1733) | (1530) | (1634) | (1092) | Weighted N |

Table 2.33
Race of Respondent

|  | 1964n | 1968n | 1972n | 1974q | 1975p | |
|---|---|---|---|---|---|---|
| Whites Only | 33.3% | 33.3% | 36.9% | 33.7% | 33.7% | Government see to it |
|  | 7.7 | 7.0 | 6.7 | 8.5 | 8.6 | Depends |
|  | 44.3 | 46.7 | 38.6 | 36.9 | 32.5 | Leave it to states or local communities |
|  | 11.1 | 10.9 | 16.7 | 19.8 | 25.2 | No interest |
|  | 3.6 | 2.1 | 1.1 | 1.2 | ** | Don't know |
|  | (4182) | (2758) | (2386) | (2530) | (1617) | Weighted N |
| Blacks Only | 89.3 | 83.8 | 84.1 | 80.3 | 85.1 | Government see to it |
|  | 2.6 | 1.4 | 0.0 | 2.1 | 1.0 | Depends |
|  | 3.6 | 8.8 | 8.3 | 7.3 | 2.1 | Leave it to states or local communities |
|  | 3.8 | 4.9 | 6.4 | 9.7 | 11.8 | No interest |
|  | 0.7 | 1.1 | 1.1 | 0.7 | ** | Don't know |
|  | (419) | (284) | (264) | (289) | (195) | Weighted N |

** Code distinction not made.

Blacks And Whites

Table 2.34
Should Government Ensure Fairness for Blacks in Jobs?
Education of Respondent

|  | | Year | | | | |
|---|---|---|---|---|---|---|
|  | 1964n | 1968n | 1972n | 1974q | 1975p | |
| Grade School Only | 45.1% | 39.0% | 41.2% | 37.1% | 40.7% | Government see to it |
|  | 4.7 | 3.5 | 5.2 | 2.5 | 6.3 | Depends |
|  | 32.1 | 39.0 | 30.0 | 28.2 | 22.4 | Leave it to states or local communities |
|  | 14.0 | 14.9 | 22.2 | 30.4 | 30.6 | No interest |
|  | 4.1 | 3.8 | 1.3 | 1.9 | ** | Don't know |
|  | (1148) | (693) | (536) | (483) | (317) | Weighted N |
| High School Only | 36.6 | 36.4 | 37.6 | 35.7 | 36.4 | Government see to it |
|  | 6.9 | 4.9 | 5.0 | 6.5 | 6.7 | Depends |
|  | 42.2 | 46.5 | 37.7 | 37.4 | 30.7 | Leave it to states or local communities |
|  | 10.6 | 10.8 | 18.4 | 19.6 | 26.2 | No interest |
|  | 3.7 | 1.5 | 1.2 | 0.9 | ** | Don't know |
|  | (2360) | (1543) | (1367) | (1405) | (925) | Weighted N |
| College Only | 36.5 | 41.2 | 49.3 | 42.8 | 43.4 | Government see to it |
|  | 11.0 | 11.4 | 7.9 | 11.5 | 9.7 | Depends |
|  | 44.6 | 40.3 | 35.0 | 30.9 | 29.9 | Leave it to states or local communities |
|  | 6.0 | 5.6 | 7.1 | 13.7 | 17.0 | No interest |
|  | 1.9 | 1.4 | 0.6 | 1.2 | ** | Don't know |
|  | (1099) | (839) | (785) | (1038) | (629) | Weighted N |

** Code distinction not made.

Blacks And Whites

Table 2.35
Should Government Ensure Fairness for Blacks in Jobs?
Age of Respondent

|  | 1964n | 1968n | 1972n | 1974q | 1975p |  |
|---|---|---|---|---|---|---|
| 18-24 Only | 39.6% | 44.6% | 51.8% | 47.2% | 45.5% | Government see to it |
|  | 4.2 | 7.3 | 2.8 | 5.6 | 9.4 | Depends |
|  | 41.8 | 38.6 | 31.3 | 25.7 | 16.5 | Leave it to states or local communities |
|  | 11.1 | 9.4 | 13.9 | 20.5 | 28.6 | No interest |
|  | 3.3 | 0.0 | 0.3 | 1.0 | ** | Don't know |
|  | (359) | (233) | (396) | (483) | (297) | Weighted N |
| 25-34 Only | 44.1 | 42.4 | 42.6 | 43.7 | 43.2 | Government see to it |
|  | 9.1 | 7.8 | 7.0 | 7.1 | 8.7 | Depends |
|  | 35.5 | 39.4 | 36.0 | 30.1 | 28.3 | Leave it to states or local communities |
|  | 8.4 | 8.8 | 13.8 | 18.8 | 19.8 | No interest |
|  | 2.8 | 1.7 | 0.7 | 0.3 | ** | Don't know |
|  | (951) | (604) | (573) | (661) | (449) | Weighted N |
| 35-44 Only | 38.3 | 38.1 | 41.0 | 37.3 | 36.0 | Government see to it |
|  | 9.1 | 7.1 | 6.2 | 7.8 | 6.5 | Depends |
|  | 39.7 | 45.8 | 37.4 | 37.7 | 41.1 | Leave it to states or local communities |
|  | 10.2 | 7.7 | 14.4 | 16.2 | 16.4 | No interest |
|  | 2.6 | 1.4 | 1.1 | 1.0 | ** | Don't know |
|  | (1020) | (651) | (439) | (501) | (292) | Weighted N |
| 45-54 Only | 40.3 | 38.2 | 38.1 | 30.5 | 34.2 | Government see to it |
|  | 6.3 | 7.5 | 8.6 | 9.2 | 5.9 | Depends |
|  | 39.7 | 42.9 | 36.0 | 41.2 | 34.9 | Leave it to states or local communities |
|  | 8.4 | 9.5 | 16.0 | 18.5 | 25.0 | No interest |
|  | 5.3 | 1.9 | 1.4 | 0.6 | ** | Don't know |
|  | (918) | (623) | (444) | (498) | (272) | Weighted N |
| 55-64 Only | 31.8 | 34.7 | 38.6 | 34.5 | 38.3 | Government see to it |
|  | 4.6 | 5.1 | 5.7 | 7.4 | 6.9 | Depends |
|  | 48.9 | 48.8 | 36.5 | 37.0 | 30.7 | Leave it to states or local communities |
|  | 11.9 | 10.4 | 17.6 | 19.0 | 24.1 | No interest |
|  | 2.8 | 1.1 | 1.6 | 2.1 | ** | Don't know |
|  | (679) | (453) | (386) | (432) | (261) | Weighted N |
| 65-74 Only | 40.3 | 40.1 | 38.2 | 33.9 | 38.9 | Government see to it |
|  | 7.8 | 1.7 | 5.1 | 7.1 | 9.1 | Depends |
|  | 35.9 | 38.0 | 35.3 | 33.9 | 23.2 | Leave it to states or local communities |
|  | 13.9 | 17.0 | 20.4 | 23.2 | 28.8 | No interest |
|  | 2.2 | 3.2 | 1.1 | 1.8 | ** | Don't know |
|  | (462) | (347) | (275) | (224) | (198) | Weighted N |
| 75 And Older Only | 26.1 | 19.4 | 37.8 | 36.2 | 33.0 | Government see to it |
|  | 7.7 | 6.3 | 4.5 | 8.5 | 4.5 | Depends |
|  | 47.4 | 46.9 | 35.3 | 23.8 | 25.0 | Leave it to states or local communities |
|  | 13.7 | 18.8 | 19.9 | 27.7 | 37.5 | No interest |
|  | 5.1 | 8.8 | 2.6 | 3.8 | ** | Don't know |
|  | (234) | (160) | (156) | (130) | (112) | Weighted N |

** Code distinction not made.

Blacks And Whites

Table 2.36
Should the Federal Government Ensure School Integration?
Total Population

QUESTION: Some people say that the government in Washington should see to it that White and Negro/Colored/Black children are allowed to go to the same schools. Others claim that this is not the (federal) government's business. Have you been concerned about this question to favor one side or the other? (IF YES) Do you think that the government in Washington should: See to it that White and Negro/Colored/Black children go to the same schools or stay out of this area (as it is none of its business)?

|  |  | 1964n | 1966n | 1968n | 1970n | 1972n | 1974q | 1975p | 1976n | 1978n |
|---|---|---|---|---|---|---|---|---|---|---|
| Government ensure integration | (5) | 41.6% | 46.3% | 38.1% | 45.3% | 36.9% | 34.0% | 33.0% | 24.2% | 28.0% |
| Depends | (3) | 7.3 | 7.5 | 6.7 | 9.5 | 6.7 | 11.7 | 13.7 | 8.3 | ** |
| Government stay out | (1) | 38.4 | 33.9 | 44.2 | 32.6 | 44.4 | 40.7 | 37.0 | 39.4 | 42.0 |
| No interest |  | 9.7 | 9.8 | 9.5 | 11.1 | 10.6 | 12.3 | 16.3 | 26.5 | 18.2 |
| Don't know |  | 3.0 | 2.5 | 1.5 | 1.4 | 1.4 | 1.4 | ** | 1.6 | 11.8 |
| Total |  | 100% | 100% | 100% | 100% | 100% | 100% | 100% | 100% | 100% |
| Weighted N |  | 4637 | 1282 | 3080 | 919 | 2700 | 2954 | 1879 | 2851 | 2200 |
| Unweighted N |  | 1769 | 1282 | 1638 | 954 | 2700 | 1501 | 1893 | 2233 | 2200 |
| Mean |  | 3.07 | 3.28 | 2.86 | 3.29 | 2.83 | 2.84 | 2.91 | 2.58 | 2.60 |
| Standard Deviation |  | 1.91 | 1.89 | 1.92 | 1.87 | 1.91 | 1.85 | 1.83 | 1.83 | 1.96 |

** Code distinction not made.
1964n, 1968n, and 1970n include Black supplement.

Figure 2.16
School Integration--Total Population

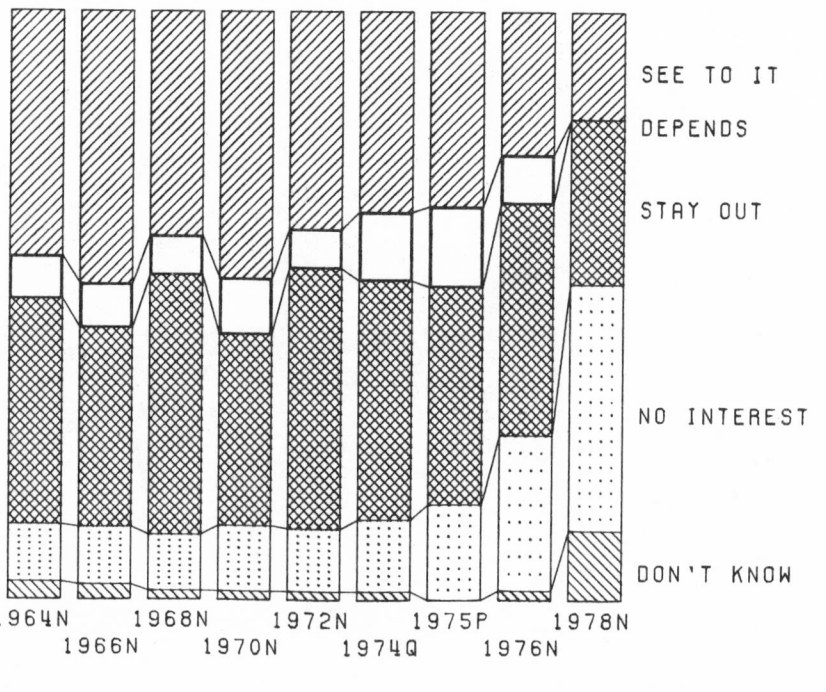

Figure 2.17
School Integration by Race of R

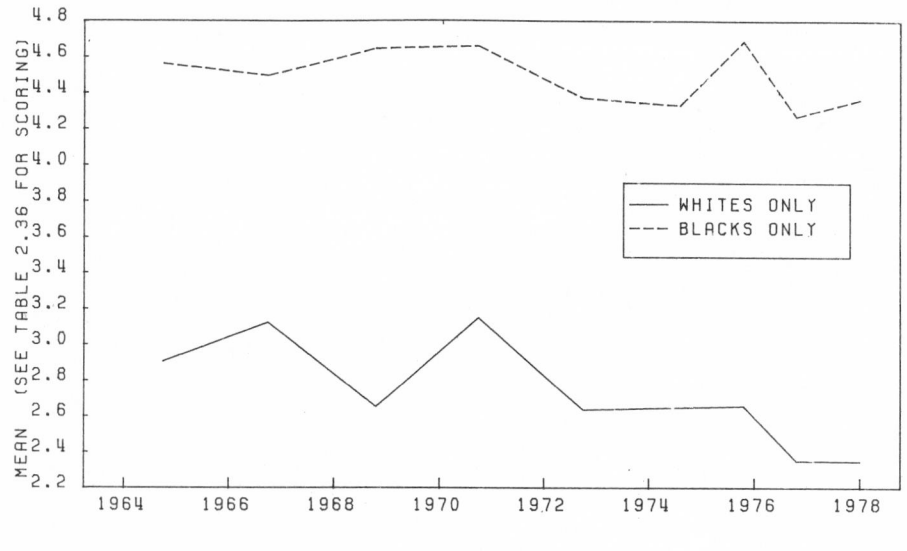

Blacks And Whites

Table 2.37
Should the Federal Government Ensure School Integration?
Sex of Respondent

|  | | | | | Year | | | | | |
|---|---|---|---|---|---|---|---|---|---|---|
|  | 1964n | 1966n | 1968n | 1970n | 1972n | 1974q | 1975p | 1976n | 1978n | |
| Males Only | 40.6% | 46.2% | 36.0% | 44.2% | 36.5% | 34.2% | 32.8% | 25.2% | 26.8% | Government ensure integration |
|  | 7.0 | 7.0 | 6.7 | 10.1 | 7.8 | 12.2 | 15.2 | 7.5 | ** | Depends |
|  | 41.3 | 33.6 | 48.9 | 34.0 | 45.5 | 42.2 | 38.1 | 43.9 | 42.8 | Government stay out |
|  | 8.6 | 11.6 | 7.3 | 10.7 | 9.2 | 10.1 | 13.9 | 22.7 | 17.2 | No interest |
|  | 2.5 | 1.6 | 1.0 | 1.0 | 1.0 | 1.3 | ** | 0.7 | 13.2 | Don't know |
|  | (2091) | (569) | (1349) | (387) | (1166) | (1323) | (790) | (1198) | (977) | Weighted N |
| Females Only | 42.4 | 46.4 | 39.6 | 46.2 | 37.1 | 33.8 | 33.2 | 23.6 | 28.9 | Government ensure integration |
|  | 7.6 | 7.9 | 6.7 | 9.1 | 5.9 | 11.2 | 12.6 | 8.9 | ** | Depends |
|  | 35.9 | 34.1 | 40.6 | 31.6 | 43.7 | 39.4 | 36.2 | 36.1 | 41.4 | Government stay out |
|  | 10.5 | 8.4 | 11.1 | 11.3 | 11.6 | 14.0 | 18.0 | 29.2 | 19.1 | No interest |
|  | 3.5 | 3.2 | 1.9 | 1.7 | 1.7 | 1.5 | ** | 2.2 | 10.6 | Don't know |
|  | (2546) | (713) | (1731) | (532) | (1534) | (1631) | (1089) | (1646) | (1223) | Weighted N |

Table 2.38
Race of Respondent

|  | 1964n | 1966n | 1968n | 1970n | 1972n | 1974q | 1975p | 1976n | 1978n | |
|---|---|---|---|---|---|---|---|---|---|---|
| Whites Only | 37.8% | 42.7% | 33.1% | 41.5% | 32.5% | 29.2% | 27.0% | 19.7% | 23.5% | Government ensure integration |
|  | 7.7 | 7.8 | 7.1 | 10.4 | 6.9 | 12.5 | 14.9 | 8.5 | ** | Depends |
|  | 41.9 | 37.3 | 48.5 | 35.1 | 48.5 | 44.3 | 41.4 | 42.7 | 46.2 | Government stay out |
|  | 9.8 | 9.6 | 9.9 | 11.5 | 10.8 | 12.5 | 16.7 | 27.6 | 17.9 | No interest |
|  | 2.9 | 2.7 | 1.5 | 1.5 | 1.4 | 1.4 | ** | 1.5 | 12.4 | Don't know |
|  | (4179) | (1130) | (2756) | (821) | (2392) | (2536) | (1617) | (2483) | (1928) | Weighted N |
| Blacks Only | 74.5 | 74.8 | 83.1 | 83.2 | 74.2 | 74.1 | 79.5 | 61.8 | 60.3 | Government ensure integration |
|  | 4.5 | 4.4 | 3.9 | 1.4 | 6.4 | 4.8 | 4.6 | 9.1 | ** | Depends |
|  | 7.2 | 8.9 | 6.3 | 7.1 | 11.2 | 13.0 | 4.6 | 10.3 | 11.4 | Government stay out |
|  | 9.5 | 11.1 | 4.2 | 6.8 | 7.5 | 6.1 | 11.3 | 16.6 | 21.5 | No interest |
|  | 4.3 | 0.7 | 2.5 | 1.4 | 0.7 | 2.0 | ** | 2.3 | 6.8 | Don't know |
|  | (419) | (135) | (284) | (84) | (267) | (293) | (195) | (287) | (219) | Weighted N |

** Code distinction not made.

Blacks And Whites

Table 2.39
Should the Federal Government Ensure School Integration?
Education of Respondent

|  | Year | | | | | | | | | |
|---|---|---|---|---|---|---|---|---|---|---|
|  | 1964n | 1966n | 1968n | 1970n | 1972n | 1974q | 1975p | 1976n | 1978n | |
| Grade School Only | 35.3% | 38.4% | 34.5% | 36.9% | 38.0% | 37.0% | 28.6% | 28.1% | 33.6% | Government ensure integration |
|  | 7.2 | 5.7 | 5.3 | 8.2 | 4.8 | 8.1 | 10.8 | 5.0 | ** | Depends |
|  | 40.3 | 37.8 | 46.0 | 33.4 | 39.7 | 30.1 | 37.1 | 35.9 | 28.9 | Government stay out |
|  | 14.4 | 14.6 | 12.7 | 19.7 | 16.0 | 23.5 | 23.5 | 29.5 | 25.7 | No interest |
|  | 2.8 | 3.6 | 1.4 | 1.8 | 1.5 | 1.2 | ** | 1.4 | 11.9 | Don't know |
|  | (1151) | (336) | (695) | (234) | (539) | (481) | (315) | (469) | (253) | Weighted N |
| High School Only | 42.5 | 47.0 | 37.7 | 44.9 | 33.8 | 34.3 | 31.1 | 21.3 | 26.0 | Government ensure integration |
|  | 6.4 | 8.2 | 6.9 | 9.8 | 6.3 | 11.4 | 12.9 | 6.3 | ** | Depends |
|  | 38.3 | 32.7 | 43.1 | 34.9 | 47.4 | 40.4 | 39.0 | 41.4 | 42.8 | Government stay out |
|  | 9.6 | 9.3 | 10.5 | 9.7 | 11.2 | 12.5 | 17.0 | 29.2 | 20.7 | No interest |
|  | 3.2 | 2.8 | 1.8 | 0.7 | 1.2 | 1.4 | ** | 1.9 | 10.4 | Don't know |
|  | (2357) | (643) | (1537) | (458) | (1370) | (1415) | (929) | (1415) | (1144) | Weighted N |
| College Only | 46.5 | 53.7 | 42.0 | 55.1 | 41.5 | 32.1 | 38.6 | 26.5 | 29.2 | Government ensure integration |
|  | 9.6 | 8.1 | 7.4 | 9.9 | 8.9 | 13.8 | 16.3 | 13.0 | ** | Depends |
|  | 35.9 | 31.9 | 44.8 | 27.5 | 42.3 | 45.9 | 33.9 | 38.7 | 45.2 | Government stay out |
|  | 5.0 | 5.7 | 4.6 | 4.9 | 5.7 | 6.7 | 11.2 | 20.6 | 12.0 | No interest |
|  | 3.0 | 0.7 | 1.2 | 2.7 | 1.6 | 1.5 | ** | 1.3 | 13.6 | Don't know |
|  | (1096) | (298) | (841) | (225) | (788) | (1042) | (625) | (952) | (797) | Weighted N |

** Code distinction not made.

Figure 2.18
School Integration by Education of R

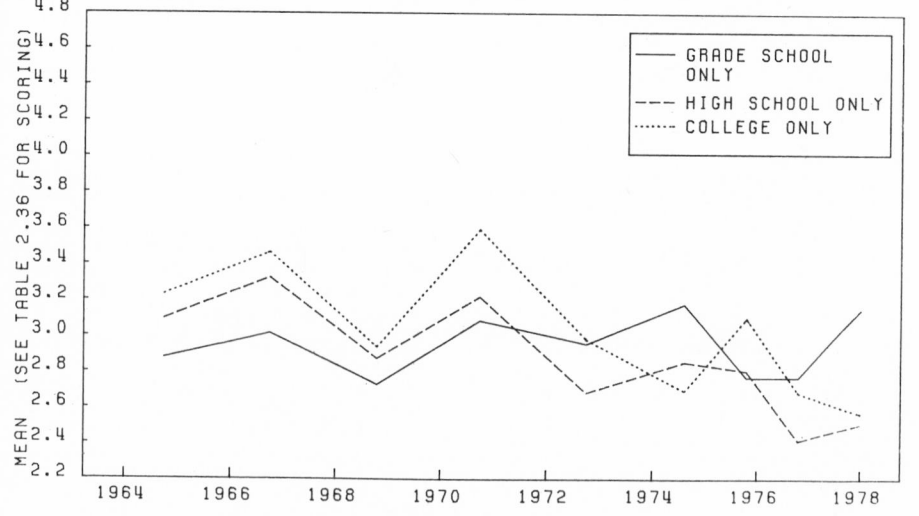

Blacks And Whites

Table 2.40
Should the Federal Government Ensure School Integration?
Age of Respondent

|  | 1964n | 1966n | 1968n | 1970n | 1972n | 1974q | 1975p | 1976n | 1978n |  |
|---|---|---|---|---|---|---|---|---|---|---|
| 18-24 Only | 43.5% | 61.9% | 47.6% | 61.7% | 47.2% | 41.8% | 43.3% | 29.2% | 37.1% | Government ensure integration |
|  | 5.3 | 8.5 | 3.0 | 9.8 | 7.3 | 10.9 | 12.3 | 7.9 | ** | Depends |
|  | 40.7 | 25.4 | 36.5 | 20.7 | 35.7 | 33.4 | 26.3 | 32.0 | 36.2 | Government stay out |
|  | 6.7 | 3.4 | 10.3 | 5.9 | 8.3 | 12.7 | 18.0 | 29.5 | 19.4 | No interest |
|  | 3.9 | 0.8 | 2.6 | 1.8 | 1.5 | 1.2 | ** | 1.4 | 7.2 | Don't know |
|  | (359) | (118) | (233) | (132) | (398) | (488) | (300) | (394) | (345) | Weighted N |
| 25-34 Only | 47.0 | 50.2 | 41.6 | 49.4 | 38.7 | 36.7 | 37.1 | 27.4 | 28.5 | Government ensure integration |
|  | 7.9 | 7.0 | 6.9 | 8.3 | 6.1 | 12.3 | 14.8 | 9.7 | ** | Depends |
|  | 33.4 | 31.0 | 41.7 | 30.6 | 46.2 | 39.3 | 34.0 | 35.3 | 41.0 | Government stay out |
|  | 8.2 | 10.0 | 6.6 | 11.1 | 7.8 | 10.2 | 14.1 | 25.7 | 16.8 | No interest |
|  | 3.4 | 1.7 | 3.1 | 0.7 | 1.2 | 1.5 | ** | 1.9 | 13.6 | Don't know |
|  | (948) | (229) | (606) | (174) | (576) | (667) | (447) | (695) | (536) | Weighted N |
| 35-44 Only | 43.6 | 47.5 | 43.4 | 40.8 | 36.0 | 31.3 | 31.3 | 17.2 | 27.0 | Government ensure integration |
|  | 7.3 | 8.7 | 7.3 | 10.6 | 10.0 | 11.6 | 15.1 | 10.1 | ** | Depends |
|  | 34.8 | 33.0 | 41.6 | 36.5 | 43.4 | 44.9 | 40.9 | 45.7 | 46.0 | Government stay out |
|  | 11.8 | 8.7 | 7.0 | 11.2 | 9.7 | 11.8 | 12.7 | 26.7 | 15.3 | No interest |
|  | 2.6 | 2.2 | 0.8 | 0.9 | 0.9 | 0.4 | ** | 0.4 | 11.7 | Don't know |
|  | (1017) | (276) | (645) | (159) | (442) | (501) | (291) | (423) | (385) | Weighted N |
| 45-54 Only | 40.4 | 44.0 | 36.6 | 42.3 | 30.1 | 27.0 | 27.8 | 25.7 | 22.8 | Government ensure integration |
|  | 6.9 | 9.3 | 7.4 | 10.3 | 6.7 | 8.4 | 15.8 | 6.9 | ** | Depends |
|  | 41.0 | 32.7 | 46.1 | 38.0 | 49.2 | 49.0 | 41.0 | 39.9 | 45.4 | Government stay out |
|  | 8.5 | 11.3 | 9.0 | 9.1 | 12.1 | 13.4 | 15.4 | 25.6 | 17.0 | No interest |
|  | 3.1 | 2.7 | 1.0 | 0.2 | 1.8 | 2.2 | ** | 1.9 | 14.8 | Don't know |
|  | (921) | (257) | (625) | (151) | (445) | (500) | (273) | (397) | (324) | Weighted N |
| 55-64 Only | 38.6 | 45.1 | 32.0 | 41.2 | 32.4 | 32.0 | 28.3 | 22.2 | 23.5 | Government ensure integration |
|  | 6.6 | 4.0 | 6.4 | 8.6 | 5.2 | 15.4 | 14.0 | 8.1 | ** | Depends |
|  | 41.1 | 37.6 | 51.7 | 35.4 | 50.8 | 40.0 | 42.6 | 43.9 | 47.8 | Government stay out |
|  | 10.2 | 9.2 | 9.1 | 13.1 | 10.6 | 11.0 | 15.1 | 25.1 | 19.4 | No interest |
|  | 3.5 | 4.0 | 0.9 | 1.8 | 1.0 | 1.6 | ** | 0.7 | 9.3 | Don't know |
|  | (679) | (173) | (453) | (154) | (386) | (435) | (258) | (409) | (289) | Weighted N |
| 65-74 Only | 37.3 | 35.3 | 30.8 | 36.6 | 34.9 | 38.0 | 28.6 | 22.8 | 27.6 | Government ensure integration |
|  | 7.0 | 5.1 | 5.2 | 10.6 | 4.0 | 13.1 | 8.0 | 7.3 | ** | Depends |
|  | 45.3 | 44.9 | 43.8 | 34.7 | 45.1 | 38.9 | 43.2 | 43.3 | 39.2 | Government stay out |
|  | 9.6 | 11.5 | 18.7 | 13.9 | 14.5 | 9.0 | 20.1 | 23.6 | 20.1 | No interest |
|  | 0.9 | 3.2 | 1.4 | 4.3 | 1.5 | 0.9 | ** | 3.0 | 13.1 | Don't know |
|  | (459) | (156) | (347) | (91) | (275) | (221) | (199) | (329) | (199) | Weighted N |
| 75 And Older Only | 30.0 | 37.1 | 28.1 | 39.1 | 38.5 | 29.5 | 25.2 | 21.2 | 28.6 | Government ensure integration |
|  | 11.4 | 9.7 | 8.8 | 6.7 | 7.1 | 10.1 | 13.5 | 3.8 | ** | Depends |
|  | 39.7 | 32.3 | 48.8 | 34.6 | 35.9 | 30.2 | 33.3 | 40.4 | 32.1 | Government stay out |
|  | 13.9 | 17.7 | 13.1 | 17.3 | 15.4 | 27.1 | 27.9 | 32.1 | 28.6 | No interest |
|  | 5.1 | 3.2 | 1.3 | 2.2 | 3.2 | 3.1 | ** | 2.5 | 10.7 | Don't know |
|  | (237) | (62) | (160) | (54) | (156) | (129) | (111) | (182) | (112) | Weighted N |

** Code distinction not made.

Blacks And Whites

Table 2.41
Racial Composition of Grade School nearest R
Total Population

QUESTION: Is the grade school nearest you: All White, Mostly White, About half and half, Mostly Negro/Black, All Negro/Black?

|  |  | Year | | | | | | |
|---|---|---|---|---|---|---|---|---|
|  |  | 1964n | 1968n | 1970n | 1972n | 1974q | 1975p | 1976n |
| All White | (1) | 53.6% | 32.5% | 32.9% | 32.9% | 24.1% | 21.2% | 28.5% |
| Mostly White | (2) | 27.9 | 43.7 | 41.8 | 34.7 | 43.3 | 43.5 | 37.9 |
| About half and half | (3) | 3.1 | 6.4 | 8.4 | 14.2 | 13.3 | 11.9 | 13.5 |
| Mostly Black | (4) | 3.7 | 4.9 | 6.6 | 5.7 | 5.1 | 6.4 | 5.6 |
| All Black | (5) | 3.8 | 2.5 | 1.0 | 1.3 | 0.8 | 1.1 | 1.3 |
| Don't know |  | 7.9 | 10.1 | 9.2 | 11.2 | 13.4 | 15.9 | 13.3 |
| Total |  | 100% | 100% | 100% | 100% | 100% | 100% | 100% |
| Weighted N |  | 4641 | 3088 | 907 | 2694 | 2954 | 1892 | 2849 |
| Unweighted N |  | 1827 | 1667 | 956 | 2694 | 1503 | 1892 | 2232 |
| Mean |  | 1.65 | 1.90 | 1.91 | 1.96 | 2.02 | 2.08 | 2.00 |
| Standard Deviation |  | 1.01 | 0.94 | 0.92 | 0.96 | 0.87 | 0.90 | 0.94 |

1964n,1968n, and 1970n include Black supplement.

Figure 2.19
Racial Composition of Grade School--Total Population

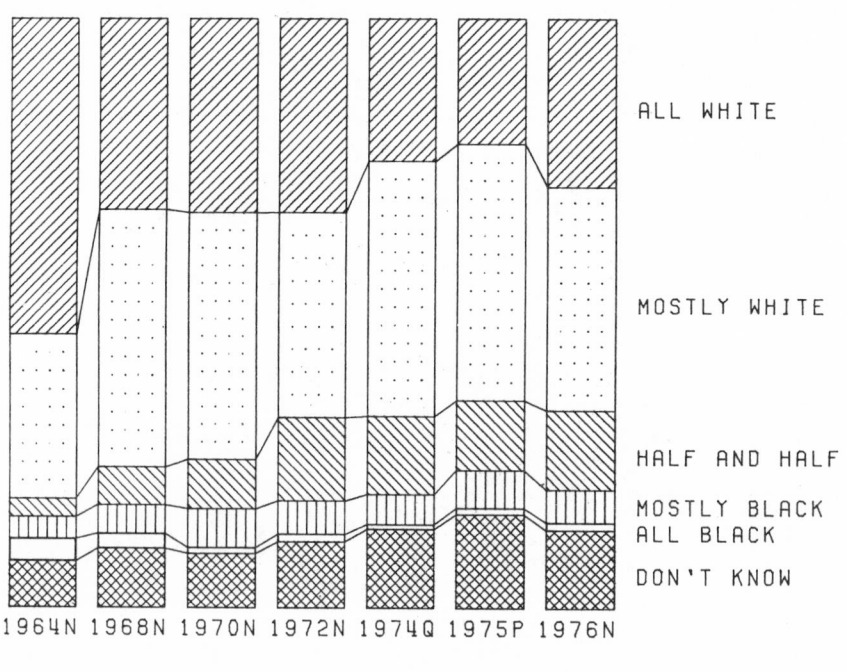

Figure 2.20
Racial Composition of Grade School by Race of R

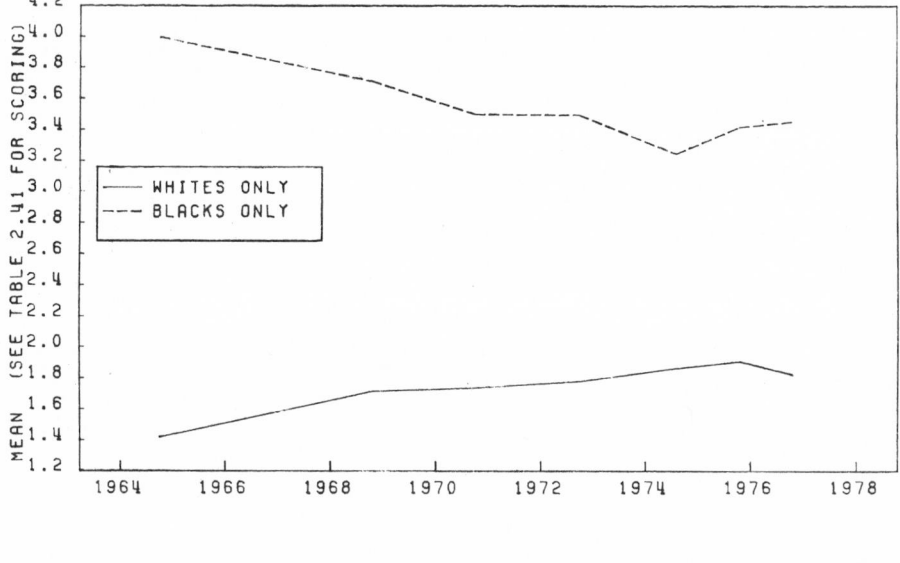

Blacks And Whites

Table 2.42
Racial Composition of Grade School nearest R
Sex of Respondent

|  | | | | Year | | | | |
|---|---|---|---|---|---|---|---|---|
|  | 1964n | 1968n | 1970n | 1972n | 1974q | 1975p | 1976n | |
| Males Only | 53.0% | 34.4% | 33.7% | 32.7% | 22.5% | 19.7% | 27.4% | All White |
|  | 29.0 | 45.0 | 41.8 | 37.0 | 46.3 | 46.5 | 40.9 | Mostly White |
|  | 3.3 | 5.3 | 9.5 | 13.0 | 12.6 | 12.1 | 13.4 | Half and half |
|  | 3.2 | 5.2 | 6.2 | 5.5 | 5.5 | 5.5 | 4.7 | Mostly Black |
|  | 3.5 | 1.4 | 0.9 | 1.1 | 0.5 | 0.9 | 0.9 | All Black |
|  | 8.0 | 8.7 | 8.1 | 10.7 | 12.6 | 15.3 | 12.7 | Don't know |
|  | (2098) | (1349) | (384) | (1164) | (1314) | (796) | (1198) | Weighted N |
| Females Only | 54.1 | 31.0 | 32.4 | 33.0 | 25.4 | 22.4 | 29.3 | All White |
|  | 27.0 | 42.7 | 41.8 | 32.9 | 40.9 | 41.3 | 35.7 | Mostly White |
|  | 2.9 | 7.2 | 7.7 | 15.2 | 13.8 | 11.8 | 13.6 | Half and half |
|  | 4.1 | 4.6 | 7.0 | 5.9 | 4.8 | 7.0 | 6.2 | Mostly Black |
|  | 4.1 | 3.3 | 1.1 | 1.5 | 1.1 | 1.3 | 1.5 | All Black |
|  | 7.9 | 11.2 | 10.1 | 11.6 | 14.1 | 16.2 | 13.7 | Don't know |
|  | (2543) | (1739) | (523) | (1530) | (1640) | (1096) | (1644) | Weighted N |

Table 2.43
Race of Respondent

|  | 1964n | 1968n | 1970n | 1972n | 1974q | 1975p | 1976n | |
|---|---|---|---|---|---|---|---|---|
| Whites Only | 58.9% | 36.2% | 36.2% | 36.8% | 27.2% | 24.1% | 32.0% | All White |
|  | 30.1 | 46.8 | 44.6 | 37.1 | 46.4 | 47.0 | 40.9 | Mostly White |
|  | 1.7 | 4.8 | 6.9 | 11.8 | 10.5 | 9.0 | 10.4 | Half and half |
|  | 1.6 | 2.1 | 2.8 | 2.6 | 2.4 | 3.3 | 2.7 | Mostly Black |
|  | 0.1 | 0.4 | 0.0 | 0.1 | 0.1 | 0.2 | 0.2 | All Black |
|  | 7.7 | 9.7 | 9.5 | 11.6 | 13.5 | 16.3 | 13.7 | Don't know |
|  | (4185) | (2766) | (812) | (2387) | (2534) | (1633) | (2478) | Weighted N |
| Blacks Only | 5.2 | 0.4 | 1.4 | 0.8 | 0.7 | 0.5 | 0.9 | All White |
|  | 6.2 | 14.2 | 15.6 | 11.3 | 21.0 | 13.9 | 10.6 | Mostly White |
|  | 13.8 | 19.1 | 22.8 | 34.6 | 31.5 | 31.4 | 36.0 | Half and half |
|  | 23.6 | 32.6 | 43.8 | 32.7 | 29.5 | 34.5 | 30.5 | Mostly Black |
|  | 41.4 | 22.7 | 10.9 | 12.8 | 7.5 | 8.8 | 11.0 | All Black |
|  | 9.8 | 11.0 | 5.4 | 7.9 | 9.8 | 10.8 | 11.1 | Don't know |
|  | (420) | (282) | (83) | (266) | (295) | (194) | (292) | Weighted N |

Blacks And Whites

Table 2.44
Racial Composition of Grade School nearest R
Education of Respondent

|  | Year | | | | | | | |
|---|---|---|---|---|---|---|---|---|
|  | 1964n | 1968n | 1970n | 1972n | 1974q | 1975p | 1976n | |
| Grade School Only | 52.4% | 27.8% | 30.7% | 36.5% | 27.0% | 18.8% | 30.4% | All White |
|  | 22.4 | 41.6 | 39.1 | 25.1 | 31.8 | 37.6 | 27.2 | Mostly White |
|  | 4.0 | 8.2 | 10.9 | 18.2 | 19.2 | 14.4 | 16.9 | Half and half |
|  | 4.8 | 9.5 | 8.7 | 7.3 | 6.8 | 6.9 | 9.5 | Mostly Black |
|  | 7.7 | 4.0 | 0.9 | 0.6 | 1.9 | 0.3 | 1.3 | All Black |
|  | 8.7 | 8.9 | 9.6 | 12.3 | 13.4 | 21.9 | 14.8 | Don't know |
|  | (1155) | (697) | (230) | (537) | (485) | (319) | (470) | Weighted N |
| High School Only | 56.6 | 36.7 | 33.6 | 33.4 | 26.6 | 22.7 | 29.4 | All White |
|  | 26.4 | 39.9 | 42.4 | 35.5 | 43.6 | 43.4 | 38.5 | Mostly White |
|  | 3.3 | 6.7 | 8.2 | 14.1 | 13.7 | 12.6 | 14.7 | Half and half |
|  | 3.5 | 4.4 | 7.1 | 5.6 | 5.0 | 7.4 | 4.5 | Mostly Black |
|  | 2.9 | 2.7 | 1.3 | 1.7 | 0.8 | 1.3 | 1.5 | All Black |
|  | 7.3 | 9.6 | 7.4 | 9.7 | 10.4 | 12.6 | 11.4 | Don't know |
|  | (2357) | (1543) | (450) | (1372) | (1412) | (937) | (1420) | Weighted N |
| College Only | 47.7 | 28.8 | 33.7 | 29.6 | 19.2 | 20.3 | 26.2 | All White |
|  | 37.8 | 52.4 | 43.6 | 39.7 | 48.6 | 46.5 | 42.4 | Mostly White |
|  | 1.7 | 4.5 | 6.4 | 11.6 | 9.6 | 9.5 | 9.6 | Half and half |
|  | 2.8 | 1.9 | 3.5 | 4.9 | 4.5 | 4.7 | 5.3 | Mostly Black |
|  | 1.4 | 0.6 | 0.3 | 1.3 | 0.4 | 1.3 | 1.0 | All Black |
|  | 8.6 | 11.8 | 12.5 | 12.9 | 17.6 | 17.7 | 15.4 | Don't know |
|  | (1096) | (841) | (225) | (783) | (1039) | (634) | (944) | Weighted N |

Blacks And Whites

Table 2.45
Racial Composition of Grade School nearest R
Age of Respondent

|  | Year | | | | | | |  |
|---|---|---|---|---|---|---|---|---|
|  | 1964n | 1968n | 1970n | 1972n | 1974q | 1975p | 1976n |  |
| 18-24 Only | 52.8% | 21.5% | 30.3% | 31.0% | 22.0% | 18.7% | 28.5% | All White |
|  | 24.7 | 41.2 | 36.4 | 30.5 | 44.1 | 42.8 | 35.1 | Mostly White |
|  | 1.7 | 10.3 | 13.2 | 16.1 | 14.8 | 15.7 | 13.6 | Half and half |
|  | 3.7 | 4.7 | 5.7 | 7.1 | 3.5 | 6.0 | 4.7 | Mostly Black |
|  | 4.8 | 3.9 | 1.6 | 1.5 | 0.6 | 1.7 | 2.8 | All Black |
|  | 12.4 | 18.5 | 12.8 | 13.9 | 15.0 | 15.1 | 15.4 | Don't know |
|  | (356) | (233) | (132) | (397) | (487) | (299) | (394) | Weighted N |
| 25-34 Only | 51.0 | 33.0 | 31.9 | 31.6 | 21.2 | 19.9 | 28.8 | All White |
|  | 30.6 | 44.8 | 47.5 | 38.5 | 45.0 | 42.9 | 39.4 | Mostly White |
|  | 3.9 | 6.6 | 6.3 | 14.9 | 13.8 | 14.4 | 12.2 | Half and half |
|  | 4.3 | 5.1 | 6.8 | 4.7 | 5.3 | 6.6 | 6.5 | Mostly Black |
|  | 4.0 | 2.3 | 1.1 | 1.6 | 1.2 | 1.5 | 1.0 | All Black |
|  | 6.2 | 8.4 | 6.5 | 8.7 | 13.5 | 14.6 | 12.1 | Don't know |
|  | (951) | (610) | (171) | (576) | (674) | (452) | (688) | Weighted N |
| 35-44 Only | 53.5 | 34.5 | 28.9 | 35.4 | 25.1 | 26.7 | 27.4 | All White |
|  | 29.4 | 44.8 | 43.7 | 38.5 | 48.8 | 52.4 | 46.9 | Mostly White |
|  | 4.2 | 7.4 | 7.6 | 13.2 | 10.9 | 6.8 | 13.3 | Half and half |
|  | 3.9 | 4.6 | 11.0 | 5.2 | 8.7 | 7.2 | 5.5 | Mostly Black |
|  | 3.9 | 2.5 | 0.8 | 2.0 | 0.6 | 0.3 | 0.9 | All Black |
|  | 5.0 | 6.2 | 8.0 | 5.7 | 5.9 | 6.5 | 5.9 | Don't know |
|  | (1018) | (649) | (150) | (441) | (494) | (292) | (424) | Weighted N |
| 45-54 Only | 55.2 | 34.9 | 32.1 | 31.2 | 25.8 | 24.9 | 29.1 | All White |
|  | 27.2 | 45.1 | 42.8 | 37.8 | 42.8 | 46.5 | 41.5 | Mostly White |
|  | 2.7 | 5.9 | 9.8 | 13.0 | 12.2 | 11.0 | 13.2 | Half and half |
|  | 3.8 | 4.3 | 5.6 | 5.8 | 5.2 | 6.6 | 4.8 | Mostly Black |
|  | 3.3 | 1.9 | 0.8 | 0.7 | 0.6 | 1.1 | 1.4 | All Black |
|  | 7.7 | 7.8 | 8.8 | 11.5 | 13.4 | 9.9 | 10.1 | Don't know |
|  | (918) | (625) | (149) | (445) | (500) | (273) | (398) | Weighted N |
| 55-64 Only | 51.8 | 34.6 | 39.3 | 35.6 | 26.5 | 18.0 | 26.9 | All White |
|  | 30.9 | 40.6 | 37.2 | 30.9 | 42.6 | 43.2 | 35.4 | Mostly White |
|  | 2.1 | 5.3 | 9.0 | 14.0 | 15.1 | 11.7 | 14.3 | Half and half |
|  | 1.8 | 4.9 | 6.1 | 5.7 | 3.9 | 8.6 | 6.0 | Mostly Black |
|  | 2.5 | 2.4 | 1.0 | 1.6 | 1.4 | 1.1 | 1.0 | All Black |
|  | 10.9 | 12.2 | 7.4 | 12.2 | 10.5 | 17.3 | 16.5 | Don't know |
|  | (679) | (451) | (153) | (385) | (437) | (266) | (407) | Weighted N |
| 65-74 Only | 53.5 | 28.7 | 32.6 | 33.2 | 28.6 | 18.9 | 29.3 | All White |
|  | 23.0 | 43.0 | 45.0 | 28.8 | 31.7 | 35.8 | 29.9 | Mostly White |
|  | 2.8 | 5.4 | 6.8 | 12.0 | 10.7 | 10.4 | 13.3 | Half and half |
|  | 5.2 | 6.6 | 3.9 | 5.1 | 2.2 | 4.0 | 7.2 | Mostly Black |
|  | 3.9 | 3.7 | 0.3 | 1.1 | 0.4 | 0.5 | 1.8 | All Black |
|  | 11.6 | 12.6 | 11.4 | 19.7 | 26.3 | 30.3 | 18.5 | Don't know |
|  | (465) | (349) | (92) | (274) | (224) | (201) | (328) | Weighted N |
| 75 And Older Only | 65.8 | 31.3 | 38.0 | 34.4 | 23.4 | 22.0 | 29.8 | All White |
|  | 19.4 | 44.4 | 40.8 | 33.1 | 34.7 | 31.2 | 30.6 | Mostly White |
|  | 1.7 | 3.8 | 3.4 | 16.9 | 15.3 | 10.1 | 16.5 | Half and half |
|  | 2.1 | 3.1 | 3.4 | 5.2 | 4.8 | 2.8 | 3.5 | Mostly Black |
|  | 5.9 | 0.6 | 0.6 | 0.0 | 0.0 | 0.9 | 0.0 | All Black |
|  | 5.1 | 16.9 | 14.0 | 10.4 | 21.8 | 33.0 | 19.7 | Don't know |
|  | (237) | (160) | (54) | (154) | (124) | (109) | (188) | Weighted N |

Blacks And Whites

Table 2.46
Racial Composition of High School nearest R
Total Population

QUESTION: Is the high school nearest you: All White, Mostly White, About half and half, Mostly Negro/Black, All Negro/Black?

|  |  | Year | | | | | |
|  |  | 1964n | 1968n | 1970n | 1972n | 1974q | 1975p |
|---|---|---|---|---|---|---|---|
| All White | (1) | 39.7% | 24.0% | 20.2% | 21.7% | 24.1% | 14.1% |
| Mostly White | (2) | 36.7 | 48.3 | 46.7 | 39.1 | 43.3 | 46.5 |
| About half and half | (3) | 5.5 | 8.8 | 12.2 | 17.9 | 13.3 | 15.0 |
| Mostly Black | (4) | 2.6 | 4.8 | 6.1 | 6.3 | 5.1 | 5.6 |
| All Black | (5) | 3.3 | 2.1 | 1.0 | 1.3 | 0.8 | 1.0 |
| Don't know |  | 12.2 | 11.9 | 13.7 | 13.7 | 13.4 | 17.7 |
| Total |  | 100% | 100% | 100% | 100% | 100% | 100% |
| Weighted N |  | 4615 | 3084 | 907 | 2693 | 2954 | 1890 |
| Unweighted N |  | 1816 | 1664 | 956 | 2693 | 1503 | 1890 |
| Mean |  | 1.78 | 2.01 | 2.08 | 2.15 | 2.02 | 2.18 |
| Standard Deviation |  | 0.96 | 0.90 | 0.87 | 0.93 | 0.87 | 0.84 |

1964n, 1968n, and 1970n include Black supplement.

Figure 2.21
Racial Composition of High School--Total Population

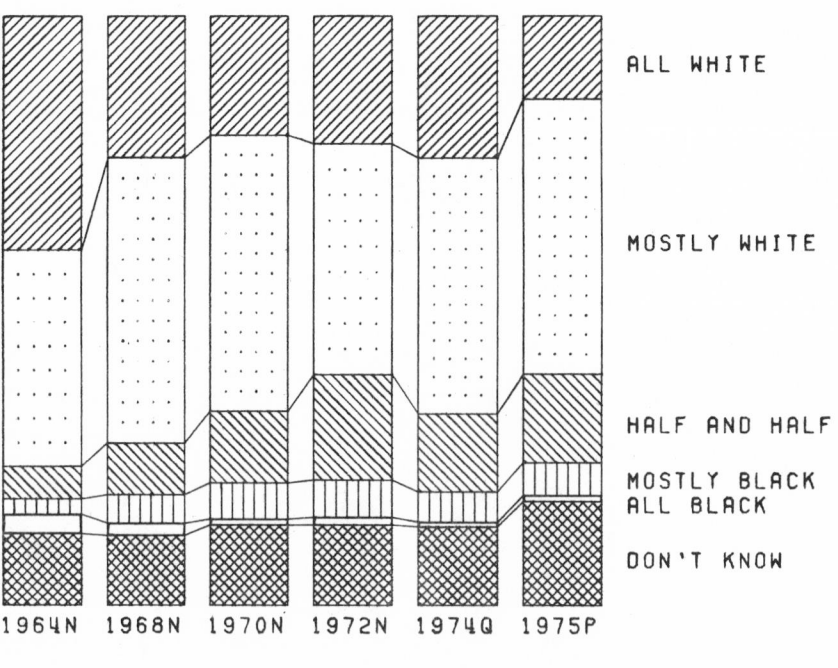

Figure 2.22
Racial Composition of High School by Race of R

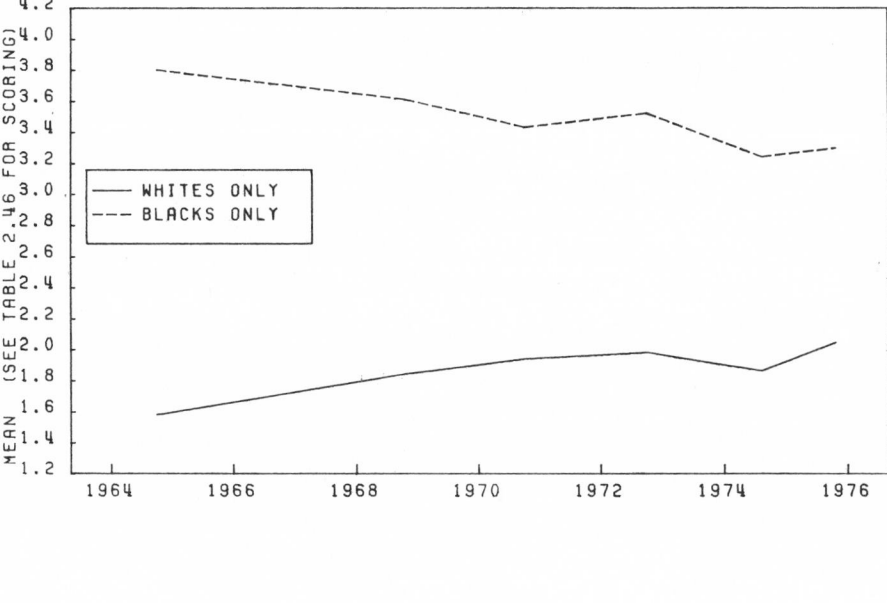

Blacks And Whites

Table 2.47
Racial Composition of High School nearest R
Sex of Respondent

|  | Year | | | | | | |
|---|---|---|---|---|---|---|---|
|  | 1964n | 1968n | 1970n | 1972n | 1974q | 1975p | |
| Males Only | 39.2% | 24.7% | 22.0% | 21.2% | 22.5% | 13.7% | All White |
|  | 38.9 | 50.5 | 46.3 | 43.1 | 46.3 | 50.4 | Mostly White |
|  | 5.4 | 8.9 | 13.7 | 16.9 | 12.6 | 14.4 | Half and half |
|  | 2.1 | 4.6 | 6.1 | 6.5 | 5.5 | 5.1 | Mostly Black |
|  | 2.8 | 1.5 | 0.8 | 1.3 | 0.5 | 0.8 | All Black |
|  | 11.6 | 9.9 | 11.0 | 11.1 | 12.6 | 15.6 | Don't know |
|  | (2097) | (1349) | (386) | (1162) | (1314) | (797) | Weighted N |
| Females Only | 40.2 | 23.5 | 18.9 | 22.1 | 25.4 | 14.5 | All White |
|  | 35.0 | 46.6 | 46.9 | 36.1 | 40.9 | 43.6 | Mostly White |
|  | 5.5 | 8.6 | 11.1 | 18.7 | 13.8 | 15.5 | Half and half |
|  | 2.9 | 5.0 | 6.1 | 6.2 | 4.8 | 5.9 | Mostly Black |
|  | 3.7 | 2.7 | 1.2 | 1.2 | 1.1 | 1.2 | All Black |
|  | 12.6 | 13.5 | 15.7 | 15.6 | 14.1 | 19.3 | Don't know |
|  | (2518) | (1735) | (521) | (1531) | (1640) | (1093) | Weighted N |

Table 2.48
Race of Respondent

|  | 1964n | 1968n | 1970n | 1972n | 1974q | 1975p | |
|---|---|---|---|---|---|---|---|
| Whites Only | 43.4% | 26.7% | 22.3% | 24.2% | 27.2% | 15.9% | All White |
|  | 39.7 | 51.7 | 50.0 | 42.5 | 46.4 | 50.3 | Mostly White |
|  | 4.2 | 7.7 | 10.8 | 15.8 | 10.5 | 12.1 | Half and half |
|  | 1.2 | 2.1 | 2.8 | 3.3 | 2.4 | 3.7 | Mostly Black |
|  | 0.0 | 0.4 | 0.3 | 0.1 | 0.1 | 0.1 | All Black |
|  | 11.5 | 11.4 | 13.8 | 14.1 | 13.5 | 17.8 | Don't know |
|  | (4161) | (2764) | (811) | (2387) | (2534) | (1631) | Weighted N |
| Blacks Only | 5.7 | 0.4 | 0.0 | 0.8 | 0.7 | 0.5 | All White |
|  | 10.3 | 17.9 | 17.0 | 8.3 | 21.0 | 14.9 | Mostly White |
|  | 15.3 | 16.4 | 25.4 | 35.5 | 31.5 | 37.6 | Half and half |
|  | 15.3 | 31.1 | 39.5 | 33.2 | 29.5 | 23.2 | Mostly Black |
|  | 36.6 | 20.0 | 8.3 | 11.7 | 7.5 | 9.3 | All Black |
|  | 16.7 | 14.3 | 9.8 | 10.6 | 9.8 | 14.4 | Don't know |
|  | (418) | (280) | (83) | (265) | (295) | (194) | Weighted N |

Blacks And Whites

Table 2.49
Racial Composition of High School nearest R
Education of Respondent

|  |  | Year |  |  |  |  |  |
|---|---|---|---|---|---|---|---|
|  | 1964n | 1968n | 1970n | 1972n | 1974q | 1975p |  |
| Grade School Only | 40.2% | 21.3% | 24.0% | 27.7% | 27.0% | 13.6% | All White |
|  | 30.6 | 44.9 | 42.2 | 28.3 | 31.8 | 37.9 | Mostly White |
|  | 5.8 | 9.1 | 12.2 | 19.5 | 19.2 | 18.0 | Half and half |
|  | 2.8 | 8.2 | 7.4 | 7.1 | 6.8 | 5.4 | Mostly Black |
|  | 6.9 | 3.7 | 1.0 | 0.7 | 1.9 | 0.3 | All Black |
|  | 13.7 | 12.8 | 13.2 | 16.7 | 13.4 | 24.9 | Don't know |
|  | (1147) | (695) | (230) | (538) | (485) | (317) | Weighted N |
| High School Only | 43.2 | 28.4 | 17.9 | 20.9 | 26.6 | 14.6 | All White |
|  | 35.0 | 45.0 | 48.1 | 39.6 | 43.6 | 45.6 | Mostly White |
|  | 6.0 | 9.1 | 12.6 | 18.5 | 13.7 | 17.2 | Half and half |
|  | 2.2 | 4.9 | 7.5 | 6.4 | 5.0 | 5.8 | Mostly Black |
|  | 2.6 | 1.9 | 1.3 | 1.6 | 0.8 | 1.1 | All Black |
|  | 11.1 | 10.6 | 12.5 | 13.1 | 10.4 | 15.8 | Don't know |
|  | (2342) | (1541) | (450) | (1371) | (1412) | (937) | Weighted N |
| College Only | 31.7 | 18.4 | 21.3 | 19.2 | 19.2 | 13.7 | All White |
|  | 47.1 | 57.2 | 48.1 | 45.8 | 48.6 | 52.2 | Mostly White |
|  | 4.2 | 8.0 | 11.6 | 15.7 | 9.6 | 10.3 | Half and half |
|  | 3.2 | 1.8 | 1.9 | 5.6 | 4.5 | 5.5 | Mostly Black |
|  | 0.8 | 1.2 | 0.3 | 1.0 | 0.4 | 1.3 | All Black |
|  | 13.0 | 13.4 | 16.8 | 12.7 | 17.6 | 17.0 | Don't know |
|  | (1093) | (841) | (225) | (782) | (1039) | (634) | Weighted N |

Blacks And Whites

Table 2.50
Racial Composition of High School nearest R
Age of Respondent

|  |  | Year |  |  |  |  |  |
|---|---|---|---|---|---|---|---|
|  | 1964n | 1968n | 1970n | 1972n | 1974q | 1975p |  |
| 18-24 Only | 36.0% | 13.7% | 17.3% | 19.9% | 22.0% | 11.7% | All White |
|  | 39.0 | 45.5 | 42.6 | 34.8 | 44.1 | 48.0 | Mostly White |
|  | 5.9 | 16.3 | 15.3 | 19.9 | 14.8 | 19.7 | Half and half |
|  | 2.2 | 5.2 | 6.4 | 10.1 | 3.5 | 7.7 | Mostly Black |
|  | 4.2 | 1.7 | 0.9 | 1.3 | 0.6 | 1.7 | All Black |
|  | 12.6 | 17.6 | 17.5 | 14.1 | 15.0 | 11.3 | Don't know |
|  | (356) | (233) | (132) | (397) | (487) | (300) | Weighted N |
| 25-34 Only | 34.3 | 26.0 | 14.7 | 19.0 | 21.2 | 11.7 | All White |
|  | 39.8 | 43.3 | 48.7 | 38.1 | 45.0 | 46.9 | Mostly White |
|  | 5.2 | 9.2 | 14.7 | 20.9 | 13.8 | 17.3 | Half and half |
|  | 2.9 | 5.1 | 5.1 | 4.5 | 5.3 | 5.3 | Mostly Black |
|  | 3.9 | 2.3 | 0.9 | 1.6 | 1.2 | 1.1 | All Black |
|  | 14.0 | 14.1 | 15.9 | 16.0 | 13.5 | 17.7 | Don't know |
|  | (945) | (608) | (171) | (575) | (674) | (452) | Weighted N |
| 35-44 Only | 39.8 | 25.7 | 18.1 | 22.4 | 25.1 | 15.8 | All White |
|  | 37.5 | 52.4 | 50.9 | 47.2 | 48.8 | 53.6 | Mostly White |
|  | 8.0 | 8.0 | 12.2 | 15.9 | 10.9 | 15.5 | Half and half |
|  | 2.4 | 5.7 | 6.3 | 6.3 | 8.7 | 3.8 | Mostly Black |
|  | 3.0 | 1.8 | 1.0 | 1.4 | 0.6 | 0.7 | All Black |
|  | 9.3 | 6.3 | 11.4 | 6.8 | 5.9 | 10.7 | Don't know |
|  | (1017) | (649) | (152) | (441) | (494) | (291) | Weighted N |
| 45-54 Only | 42.6 | 25.3 | 19.3 | 19.8 | 25.8 | 19.0 | All White |
|  | 37.8 | 51.0 | 51.2 | 44.9 | 42.8 | 49.8 | Mostly White |
|  | 5.5 | 7.9 | 11.4 | 17.3 | 12.2 | 13.2 | Half and half |
|  | 2.9 | 5.4 | 7.0 | 4.9 | 5.2 | 6.2 | Mostly Black |
|  | 2.4 | 1.3 | 1.6 | 0.9 | 0.6 | 1.1 | All Black |
|  | 8.8 | 9.1 | 9.4 | 12.1 | 13.4 | 10.6 | Don't know |
|  | (908) | (624) | (149) | (445) | (500) | (273) | Weighted N |
| 55-64 Only | 41.9 | 23.1 | 24.7 | 25.3 | 26.5 | 13.2 | All White |
|  | 38.0 | 48.7 | 45.5 | 35.9 | 42.6 | 45.7 | Mostly White |
|  | 4.1 | 8.7 | 10.3 | 17.4 | 15.1 | 11.3 | Half and half |
|  | 2.2 | 3.3 | 7.8 | 6.5 | 3.9 | 7.5 | Mostly Black |
|  | 2.1 | 3.3 | 0.6 | 1.3 | 1.4 | 1.1 | All Black |
|  | 11.7 | 12.9 | 11.1 | 13.5 | 10.5 | 21.1 | Don't know |
|  | (676) | (450) | (151) | (384) | (437) | (265) | Weighted N |
| 65-74 Only | 39.2 | 21.8 | 26.1 | 26.0 | 28.6 | 13.5 | All White |
|  | 30.7 | 47.3 | 42.3 | 32.6 | 31.7 | 39.5 | Mostly White |
|  | 4.8 | 7.4 | 10.4 | 13.6 | 10.7 | 13.0 | Half and half |
|  | 3.1 | 4.6 | 4.6 | 5.9 | 2.2 | 4.5 | Mostly Black |
|  | 3.9 | 3.4 | 1.3 | 1.1 | 0.4 | 0.0 | All Black |
|  | 18.3 | 15.5 | 15.3 | 20.9 | 26.3 | 29.5 | Don't know |
|  | (459) | (349) | (92) | (273) | (224) | (200) | Weighted N |
| 75 And Older Only | 50.6 | 26.3 | 33.5 | 25.0 | 23.4 | 17.4 | All White |
|  | 23.2 | 46.9 | 36.3 | 36.5 | 34.7 | 28.4 | Mostly White |
|  | 0.8 | 6.3 | 8.4 | 17.3 | 15.3 | 9.2 | Half and half |
|  | 1.7 | 2.5 | 2.8 | 5.8 | 4.8 | 1.8 | Mostly Black |
|  | 5.9 | 0.6 | 0.0 | 0.6 | 0.0 | 0.9 | All Black |
|  | 17.7 | 17.5 | 19.0 | 14.7 | 21.8 | 42.2 | Don't know |
|  | (237) | (160) | (54) | (156) | (124) | (109) | Weighted N |

Blacks And Whites

## Chapter 3. Women

Another major change in the past two decades in the United States has involved the role of women. The concept of "women's role" has a great multiplicity of facets, and the potential set of indicators which might have been measured to capture the evolution of role assumptions is very large indeed. Most of the measures in this chapter are limited to the role of women vis-a-vis work, including housework, on one hand, and paid work outside the home, on the other.

Although we open the chapter with an item concerning the engagement of married women in paid work outside the home, which shows a major advance in the reported incidence of such work on the part of wives between 1962 and 1978, the best data on the proportion of women in the labor force naturally come from government Census sources. These figures indicate that the proportion of women ages eighteen to sixty-five in the labor force has increased from 31 percent in 1950 to about 50 percent in 1978. This chapter captures some of the concomitants of this change.

It is wise to read the tables below with particular caution from several points of view. One is that many of the tables deal with responses from women alone and some from only those women who are housewives (not engaged in any major paid work outside the home). With case numbers thus restricted, sampling variability rises considerably. Moreover numbers vary widely by study. Thus for example, the item asking housewives about plans for a job in the future presented in table 3.21, was asked twice in 1976, the final year of the series. However, the final distribution to which the eye naturally gravitates in assessing change was only about a quarter of the size of the earlier 1976 study. In this case it is worth mentally merging the two 1976 distributions, rather than depending on the final 1976 value alone.

Caution is also in order from another point of view. Precisely because of the swelling tide of women in the labor force, the slice of the population represented by the housewife category in 1957, where several of our series begin is quite different from the membership of that category by 1976. Consider the item asking whether the housewife has ever wanted a career (table 3.17). At first glance, it appears that there has been little or no change in these aspirations since 1957, a judgement which would seem quite contrary to most of the other data showing widespread shifts in assumptions about women's roles. However, one must keep in mind the fact that more and more women coveting careers have actually gone about adopting them, thereby selecting themselves out of the pure housewife category. Thus the category has over time been progressively stripped back to women who are, as it were, "hard-core" housewives, and, within this dwindling set, desires for a career appear to remain at something of an equilibrium.

By the same token, however, the substantial changes reflected in some other tables dealing with housewives are the more impressive because they register despite the shrinkage in the housewife set. Thus, for example, although the item concerning reactions to housework as a job (table 3.13) is based on limited case numbers and shows some irregularities, it appears that many fewer housewives are professing to like housework than said so years ago. It is still true that few express actual dislike, but ambivalence has increased. Such change must be evaluated keeping in mind the fact that self-selection out of the housewife category has been occurring in the interim, presumably among those who have found housework least satisfying.

In the preceding chapter we noted that change in racial attitudes in the past two decades has been spearheaded by the young and well-educated. The same message is embedded in virtually all of the tables involving changes in women's roles. Indeed, in this case it frequently appears as though new conceptions of women's roles have as yet failed to affect at all those women whose educational backgrounds are limited to grade school completion or less. Of course, this apparent immunity must again be evaluated against the joint facts that the proportion of women with grade-school education only has itself been dwindling in the past two decades, and that, for the housewife tables, there has been some self-selection out into the labor force in any event. Nonetheless, it is clear that movement into the labor force has been most marked among college women, and least marked at the grade-school level.

The item starting in table 3.26 suggests some change in the motivations women have for working. The code categories here, compressing a wide range of reasons expressed, are a bit cryptic and require brief explanation. The category "Positive: extrinsic" simply encompasses all of those reasons which are purely economic, such as money or retirement benefits as well as a minuscule admixture of reasons for working that have to do with the pleasant surroundings of the particualr job. The modest recent decline in frequency of these references may fruitfully be compared with cognate data in our later chapter on work. The ego satisfaction category includes such things as feelings of usefulness, the challenge of the job, the demonstration of skills, and the like. The negative states that work prevents include boredom, preoccupation with personal problems and even emotional upset.

Women

Table 3.1
Did Wife Work for Money in Previous Year?
Total Population

QUESTION: Did your wife/Did you (wife) do any work for money during the previous year?

|  | Year | | | | | | | |
|---|---|---|---|---|---|---|---|---|
|  | 1962f | 1965b | 1966a | 1967a | 1968e | 1969e | 1970a | 1970e |
| Yes (1) | 36.8% | 45.4% | 42.2% | 44.5% | 44.6% | 48.6% | 48.6% | 51.4% |
| No (5) | 63.2 | 54.6 | 57.8 | 55.5 | 55.4 | 51.4 | 51.4 | 48.6 |
| Total | 100% | 100% | 100% | 100% | 100% | 100% | 100% | 100% |
| Weighted N | 989 | 1619 | 1748 | 2661 | 81394 | 83286 | 1838 | 86976 |
| Unweighted N | 989 | 1619 | 1748 | 2365 | 2397 | 2514 | 1838 | 2693 |
| Mean | 3.53 | 3.18 | 3.31 | 3.22 | 3.22 | 3.05 | 3.06 | 2.94 |
| Standard Deviation | 1.93 | 1.99 | 1.98 | 1.99 | 1.99 | 2.00 | 2.00 | 2.00 |

Table 3.2

|  | 1971e | 1972e | 1972f | 1973e | 1974e | 1975e | 1976e | 1978n |
|---|---|---|---|---|---|---|---|---|
| Yes (1) | 51.5% | 52.3% | 46.2% | 49.7% | 52.2% | 52.5% | 56.3% | 57.7% |
| No (5) | 48.5 | 47.7 | 53.8 | 50.3 | 47.8 | 47.5 | 43.7 | 42.3 |
| Total | 100% | 100% | 100% | 100% | 100% | 100% | 100% | 100% |
| Weighted N | 76356 | 79633 | 914 | 82777 | 85224 | 87511 | 179710 | 1886 |
| Unweighted N | 2453 | 2658 | 914 | 2863 | 3058 | 3265 | 179710 | 1886 |
| Mean | 2.94 | 2.91 | 3.15 | 3.01 | 2.91 | 2.90 | 2.75 | 2.69 |
| Standard Deviation | 2.00 | 2.00 | 1.99 | 2.00 | 2.00 | 2.00 | 1.98 | 1.98 |

Figure 3.1
Did Wife Work Last Year?--Total Population

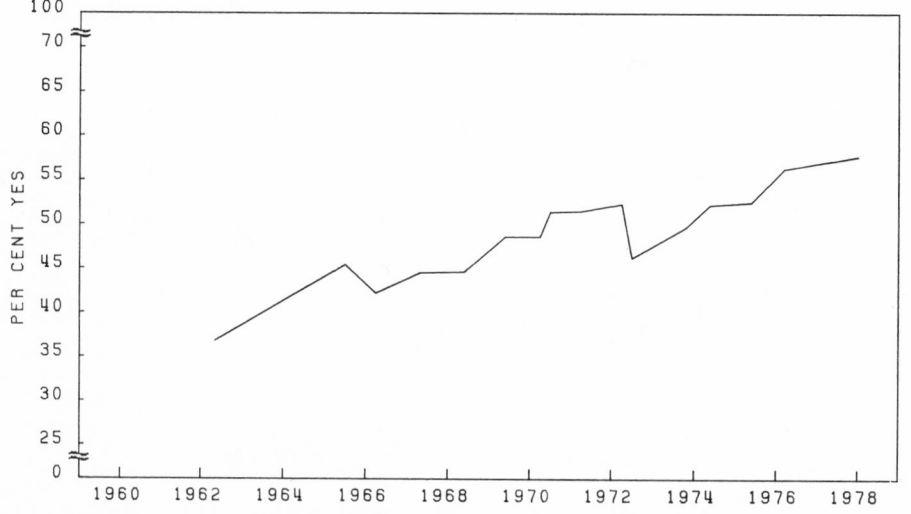

Women

Table 3.3
Did Wife Work for Money in Previous Year?
Sex of Respondent

% Yes

|  |  | Year |  |  |  |  |  |  |  |
|---|---|---|---|---|---|---|---|---|---|
|  |  | 1962f | 1965b | 1966a | 1967a | 1968e | 1969e | 1970a | 1970e |  |
| Males Only |  | 37.5% | 45.4% | 42.3% | 44.9% | 44.2% | 48.3% | 48.3% | 51.2% | Yes |
|  |  | (477) | (1442) | (1661) | (2456) | (75223) | (76627) | (1600) | (79173) | Weighted N |
| Females Only |  | 36.1 | 45.8 | 41.4 | 40.5 | 49.3 | 52.3 | 50.8 | 53.9 | Yes |
|  |  | (512) | (177) | (87) | (205) | (6171) | (6659) | (238) | (7803) | Weighted N |

Table 3.4

|  |  | 1971e | 1972e | 1972f | 1973e | 1974e | 1975e | 1976e | 1978n |  |
|---|---|---|---|---|---|---|---|---|---|---|
| Males Only |  | 51.6% | 52.5% | 43.5% | 50.2% | 52.6% | 52.6% | 55.6% | 57.0% | Yes |
|  |  | (69268) | (72266) | (434) | (73066) | (73425) | (74555) | (91226) | (700) | Weighted N |
| Females Only |  | 50.8 | 50.0 | 48.5 | 46.6 | 49.4 | 52.0 | 56.9 | 58.2 | Yes |
|  |  | (7088) | (7260) | (480) | (9385) | (11606) | (12885) | (88484) | (1186) | Weighted N |

Sex coded for head of household and wife only in 1962f,1968e,1969e,1970e,1971e,1972e,1974e,and 1975e.

Table 3.5
Race of Respondent

|  |  | 1962f | 1965b | 1966a | 1967a | 1968e | 1969e | 1970a | 1970e |  |
|---|---|---|---|---|---|---|---|---|---|---|
| Whites Only |  | 36.0% | 44.3% | 40.4% | 43.7% | 43.0% | 47.2% | 47.4% | 50.5% | Yes |
|  |  | (889) | (1465) | (1607) | (2394) | (73293) | (74864) | (1681) | (77636) | Weighted N |
| Blacks Only |  | 51.3 | 61.6 | 63.8 | 55.2 | 62.2 | 63.2 | 62.1 | 63.1 | Yes |
|  |  | (78) | (138) | (116) | (212) | (6304) | (6568) | (140) | (6820) | Weighted N |

Table 3.6

|  |  | 1971e | 1972e | 1972f | 1973e | 1974e | 1975e | 1976e | 1978n |  |
|---|---|---|---|---|---|---|---|---|---|---|
| Whites Only |  | 50.5% | 51.7% | 45.0% | 48.9% | 51.0% | 51.6% | 55.7% | 57.3% | Yes |
|  |  | (68614) | (71344) | (834) | (73975) | (76220) | (78125) | (160260) | (1678) | Weighted N |
| Blacks Only |  | 62.0 | 61.8 | 61.2 | 59.5 | 62.2 | 60.2 | 63.4 | 64.9 | Yes |
|  |  | (5492) | (5944) | (67) | (6270) | (6394) | (6611) | (13772) | (171) | Weighted N |

Race coded for head of household and wife only in 1971e.

Table 3.7
Did Wife Work for Money in Previous Year?
Education of Respondent

% Yes

| | | | | Year | | | | |
|---|---|---|---|---|---|---|---|---|
| | 1962f | 1965b | 1966a | 1967a | 1968e | 1969e | 1970a | 1970e |
| Grade School Only | 34.0% | 39.8% | 33.9% | 35.5% | 36.9% | 41.3% | 33.9% | 41.7% Yes |
| | (153) | (450) | (457) | (708) | (18760) | (19577) | (274) | (18607) Weighted N |
| High School Only | 38.0 | 49.5 | 46.8 | 47.0 | 47.9 | 50.4 | 49.6 | 54.1 Yes |
| | (208) | (778) | (757) | (1269) | (38000) | (37979) | (1106) | (41306) Weighted N |
| College Only | 37.7 | 44.2 | 43.2 | 49.4 | 45.0 | 51.2 | 57.4 | 53.5 Yes |
| | (130) | (391) | (442) | (664) | (24159) | (25119) | (408) | (25928) Weighted N |

Table 3.8

| | 1971e | 1972e | 1972f | 1973e | 1974e | 1975e | 1976e | 1978n |
|---|---|---|---|---|---|---|---|---|
| Grade School Only | 40.9% | 40.2% | 29.0% | 41.5% | 40.9% | 41.3% | 38.0% | 34.1% Yes |
| | (12384) | (13337) | (162) | (13191) | (13015) | (12993) | (23525) | (229) Weighted N |
| High School Only | 53.4 | 53.9 | 45.2 | 49.9 | 53.1 | 52.3 | 56.6 | 58.4 Yes |
| | (32543) | (39183) | (482) | (40915) | (42256) | (44422) | (101390) | (1006) Weighted N |
| College Only | 55.2 | 56.6 | 58.8 | 53.8 | 55.9 | 58.5 | 64.5 | 65.1 Yes |
| | (23123) | (25324) | (267) | (26271) | (27540) | (28720) | (52452) | (648) Weighted N |

Education coded for head of household only in 1962f,1966a,and 1971e, and for head and wife only in 1965b,1967a, 1968e,1969e,1970a,1970e,1972e,1974e,and 1975e.

Figure 3.2
Did Wife Work Last Year? by Race of R

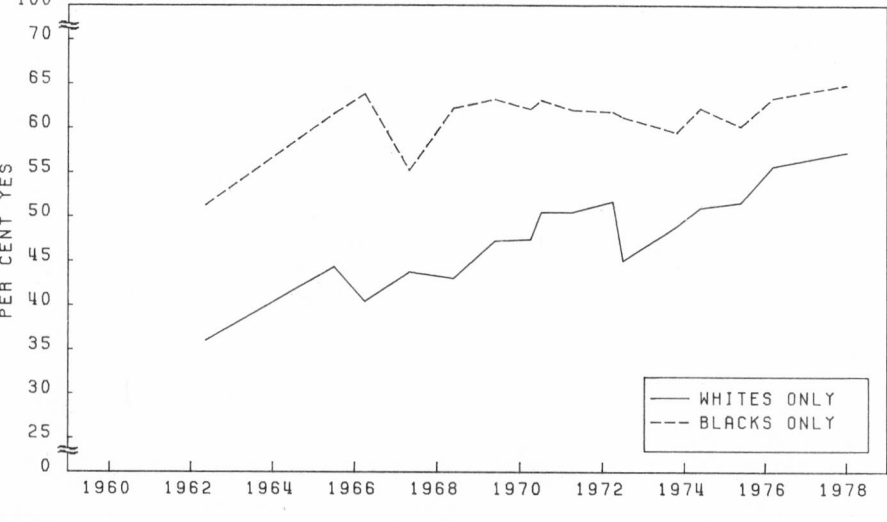

Figure 3.3
Did Wife Work Last Year? by Education of R

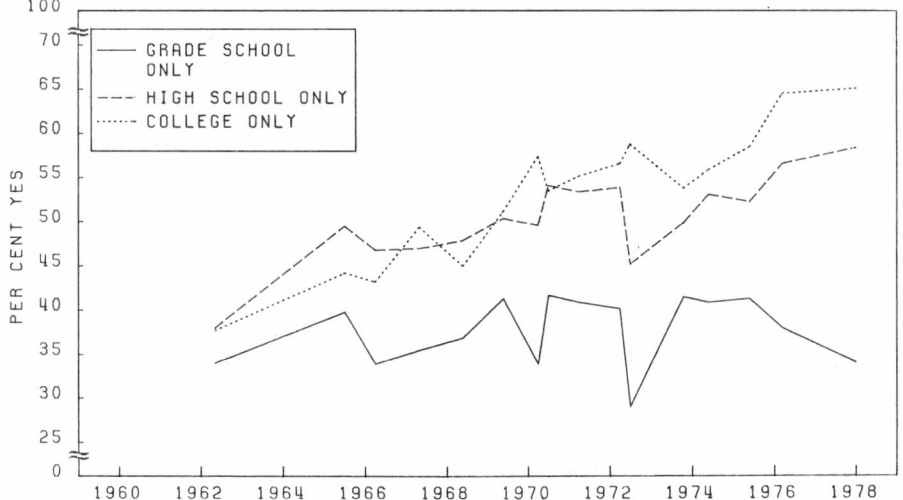

Women

Table 3.9
Did Wife Work for Money in Previous Year?
Age of Respondent

% Yes

|  | | Year | | | | | | |
|---|---|---|---|---|---|---|---|---|
|  | 1962f | 1965b | 1966a | 1967a | 1968e | 1969e | 1970a | 1970e |
| 18-24 Only | 22.2% | 65.6% | 59.4% | 63.4% | 60.8% | 65.5% | 65.6% | 74.5% Yes |
|  | (27) | (93) | (106) | (164) | (6460) | (6033) | (131) | (7163) Weighted N |
| 25-34 Only | 42.7 | 45.7 | 43.0 | 51.8 | 49.4 | 55.6 | 52.0 | 55.2 Yes |
|  | (103) | (304) | (363) | (527) | (17189) | (18231) | (333) | (19297) Weighted N |
| 35-44 Only | 35.9 | 46.4 | 48.0 | 51.0 | 43.6 | 50.5 | 50.0 | 52.9 Yes |
|  | (117) | (375) | (400) | (590) | (21043) | (20747) | (348) | (20203) Weighted N |
| 45-54 Only | 40.6 | 54.9 | 47.5 | 49.0 | 46.5 | 50.7 | 51.0 | 53.2 Yes |
|  | (106) | (375) | (379) | (561) | (15920) | (16415) | (361) | (17377) Weighted N |
| 55-64 Only | 41.7 | 43.9 | 39.2 | 41.2 | 45.5 | 43.3 | 50.0 | 49.0 Yes |
|  | (72) | (269) | (268) | (413) | (12332) | (12822) | (244) | (12749) Weighted N |
| 65-74 Only | 27.1 | 21.7 | 18.1 | 18.8 | 22.7 | 27.9 | 19.7 | 29.9 Yes |
|  | (48) | (157) | (232) | (276) | (6289) | (6533) | (142) | (7447) Weighted N |
| 75 And Older Only | 5.9 | 10.6 | ** | 6.3 | 13.4 | 12.0 | 13.0 | 11.8 Yes |
|  | (17) | (47) | ** | (128) | (2080) | (2546) | (46) | (2715) Weighted N |

** Code distinction not made--oldest age group coded "65 And Older" in 1966a.
Age coded for head of household only in 1962f, and for head and wife only in 1965b,1966a,1967a,1968e,1969e,1970a,
   and 1970e.


Table 3.10

|  | 1971e | 1972e | 1972f | 1973e | 1974e | 1975e | 1976e | 1978n |
|---|---|---|---|---|---|---|---|---|
| 18-24 Only | 68.4% | 71.7% | 58.1% | 68.1% | 71.7% | 70.2% | 70.8% | 80.6% Yes |
|  | (6714) | (7124) | (155) | (7309) | (7022) | (7327) | (18244) | (196) Weighted N |
| 25-34 Only | 55.5 | 60.5 | 49.8 | 56.6 | 61.2 | 60.7 | 66.4 | 69.2 Yes |
|  | (17118) | (18492) | (215) | (19514) | (21148) | (22126) | (45742) | (474) Weighted N |
| 35-44 Only | 53.6 | 54.1 | 54.3 | 48.7 | 53.7 | 55.2 | 62.9 | 64.0 Yes |
|  | (18813) | (17980) | (184) | (17495) | (16901) | (16634) | (33841) | (358) Weighted N |
| 45-54 Only | 54.2 | 51.7 | 51.1 | 53.1 | 52.8 | 55.9 | 58.5 | 66.0 Yes |
|  | (15252) | (16214) | (139) | (17777) | (18694) | (19111) | (37092) | (300) Weighted N |
| 55-64 Only | 45.6 | 48.3 | 31.3 | 43.9 | 47.7 | 45.0 | 44.8 | 47.1 Yes |
|  | (10577) | (10972) | (112) | (11065) | (11026) | (11197) | (24142) | (272) Weighted N |
| 65-74 Only | 27.2 | 23.1 | 20.3 | 26.2 | 23.8 | 25.6 | 21.9 | 18.8 Yes |
|  | (6570) | (6793) | (74) | (7083) | (8047) | (8245) | (15590) | (192) Weighted N |
| 75 And Older Only | 21.8 | 15.7 | 9.7 | 15.1 | 10.4 | 11.4 | 10.3 | 6.9 Yes |
|  | (1308) | (1869) | (31) | (2099) | (2061) | (2747) | (4790) | (87) Weighted N |

Age coded for head and wife only in 1971e,1972e,1974e,and 1975e.

Women

Table 3.11
Did Wife Work for Money in Previous Year?
Income of Respondent

% Yes

|  | | | | | Year | | | | |
|---|---|---|---|---|---|---|---|---|---|
|  | 1962f | 1965b | 1966a | 1967a | 1968e | 1969e | 1970a | 1970e | |
| Income 1 (0-16%) | 22.8% | 26.9% | 22.6% | 22.5% | 25.1% | 23.8% | 22.9% | 27.4% | Yes |
|  | (79) | (108) | (168) | (280) | (7202) | (7316) | (157) | (6686) | Weighted N |
| Income 2 (17-33%) | 26.6 | 34.5 | 35.3 | 34.9 | 37.1 | 40.8 | 33.1 | 42.1 | Yes |
|  | (154) | (197) | (317) | (347) | (12778) | (12281) | (245) | (12369) | Weighted N |
| Income 3 (34-67%) | 38.1 | 45.3 | 42.0 | 45.3 | 45.1 | 48.9 | 47.6 | 50.2 | Yes |
|  | (383) | (592) | (690) | (1110) | (30549) | (31182) | (718) | (33280) | Weighted N |
| Income 4 (68-95%) | 45.1 | 53.5 | 56.1 | 57.1 | 53.4 | 58.2 | 61.8 | 63.9 | Yes |
|  | (295) | (636) | (437) | (641) | (25994) | (27478) | (631) | (29493) | Weighted N |
| Income 5 (96-100%) | 38.0 | 40.8 | 38.6 | 46.4 | 43.5 | 50.4 | 49.5 | 41.7 | Yes |
|  | (50) | (103) | (140) | (295) | (4871) | (5090) | (103) | (5349) | Weighted N |

Table 3.12

|  | 1971e | 1972e | 1972f | 1973e | 1974e | 1975e | 1976e | 1978n | |
|---|---|---|---|---|---|---|---|---|---|
| Income 1 (0-16%) | 26.5% | 22.3% | 12.1% | 23.0% | 20.3% | 27.0% | 27.7% | 42.7% | Yes |
|  | (4749) | (4654) | (91) | (5556) | (4433) | (4722) | (13835) | (267) | Weighted N |
| Income 2 (17-33%) | 36.7 | 39.6 | 33.3 | 33.8 | 37.3 | 33.2 | 41.1 | 56.0 | Yes |
|  | (9768) | (9469) | (84) | (9390) | (9911) | (10280) | (25285) | (298) | Weighted N |
| Income 3 (34-67%) | 49.4 | 50.6 | 42.7 | 48.8 | 50.0 | 49.8 | 57.7 | 60.0 | Yes |
|  | (28690) | (29718) | (335) | (28793) | (31994) | (31106) | (65635) | (505) | Weighted N |
| Income 4 (68-95%) | 64.3 | 63.3 | 64.8 | 58.5 | 62.3 | 63.8 | 66.4 | 67.2 | Yes |
|  | (28094) | (30227) | (290) | (30351) | (33023) | (35163) | (64042) | (463) | Weighted N |
| Income 5 (96-100%) | 44.7 | 49.1 | 48.6 | 57.1 | 53.3 | 54.1 | 59.6 | 55.7 | Yes |
|  | (5055) | (5565) | (74) | (8455) | (6263) | (6240) | (10913) | (122) | Weighted N |

Table 3.13
Is Housekeeping Just a Job or Is It Enjoyable?
Total Population

QUESTION: Different people feel differently about taking care of a home--I don't mean taking care of the children, but things like cooking and sewing and keeping house.  Some women look on these things as just a job that has to be done-- other women really enjoy them. How do you feel about this?

| Housewives Only | | Year | | |
|---|---|---|---|---|
| | | 1957h | 1971j | 1976h |
| Like | (5) | 70.0% | 74.2% | 55.3% |
| Ambivalent or other | (3) | 24.4 | 19.8 | 39.1 |
| Dislike | (1) | 5.6 | 6.0 | 5.6 |
| Total | | 100% | 100% | 100% |
| Weighted N | | 864 | 2340 | 924 |
| Unweighted N | | 864 | 577 | 498 |
| Mean | | 4.29 | 4.36 | 3.99 |
| Standard Deviation | | 1.17 | 1.16 | 1.20 |

Figure 3.4
Is Housekeeping a Job?--Total Population

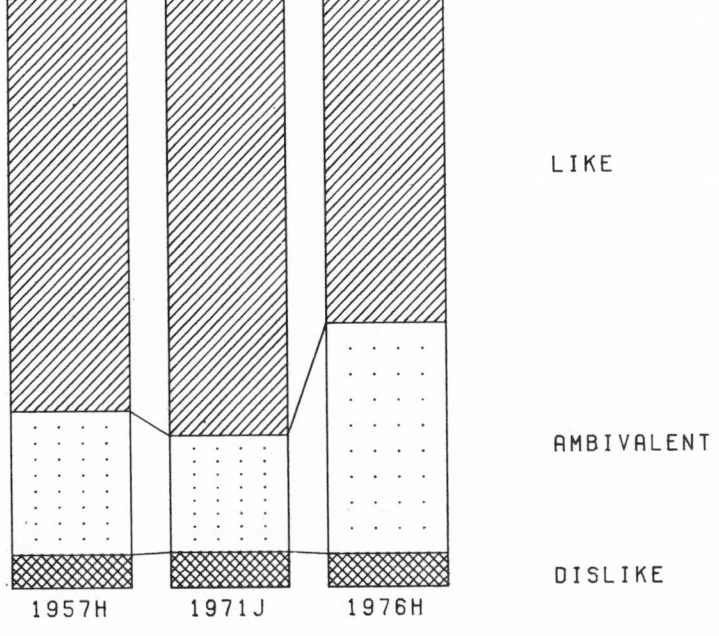

Figure 3.5
Is Housekeeping a Job? by Education of R

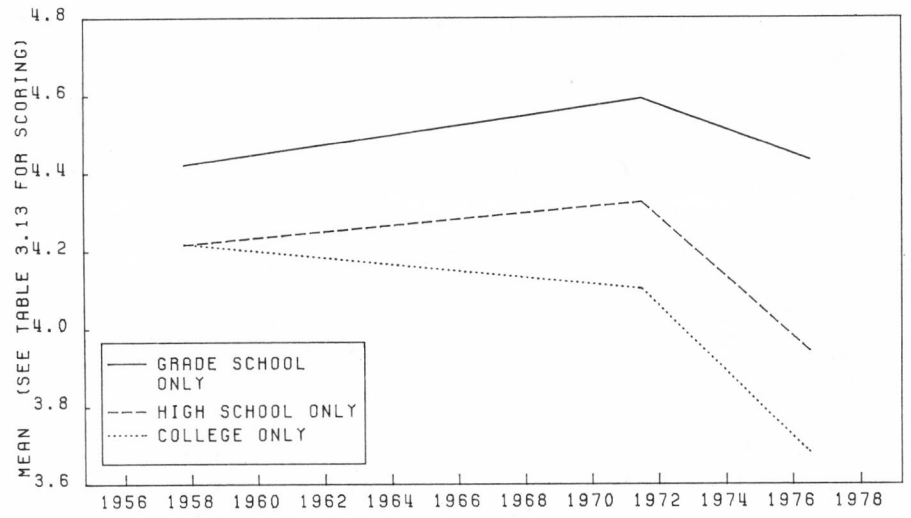

Table 3.14
Is Housekeeping Just a Job or Is It Enjoyable?
Race of Respondent

Housewives Only

| | Year | | | |
|---|---|---|---|---|
| | 1957h | 1971j | 1976h | |
| Whites Only | 69.9% | 73.3% | 53.4% | Like |
| | 24.7 | 20.7 | 40.9 | Ambivalent or other |
| | 5.4 | 6.0 | 5.8 | Dislike |
| | (774) | (2140) | (847) | Weighted N |
| Blacks Only | 71.2 | 82.1 | 78.6 | Like |
| | 19.2 | 10.3 | 21.4 | Ambivalent or other |
| | 9.6 | 7.7 | 0.0 | Dislike |
| | (52) | (156) | (42) | Weighted N |

Table 3.15
Education of Respondent

Housewives Only

| | 1957h | 1971j | 1976h | |
|---|---|---|---|---|
| Grade School Only | 76.7% | 82.9% | 76.3% | Like |
| | 17.8 | 13.8 | 19.2 | Ambivalent or other |
| | 5.6 | 3.3 | 4.5 | Dislike |
| | (287) | (608) | (198) | Weighted N |
| High School Only | 66.4 | 73.0 | 54.0 | Like |
| | 28.1 | 20.2 | 39.2 | Ambivalent or other |
| | 5.5 | 6.7 | 6.8 | Dislike |
| | (455) | (1364) | (500) | Weighted N |
| College Only | 66.9 | 63.2 | 38.2 | Like |
| | 27.1 | 28.7 | 57.6 | Ambivalent or other |
| | 5.9 | 8.0 | 4.1 | Dislike |
| | (118) | (348) | (217) | Weighted N |

Table 3.16
Is Housekeeping Just a Job or Is It Enjoyable?
Age of Respondent

Housewives Only

|  | Year | | | |
|---|---|---|---|---|
|  | 1957h | 1971j | 1976h | |
| 18-24 Only | 68.2% | 78.0% | 42.2% | Like |
|  | 27.3 | 20.0 | 48.4 | Ambivalent or other |
|  | 4.5 | 2.0 | 9.4 | Dislike |
|  | (66) | (200) | (64) | Weighted N |
| 25-34 Only | 61.5 | 68.2 | 43.2 | Like |
|  | 33.2 | 24.0 | 52.6 | Ambivalent or other |
|  | 5.3 | 7.8 | 4.2 | Dislike |
|  | (226) | (516) | (213) | Weighted N |
| 35-44 Only | 63.6 | 67.7 | 51.7 | Like |
|  | 29.5 | 24.2 | 45.5 | Ambivalent or other |
|  | 6.8 | 8.1 | 2.8 | Dislike |
|  | (176) | (396) | (145) | Weighted N |
| 45-54 Only | 76.3 | 78.9 | 55.3 | Like |
|  | 18.5 | 13.3 | 36.8 | Ambivalent or other |
|  | 5.2 | 7.8 | 7.9 | Dislike |
|  | (135) | (360) | (152) | Weighted N |
| 55-64 Only | 84.3 | 76.4 | 64.2 | Like |
|  | 12.2 | 20.8 | 31.4 | Ambivalent or other |
|  | 3.5 | 2.8 | 4.4 | Dislike |
|  | (115) | (288) | (159) | Weighted N |
| 65-74 Only | 74.1 | 74.7 | 67.3 | Like |
|  | 18.9 | 20.5 | 25.7 | Ambivalent or other |
|  | 7.0 | 4.8 | 6.9 | Dislike |
|  | (143) | (332) | (101) | Weighted N |
| 75 And Older Only | ** | 86.4 | 70.0 | Like |
|  | ** | 10.2 | 22.2 | Ambivalent or other |
|  | ** | 3.4 | 7.8 | Dislike |
|  | ** | (236) | (90) | Weighted N |

** Code distinction not made.
Youngest age group coded "21-24" in 1957h.
Oldest age group coded "65 And Older" in 1957h.

Table 3.17
Housewives' Desire for a Career
Total Population

QUESTION: Have you ever wanted a career?

|  | | | Year | | |
|---|---|---|---|---|
| Housewives Only | | 1957h | 1971j | 1972n | 1976h |
| Wanted a career | (5) | 36.3% | 32.4% | 29.5% | 39.6% |
| Ambivalent | (3) | ** | 8.8 | 7.9 | ** |
| Didn't want a career | (1) | 63.7 | 58.7 | 62.6 | 60.4 |
| Total | | 100% | 100% | 100% | 100% |
| Weighted N | | 865 | 2356 | 645 | 926 |
| Unweighted N | | 865 | 589 | 645 | 499 |
| Mean | | 2.45 | 2.47 | 2.34 | 2.58 |
| Standard Deviation | | 1.92 | 1.84 | 1.80 | 1.96 |

** Code distinction not made.

Figure 3.6
Desire for Career--Total Population

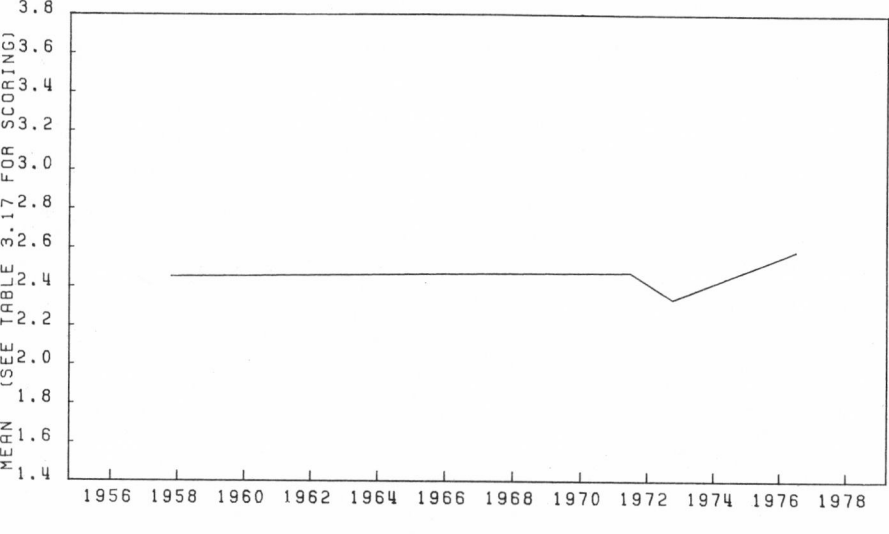
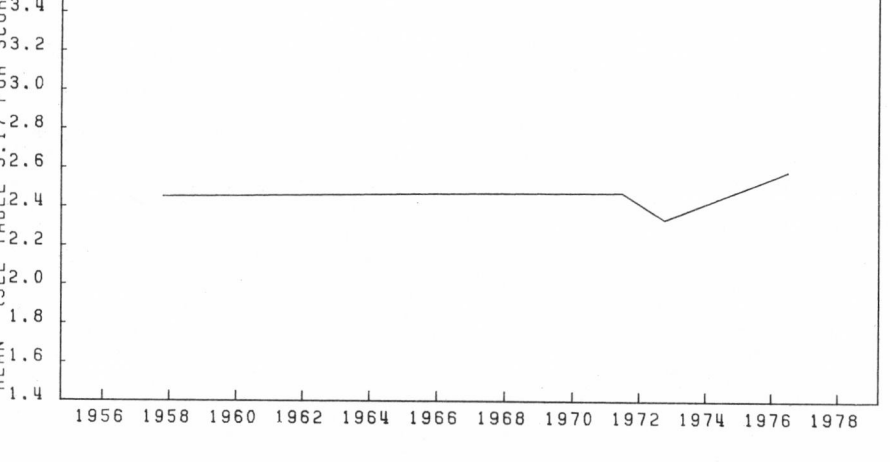

Figure 3.7
Desire for Career by Education of R

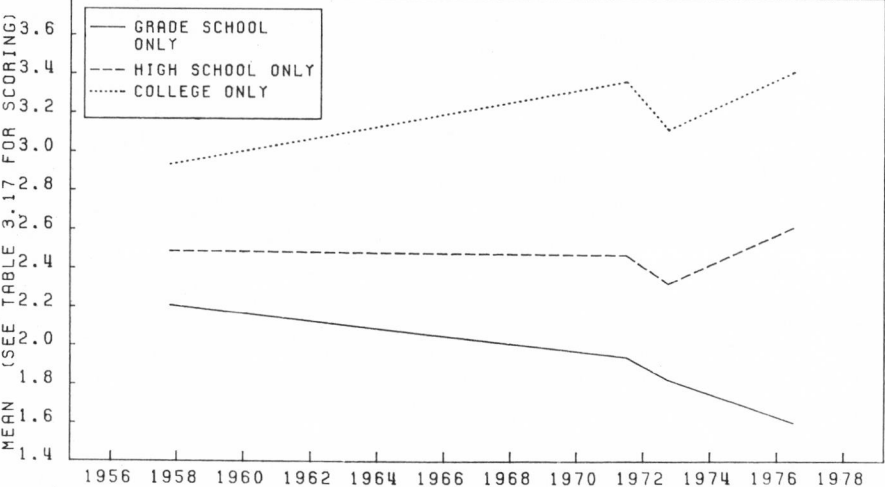

Table 3.18
Housewives' Desire for a Career
Race of Respondent

Housewives Only

| | | Year | | | |
|---|---|---|---|---|---|
| | 1957h | 1971j | 1972n | 1976h | |
| Whites Only | 35.4% | 30.0% | 29.2% | 39.3% | Wanted a career |
| | ** | 9.1 | 7.2 | ** | Ambivalent |
| | 64.6 | 60.9 | 63.6 | 60.7 | Didn't want a career |
| | (775) | (2160) | (585) | (849) | Weighted N |
| Blacks Only | 51.9 | 60.5 | 34.0 | 50.0 | Wanted a career |
| | ** | 5.3 | 18.0 | ** | Ambivalent |
| | 48.1 | 34.2 | 48.0 | 50.0 | Didn't want a career |
| | (52) | (152) | (50) | (42) | Weighted N |

Table 3.19
Education of Respondent

Housewives Only

| | 1957h | 1971j | 1972n | 1976h | |
|---|---|---|---|---|---|
| Grade School Only | 30.2% | 19.6% | 16.5% | 15.1% | Wanted a career |
| | ** | 7.8 | 8.2 | ** | Ambivalent |
| | 69.8 | 72.5 | 75.3 | 84.9 | Didn't want a career |
| | (288) | (612) | (170) | (199) | Weighted N |
| High School Only | 37.1 | 31.8 | 29.7 | 40.3 | Wanted a career |
| | ** | 9.9 | 6.8 | ** | Ambivalent |
| | 62.9 | 58.3 | 63.6 | 59.7 | Didn't want a career |
| | (455) | (1372) | (354) | (501) | Weighted N |
| College Only | 48.3 | 55.7 | 47.5 | 60.4 | Wanted a career |
| | ** | 6.8 | 10.8 | ** | Ambivalent |
| | 51.7 | 37.5 | 41.7 | 39.6 | Didn't want a career |
| | (118) | (352) | (120) | (217) | Weighted N |

** Code distinction not made.

Table 3.20
Housewives' Desire for a Career
Age of Respondent

Housewives Only

| | Year | | | | |
|---|---|---|---|---|---|
| | 1957h | 1971j | 1972n | 1976h | |
| 18-24 Only | 50.0% | 45.1% | 47.5% | 65.6% | Wanted a career |
| | ** | 9.8 | 10.2 | ** | Ambivalent |
| | 50.0 | 45.1 | 42.4 | 34.4 | Didn't want a career |
| | (66) | (204) | (59) | (64) | Weighted N |
| 25-34 Only | 39.4 | 39.2 | 37.3 | 57.7 | Wanted a career |
| | ** | 8.5 | 6.0 | ** | Ambivalent |
| | 60.6 | 52.3 | 56.7 | 42.3 | Didn't want a career |
| | (226) | (520) | (134) | (213) | Weighted N |
| 35-44 Only | 39.2 | 41.8 | 26.4 | 35.9 | Wanted a career |
| | ** | 6.1 | 14.9 | ** | Ambivalent |
| | 60.8 | 52.0 | 58.6 | 64.1 | Didn't want a career |
| | (176) | (392) | (87) | (145) | Weighted N |
| 45-54 Only | 30.4 | 23.1 | 23.7 | 34.2 | Wanted a career |
| | ** | 14.3 | 6.2 | ** | Ambivalent |
| | 69.6 | 62.6 | 70.1 | 65.8 | Didn't want a career |
| | (135) | (364) | (97) | (152) | Weighted N |
| 55-64 Only | 33.9 | 39.7 | 29.2 | 28.6 | Wanted a career |
| | ** | 4.1 | 10.4 | ** | Ambivalent |
| | 66.1 | 56.2 | 60.4 | 71.4 | Didn't want a career |
| | (115) | (292) | (96) | (161) | Weighted N |
| 65-74 Only | 28.5 | 21.7 | 25.5 | 30.0 | Wanted a career |
| | ** | 13.3 | 3.1 | ** | Ambivalent |
| | 71.5 | 65.1 | 71.4 | 70.0 | Didn't want a career |
| | (144) | (332) | (98) | (100) | Weighted N |
| 75 And Older Only | ** | 11.7 | 17.6 | 24.2 | Wanted a career |
| | ** | 3.3 | 5.9 | ** | Ambivalent |
| | ** | 85.0 | 76.5 | 75.8 | Didn't want a career |
| | ** | (240) | (68) | (91) | Weighted N |

** Code distinction not made.
Youngest age group coded "21-24" in 1957h.
Oldest age group coded "65 And Older" in 1957h.

Table 3.21
Does Housewife Plan on Getting a Job?
Total Population

QUESTION:Are you planning to go to work/thinking of getting a job in the future?

| Housewives Only | | | Year | | | |
|---|---|---|---|---|---|---|
| | 1957h | 1971j | 1972f | 1972n | 1976e | 1976h |
| Yes (5) | 16.6% | 24.3% | 24.2% | 24.4% | 28.5% | 29.9% |
| Depends (3) | ** | 12.2 | 13.9 | 12.7 | ** | 2.0 |
| No (1) | 83.4 | 63.3 | 57.1 | 62.7 | 71.5 | 68.1 |
| Don't know | ** | 0.2 | 4.8 | 0.3 | ** | ** |
| Total | 100% | 100% | 100% | 100% | 100% | 100% |
| Weighted N | 842 | 2352 | 273 | 648 | 55717 | 923 |
| Unweighted N | 842 | 588 | 273 | 648 | 2089 | 498 |
| Mean | 1.66 | 2.22 | 2.31 | 2.23 | 2.14 | 2.23 |
| Standard Deviation | 1.49 | 1.70 | 1.72 | 1.70 | 1 80 | 1.83 |

** Code distinction not made.

Figure 3.8
Future Job Plans--Total Population

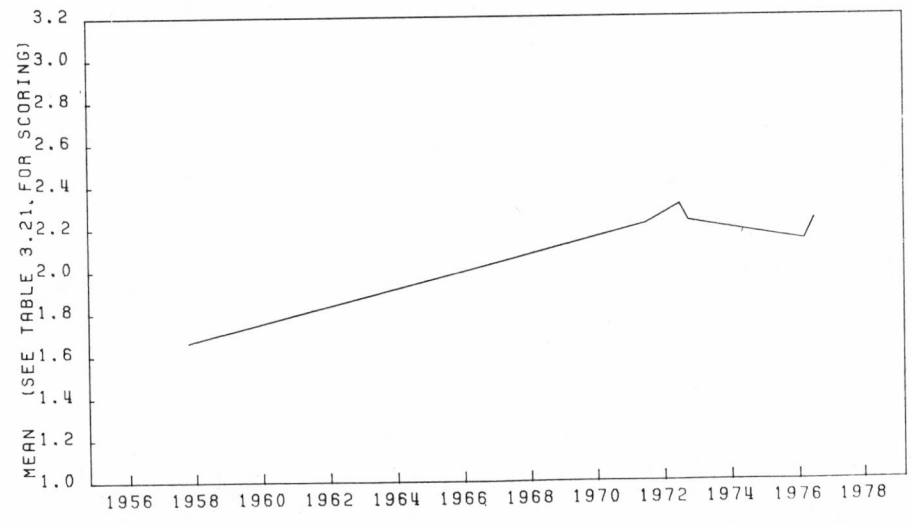

Figure 3.9
Future Job Plans by Education of R

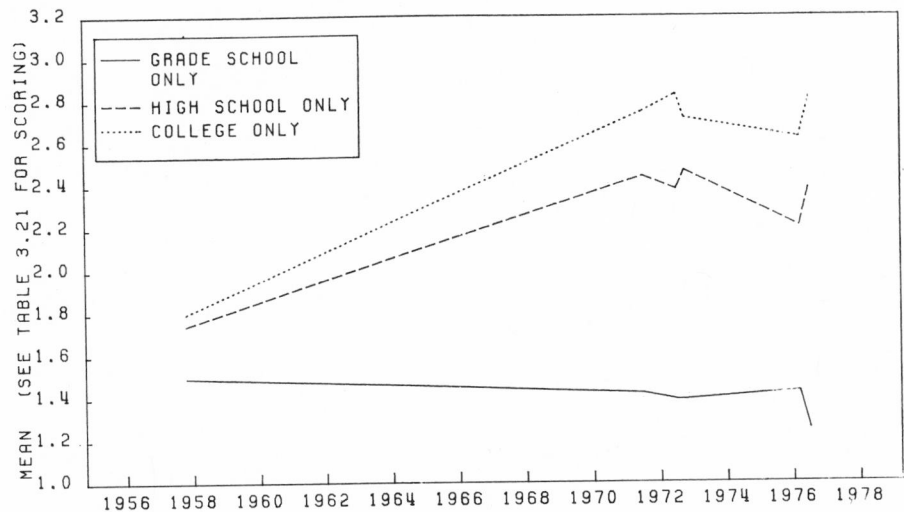

Women

Table 3.22
Does Housewife Plan on Getting a Job?
Race of Respondent

Housewives Only

|  |  | Year | | | | | |
| --- | --- | --- | --- | --- | --- | --- | --- |
|  | 1957h | 1971j | 1972f | 1972n | 1976e | 1976h | |
| Whites Only | 15.4% | 22.3% | 24.8% | 23.5% | 26.9% | 28.7% | Yes |
|  | ** | 13.0 | 15.4 | 13.1 | ** | 2.0 | Depends |
|  | 84.6 | 64.7 | 59.8 | 63.3 | 73.1 | 69.3 | No |
|  | (753) | (2152) | (246) | (586) | (49904) | (846) | Weighted N |
| Blacks Only | 32.7 | 47.4 | 45.5 | 32.0 | 41.7 | 40.5 | Yes |
|  | ** | 5.3 | 0.0 | 10.0 | ** | 0.0 | Depends |
|  | 67.3 | 47.4 | 54.5 | 58.0 | 58.3 | 59.5 | No |
|  | (52) | (152) | (11) | (50) | (4186) | (42) | Weighted N |

Table 3.23
Education of Respondent

Housewives Only

|  | 1957h | 1971j | 1972f | 1972n | 1976e | 1976h | |
| --- | --- | --- | --- | --- | --- | --- | --- |
| Grade School Only | 12.4% | 7.2% | 6.5% | 7.7% | 10.7% | 6.0% | Yes |
|  | ** | 6.6 | 6.5 | 4.1 | ** | 0.5 | Depends |
|  | 87.6 | 86.2 | 87.0 | 88.2 | 89.3 | 93.5 | No |
|  | (282) | (608) | (46) | (169) | (10334) | (199) | Weighted N |
| High School Only | 18.6 | 28.4 | 25.2 | 29.0 | 30.2 | 33.9 | Yes |
|  | ** | 15.5 | 18.7 | 15.5 | ** | 2.2 | Depends |
|  | 81.4 | 56.1 | 56.1 | 55.5 | 69.8 | 63.9 | No |
|  | (441) | (1368) | (155) | (355) | (34994) | (499) | Weighted N |
| College Only | 20.0 | 38.6 | 40.7 | 34.7 | 40.7 | 44.0 | Yes |
|  | ** | 10.2 | 10.2 | 16.5 | ** | 2.8 | Depends |
|  | 80.0 | 51.1 | 49.2 | 48.8 | 59.3 | 53.2 | No |
|  | (115) | (352) | (59) | (121) | (9634) | (216) | Weighted N |

** Code distinction not made.

Table 3.24
Does Housewife Plan on Getting a Job?
Age of Respondent

| Housewives Only | | | Year | | | | |
|---|---|---|---|---|---|---|---|
| | 1957h | 1971j | 1972f | 1972n | 1976e | 1976h | |
| 18-24 Only | 33.8% | 39.2% | 56.4% | 40.7% | 57.3% | 60.9% | Yes |
| | ** | 23.5 | 23.1 | 20.3 | ** | 0.0 | Depends |
| | 66.2 | 37.3 | 20.5 | 39.0 | 42.7 | 39.1 | No |
| | (65) | (204) | (39) | (59) | (6590) | (64) | Weighted N |
| 25-34 Only | 23.5 | 48.5 | 36.4 | 54.5 | 49.8 | 61.8 | Yes |
| | ** | 18.5 | 21.2 | 14.9 | ** | 4.7 | Depends |
| | 76.5 | 33.1 | 42.4 | 30.6 | 50.2 | 33.5 | No |
| | (221) | (520) | (66) | (134) | (11656) | (212) | Weighted N |
| 35-44 Only | 23.7 | 44.4 | 33.3 | 40.9 | 38.9 | 36.6 | Yes |
| | ** | 15.2 | 14.6 | 20.5 | ** | 2.1 | Depends |
| | 76.3 | 40.4 | 52.1 | 38.6 | 61.1 | 61.4 | No |
| | (173) | (396) | (48) | (88) | (7741) | (145) | Weighted N |
| 45-54 Only | 10.8 | 12.4 | 9.1 | 15.6 | 25.5 | 24.2 | Yes |
| | ** | 11.2 | 15.2 | 22.9 | ** | 1.3 | Depends |
| | 89.2 | 76.4 | 75.8 | 61.5 | 74.5 | 74.5 | No |
| | (130) | (356) | (33) | (96) | (9418) | (149) | Weighted N |
| 55-64 Only | 8.1 | 2.8 | 2.8 | 8.3 | 8.9 | 8.1 | Yes |
| | ** | 8.3 | 8.3 | 7.3 | ** | 1.9 | Depends |
| | 91.9 | 88.9 | 88.9 | 84.4 | 91.1 | 90.1 | No |
| | (111) | (288) | (36) | (96) | (8660) | (161) | Weighted N |
| 65-74 Only | 0.7 | 2.4 | 0.0 | 1.0 | 0.9 | 0.0 | Yes |
| | ** | 4.8 | 0.0 | 3.0 | ** | 0.0 | Depends |
| | 99.3 | 92.9 | 100.0 | 96.0 | 99.1 | 100.0 | No |
| | (140) | (336) | (32) | (99) | (7585) | (101) | Weighted N |
| 75 And Older Only | ** | 0.0 | 0.0 | 0.0 | 1.0 | 4.4 | Yes |
| | ** | 0.0 | 0.0 | 0.0 | ** | 0.0 | Depends |
| | ** | 100.0 | 100.0 | 100.0 | 99.0 | 95.6 | No |
| | ** | (236) | (5) | (68) | (4067) | (91) | Weighted N |

** Code distinction not made.
Youngest age group coded "21-24" in 1957h.
Oldest age group coded "65 And Older" in 1957h.

Table 3.25
Does Housewife Plan on Getting a Job?
Income of Respondent

Housewives Only

|  | 1957h | 1971j | 1972f | 1972n | 1976e | 1976h |  |
|---|---|---|---|---|---|---|---|
| Income 1 (0-16%) | 12.0% | 10.9% | 15.8% | 8.9% | 18.7% | 18.7% | Yes |
|  | ** | 7.1 | 5.3 | 8.9 | ** | 0.6 | Depends |
|  | 88.0 | 82.1 | 78.9 | 82.3 | 81.3 | 80.7 | No |
|  | (166) | (624) | (38) | (158) | (11235) | (166) | Weighted N |
| Income 2 (17-33%) | 19.4 | 27.3 | 28.0 | 25.0 | 23.4 | 27.3 | Yes |
|  | ** | 14.3 | 28.0 | 6.3 | ** | 0.8 | Depends |
|  | 80.6 | 58.4 | 44.0 | 68.8 | 76.6 | 71.9 | No |
|  | (93) | (616) | (25) | (112) | (10081) | (128) | Weighted N |
| Income 3 (34-67%) | 19.8 | 30.6 | 26.7 | 34.6 | 31.4 | 40.8 | Yes |
|  | ** | 15.9 | 18.1 | 15.2 | ** | 3.2 | Depends |
|  | 80.2 | 53.5 | 55.2 | 50.3 | 68.6 | 56.1 | No |
|  | (247) | (680) | (116) | (191) | (18723) | (314) | Weighted N |
| Income 4 (68-95%) | 19.6 | 45.9 | 28.8 | 27.7 | 35.7 | 30.8 | Yes |
|  | ** | 21.6 | 11.5 | 21.0 | ** | 0.0 | Depends |
|  | 80.4 | 32.4 | 59.6 | 51.3 | 64.3 | 69.2 | No |
|  | (250) | (148) | (52) | (119) | (13138) | (169) | Weighted N |
| Income 5 (96-100%) | 7.8 | 30.3 | 23.5 | 34.3 | 33.1 | 20.9 | Yes |
|  | ** | 3.0 | 11.8 | 8.6 | ** | 4.7 | Depends |
|  | 92.2 | 66.7 | 64.7 | 57.1 | 66.9 | 74.4 | No |
|  | (51) | (132) | (17) | (35) | (2540) | (43) | Weighted N |

** Code distinction not made.

Table 3.26
Women's Reasons for Working
Total Population

QUESTION: Women have different reasons for working  what would be your main reason for working?

| Women Only | Year | | | |
|---|---|---|---|---|
| | 1957h | 1971j | 1972n | 1976h |
| Positive: extrinsic | 62.7% | 59.2% | 61.3% | 49.1% |
| Positive: ego satisfaction | 16.9 | 20.9 | 22.2 | 27.3 |
| Work is moral | ** | 0.5 | 1.3 | 2.0 |
| Work prevents negative states | 18.3 | 19.4 | 14.3 | 20.5 |
| Other | 2.1 | ** | 0.9 | 1.0 |
| Total | 100% | 100% | 100% | 100% |
| Weighted N | 142 | 844 | 230 | 293 |
| Unweighted N | 142 | 211 | 230 | 151 |

** Code distinction not made

Figure 3.10
Reasons for Working--Total Population

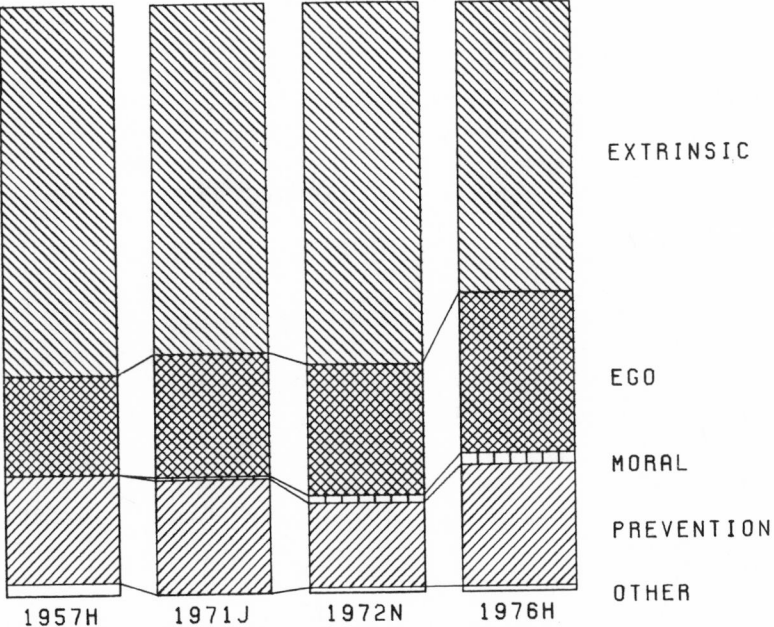

EXTRINSIC

EGO

MORAL

PREVENTION

OTHER

1957H    1971J    1972N    1976H

Women

Table 3.27
Women's Reasons for Working
Race of Respondent

Women Only

|  | Year | | | | |
| --- | --- | --- | --- | --- | --- |
|  | 1957h | 1971j | 1972n | 1976h | |
| Whites Only | 59 6% | 57.0% | 61.0% | 49 8% | Positive: extrinsic |
|  | 19.3 | 21.0 | 22.4 | 28.0 | Positive: ego satisfaction |
|  | ** | 0.5 | 1.5 | 2.3 | Work is moral |
|  | 21.1 | 21.5 | 15.1 | 19.8 | Work prevents negative states |
|  | (114) | (744) | (205) | (257) | Weighted N |
| Blacks Only | 94.1 | 80.0 | 78.9 | 50.0 | Positive: extrinsic |
|  | 0.0 | 20.0 | 15.8 | 50.0 | Positive: ego satisfaction |
|  | ** | 0.0 | 0.0 | 0.0 | Work is moral |
|  | 5.9 | 0.0 | 5.3 | 0.0 | Work prevents negative states |
|  | (17) | (80) | (19) | (16) | Weighted N |

Table 3.28
Education of Respondent

Women Only

|  | 1957h | 1971j | 1972n | 1976h | |
| --- | --- | --- | --- | --- | --- |
| Grade School Only | 73.5% | 85.0% | 78.9% | 100.0% | Positive: extrinsic |
|  | 11.8 | 10.0 | 0.0 | 0.0 | Positive: ego satisfaction |
|  | ** | 0.0 | 0.0 | 0.0 | Work is moral |
|  | 14.7 | 5.0 | 21.1 | 0.0 | Work prevents negative states |
|  | (34) | (80) | (19) | (13) | Weighted N |
| High School Only | 63.9 | 62.3 | 64.9 | 50.0 | Positive: extrinsic |
|  | 19.3 | 15.8 | 17.2 | 26.4 | Positive: ego satisfaction |
|  | ** | 0.7 | 2.0 | 2.2 | Work is moral |
|  | 16.9 | 21.2 | 15.9 | 21.3 | Work prevents negative states |
|  | (83) | (584) | (151) | (178) | Weighted N |
| College Only | 50 0 | 38.6 | 48.3 | 42.4 | Positive: extrinsic |
|  | 18.2 | 40.9 | 43.1 | 33.3 | Positive: ego satisfaction |
|  | ** | 0.0 | 0.0 | 2.0 | Work is moral |
|  | 31.8 | 20.5 | 8.6 | 22.2 | Work prevents negative states |
|  | (22) | (176) | (58) | (99) | Weighted N |

** Code distinction not made.

Table 3.29
Women's Reasons for Working
Age of Respondent

| Women Only | | Year | | | | |
|---|---|---|---|---|---|---|
| | | 1957h | 1971j | 1972n | 1976h | |
| 18-24 Only | | 68.2% | 62.5% | 82.4% | 61.5% | Positive: extrinsic |
| | | 18.2 | 18.8 | 14.7 | 23.1 | Positive: ego satisfaction |
| | | ** | 0.0 | 0.0 | 0.0 | Work is moral |
| | | 13.6 | 18.8 | 2.9 | 15.4 | Work prevents negative states |
| | | (22) | (128) | (34) | (39) | Weighted N |
| 25-34 Only | | 66.0 | 58.3 | 57.1 | 51.8 | Positive: extrinsic |
| | | 11.3 | 21.4 | 26.4 | 26.2 | Positive: ego satisfaction |
| | | ** | 0.0 | 1.1 | 2.8 | Work is moral |
| | | 22.6 | 20.2 | 15.4 | 19.1 | Work prevents negative states |
| | | (53) | (336) | (91) | (141) | Weighted N |
| 35-44 Only | | 60.0 | 53.4 | 61.5 | 34.6 | Positive: extrinsic |
| | | 17.5 | 22.4 | 23.1 | 34.6 | Positive: ego satisfaction |
| | | ** | 0.0 | 1.9 | 0.0 | Work is moral |
| | | 22.5 | 24.1 | 13.5 | 30.8 | Work prevents negative states |
| | | (40) | (232) | (52) | (52) | Weighted N |
| 45-54 Only | | 83.3 | 68.2 | 55.9 | 42.1 | Positive: extrinsic |
| | | 16.7 | 22.7 | 17.6 | 36.8 | Positive: ego satisfaction |
| | | ** | 0.0 | 2.9 | 5.3 | Work is moral |
| | | 0.0 | 9.1 | 23.5 | 15.8 | Work prevents negative states |
| | | (12) | (88) | (34) | (38) | Weighted N |
| 55-64 Only | | 44.4 | 42.9 | 58.3 | 56.3 | Positive: extrinsic |
| | | 44.4 | 14.3 | 25.0 | 12.5 | Positive: ego satisfaction |
| | | ** | 14.3 | 0.0 | 0.0 | Work is moral |
| | | 11.1 | 28.6 | 16.7 | 31.3 | Work prevents negative states |
| | | (9) | (28) | (12) | (16) | Weighted N |
| 65 And Older Only | | 0.0 | 83.3 | 50.0 | 100.0 | Positive: extrinsic |
| | | 100.0 | 16.7 | 25.0 | 0.0 | Positive: ego satisfaction |
| | | ** | 0.0 | 0.0 | 0.0 | Work is moral |
| | | 0.0 | 0.0 | 25.0 | 0.0 | Work prevents negative states |
| | | (1) | (24) | (4) | (4) | Weighted N |

** Code distinction not made.
Youngest age group coded "21-24" in 1957h.

Table 3.30
Women's Reasons for Working
Income of Respondent

| Women Only | Year | | | | |
|---|---|---|---|---|---|
| | 1957h | 1971j | 1972n | 1976h | |
| Income 1 (0-16%) | 76.2% | 76.9% | 91.7% | 71.0% | Positive: extrinsic |
| | 4.8 | 3.8 | 4.2 | 9.7 | Positive: ego satisfaction |
| | ** | 0.0 | 0.0 | 0.0 | Work is moral |
| | 19.0 | 19.2 | 4.2 | 19.4 | Work prevents negative states |
| | (21) | (104) | (24) | (31) | Weighted N |
| | | | | | |
| Income 2 (17-33%) | 88.2 | 73.4 | 77.1 | 65.7 | Positive: extrinsic |
| | 11.8 | 14.1 | 11.4 | 17.1 | Positive: ego satisfaction |
| | ** | 1.6 | 0.0 | 0.0 | Work is moral |
| | 0.0 | 10.9 | 11.4 | 17.1 | Work prevents negative states |
| | (17) | (256) | (35) | (35) | Weighted N |
| | | | | | |
| Income 3 (34-67%) | 68.0 | 55.8 | 60.9 | 44.1 | Positive: extrinsic |
| | 20.0 | 26.0 | 23.9 | 33.8 | Positive: ego satisfaction |
| | ** | 0.0 | 2.2 | 1.5 | Work is moral |
| | 12.0 | 18.2 | 13.0 | 20.6 | Work prevents negative states |
| | (50) | (308) | (92) | (136) | Weighted N |
| | | | | | |
| Income 4 (68-95%) | 51.1 | 36.0 | 47.3 | 42.3 | Positive: extrinsic |
| | 19.1 | 32.0 | 34.5 | 26.9 | Positive: ego satisfaction |
| | ** | 0.0 | 1.8 | 3.8 | Work is moral |
| | 29.8 | 32.0 | 16.4 | 26.9 | Work prevents negative states |
| | (47) | (100) | (55) | (52) | Weighted N |
| | | | | | |
| Income 5 (96-100%) | 0.0 | 9.1 | 35.7 | 63.6 | Positive: extrinsic |
| | 50.0 | 45.5 | 28.6 | 18.2 | Positive: ego satisfaction |
| | ** | 0.0 | 0.0 | 0.0 | Work is moral |
| | 50.0 | 45.5 | 35.7 | 18.2 | Work prevents negative states |
| | (4) | (44) | (14) | (11) | Weighted N |

** Code distinction not made

Table 3.31
Should Women Stay Out of Politics?
Total Population

QUESTION: Women should stay out of politics.  Do you agree or disagree?

|  | Year | |
| --- | --- | --- |
|  | 1952n | 1972n |
| Agree (1) | 29.4% | 19.6% |
| Disagree (5) | 69.5 | 79.5 |
| Don't know | 1.1 | 0.9 |
| Total | 100% | 100% |
| Weighted N | 534 | 2686 |
| Unweighted N | 534 | 2686 |
| Mean | 3.81 | 4.21 |
| Standard Deviation | 1.83 | 1.59 |

Figure 3.11
Women in Politics--Total Population

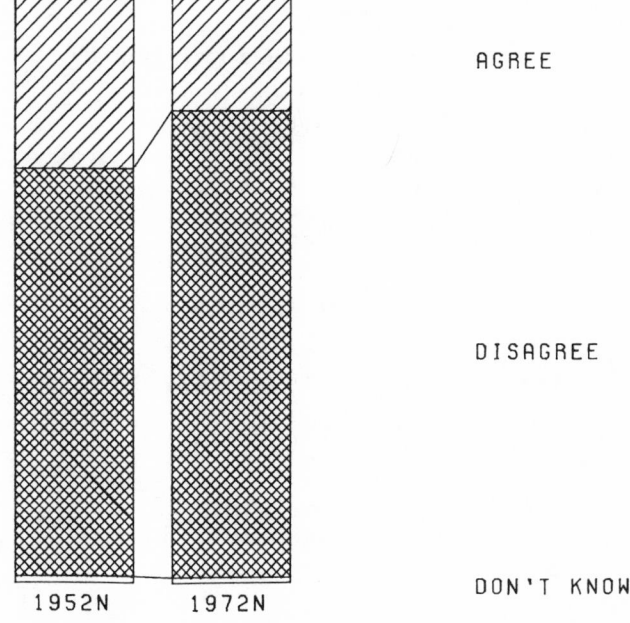

AGREE

DISAGREE

DON'T KNOW

1952N     1972N

Women

Table 3.32
Should Women Stay Out of Politics?
Social Groups

| % Agree | Year | | |
|---|---|---|---|
| | 1952n | 1972n | |
| Males Only | 27.0 | 18.5 | Agree |
| | (234) | (1149) | Weighted N |
| Females Only | 31.3 | 20.5 | Agree |
| | (294) | (1513) | Weighted N |
| Whites Only | 27.6 | 19.4 | Agree |
| | (474) | (2362) | Weighted N |
| Blacks Only | 46.3 | 19.7 | Agree |
| | (53) | (261) | Weighted N |
| Grade School Only | 38.4 | 38.0 | Agree |
| | (211) | (514) | Weighted N |
| High School Only | 28.0 | 20.6 | Agree |
| | (238) | (1360) | Weighted N |
| College Only | 7.7 | 5.5 | Agree |
| | (78) | (785) | Weighted N |
| 18-24 Only | 32.3 | 13.4 | Agree |
| | (30) | (392) | Weighted N |
| 25-34 Only | 20.9 | 16.4 | Agree |
| | (128) | (570) | Weighted N |
| 35-44 Only | 37.0 | 16.8 | Agree |
| | (125) | (438) | Weighted N |
| 45-54 Only | 18.9 | 20.3 | Agree |
| | (95) | (439) | Weighted N |
| 55-64 Only | 27.8 | 21.6 | Agree |
| | (71) | (381) | Weighted N |
| 65-74 Only | 36.2 | 22.3 | Agree |
| | (46) | (271) | Weighted N |
| 75 And Older Only | 46.2 | 43.6 | Agree |
| | (26) | (152) | Weighted N |

Percentages based on content categories "Agree" and "Disagree"

Chapter 4. Family Living

As the title may imply, this chapter is something of a potpourri. It encompasses a set of items which are very disparate in their topical focus, although most of them refer to expectations, behaviors, or relationships that center in the family. The items are also more disparate than usual in their time scope, with some series being of very satisfying length and others frustratingly short.

The first item mirrors in fragmentary form the shrinkage which has been occurring in American perspectives on ideal family size. Much fuller series exist elsewhere, especially with respect to family planning on the part of women of childbearing ages, but the glimpse afforded here, which is little more than two time points, conforms to trends that are clear in fuller data. Less familiar are the data that follow on assumptions about ultimate education levels to be achieved by one's children, a series which is regrettably brief. Both of these items should be read with special attention to the breakdowns by age, since they have rather different portent across the life cycle.

The next series, on frequency of newspaper reading, is more satisfying in its length. Given the fact that these data span much of the period in which television use has increased most dramatically, we might have suspected more of a decline in newspaper use than actually registers for the population as a whole. Examination of the finer partitions suggests that the very faint overall decline in newspaper use masks a few modest changes in the social distribution of readership. Newspaper readership among blacks has clearly risen since 1957 (table 4.10), and it seems more generally true that differences in newspaper use by education have been flattening out somewhat over this period. Moreover, given the strong association between education and newspaper reading, it is noteworthy that the slight decline in newspaper use since 1956 has taken place despite major advances in adult education levels in the interim. At each point of the series, the young use newspapers least, and the middle-aged the most. But it is also clear that one source of the secular decline is the fact that the young of the 1970s read newspapers less than the young of the 1950s did.

The next two items, involving familiarity with neighbors and the residential proximity of relatives (tables 4.13-4.19), show no particular trends over time, but the span of observations is too small to expect much.

Reports of church-attendance habits form a series of highly satisfying length, marred only by the fact that the item form was changed between 1968 and 1970. We can mentally splice the two series, however, to derive a general impression of long-term trends. The first segment (1952-68, in tables 4.20-4.25) suggests that attendance inched upward over much of this period, but then fell off visibly after 1964. With the new item in 1970 (tables 4.26-4.31), considerably fewer (27 percent, instead of 39 percent) people claimed to attend church "every week," as opposed to the earlier reports of "regularly," but it is likely that some "regular" church-goers might still not want to claim they went every week. At the other end of the spectrum, however, the "never" response exists in both question forms and seems clear-cut. Proportions in this category have continued to advance since 1964, and it seems likely that overall attendance has declined since that time. While the decline has registered for all creeds, it seems to have been sharper among Catholics and Jews than among Protestants.

The final series, dealing with the carriage of life insurance, is also very lengthy but displays rather little trend over time. What this overall constancy masks, however, is the fact that the probability of the young carrying insurance has declined while it has risen for older people.

Table 4.1
The Ideal Number of Children for the Average Family
Total Population

QUESTION: What do you think is the ideal number of children for the average family?

|  | Year | | | |
|---|---|---|---|---|
|  | 1954m | 1970e | 1971e | |
| Total Population | 3.6 | 3.0 | 2.8 | Mean |
|  | 1.2 | 1.0 | 1.1 | Standard Deviation |
|  | (872) | (95061) | (101866) | Weighted N |
| Unweighted Total | 872 | 3231 | 3528 | |

Figure 4.1
Ideal Number of Children--Total Population

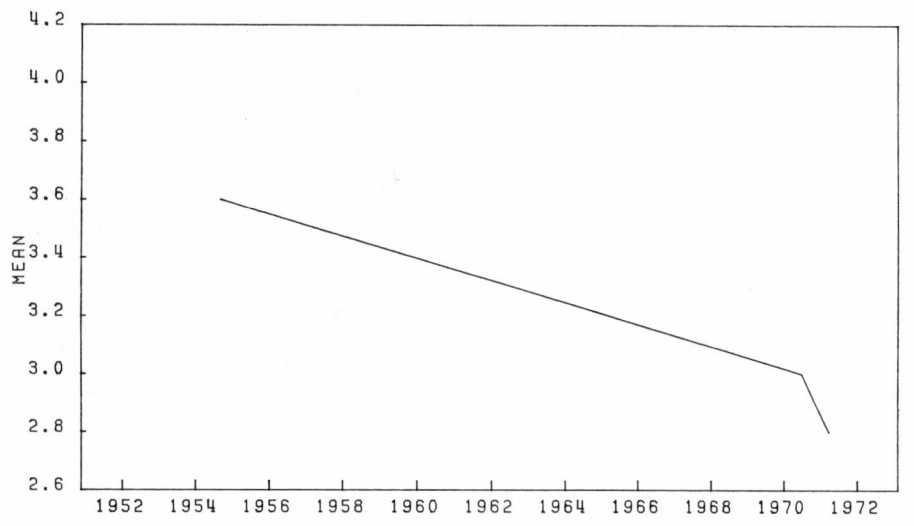

Table 4.2
The Ideal Number of Children for the Average Family

|                    | Year    |         |         |                    |
|                    | 1954m   | 1970e   | 1971e   |                    |
|--------------------|---------|---------|---------|--------------------|
| Males Only         | 3.5     | 2.9     | 2.8     | Mean               |
|                    | 1.2     | 1.0     | 1.0     | Standard Deviation |
|                    | (409)   | (71050) | (74160) | Weighted N         |
| Females Only       | 3.7     | 3.1     | 2.9     | Mean               |
|                    | 1.1     | 1.1     | 1.1     | Standard Deviation |
|                    | (463)   | (24011) | (27706) | Weighted N         |
| Whites Only        | 3.6     | 2.9     | 2.8     | Mean               |
|                    | 1.1     | 1.0     | 1.0     | Standard Deviation |
|                    | (789)   | (83284) | (88720) | Weighted N         |
| Blacks Only        | 4.0     | 3.3     | 3.4     | Mean               |
|                    | 1.5     | 1.4     | 1.5     | Standard Deviation |
|                    | (75)    | (9397)  | (10445) | Weighted N         |
| Grade School Only  | 4.0     | 3.2     | 3.2     | Mean               |
|                    | 1.3     | 1.1     | 1.2     | Standard Deviation |
|                    | (301)   | (18422) | (18821) | Weighted N         |
| High School Only   | 3.4     | 2.9     | 2.8     | Mean               |
|                    | 1.0     | 1.0     | 1.0     | Standard Deviation |
|                    | (413)   | (41418) | (44316) | Weighted N         |
| College Only       | 3.4     | 2.7     | 2.6     | Mean               |
|                    | 1.0     | 0.9     | 0.9     | Standard Deviation |
|                    | (156)   | (27540) | (29688) | Weighted N         |
| 18-24 Only         | 3.6     | 2.7     | 2.5     | Mean               |
|                    | 1.0     | 0.9     | 0.9     | Standard Deviation |
|                    | (58)    | (8391)  | (10479) | Weighted N         |
| 25-34 Only         | 3.5     | 2.8     | 2.6     | Mean               |
|                    | 1.0     | 0.9     | 0.9     | Standard Deviation |
|                    | (247)   | (18565) | (20219) | Weighted N         |
| 35-44 Only         | 3.5     | 3.1     | 2.9     | Mean               |
|                    | 1.2     | 1.1     | 1.0     | Standard Deviation |
|                    | (215)   | (21255) | (21374) | Weighted N         |
| 45-54 Only         | 3.7     | 3.0     | 3.0     | Mean               |
|                    | 1.3     | 1.1     | 1.1     | Standard Deviation |
|                    | (158)   | (18447) | (18642) | Weighted N         |
| 55-64 Only         | 4.0     | 3.0     | 3.0     | Mean               |
|                    | 1.3     | 1.1     | 1.2     | Standard Deviation |
|                    | (88)    | (15732) | (16282) | Weighted N         |
| 65-74 Only         | 3.7     | 3.0     | 3.0     | Mean               |
|                    | 1.2     | 1.1     | 1.0     | Standard Deviation |
|                    | (104)   | (9648)  | (11122) | Weighted N         |
| 75 And Older Only  | **      | 3.0     | 3.1     | Mean               |
|                    | **      | 1.0     | 1.2     | Standard Deviation |
|                    | **      | (2994)  | (3744)  | Weighted N         |

** Code distinction not made--oldest age group coded "65 And Older" in 1954m.
Youngest age group coded "21-24" in 1954m.
Sex and age coded for head of household and wife only in 1970e and 1971e.
Race coded for head of household and wife only in 1971e.
Education coded for head of household only in 1971e, and for head and wife only in 1970e.

Table 4.3
Education Plans for Children
Total Population

QUESTION: (About) how much education do you think your children will have when they stop going to school?

|                      |        |        | Year   |        |        |
|----------------------|--------|--------|--------|--------|--------|
|                      | 1968e  | 1969e  | 1970e  | 1971e  | 1972e  |
| All to college       | 33.0%  | 33.3%  | 34.4%  | 33.0%  | 35.3%  |
| Some to college      | 26.4   | 26.5   | 22.0   | 22.0   | 28.9   |
| All finish high school | 29.3 | 31.6   | 36.3   | 35.8   | 27.6   |
| Other,Don't know     | 11.3   | 8.6    | 7.4    | 9.2    | 8.2    |
| Total                | 100%   | 100%   | 100%   | 100%   | 100%   |
| Weighted N           | 45807  | 50602  | 51523  | 45405  | 47605  |
| Unweighted N         | 1762   | 1945   | 2001   | 1801   | 1896   |

Figure 4.2
Education Plans for Children--Total Population

Family Living

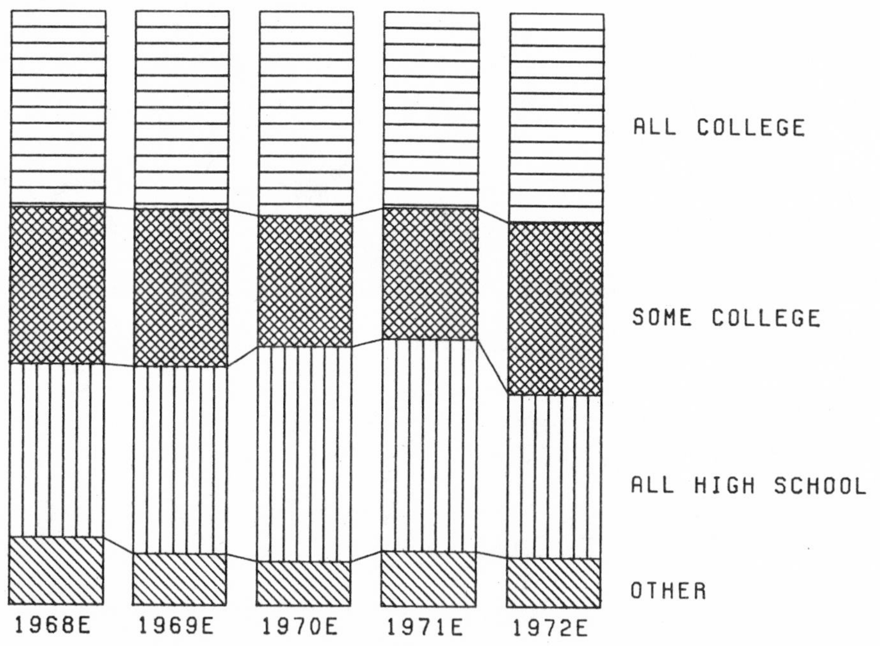

Table 4.4
Education Plans for Children
Sex of Respondent

|  | | | Year | | | |
|---|---|---|---|---|---|---|
|  | 1968e | 1969e | 1970e | 1971e | 1972e | |
| Males Only | 33.5% | 35.3% | 37.0% | 34.2% | 37.7% | All to college |
|  | 28.4 | 26.4 | 23.3 | 23.0 | 28.5 | Some to college |
|  | 28.1 | 31.2 | 34.2 | 34.9 | 27.6 | All finish high school |
|  | 10.1 | 7.2 | 5.5 | 7.9 | 6.3 | Other, Don't know |
|  | (37120) | (40006) | (39798) | (35259) | (36424) | Weighted N |
| Females Only | 31.3 | 25.8 | 25.3 | 28.8 | 27.7 | All to college |
|  | 18.1 | 26.8 | 17.6 | 18.6 | 30.7 | Some to college |
|  | 34.5 | 33.3 | 43.3 | 38.8 | 27.3 | All finish high school |
|  | 16.1 | 14.2 | 13.7 | 13.8 | 14.4 | Other, Don't know |
|  | (8687) | (10596) | (11725) | (10146) | (11094) | Weighted N |

Sex coded for head of household and wife only.

Table 4.5
Race of Respondent

|  | 1968e | 1969e | 1970e | 1971e | 1972e | |
|---|---|---|---|---|---|---|
| Whites Only | 35.3% | 36.0% | 36.6% | 35.2% | 37.3% | All to college |
|  | 28.4 | 27.5 | 22.7 | 22.5 | 29.6 | Some to college |
|  | 27.2 | 29.6 | 35.2 | 34.9 | 26.6 | All finish high school |
|  | 9.1 | 6.8 | 5.5 | 7.4 | 6.5 | Other, Don't know |
|  | (38946) | (43030) | (43319) | (38222) | (39829) | Weighted N |
| Blacks Only | 18.9 | 16.4 | 19.9 | 22.1 | 20.6 | All to college |
|  | 16.6 | 18.1 | 19.4 | 17.1 | 23.4 | Some to college |
|  | 41.0 | 45.2 | 42.0 | 40.4 | 36.2 | All finish high school |
|  | 23.6 | 20.3 | 18.7 | 20.4 | 19.9 | Other, Don't know |
|  | (5885) | (6457) | (6607) | (5565) | (6062) | Weighted N |

Race coded for head of household and wife only in 1971e.

Figure 4.3
Education Plans for Children--Males Only

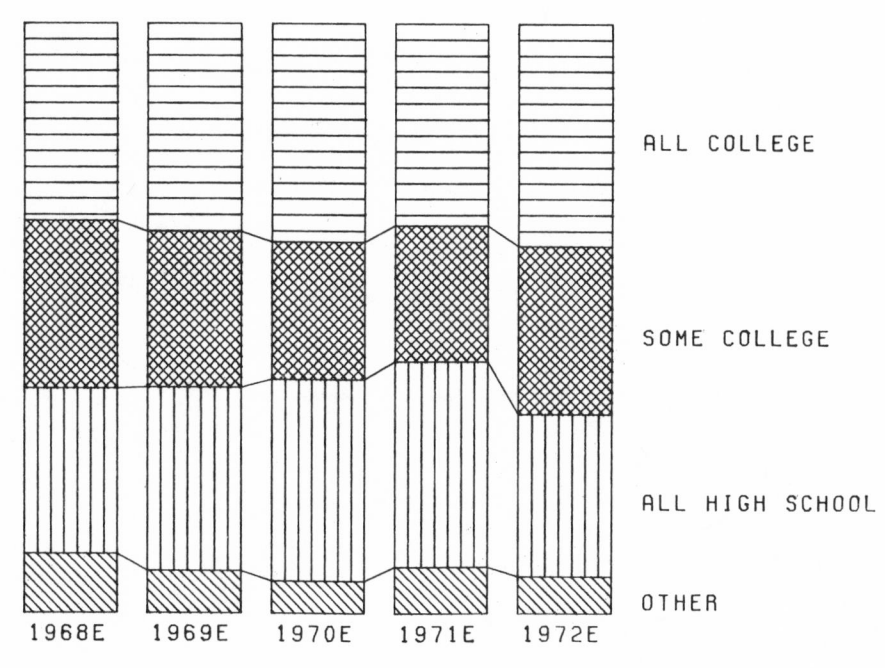

Figure 4.5
Education Plans for Children--Females Only

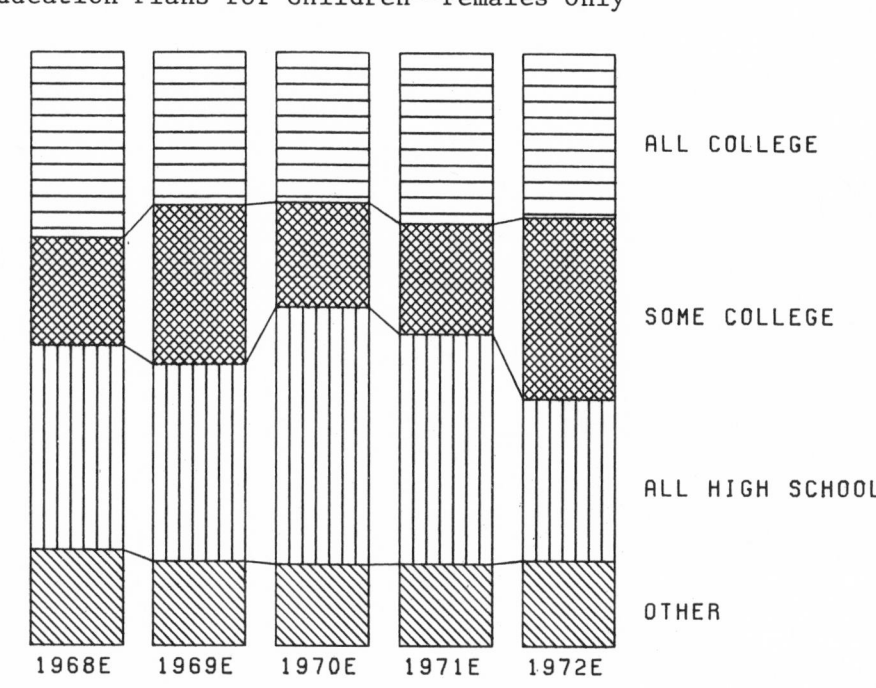

Figure 4.4
Education Plans for Children--Whites Only

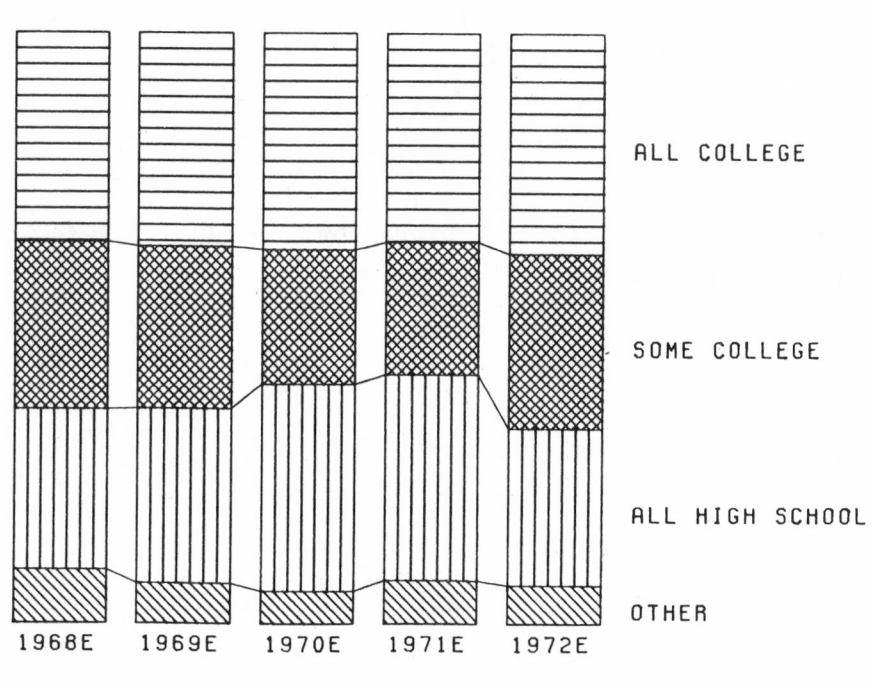

Figure 4.6
Education Plans for Children--Blacks Only

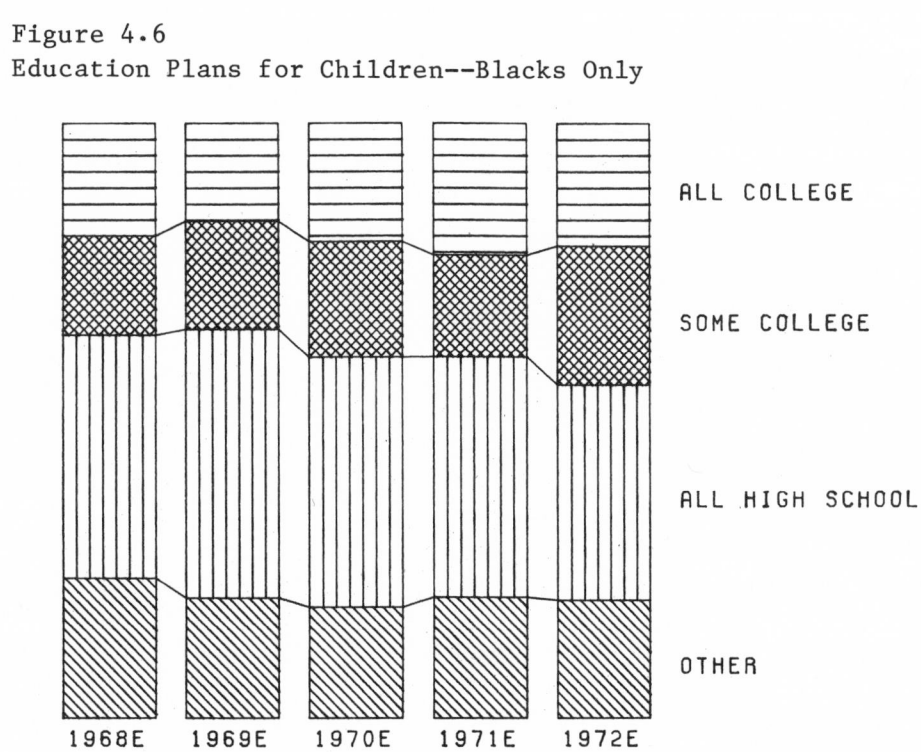

Family Living

Table 4.6
Education Plans for Children
Education of Respondent

|  | | | Year | | | |
|---|---|---|---|---|---|---|
|  | 1968e | 1969e | 1970e | 1971e | 1972e | |
| Grade School Only | 12.6% | 15.2% | 14.0% | 15.0% | 15.4% | All to college |
|  | 14.7 | 16.3 | 12.8 | 16.1 | 18.8 | Some to college |
|  | 41.3 | 47.7 | 54.0 | 44.4 | 43.4 | All finish high school |
|  | 31.3 | 20.9 | 19.2 | 24.5 | 22.4 | Other, Don't know |
|  | (9434) | (10671) | (9802) | (6808) | (7476) | Weighted N |
| High School Only | 28.0 | 27.6 | 29.6 | 26.9 | 29.9 | All to college |
|  | 29.8 | 29.1 | 23.7 | 22.6 | 30.2 | Some to college |
|  | 33.7 | 35.6 | 40.5 | 41.6 | 32.6 | All finish high school |
|  | 8.5 | 7.7 | 6.1 | 8.8 | 7.3 | Other, Don't know |
|  | (23998) | (25501) | (27529) | (21257) | (25240) | Weighted N |
| College Only | 59.3 | 57.6 | 58.2 | 55.4 | 58.0 | All to college |
|  | 29.2 | 28.9 | 25.1 | 26.2 | 32.8 | Some to college |
|  | 10.4 | 12.6 | 15.4 | 17.1 | 7.7 | All finish high school |
|  | 1.1 | 0.9 | 1.3 | 1.3 | 1.6 | Other, Don't know |
|  | (12165) | (14153) | (13907) | (12368) | (13797) | Weighted N |

Education coded for head of household only in 1971e, and for head and wife only in 1968e, 1969e, 1970e, and 1972e.

Figure 4.7
Education Plans for Children--Grade School Only

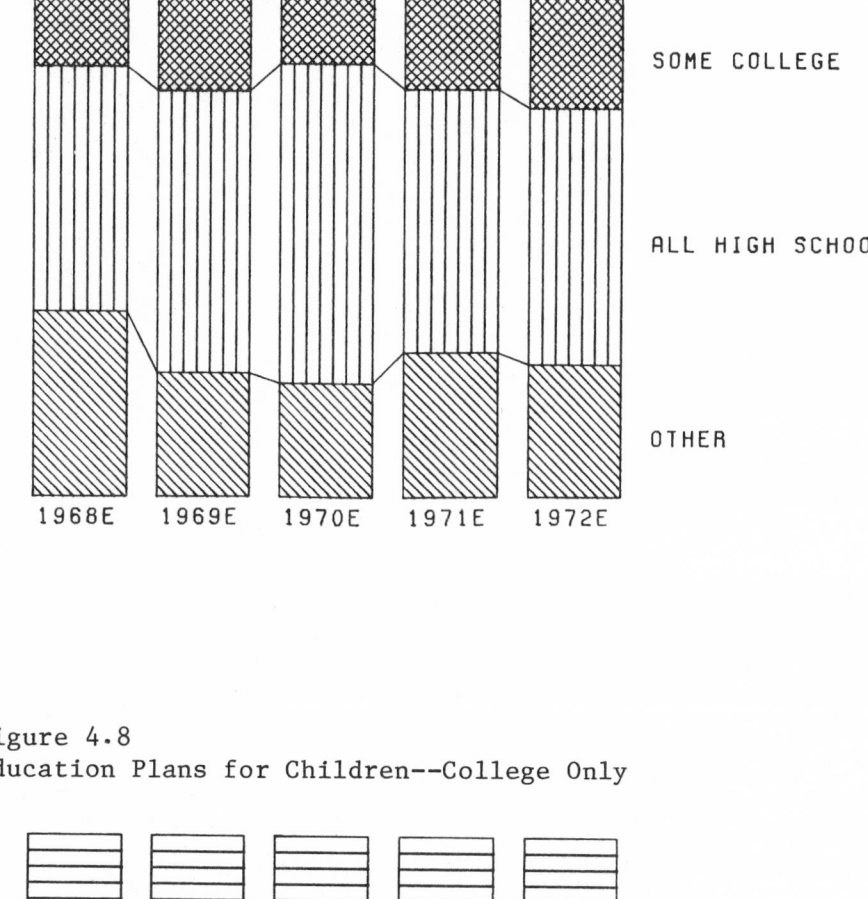

Figure 4.9
Education Plans for Children--High School Only

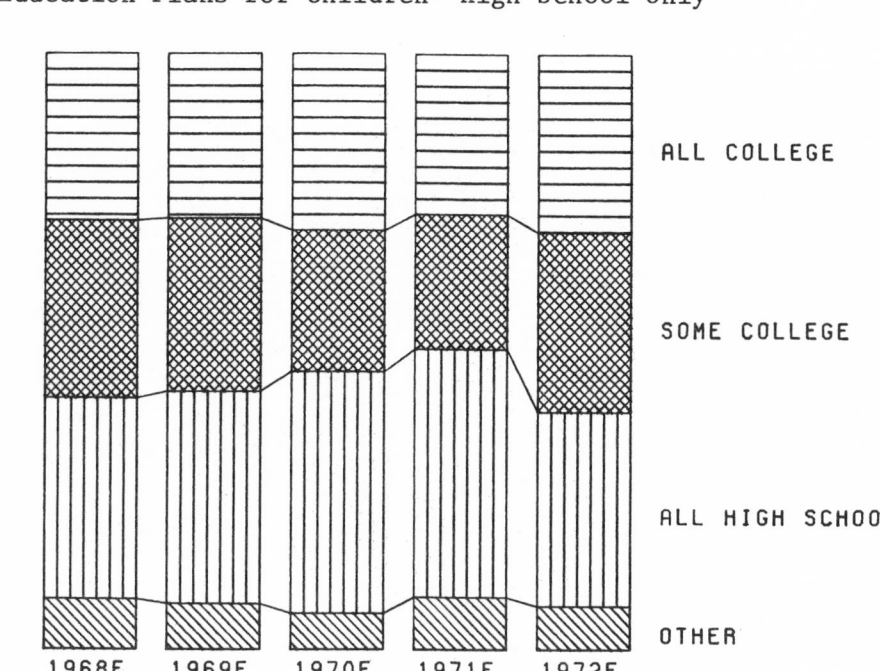

Figure 4.8
Education Plans for Children--College Only

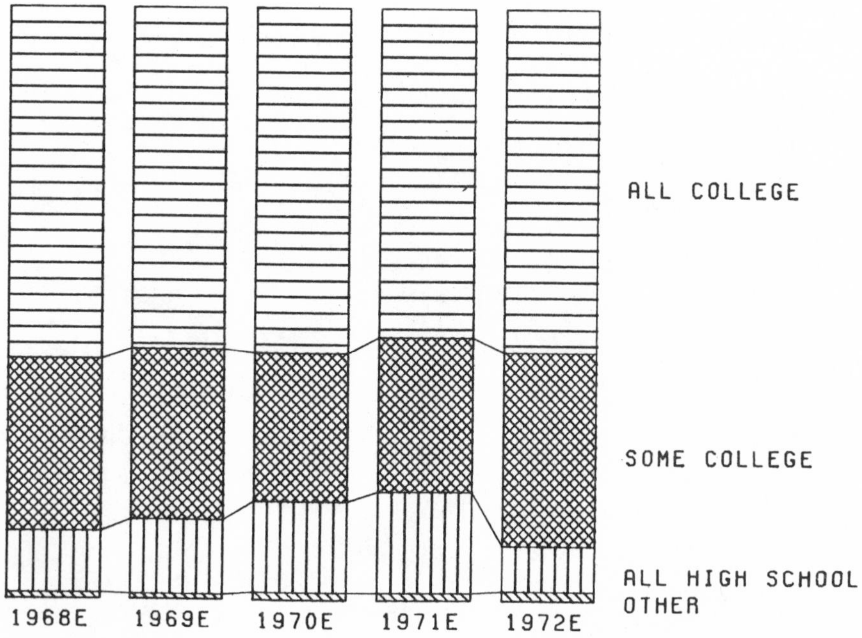

Table 4.7
Education Plans for Children
Age of Respondent

|  | | | Year | | | |
|---|---|---|---|---|---|---|
|  | 1968e | 1969e | 1970e | 1971e | 1972e | |
| 18-24 Only | 19.8% | 25.2% | 26.0% | 40.4% | 14.7% | All to college |
|  | 12.4 | 16.9 | 10.1 | 0.0 | 39.4 | Some to college |
|  | 64.9 | 38.2 | 51.9 | 47.5 | 35.4 | All finish high school |
|  | 2.9 | 19.7 | 12.0 | 12.1 | 10.5 | Other, Don't know |
|  | (242) | (836) | (832) | (354) | (667) | Weighted N |
| 25-34 Only | 32.9 | 35.2 | 36.4 | 34.3 | 36.4 | All to college |
|  | 27.6 | 24.6 | 20.2 | 21.8 | 31.5 | Some to college |
|  | 30.3 | 35.5 | 37.8 | 34.6 | 23.8 | All finish high school |
|  | 9.2 | 4.7 | 5.6 | 9.3 | 8.3 | Other, Don't know |
|  | (8874) | (10657) | (11413) | (10227) | (11376) | Weighted N |
| 35-44 Only | 30.9 | 29.8 | 32.6 | 32.8 | 33.6 | All to college |
|  | 27.3 | 31.5 | 26.7 | 21.9 | 32.8 | Some to college |
|  | 31.4 | 31.6 | 35.0 | 37.8 | 27.3 | All finish high school |
|  | 10.4 | 7.1 | 5.7 | 7.5 | 6.3 | Other, Don't know |
|  | (20408) | (20515) | (20262) | (18629) | (17750) | Weighted N |
| 45-54 Only | 35.9 | 37.3 | 38.1 | 31.7 | 37.1 | All to college |
|  | 27.0 | 24.7 | 19.7 | 24.2 | 25.3 | Some to college |
|  | 25.6 | 28.6 | 34.2 | 35.6 | 30.7 | All finish high school |
|  | 11.5 | 9.4 | 8.1 | 8.5 | 6.9 | Other, Don't know |
|  | (12010) | (13555) | (13389) | (11851) | (13076) | Weighted N |
| 55-64 Only | 39.2 | 40.9 | 32.1 | 30.4 | 40.4 | All to college |
|  | 20.7 | 11.6 | 18.4 | 23.6 | 17.7 | Some to college |
|  | 24.3 | 30.9 | 37.7 | 30.4 | 24.8 | All finish high school |
|  | 15.7 | 16.5 | 11.8 | 15.5 | 17.2 | Other, Don't know |
|  | (3356) | (4087) | (4430) | (3335) | (3551) | Weighted N |
| 65-74 Only | 29.9 | 14.1 | 26.2 | 47.7 | 36.1 | All to college |
|  | 13.3 | 34.1 | 1.0 | 4.3 | 19.2 | Some to college |
|  | 29.2 | 21.9 | 49.0 | 21.2 | 19.6 | All finish high school |
|  | 27.6 | 29.9 | 23.7 | 26.7 | 25.1 | Other, Don't know |
|  | (757) | (775) | (889) | (920) | (843) | Weighted N |
| 75 And Older Only | 0.0 | 0.0 | 0.0 | 0.0 | 0.0 | All to college |
|  | 0.0 | 22.7 | 22.7 | 0.0 | 0.0 | Some to college |
|  | 0.0 | 44.6 | 46.9 | 100.0 | 90.4 | All finish high school |
|  | 100.0 | 32.7 | 30.3 | 0.0 | 9.6 | Other, Don't know |
|  | (39) | (278) | (277) | (84) | (249) | Weighted N |

Age coded for head of household and wife only.

Table 4.8
How Often Does R [Head] Read Newspaper?
Total Population

QUESTION: How often do you [head] read a newspaper--every day, once a week, or what?

|  |  | Year | | | | | | |
|---|---|---|---|---|---|---|---|---|
|  |  | 1957g | 1958g | 1968e | 1969e | 1970e | 1971e | 1972e |
| Never | (1) | 8.9% | 9.7% | 8.0% | 7.7% | 7.9% | 7.4% | 7.7% |
| Occasionally | (2) | 2.3 | 2.0 | 2.2 | 2.9 | 3.0 | 2.2 | 2.5 |
| One to five times a week | (3) | 10.9 | 13.1 | 13.0 | 13.7 | 15.3 | 14.9 | 16.8 |
| Every day | (4) | 77.9 | 75.3 | 76.9 | 75.6 | 73.8 | 75.4 | 73.0 |
| Total |  | 100% | 100% | 100% | 100% | 100% | 100% | 100% |
| Weighted N |  | 1886 | 1568 | 107339 | 113964 | 123188 | 106640 | 114016 |
| Unweighted N |  | 1886 | 1568 | 3500 | 3762 | 4132 | 3703 | 4054 |
| Mean |  | 3.58 | 3.54 | 3.59 | 3.57 | 3.55 | 3.58 | 3.55 |
| Standard Deviation |  | 0.91 | 0.93 | 0.87 | 0.88 | 0.88 | 0.86 | 0.87 |

"Occasionally" includes "Hardly ever" and "Less than once a week".
"One to five times a week" includes "Weekly", "Weekdays", "Several times a week", "Once or twice a week".

Figure 4.10                                    Figure 4.11
Newspaper Reading--Total Population             Newspaper Reading by Race of R

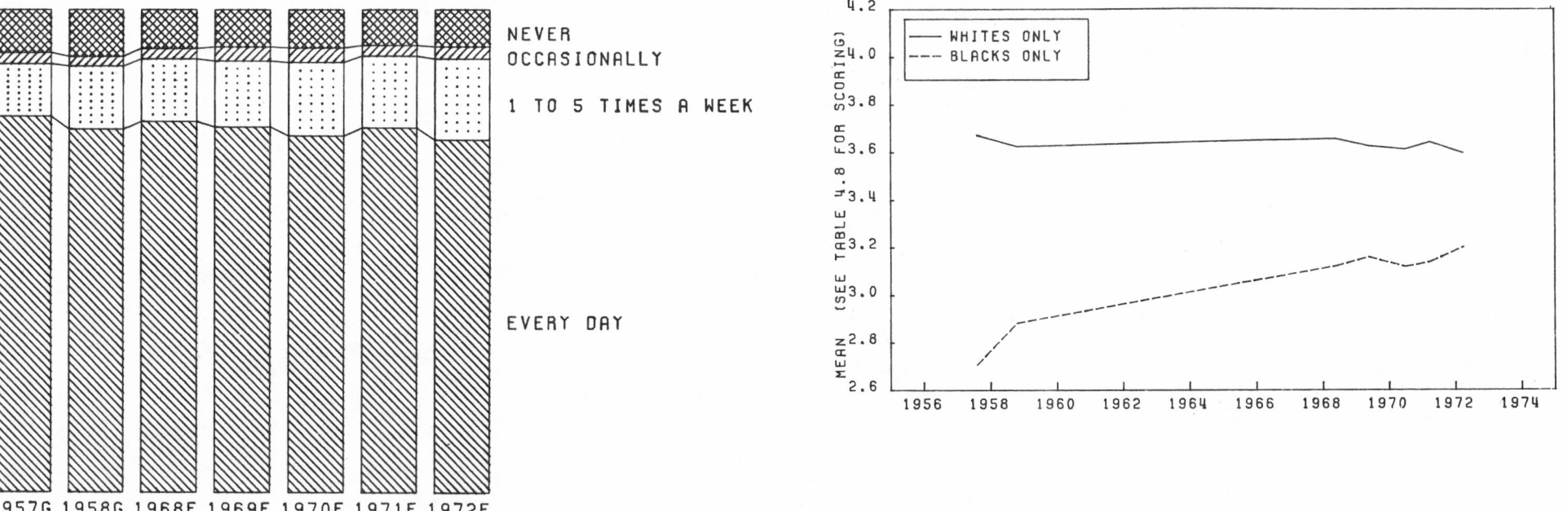

Table 4.9
How Often Does R [Head] Read Newspaper?
Sex of Respondent

|  | Year | | | | | | | |
|---|---|---|---|---|---|---|---|---|
|  | 1957g | 1958g | 1968e | 1969e | 1970e | 1971e | 1972e |  |
| Males Only | 8.6% | 8.8% | 6.8% | 6.7% | 6.8% | 6.4% | 6.8% | Never |
|  | 2.8 | 1.4 | 2.2 | 2.4 | 2.7 | 1.8 | 2.3 | Occasionally |
|  | 9.8 | 12.5 | 13.0 | 13.3 | 14.8 | 14.8 | 16.1 | One to five times a week |
|  | 78.7 | 77.2 | 78.0 | 77.6 | 75.7 | 76.9 | 74.8 | Every day |
|  | (814) | (690) | (81369) | (84992) | (89647) | (77216) | (81691) | Weighted N |
| Females Only | 9.1 | 10.4 | 11.6 | 10.7 | 10.9 | 9.9 | 9.8 | Never |
|  | 2.0 | 2.4 | 1.9 | 4.4 | 3.9 | 3.3 | 2.9 | Occasionally |
|  | 11.7 | 13.6 | 13.1 | 14.9 | 16.6 | 15.5 | 18.7 | One to five times a week |
|  | 77.2 | 73.7 | 73.4 | 69.9 | 68.6 | 71.3 | 68.6 | Every day |
|  | (1072) | (878) | (25970) | (28972) | (33541) | (29514) | (32169) | Weighted N |

Sex coded for head of household and wife only.

Table 4.10
Race of Respondent

|  | 1957g | 1958g | 1968e | 1969e | 1970e | 1971e | 1972e |  |
|---|---|---|---|---|---|---|---|---|
| Whites Only | 6.7% | 7.1% | 6.1% | 6.5% | 6.3% | 6.0% | 6.5% | Never |
|  | 1.4 | 1.8 | 1.9 | 2.4 | 2.8 | 1.7 | 2.5 | Occasionally |
|  | 10.0 | 12.5 | 12.3 | 13.0 | 14.4 | 14.4 | 16.0 | One to five times a week |
|  | 81.9 | 78.6 | 79.7 | 78.0 | 76.5 | 77.9 | 75.1 | Every day |
|  | (1681) | (1371) | (94226) | (99707) | (106820) | (92771) | (98545) | Weighted N |
| Blacks Only | 29.9 | 29.1 | 20.9 | 17.3 | 19.7 | 18.2 | 17.5 | Never |
|  | 10.3 | 4.1 | 3.8 | 7.5 | 4.9 | 5.7 | 2.7 | Occasionally |
|  | 19.0 | 16.3 | 17.4 | 17.2 | 19.2 | 20.3 | 21.9 | One to five times a week |
|  | 40.8 | 50.6 | 57.9 | 58.0 | 56.2 | 55.9 | 57.9 | Every day |
|  | (174) | (172) | (11309) | (12029) | (13297) | (11288) | (12376) | Weighted N |

Race coded for head of household and wife only in 1971e.

Table 4.11
How Often Does R [Head] Read Newspaper?
Education of Respondent

|  | Year | | | | | | | |
|---|---|---|---|---|---|---|---|---|
|  | 1957g | 1958g | 1968e | 1969e | 1970e | 1971e | 1972e | |
| Grade School Only | 19.9% | 18.9% | 20.3% | 18.9% | 18.3% | 15.3% | 14.4% | Never |
|  | 5.2 | 2.8 | 3.3 | 5.4 | 4.6 | 4.0 | 3.6 | Occasionally |
|  | 13.3 | 17.7 | 17.2 | 17.4 | 17.6 | 17.1 | 21.0 | One to five times a week |
|  | 61.6 | 60.6 | 59.2 | 58.3 | 59.5 | 63.7 | 61.0 | Every day |
|  | (675) | (530) | (27678) | (29946) | (29916) | (20188) | (21774) | Weighted N |
| High School Only | 3.3 | 5.7 | 4.7 | 4.6 | 5.3 | 4.8 | 6.1 | Never |
|  | 0.7 | 2.0 | 2.0 | 2.9 | 3.1 | 2.6 | 2.6 | Occasionally |
|  | 10.1 | 12.7 | 12.4 | 12.8 | 15.4 | 15.1 | 16.8 | One to five times a week |
|  | 85.8 | 79.6 | 80.9 | 79.7 | 76.2 | 77.5 | 74.5 | Every day |
|  | (869) | (740) | (49073) | (51206) | (57283) | (46185) | (54056) | Weighted N |
| College Only | 1.2 | 1.1 | 2.0 | 2.5 | 3.4 | 2.9 | 2.9 | Never |
|  | 0.9 | 0.4 | 1.4 | 0.6 | 1.5 | 0.6 | 1.7 | Occasionally |
|  | 8.0 | 5.4 | 9.9 | 11.6 | 13.2 | 13.1 | 14.4 | One to five times a week |
|  | 89.9 | 93.1 | 86.7 | 85.2 | 81.9 | 83.4 | 81.1 | Every day |
|  | (337) | (277) | (30066) | (32144) | (34370) | (30803) | (34650) | Weighted N |

Education coded for head of household only in 1971e, and for head and wife only in 1968e,1969e,1970e,and 1972e.

Figure 4.12
Newspaper Reading by Education of R

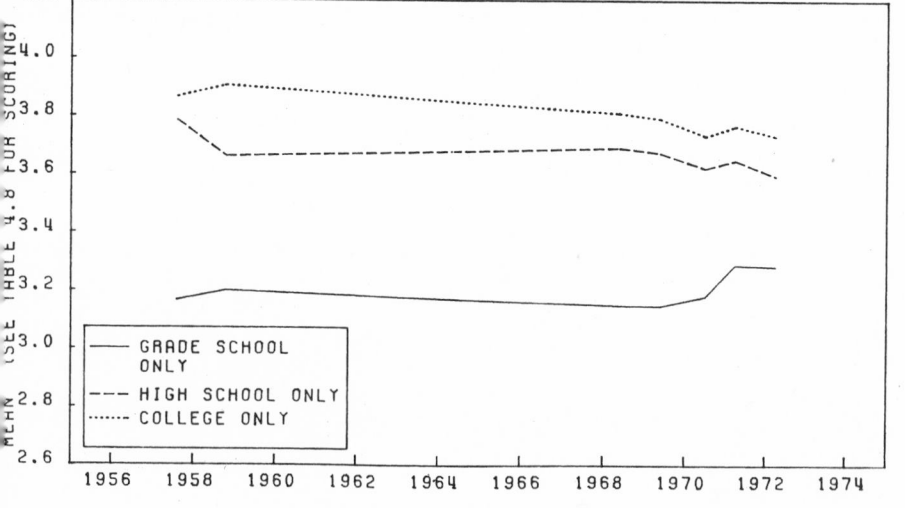

Table 4.12
How Often Does R [Head] Read Newspaper?
Age of Respondent

|  | Year | | | | | | | |
|---|---|---|---|---|---|---|---|---|
|  | 1957g | 1958g | 1968e | 1969e | 1970e | 1971e | 1972e | |
| 18-24 Only | 5.5% | 14.6% | 6.7% | 14.7% | 9.6% | 8.4% | 6.8% | Never |
|  | 3.1 | 4.6 | 6.7 | 4.6 | 6.3 | 4.4 | 4.8 | Occasionally |
|  | 20.5 | 20.8 | 26.1 | 22.0 | 28.3 | 26.0 | 33.6 | One to five times a week |
|  | 70.9 | 60.0 | 60.5 | 58.7 | 55.8 | 61.2 | 54.8 | Every day |
|  | (127) | (130) | (8431) | (8994) | (11900) | (10582) | (11810) | Weighted N |
| 25-34 Only | 8.2 | 7.3 | 6.7 | 5.2 | 6.5 | 6.6 | 6.7 | Never |
|  | 2.2 | 1.8 | 2.7 | 3.5 | 2.7 | 1.6 | 2.3 | Occasionally |
|  | 12.6 | 16.4 | 15.8 | 19.9 | 22.1 | 21.2 | 23.9 | One to five times a week |
|  | 76.9 | 74.5 | 74.9 | 71.4 | 68.7 | 70.6 | 67.2 | Every day |
|  | (451) | (330) | (19601) | (21617) | (23402) | (20900) | (22994) | Weighted N |
| 35-44 Only | 8.1 | 6.5 | 6.2 | 6.1 | 5.9 | 5.8 | 5.3 | Never |
|  | 1.9 | 1.0 | 2.0 | 2.5 | 3.1 | 2.7 | 3.0 | Occasionally |
|  | 8.9 | 11.8 | 11.5 | 12.0 | 13.8 | 14.7 | 14.6 | One to five times a week |
|  | 81.1 | 80.6 | 80.3 | 79.5 | 77.2 | 76.9 | 77.1 | Every day |
|  | (470) | (397) | (24517) | (24721) | (24979) | (22615) | (22412) | Weighted N |
| 45-54 Only | 7.0 | 10.8 | 8.1 | 6.5 | 6.6 | 5.9 | 5.5 | Never |
|  | 2.4 | 3.4 | 1.6 | 1.7 | 2.1 | 1.1 | 2.1 | Occasionally |
|  | 8.4 | 10.4 | 10.5 | 10.9 | 11.9 | 10.2 | 11.9 | One to five times a week |
|  | 82.2 | 75.4 | 79.7 | 80.8 | 79.4 | 82.7 | 80.5 | Every day |
|  | (370) | (297) | (20757) | (21612) | (22862) | (19927) | (21154) | Weighted N |
| 55-64 Only | 10.6 | 10.9 | 8.2 | 8.2 | 9.5 | 9.6 | 11.0 | Never |
|  | 1.7 | 1.6 | 1.0 | 3.1 | 3.1 | 2.6 | 1.5 | Occasionally |
|  | 9.4 | 10.9 | 11.2 | 11.2 | 11.3 | 10.9 | 11.7 | One to five times a week |
|  | 78.3 | 76.5 | 79.6 | 77.5 | 76.1 | 76.9 | 75.8 | Every day |
|  | (235) | (183) | (18126) | (19584) | (20020) | (16726) | (17432) | Weighted N |
| 65-74 Only | 15.2 | 13.2 | 10.0 | 8.2 | 10.0 | 7.8 | 9.7 | Never |
|  | 3.6 | 0.9 | 1.5 | 4.1 | 2.1 | 2.3 | 2.9 | Occasionally |
|  | 11.7 | 11.9 | 10.1 | 9.0 | 10.2 | 10.8 | 10.8 | One to five times a week |
|  | 69.5 | 74.0 | 78.4 | 78.8 | 77.7 | 79.1 | 76.7 | Every day |
|  | (223) | (219) | (11078) | (12024) | (13625) | (11922) | (12761) | Weighted N |
| 75 And Older Only | ** | ** | 18.4 | 17.5 | 12.8 | 14.7 | 15.1 | Never |
|  | ** | ** | 0.9 | 0.8 | 2.7 | 1.2 | 0.0 | Occasionally |
|  | ** | ** | 11.3 | 13.5 | 7.9 | 8.5 | 9.7 | One to five times a week |
|  | ** | ** | 69.4 | 68.2 | 76.7 | 75.6 | 75.2 | Every day |
|  | ** | ** | (4628) | (5541) | (6336) | (4049) | (5208) | Weighted N |

** Code distinction not made.
Oldest age group coded "65 And Older" in 1957g and 1958g.
Age coded for head of household and wife only in 1968e,1969e,1970e,1971e,and 1972e.

Family Living

Table 4.13
How Many Neighbors Does R Know
Total Population

QUESTION: About how many people in this neighborhood do you know by name?

|  |  | Year | | | |
|---|---|---|---|---|---|
|  |  | 1969e | 1970e | 1971e | 1972e |
| None to two | (1) | 9.3% | 8.3% | 8.2% | 8.2% |
| Three to nine | (2) | 22.2 | 22.6 | 23.7 | 22.3 |
| Ten to nineteen | (3) | 22.5 | 23.1 | 21.4 | 23.3 |
| Twenty or more | (4) | 45.9 | 46.0 | 46.8 | 46.2 |
| Total | | 100% | 100% | 100% | 100% |
| Weighted N | | 113195 | 123003 | 106973 | 114421 |
| Unweighted N | | 3744 | 4127 | 3714 | 4070 |
| Mean | | 3.05 | 3.07 | 3.07 | 3.07 |
| Standard Deviation | | 1.02 | 1.01 | 1.01 | 1.00 |

Figure 4.13
Neighbors Known--Total Population

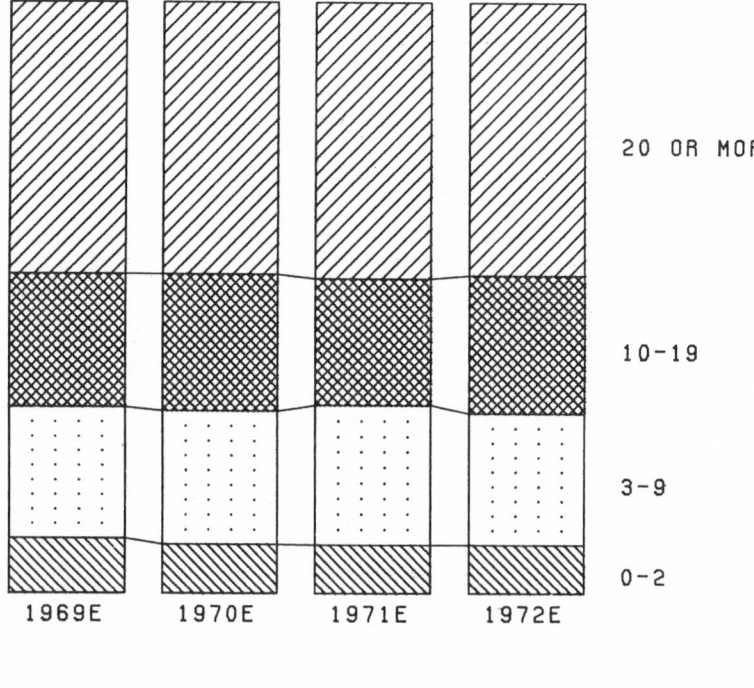

Figure 4.14
Neighbors Known by Race of R

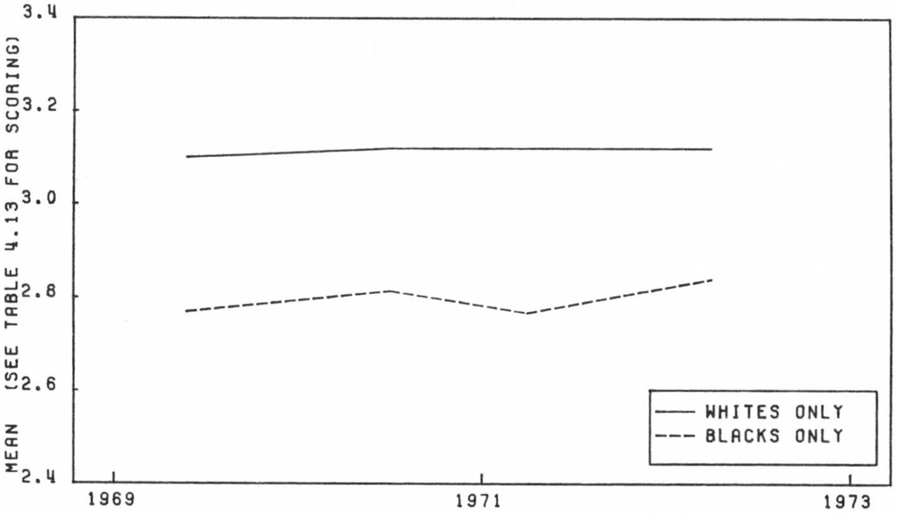

Table 4.14
How Many Neighbors Does R Know
Sex of Respondent

|  | Year | | | | |
|---|---|---|---|---|---|
|  | 1969e | 1970e | 1971e | 1972e | |
| Males Only | 8.3% | 8.2% | 7.4% | 7.7% | None to two |
|  | 22.0 | 20.7 | 23.2 | 21.3 | Three to nine |
|  | 22.6 | 23.0 | 21.1 | 23.7 | Ten to nineteen |
|  | 47.1 | 48.1 | 48.3 | 47.2 | Twenty or more |
|  | (84236) | (89329) | (77314) | (81805) | Weighted N |
| Females Only | 12.2 | 8.6 | 10.2 | 9.2 | None to two |
|  | 22.8 | 29.6 | 24.8 | 24.9 | Three to nine |
|  | 22.5 | 22.7 | 22.2 | 22.4 | Ten to nineteen |
|  | 42.5 | 39.2 | 42.9 | 43.5 | Twenty or more |
|  | (28959) | (34674) | (29659) | (32460) | Weighted N |

Sex coded for head of household and wife only.

Table 4.15
Race of Respondent

|  | 1969e | 1970e | 1971e | 1972e | |
|---|---|---|---|---|---|
| Whites Only | 8.2% | 7.2% | 7.0% | 7.2% | None to two |
|  | 21.2 | 21.3 | 22.4 | 21.0 | Three to nine |
|  | 23.0 | 23.7 | 22.2 | 24.3 | Ten to nineteen |
|  | 47.7 | 47.7 | 48.4 | 47.5 | Twenty or more |
|  | (99133) | (106551) | (92667) | (98976) | Weighted N |
| Blacks Only | 16.2 | 12.7 | 16.4 | 14.1 | None to two |
|  | 26.8 | 30.4 | 28.5 | 28.1 | Three to nine |
|  | 20.7 | 19.5 | 17.2 | 17.5 | Ten to nineteen |
|  | 36.3 | 37.3 | 38.0 | 40.3 | Twenty or more |
|  | (11874) | (13390) | (11430) | (12415) | Weighted N |

Race coded for head of household and wife only in 1971e.

Table 4.16
How Many Neighbors Does R Know
Education of Respondent

|  | Year | | | | |
|---|---|---|---|---|---|
|  | 1969e | 1970e | 1971e | 1972e | |
| Grade School Only | 9.0% | 7.9% | 8.4% | 7.4% | None to two |
|  | 23.7 | 23.1 | 25.2 | 21.9 | Three to nine |
|  | 20.0 | 22.1 | 17.7 | 22.0 | Ten to nineteen |
|  | 47.3 | 46.9 | 48.7 | 48.8 | Twenty or more |
|  | (29766) | (29839) | (20303) | (21839) | Weighted N |
|  |  |  |  |  |  |
| High School Only | 9.6 | 8.9 | 8.5 | 9.4 | None to two |
|  | 22.1 | 22.1 | 22.7 | 23.1 | Three to nine |
|  | 22.3 | 23.3 | 22.6 | 23.7 | Ten to nineteen |
|  | 46.1 | 45.7 | 46.2 | 43.9 | Twenty or more |
|  | (50914) | (57131) | (46220) | (54382) | Weighted N |
|  |  |  |  |  |  |
| College Only | 8.9 | 7.4 | 7.5 | 6.3 | None to two |
|  | 20.9 | 22.3 | 23.9 | 21.9 | Three to nine |
|  | 25.5 | 24.0 | 22.0 | 23.4 | Ten to nineteen |
|  | 44.8 | 46.2 | 46.6 | 48.4 | Twenty or more |
|  | (31844) | (34414) | (30741) | (34658) | Weighted N |

Education coded for head of household only in 1971e, and for head and wife only in 1969e,1970e,and 1972e.

Figure 4.15
Neighbors Known by Age of R

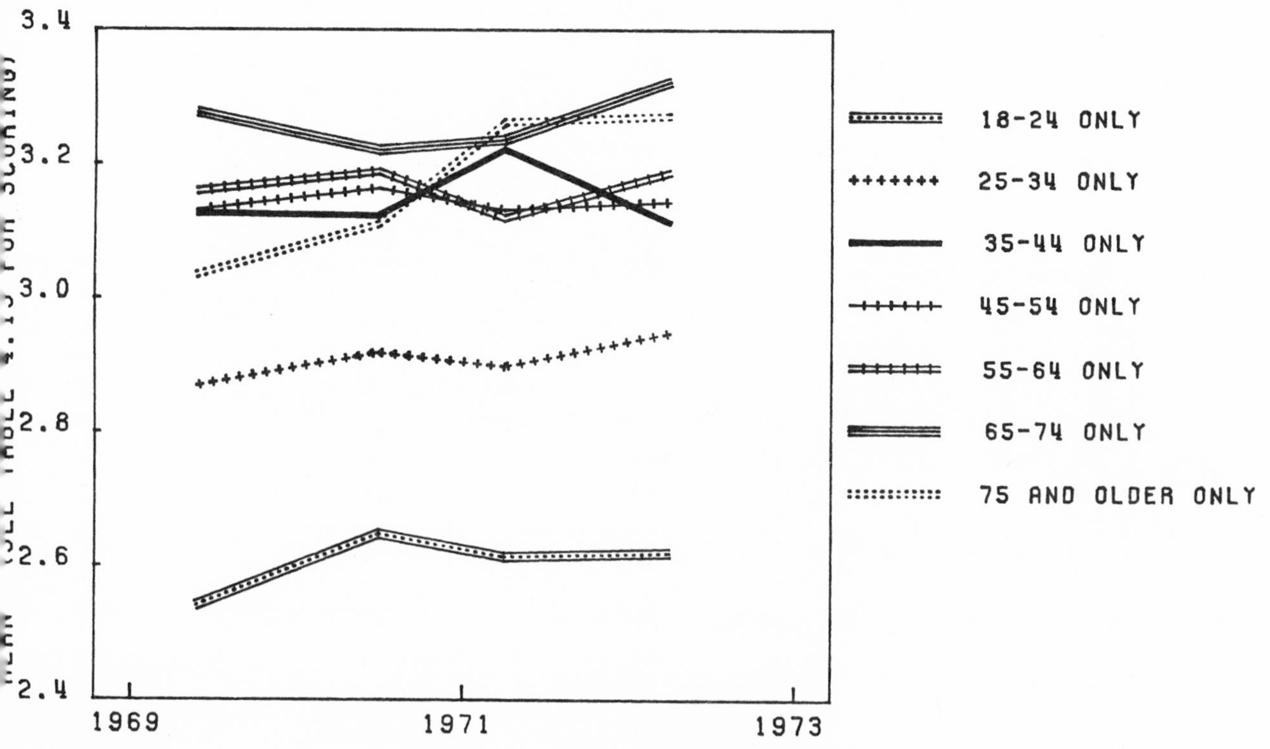

| | |
|---|---|
| ▦▦▦▦▦ ·········· | 18-24 ONLY |
| ++++++ | 25-34 ONLY |
| ▬▬▬▬▬ | 35-44 ONLY |
| -+++++- | 45-54 ONLY |
| ▦▦▦▦▦▦ | 55-64 ONLY |
| ▬▬▬▬▬ | 65-74 ONLY |
| ·········· | 75 AND OLDER ONLY |

Table 4.17
How Many Neighbors Does R Know
Age of Respondent

|                   | Year    |         |         |         |                |
|                   | 1969e   | 1970e   | 1971e   | 1972e   |                |
|-------------------|---------|---------|---------|---------|----------------|
| 18–24 Only        | 23.4%   | 18.8%   | 21.3%   | 20.4%   | None to two    |
|                   | 26.7    | 27.4    | 29.2    | 28.5    | Three to nine  |
|                   | 22.4    | 24.2    | 16.1    | 19.8    | Ten to nineteen |
|                   | 27.5    | 29.7    | 33.4    | 31.3    | Twenty or more |
|                   | (8837)  | (11824) | (10511) | (11793) | Weighted N     |
|                   |         |         |         |         |                |
| 25–34 Only        | 12.5    | 10.9    | 9.2     | 8.6     | None to two    |
|                   | 25.7    | 26.9    | 29.3    | 26.4    | Three to nine  |
|                   | 24.1    | 21.7    | 23.9    | 26.8    | Ten to nineteen |
|                   | 37.6    | 40.5    | 37.6    | 38.3    | Twenty or more |
|                   | (21537) | (23349) | (20950) | (23004) | Weighted N     |
|                   |         |         |         |         |                |
| 35–44 Only        | 9.8     | 8.2     | 6.4     | 7.9     | None to two    |
|                   | 18.3    | 20.5    | 18.3    | 21.4    | Three to nine  |
|                   | 21.6    | 22.2    | 22.0    | 22.4    | Ten to nineteen |
|                   | 50.4    | 49.2    | 53.3    | 48.3    | Twenty or more |
|                   | (24467) | (24982) | (22781) | (22480) | Weighted N     |
|                   |         |         |         |         |                |
| 45–54 Only        | 7.4     | 6.9     | 7.4     | 7.9     | None to two    |
|                   | 22.8    | 19.5    | 21.5    | 18.9    | Three to nine  |
|                   | 19.1    | 23.9    | 21.6    | 24.4    | Ten to nineteen |
|                   | 50.7    | 49.7    | 49.5    | 48.9    | Twenty or more |
|                   | (21612) | (22832) | (19940) | (21269) | Weighted N     |
|                   |         |         |         |         |                |
| 55–64 Only        | 5.4     | 5.2     | 5.1     | 3.7     | None to two    |
|                   | 22.6    | 20.6    | 26.5    | 23.7    | Three to nine  |
|                   | 22.8    | 24.5    | 19.9    | 22.9    | Ten to nineteen |
|                   | 49.3    | 49.7    | 48.5    | 49.8    | Twenty or more |
|                   | (19310) | (19938) | (16787) | (17441) | Weighted N     |
|                   |         |         |         |         |                |
| 65–74 Only        | 5.0     | 4.3     | 6.3     | 4.7     | None to two    |
|                   | 16.6    | 21.6    | 18.3    | 16.0    | Three to nine  |
|                   | 24.3    | 21.9    | 21.1    | 21.7    | Ten to nineteen |
|                   | 54.1    | 52.2    | 54.4    | 57.6    | Twenty or more |
|                   | (12073) | (13701) | (11930) | (12878) | Weighted N     |
|                   |         |         |         |         |                |
| 75 And Older Only | 4.9     | 4.0     | 0.0     | 3.9     | None to two    |
|                   | 25.6    | 25.7    | 24.4    | 19.4    | Three to nine  |
|                   | 30.9    | 25.6    | 25.0    | 22.3    | Ten to nineteen |
|                   | 38.7    | 44.7    | 50.6    | 54.4    | Twenty or more |
|                   | (5488)  | (6313)  | (4069)  | (5311)  | Weighted N     |

Age coded for head of household and wife only in 1969e,1970e,1971e,and 1972e.

Table 4.18
Are Relatives within Walking Distance?
Total Population

QUESTION: Do you (family) have any relatives who live within walking distance of here?

|  | Year | | | |
|---|---|---|---|---|
|  | 1969e | 1970e | 1971e | 1972e |
| Yes (1) | 42.2% | 42.3% | 42.8% | 43.7% |
| No (5) | 57.8 | 57.7 | 57.2 | 56.3 |
| Total | 100% | 100% | 100% | 100% |
| Weighted N | 113990 | 123288 | 106979 | 114368 |
| Unweighted N | 3758 | 4133 | 3718 | 4054 |
| Mean | 3.31 | 3.31 | 3.29 | 3.25 |
| Standard Deviation | 1.98 | 1.98 | 1.98 | 1.98 |

Figure 4.16
Are Relatives Near? by Education of R

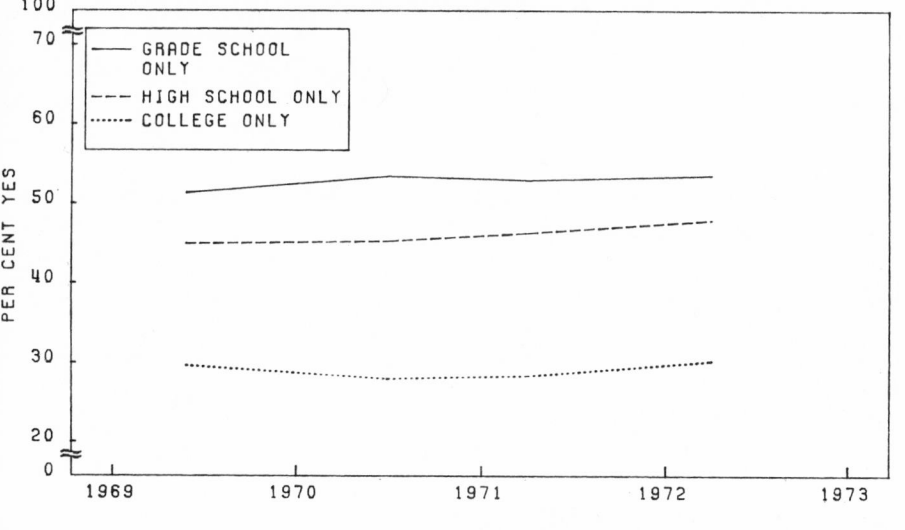

Table 4.19
re Relatives within Walking Distance?

| % Yes | Year | | | | |
|---|---|---|---|---|---|
| | 1969e | 1970e | 1971e | 1972e | |
| Males Only | 41.8 | 42.1 | 41.1 | 42.7 | Yes |
| | (84858) | (89525) | (77210) | (81801) | Weighted N |
| Females Only | 43.4 | 43.1 | 47.1 | 46.2 | Yes |
| | (29132) | (33763) | (29769) | (32411) | Weighted N |
| | | | | | |
| Whites Only | 40.7 | 40.9 | 40.9 | 42.0 | Yes |
| | (99721) | (106888) | (92775) | (98931) | Weighted N |
| Blacks Only | 54.1 | 54.0 | 56.3 | 56.3 | Yes |
| | (12093) | (13338) | (11376) | (12361) | Weighted N |
| | | | | | |
| Grade School Only | 51.3 | 53.4 | 52.9 | 53.5 | Yes |
| | (30110) | (29890) | (20227) | (21841) | Weighted N |
| High School Only | 44.9 | 45.2 | 46.3 | 47.9 | Yes |
| | (51113) | (57325) | (46171) | (54330) | Weighted N |
| College Only | 29.6 | 27.9 | 28.3 | 30.2 | Yes |
| | (32096) | (34454) | (30830) | (34693) | Weighted N |
| | | | | | |
| 18-24 Only | 42.3 | 39.1 | 43.5 | 42.2 | Yes |
| | (8959) | (11836) | (10475) | (11774) | Weighted N |
| 25-34 Only | 45.6 | 43.0 | 43.3 | 41.5 | Yes |
| | (21466) | (23462) | (20975) | (22963) | Weighted N |
| 35-44 Only | 39.7 | 40.6 | 40.6 | 43.9 | Yes |
| | (24771) | (25043) | (22733) | (22533) | Weighted N |
| 45-54 Only | 39.3 | 39.2 | 40.3 | 42.4 | Yes |
| | (21746) | (22901) | (19936) | (21223) | Weighted N |
| 55-64 Only | 42.5 | 44.3 | 44.1 | 42.5 | Yes |
| | (19481) | (19906) | (16729) | (17486) | Weighted N |
| 65-74 Only | 41.5 | 43.7 | 43.0 | 48.4 | Yes |
| | (12073) | (13701) | (12012) | (12833) | Weighted N |
| 75 And Older Only | 53.9 | 54.4 | 55.8 | 53.2 | Yes |
| | (5623) | (6375) | (4110) | (5311) | Weighted N |

ex coded for head of household and wife only.
ace coded for head of household and wife only in 1971e.
ducation coded for head of household only in 1971e, and for head and wife only in 1969e,1970e,and 1972e.
ge coded for head of household and wife only in 1969e,1970e,1971e,and 1972e.

Table 4.20
Does R Attend Church Regularly?
Total Population

QUESTION: Would you say you go to church regularly, often, seldom, or never?

|  | | Year | | | | | | | |
|---|---|---|---|---|---|---|---|---|---|
| | | 1952n | 1956n | 1958n | 1960n | 1962n | 1964n | 1965b | 1966n | 1968n |
| Regularly | (4) | 38.4% | 42.5% | 43.0% | 44.1% | 44.6% | 44.0% | 40.0% | 39.8% | 38.3% |
| Often | (3) | 17.9 | 18.3 | 18.4 | 17.7 | 16.3 | 17.4 | 14.3 | 17.8 | 15.3 |
| Seldom | (2) | 35.7 | 33.5 | 32.3 | 33.1 | 31.3 | 32.1 | 34.4 | 31.0 | 35.6 |
| Never | (1) | 8.0 | 5.6 | 6.2 | 5.1 | 7.9 | 6.5 | 11.3 | 11.4 | 10.7 |
| Total | | 100% | 100% | 100% | 100% | 100% | 100% | 100% | 100% | 100% |
| Weighted N | | 1782 | 1753 | 1796 | 1794 | 1286 | 4396 | 2199 | 1283 | 3036 |
| Unweighted N | | 1782 | 1753 | 1428 | 1088 | 1286 | 1730 | 2199 | 1283 | 1639 |
| Mean | | 2.87 | 2.98 | 2.98 | 3.01 | 2.97 | 2.99 | 2.83 | 2.86 | 2.81 |
| Standard Deviation | | 1.02 | 0.99 | 1.00 | 0.99 | 1.04 | 1.01 | 1.08 | 1.07 | 1.06 |

1964n and 1968n include Black supplement.

Figure 4.17
Does R Attend Church Regularly?--Total Population

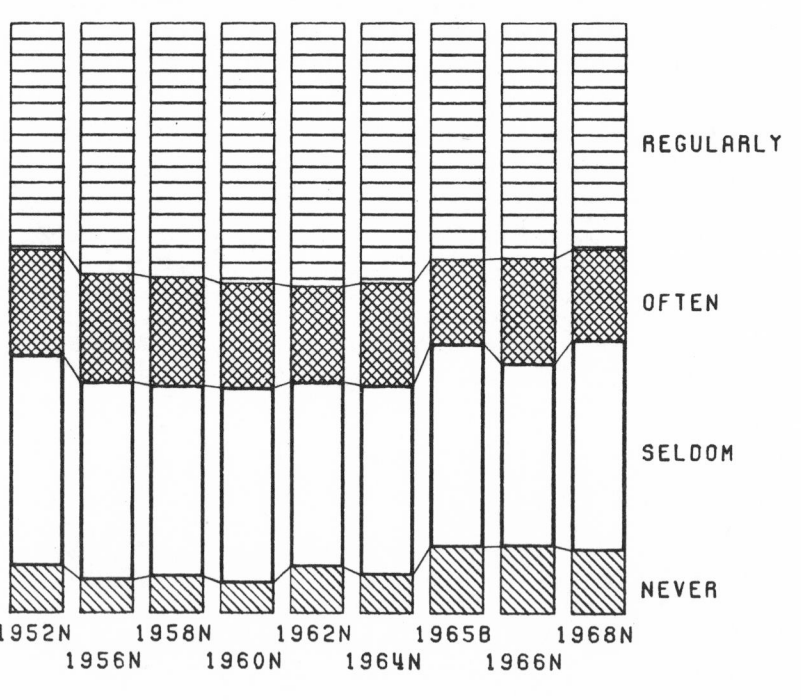

Figure 4.18
Does R Attend Church Regularly? by Sex of R

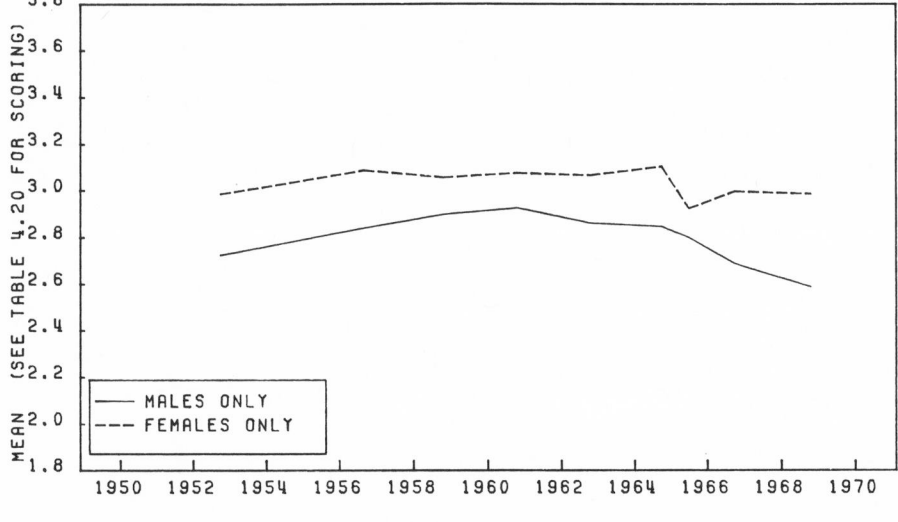

Table 4.21
Does R Attend Church Regularly?
Sex of Respondent

|  | Year | | | | | | | | | |
|---|---|---|---|---|---|---|---|---|---|---|
|  | 1952n | 1956n | 1958n | 1960n | 1962n | 1964n | 1965b | 1966n | 1968n | |
| Males Only | 32.6% | 37.5% | 38.8% | 38.5% | 40.2% | 39.2% | 38.9% | 34.6% | 30.1% | Regularly |
|  | 16.6 | 16.2 | 18.9 | 20.3 | 14.9 | 15.4 | 14.0 | 14.9 | 14.4 | Often |
|  | 41.6 | 39.2 | 35.6 | 36.5 | 35.8 | 36.4 | 35.4 | 35.4 | 40.0 | Seldom |
|  | 9.2 | 7.1 | 6.7 | 4.7 | 9.2 | 9.0 | 11.7 | 15.1 | 15.6 | Never |
|  | (813) | (784) | (832) | (808) | (579) | (1950) | (1616) | (570) | (1330) | Weighted N |
| Females Only | 43.2 | 46.5 | 46.7 | 48.7 | 48.1 | 47.9 | 43.5 | 44.0 | 44.8 | Regularly |
|  | 19.0 | 20.0 | 18.0 | 15.6 | 17.4 | 18.9 | 15.2 | 20.1 | 16.0 | Often |
|  | 30.9 | 29.0 | 29.5 | 30.2 | 27.6 | 28.7 | 31.6 | 27.5 | 32.2 | Seldom |
|  | 6.9 | 4.4 | 5.8 | 5.5 | 6.9 | 4.5 | 9.7 | 8.4 | 7.0 | Never |
|  | (969) | (969) | (964) | (986) | (707) | (2446) | (566) | (713) | (1706) | Weighted N |

Table 4.22
Race of Respondent

|  | 1952n | 1956n | 1958n | 1960n | 1962n | 1964n | 1965b | 1966n | 1968n | |
|---|---|---|---|---|---|---|---|---|---|---|
| Whites Only | 37.5% | 41.7% | 42.8% | 44.3% | 44.8% | 44.5% | 40.0% | 40.3% | 37.8% | Regularly |
|  | 17.7 | 18.1 | 18.1 | 18.1 | 15.8 | 16.9 | 13.6 | 17.4 | 14.7 | Often |
|  | 36.2 | 34.0 | 32.5 | 32.2 | 31.2 | 31.9 | 34.7 | 30.5 | 36.5 | Seldom |
|  | 8.6 | 6.1 | 6.6 | 5.3 | 8.2 | 6.7 | 11.8 | 11.7 | 11.0 | Never |
|  | (1607) | (1601) | (1620) | (1629) | (1165) | (3969) | (1947) | (1133) | (2716) | Weighted N |
| Blacks Only | 48.2 | 50.7 | 45.9 | 45.6 | 42.3 | 40.3 | 40.6 | 39.1 | 43.6 | Regularly |
|  | 19.6 | 19.9 | 21.4 | 12.9 | 20.7 | 22.9 | 20.8 | 21.1 | 22.1 | Often |
|  | 30.4 | 28.8 | 29.6 | 38.1 | 32.4 | 33.2 | 32.9 | 33.1 | 27.1 | Seldom |
|  | 1.8 | 0.7 | 3.1 | 3.4 | 4.5 | 3.5 | 5.8 | 6.8 | 7.1 | Never |
|  | (168) | (146) | (159) | (147) | (111) | (397) | (207) | (133) | (280) | Weighted N |

Table 4.23
Does R Attend Church Regularly?
Education of Respondent

|  | | | | | Year | | | | | |
|---|---|---|---|---|---|---|---|---|---|---|
|  | 1952n | 1956n | 1958n | 1960n | 1962n | 1964n | 1965b | 1966n | 1968n | |
| Grade School Only | 37.8% | 37.9% | 39.5% | 35.9% | 41.5% | 39.2% | 37.5% | 34.9% | 36.4% | Regularly |
|  | 18.4 | 19.7 | 19.1 | 16.2 | 14.8 | 15.8 | 14.5 | 19.1 | 15.8 | Often |
|  | 34.3 | 33.6 | 32.3 | 41.7 | 31.9 | 34.7 | 33.5 | 30.7 | 32.5 | Seldom |
|  | 9.4 | 8.7 | 9.1 | 6.2 | 11.8 | 10.3 | 14.5 | 15.2 | 15.4 | Never |
|  | (732) | (538) | (539) | (532) | (357) | (1098) | (662) | (335) | (684) | Weighted N |
| High School Only | 39.2 | 42.7 | 43.0 | 46.2 | 43.0 | 42.5 | 39.6 | 39.4 | 37.6 | Regularly |
|  | 17.7 | 18.3 | 17.1 | 15.4 | 16.9 | 19.2 | 14.2 | 19.1 | 16.0 | Often |
|  | 36.4 | 34.5 | 33.8 | 33.2 | 33.9 | 32.7 | 36.6 | 32.1 | 36.9 | Seldom |
|  | 6.8 | 4.4 | 6.0 | 5.2 | 6.2 | 5.6 | 9.6 | 9.5 | 9.5 | Never |
|  | (784) | (878) | (881) | (862) | (616) | (2241) | (1006) | (645) | (1520) | Weighted N |
| College Only | 38.3 | 49.2 | 49.3 | 51.1 | 51.1 | 52.8 | 43.8 | 46.5 | 41.6 | Regularly |
|  | 16.1 | 16.1 | 19.9 | 24.8 | 16.9 | 14.8 | 14.2 | 13.6 | 13.5 | Often |
|  | 38.3 | 30.7 | 28.0 | 20.5 | 24.8 | 28.6 | 31.5 | 28.6 | 35.9 | Seldom |
|  | 7.3 | 4.0 | 2.8 | 3.5 | 7.2 | 3.9 | 10.4 | 11.3 | 8.9 | Never |
|  | (261) | (329) | (357) | (395) | (307) | (1029) | (527) | (301) | (827) | Weighted N |

Education coded for head of household and wife only in 1965b.

Table 4.24
Does R Attend Church Regularly?
Age of Respondent

| | | | | | Year | | | | | |
|---|---|---|---|---|---|---|---|---|---|---|
| | 1952n | 1956n | 1958n | 1960n | 1962n | 1964n | 1965b | 1966n | 1968n | |
| 18-24 Only | 37.3% | 32.4% | 32.6% | 56.9% | 40.0% | 19.3% | 32.3% | 33.9% | 31.8% | Regularly |
| | 17.8 | 27.0 | 12.4 | 20.7 | 17.3 | 22.4 | 18.8 | 15.3 | 18.0 | Often |
| | 37.3 | 38.7 | 47.2 | 22.4 | 36.0 | 46.2 | 41.4 | 37.3 | 39.5 | Seldom |
| | 7.6 | 1.8 | 7.9 | 0.0 | 6.7 | 12.1 | 7.5 | 13.6 | 10.7 | Never |
| | (118) | (111) | (89) | (58) | (75) | (331) | (133) | (118) | (233) | Weighted N |
| 25-34 Only | 34.4 | 46.9 | 41.5 | 41.1 | 39.4 | 44.2 | 32.3 | 33.9 | 34.6 | Regularly |
| | 17.3 | 17.5 | 20.0 | 16.5 | 15.8 | 16.9 | 13.3 | 19.1 | 15.7 | Often |
| | 41.5 | 31.4 | 31.8 | 35.1 | 37.1 | 34.2 | 42.8 | 39.1 | 40.7 | Seldom |
| | 6.8 | 4.2 | 6.8 | 7.3 | 7.7 | 4.8 | 11.6 | 7.8 | 9.0 | Never |
| | (427) | (424) | (400) | (382) | (259) | (901) | (362) | (230) | (592) | Weighted N |
| 35-44 Only | 40.5 | 44.4 | 46.0 | 48.4 | 49.3 | 47.3 | 42.0 | 38.6 | 43.1 | Regularly |
| | 19.2 | 17.3 | 18.1 | 21.1 | 19.5 | 15.8 | 14.4 | 20.6 | 19.0 | Often |
| | 34.6 | 34.4 | 32.5 | 27.5 | 26.2 | 31.3 | 35.1 | 31.4 | 31.2 | Seldom |
| | 5.7 | 3.9 | 3.4 | 3.1 | 5.0 | 5.6 | 8.5 | 9.4 | 6.7 | Never |
| | (422) | (439) | (465) | (455) | (282) | (948) | (436) | (277) | (641) | Weighted N |
| 45-54 Only | 37.9 | 40.4 | 42.5 | 46.0 | 41.8 | 41.7 | 41.1 | 41.4 | 35.4 | Regularly |
| | 18.4 | 16.9 | 19.5 | 19.9 | 16.0 | 21.0 | 14.6 | 14.8 | 11.5 | Often |
| | 35.0 | 36.7 | 31.6 | 30.3 | 35.0 | 32.0 | 36.1 | 31.6 | 41.4 | Seldom |
| | 8.7 | 6.0 | 6.3 | 3.8 | 7.2 | 5.3 | 8.3 | 12.1 | 11.7 | Never |
| | (309) | (332) | (348) | (346) | (263) | (875) | (460) | (256) | (616) | Weighted N |
| 55-64 Only | 42.5 | 41.9 | 49.2 | 42.0 | 43.4 | 45.6 | 43.3 | 45.1 | 42.4 | Regularly |
| | 16.3 | 19.4 | 15.4 | 15.4 | 13.8 | 15.4 | 11.0 | 21.1 | 14.3 | Often |
| | 31.3 | 32.6 | 28.3 | 39.5 | 31.6 | 31.3 | 31.0 | 25.1 | 33.3 | Seldom |
| | 9.9 | 6.2 | 7.1 | 3.1 | 11.2 | 7.7 | 14.7 | 8.6 | 10.0 | Never |
| | (252) | (227) | (254) | (286) | (196) | (636) | (381) | (175) | (448) | Weighted N |
| 65-74 Only | 38.5 | 39.4 | 41.8 | 42.6 | 55.5 | 55.8 | 43.2 | 47.1 | 38.4 | Regularly |
| | 19.9 | 19.7 | 20.9 | 16.2 | 13.9 | 15.5 | 17.0 | 15.9 | 15.2 | Often |
| | 36.0 | 30.7 | 32.3 | 38.6 | 23.4 | 23.0 | 25.8 | 21.0 | 31.1 | Seldom |
| | 5.6 | 10.2 | 5.1 | 2.5 | 7.3 | 5.8 | 14.0 | 15.9 | 15.2 | Never |
| | (161) | (137) | (158) | (197) | (137) | (452) | (271) | (157) | (341) | Weighted N |
| 75 And Older Only | 35.7 | 44.4 | 30.5 | 25.7 | 43.3 | 48.9 | 43.9 | 35.5 | 43.6 | Regularly |
| | 14.3 | 14.3 | 19.5 | 2.9 | 14.9 | 13.1 | 15.9 | 12.9 | 11.5 | Often |
| | 24.3 | 23.8 | 32.9 | 38.6 | 26.9 | 27.8 | 24.2 | 27.4 | 23.1 | Seldom |
| | 25.7 | 17.5 | 17.1 | 32.9 | 14.9 | 10.1 | 15.9 | 24.2 | 21.8 | Never |
| | (70) | (63) | (82) | (70) | (67) | (237) | (132) | (62) | (156) | Weighted N |

Age coded for head of household and wife only in 1965b.

Table 4.25
Does R Attend Church Regularly?
Religion of Respondent

| | Year | | | | | | | | | |
|---|---|---|---|---|---|---|---|---|---|---|
| | 1952n | 1956n | 1958n | 1960n | 1962n | 1964n | 1965b | 1966n | 1968n | |
| Protestants Only | 34.0% | 36.0% | 37.5% | 38.1% | 39.2% | 39.0% | 34.9% | 35.7% | 34.5% | Regularly |
| | 19.2 | 20.2 | 18.9 | 18.5 | 17.3 | 17.8 | 16.3 | 20.2 | 16.7 | Often |
| | 39.3 | 37.8 | 36.8 | 37.1 | 36.1 | 35.7 | 38.5 | 32.9 | 39.5 | Seldom |
| | 7.5 | 6.0 | 6.8 | 6.4 | 7.4 | 7.5 | 10.3 | 11.2 | 9.3 | Never |
| | (1274) | (1280) | (1329) | (1349) | (943) | (3192) | (1548) | (911) | (2153) | Weighted N |
| Catholics Only | 62.4 | 71.0 | 66.3 | 73.0 | 73.5 | 64.2 | 65.6 | 63.8 | 60.8 | Regularly |
| | 13.2 | 13.2 | 17.2 | 14.2 | 12.3 | 14.9 | 9.7 | 11.5 | 12.9 | Often |
| | 21.2 | 14.8 | 13.3 | 11.4 | 11.5 | 18.3 | 20.1 | 20.8 | 20.2 | Seldom |
| | 3.1 | 1.1 | 3.1 | 1.4 | 2.7 | 2.7 | 4.6 | 3.9 | 6.1 | Never |
| | (386) | (372) | (383) | (367) | (260) | (1030) | (497) | (279) | (673) | Weighted N |
| Jews Only | 6.9 | 12.5 | 14.5 | 3.2 | 15.9 | 14.0 | 8.3 | 11.6 | 0.0 | Regularly |
| | 27.6 | 21.4 | 21.8 | 24.2 | 29.5 | 25.6 | 12.5 | 20.9 | 17.9 | Often |
| | 51.7 | 60.7 | 58.2 | 71.0 | 43.2 | 53.5 | 63.9 | 51.2 | 64.1 | Seldom |
| | 13.8 | 5.4 | 5.5 | 1.6 | 11.4 | 7.0 | 15.3 | 16.3 | 17.9 | Never |
| | (58) | (56) | (55) | (62) | (44) | (129) | (72) | (43) | (78) | Weighted N |

Figure 4.19
Does R Attend Church Regularly? by Religion of R

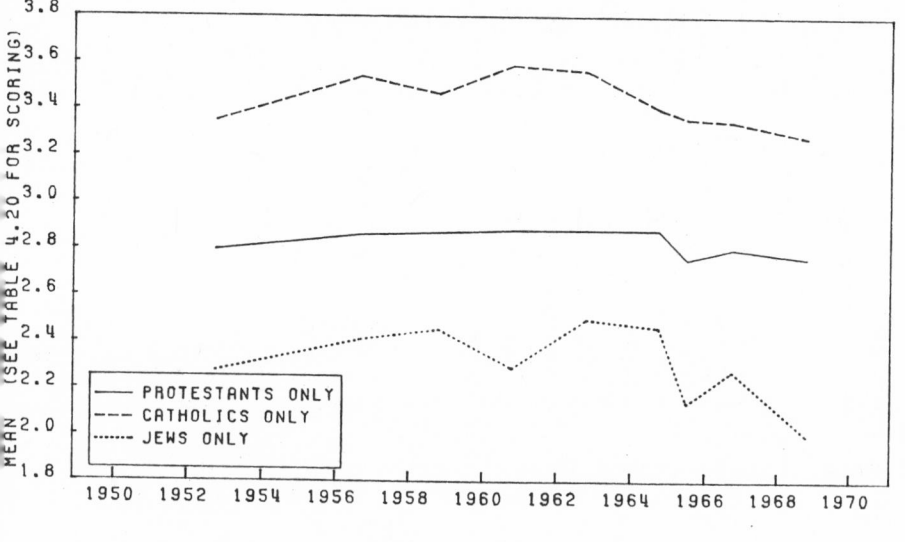

Table 4.26
Does R Attend Church Weekly?
Total Population

QUESTION: Would you say you go to church every week, almost every week, once or twice a month, a few times a year or never?

|  |  | Year | | | | |
|---|---|---|---|---|---|---|
|  |  | 1970n | 1972n | 1974n | 1976n | 1978n |
| Every week | (5) | ** | 27.3% | 27.0% | 27.1% | 27.3% |
| Almost every week | (4) | 39.5 | 11.9 | 13.1 | 12.9 | 11.9 |
| Once or twice a month | (3) | 16.9 | 12.2 | 13.0 | 15.1 | 13.0 |
| A few times a year | (2) | 31.2 | 33.6 | 32.7 | 30.6 | 32.8 |
| Never | (1) | 12.4 | 15.0 | 14.2 | 14.3 | 15.0 |
| Total |  | 100% | 100% | 100% | 100% | 100% |
| Weighted N |  | 1743 | 2560 | 2316 | 26505 | 2079 |
| Unweighted N |  | 1577 | 2560 | 1470 | 2084 | 2079 |
| Mean |  | 2.83 | 3.03 | 3.06 | 3.08 | 3.04 |
| Standard Deviation |  | 1.08 | 1.46 | 1.45 | 1.44 | 1.46 |

** Code distinction not made.
1970n includes Black supplement.

Figure 4.20
Does R Attend Church Weekly?--Total Population

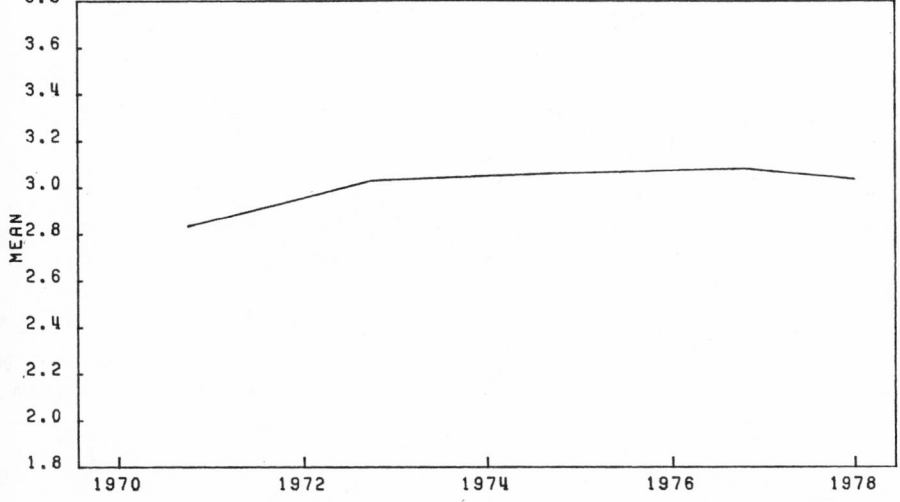

Figure 4.21
Does R Attend Church Weekly? by Sex of R

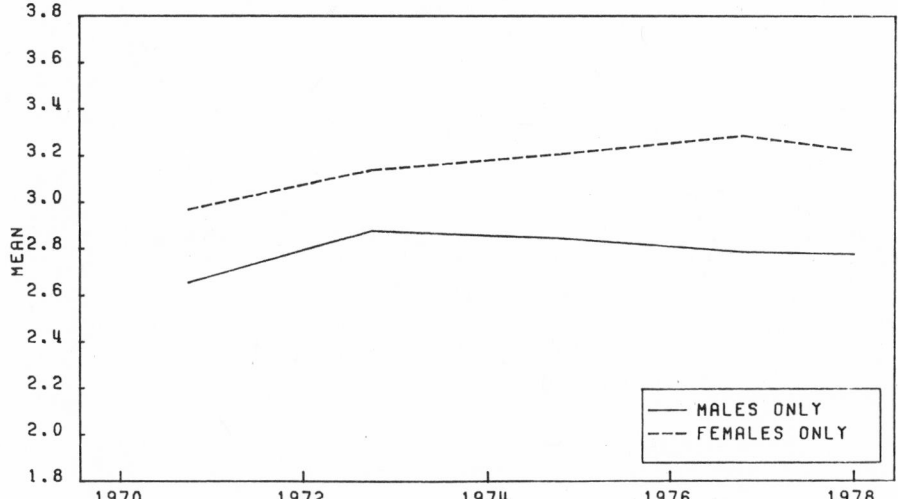

Table 4.27
Does R Attend Church Weekly?
Sex of Respondent

|  | | Year | | | | |
|---|---|---|---|---|---|---|
|  | 1970n | 1972n | 1974n | 1976n | 1978n | |
| Males Only | ** | 24.0% | 21.4% | 21.0% | 21.4% | Every week |
|  | 33.1 | 10.6 | 13.1 | 10.4 | 9.6 | Almost every week |
|  | 15.9 | 12.0 | 11.5 | 13.1 | 13.6 | Once or twice a month |
|  | 34.5 | 36.1 | 36.6 | 37.1 | 36.2 | A few times a year |
|  | 16.5 | 17.3 | 17.4 | 18.3 | 19.2 | Never |
|  | (748) | (1084) | (939) | (10865) | (875) | Weighted N |
| Females Only | ** | 29.7 | 30.9 | 31.5 | 31.6 | Every week |
|  | 44.3 | 12.9 | 13.1 | 14.6 | 13.5 | Almost every week |
|  | 17.7 | 12.4 | 13.9 | 16.5 | 12.6 | Once or twice a month |
|  | 28.6 | 31.8 | 30.1 | 26.0 | 30.3 | A few times a year |
|  | 9.3 | 13.2 | 12.0 | 11.4 | 12.0 | Never |
|  | (995) | (1476) | (1377) | (15590) | (1204) | Weighted N |

Table 4.28
Race of Respondent

|  | 1970n | 1972n | 1974n | 1976n | 1978n | |
|---|---|---|---|---|---|---|
| Whites Only | ** | 28.3% | 27.2% | 27.7% | 28.2% | Every week |
|  | 40.0 | 11.8 | 12.6 | 12.9 | 11.1 | Almost every week |
|  | 15.4 | 10.8 | 12.1 | 13.1 | 11.3 | Once or twice a month |
|  | 31.2 | 33.5 | 33.6 | 31.1 | 33.2 | A few times a year |
|  | 13.5 | 15.7 | 14.5 | 15.2 | 16.2 | Never |
|  | (1559) | (2269) | (2050) | (23050) | (1817) | Weighted N |
| Blacks Only | ** | 20.6 | 24.9 | 23.2 | 19.7 | Every week |
|  | 36.0 | 13.4 | 17.5 | 14.1 | 17.4 | Almost every week |
|  | 31.8 | 24.5 | 19.8 | 31.6 | 27.2 | Once or twice a month |
|  | 28.8 | 34.4 | 26.7 | 25.3 | 31.5 | A few times a year |
|  | 3.4 | 7.1 | 11.1 | 5.8 | 4.2 | Never |
|  | (160) | (253) | (217) | (2690) | (213) | Weighted N |

** Code distinction not made.

Table 4.29
Does R Attend Church Weekly?
Education of Respondent

|                    |       |       | Year  |        |       |                     |
|--------------------|-------|-------|-------|--------|-------|---------------------|
|                    | 1970n | 1972n | 1974n | 1976n  | 1978n |                     |
| Grade School Only  | **    | 27.8% | 31.9% | 31.0%  | 30.8% | Every week          |
|                    | 39.4  | 11.0  | 14.8  | 15.0   | 9.9   | Almost every week   |
|                    | 15.6  | 11.8  | 12.4  | 13.1   | 17.4  | Once or twice a month |
|                    | 29.1  | 31.7  | 25.2  | 25.7   | 28.9  | A few times a year  |
|                    | 15.9  | 17.8  | 15.7  | 15.2   | 13.0  | Never               |
|                    | (416) | (518) | (420) | (4435) | (253) | Weighted N          |
| High School Only   | **    | 25.2  | 25.9  | 25.4   | 26.9  | Every week          |
|                    | 37.1  | 11.5  | 12.0  | 13.1   | 11.3  | Almost every week   |
|                    | 19.0  | 12.3  | 11.9  | 15.7   | 11.4  | Once or twice a month |
|                    | 32.4  | 36.8  | 34.1  | 31.7   | 34.2  | A few times a year  |
|                    | 11.5  | 14.3  | 16.1  | 14.0   | 16.3  | Never               |
|                    | (898) | (1312)| (1206)| (13390)| (1091)| Weighted N          |
| College Only       | **    | 30.6  | 25.3  | 28.1   | 26.8  | Every week          |
|                    | 44.9  | 13.3  | 14.4  | 11.4   | 13.5  | Almost every week   |
|                    | 14.0  | 12.4  | 15.2  | 15.2   | 13.9  | Once or twice a month |
|                    | 30.6  | 29.4  | 35.3  | 30.9   | 32.0  | A few times a year  |
|                    | 10.6  | 14.3  | 9.8   | 14.4   | 13.8  | Never               |
|                    | (425) | (728) | (672) | (8580) | (732) | Weighted N          |

** Code distinction not made.

Table 4.30
Does R Attend Church Weekly?
Age of Respondent

|  |  |  | Year |  |  |  |
|---|---|---|---|---|---|---|
|  | 1970n | 1972n | 1974n | 1976n | 1978n |  |
| 18-24 Only | ** | 16.9% | 16.3% | 24.3% | 17.0% | Every week |
|  | 30.2 | 11.5 | 11.2 | 7.4 | 8.8 | Almost every week |
|  | 21.8 | 14.0 | 11.5 | 22.4 | 18.6 | Once or twice a month |
|  | 35.3 | 40.7 | 42.3 | 33.9 | 39.5 | A few times a year |
|  | 12.7 | 16.9 | 18.6 | 11.9 | 16.0 | Never |
|  | (226) | (356) | (312) | (3435) | (306) | Weighted N |
| 25-34 Only | ** | 22.0 | 22.7 | 20.1 | 23.2 | Every week |
|  | 37.1 | 13.6 | 10.2 | 11.6 | 12.3 | Almost every week |
|  | 21.7 | 13.4 | 16.8 | 16.1 | 11.3 | Once or twice a month |
|  | 31.0 | 37.2 | 36.0 | 35.1 | 36.5 | A few times a year |
|  | 10.2 | 13.8 | 14.2 | 17.1 | 16.8 | Never |
|  | (337) | (537) | (541) | (6285) | (488) | Weighted N |
| 35-44 Only | ** | 29.1 | 24.3 | 25.5 | 25.9 | Every week |
|  | 36.9 | 12.8 | 17.3 | 14.5 | 13.8 | Almost every week |
|  | 15.5 | 11.6 | 11.2 | 15.0 | 13.2 | Once or twice a month |
|  | 34.3 | 32.9 | 35.8 | 33.5 | 32.2 | A few times a year |
|  | 13.3 | 13.7 | 11.5 | 11.4 | 14.9 | Never |
|  | (298) | (423) | (313) | (3955) | (370) | Weighted N |
| 45-54 Only | ** | 27.3 | 30.4 | 25.1 | 31.4 | Every week |
|  | 39.7 | 11.3 | 11.8 | 14.9 | 12.1 | Almost every week |
|  | 16.8 | 12.2 | 11.8 | 13.5 | 13.1 | Once or twice a month |
|  | 31.3 | 34.4 | 36.5 | 30.9 | 28.8 | A few times a year |
|  | 12.1 | 14.8 | 9.4 | 15.7 | 14.7 | Never |
|  | (307) | (433) | (381) | (3865) | (306) | Weighted N |
| 55-64 Only | ** | 33.3 | 32.7 | 36.3 | 32.1 | Every week |
|  | 44.8 | 13.9 | 16.0 | 14.6 | 11.3 | Almost every week |
|  | 13.5 | 11.5 | 11.1 | 10.5 | 12.6 | Once or twice a month |
|  | 33.0 | 28.5 | 25.4 | 25.8 | 30.0 | A few times a year |
|  | 8.7 | 12.8 | 14.9 | 12.8 | 14.0 | Never |
|  | (275) | (375) | (343) | (3825) | (293) | Weighted N |
| 65-74 Only | ** | 33.5 | 33.2 | 32.6 | 37.2 | Every week |
|  | 46.9 | 9.9 | 14.0 | 13.5 | 10.6 | Almost every week |
|  | 13.8 | 10.3 | 12.8 | 14.1 | 9.0 | Once or twice a month |
|  | 24.4 | 29.3 | 26.0 | 24.7 | 31.2 | A few times a year |
|  | 14.8 | 17.1 | 14.0 | 15.2 | 12.1 | Never |
|  | (187) | (263) | (265) | (3195) | (199) | Weighted N |
| 75 And Older Only | ** | 40.6 | 36.4 | 34.7 | 37.0 | Every week |
|  | 46.3 | 5.2 | 14.0 | 13.3 | 13.9 | Almost every week |
|  | 10.3 | 11.0 | 14.0 | 13.8 | 13.9 | Once or twice a month |
|  | 21.7 | 23.2 | 14.0 | 22.9 | 21.3 | A few times a year |
|  | 21.7 | 20.0 | 21.7 | 15.3 | 13.9 | Never |
|  | (105) | (155) | (143) | (1770) | (108) | Weighted N |

** Code distinction not made.

Table 4.31
Does R Attend Church Weekly?
Religion of Respondent

|  | Year | | | | | |
|---|---|---|---|---|---|---|
|  | 1970n | 1972n | 1974n | 1976n | 1978n | |
| Protestants Only | ** | 22.8% | 23.4% | 23.8% | 23.3% | Every week |
|  | 36.2 | 13.1 | 14.2 | 14.8 | 12.8 | Almost every week |
|  | 18.3 | 12.8 | 13.3 | 16.6 | 14.7 | Once or twice a month |
|  | 32.5 | 35.3 | 33.5 | 29.4 | 32.7 | A few times a year |
|  | 13.0 | 16.1 | 15.5 | 15.3 | 16.5 | Never |
|  | (1283) | (1835) | (1685) | (18415) | (1431) | Weighted N |
| Catholics Only | ** | 42.0 | 41.5 | 38.1 | 40.8 | Every week |
|  | 55.5 | 9.6 | 10.2 | 9.2 | 10.6 | Almost every week |
|  | 13.9 | 11.1 | 12.4 | 11.1 | 9.7 | Once or twice a month |
|  | 24.5 | 26.6 | 28.1 | 31.8 | 29.3 | A few times a year |
|  | 6.1 | 10.7 | 7.8 | 9.7 | 9.5 | Never |
|  | (362) | (638) | (540) | (6975) | (546) | Weighted N |
| Jews Only | ** | 3.3 | 1.7 | 3.8 | 4.5 | Every week |
|  | 9.0 | 3.3 | 6.7 | 7.6 | 6.0 | Almost every week |
|  | 11.2 | 10.0 | 13.3 | 13.6 | 6.0 | Once or twice a month |
|  | 52.8 | 61.7 | 60.0 | 50.0 | 65.7 | A few times a year |
|  | 27.0 | 21.7 | 18.3 | 25.0 | 17.9 | Never |
|  | (53) | (60) | (60) | (660) | (67) | Weighted N |

** Code distinction not made.

Figure 4.22
Does R Attend Church Weekly? by Religion of R

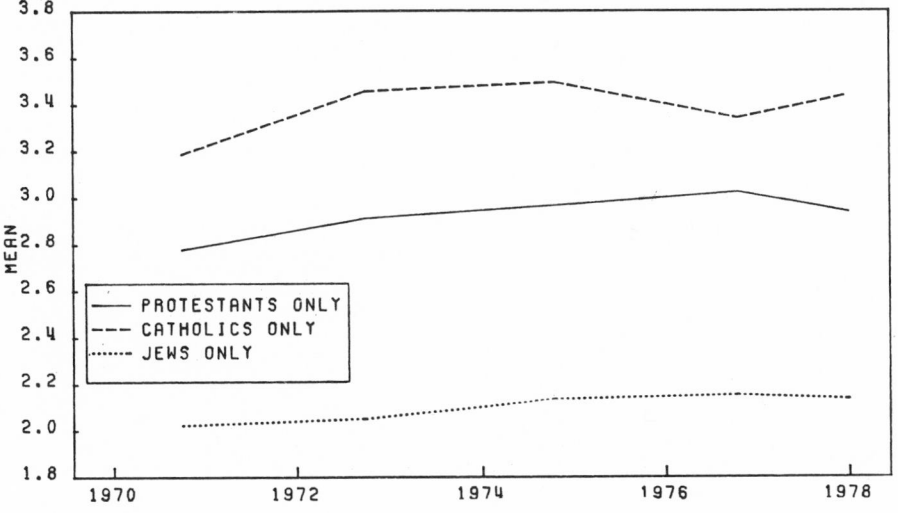

Family Living

Table 4.32
Does Household Member Carry Life Insurance?
Total Population

QUESTION: Do you (or any other member of your family) carry any life insurance (which you purchase yourself or which your employer provides as part of employment benefits)?

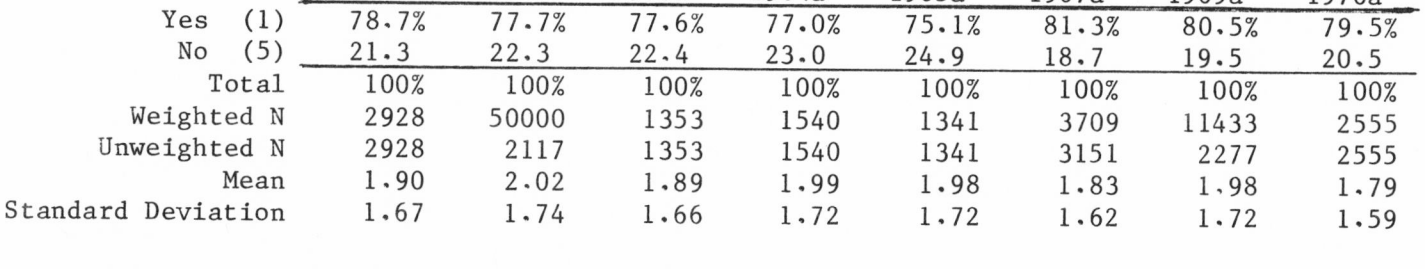

|  |  | Year |  |  |  |  |  |  |
|---|---|---|---|---|---|---|---|---|
|  |  | 1947a | 1948a | 1949a | 1950a | 1951a | 1952k | 1953a | 1957a |
| Yes | (1) | 78.7% | 77.7% | 77.6% | 77.0% | 75.1% | 81.3% | 80.5% | 79.5% |
| No | (5) | 21.3 | 22.3 | 22.4 | 23.0 | 24.9 | 18.7 | 19.5 | 20.5 |
| Total |  | 100% | 100% | 100% | 100% | 100% | 100% | 100% | 100% |
| Weighted N |  | 884659 | 873348 | 914300 | 99958 | 99856 | 926 | 90337 | 99827 |
| Unweighted N |  | 2712 | 3100 | 3210 | 3509 | 3410 | 926 | 2814 | 3036 |
| Mean |  | 1.85 | 1.89 | 1.90 | 1.92 | 1.99 | 1.75 | 1.78 | 1.82 |
| Standard Deviation |  | 1.64 | 1.66 | 1.67 | 1.68 | 1.73 | 1.56 | 1.58 | 1.61 |

Table 4.33

|  |  | 1960a | 1962a | 1963k | 1964a | 1965a | 1967a | 1969a | 1970a |
|---|---|---|---|---|---|---|---|---|---|
| Yes | (1) | 78.7% | 77.7% | 77.6% | 77.0% | 75.1% | 81.3% | 80.5% | 79.5% |
| No | (5) | 21.3 | 22.3 | 22.4 | 23.0 | 24.9 | 18.7 | 19.5 | 20.5 |
| Total |  | 100% | 100% | 100% | 100% | 100% | 100% | 100% | 100% |
| Weighted N |  | 2928 | 50000 | 1353 | 1540 | 1341 | 3709 | 11433 | 2555 |
| Unweighted N |  | 2928 | 2117 | 1353 | 1540 | 1341 | 3151 | 2277 | 2555 |
| Mean |  | 1.90 | 2.02 | 1.89 | 1.99 | 1.98 | 1.83 | 1.98 | 1.79 |
| Standard Deviation |  | 1.67 | 1.74 | 1.66 | 1.72 | 1.72 | 1.62 | 1.72 | 1.59 |

Figure 4.23
Does Household Member Carry Life Insurance?--Total Population

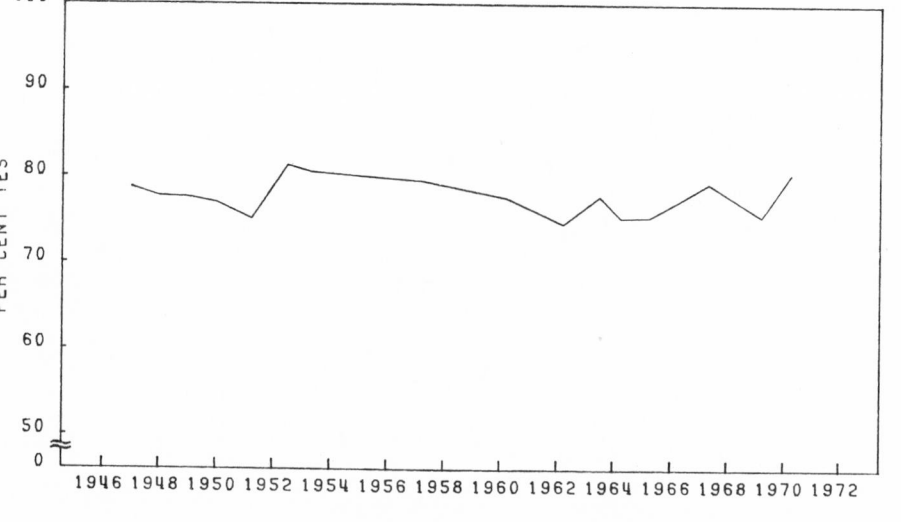

Table 4.34
Does Household Member Carry Life Insurance?
Sex of Respondent

% Yes

|  | | Year | | | | | | | |
|---|---|---|---|---|---|---|---|---|---|
|  | 1947a | 1948a | 1949a | 1950a | 1951a | 1952k | 1953a | 1957a | |
| Males Only | 80.1% | 79.3% | 78.3% | 79.2% | 76.9% | 82.9% | 82.3% | 81.8% | Yes |
|  | (596924) | (557987) | (553096) | (68705) | (63360) | (404) | (62772) | (65365) | Weighted N |
| Females Only | 75.7 | 74.9 | 76.4 | 72.1 | 71.1 | 80.1 | 76.5 | 74.9 | Yes |
|  | (287735) | (315361) | (361204) | (31096) | (33835) | (522) | (27565) | (33659) | Weighted N |

Table 4.35

|  | 1960a | 1962a | 1963k | 1964a | 1965a | 1967a | 1969a | 1970a | |
|---|---|---|---|---|---|---|---|---|---|
| Males Only | 81.7% | 79.0% | 80.2% | 78.6% | 80.1% | 83.1% | 81.9% | 84.4% | Yes |
|  | (1963) | (33010) | (581) | (1168) | (947) | (2809) | (8297) | (1846) | Weighted N |
| Females Only | 69.3 | 65.6 | 76.1 | 64.7 | 64.0 | 67.7 | 58.4 | 69.8 | Yes |
|  | (965) | (16642) | (769) | (368) | (394) | (900) | (3136) | (709) | Weighted N |

Sex coded for head of household and wife only in 1963k.

Table 4.36
Race of Respondent

% Yes

|  | 1947a | 1948a | 1949a | 1950a | 1951a | 1952k | 1953a | 1957a | |
|---|---|---|---|---|---|---|---|---|---|
| Whites Only | 78.7% | 77.9% | 78.3% | 77.4% | 76.4% | 82.4% | 81.4% | 80.6% | Yes |
|  | (812987) | (799845) | (837114) | (92201) | (90294) | (822) | (82122) | (89517) | Weighted N |
| Blacks Only | 79.1 | 76.6 | 72.7 | 72.1 | 63.8 | 72.3 | 75.2 | 69.0 | Yes |
|  | (69410) | (80051) | (80451) | (6756) | (7834) | (94) | (9752) | (8867) | Weighted N |

Table 4.37

|  | 1960a | 1962a | 1963k | 1964a | 1965a | 1967a | 1969a | 1970a | |
|---|---|---|---|---|---|---|---|---|---|
| Whites Only | 78.7% | 75.2% | 79.2% | 77.2% | 76.9% | 80.7% | 76.6% | 81.6% | Yes |
|  | (2618) | (44252) | (1216) | (1355) | (1188) | (3260) | (10124) | (2247) | Weighted N |
| Blacks Only | 72.0 | 70.8 | 68.0 | 58.7 | 61.7 | 73.2 | 69.1 | 74.2 | Yes |
|  | (314) | (4964) | (103) | (138) | (120) | (366) | (1132) | (279) | Weighted N |

Table 4.38
Does Household Member Carry Life Insurance?
Education of Respondent

% Yes

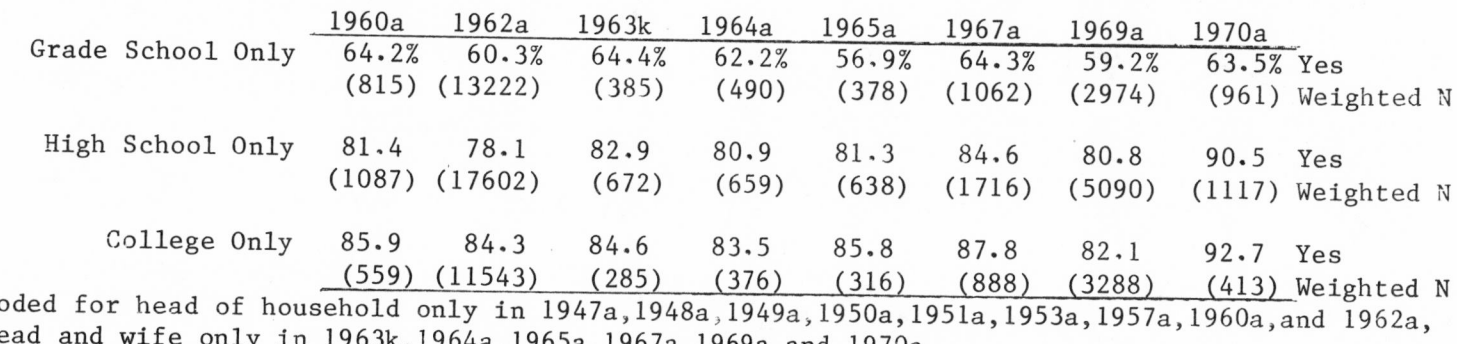

| | | | | Year | | | | |
|---|---|---|---|---|---|---|---|---|
| | 1947a | 1948a | 1949a | 1950a | 1951a | 1952k | 1953a | 1957a |
| Grade School Only | 68.9% | 66.7% | 68.8% | 70.1% | 64.1% | 72.1% | 69.3% | 68.2% Yes |
| | (322640) | (311067) | (301159) | (36871) | (34331) | (366) | (32250) | (28846) Weighted N |
| High School Only | 83.8 | 80.8 | 80.2 | 79.6 | 78.6 | 86.9 | 86.1 | 82.8 Yes |
| | (290662) | (277946) | (289402) | (33393) | (31091) | (375) | (31634) | (36056) Weighted N |
| College Only | 83.9 | 85.3 | 82.8 | 83.1 | 83.7 | 89.4 | 87.9 | 86.1 Yes |
| | (113418) | (122093) | (127050) | (14337) | (13898) | (180) | (15035) | (16620) Weighted N |

Table 4.39

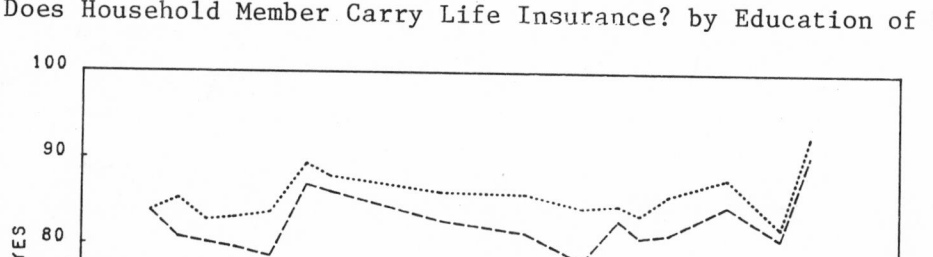

| | 1960a | 1962a | 1963k | 1964a | 1965a | 1967a | 1969a | 1970a |
|---|---|---|---|---|---|---|---|---|
| Grade School Only | 64.2% | 60.3% | 64.4% | 62.2% | 56.9% | 64.3% | 59.2% | 63.5% Yes |
| | (815) | (13222) | (385) | (490) | (378) | (1062) | (2974) | (961) Weighted N |
| High School Only | 81.4 | 78.1 | 82.9 | 80.9 | 81.3 | 84.6 | 80.8 | 90.5 Yes |
| | (1087) | (17602) | (672) | (659) | (638) | (1716) | (5090) | (1117) Weighted N |
| College Only | 85.9 | 84.3 | 84.6 | 83.5 | 85.8 | 87.8 | 82.1 | 92.7 Yes |
| | (559) | (11543) | (285) | (376) | (316) | (888) | (3288) | (413) Weighted N |

Education coded for head of household only in 1947a,1948a,1949a,1950a,1951a,1953a,1957a,1960a,and 1962a,
   and for head and wife only in 1963k,1964a,1965a,1967a,1969a,and 1970a.

Figure 4.24
Does Household Member Carry Life Insurance? by Education of R

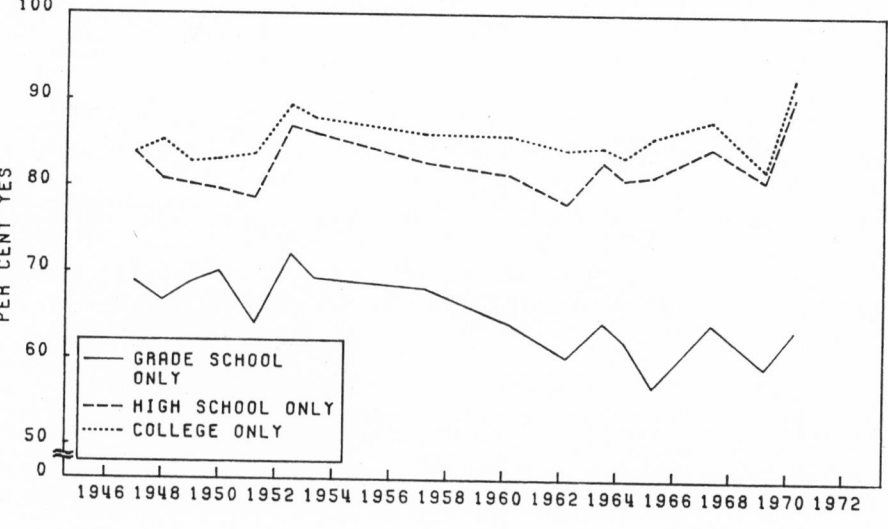

Table 4.40
Does Household Member Carry Life Insurance?
Age of Respondent

% Yes

| | | | | Year | | | | | |
|---|---|---|---|---|---|---|---|---|---|
| | 1947a | 1948a | 1949a | 1950a | 1951a | 1952k | 1953a | 1957a | |
| 18-24 Only | 73.0% | 72.7% | 75.1% | 68.1% | 71.1% | 81.1% | 75.6% | 70.2% | Yes |
| | (80551) | (85690) | (88986) | (9354) | (7654) | (53) | (8260) | (8906) | Weighted N |
| 25-34 Only | 82.6 | 85.1 | 80.7 | 82.6 | 82.9 | 88.7 | 88.4 | 87.1 | Yes |
| | (166535) | (155337) | (150514) | (19147) | (16522) | (231) | (18776) | (16272) | Weighted N |
| 35-44 Only | 83.7 | 84.0 | 81.2 | 84.8 | 83.0 | 87.9 | 86.2 | 85.8 | Yes |
| | (167518) | (153445) | (151051) | (18186) | (17480) | (248) | (16086) | (16644) | Weighted N |
| 45-54 Only | 79.4 | 78.2 | 80.3 | 80.1 | 73.9 | 82.5 | 81.3 | 83.5 | Yes |
| | (231534) | (128971) | (135962) | (15718) | (13889) | (160) | (14454) | (14831) | Weighted N |
| 55-64 Only | ** | 72.3 | 74.2 | 71.2 | 69.8 | 74.4 | 78.9 | 78.7 | Yes |
| | ** | (103314) | (107281) | (11621) | (12099) | (117) | (10665) | (11825) | Weighted N |
| 65 And Older Only | 49.9 | 44.3 | 53.7 | 54.2 | 48.9 | 57.5 | 55.8 | 55.7 | Yes |
| | (82410) | (84349) | (83817) | (10184) | (11486) | (113) | (10678) | (12446) | Weighted N |

Table 4.41

| | 1960a | 1962a | 1963k | 1964a | 1965a | 1967a | 1969a | 1970a | |
|---|---|---|---|---|---|---|---|---|---|
| 18-24 Only | 62.6% | 56.8% | 74.5% | 66.7% | 64.0% | 73.3% | 62.5% | 66.5% | Yes |
| | (203) | (4465) | (94) | (108) | (125) | (251) | (1092) | (239) | Weighted N |
| 25-34 Only | 83.0 | 83.8 | 80.3 | 79.5 | 77.6 | 86.3 | 86.8 | 83.9 | Yes |
| | (487) | (8046) | (228) | (263) | (245) | (665) | (2291) | (415) | Weighted N |
| 35-44 Only | 84.0 | 83.7 | 84.2 | 83.3 | 83.3 | 89.1 | 88.4 | 88.1 | Yes |
| | (545) | (9574) | (228) | (330) | (275) | (714) | (1971) | (438) | Weighted N |
| 45-54 Only | 83.0 | 80.0 | 84.7 | 84.8 | 85.5 | 84.4 | 83.7 | 88.4 | Yes |
| | (489) | (7781) | (170) | (315) | (248) | (710) | (1944) | (457) | Weighted N |
| 55-64 Only | 77.7 | 72.4 | 82.5 | 73.9 | 79.5 | 81.3 | 77.2 | 82.2 | Yes |
| | (372) | (5318) | (439) | (245) | (220) | (592) | (1759) | (371) | Weighted N |
| 65 And Older Only | 55.9 | 56.8 | 52.7 | 55.3 | 54.3 | 60.5 | 50.9 | 59.9 | Yes |
| | (379) | (7258) | (186) | (275) | (223) | (755) | (2316) | (384) | Weighted N |

** Code distinction not made.
Age group coded "45-64" in 1947a.
Age coded for head of household only in 1947a,1948a,1949a,1950a,1951a,1953a,1957a,1960a,and
   1962a, and for head and wife only in 1963k,1964a,1965a,1967a,1969a,and 1970a.

Table 4.42
Does Household Member Carry Life Insurance?
Income of Respondent

% Yes

|  | | | | Year | | | | | |
|---|---|---|---|---|---|---|---|---|---|
|  | 1947a | 1948a | 1949a | 1950a | 1951a | 1952k | 1953a | 1957a | |
| Income 1 (0-16%) | 52.8% | 42.8% | 53.4% | 47.7% | 43.2% | 42.9% | 61.2% | 49.0% | Yes |
|  | (145471) | (120058) | (139909) | (14131) | (12556) | (91) | (21999) | (20659) | Weighted N |
| Income 2 (17-33%) | 68.8 | 67.0 | 65.6 | 61.9 | 60.3 | 74.3 | 74.9 | 66.7 | Yes |
|  | (134643) | (139370) | (133500) | (18764) | (17322) | (261) | (14776) | (11924) | Weighted N |
| Income 3 (34-67%) | 82.8 | 82.7 | 81.0 | 84.1 | 78.8 | 88.3 | 87.5 | 87.7 | Yes |
|  | (304612) | (299557) | (340539) | (39408) | (37296) | (299) | (30464) | (38481) | Weighted N |
| Income 4 (68-95%) | 91.2 | 90.4 | 89.8 | 93.6 | 90.8 | 95.0 | 94.2 | 95.8 | Yes |
|  | (253058) | (247115) | (259345) | (21414) | (26132) | (200) | (20381) | (20692) | Weighted N |
| Income 5 (96-100%) | 92.3 | 91.8 | 92.3 | 92.9 | 93.6 | 100.0 | 90.1 | 95.9 | Yes |
|  | (46875) | (75104) | (48794) | (5072) | (5624) | (41) | (4254) | (8044) | Weighted N |

Table 4.43

|  | 1960a | 1962a | 1963k | 1964a | 1965a | 1967a | 1969a | 1970a | |
|---|---|---|---|---|---|---|---|---|---|
| Income 1 (0-16%) | 44.6% | 41.9% | 49.1% | 39.6% | 39.5% | 49.7% | 38.1% | 47.9% | Yes |
|  | (556) | (9059) | (320) | (225) | (172) | (726) | (2453) | (474) | Weighted N |
| Income 2 (17-33%) | 68.9 | 67.7 | 74.0 | 61.0 | 58.9 | 69.9 | 68.2 | 69.1 | Yes |
|  | (617) | (10001) | (208) | (254) | (224) | (555) | (2210) | (418) | Weighted N |
| Income 3 (34-67%) | 88.8 | 75.2 | 86.8 | 80.9 | 78.2 | 86.0 | 87.7 | 89.1 | Yes |
|  | (1127) | (11430) | (311) | (538) | (426) | (1422) | (3817) | (891) | Weighted N |
| Income 4 (68-95%) | 94.6 | 93.0 | 93.5 | 91.1 | 91.9 | 97.1 | 96.6 | 96.0 | Yes |
|  | (557) | (17668) | (370) | (448) | (421) | (694) | (2617) | (681) | Weighted N |
| Income 5 (96-100%) | 92.0 | 92.3 | 100.0 | 97.3 | 91.5 | 95.4 | 89.5 | 96.3 | Yes |
|  | (113) | (1842) | (81) | (75) | (106) | (324) | (420) | (109) | Weighted N |

## Chapter 5. Work And Retirement

The first item in this chapter involves a simple and relatively routine item concerning the respondent's job satisfaction asked of all employed persons During the past twenty-five years the overall distribution on this measure has shown remarkably little change although the final observations in 1975 and 1976 hint at some downturn in the degree of job satisfaction expressed.

The backbone of this chapter, and in some ways one of the most fascinating clusters of series in this whole volume is made up of a set of six characteristics which respondents have been asked to rank for personal importance to them in evaluating a job (tables 5.7-5.78). Although this battery of data begins only in 1958, the relative position of factors that concern people in their jobs has shown marked and majestic change in the intervening period, such that merged rankings for the total population have taken on a very different cast.

Across the six factors ranked, the most extreme change has been registered in the importance attached to the steadiness of the income the job supplies. Although a full six factors were available, over half of the employed population (56 percent) placed the steady income criterion at the top of the list in 1958. By 1974 less that one quarter (24 percent) of the respondents did so and a majority placed it third or lower. Nearly the same fate has befallen job security--the danger of being fired--as a criterion. While it was not as popular a response as income steadiness at the outset of the series, nearly half (over 44 percent) ranked this criterion at least as high as second, if not first, but the same proportion has dwindled to a mere 18 percent by the end of the series. Thus both security factors (job and income), which dominated the series in the late 1950s, have faded enormously in the interim. The fact that the first observation was drawn in 1958 at the time of a major recession when risk was salient, may have helped to exaggerate one's sense of change over this period. Nonetheless, the change has remained quite progressive even in the 1962-74 segment of the series and seems to be more than situational.

Since relative ranks are being asked for here, the vacuum created by the fading salience of security concerns must be filled by other criteria. Although some gains are registered by the infrequently cited criterion of a high and increasing income, the most noteworthy advance is registered by the criterion "Work is important, gives a feeling of accomplishment." It seems likely that this sea change from a concern with security to a demand for

challenge reflects the joint effects of the progressive obliteration of memories of the Great Depression and the rising tide of public affluence over the period monitored.

The remainder of the chapter is given over to more modest series involving such matters as job disability presumed job mobility, and questions concerning retirement. Some of these items show little change, although the question of retirement plans, asked only of household heads thirty-five years of age and older, captures the trend during the 1960s toward increasing hopes of early retirement (tables 5.90-5.95).

Table 5.1
How Satisfied Is R with Job?
Total Population

QUESTION: All things considered, how satisfied are you with your job? (How do you feel about your job?)

Employed Respondents

| | Year | | | | | | |
|---|---|---|---|---|---|---|---|
| | 1953m | 1957h | 1971j | 1973g | 1974q | 1975q | 1976h |
| Satisfied (5) | 80.1% | 77.6% | 79.4% | 80.8% | 80.1% | 77.5% | 74.1% |
| Neutral or Ambivalent (3) | 9.1 | 14.1 | 12.4 | 12.2 | 11.9 | 13.1 | 13.4 |
| Dissatisfied (1) | 6.9 | 8.3 | 8.2 | 7.0 | 7.8 | 9.4 | 12.5 |
| Don't Know/no feelings | 3.9 | ** | ** | ** | 0.2 | ** | ** |
| Total | 100% | 100% | 100% | 100% | 100% | 100% | 100% |
| Weighted N | 584 | 1361 | 5634 | 1587 | 1878 | 1535 | 2517 |
| Unweighted N | 584 | 1361 | 1231 | 725 | 929 | 786 | 1363 |
| Mean | 4.53 | 4.39 | 4.42 | 4.48 | 4.45 | 4.36 | 4.23 |
| Standard Deviation | 1.14 | 1.23 | 1.22 | 1.15 | 1.19 | 1.28 | 1.40 |

** Code distinction not made.

Figure 5.1
Satisfaction with Job--Total Population

SATISFIED
AMBIVALENT
DISSATISFIED
DON'T KNOW

1953M 1957H 1971J 1973G 1974Q 1975Q 1976H

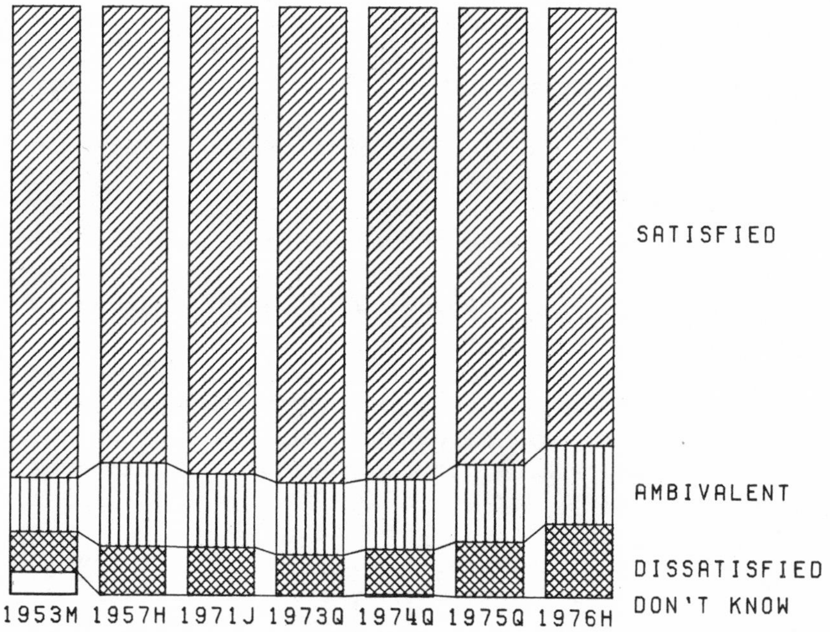

Table 5.2
How Satisfied Is R with Job?
Sex of Respondent

| | | | Year | | | | | |
|---|---|---|---|---|---|---|---|---|
| | 1953m | 1957h | 1971j | 1973q | 1974q | 1975q | 1976h | |
| Males Only | 82.6% | 76.7% | 79.4% | 80.6% | 79.7% | 75.4% | 75.2% | Satisfied |
| | 9.7 | 14.9 | 11.7 | 11.8 | 12.6 | 15.0 | 12.7 | Neutral or Ambivalent |
| | 7.7 | 8.3 | 8.9 | 7.6 | 7.7 | 9.6 | 12.1 | Dissatisfied |
| | (390) | (911) | (3550) | (991) | (1066) | (940) | (1463) | Weighted N |
| Females Only | 85.4 | 79.3 | 79.3 | 81.2 | 80.9 | 80.7 | 72.6 | Satisfied |
| | 8.8 | 12.4 | 13.6 | 12.8 | 11.1 | 10.1 | 14.3 | Neutral or Ambivalent |
| | 5.8 | 8.2 | 7.1 | 6.0 | 7.9 | 9.2 | 13.1 | Dissatisfied |
| | (171) | (450) | (2084) | (596) | (808) | (595) | (1054) | Weighted N |

Table 5.3
Race of Respondent

| | 1953m | 1957h | 1971j | 1973q | 1974q | 1975q | 1976h | |
|---|---|---|---|---|---|---|---|---|
| Whites Only | 83.4% | 77.7% | 80.9% | 82.6% | 80.6% | 78.3% | 74.3% | Satisfied |
| | 9.7 | 14.6 | 11.0 | 10.8 | 12.0 | 12.4 | 13.1 | Neutral or Ambivalent |
| | 6.8 | 7.7 | 8.1 | 6.6 | 7.5 | 9.3 | 12.6 | Dissatisfied |
| | (513) | (1195) | (4836) | (1399) | (1597) | (1348) | (2198) | Weighted N |
| Blacks Only | 82.2 | 73.7 | 68.8 | 67.6 | 79.1 | 75.5 | 71.0 | Satisfied |
| | 6.7 | 11.4 | 21.8 | 25.7 | 11.7 | 15.8 | 15.9 | Neutral or Ambivalent |
| | 11.1 | 14.9 | 9.4 | 6.6 | 9.2 | 8.6 | 13.1 | Dissatisfied |
| | (45) | (114) | (637) | (136) | (206) | (139) | (252) | Weighted N |

Table 5.4
How Satisfied Is R with Job?
Education of Respondent

|  | Year | | | | | | | |
|---|---|---|---|---|---|---|---|---|
|  | 1953m | 1957h | 1971j | 1973q | 1974q | 1975q | 1976h |  |
| Grade School Only | 83.2% | 79.8% | 78.9% | 79.9% | 77.8% | 80.3% | 77.9% | Satisfied |
|  | 9.5 | 12.4 | 13.0 | 11.8 | 10.8 | 9.6 | 11.3 | Neutral or Ambivalent |
|  | 7.4 | 7.8 | 8.1 | 8.3 | 11.3 | 10.2 | 10.8 | Dissatified |
|  | (190) | (396) | (844) | (169) | (194) | (157) | (204) | Weighted N |
| High School Only | 84.3 | 75.0 | 79.3 | 80.4 | 80.6 | 77.6 | 72.5 | Satisfied |
|  | 7.7 | 16.1 | 13.3 | 12.4 | 12.7 | 11.2 | 14.6 | Neutral or Ambivalent |
|  | 8.0 | 8.9 | 7.4 | 7.2 | 6.7 | 11.2 | 12.9 | Dissatified |
|  | (274) | (660) | (2973) | (895) | (905) | (805) | (1285) | Weighted N |
| College Only | 80.6 | 80.1 | 79.7 | 81.6 | 80.8 | 76.4 | 75.2 | Satisfied |
|  | 15.1 | 12.2 | 10.8 | 12.0 | 11.5 | 16.8 | 12.4 | Neutral or Ambivalent |
|  | 4.3 | 7.8 | 9.5 | 6.4 | 7.7 | 6.8 | 12.4 | Dissatified |
|  | (93) | (296) | (1800) | (516) | (766) | (572) | (1026) | Weighted N |

Work And Retirement

Table 5.5
How Satisfied Is R with Job?
Age of Respondent

|  | Year | | | | | | |  |
|---|---|---|---|---|---|---|---|---|
|  | 1953m | 1957h | 1971j | 1973q | 1974q | 1975q | 1976h |  |
| 18-24 Only | 95.2% | 68.8% | 72.1% | 74.7% | 68.7% | 65.8% | 57.3% | Satisfied |
|  | 0.0 | 17.5 | 13.8 | 13.4 | 19.8 | 11.1 | 20.3 | Neutral or Ambivalent |
|  | 4.8 | 13.8 | 14.1 | 11.9 | 11.5 | 23.1 | 22.4 | Dissatified |
|  | (21) | (80) | (970) | (328) | (348) | (234) | (281) | Weighted N |
| 25-34 Only | 79.9 | 75.6 | 76.8 | 76.2 | 77.2 | 73.4 | 73.0 | Satisfied |
|  | 9.4 | 14.9 | 13.2 | 17.1 | 14.7 | 17.0 | 13.4 | Neutral or Ambivalent |
|  | 10.8 | 9.5 | 10.1 | 6.7 | 8.1 | 9.5 | 13.6 | Dissatified |
|  | (139) | (348) | (1351) | (374) | (496) | (440) | (792) | Weighted N |
| 35-44 Only | 86.8 | 75.4 | 81.3 | 85.2 | 91.7 | 80.4 | 75.6 | Satisfied |
|  | 8.8 | 16.2 | 12.6 | 12.3 | 3.6 | 13.5 | 11.8 | Neutral or Ambivalent |
|  | 4.4 | 8.4 | 6.1 | 2.5 | 4.7 | 6.2 | 12.6 | Dissatified |
|  | (159) | (357) | (1192) | (325) | (362) | (341) | (508) | Weighted N |
| 45-54 Only | 83.5 | 79.2 | 79.4 | 83.7 | 81.0 | 83.6 | 81.0 | Satisfied |
|  | 11.3 | 13.8 | 14.1 | 7.5 | 12.8 | 12.2 | 9.6 | Neutral or Ambivalent |
|  | 5.2 | 7.1 | 6.5 | 8.7 | 6.3 | 4.2 | 9.4 | Dissatified |
|  | (115) | (312) | (1079) | (332) | (384) | (286) | (448) | Weighted N |
| 55-64 Only | 84.6 | 83.0 | 87.0 | 87.4 | 85.7 | 85.6 | 74.7 | Satisfied |
|  | 7.7 | 9.6 | 8.6 | 9.5 | 6.5 | 8.2 | 16.4 | Neutral or Ambivalent |
|  | 7.7 | 7.4 | 4.5 | 3.2 | 7.8 | 6.2 | 8.9 | Dissatified |
|  | (78) | (188) | (830) | (190) | (245) | (195) | (372) | Weighted N |
| 65-74 Only | 73.9 | 85.7 | 89.1 | 81.8 | 76.7 | 83.9 | 86.3 | Satisfied |
|  | 15.2 | 10.0 | 8.0 | 6.1 | 10.0 | 9.7 | 9.8 | Neutral or Ambivalent |
|  | 10.9 | 4.3 | 2.9 | 12.1 | 13.3 | 6.5 | 3.9 | Dissatified |
|  | (46) | (70) | (175) | (33) | (30) | (31) | (102) | Weighted N |
| 75 And Older Only | ** | ** | 100.0 | 100.0 | 66.7 | 100.0 | 90.9 | Satisfied |
|  | ** | ** | 0.0 | 0.0 | 0.0 | 0.0 | 0.0 | Neutral or Ambivalent |
|  | ** | ** | 0.0 | 0.0 | 33.3 | 0.0 | 9.1 | Dissatified |
|  | ** | ** | (32) | (2) | (3) | (3) | (11) | Weighted N |

** Code distinction not made.
Youngest age group coded "21-24" in 1953m and 1957h.
Oldest age group coded "65 And Older" in 1953m and 1957h.

Table 5.6
How Satisfied Is R with Job?
Income of Respondent

| | 1953m | 1957h | 1971j | 1973q | 1974q | 1975q | 1976h | |
|---|---|---|---|---|---|---|---|---|
| Income 1 (0-16%) | 70.8% | 80.9% | 72.2% | 68.8% | 66.4% | 77.6% | 80.4% | Satisfied |
| | 12.5 | 7.6 | 17.9 | 18.8 | 27.2 | 7.5 | 9.5 | Neutral or Ambivalent |
| | 16.7 | 11.5 | 9.9 | 12.5 | 6.4 | 15.0 | 10.1 | Dissatisfied |
| | (72) | (131) | (637) | (112) | (125) | (107) | (168) | Weighted N |
| Income 2 (17-33%) | 88.3 | 67.5 | 76.2 | 68.6 | 78.3 | 73.1 | 67.5 | Satisfied |
| | 7.8 | 18.8 | 15.0 | 26.4 | 13.2 | 15.9 | 17.0 | Neutral or Ambivalent |
| | 3.9 | 13.7 | 8.8 | 5.0 | 8.5 | 11.0 | 15.5 | Dissatisfied |
| | (77) | (117) | (1736) | (121) | (318) | (227) | (335) | Weighted N |
| Income 3 (34-67%) | 85.7 | 75.5 | 81.4 | 76.1 | 77.9 | 73.5 | 70.7 | Satisfied |
| | 10.3 | 16.4 | 11.5 | 13.2 | 12.6 | 14.4 | 14.7 | Neutral or Ambivalent |
| | 3.9 | 8.1 | 7.2 | 10.7 | 9.5 | 12.1 | 14.6 | Dissatisfied |
| | (203) | (603) | (2265) | (522) | (673) | (506) | (925) | Weighted N |
| Income 4 (68-95%) | 82.0 | 80.3 | 84.3 | 86.7 | 85.7 | 81.2 | 78.0 | Satisfied |
| | 9.0 | 13.0 | 10.7 | 9.0 | 7.9 | 13.7 | 12.8 | Neutral or Ambivalent |
| | 9.0 | 6.8 | 5.0 | 4.3 | 6.4 | 5.1 | 9.2 | Dissatisfied |
| | (167) | (370) | (560) | (611) | (482) | (431) | (806) | Weighted N |
| Income 5 (96-100%) | 93.1 | 85.5 | 89.7 | 93.7 | 97.1 | 90.6 | 83.2 | Satisfied |
| | 3.4 | 7.7 | 1.9 | 4.7 | 2.9 | 6.3 | 4.8 | Neutral or Ambivalent |
| | 3.4 | 6.8 | 8.4 | 1.6 | 0.0 | 3.1 | 12.0 | Dissatisfied |
| | (29) | (117) | (261) | (127) | (68) | (96) | (167) | Weighted N |

Figure 5.2
Satisfaction with Job by Income of R

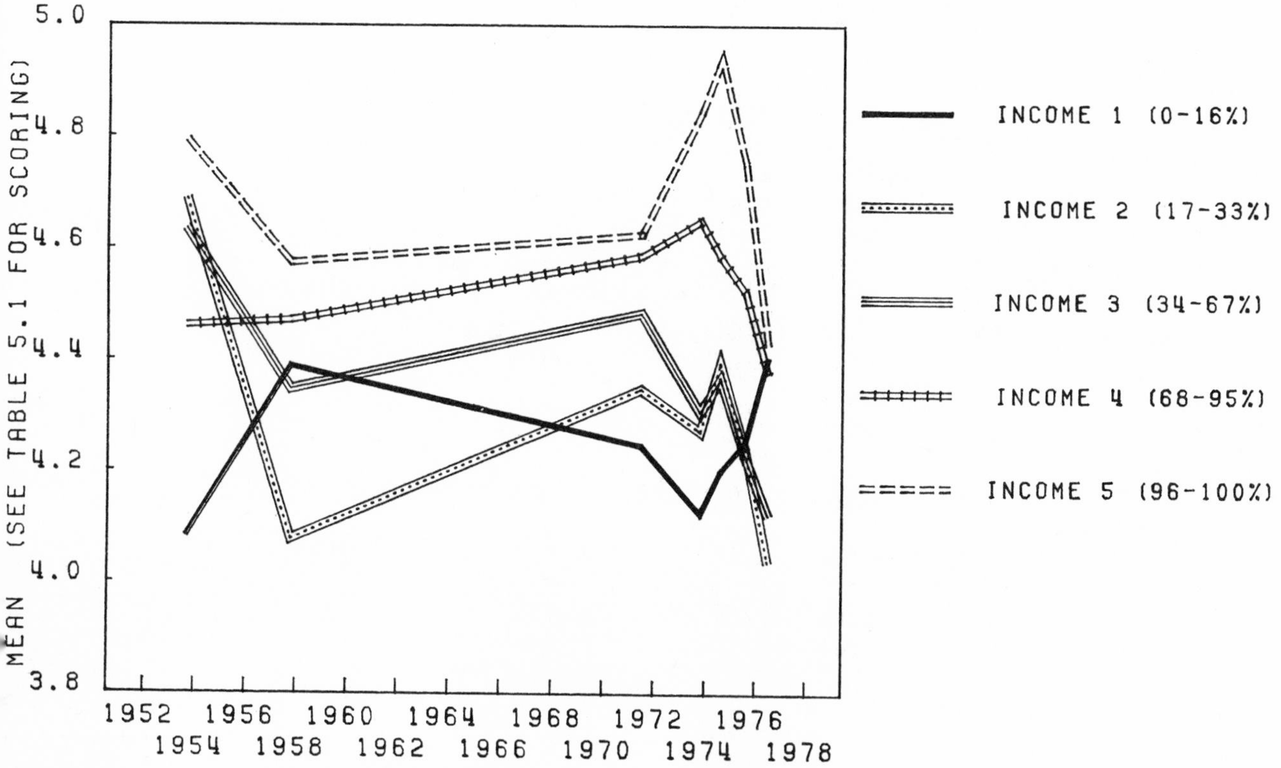

Work And Retirement

Table 5-7
Preference in a Job: Income Is Steady
Total Population--Employed and Unemployed Respondents

QUESTION. Would you look at this card and tell me which thing on this list about a job(occupation) you would most prefer, which comes next and so forth? (Would you please look at this card and tell me which things about your job you are most concerned about these days? Anything else? Of the things you mentioned, which is most important to you these days,which comes next and so forth?) (A) Income is steady (Maintaining a steady income), (B) Income is high (Increasing my income), (C) There's no danger of being fired or unemployed, (D) Working hours are short (Not working too long or too hard), (E) Chances for advancement are good, (F) The work is important, gives a feeling of accomplishment.

Employed Respondents

|  | | Year | | | | | | |
| --- | --- | 1958m | 1962k | 1963m | 1965b | 1966a | 1973q | 1974q |
| Ranked 1st | (5) | 55.6% | 43.7% | 42.5% | 44.6% | 35.0% | 25.3% | 24.2% |
| Ranked 2nd | (3) | 19.6 | 21.0 | 21.6 | 22.3 | 26.9 | 16.6 | 19.1 |
| Ranked 3rd to 6th/not ranked | (1) | 24.8 | 35 3 | 35.9 | 33.1 | 38.1 | 58.1 | 56.7 |
| Total | | 100% | 100% | 100% | 100% | 100% | 100% | 100% |
| Weighted N | | 576 | 510 | 529 | 1447 | 1694 | 1580 | 1753 |
| Unweighted N | | 576 | 510 | 529 | 1447 | 1694 | 797 | 868 |

Table 5-8

Unemployed Respondents

|  | | 1958m | 1962k | 1963m | 1965b | 1966a | 1973q | 1974q |
| --- | --- | --- | --- | --- | --- | --- | --- | --- |
| Ranked 1st | (5) | 60.2% | 52.1% | 47.9% | 50.2% | 34.0% | ** | ** |
| Ranked 2nd | (3) | 21.5 | 20.1 | 24.2 | 20.3 | 24.5 | ** | ** |
| Ranked 3rd to 6th/not ranked | (1) | 18.2 | 27.8 | 27.9 | 29.5 | 41.5 | ** | ** |
| Total | | 100% | 100% | 100% | 100% | 100% | ** | ** |
| Weighted N | | 181 | 234 | 240 | 508 | 94 | ** | ** |
| Unweighted N | | 181 | 234 | 240 | 508 | 94 | ** | ** |

** Data not available.
Question asked of head of households only in 1958m 1962k,1963m,1965b,and 1966a.

Table 5.9
Preference in a Job: Income Is Steady
Sex of Respondent

Employed Respondents

| | Year | | | | | | | |
|---|---|---|---|---|---|---|---|---|
| | 1958m | 1962k | 1963m | 1965b | 1966a | 1973q | 1974q | |
| Males Only | 54.0% | 43.0% | 40.7% | 45.1% | 35.0% | 27.1% | 26.8% | Ranked 1st |
| | 19.6 | 19.8 | 20.7 | 21.8 | 25.3 | 15.4 | 19.4 | Ranked 2nd |
| | 26.3 | 37.1 | 38.6 | 33.1 | 39.7 | 57.5 | 53.8 | Ranked 3rd to 6th/not ranked |
| | (448) | (388) | (415) | (1280) | (1437) | (988) | (1026) | Weighted N |
| Females Only | 60.9 | 46.3 | 49.1 | 40.4 | 34.9 | 22.1 | 20.5 | Ranked 1st |
| | 19.5 | 24.0 | 24.6 | 26.5 | 35.3 | 18.8 | 18.7 | Ranked 2nd |
| | 19.5 | 29.8 | 26.3 | 33.1 | 29.8 | 59.1 | 60.8 | Ranked 3rd to 6th/not ranked |
| | (128) | (121) | (114) | (166) | (255) | (592) | (727) | Weighted N |

Table 5.10

Unemployed Respondents

| | 1958m | 1962k | 1963m | 1965b | 1966a | 1973q | 1974q | |
|---|---|---|---|---|---|---|---|---|
| Males Only | 61.4% | 54.3% | 47.7% | 48.5% | 29.9% | ** | ** | Ranked 1st |
| | 22.7 | 15.2 | 22.5 | 20.7 | 27.3 | ** | ** | Ranked 2nd |
| | 15.9 | 30.5 | 29.7 | 30.8 | 42.9 | ** | ** | Ranked 3rd to 6th/not ranked |
| | (88) | (105) | (111) | (299) | (77) | ** | ** | Weighted N |
| Females Only | 59.1 | 50.0 | 48.1 | 52.6 | 52.9 | ** | ** | Ranked 1st |
| | 20.4 | 24.2 | 25.6 | 19.6 | 11.8 | ** | ** | Ranked 2nd |
| | 20.4 | 25.8 | 26.4 | 27.8 | 35.3 | ** | ** | Ranked 3rd to 6th/not ranked |
| | (93) | (128) | (129) | (209) | (17) | ** | ** | Weighted N |

** Data not available.

Table 5.11
Preference in a Job: Income Is Steady
Race of Respondent

Employed Respondents

|  | | Year | | | | | | |
|---|---|---|---|---|---|---|---|---|
|  | 1958m | 1962k | 1963m | 1965b | 1966a | 1973q | 1974q | |
| Whites Only | 54.9% | 42.1% | 43.2% | 44.9% | 34.2% | 24.9% | 25.6% | Ranked 1st |
|  | 19.9 | 21.4 | 21.3 | 22.1 | 27.0 | 17.2 | 19.1 | Ranked 2nd |
|  | 25.2 | 36.6 | 35.6 | 33.0 | 38.8 | 58.0 | 55.2 | Ranked 3rd to 6th/not ranked |
|  | (503) | (454) | (475) | (1283) | (1543) | (1396) | (1490) | Weighted N |
| Blacks Only | 59.7 | 60.4 | 35.6 | 43.3 | 43.3 | 25.0 | 15.3 | Ranked 1st |
|  | 16.4 | 18.8 | 22.2 | 22.4 | 27.5 | 10.6 | 16.8 | Ranked 2nd |
|  | 23.9 | 20.8 | 42.2 | 34.3 | 29.2 | 64.4 | 67.9 | Ranked 3rd to 6th/not ranked |
|  | (67) | (48) | (45) | (134) | (120) | (132) | (196) | Weighted N |

Table 5.12

Unemployed Respondents

|  | 1958m | 1962k | 1963m | 1965b | 1966a | 1973q | 1974q | |
|---|---|---|---|---|---|---|---|---|
| Whites Only | 60.8% | 53.8% | 49.0% | 51.1% | 34.8% | ** | ** | Ranked 1st |
|  | 19.6 | 19.2 | 25.5 | 20.0 | 23.2 | ** | ** | Ranked 2nd |
|  | 19.6 | 26.9 | 25.5 | 28.9 | 42.0 | ** | ** | Ranked 3rd to 6th/not ranked |
|  | (153) | (208) | (204) | (450) | (69) | ** | ** | Weighted N |
| Blacks Only | 52.0 | 34.8 | 41.2 | 47.9 | 33.3 | ** | ** | Ranked 1st |
|  | 36.0 | 26.1 | 17.6 | 20.8 | 29.2 | ** | ** | Ranked 2nd |
|  | 12.0 | 39.1 | 41.2 | 31.3 | 37.5 | ** | ** | Ranked 3rd to 6th/not ranked |
|  | (25) | (23) | (34) | (48) | (24) | ** | ** | Weighted N |

* Data not available.

Table 5.13
Preference in a Job: Income Is Steady
Education of Respondent

Employed Respondents

| | | | | Year | | | | |
|---|---|---|---|---|---|---|---|---|
| | 1958m | 1962k | 1963m | 1965b | 1966a | 1973q | 1974q | |
| Grade School Only | 62.4% | 53.7% | 51.4% | 57.8% | 51.3% | 35.9% | 28.7% | Ranked 1st |
| | 19.7 | 22.8 | 21.1 | 22.3 | 24.4 | 18.0 | 19.5 | Ranked 2nd |
| | 17.9 | 23.5 | 27.5 | 19.9 | 24.4 | 46.1 | 51.7 | Ranked 3rd to 6th/not ranked |
| | (173) | (136) | (109) | (332) | (349) | (167) | (174) | Weighted N |
| High School Only | 57.0 | 49.4 | 50.0 | 48.0 | 39.3 | 27.8 | 29.9 | Ranked 1st |
| | 20.1 | 19.5 | 20.5 | 22.7 | 28.2 | 18.5 | 17.8 | Ranked 2nd |
| | 22.9 | 31.2 | 29.5 | 29.3 | 32.5 | 53.6 | 52.3 | Ranked 3rd to 6th/not ranked |
| | (279) | (231) | (254) | (731) | (798) | (891) | (847) | Weighted N |
| College Only | 42.6 | 25.2 | 20.3 | 26.6 | 15.5 | 17.7 | 16.7 | Ranked 1st |
| | 18.9 | 21.7 | 21.7 | 21.6 | 24.7 | 13.0 | 20.6 | Ranked 2nd |
| | 38.5 | 53.1 | 58.0 | 51.8 | 59.8 | 69.3 | 62.7 | Ranked 3rd to 6th/not ranked |
| | (122) | (143) | (143) | (384) | (465) | (515) | (723) | Weighted N |

Table 5.14

Unemployed Respondents

| | 1958m | 1962k | 1963m | 1965b | 1966a | 1973q | 1974q | |
|---|---|---|---|---|---|---|---|---|
| Grade School Only | 68.4% | 51.9% | 54.3% | 53.0% | 25.7% | ** | ** | Ranked 1st |
| | 16.3 | 26.0 | 29.3 | 22.9 | 28.6 | ** | ** | Ranked 2nd |
| | 15.3 | 22.1 | 16.4 | 24.2 | 45.7 | ** | ** | Ranked 3rd to 6th/not ranked |
| | (98) | (104) | (116) | (236) | (35) | ** | ** | Weighted N |
| High School Only | 50.9 | 53.4 | 46.2 | 52.3 | 40.9 | ** | ** | Ranked 1st |
| | 28.3 | 21.6 | 19.2 | 15.7 | 22.7 | ** | ** | Ranked 2nd |
| | 20.8 | 25.0 | 34.6 | 32.0 | 36.4 | ** | ** | Ranked 3rd to 6th/not ranked |
| | (53) | (88) | (78) | (172) | (44) | ** | ** | Weighted N |
| College Only | 48.1 | 44.7 | 33.3 | 38.8 | 23.1 | ** | ** | Ranked 1st |
| | 25.9 | 2.6 | 20.0 | 22.4 | 23.1 | ** | ** | Ranked 2nd |
| | 25.9 | 52.6 | 46.7 | 38.8 | 53.8 | ** | ** | Ranked 3rd to 6th/not ranked |
| | (27) | (38) | (30) | (98) | (13) | ** | ** | Weighted N |

** Data not available.

Table 5.15
Preference in a Job: Income Is Steady
Age of Respondent

Employed Respondents

| | 1958m | 1962k | 1963m | 1965b | 1966a | 1973q | 1974q | |
|---|---|---|---|---|---|---|---|---|
| | | | | Year | | | | |
| 18-24 Only | 37.1% | 42.9% | 27.5% | 33.3% | 26.8% | 19.2% | 22.3% | Ranked 1st |
| | 37.1 | 14.3 | 20.0 | 12.0 | 27.7 | 16.2 | 19.0 | Ranked 2nd |
| | 25.7 | 42.9 | 52.5 | 54.7 | 45.5 | 64.6 | 58.8 | Ranked 3rd to 6th/not ranked |
| | (35) | (21) | (40) | (75) | (112) | (328) | (337) | Weighted N |
| 25-34 Only | 43.5 | 34.9 | 32.4 | 38.8 | 31.1 | 23.4 | 25.0 | Ranked 1st |
| | 21.8 | 24.6 | 23.1 | 20.1 | 22.7 | 17.2 | 17.3 | Ranked 2nd |
| | 34.7 | 40.5 | 44.4 | 41.1 | 46.2 | 59.4 | 57.7 | Ranked 3rd to 6th/not ranked |
| | (124) | (126) | (108) | (304) | (392) | (372) | (468) | Weighted N |
| 35-44 Only | 59.1 | 43.5 | 39.7 | 40.9 | 35.1 | 25.3 | 25.8 | Ranked 1st |
| | 16.2 | 20.3 | 17.4 | 25.8 | 25.1 | 16.7 | 15.5 | Ranked 2nd |
| | 24.7 | 36.2 | 43.0 | 33.2 | 39.8 | 58.0 | 58.7 | Ranked 3rd to 6th/not ranked |
| | (154) | (138) | (121) | (364) | (422) | (324) | (341) | Weighted N |
| 45-54 Only | 58.5 | 49.1 | 51.1 | 50.3 | 38.5 | 29.4 | 22.0 | Ranked 1st |
| | 20.8 | 16.4 | 27.0 | 22.7 | 27.7 | 12.7 | 22.3 | Ranked 2nd |
| | 20.8 | 34.5 | 21.9 | 27.0 | 33.8 | 57.9 | 55.8 | Ranked 3rd to 6th/not ranked |
| | (130) | (110) | (137) | (370) | (408) | (330) | (355) | Weighted N |
| 55-64 Only | 61.1 | 47.8 | 52.8 | 48.9 | 37.9 | 30.5 | 28.3 | Ranked 1st |
| | 15.8 | 21.1 | 19.1 | 24.6 | 33.2 | 22.6 | 21.7 | Ranked 2nd |
| | 23.2 | 31.1 | 28.1 | 26.5 | 28.9 | 46.8 | 50.0 | Ranked 3rd to 6th/not ranked |
| | (95) | (90) | (89) | (268) | (298) | (190) | (226) | Weighted N |
| 65-74 Only | 73.7 | 43.8 | 37.0 | 52.6 | 40.4 | 29.0 | 0.0 | Ranked 1st |
| | 15.8 | 37.5 | 22.2 | 14.0 | 23.4 | 22.6 | 36.8 | Ranked 2nd |
| | 10.5 | 18.8 | 40.7 | 33.3 | 36.2 | 48.4 | 63.2 | Ranked 3rd to 6th/not ranked |
| | (38) | (16) | (27) | (57) | (47) | (31) | (19) | Weighted N |
| 75 And Older Only | ** | 80.0 | 80.0 | 66.7 | 33.3 | 0.0 | 50.0 | Ranked 1st |
| | ** | 20.0 | 0.0 | 11.1 | 50.0 | 0.0 | 50.0 | Ranked 2nd |
| | ** | 0.0 | 20.0 | 22.2 | 16.7 | 100.0 | 0.0 | Ranked 3rd to 6th/not ranked |
| | ** | (5) | (5) | (9) | (6) | (2) | (2) | Weighted N |

** Code distinction not made.
Oldest age group coded "65 And Older" in 1958m.

Table 5.16
Preference in a Job: Income Is Steady
Age of Respondent

Unemployed Respondents

| | 1958m | 1962k | 1963m | 1965b | 1966a | 1973q | 1974q | |
|---|---|---|---|---|---|---|---|---|
| 18-24 Only | 25.0% | 30.0% | 15.4% | 30.0% | 28.6% | ** | ** | Ranked 1st |
| | 50.0 | 10.0 | 15.4 | 20.0 | 42.9 | ** | ** | Ranked 2nd |
| | 25.0 | 60.0 | 69.2 | 50.0 | 28.6 | ** | ** | Ranked 3rd to 6th/not ranked |
| | (4) | (10) | (13) | (40) | (7) | ** | ** | Weighted N |
| 25-34 Only | 35.3 | 37.5 | 40.0 | 42.1 | 33.3 | ** | ** | Ranked 1st |
| | 35.3 | 18.8 | 20.0 | 31.6 | 16.7 | ** | ** | Ranked 2nd |
| | 29.4 | 43.8 | 40.0 | 26.3 | 50.0 | ** | ** | Ranked 3rd to 6th/not ranked |
| | (17) | (16) | (15) | (19) | (12) | ** | ** | Weighted N |
| 35-44 Only | 76.5 | 43.8 | 46.7 | 39.3 | 50.0 | ** | ** | Ranked 1st |
| | 5.9 | 25.0 | 26.7 | 25.0 | 33.3 | ** | ** | Ranked 2nd |
| | 17.6 | 31.3 | 26.7 | 35.7 | 16.7 | ** | ** | Ranked 3rd to 6th/not ranked |
| | (17) | (16) | (15) | (28) | (12) | ** | ** | Weighted N |
| 45-54 Only | 41.2 | 34.8 | 58.8 | 55.6 | 28.6 | ** | ** | Ranked 1st |
| | 41.2 | 21.7 | 23.5 | 15.6 | 28.6 | ** | ** | Ranked 2nd |
| | 17.6 | 43.5 | 17.6 | 28.9 | 42.9 | ** | ** | Ranked 3rd to 6th/not ranked |
| | (17) | (23) | (17) | (45) | (28) | ** | ** | Weighted N |
| 55-64 Only | 52.4 | 63.0 | 51.4 | 45.1 | 47.4 | ** | ** | Ranked 1st |
| | 23.8 | 14.8 | 27.0 | 24.4 | 15.8 | ** | ** | Ranked 2nd |
| | 23.8 | 22.2 | 21.6 | 30.5 | 36.8 | ** | ** | Ranked 3rd to 6th/not ranked |
| | (21) | (27) | (37) | (82) | (19) | ** | ** | Weighted N |
| 65-74 Only | 67.6 | 57.0 | 47.4 | 56.8 | 18.2 | ** | ** | Ranked 1st |
| | 17.1 | 17.4 | 25.0 | 15.1 | 18.2 | ** | ** | Ranked 2nd |
| | 15.2 | 25.6 | 27.6 | 28.1 | 63.6 | ** | ** | Ranked 3rd to 6th/not ranked |
| | (105) | (86) | (76) | (185) | (11) | ** | ** | Weighted N |
| 75 And Older Only | ** | 58.5 | 53.2 | 52.3 | 0.0 | ** | ** | Ranked 1st |
| | ** | 28.3 | 24.2 | 24.8 | 33.3 | ** | ** | Ranked 2nd |
| | ** | 13.2 | 22.6 | 22.9 | 66.7 | ** | ** | Ranked 3rd to 6th/not ranked |
| | ** | (53) | (62) | (109) | (3) | ** | ** | Weighted N |

** Data not available in 1973q and 1974q.
** Code distinction not made in 1958m--oldest age group coded "65 And Older".

Table 5.17
Preference in a Job: Income Is Steady
Income of Respondent

Employed Respondents

|  | Year | | | | | | | |
|---|---|---|---|---|---|---|---|---|
|  | 1958m | 1962k | 1963m | 1965b | 1966a | 1973q | 1974q | |
| Income 1 (0-16%) | 60.7% | 52.8% | 47.8% | 48.4% | 45.3% | 27.3% | 22.9% | Ranked 1st |
|  | 21.3 | 22.2 | 30.4 | 18.8 | 24.2 | 18.2 | 13.6 | Ranked 2nd |
|  | 18.0 | 25.0 | 21.7 | 32.8 | 30.5 | 54.5 | 63.6 | Ranked 3rd to 6th/not ranked |
|  | (61) | (36) | (23) | (64) | (128) | (110) | (118) | Weighted N |
| Income 2 (17-33%) | 63.2 | 46.1 | 41.1 | 50.6 | 41.4 | 26.0 | 28.8 | Ranked 1st |
|  | 20.6 | 22.4 | 26.0 | 22.0 | 26.4 | 14.5 | 17.4 | Ranked 2nd |
|  | 16.2 | 31.6 | 32.9 | 27.4 | 32.2 | 59.5 | 53.8 | Ranked 3rd to 6th/not ranked |
|  | (68) | (76) | (73) | (164) | (292) | (131) | (299) | Weighted N |
| Income 3 (34-67%) | 56.7 | 48.9 | 47.9 | 51.5 | 38.9 | 32.5 | 27.5 | Ranked 1st |
|  | 20.6 | 21.8 | 20.6 | 21.4 | 28.9 | 17.4 | 17.0 | Ranked 2nd |
|  | 22.7 | 29.3 | 31.4 | 27.1 | 32.2 | 50.1 | 55.5 | Ranked 3rd to 6th/not ranked |
|  | (233) | (225) | (194) | (538) | (696) | (517) | (625) | Weighted N |
| Income 4 (68-95%) | 51.4 | 35.9 | 38.3 | 39.5 | 27.3 | 21.4 | 20.8 | Ranked 1st |
|  | 16.2 | 16.9 | 20.6 | 22.9 | 27.3 | 17.2 | 21.4 | Ranked 2nd |
|  | 32.4 | 47.2 | 41.1 | 37.5 | 45.3 | 61.4 | 57.8 | Ranked 3rd to 6th/not ranked |
|  | (148) | (142) | (180) | (597) | (450) | (611) | (462) | Weighted N |
| Income 5 (96-100%) | 49.1 | 20.8 | 31.0 | 21.4 | 15.0 | 14.4 | 13.6 | Ranked 1st |
|  | 22.6 | 29.2 | 19.0 | 27.4 | 18.1 | 17.6 | 13.6 | Ranked 2nd |
|  | 28.3 | 50.0 | 50.0 | 51.2 | 66.9 | 68.0 | 72.7 | Ranked 3rd to 6th/not ranked |
|  | (53) | (24) | (42) | (84) | (127) | (125) | (66) | Weighted N |

Figure 5.3
Steady Income by Income of Employed R

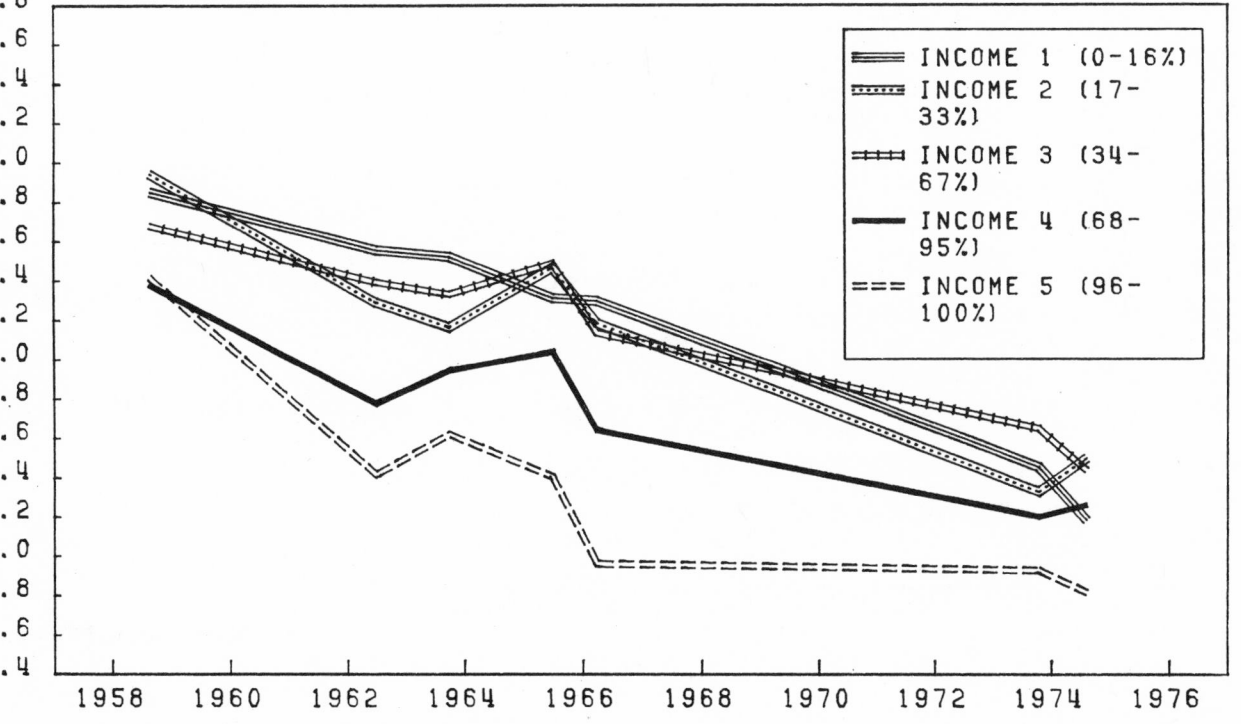

Work And Retirement

Table 5.18
Preference in a Job  Income Is Steady
Income of Respondent

Unemployed Respondents

| | 1958m | 1962k | 1963m | 1965b | 1966a | 1973q | 1974q | |
|---|---|---|---|---|---|---|---|---|
| Income 1 (0-16%) | 63.2% | 48.4% | 55.1% | 46.7% | 50.0% | ** | ** | Ranked 1st |
| | 23.0 | 22.1 | 18.7 | 22.1 | 22.7 | ** | ** | Ranked 2nd |
| | 13.8 | 29.5 | 26.2 | 31.2 | 27.3 | ** | ** | Ranked 3rd to 6th/not ranked |
| | (87) | (95) | (107) | (199) | (22) | ** | ** | Weighted N |
| | | | | | | | | |
| Income 2 (17-33%) | 58.1 | 50.7 | 41.7 | 56.9 | 23.1 | ** | ** | Ranked 1st |
| | 19.4 | 23.9 | 28.3 | 19.0 | 38.5 | ** | ** | Ranked 2nd |
| | 22.6 | 25.4 | 30.0 | 24.1 | 38.5 | ** | ** | Ranked 3rd to 6th/not ranked |
| | (31) | (71) | (60) | (137) | (26) | ** | ** | Weighted N |
| | | | | | | | | |
| Income 3 (34-67%) | 56.8 | 64.1 | 58.3 | 51.3 | 40.6 | ** | ** | Ranked 1st |
| | 13.5 | 15.4 | 25.0 | 17.1 | 12.5 | ** | ** | Ranked 2nd |
| | 29.7 | 20.5 | 16.7 | 31.6 | 46.9 | ** | ** | Ranked 3rd to 6th/not ranked |
| | (37) | (39) | (36) | (117) | (32) | ** | ** | Weighted N |
| | | | | | | | | |
| Income 4 (68-95%) | 53.8 | 50.0 | 33.3 | 41.3 | 22.2 | ** | ** | Ranked 1st |
| | 38.5 | 10.0 | 20.0 | 23.9 | 22.2 | ** | ** | Ranked 2nd |
| | 7.7 | 40.0 | 46.7 | 34.8 | 55.6 | ** | ** | Ranked 3rd to 6th/not ranked |
| | (13) | (10) | (15) | (46) | (9) | ** | ** | Weighted N |
| | | | | | | | | |
| Income 5 (96-100%) | 66.7 | 66.7 | 0.0 | 55.6 | 0.0 | ** | ** | Ranked 1st |
| | 33.3 | 0.0 | 50.0 | 22.2 | 40.0 | ** | ** | Ranked 2nd |
| | 0.0 | 33.3 | 50.0 | 22.2 | 60.0 | ** | ** | Ranked 3rd to 6th/not ranked |
| | (3) | (6) | (2) | (9) | (5) | ** | ** | Weighted N |

* Data not available.

Table 5.19
Preference in a Job: Income Is High, Increasing
Total Population--Employed and Unemployed Respondents

Employed Respondents

| | | Year | | | | | | |
|---|---|---|---|---|---|---|---|---|
| | | 1958m | 1962k | 1963m | 1965b | 1966a | 1973q | 1974q |
| Ranked 1st | (5) | 6.0% | 10.2% | 8.0% | 10.5% | 8.9% | 15.3% | 17.9% |
| Ranked 2nd | (3) | 13.9 | 14.7 | 15.5 | 14.1 | 16.8 | 21.4 | 17.9 |
| Ranked 3rd-6th/not ranked | (1) | 80.2 | 75.1 | 76.5 | 75.4 | 74.3 | 63.4 | 64.2 |
| Total | | 100% | 100% | 100% | 100% | 100% | 100% | 100% |
| Weighted N | | 570 | 502 | 528 | 1426 | 1669 | 1580 | 1753 |
| Unweighted N | | 570 | 502 | 528 | 1426 | 1669 | 797 | 868 |

Table 5.20

Unemployed Respondents

| | | 1958m | 1962k | 1963m | 1965b | 1966a | 1973q | 1974q |
|---|---|---|---|---|---|---|---|---|
| Ranked 1st | (5) | 3.6% | 8.4% | 6.8% | 9.2% | 10.8% | ** | ** |
| Ranked 2nd | (3) | 11.2 | 14.6 | 9.7 | 10.0 | 15.1 | ** | ** |
| Ranked 3rd-6th/not ranked | (1) | 85.2 | 77.0 | 83.5 | 80.8 | 74.2 | ** | ** |
| Total | | 100% | 100% | 100% | 100% | 100% | ** | ** |
| Weighted N | | 169 | 226 | 237 | 499 | 93 | ** | ** |
| Unweighted N | | 169 | 226 | 237 | 499 | 93 | ** | ** |

** Data not available.
Question asked of head of households only in 1958m,1962k,1963m,1965b,and 1966a.

Table 5.21

Preference in a Job: Income Is High, Increasing
Sex of Respondent

Employed Respondents

| | | | | Year | | | | |
|---|---|---|---|---|---|---|---|---|
| | 1958m | 1962k | 1963m | 1965b | 1966a | 1973q | 1974q | |
| Males Only | 6.6% | 10.4% | 8.7% | 10.4% | 9.4% | 15.5% | 18.7% | Ranked 1st |
| | 15.4 | 14.4 | 15.2 | 14.0 | 17.0 | 22.3 | 17.6 | Ranked 2nd |
| | 78.0 | 75 2 | 76.1 | 75.6 | 73.6 | 62.2 | 63.6 | Ranked 3rd-6th/not ranked |
| | (441) | (383) | (414) | (1261) | (1416) | (988) | (1026) | Weighted N |
| Females Only | 3.9 | 8.5 | 5.3 | 11.6 | 6.4 | 14.9 | 16.6 | Ranked 1st |
| | 8.5 | 16.1 | 16.7 | 14.6 | 15.5 | 19.9 | 18.3 | Ranked 2nd |
| | 87.6 | 75.4 | 78.1 | 73.8 | 78.1 | 65.2 | 65.1 | Ranked 3rd-6th/not ranked |
| | (129) | (118) | (114) | (164) | (251) | (592) | (727) | Weighted N |

Table 5.22

Unemployed Respondents

| | 1958m | 1962k | 1963m | 1965b | 1966a | 1973q | 1974q | |
|---|---|---|---|---|---|---|---|---|
| Males Only | 2.4% | 8.9% | 10.1% | 10.1% | 13.2% | ** | ** | Ranked 1st |
| | 8.5 | 16.8 | 12.8 | 10.8 | 17.1 | ** | ** | Ranked 2nd |
| | 89.0 | 74.3 | 77.1 | 79.1 | 69.7 | ** | ** | Ranked 3rd-6th/not ranked |
| | (82) | (101) | (109) | (296) | (76) | ** | ** | Weighted N |
| Females Only | 4.6 | 8.1 | 3.9 | 7.9 | 0.0 | ** | ** | Ranked 1st |
| | 13.8 | 12.1 | 7.0 | 8.9 | 5.9 | ** | ** | Ranked 2nd |
| | 81.6 | 79.8 | 89.1 | 83.3 | 94.1 | ** | ** | Ranked 3rd-6th/not ranked |
| | (87) | (124) | (128) | (203) | (17) | ** | ** | Weighted N |

** Data not available.

Table 5.23
Preference in a Job: Income Is High, Increasing
Race of Respondent

Employed Respondents

| | 1958m | 1962k | 1963m | 1965b | 1966a | 1973q | 1974q | |
|---|---|---|---|---|---|---|---|---|
| Whites Only | 6.2% | 8.7% | 7.4% | 10.0% | 8.6% | 14.7% | 16.6% | Ranked 1st |
| | 13.3 | 13.4 | 15.2 | 13.5 | 16.5 | 20.7 | 17.2 | Ranked 2nd |
| | 80.5 | 78.0 | 77.4 | 76.5 | 74.9 | 64.6 | 66.2 | Ranked 3rd-6th/not ranked |
| | (497) | (449) | (474) | (1265) | (1520) | (1396) | (1490) | Weighted N |
| Blacks Only | 3.0 | 22.2 | 15.6 | 17.3 | 11.8 | 22.0 | 26.0 | Ranked 1st |
| | 17.9 | 31.1 | 22.2 | 21.1 | 21.0 | 21.2 | 26.0 | Ranked 2nd |
| | 79.1 | 46.7 | 62.2 | 61.7 | 67.2 | 56.8 | 48.0 | Ranked 3rd-6th/not ranked |
| | (67) | (45) | (45) | (133) | (119) | (132) | (196) | Weighted N |

Table 5.24

Unemployed Respondents

| | 1958m | 1962k | 1963m | 1965b | 1966a | 1973q | 1974q | |
|---|---|---|---|---|---|---|---|---|
| Whites Only | 2.8% | 7.0% | 5.9% | 8.4% | 4.4% | ** | ** | Ranked 1st |
| | 12.1 | 13.9 | 8.9 | 9.3 | 19.1 | ** | ** | Ranked 2nd |
| | 85.1 | 79.1 | 85.2 | 82.3 | 76.5 | ** | ** | Ranked 3rd-6th/not ranked |
| | (141) | (201) | (203) | (441) | (68) | ** | ** | Weighted N |
| Blacks Only | 8.0 | 22.7 | 12.5 | 16.7 | 29.2 | ** | ** | Ranked 1st |
| | 4.0 | 22.7 | 15.6 | 16.7 | 4.2 | ** | ** | Ranked 2nd |
| | 88.0 | 54.5 | 71.9 | 66.7 | 66.7 | ** | ** | Ranked 3rd-6th/not ranked |
| | (25) | (22) | (32) | (48) | (24) | ** | ** | Weighted N |

** Data not available.

Table 5.25
Preference in a Job: Income Is High, Increasing
Education of Respondent

Employed Respondents

|  | | | | Year | | | | |
|---|---|---|---|---|---|---|---|---|
|  | 1958m | 1962k | 1963m | 1965b | 1966a | 1973q | 1974q | |
| Grade School Only | 6.4% | 13.3% | 5.6% | 10.6% | 9.5% | 9.0% | 21.3% | Ranked 1st |
|  | 14.5 | 18.5 | 20.4 | 17.7 | 12.5 | 26.9 | 23.0 | Ranked 2nd |
|  | 79.2 | 68.1 | 74.1 | 71.7 | 78.0 | 64.1 | 55.7 | Ranked 3rd-6th/not ranked |
|  | (173) | (135) | (108) | (322) | (336) | (167) | (174) | Weighted N |
| High School Only | 6.9 | 10.1 | 8.3 | 9.3 | 8.1 | 16.5 | 17.4 | Ranked 1st |
|  | 11.3 | 13.2 | 13.8 | 13.5 | 18.1 | 19.4 | 18.8 | Ranked 2nd |
|  | 81.8 | 76.7 | 78.0 | 77.2 | 73.7 | 64.1 | 63.9 | Ranked 3rd-6th/not ranked |
|  | (274) | (227) | (254) | (724) | (788) | (891) | (847) | Weighted N |
| College Only | 3.3 | 7.1 | 8.4 | 12.9 | 9.7 | 15.3 | 17.3 | Ranked 1st |
|  | 19.0 | 13.6 | 16.1 | 12.1 | 17.9 | 23.3 | 15.2 | Ranked 2nd |
|  | 77.7 | 79.3 | 75.5 | 75.0 | 72.4 | 61.4 | 67.5 | Ranked 3rd-6th/not ranked |
|  | (121) | (140) | (143) | (380) | (464) | (515) | (723) | Weighted N |

Table 5.26

Unemployed Respondents

|  | 1958m | 1962k | 1963m | 1965b | 1966a | 1973q | 1974q | |
|---|---|---|---|---|---|---|---|---|
| Grade School Only | 4.5% | 11.3% | 7.1% | 11.6% | 8.6% | ** | ** | Ranked 1st |
|  | 9.0 | 14.4 | 10.6 | 12.4 | 17.1 | ** | ** | Ranked 2nd |
|  | 86.5 | 74.2 | 82.3 | 76.0 | 74.3 | ** | ** | Ranked 3rd-6th/not ranked |
|  | (89) | (97) | (113) | (233) | (35) | ** | ** | Weighted N |
| High School Only | 3.9 | 4.7 | 7.7 | 8.3 | 9.3 | ** | ** | Ranked 1st |
|  | 11.8 | 16.3 | 10.3 | 6.5 | 9.3 | ** | ** | Ranked 2nd |
|  | 84.3 | 79.1 | 82.1 | 85.1 | 81.4 | ** | ** | Ranked 3rd-6th/not ranked |
|  | (51) | (86) | (78) | (168) | (43) | ** | ** | Weighted N |
| College Only | 0.0 | 10.3 | 3.3 | 5.2 | 23.1 | ** | ** | Ranked 1st |
|  | 19.2 | 10.3 | 3.3 | 10.4 | 30.8 | ** | ** | Ranked 2nd |
|  | 80.8 | 79.5 | 93.3 | 84.4 | 46.2 | ** | ** | Ranked 3rd-6th/not ranked |
|  | (26) | (39) | (30) | (96) | (13) | ** | ** | Weighted N |

** Data not available.

Table 5.27
Preference in a Job: Income Is High, Increasing
Age of Respondent

Employed Respondents

| | | | | Year | | | | |
|---|---|---|---|---|---|---|---|---|
| | 1958m | 1962k | 1963m | 1965b | 1966a | 1973q | 1974q | |
| 18-24 Only | 11.4% | 4.8% | 10.0% | 9.3% | 7.1% | 14.0% | 16.0% | Ranked 1st |
| | 17.1 | 9.5 | 17.5 | 17.3 | 16.1 | 18.0 | 20.2 | Ranked 2nd |
| | 71.4 | 85.7 | 72.5 | 73.3 | 76.8 | 68.0 | 63.8 | Ranked 3rd-6th/not ranked |
| | (35) | (21) | (40) | (75) | (112) | (328) | (337) | Weighted N |
| | | | | | | | | |
| 25-34 Only | 8.8 | 13.6 | 8.3 | 15.2 | 11.3 | 17.7 | 20.5 | Ranked 1st |
| | 18.4 | 10.4 | 17.6 | 15.2 | 18.4 | 21.0 | 18.2 | Ranked 2nd |
| | 72.8 | 76.0 | 74.1 | 69.5 | 70.3 | 61.3 | 61.3 | Ranked 3rd-6th/not ranked |
| | (125) | (125) | (108) | (302) | (391) | (372) | (468) | Weighted N |
| | | | | | | | | |
| 35-44 Only | 4.6 | 11.7 | 8.3 | 13.6 | 11.2 | 17.9 | 18.5 | Ranked 1st |
| | 12.5 | 21.2 | 13.2 | 13.6 | 20.3 | 17.9 | 18.8 | Ranked 2nd |
| | 82.9 | 67.2 | 78.5 | 72.9 | 68.5 | 64.2 | 62.8 | Ranked 3rd-6th/not ranked |
| | (152) | (137) | (121) | (361) | (419) | (324) | (341) | Weighted N |
| | | | | | | | | |
| 45-54 Only | 5.4 | 10.2 | 9.4 | 7.5 | 7.1 | 15.5 | 16.6 | Ranked 1st |
| | 12.4 | 14.8 | 15.2 | 14.4 | 15.5 | 26.4 | 15.5 | Ranked 2nd |
| | 82.2 | 75.0 | 75.4 | 78.2 | 77.4 | 58.2 | 67.9 | Ranked 3rd-6th/not ranked |
| | (129) | (108) | (138) | (362) | (394) | (330) | (355) | Weighted N |
| | | | | | | | | |
| 55-64 Only | 5.5 | 5.7 | 3.4 | 6.4 | 6.1 | 8.4 | 17.7 | Ranked 1st |
| | 9.9 | 13.8 | 17.2 | 12.1 | 11.2 | 26.8 | 17.3 | Ranked 2nd |
| | 84.6 | 80.5 | 79.3 | 81.5 | 82.7 | 64.7 | 65.0 | Ranked 3rd-6th/not ranked |
| | (91) | (87) | (87) | (265) | (294) | (190) | (226) | Weighted N |
| | | | | | | | | |
| 65-74 Only | 0.0 | 0.0 | 11.1 | 7.5 | 4.5 | 12.9 | 0.0 | Ranked 1st |
| | 15.8 | 13.3 | 14.8 | 15.1 | 22.7 | 12.9 | 15.8 | Ranked 2nd |
| | 84.2 | 86.7 | 74.1 | 77.4 | 72.7 | 74.2 | 84.2 | Ranked 3rd-6th/not ranked |
| | (38) | (15) | (27) | (53) | (44) | (31) | (19) | Weighted N |
| | | | | | | | | |
| 75 And Older Only | ** | 0.0 | 0.0 | 0.0 | 0.0 | 0.0 | 0.0 | Ranked 1st |
| | ** | 0.0 | 0.0 | 12.5 | 16.7 | 0.0 | 0.0 | Ranked 2nd |
| | ** | 100.0 | 100.0 | 87.5 | 83.3 | 100.0 | 100.0 | Ranked 3rd-6th/not ranked |
| | ** | (5) | (5) | (8) | (6) | (2) | (2) | Weighted N |

** Code distinction not made.
Oldest age group coded "65 And Older" in 1958m.

Table 5.28
Preference in a Job: Income Is High, Increasing
Age of Respondent

| Unemployed Respondents | Year | | | | | | | |
|---|---|---|---|---|---|---|---|---|
| | 1958m | 1962k | 1963m | 1965b | 1966a | 1973q | 1974q | |
| 18-24 Only | 0.0% | 20.0% | 15.4% | 12.5% | 0.0% | ** | ** | Ranked 1st |
| | 0.0 | 10.0 | 0.0 | 10.0 | 14.3 | ** | ** | Ranked 2nd |
| | 100.0 | 70.0 | 84.6 | 77.5 | 85.7 | ** | ** | Ranked 3rd-6th/not ranked |
| | (4) | (10) | (13) | (40) | (7) | ** | ** | Weighted N |
| 25-34 Only | 5.9 | 18.8 | 26.7 | 15.8 | 16.7 | ** | ** | Ranked 1st |
| | 23.5 | 18.8 | 0.0 | 10.5 | 25.0 | ** | ** | Ranked 2nd |
| | 70.6 | 62.5 | 73.3 | 73.7 | 58.3 | ** | ** | Ranked 3rd-6th/not ranked |
| | (17) | (16) | (15) | (19) | (12) | ** | ** | Weighted N |
| 35-44 Only | 6.3 | 0.0 | 6.7 | 3.6 | 16.7 | ** | ** | Ranked 1st |
| | 12.5 | 12.5 | 20.0 | 7.1 | 8.3 | ** | ** | Ranked 2nd |
| | 81.3 | 87.5 | 73.3 | 89.3 | 75.0 | ** | ** | Ranked 3rd-6th/not ranked |
| | (16) | (16) | (15) | (28) | (12) | ** | ** | Weighted N |
| 45-54 Only | 5.9 | 8.7 | 0.0 | 13.3 | 17.9 | ** | ** | Ranked 1st |
| | 17.6 | 21.7 | 11.8 | 13.3 | 21.4 | ** | ** | Ranked 2nd |
| | 76.5 | 69.6 | 88.2 | 73.3 | 60.7 | ** | ** | Ranked 3rd-6th/not ranked |
| | (17) | (23) | (17) | (45) | (28) | ** | ** | Weighted N |
| 55-64 Only | 5.0 | 11.5 | 8.6 | 9.8 | 5.3 | ** | ** | Ranked 1st |
| | 5.0 | 19.2 | 11.4 | 12.2 | 10.5 | ** | ** | Ranked 2nd |
| | 90.0 | 69.2 | 80.0 | 78.0 | 84.2 | ** | ** | Ranked 3rd-6th/not ranked |
| | (20) | (26) | (35) | (82) | (19) | ** | ** | Weighted N |
| 65-74 Only | 2.1 | 7.3 | 6.7 | 8.4 | 0.0 | ** | ** | Ranked 1st |
| | 9.5 | 17.1 | 9.3 | 9.6 | 10.0 | ** | ** | Ranked 2nd |
| | 88.4 | 75.6 | 84.0 | 82.0 | 90.0 | ** | ** | Ranked 3rd-6th/not ranked |
| | (95) | (82) | (75) | (178) | (10) | ** | ** | Weighted N |
| 75 And Older Only | ** | 6.0 | 1.6 | 7.5 | 0.0 | ** | ** | Ranked 1st |
| | ** | 6.0 | 11.3 | 8.4 | 0.0 | ** | ** | Ranked 2nd |
| | ** | 88.0 | 87.1 | 84.1 | 100.0 | ** | ** | Ranked 3rd-6th/not ranked |
| | ** | (50) | (62) | (107) | (3) | ** | ** | Weighted N |

** Data not available in 1973q and 1974q.
** Code distinction not made in 1958m--oldest age group coded "65 And Older".

Table 5.29
Preference in a Job: Income Is High   Increasing
Income of Respondent

| Employed Respondents | | | | Year | | | | |
|---|---|---|---|---|---|---|---|---|
| | 1958m | 1962k | 1963m | 1965b | 1966a | 1973q | 1974q | |
| Income 1 (0-16%) | 1.7% | 20.0% | 13.0% | 16.4% | 4.8% | 16.4% | 18.6% | Ranked 1st |
| | 15.0 | 20.0 | 26.1 | 14.8 | 15.1 | 17.3 | 27.1 | Ranked 2nd |
| | 83.3 | 60.0 | 60.9 | 68.9 | 80.2 | 66.4 | 54.2 | Ranked 3rd-6th/not ranked |
| | (60) | (35) | (23) | (61) | (126) | (110) | (118) | Weighted N |
| Income 2 (17-33%) | 5.8 | 16.2 | 12.3 | 10.6 | 8.1 | 8.3 | 19.7 | Ranked 1st |
| | 17.4 | 9.5 | 11.0 | 18.8 | 13.8 | 27.3 | 19.4 | Ranked 2nd |
| | 76.8 | 74.3 | 76.7 | 70.6 | 78.1 | 64.5 | 60.9 | Ranked 3rd-6th/not ranked |
| | (69) | (74) | (73) | (160) | (283) | (121) | (299) | Weighted N |
| Income 3 (34-67%) | 7.9 | 9.4 | 5.7 | 9.8 | 7.7 | 15.3 | 16.6 | Ranked 1st |
| | 10.9 | 15.2 | 16.6 | 13.2 | 14.9 | 22.6 | 20.2 | Ranked 2nd |
| | 81.2 | 75.4 | 77.7 | 77.0 | 77.4 | 62.1 | 63.2 | Ranked 3rd-6th/not ranked |
| | (229) | (224) | (193) | (530) | (686) | (517) | (625) | Weighted N |
| Income 4 (68-95%) | 5.5 | 7.1 | 7.2 | 9.8 | 11.2 | 14.9 | 17.5 | Ranked 1st |
| | 17.9 | 16.3 | 13.3 | 13.2 | 20.4 | 20.0 | 13.0 | Ranked 2nd |
| | 76.6 | 76.6 | 79.4 | 77.1 | 68.3 | 65.1 | 69.5 | Ranked 3rd-6th/not ranked |
| | (145) | (141) | (180) | (593) | (445) | (611) | (462) | Weighted N |
| Income 5 (96-100%) | 3.8 | 4.5 | 11.9 | 15.9 | 13.3 | 18.4 | 13.6 | Ranked 1st |
| | 9.4 | 13.6 | 21.4 | 17.1 | 22.7 | 21.6 | 15.2 | Ranked 2nd |
| | 86.8 | 81.8 | 66.7 | 67.1 | 64.1 | 60.0 | 71.2 | Ranked 3rd-6th/not ranked |
| | (53) | (22) | (42) | (82) | (128) | (125) | (66) | Weighted N |

Table 5.30
Preference in a Job  Income Is High, Increasing
Income of Respondent

Unemployed Respondents

| | 1958m | 1962k | 1963m | 1965b | 1966a | 1973q | 1974q | |
|---|---|---|---|---|---|---|---|---|
| **Income 1 (0-16%)** | 2.5% | 11.4% | 6.7% | 10.9% | 13.6% | ** | ** | Ranked 1st |
| | 12.3 | 10.2 | 10.6 | 11.5 | 13.6 | ** | ** | Ranked 2nd |
| | 85.2 | 78.4 | 82.7 | 77.6 | 72.7 | ** | ** | Ranked 3rd-6th/not ranked |
| | (81) | (88) | (104) | (192) | (22) | ** | ** | Weighted N |
| **Income 2 (17-33%)** | 6.7 | 5.6 | 8.3 | 6.6 | 15.4 | ** | ** | Ranked 1st |
| | 10.0 | 21.1 | 13.3 | 8.8 | 11.5 | ** | ** | Ranked 2nd |
| | 83.3 | 73.2 | 78.3 | 84.6 | 73.1 | ** | ** | Ranked 3rd-6th/not ranked |
| | (30) | (71) | (60) | (136) | (26) | ** | ** | Weighted N |
| **Income 3 (34-67%)** | 2.9 | 2.6 | 5.6 | 10.3 | 3.1 | ** | ** | Ranked 1st |
| | 8.8 | 13.2 | 2.8 | 11.1 | 12.5 | ** | ** | Ranked 2nd |
| | 88.2 | 84.2 | 91.7 | 78.6 | 84.4 | ** | ** | Ranked 3rd-6th/not ranked |
| | (34) | (38) | (36) | (117) | (32) | ** | ** | Weighted N |
| **Income 4 (68-95%)** | 0.0 | 10.0 | 0.0 | 6.5 | 0.0 | ** | ** | Ranked 1st |
| | 0.0 | 20.0 | 13.3 | 6.5 | 50.0 | ** | ** | Ranked 2nd |
| | 100.0 | 70.0 | 86.7 | 87.0 | 50.0 | ** | ** | Ranked 3rd-6th/not ranked |
| | (11) | (10) | (15) | (46) | (8) | ** | ** | Weighted N |
| **Income 5 (96-100%)** | 0.0 | 16.7 | 0.0 | 12.5 | 40.0 | ** | ** | Ranked 1st |
| | 0.0 | 16 7 | 0.0 | 0.0 | 0.0 | ** | ** | Ranked 2nd |
| | 100.0 | 66.7 | 100.0 | 87.5 | 60.0 | ** | ** | Ranked 3rd-6th/not ranked |
| | (3) | (6) | (2) | (8) | (5) | ** | ** | Weighted N |

** Data not available.

Table 5.31
Preference in a Job: No Danger of Being Fired
Total Population--Employed and Unemployed Respondents

Employed Respondents

|  | | | | | Year | | | |
| --- | --- | --- | --- | --- | --- | --- | --- | --- |
|  | | 1958m | 1962k | 1963m | 1965b | 1966a | 1973q | 1974q |
| Ranked 1st | (5) | 14.0% | 10.4% | 11.6% | 10.0% | 8.7% | 10.8% | 10.3% |
| Ranked 2nd | (3) | 30.4 | 17.1 | 17.4 | 20.0 | 15.0 | 7.4 | 7.8 |
| Ranked 3rd-6th/not ranked | (1) | 55.6 | 72.5 | 71.0 | 70.0 | 76.3 | 81.8 | 81.9 |
| Total | | 100% | 100% | 100% | 100% | 100% | 100% | 100% |
| Weighted N | | 570 | 502 | 528 | 1430 | 1672 | 1578 | 1753 |
| Unweighted N | | 570 | 502 | 528 | 1430 | 1672 | 796 | 868 |

Table 5.32

Unemployed Respondents

|  | | 1958m | 1962k | 1963m | 1965b | 1966a | 1973q | 1974q |
| --- | --- | --- | --- | --- | --- | --- | --- | --- |
| Ranked 1st | (5) | 13.6% | 14.0% | 16.0% | 11.8% | 12.8% | ** | ** |
| Ranked 2nd | (3) | 35.8 | 27.6 | 24.8 | 26.5 | 21.3 | ** | ** |
| Ranked 3rd-6th/not ranked | (1) | 50.6 | 58.3 | 59.2 | 61.7 | 66.0 | ** | ** |
| Total | | 100% | 100% | 100% | 100% | 100% | ** | ** |
| Weighted N | | 176 | 228 | 238 | 499 | 94 | ** | ** |
| Unweighted N | | 176 | 228 | 238 | 499 | 94 | ** | ** |

** Data not available.
Question asked of head of households only in 1958m,1962k,1963m,1965b,and 1966a.

Table 5.33
Preference in a Job: No Danger of Being Fired
Sex of Respondent

Employed Respondents

|  | | | | Year | | | | |
|---|---|---|---|---|---|---|---|---|
|  | 1958m | 1962k | 1963m | 1965b | 1966a | 1973q | 1974q | |
| Males Only | 15.4% | 11.8% | 11.6% | 9.0% | 8.8% | 11.9% | 11.1% | Ranked 1st |
|  | 29.0 | 17.9 | 16.7 | 20.0 | 15.3 | 6.6 | 7.9 | Ranked 2nd |
|  | 55.7 | 70.3 | 71.7 | 71.0 | 75.9 | 81.5 | 81.0 | Ranked 3rd-6th/not ranked |
|  | (442) | (380) | (414) | (1263) | (1419) | (986) | (1026) | Weighted N |
| Females Only | 9.4 | 5.8 | 11.4 | 17.5 | 8.0 | 9.1 | 9.1 | Ranked 1st |
|  | 35.2 | 14.9 | 20.2 | 19.9 | 13.5 | 8.6 | 7.7 | Ranked 2nd |
|  | 55.5 | 79.3 | 68.4 | 62.7 | 78.5 | 82.3 | 83.2 | Ranked 3rd-6th/not ranked |
|  | (128) | (121) | (114) | (166) | (251) | (592) | (727) | Weighted N |

Table 5.34

Unemployed Respondents

|  | 1958m | 1962k | 1963m | 1965b | 1966a | 1973q | 1974q | |
|---|---|---|---|---|---|---|---|---|
| Males Only | 9.3% | 12.6% | 14.5% | 11.2% | 13.0% | ** | ** | Ranked 1st |
|  | 31.4 | 33.0 | 22.7 | 24.1 | 19.5 | ** | ** | Ranked 2nd |
|  | 59.3 | 54.4 | 62.7 | 64.7 | 67.5 | ** | ** | Ranked 3rd-6th/not ranked |
|  | (86) | (103) | (110) | (295) | (77) | ** | ** | Weighted N |
| Females Only | 17.8 | 15.3 | 17.2 | 12.7 | 11.8 | ** | ** | Ranked 1st |
|  | 40.0 | 23.4 | 26.6 | 29.9 | 29.4 | ** | ** | Ranked 2nd |
|  | 42.2 | 61.3 | 56.3 | 57.4 | 58.8 | ** | ** | Ranked 3rd-6th/not ranked |
|  | (90) | (124) | (128) | (204) | (17) | ** | ** | Weighted N |

** Data not available.

Table 5.35
Preference in a Job: No Danger of Being Fired
Race of Respondent

Employed Respondents

|  | | Year | | | | | | |
|---|---|---|---|---|---|---|---|---|
|  | 1958m | 1962k | 1963m | 1965b | 1966a | 1973q | 1974q | |
| Whites Only | 11.9% | 10.5% | 10.5% | 8.8% | 7.9% | 10.0% | 8.7% | Ranked 1st |
|  | 29.6 | 16.7 | 17.1 | 19.3 | 15.0 | 6.0 | 7.4 | Ranked 2nd |
|  | 58.6 | 72.8 | 72.4 | 71.9 | 77.1 | 84.0 | 83.9 | Ranked 3rd-6th/not ranked |
|  | (497) | (449) | (474) | (1267) | (1524) | (1394) | (1490) | Weighted N |
| Blacks Only | 28.8 | 8.9 | 22.2 | 17.3 | 17.6 | 15.9 | 18.4 | Ranked 1st |
|  | 34.8 | 22.2 | 22.2 | 23.3 | 16.0 | 18.2 | 11.2 | Ranked 2nd |
|  | 36.4 | 68.9 | 55.6 | 59.4 | 66.4 | 65.9 | 70.4 | Ranked 3rd-6th/not ranked |
|  | (66) | (45) | (45) | (133) | (119) | (132) | (196) | Weighted N |

Table 5.36

Unemployed Respondents

|  | 1958m | 1962k | 1963m | 1965b | 1966a | 1973q | 1974q | |
|---|---|---|---|---|---|---|---|---|
| Whites Only | 12.9% | 13.9% | 13.8% | 11.1% | 13.0% | ** | ** | Ranked 1st |
|  | 33.3 | 28.2 | 22.7 | 26.9 | 15.9 | ** | ** | Ranked 2nd |
|  | 53.7 | 57.9 | 63.5 | 62.0 | 71.0 | ** | ** | Ranked 3rd-6th/not ranked |
|  | (147) | (202) | (203) | (442) | (69) | ** | ** | Weighted N |
| Blacks Only | 19.2 | 17.4 | 30.3 | 14.9 | 12.5 | ** | ** | Ranked 1st |
|  | 46.2 | 21.7 | 39.4 | 25.5 | 37.5 | ** | ** | Ranked 2nd |
|  | 34.6 | 60.9 | 30.3 | 59.6 | 50.0 | ** | ** | Ranked 3rd-6th/not ranked |
|  | (26) | (23) | (33) | (47) | (24) | ** | ** | Weighted N |

** Data not available.

Table 5.37
Preference in a Job: No Danger of Being Fired
Education of Respondent

Employed Respondents

| | | | Year | | | | | |
|---|---|---|---|---|---|---|---|---|
| | 1958m | 1962k | 1963m | 1965b | 1966a | 1973q | 1974q | |
| Grade School Only | 19.8% | 17.9% | 15.6% | 12.0% | 10.9% | 15.6% | 19.0% | Ranked 1st |
| | 40.1 | 26.9 | 25.7 | 29.1 | 24.6 | 9.0 | 14.9 | Ranked 2nd |
| | 40.1 | 55.2 | 58.7 | 58.9 | 64.5 | 75.4 | 66.1 | Ranked 3rd-6th/not ranked |
| | (172) | (134) | (109) | (326) | (341) | (167) | (174) | Weighted N |
| High School Only | 14.1 | 9.6 | 14.2 | 11.5 | 9.9 | 13.5 | 11.3 | Ranked 1st |
| | 30.3 | 17.9 | 19.0 | 22.0 | 14.6 | 9.0 | 8.9 | Ranked 2nd |
| | 55.6 | 72.5 | 66.8 | 66.5 | 75.5 | 77.5 | 79.8 | Ranked 3rd-6th/not ranked |
| | (277) | (229) | (253) | (723) | (788) | (889) | (847) | Weighted N |
| College Only | 5.9 | 4.3 | 4.2 | 5.5 | 4.1 | 4.7 | 6.4 | Ranked 1st |
| | 16.8 | 6.5 | 7.0 | 8.4 | 8.7 | 4.1 | 5.0 | Ranked 2nd |
| | 77.3 | 89.2 | 88.8 | 86.1 | 87.2 | 91.3 | 88.7 | Ranked 3rd-6th/not ranked |
| | (119) | (139) | (143) | (381) | (462) | (515) | (723) | Weighted N |

Table 5.38

Unemployed Respondents

| | 1958m | 1962k | 1963m | 1965b | 1966a | 1973q | 1974q | |
|---|---|---|---|---|---|---|---|---|
| Grade School Only | 14.6% | 19.2% | 19.3% | 14.7% | 17.1% | ** | ** | Ranked 1st |
| | 45.8 | 30.3 | 32.5 | 29.0 | 25.7 | ** | ** | Ranked 2nd |
| | 39.6 | 50.5 | 48.2 | 56.3 | 57.1 | ** | ** | Ranked 3rd-6th/not ranked |
| | (96) | (99) | (114) | (231) | (35) | ** | ** | Weighted N |
| High School Only | 15.7 | 12.6 | 12.8 | 11.2 | 13.6 | ** | ** | Ranked 1st |
| | 27.5 | 24.1 | 23.1 | 27.2 | 22.7 | ** | ** | Ranked 2nd |
| | 56.9 | 63.2 | 64.1 | 61.5 | 63.6 | ** | ** | Ranked 3rd-6th/not ranked . |
| | (51) | (87) | (78) | (169) | (44) | ** | ** | Weighted N |
| College Only | 3.8 | 5.3 | 10.0 | 6.2 | 0.0 | ** | ** | Ranked 1st |
| | 11.5 | 26.3 | 6.7 | 19.6 | 7.7 | ** | ** | Ranked 2nd |
| | 84.6 | 68.4 | 83.3 | 74.2 | 92.3 | ** | ** | Ranked 3rd-6th/not ranked |
| | (26) | (38) | (30) | (97) | (13) | ** | ** | Weighted N |

** Data not available.

Table 5.39
Preference in a Job  No Danger of Being Fired
Age of Respondent

Employed Respondents

| | | | | Year | | | | |
|---|---|---|---|---|---|---|---|---|
| | 1958m | 1962k | 1963m | 1965b | 1966a | 1973q | 1974q | |
| **18-24 Only** | 20.0% | 4.8% | 12.5% | 16.0% | 8.9% | 13.2% | 12.2% | Ranked 1st |
| | 17.1 | 14.3 | 7.5 | 18.7 | 8.0 | 9.2 | 7.4 | Ranked 2nd |
| | 62.9 | 81.0 | 80.0 | 65.3 | 83.0 | 77.6 | 80.4 | Ranked 3rd-6th/not ranked |
| | (35) | (21) | (40) | (75) | (112) | (326) | (337) | Weighted N |
| **25-34 Only** | 16.1 | 11.1 | 8.4 | 7.3 | 7.9 | 8.6 | 11.5 | Ranked 1st |
| | 18.5 | 16.7 | 14.0 | 16.5 | 15.1 | 5.6 | 7.3 | Ranked 2nd |
| | 65.3 | 72.2 | 77.6 | 76.2 | 76.9 | 85.8 | 81.2 | Ranked 3rd-6th/not ranked |
| | (124) | (126) | (107) | (303) | (390) | (372) | (468) | Weighted N |
| **35-44 Only** | 13.2 | 8.2 | 9.9 | 11.1 | 7.6 | 13.6 | 7.9 | Ranked 1st |
| | 32.5 | 16.4 | 17.4 | 15.5 | 14.7 | 6.8 | 8.5 | Ranked 2nd |
| | 54.3 | 75.4 | 72.7 | 73.4 | 77.7 | 79.6 | 83.6 | Ranked 3rd-6th/not ranked |
| | (151) | (134) | (121) | (361) | (421) | (324) | (341) | Weighted N |
| **45-54 Only** | 13.4 | 9.3 | 10.9 | 9.1 | 8.1 | 8.2 | 11.5 | Ranked 1st |
| | 33.9 | 14.8 | 22.6 | 22.3 | 15.4 | 6.1 | 7.6 | Ranked 2nd |
| | 52.8 | 75.9 | 66.4 | 68.7 | 76.6 | 85.8 | 80.8 | Ranked 3rd-6th/not ranked |
| | (127) | (108) | (137) | (364) | (397) | (330) | (355) | Weighted N |
| **55-64 Only** | 11.6 | 9.2 | 14.6 | 12.5 | 11.3 | 10.0 | 6.6 | Ranked 1st |
| | 41.1 | 23.0 | 15.7 | 25.7 | 16.8 | 11.6 | 8.8 | Ranked 2nd |
| | 47.4 | 67.8 | 69.7 | 61.9 | 71.9 | 78.4 | 84.5 | Ranked 3rd-6th/not ranked |
| | (95) | (87) | (89) | (265) | (292) | (190) | (226) | Weighted N |
| **65-74 Only** | 13.2 | 35.3 | 22.2 | 5.6 | 13.3 | 16.1 | 10.5 | Ranked 1st |
| | 34.2 | 17.6 | 14.8 | 25.9 | 20.0 | 3.2 | 0.0 | Ranked 2nd |
| | 52.6 | 47.1 | 63.0 | 68.5 | 66.7 | 80.6 | 89.5 | Ranked 3rd-6th/not ranked |
| | (38) | (17) | (27) | (54) | (45) | (31) | (19) | Weighted N |
| **75 And Older Only** | ** | 20.0 | 0.0 | 0.0 | 0.0 | 50.0 | 0.0 | Ranked 1st |
| | ** | 20.0 | 80.0 | 37.5 | 0.0 | 0.0 | 50.0 | Ranked 2nd |
| | ** | 60.0 | 20.0 | 62.5 | 100.0 | 50.0 | 50.0 | Ranked 3rd-6th/not ranked |
| | ** | (5) | (5) | (8) | (6) | (2) | (2) | Weighted N |

** Code distinction not made.
Oldest age group coded "65 And Older" in 1958m.

Table 5.40
Preference in a Job: No Danger of Being Fired
Age of Respondent

Unemployed Respondents

| | 1958m | 1962k | 1963m | 1965b | 1966a | 1973q | 1974q | |
|---|---|---|---|---|---|---|---|---|
| 18-24 Only | 50.0% | 10 0% | 23.1% | 17.5% | 28.6% | ** | ** | Ranked 1st |
| | 0.0 | 30.0 | 7.7 | 20.0 | 0.0 | ** | ** | Ranked 2nd |
| | 50.0 | 60.0 | 69.2 | 62.5 | 71.4 | ** | ** | Ranked 3rd-6th/not ranked |
| | (4) | (10) | (13) | (40) | (7) | ** | ** | Weighted N |
| 25-34 Only | 5.9 | 0.0 | 6.7 | 0.0 | 8.3 | ** | ** | Ranked 1st |
| | 23.5 | 20.0 | 13.3 | 15.8 | 33.3 | ** | ** | Ranked 2nd |
| | 70.6 | 80.0 | 80.0 | 84.2 | 58.3 | ** | ** | Ranked 3rd-6th/not ranked |
| | (17) | (15) | (15) | (19) | (12) | ** | ** | Weighted N |
| 35-44 Only | 5.9 | 6.3 | 26.7 | 25.0 | 8.3 | ** | ** | Ranked 1st |
| | 52.9 | 37.5 | 13.3 | 28.6 | 25.0 | ** | ** | Ranked 2nd |
| | 41.2 | 56.3 | 60.0 | 46.4 | 66.7 | ** | ** | Ranked 3rd-6th/not ranked |
| | (17) | (16) | (15) | (28) | (12) | ** | ** | Weighted N |
| 45-54 Only | 23.5 | 13.0 | 17.6 | 6.7 | 10.7 | ** | ** | Ranked 1st |
| | 23.5 | 8.7 | 35.3 | 22.2 | 17.9 | ** | ** | Ranked 2nd |
| | 52.9 | 78.3 | 47.1 | 71.1 | 71.4 | ** | ** | Ranked 3rd-6th/not ranked |
| | (17) | (23) | (17) | (45) | (28) | ** | ** | Weighted N |
| 55-64 Only | 4.8 | 7.4 | 13.9 | 12.3 | 15.8 | ** | ** | Ranked 1st |
| | 42.9 | 33.3 | 30.6 | 19.8 | 21.1 | ** | ** | Ranked 2nd |
| | 52.4 | 59.3 | 55.6 | 67.9 | 63.2 | ** | ** | Ranked 3rd-6th/not ranked |
| | (21) | (27) | (36) | (81) | (19) | ** | ** | Weighted N |
| 65-74 Only | 15.0 | 17.1 | 12.0 | 10.5 | 9.1 | ** | ** | Ranked 1st |
| | 37.0 | 31.7 | 22.7 | 33.1 | 18.2 | ** | ** | Ranked 2nd |
| | 48.0 | 51.2 | 65.3 | 56.4 | 72.7 | ** | ** | Ranked 3rd-6th/not ranked |
| | (100) | (82) | (75) | (181) | (11) | ** | ** | Weighted N |
| 75 And Older Only | ** | 19.2 | 16.1 | 12.4 | 33.3 | ** | ** | Ranked 1st |
| | ** | 26 9 | 29.0 | 25.7 | 33.3 | ** | ** | Ranked 2nd |
| | ** | 53.8 | 54.8 | 61.9 | 33.3 | ** | ** | Ranked 3rd-6th/not ranked |
| | ** | (52) | (62) | (105) | (3) | ** | ** | Weighted N |

** Data not available in 1973q and 1974q.
** Code distinction not made in 1958m--oldest age group coded "65 And Older".

Table 5.41
Preference in a Job: No Danger of Being Fired
Income of Respondent

| Employed Respondents | Year | | | | | | | |
| --- | --- | --- | --- | --- | --- | --- | --- | --- |
| | 1958m | 1962k | 1963m | 1965b | 1966a | 1973q | 1974q | |
| Income 1 (0-16%) | 19.7% | 16.7% | 21.7% | 16.1% | 13.5% | 14.5% | 16.9% | Ranked 1st |
| | 44.3 | 25.0 | 21.7 | 27.4 | 19.8 | 10.9 | 16.9 | Ranked 2nd |
| | 36.1 | 58.3 | 56.5 | 56.5 | 66.7 | 74.5 | 66.1 | Ranked 3rd-6th/not ranked |
| | (61) | (36) | (23) | (62) | (126) | (110) | (118) | Weighted N |
| Income 2 (17-33%) | 15.7 | 14.7 | 16.4 | 17.9 | 11.3 | 10.7 | 11.7 | Ranked 1st |
| | 38.6 | 16.0 | 24.7 | 23.5 | 21.8 | 4.1 | 9.4 | Ranked 2nd |
| | 45.7 | 69.3 | 58.9 | 58.6 | 66.9 | 85.1 | 78.9 | Ranked 3rd-6th/not ranked |
| | (70) | (75) | (73) | (162) | (284) | (121) | (299) | Weighted N |
| Income 3 (34-67%) | 14.4 | 8.6 | 13.4 | 8.5 | 8.6 | 12.4 | 10.4 | Ranked 1st |
| | 29.7 | 20.3 | 19.6 | 24.1 | 15.8 | 10.3 | 8.3 | Ranked 2nd |
| | 55.9 | 71.2 | 67.0 | 67.4 | 75.6 | 77.3 | 81.3 | Ranked 3rd-6th/not ranked |
| | (229) | (222) | (194) | (531) | (689) | (515) | (625) | Weighted N |
| Income 4 (68-95%) | 13.3 | 9.3 | 7.3 | 9.3 | 6.3 | 11.3 | 7.4 | Ranked 1st |
| | 23.8 | 12.1 | 13.4 | 16.0 | 10.3 | 5.9 | 3.0 | Ranked 2nd |
| | 62.9 | 78.6 | 79.3 | 74.7 | 83.4 | 82.8 | 89.6 | Ranked 3rd-6th/not ranked |
| | (143) | (140) | (179) | (593) | (445) | (611) | (462) | Weighted N |
| Income 5 (96-100%) | 7.4 | 4.8 | 7.1 | 4.9 | 7.1 | 0.0 | 12.1 | Ranked 1st |
| | 22.2 | 0.0 | 9.5 | 9.8 | 7.1 | 0.0 | 4.5 | Ranked 2nd |
| | 70.4 | 95.2 | 83.3 | 85.4 | 85.8 | 100.0 | 83.3 | Ranked 3rd-6th/not ranked |
| | (54) | (21) | (42) | (82) | (127) | (125) | (66) | Weighted N |

Figure 5.4
No Danger of Being Fired by Income of Employed R

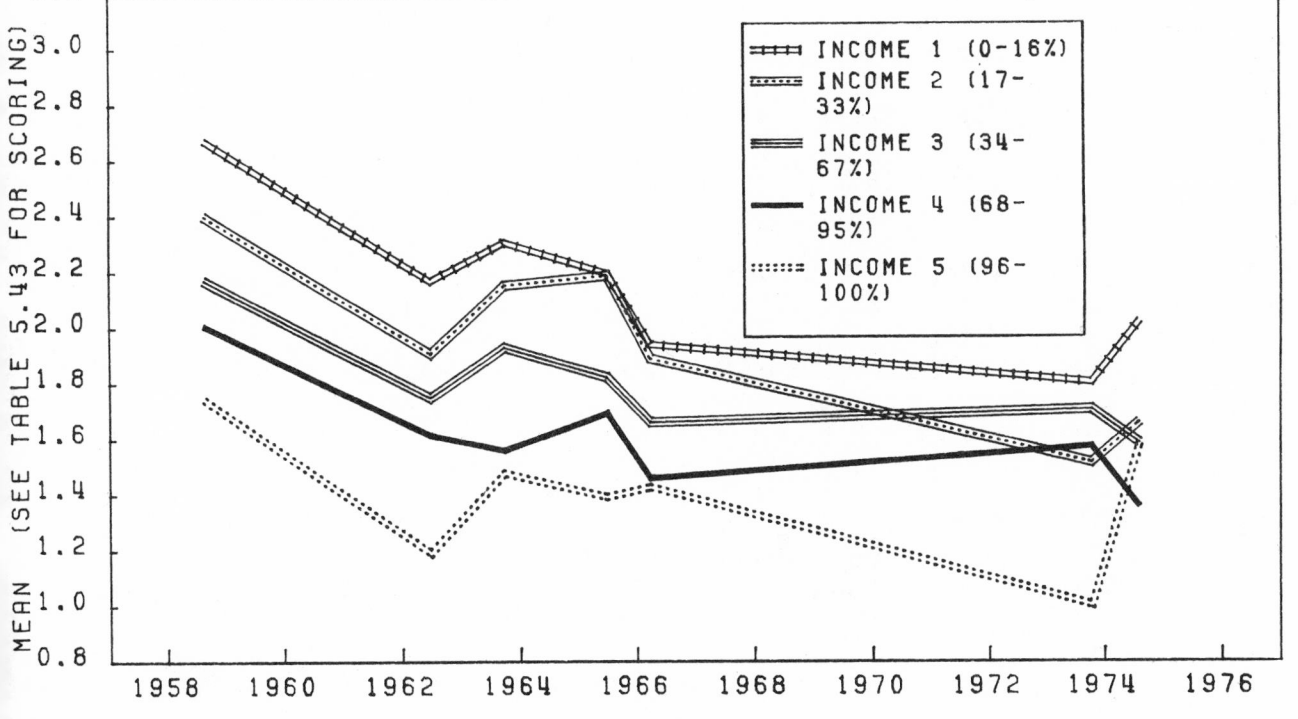

Work And Retirement

Table 5.42
Preference in a Job: No Danger of Being Fired
Income of Respondent

Unemployed Respondents

|  | Year | | | | | | | |
|---|---|---|---|---|---|---|---|---|
|  | 1958m | 1962k | 1963m | 1965b | 1966a | 1973q | 1974q | |
| Income 1 (0-16%) | 16.5% | 18.7% | 16.2% | 13.3% | 9.1% | ** | ** | Ranked 1st |
|  | 41.2 | 29.7 | 33.3 | 28.7 | 27.3 | ** | ** | Ranked 2nd |
|  | 42.4 | 51.6 | 50.5 | 57.9 | 63.6 | ** | ** | Ranked 3rd-6th/not ranked |
|  | (85) | (91) | (105) | (195) | (22) | ** | ** | Weighted N |
| Income 2 (17-33%) | 9.7 | 13.0 | 15.0 | 11.2 | 15.4 | ** | ** | Ranked 1st |
|  | 35.5 | 27.5 | 18.3 | 27.6 | 19.2 | ** | ** | Ranked 2nd |
|  | 54.8 | 59.4 | 66.7 | 61.2 | 65.4 | ** | ** | Ranked 3rd-6th/not ranked |
|  | (31) | (69) | (60) | (134) | (26) | ** | ** | Weighted N |
| Income 3 (34-67%) | 17.1 | 10.3 | 16.7 | 11.1 | 12.5 | ** | ** | Ranked 1st |
|  | 31.4 | 35.9 | 19.4 | 24.8 | 25.0 | ** | ** | Ranked 2nd |
|  | 51.4 | 53.8 | 63.9 | 64.1 | 62.5 | ** | ** | Ranked 3rd-6th/not ranked |
|  | (35) | (39) | (36) | (117) | (32) | ** | ** | Weighted N |
| Income 4 (68-95%) | 0.0 | 20.0 | 13.3 | 8.9 | 22.2 | ** | ** | Ranked 1st |
|  | 41.7 | 10.0 | 13.3 | 22.2 | 0.0 | ** | ** | Ranked 2nd |
|  | 58.3 | 70.0 | 73.3 | 68.9 | 77.8 | ** | ** | Ranked 3rd-6th/not ranked |
|  | (12) | (10) | (15) | (45) | (9) | ** | ** | Weighted N |
| Income 5 (96-100%) | 0.0 | 0.0 | 0.0 | 12.5 | 0.0 | ** | ** | Ranked 1st |
|  | 0.0 | 16.7 | 0.0 | 0.0 | 20.0 | ** | ** | Ranked 2nd |
|  | 100.0 | 83.3 | 100.0 | 87.5 | 80.0 | ** | ** | Ranked 3rd-6th/not ranked |
|  | (3) | (6) | (2) | (8) | (5) | ** | ** | Weighted N |

* Data not available.

Table 5.43
Preference in a Job: Work Not Hard, Hours Not Long
Total Population--Employed and Unemployed Respondents

Employed Respondents

|  |  |  | Year |  |  |  |  |  |
|---|---|---|---|---|---|---|---|---|
|  |  | 1958m | 1962k | 1963m | 1965b | 1966a | 1973q | 1974q |
| Ranked 1st | (5) | 2.1% | 3.0% | 2.3% | 2.2% | 1.9% | 3.4% | 2.6% |
| Ranked 2nd | (3) | 2.7 | 4.8 | 3.6 | 4.2 | 6.0 | 6.4 | 4.4 |
| Ranked 3rd-6th/not ranked | (1) | 95.2 | 92.2 | 94.1 | 93.5 | 92.1 | 90.3 | 93.0 |
| Total |  | 100% | 100% | 100% | 100% | 100% | 100% | 100% |
| Weighted N |  | 518 | 498 | 527 | 1425 | 1661 | 1580 | 1753 |
| Unweighted N |  | 518 | 498 | 527 | 1425 | 1661 | 797 | 868 |

Table 5.44

Unemployed Respondents

|  |  | 1958m | 1962k | 1963m | 1965b | 1966a | 1973q | 1974q |
|---|---|---|---|---|---|---|---|---|
| Ranked 1st | (5) | 2.5% | 2.7% | 1.7% | 3.2% | 5.3% | ** | ** |
| Ranked 2nd | (3) | 5.6 | 5.4 | 5.1 | 3.8 | 11.7 | ** | ** |
| Ranked 3rd-6th/not ranked | (1) | 92.0 | 91.9 | 93.2 | 93.0 | 83.0 | ** | ** |
| Total |  | 100% | 100% | 100% | 100% | 100% | ** | ** |
| Weighted N |  | 162 | 223 | 237 | 497 | 94 | ** | ** |
| Unweighted N |  | 162 | 223 | 237 | 497 | 94 | ** | ** |

** Data not available.
Question asked of head of households only in 1958m,1962k,1963m,1965b,and 1966a.

Table 5.45
Preference in a Job: Work Not Hard, Hours Not Long
Sex of Respondent

Employed Respondents

| | | | | Year | | | | |
|---|---|---|---|---|---|---|---|---|
| | 1958m | 1962k | 1963m | 1965b | 1966a | 1973q | 1974q | |
| Males Only | 1.7% | 2.9% | 2.2% | 2.2% | 1.8% | 2.6% | 2.5% | Ranked 1st |
| | 2.0 | 5.0 | 3.9 | 4.0 | 5.7 | 5.4 | 3.5 | Ranked 2nd |
| | 96.3 | 92.1 | 93.9 | 93.7 | 92.5 | 92.0 | 94.0 | Ranked 3rd-6th/not ranked |
| | (403) | (378) | (413) | (1260) | (1409) | (988) | (1026) | Weighted N |
| Females Only | 3.5 | 3.4 | 2.6 | 2.4 | 2.0 | 4.6 | 2.6 | Ranked 1st |
| | 5.2 | 4.2 | 2.6 | 5.5 | 7.6 | 8.1 | 5.6 | Ranked 2nd |
| | 91.3 | 92.4 | 94.7 | 92.1 | 90.4 | 87.3 | 91.7 | Ranked 3rd-6th/not ranked |
| | (115) | (119) | (114) | (164) | (250) | (592) | (727) | Weighted N |

Table 5.46

Unemployed Respondents

| | 1958m | 1962k | 1963m | 1965b | 1966a | 1973q | 1974q | |
|---|---|---|---|---|---|---|---|---|
| Males Only | 3.8% | 4.0% | 2.8% | 4.1% | 5.2% | ** | ** | Ranked 1st |
| | 8.9 | 3.0 | 5.5 | 3.1 | 11.7 | ** | ** | Ranked 2nd |
| | 87.3 | 92.9 | 91.7 | 92.9 | 83.1 | ** | ** | Ranked 3rd-6th/not ranked |
| | (79) | (99) | (109) | (295) | (77) | ** | ** | Weighted N |
| Females Only | 1.2 | 1.6 | 0.8 | 2.0 | 5.9 | ** | ** | Ranked 1st |
| | 2.4 | 7.3 | 4.7 | 5.0 | 11.8 | ** | ** | Ranked 2nd |
| | 96.4 | 91.1 | 94.5 | 93.1 | 82.4 | ** | ** | Ranked 3rd-6th/not ranked |
| | (83) | (123) | (128) | (202) | (17) | ** | ** | Weighted N |

** Data not available.

Work And Retirement

Table 5.47
Preference in a Job: Work Not Hard, Hours Not Long
Race of Respondent

Employed Respondents

|  |  | 1958m | 1962k | 1963m | 1965b | 1966a | 1973q | 1974q |  |
|---|---|---|---|---|---|---|---|---|---|
| Whites Only |  | 2.2% | 2.9% | 2.1% | 2.0% | 1.8% | 3.2% | 2.6% | Ranked 1st |
|  |  | 2.2 | 4.5 | 3.4 | 3.9 | 5.5 | 6.7 | 4.5 | Ranked 2nd |
|  |  | 95.6 | 92.6 | 94.5 | 94.1 | 92.7 | 90.2 | 92.9 | Ranked 3rd-6th/not ranked |
|  |  | (453) | (446) | (473) | (1264) | (1512) | (1396) | (1490) | Weighted N |
| Blacks Only |  | 1.7 | 4.5 | 4.4 | 3.8 | 3.4 | 6.8 | 3.1 | Ranked 1st |
|  |  | 6.7 | 6.8 | 6.7 | 6.1 | 10.9 | 4.5 | 3.6 | Ranked 2nd |
|  |  | 91.7 | 88.6 | 88.9 | 90.2 | 85.7 | 88.6 | 93.4 | Ranked 3rd-6th/not ranked |
|  |  | (60) | (44) | (45) | (132) | (119) | (132) | (196) | Weighted N |

Table 5.48

Unemployed Respondents

|  |  | 1958m | 1962k | 1963m | 1965b | 1966a | 1973q | 1974q |  |
|---|---|---|---|---|---|---|---|---|---|
| Whites Only |  | 1.5% | 2.0% | 2.0% | 3.2% | 7.2% | ** | ** | Ranked 1st |
|  |  | 6.0 | 4.5 | 4.9 | 3.2 | 10.1 | ** | ** | Ranked 2nd |
|  |  | 92.5 | 93.4 | 93.1 | 93.6 | 82.6 | ** | ** | Ranked 3rd-6th/not ranked |
|  |  | (134) | (198) | (203) | (440) | (69) | ** | ** | Weighted N |
| Blacks Only |  | 8.0 | 9.1 | 0.0 | 4.3 | 0.0 | ** | ** | Ranked 1st |
|  |  | 4.0 | 9.1 | 6.3 | 8.5 | 16.7 | ** | ** | Ranked 2nd |
|  |  | 88.0 | 81.8 | 93.8 | 87.2 | 83.3 | ** | ** | Ranked 3rd-6th/not ranked |
|  |  | (25) | (22) | (32) | (47) | (24) | ** | ** | Weighted N |

** Data not available.

Table 5.49
Preference in a Job: Work Not Hard, Hours Not Long
Education of Respondent

Employed Respondents

| | 1958m | 1962k | 1963m | 1965b | 1966a | 1973q | 1974q | |
|---|---|---|---|---|---|---|---|---|
| Grade School Only | 1.9% | 4.5% | 7.4% | 5.3% | 2.7% | 2.4% | 1.1% | Ranked 1st |
| | 3.8 | 7.6 | 5.6 | 4.3 | 11.9 | 9.0 | 7.5 | Ranked 2nd |
| | 94.3 | 87.9 | 87.0 | 90.4 | 85.5 | 88.6 | 91.4 | Ranked 3rd-6th/not ranked |
| | (158) | (132) | (108) | (323) | (337) | (167) | (174) | Weighted N |
| High School Only | 1.2 | 1.8 | 1.2 | 1.4 | 1.8 | 3.7 | 1.4 | Ranked 1st |
| | 2.8 | 4.8 | 3.6 | 3.7 | 4.6 | 7.0 | 4.5 | Ranked 2nd |
| | 96.0 | 93.4 | 95.3 | 94.9 | 93.6 | 89.3 | 94.1 | Ranked 3rd-6th/not ranked |
| | (249) | (227) | (253) | (721) | (786) | (891) | (847) | Weighted N |
| College Only | 4.6 | 3.6 | 0.7 | 1.3 | 1.1 | 3.1 | 4.3 | Ranked 1st |
| | 0.9 | 2.2 | 2.1 | 5.0 | 4.2 | 4.7 | 3.3 | Ranked 2nd |
| | 94.5 | 94.2 | 97.2 | 93.7 | 94.7 | 92.2 | 92.4 | Ranked 3rd-6th/not ranked |
| | (109) | (139) | (143) | (381) | (456) | (515) | (723) | Weighted N |

Table 5.50

Unemployed Respondents

| | 1958m | 1962k | 1963m | 1965b | 1966a | 1973q | 1974q | |
|---|---|---|---|---|---|---|---|---|
| Grade School Only | 1.2% | 2.1% | 2.7% | 2.6% | 5.7% | ** | ** | Ranked 1st |
| | 5.9 | 6.3 | 7.1 | 3.0 | 8.6 | ** | ** | Ranked 2nd |
| | 92.9 | 91.7 | 90.3 | 94.4 | 85.7 | ** | ** | Ranked 3rd-6th/not ranked |
| | (85) | (96) | (113) | (231) | (35) | ** | ** | Weighted N |
| High School Only | 5.9 | 4.7 | 0.0 | 4.2 | 4.5 | ** | ** | Ranked 1st |
| | 5.9 | 3.5 | 2.6 | 6.0 | 13.6 | ** | ** | Ranked 2nd |
| | 88.2 | 91.8 | 97.4 | 89.8 | 81.8 | ** | ** | Ranked 3rd-6th/not ranked |
| | (51) | (85) | (78) | (167) | (44) | ** | ** | Weighted N |
| College Only | 0.0 | 0.0 | 3.3 | 3.1 | 7.7 | ** | ** | Ranked 1st |
| | 4.3 | 7.9 | 3.3 | 2.1 | 15.4 | ** | ** | Ranked 2nd |
| | 95.7 | 92.1 | 93.3 | 94.8 | 76.9 | ** | ** | Ranked 3rd-6th/not ranked |
| | (23) | (38) | (30) | (97) | (13) | ** | ** | Weighted N |

** Data not available.

Table 5.51

Preference in a Job: Work Not Hard, Hours Not Long

Age of Respondent

| Employed Respondents | | | | Year | | | | |
|---|---|---|---|---|---|---|---|---|
| | 1958m | 1962k | 1963m | 1965b | 1966a | 1973q | 1974q | |
| 18-24 Only | 0.0% | 9.5% | 5.0% | 1.3% | 2.7% | 10.4% | 1.5% | Ranked 1st |
| | 3.0 | 0.0 | 2.5 | 6.7 | 4.5 | 25.0 | 1.5 | Ranked 2nd |
| | 97.0 | 90.5 | 92.5 | 92.0 | 92.9 | 64.6 | 97.0 | Ranked 3rd-6th/not ranked |
| | (33) | (21) | (40) | (75) | (112) | (48) | (337) | Weighted N |
| 25-34 Only | 1.8 | 4.0 | 0.9 | 1.3 | 1.0 | 1.9 | 2.6 | Ranked 1st |
| | 0.9 | 4.8 | 1.9 | 3.0 | 5.4 | 6.7 | 3.2 | Ranked 2nd |
| | 97.3 | 91.2 | 97.2 | 95.7 | 93.6 | 91.4 | 94.2 | Ranked 3rd-6th/not ranked |
| | (111) | (125) | (107) | (302) | (390) | (372) | (468) | Weighted N |
| 35-44 Only | 0.7 | 1.5 | 0.0 | 1.1 | 1.4 | 2.8 | 1.2 | Ranked 1st |
| | 1.5 | 3.0 | 0.8 | 4.7 | 4.1 | 4.3 | 3.5 | Ranked 2nd |
| | 97.8 | 95.6 | 99.2 | 94.1 | 94.4 | 92.9 | 95.3 | Ranked 3rd-6th/not ranked |
| | (137) | (135) | (121) | (358) | (414) | (324) | (341) | Weighted N |
| 45-54 Only | 2.5 | 1.9 | 2.9 | 1.4 | 2.0 | 6.1 | 2.8 | Ranked 1st |
| | 1.6 | 3.8 | 5.8 | 3.9 | 6.4 | 7.0 | 5.6 | Ranked 2nd |
| | 95.9 | 94.3 | 91.3 | 94.8 | 91.6 | 87.0 | 91.5 | Ranked 3rd-6th/not ranked |
| | (122) | (106) | (138) | (363) | (392) | (330) | (355) | Weighted N |
| 55-64 Only | 4.9 | 3.5 | 3.4 | 5.6 | 3.1 | 4.7 | 4.9 | Ranked 1st |
| | 6.1 | 5.9 | 5.7 | 3.8 | 9.2 | 9.5 | 9.3 | Ranked 2nd |
| | 89.0 | 90.6 | 90.8 | 90.6 | 87.8 | 85.8 | 85.8 | Ranked 3rd-6th/not ranked |
| | (82) | (85) | (87) | (266) | (294) | (190) | (226) | Weighted N |
| 65-74 Only | 3.0 | 5.9 | 3.7 | 3.8 | 0.0 | 9.7 | 15.8 | Ranked 1st |
| | 9.1 | 17.6 | 7.4 | 9.4 | 11.4 | 29.0 | 21.1 | Ranked 2nd |
| | 87.9 | 76.5 | 88.9 | 86.8 | 88.6 | 61.3 | 63.2 | Ranked 3rd-6th/not ranked |
| | (33) | (17) | (27) | (53) | (44) | (31) | (19) | Weighted N |
| 75 And Older Only | ** | 0.0 | 20.0 | 12.5 | 0.0 | 0.0 | 0.0 | Ranked 1st |
| | ** | 0.0 | 0.0 | 0.0 | 0.0 | 0.0 | 0.0 | Ranked 2nd |
| | ** | 100.0 | 80.0 | 87.5 | 100.0 | 100.0 | 100.0 | Ranked 3rd-6th/not ranked |
| | ** | (5) | (5) | (8) | (6) | (2) | (2) | Weighted N |

** Code distinction not made.

Oldest age group coded "65 And Older" in 1958m.

Table 5.52
Preference in a Job: Work Not Hard, Hours Not Long
Age of Respondent

Unemployed Respondents

|  | Year | | | | | | | |
|---|---|---|---|---|---|---|---|---|
|  | 1958m | 1962k | 1963m | 1965b | 1966a | 1973q | 1974q | |
| 18-24 Only | 0.0% | 0.0% | 0.0% | 0.0% | 0.0% | ** | ** | Ranked 1st |
|  | 0.0 | 0.0 | 0.0 | 5.0 | 0.0 | ** | ** | Ranked 2nd |
|  | 100.0 | 100.0 | 100.0 | 95.0 | 100.0 | ** | ** | Ranked 3rd-6th/not ranked |
|  | (3) | (10) | (13) | (40) | (7) | ** | ** | Weighted N |
| 25-34 Only | 0.0 | 0.0 | 0.0 | 5.3 | 0.0 | ** | ** | Ranked 1st |
|  | 0.0 | 0.0 | 6.7 | 5.3 | 16.7 | ** | ** | Ranked 2nd |
|  | 100.0 | 100.0 | 93.3 | 89.5 | 83.3 | ** | ** | Ranked 3rd-6th/not ranked |
|  | (16) | (15) | (15) | (19) | (12) | ** | ** | Weighted N |
| 35-44 Only | 6.7 | 0.0 | 0.0 | 0.0 | 0.0 | ** | ** | Ranked 1st |
|  | 13.3 | 0.0 | 6.7 | 0.0 | 0.0 | ** | ** | Ranked 2nd |
|  | 80.0 | 100.0 | 93.3 | 100.0 | 100.0 | ** | ** | Ranked 3rd-6th/not ranked |
|  | (15) | (15) | (15) | (28) | (12) | ** | ** | Weighted N |
| 45-54 Only | 12.5 | 4.3 | 0.0 | 6.7 | 3.6 | ** | ** | Ranked 1st |
|  | 6.3 | 13.0 | 0.0 | 4.4 | 7.1 | ** | ** | Ranked 2nd |
|  | 81.3 | 82.6 | 100.0 | 88.9 | 89.3 | ** | ** | Ranked 3rd-6th/not ranked |
|  | (16) | (23) | (17) | (45) | (28) | ** | ** | Weighted N |
| 55-64 Only | 0.0 | 7.4 | 0.0 | 7.2 | 10.5 | ** | ** | Ranked 1st |
|  | 10.0 | 11.1 | 2.9 | 6.0 | 10.5 | ** | ** | Ranked 2nd |
|  | 90.0 | 81.5 | 97.1 | 86.7 | 78.9 | ** | ** | Ranked 3rd-6th/not ranked |
|  | (20) | (27) | (35) | (83) | (19) | ** | ** | Weighted N |
| 65-74 Only | 1.1 | 2.5 | 2.7 | 2.8 | 18.2 | ** | ** | Ranked 1st |
|  | 4.3 | 5.0 | 9.3 | 2.8 | 45.5 | ** | ** | Ranked 2nd |
|  | 94.6 | 92.5 | 88.0 | 94.4 | 36.4 | ** | ** | Ranked 3rd-6th/not ranked |
|  | (92) | (80) | (75) | (178) | (11) | ** | ** | Weighted N |
| 75 And Older Only | ** | 2.0 | 3.2 | 1.0 | 0.0 | ** | ** | Ranked 1st |
|  | ** | 2.0 | 3.2 | 3.8 | 0.0 | ** | ** | Ranked 2nd |
|  | ** | 96.0 | 93.5 | 95.2 | 100.0 | ** | ** | Ranked 3rd-6th/not ranked |
|  | ** | (50) | (62) | (104) | (3) | ** | ** | Weighted N |

* Data not available in 1973q and 1974q.
* Code distinction not made in 1958m--oldest age group coded "65 And Older".

Table 5.53
Preference in a Job: Work Not Hard, Hours Not Long
Income of Respondent

| Employed Respondents | | | | Year | | | | |
|---|---|---|---|---|---|---|---|---|
| | 1958m | 1962k | 1963m | 1965b | 1966a | 1973q | 1974q | |
| Income 1 (0-16%) | 1.8% | 5.7% | 4.3% | 6.6% | 1.6% | 4.5% | 3.4% | Ranked 1st |
| | 5.5 | 5.7 | 13.0 | 11.5 | 13.4 | 8.2 | 1.7 | Ranked 2nd |
| | 92.7 | 88.6 | 82.6 | 82.0 | 85.0 | 87.3 | 94.9 | Ranked 3rd-6th/not ranked |
| | (55) | (35) | (23) | (61) | (127) | (110) | (118) | Weighted N |
| Income 2 (17-33%) | 3.3 | 1.4 | 4.1 | 3.8 | 2.8 | 1.7 | 2.7 | Ranked 1st |
| | 1.6 | 10.8 | 2.7 | 3.8 | 8.5 | 3.3 | 5.0 | Ranked 2nd |
| | 95.1 | 87.8 | 93.2 | 92.5 | 88 7 | 95.0 | 92.3 | Ranked 3rd-6th/not ranked |
| | (61) | (74) | (73) | (160) | (283) | (121) | (299) | Weighted N |
| Income 3 (34-67%) | 1.4 | 3.6 | 3.6 | 1.5 | 1.8 | 2.9 | 1.1 | Ranked 1st |
| | 2.4 | 4.5 | 3.6 | 3.8 | 5.6 | 4.8 | 5.1 | Ranked 2nd |
| | 96.1 | 91.9 | 92.7 | 94.7 | 92.7 | 92.3 | 93.8 | Ranked 3rd-6th/not ranked |
| | (207) | (223) | (193) | (529) | (682) | (517) | (625) | Weighted N |
| Income 4 (68-95%) | 3.8 | 2.2 | 0.0 | 2.4 | 2.0 | 3.8 | 2.4 | Ranked 1st |
| | 2.3 | 1.4 | 2.2 | 4.0 | 4.1 | 7.9 | 5.0 | Ranked 2nd |
| | 93.8 | 96.4 | 97.8 | 93.6 | 93.9 | 88.4 | 92.6 | Ranked 3rd-6th/not ranked |
| | (130) | (139) | (179) | (593) | (444) | (611) | (462) | Weighted N |
| Income 5 (96-100%) | 0.0 | 5.0 | 0.0 | 0.0 | 0.0 | 2.4 | 9.1 | Ranked 1st |
| | 3.9 | 5.0 | 4.8 | 3.7 | 2.4 | 7.2 | 0.0 | Ranked 2nd |
| | 96.1 | 90.0 | 95.2 | 96.3 | 97.6 | 90.4 | 90.9 | Ranked 3rd-6th/not ranked |
| | (51) | (20) | (42) | (82) | (124) | (125) | (66) | Weighted N |

Table 5.54
Preference in a Job: Work Not Hard  Hours Not Long
Income of Respondent

Unemployed Respondents

| | 1958m | 1962k | 1963m | 1965b | 1966a | 1973q | 1974q | |
|---|---|---|---|---|---|---|---|---|
| Income 1 (0-16%) | 3.7% | 3.4% | 2.9% | 3.1% | 0.0% | ** | ** | Ranked 1st |
| | 1.2 | 7.9 | 7.7 | 5.2 | 13.6 | ** | ** | Ranked 2nd |
| | 95.1 | 88.8 | 89.4 | 91.7 | 86.4 | ** | ** | Ranked 3rd-6th/not ranked |
| | (81) | (89) | (104) | (192) | (22) | ** | ** | Weighted N |
| Income 2 (17-33%) | 0.0 | 1.4 | 1.7 | 5.2 | 0.0 | ** | ** | Ranked 1st |
| | 18.5 | 1.4 | 6.7 | 4.5 | 15.4 | ** | ** | Ranked 2nd |
| | 81.5 | 97.1 | 91.7 | 90.3 | 84.6 | ** | ** | Ranked 3rd-6th/not ranked |
| | (27) | (69) | (60) | (134) | (26) | ** | ** | Weighted N |
| Income 3 (34-67%) | 3.1 | 2.7 | 0.0 | 2.5 | 9.4 | ** | ** | Ranked 1st |
| | 9.4 | 2.7 | 0.0 | 1.7 | 6.3 | ** | ** | Ranked 2nd |
| | 87.5 | 94.6 | 100.0 | 95.8 | 84.4 | ** | ** | Ranked 3rd-6th/not ranked |
| | (32) | (37) | (36) | (118) | (32) | ** | ** | Weighted N |
| Income 4 (68-95%) | 0.0 | 0.0 | 0.0 | 0.0 | 22.2 | ** | ** | Ranked 1st |
| | 0.0 | 0.0 | 0.0 | 2.2 | 11.1 | ** | ** | Ranked 2nd |
| | 100.0 | 100.0 | 100.0 | 97.8 | 66.7 | ** | ** | Ranked 3rd-6th/not ranked |
| | (10) | (10) | (15) | (45) | (9) | ** | ** | Weighted N |
| Income 5 (96-100%) | 0.0 | 0.0 | 0.0 | 0.0 | 0.0 | ** | ** | Ranked 1st |
| | 0.0 | 33.3 | 0.0 | 0.0 | 20.0 | ** | ** | Ranked 2nd |
| | 100.0 | 66.7 | 100.0 | 100.0 | 80.0 | ** | ** | Ranked 3rd-6th/not ranked |
| | (3) | (6) | (2) | (8) | (5) | ** | ** | Weighted N |

* Data not available.

Table 5.55
Preference in a Job: Chances for Advancement Are Good
Total Population--Employed and Unemployed Respondents

Employed Respondents

| | | Year | | | | | | |
|---|---|---|---|---|---|---|---|---|
| | | 1958m | 1962k | 1963m | 1965b | 1966a | 1973q | 1974q |
| Ranked 1st | (5) | 10.7% | 12.7% | 10.3% | 10.8% | 11.7% | 9.9% | 8.7% |
| Ranked 2nd | (3) | 21.5 | 24.7 | 25.1 | 23.1 | 21.5 | 17.7 | 17.8 |
| Ranked 3rd-6th/not ranked | (1) | 67.8 | 62.5 | 64.6 | 66.0 | 66.8 | 72.5 | 73.6 |
| Total | | 100% | 100% | 100% | 100% | 100% | 100% | 100% |
| Weighted N | | 571 | 502 | 526 | 1422 | 1673 | 1580 | 1751 |
| Unweighted N | | 571 | 502 | 526 | 1422 | 1673 | 797 | 867 |

Table 5.56

Unemployed Respondents

| | | 1958m | 1962k | 1963m | 1965b | 1966a | 1973q | 1974q |
|---|---|---|---|---|---|---|---|---|
| Ranked 1st | (5) | 4.0% | 5.4% | 10.1% | 9.9% | 6.5% | ** | ** |
| Ranked 2nd | (3) | 19.5 | 20.1 | 22.4 | 25.6 | 15.1 | ** | ** |
| Ranked 3rd-6th/not ranked | (1) | 76.4 | 74.6 | 67.5 | 64.6 | 78.5 | ** | ** |
| Total | | 100% | 100% | 100% | 100% | 100% | ** | ** |
| Weighted N | | 174 | 224 | 237 | 497 | 93 | ** | ** |
| Unweighted N | | 174 | 224 | 237 | 497 | 93 | ** | ** |

** Data not available.
Question asked of head of households only in 1958m,1962k,1963m,1965b,and 1966a.

Table 5.57
Preference in a Job  Chances for Advancement Are Good
Sex of Respondent

Employed Respondents

|  |  | Year | | | | | | | |
|---|---|---|---|---|---|---|---|---|---|
|  |  | 1958m | 1962k | 1963m | 1965b | 1966a | 1973q | 1974q |  |
| Males Only |  | 12.2% | 13.8% | 12.4% | 11.8% | 12.5% | 11.4% | 9.0% | Ranked 1st |
|  |  | 22.9 | 25.8 | 25.7 | 23.8 | 22.6 | 18.0 | 16.6 | Ranked 2nd |
|  |  | 64.9 | 60.3 | 61.9 | 64.5 | 65.0 | 70.5 | 74.4 | Ranked 3rd-6th/not ranked |
|  |  | (442) | (383) | (412) | (1258) | (1418) | (988) | (1024) | Weighted N |
| Females Only |  | 5.4 | 9.3 | 2.6 | 3.7 | 7.1 | 7.3 | 8.3 | Ranked 1st |
|  |  | 17.1 | 21.2 | 22.8 | 18.4 | 15.8 | 17.1 | 19.4 | Ranked 2nd |
|  |  | 77.5 | 69.5 | 74.6 | 77.9 | 77.1 | 75.7 | 72.4 | Ranked 3rd-6th/not ranked |
|  |  | (129) | (118) | (114) | (163) | (253) | (592) | (727) | Weighted N |

Table 5.58

Unemployed Respondents

|  |  | 1958m | 1962k | 1963m | 1965b | 1966a | 1973q | 1974q |  |
|---|---|---|---|---|---|---|---|---|---|
| Males Only |  | 7.1% | 6.9% | 10.1% | 12.2% | 5.3% | ** | ** | Ranked 1st |
|  |  | 22.4 | 19.8 | 23.9 | 26.0 | 15.8 | ** | ** | Ranked 2nd |
|  |  | 70.6 | 73.3 | 66.1 | 61.8 | 78.9 | ** | ** | Ranked 3rd-6th/not ranked |
|  |  | (85) | (101) | (109) | (296) | (76) | ** | ** | Weighted N |
| Females Only |  | 1.1 | 4.1 | 10.2 | 6.5 | 11.8 | ** | ** | Ranked 1st |
|  |  | 16.9 | 20.5 | 21.1 | 24.9 | 11.8 | ** | ** | Ranked 2nd |
|  |  | 82.0 | 75.4 | 68.8 | 68.7 | 76.5 | ** | ** | Ranked 3rd-6th/not ranked |
|  |  | (89) | (122) | (128) | (201) | (17) | ** | ** | Weighted N |

** Data not available.

Figure 5 5
Good Chances for Advancement by Sex of Employed R

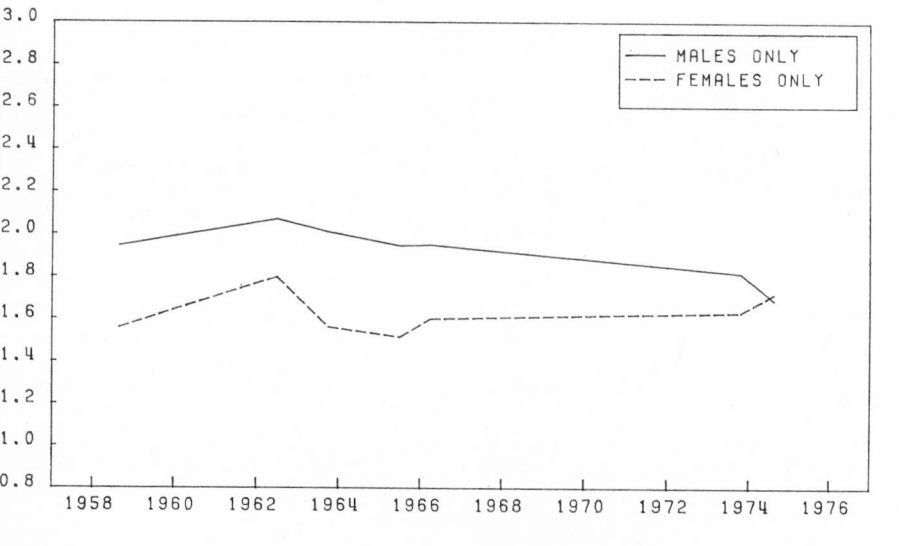

Table 5-59
Preference in a Job: Chances for Advancement Are Good
Race of Respondent

Employed Respondents

|  | 1958m | 1962k | 1963m | 1965b | 1966a | 1973q | 1974q |  |
|---|---|---|---|---|---|---|---|---|
| Whites Only | 11.8% | 13.8% | 10.0% | 11.0% | 11.9% | 10.1% | 8.1% | Ranked 1st |
|  | 21.6 | 25.8 | 26.3 | 24.2 | 22.0 | 17.8 | 16.8 | Ranked 2nd |
|  | 66.5 | 60.4 | 63.8 | 64.7 | 66.1 | 72.1 | 75.1 | Ranked 3rd-6th/not ranked |
|  | (499) | (449) | (472) | (1262) | (1524) | (1396) | (1488) | Weighted N |
| Blacks Only | 3.0 | 4.4 | 13.3 | 9.2 | 6.7 | 10.6 | 12.8 | Ranked 1st |
|  | 22.7 | 11.1 | 13.3 | 15.3 | 15.8 | 18.9 | 19.9 | Ranked 2nd |
|  | 74.2 | 84.4 | 73.3 | 75.6 | 77.5 | 70.5 | 67.3 | Ranked 3rd-6th/not ranked |
|  | (66) | (45) | (45) | (131) | (120) | (132) | (196) | Weighted N |

Table 5-60

Unemployed Respondents

|  | 1958m | 1962k | 1963m | 1965b | 1966a | 1973q | 1974q |  |
|---|---|---|---|---|---|---|---|---|
| Whites Only | 3.4% | 5.5% | 10.3% | 9.8% | 8.8% | ** | ** | Ranked 1st |
|  | 21.2 | 21.1 | 22.2 | 25.9 | 16.2 | ** | ** | Ranked 2nd |
|  | 75.3 | 73.4 | 67.5 | 64.3 | 75.0 | ** | ** | Ranked 3rd-6th/not ranked |
|  | (146) | (199) | (203) | (440) | (68) | ** | ** | Weighted N |
| Blacks Only | 8.0 | 4.5 | 6.3 | 8.5 | 0.0 | ** | ** | Ranked 1st |
|  | 12.0 | 13.6 | 21.9 | 23.4 | 8.3 | ** | ** | Ranked 2nd |
|  | 80.0 | 81.8 | 71.9 | 68.1 | 91.7 | ** | ** | Ranked 3rd-6th/not ranked |
|  | (25) | (22) | (32) | (47) | (24) | ** | ** | Weighted N |

** Data not available.

Figure 5.6
Good Chances for Advancement by Race of Employed R

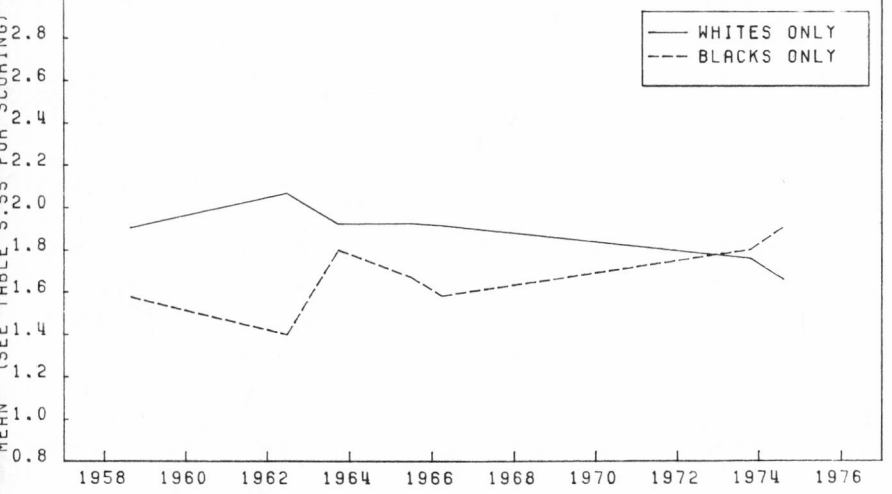

Table 5.61
Preference in a Job. Chances for Advancement Are Good
Education of Respondent

Employed Respondents

|  | | | | Year | | | | |
|---|---|---|---|---|---|---|---|---|
|  | 1958m | 1962k | 1963m | 1965b | 1966a | 1973q | 1974q | |
| Grade School Only | 4.7% | 5.3% | 3.7% | 3.1% | 5.9% | 6.6% | 6.3% | Ranked 1st |
|  | 17.5 | 13.5 | 18.5 | 13.1 | 12.7 | 12.0 | 17.8 | Ranked 2nd |
|  | 77.8 | 81.2 | 77.8 | 83.8 | 81.4 | 81.4 | 75.9 | Ranked 3rd-6th/not ranked |
|  | (171) | (133) | (108) | (320) | (339) | (167) | (174) | Weighted N |
| High School Only | 9.7 | 11.4 | 9.9 | 12.1 | 11.4 | 9.4 | 8.0 | Ranked 1st |
|  | 23.1 | 25.9 | 23.0 | 21.8 | 20.3 | 17.2 | 17.1 | Ranked 2nd |
|  | 67.1 | 62.7 | 67.1 | 66.2 | 68.3 | 73.4 | 74.9 | Ranked 3rd-6th/not ranked |
|  | (277) | (228) | (252) | (721) | (788) | (891) | (847) | Weighted N |
| College Only | 21.5 | 22.0 | 16.8 | 15.0 | 16.8 | 11.8 | 10.1 | Ranked 1st |
|  | 22.3 | 33.3 | 35.0 | 34.1 | 31.6 | 19.4 | 18.7 | Ranked 2nd |
|  | 56.2 | 44.7 | 48.3 | 50.9 | 51.6 | 68.7 | 71.2 | Ranked 3rd-6th/not ranked |
|  | (121) | (141) | (143) | (381) | (465) | (515) | (721) | Weighted N |

Table 5.62

Unemployed Respondents

|  | 1958m | 1962k | 1963m | 1965b | 1966a | 1973q | 1974q | |
|---|---|---|---|---|---|---|---|---|
| Grade School Only | 1.1% | 5.2% | 5.3% | 8.7% | 5.7% | ** | ** | Ranked 1st |
|  | 18.3 | 12.4 | 12.4 | 21.6 | 17.1 | ** | ** | Ranked 2nd |
|  | 80.6 | 82.5 | 82.3 | 69.7 | 77.1 | ** | ** | Ranked 3rd-6th/not ranked |
|  | (93) | (97) | (113) | (231) | (35) | ** | ** | Weighted N |
| High School Only | 9.6 | 2.3 | 14.1 | 8.4 | 9.3 | ** | ** | Ranked 1st |
|  | 21.2 | 24.4 | 29.5 | 24.6 | 16.3 | ** | ** | Ranked 2nd |
|  | 69.2 | 73.3 | 56.4 | 67.1 | 74.4 | ** | ** | Ranked 3rd-6th/not ranked |
|  | (52) | (86) | (78) | (167) | (43) | ** | ** | Weighted N |
| College Only | 3.8 | 13.2 | 20.0 | 15.5 | 0.0 | ** | ** | Ranked 1st |
|  | 23.1 | 31.6 | 36.7 | 37.1 | 7.7 | ** | ** | Ranked 2nd |
|  | 73.1 | 55.3 | 43.3 | 47.4 | 92.3 | ** | ** | Ranked 3rd-6th/not ranked |
|  | (26) | (38) | (30) | (97) | (13) | ** | ** | Weighted N |

** Data not available.

Work And Retirement

Figure 5.7
Good Chances for Advancement by Education of Employed R

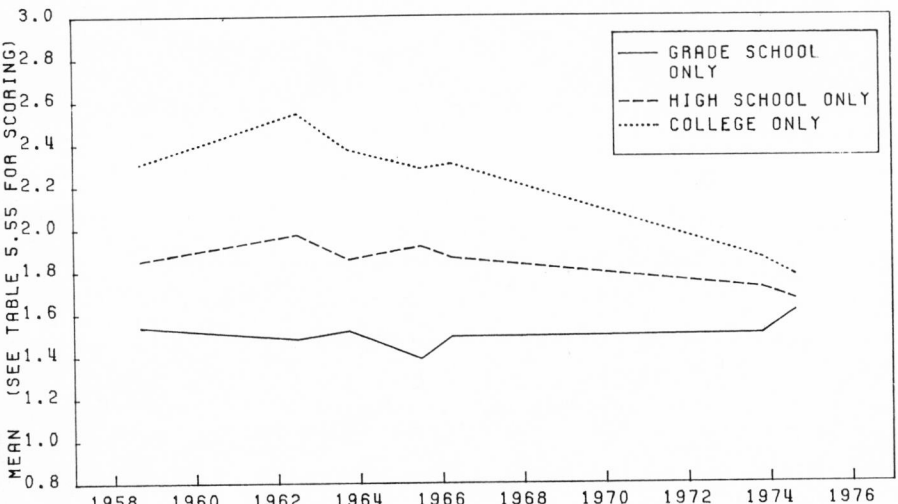

Table 5.63
Preference in a Job: Chances for Advancement Are Good
Age of Respondent

Employed Respondents

| | | | | Year | | | | |
|---|---|---|---|---|---|---|---|---|
| | 1958m | 1962k | 1963m | 1965b | 1966a | 1973q | 1974q | |
| 18-24 Only | 11.4% | 14.3% | 12.5% | 24.0% | 14.3% | 19.2% | 10.7% | Ranked 1st |
| | 17.1 | 47.6 | 32.5 | 25.3 | 29.5 | 24.1 | 25.5 | Ranked 2nd |
| | 71.4 | 38.1 | 55.0 | 50.7 | 56.3 | 56.7 | 63.8 | Ranked 3rd-6th/not ranked |
| | (35) | (21) | (40) | (75) | (112) | (328) | (337) | Weighted N |
| 25-34 Only | 16.8 | 13.6 | 17.8 | 15.0 | 19.4 | 12.4 | 12.0 | Ranked 1st |
| | 24.0 | 28.8 | 30.8 | 33.6 | 23.2 | 21.5 | 20.6 | Ranked 2nd |
| | 59.2 | 57.6 | 51.4 | 51.5 | 57.4 | 66.1 | 67.4 | Ranked 3rd-6th/not ranked |
| | (125) | (125) | (107) | (301) | (392) | (372) | (466) | Weighted N |
| 35-44 Only | 13.0 | 14.1 | 9.9 | 12.5 | 11.7 | 5.2 | 6.2 | Ranked 1st |
| | 26.6 | 23.7 | 33.9 | 22.3 | 24.1 | 19.1 | 19.9 | Ranked 2nd |
| | 60.4 | 62.2 | 56.2 | 65.2 | 64.2 | 75.6 | 73.9 | Ranked 3rd-6th/not ranked |
| | (154) | (135) | (121) | (359) | (419) | (324) | (341) | Weighted N |
| 45-54 Only | 8.7 | 11.9 | 6.6 | 6.9 | 8.3 | 7.0 | 8.5 | Ranked 1st |
| | 21.3 | 25.7 | 16.8 | 21.9 | 19.9 | 12.4 | 9.0 | Ranked 2nd |
| | 70.1 | 62.4 | 76.6 | 71.2 | 71.7 | 80.6 | 82.5 | Ranked 3rd-6th/not ranked |
| | (127) | (109) | (137) | (361) | (396) | (330) | (355) | Weighted N |
| 55-64 Only | 4.3 | 13.6 | 8.0 | 6.8 | 5.8 | 3.7 | 4.0 | Ranked 1st |
| | 15.2 | 14.8 | 18.4 | 16.2 | 16.0 | 8.9 | 11.9 | Ranked 2nd |
| | 80.4 | 71.6 | 73.6 | 77.1 | 78.2 | 87.4 | 84.1 | Ranked 3rd-6th/not ranked |
| | (92) | (88) | (87) | (266) | (294) | (190) | (226) | Weighted N |
| 65-74 Only | 2.6 | 0.0 | 7.4 | 5.8 | 6.7 | 0.0 | 0.0 | Ranked 1st |
| | 13.2 | 20.0 | 18.5 | 9.6 | 13.3 | 0.0 | 10.5 | Ranked 2nd |
| | 84.2 | 80.0 | 74.1 | 84.6 | 80.0 | 100.0 | 89.5 | Ranked 3rd-6th/not ranked |
| | (38) | (15) | (27) | (52) | (45) | (31) | (19) | Weighted N |
| 75 And Older Only | ** | 0.0 | 0.0 | 0.0 | 16.7 | 0.0 | 0.0 | Ranked 1st |
| | ** | 40.0 | 0.0 | 25.0 | 16.7 | 0.0 | 0.0 | Ranked 2nd |
| | ** | 60.0 | 100.0 | 75.0 | 66.7 | 100.0 | 100.0 | Ranked 3rd-6th/not ranked |
| | ** | (5) | (5) | (8) | (6) | (2) | (2) | Weighted N |

* Code distinction not made.
Oldest age group coded "65 And Older" in 1958m.

Table 5.64
Preference in a Job: Chances for Advancement Are Good
Age of Respondent

**Unemployed Respondents**

| | 1958m | 1962k | 1963m | 1965b | 1966a | 1973q | 1974q | |
|---|---|---|---|---|---|---|---|---|
| **18-24 Only** | 0.0% | 10.0% | 23.1% | 17.5% | 42.9% | ** | ** | Ranked 1st |
| | 50.0 | 40.0 | 53.8 | 27.5 | 14.3 | ** | ** | Ranked 2nd |
| | 50.0 | 50.0 | 23.1 | 55.0 | 42.9 | ** | ** | Ranked 3rd-6th/not ranked |
| | (4) | (10) | (13) | (40) | (7) | ** | ** | Weighted N |
| **25-34 Only** | 23.5 | 12.5 | 13.3 | 5.3 | 8.3 | ** | ** | Ranked 1st |
| | 17.6 | 18.8 | 46.7 | 26.3 | 8.3 | ** | ** | Ranked 2nd |
| | 58.8 | 68.8 | 40.0 | 68.4 | 83.3 | ** | ** | Ranked 3rd-6th/not ranked |
| | (17) | (16) | (15) | (19) | (12) | ** | ** | Weighted N |
| **35-44 Only** | 0.0 | 6.3 | 6.7 | 17.9 | 8.3 | ** | ** | Ranked 1st |
| | 17.6 | 18.8 | 13.3 | 21.4 | 16.7 | ** | ** | Ranked 2nd |
| | 82.4 | 75.0 | 80.0 | 60.7 | 75.0 | ** | ** | Ranked 3rd-6th/not ranked |
| | (17) | (16) | (15) | (28) | (12) | ** | ** | Weighted N |
| **45-54 Only** | 5.9 | 4.3 | 0.0 | 6.5 | 3.6 | ** | ** | Ranked 1st |
| | 5.9 | 26.1 | 23.5 | 21.7 | 14.3 | ** | ** | Ranked 2nd |
| | 88.2 | 69.6 | 76.5 | 71.7 | 82.1 | ** | ** | Ranked 3rd-6th/not ranked |
| | (17) | (23) | (17) | (46) | (28) | ** | ** | Weighted N |
| **55-64 Only** | 0.0 | 0.0 | 14.3 | 6.3 | 0.0 | ** | ** | Ranked 1st |
| | 14.3 | 7.7 | 14.3 | 26.3 | 26.3 | ** | ** | Ranked 2nd |
| | 85.7 | 92.3 | 71.4 | 67.5 | 73.7 | ** | ** | Ranked 3rd-6th/not ranked |
| | (21) | (26) | (35) | (80) | (19) | ** | ** | Weighted N |
| **65-74 Only** | 2.0 | 6.3 | 9.3 | 8.9 | 0.0 | ** | ** | Ranked 1st |
| | 22.4 | 17.5 | 21.3 | 25.0 | 0.0 | ** | ** | Ranked 2nd |
| | 75.5 | 76.3 | 69.3 | 66.1 | 100.0 | ** | ** | Ranked 3rd-6th/not ranked |
| | (98) | (80) | (75) | (180) | (10) | ** | ** | Weighted N |
| **75 And Older Only** | ** | 4.0 | 9.7 | 11.5 | 0.0 | ** | ** | Ranked 1st |
| | ** | 24.0 | 17.7 | 27.9 | 33.3 | ** | ** | Ranked 2nd |
| | ** | 72.0 | 72.6 | 60.6 | 66.7 | ** | ** | Ranked 3rd-6th/not ranked |
| | ** | (50) | (62) | (104) | (3) | ** | ** | Weighted N |

** Data not available in 1973q and 1974q.
** Code distinction not made in 1958m--oldest age group coded "65 And Older".

Table 5.65
Preference in a Job: Chances for Advancement Are Good
Income of Respondent

Employed Respondents

| | Year | | | | | | | |
|---|---|---|---|---|---|---|---|---|
| | 1958m | 1962k | 1963m | 1965b | 1966a | 1973q | 1974q | |
| Income 1 (0-16%) | 5.0% | 0.0% | 0.0% | 1.7% | 8.7% | 10.0% | 6.8% | Ranked 1st |
| | 13.3 | 13.9 | 0.0 | 13.3 | 15.1 | 18.2 | 24.6 | Ranked 2nd |
| | 81.7 | 86.1 | 100.0 | 85.0 | 76.2 | 71.8 | 68.6 | Ranked 3rd-6th/not ranked |
| | (60) | (36) | (23) | (60) | (126) | (110) | (118) | Weighted N |
| Income 2 (17-33%) | 4.4 | 9.5 | 6.8 | 6.3 | 8.7 | 19.8 | 5.4 | Ranked 1st |
| | 13.2 | 25.7 | 23.3 | 17.7 | 16.7 | 14.0 | 23.1 | Ranked 2nd |
| | 82.4 | 64.9 | 69.9 | 75.9 | 74.7 | 66.1 | 71.6 | Ranked 3rd-6th/not ranked |
| | (68) | (74) | (73) | (158) | (288) | (121) | (299) | Weighted N |
| Income 3 (34-67%) | 8.2 | 13.0 | 9.3 | 11.2 | 12.5 | 9.3 | 9.3 | Ranked 1st |
| | 24.7 | 19.7 | 22.8 | 21.9 | 20.4 | 17.8 | 19.4 | Ranked 2nd |
| | 67.1 | 67.3 | 67.9 | 66.9 | 67.1 | 72.9 | 71.4 | Ranked 3rd-6th/not ranked |
| | (231) | (223) | (193) | (529) | (686) | (517) | (625) | Weighted N |
| Income 4 (68-95%) | 16.0 | 16.3 | 15.2 | 12.0 | 13.3 | 9.4 | 8.3 | Ranked 1st |
| | 24.3 | 32.6 | 31.5 | 26.2 | 24.0 | 17.6 | 11.7 | Ranked 2nd |
| | 59.7 | 51.1 | 53.4 | 61.8 | 62.7 | 73.0 | 80.0 | Ranked 3rd-6th/not ranked |
| | (144) | (141) | (178) | (592) | (445) | (615) | (460) | Weighted N |
| Income 5 (96-100%) | 20.4 | 22.7 | 9.5 | 15.7 | 11.0 | 4.0 | 6.1 | Ranked 1st |
| | 20.4 | 36.4 | 23.8 | 26.5 | 35.4 | 20.0 | 25.8 | Ranked 2nd |
| | 59.3 | 40.9 | 66.7 | 57.8 | 53.5 | 76.0 | 68.2 | Ranked 3rd-6th/not ranked |
| | (54) | (22) | (42) | (83) | (127) | (125) | (66) | Weighted N |

Figure 5.8
Good Chances for Advancement by Income of Employed R

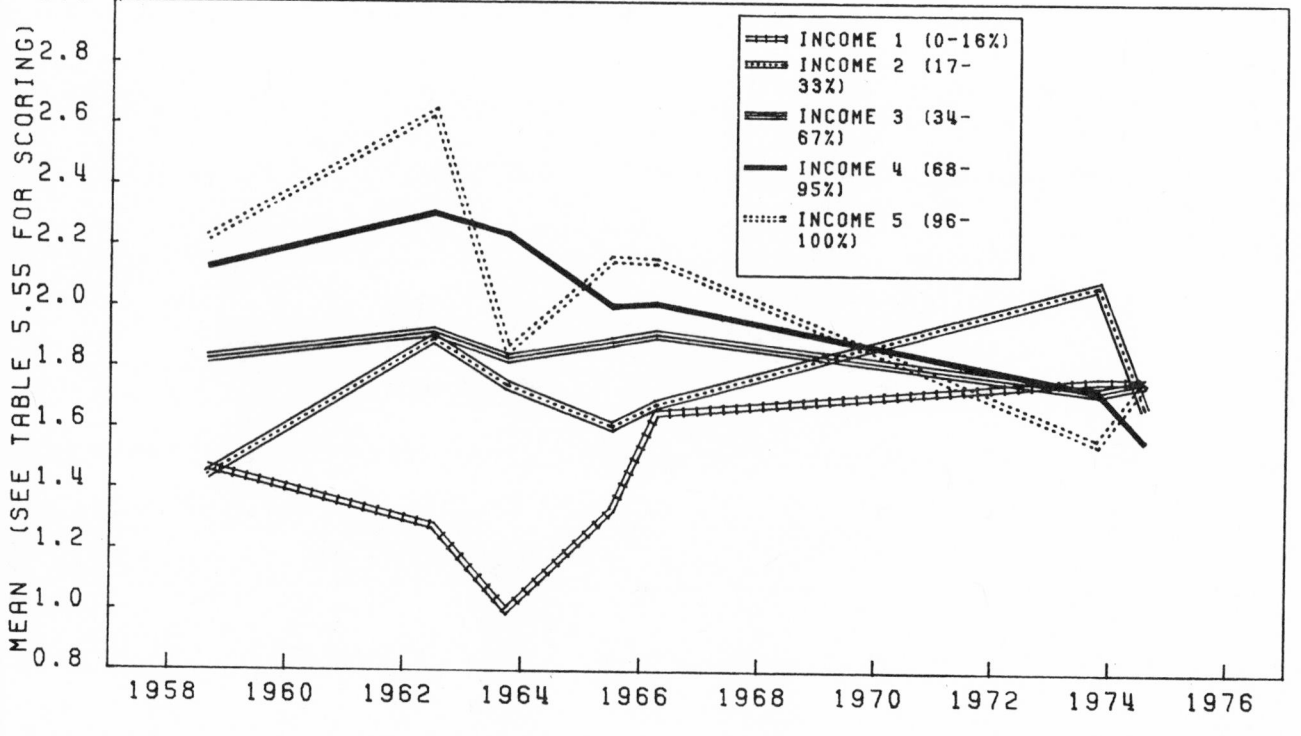

Work And Retirement

Table 5.66
Preference in a Job  Chances for Advancement Are Good
Income of Respondent

| Unemployed Respondents | | | | Year | | | | |
|---|---|---|---|---|---|---|---|---|
| | 1958m | 1962k | 1963m | 1965b | 1966a | 1973q | 1974q | |
| Income 1 (0–16%) | 2.4% | 3.4% | 7.7% | 10.5% | 0.0% | ** | ** | Ranked 1st |
| | 15.5 | 20.2 | 18.3 | 20.4 | 13.6 | ** | ** | Ranked 2nd |
| | 82.1 | 76.4 | 74.0 | 69.1 | 86.4 | ** | ** | Ranked 3rd–6th/not ranked |
| | (84) | (89) | (104) | (191) | (22) | ** | ** | Weighted N |
| Income 2 (17–33%) | 6.7 | 7.1 | 6.7 | 7.4 | 7.7 | ** | ** | Ranked 1st |
| | 20.0 | 15.7 | 21.7 | 25.2 | 7.7 | ** | ** | Ranked 2nd |
| | 73.3 | 77.1 | 71.7 | 67.4 | 84.6 | ** | ** | Ranked 3rd–6th/not ranked |
| | (30) | (70) | (60) | (135) | (26) | ** | ** | Weighted N |
| Income 3 (34–67%) | 5.7 | 2.7 | 11.1 | 6.9 | 12.5 | ** | ** | Ranked 1st |
| | 22.9 | 18.9 | 36.1 | 29.3 | 25.0 | ** | ** | Ranked 2nd |
| | 71.4 | 78.4 | 52.8 | 63.8 | 62.5 | ** | ** | Ranked 3rd–6th/not ranked |
| | (35) | (37) | (36) | (116) | (32) | ** | ** | Weighted N |
| Income 4 (68–95%) | 8.3 | 10.0 | 20.0 | 20.0 | 0.0 | ** | ** | Ranked 1st |
| | 16.7 | 40.0 | 40.0 | 31.1 | 12.5 | ** | ** | Ranked 2nd |
| | 75.0 | 50.0 | 40.0 | 48.9 | 87.5 | ** | ** | Ranked 3rd–6th/not ranked |
| | (12) | (10) | (15) | (45) | (8) | ** | ** | Weighted N |
| Income 5 (96–100%) | 0.0 | 16.7 | 50.0 | 20.0 | 0.0 | ** | ** | Ranked 1st |
| | 66.7 | 16.7 | 0.0 | 60.0 | 0.0 | ** | ** | Ranked 2nd |
| | 33.3 | 66.7 | 50.0 | 20.0 | 100.0 | ** | ** | Ranked 3rd–6th/not ranked |
| | (3) | (6) | (2) | (10) | (5) | ** | ** | Weighted N |

** Data not available

Table 5.67
Preference in a Job: Work Is Important, Gives Feeling of Accomplishment
Total Population--Employed and Unemployed Respondents

Employed Respondents

| | | Year | | | | | | |
|---|---|---|---|---|---|---|---|---|
| | | 1958m | 1962k | 1963m | 1965b | 1966a | 1973q | 1974q |
| Ranked 1st | (5) | 13.3% | 21.6% | 26.4% | 22.7% | 35.7% | 31.9% | 35.1% |
| Ranked 2nd | (3) | 13.3 | 19.2 | 17.2 | 17.1 | 14.9 | 17.2 | 18.8 |
| Ranked 3rd-6th/not ranked | (1) | 73.5 | 59.2 | 56.4 | 60.2 | 49.4 | 50.9 | 46.1 |
| Total | | 100% | 100% | 100% | 100% | 100% | 100% | 100% |
| Weighted N | | 573 | 505 | 530 | 1442 | 1696 | 1576 | 1753 |
| Unweighted N | | 573 | 505 | 530 | 1442 | 1696 | 795 | 868 |

Table 5.68

Unemployed Respondents

| | | 1958m | 1962k | 1963m | 1965b | 1966a | 1973q | 1974q |
|---|---|---|---|---|---|---|---|---|
| Ranked 1st | (5) | 18.7% | 21.8% | 18.1% | 17.4% | 31.6% | ** | ** |
| Ranked 2nd | (3) | 8.8 | 13.8 | 14.3 | 15.2 | 12.6 | ** | ** |
| Ranked 3rd-6th/not ranked | (1) | 72.5 | 64.4 | 67.6 | 67.3 | 55.8 | ** | ** |
| Total | | 100% | 100% | 100% | 100% | 100% | ** | ** |
| Weighted N | | 171 | 225 | 238 | 505 | 95 | ** | ** |
| Unweighted N | | 171 | 225 | 238 | 505 | 95 | ** | ** |

** Data not available
Question asked of head of households only in 1958m, 1962k, 1963m, 1965b, and 1966a.

Table 5.69
Preference in a Job: Work Is Important, Gives Feeling of Accomplishment
Sex of Respondent

Employed Respondents

|  |  | | | | Year | | | |
|---|---|---|---|---|---|---|---|---|
|  |  | 1958m | 1962k | 1963m | 1965b | 1966a | 1973q | 1974q |
| Males Only | | 12.4% | 19.8% | 25.7% | 22.5% | 34.4% | 27.2% | 31.2% | Ranked 1st |
| | | 12.8 | 18.8 | 18.3 | 17.2 | 15.3 | 18.2 | 20.8 | Ranked 2nd |
| | | 74.8 | 61.4 | 56.0 | 60.3 | 50.2 | 54.7 | 48.1 | Ranked 3rd-6th/not ranked |
| | | (445) | (383) | (416) | (1277) | (1437) | (986) | (1026) | Weighted N |
| Females Only | | 16.4 | 27.3 | 28.9 | 25.0 | 42.8 | 39.8 | 40.6 | Ranked 1st |
| | | 14.8 | 20.7 | 13.2 | 15.9 | 12.5 | 15.6 | 16.1 | Ranked 2nd |
| | | 68.8 | 52.1 | 57.9 | 59.1 | 44.7 | 44.6 | 43.3 | Ranked 3rd-6th/not ranked |
| | | (128) | (121) | (114) | (164) | (257) | (590) | (727) | Weighted N |

Table 5.70

Unemployed Respondents

|  | 1958m | 1962k | 1963m | 1965b | 1966a | 1973q | 1974q | |
|---|---|---|---|---|---|---|---|---|
| Males Only | 19.3% | 18.8% | 15.6% | 15.4% | 34.6% | ** | ** | Ranked 1st |
| | 8.4 | 13.9 | 12.8 | 16.4 | 9.0 | ** | ** | Ranked 2nd |
| | 72.3 | 67.3 | 71.6 | 68.2 | 56.4 | ** | ** | Ranked 3rd-6th/not ranked |
| | (83) | (101) | (109) | (299) | (78) | ** | ** | Weighted N |
| Females Only | 18.2 | 24.4 | 20.2 | 20.4 | 17.6 | ** | ** | Ranked 1st |
| | 9.1 | 13.8 | 15.5 | 13.6 | 29.4 | ** | ** | Ranked 2nd |
| | 72.7 | 61.8 | 64.3 | 66.0 | 52.9 | ** | ** | Ranked 3rd-6th/not ranked |
| | (88) | (123) | (129) | (206) | (17) | ** | ** | Weighted N |

** Data not available.

Table 5.71
Preference in a Job: Work Is Important, Gives Feeling of Accomplishment
Race of Respondent

Employed Respondents

|  | 1958m | 1962k | 1963m | 1965b | 1966a | 1973q | 1974q | |
|---|---|---|---|---|---|---|---|---|
| Whites Only | 14.6% | 23.5% | 27.9% | 24.2% | 37.4% | 33.1% | 36.7% | Ranked 1st |
|  | 14.8 | 19.7 | 17.2 | 17.7 | 15.3 | 17.8 | 19.7 | Ranked 2nd |
|  | 70.7 | 56.8 | 54.8 | 58.1 | 47.4 | 49.1 | 43.6 | Ranked 3rd-6th/not ranked |
|  | (501) | (451) | (476) | (1281) | (1547) | (1392) | (1490) | Weighted N |
| Blacks Only | 4.5 | 2.2 | 8.9 | 9.8 | 17.6 | 21.2 | 23.5 | Ranked 1st |
|  | 3.0 | 13.0 | 13.3 | 12.1 | 9.2 | 14.4 | 12.2 | Ranked 2nd |
|  | 92.4 | 84.8 | 77.8 | 78.0 | 73.1 | 64.4 | 64.3 | Ranked 3rd-6th/not ranked |
|  | (66) | (46) | (45) | (132) | (119) | (132) | (196) | Weighted N |

Table 5.72

Unemployed Respondents

|  | 1958m | 1962k | 1963m | 1965b | 1966a | 1973q | 1974q | |
|---|---|---|---|---|---|---|---|---|
| Whites Only | 20.8% | 22.5% | 19.2% | 18.3% | 32.9% | ** | ** | Ranked 1st |
|  | 10.4 | 14.5 | 15.8 | 16.1 | 15.7 | ** | ** | Ranked 2nd |
|  | 68.8 | 63.0 | 65.0 | 65.6 | 51.4 | ** | ** | Ranked 3rd-6th/not ranked |
|  | (144) | (200) | (203) | (448) | (70) | ** | ** | Weighted N |
| Blacks Only | 8.3 | 13.6 | 12.1 | 8.5 | 25.0 | ** | ** | Ranked 1st |
|  | 0.0 | 9.1 | 3.0 | 6.4 | 4.2 | ** | ** | Ranked 2nd |
|  | 91.7 | 77.3 | 84.8 | 85.1 | 70.8 | ** | ** | Ranked 3rd-6th/not ranked |
|  | (24) | (22) | (33) | (47) | (24) | ** | ** | Weighted N |

** Data not available.

Figure 5.9
Work Is Important by Race of Employed R

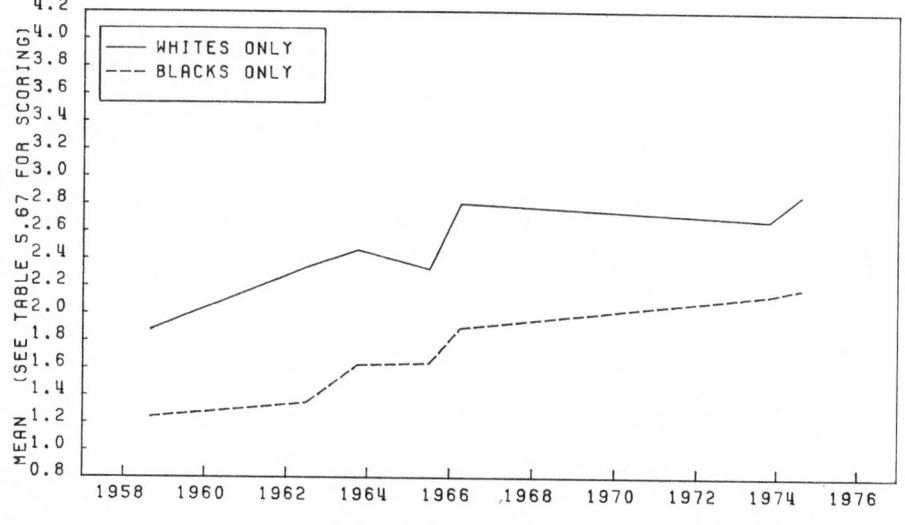

Table 5.73
Preference in a Job: Work Is Important, Gives Feeling of Accomplishment
Education of Respondent

**Employed Respondents**

| | 1958m | 1962k | 1963m | 1965b | 1966a | 1973q | 1974q | |
|---|---|---|---|---|---|---|---|---|
| **Grade School Only** | 8.1% | 8.3% | 16.7% | 12.3% | 22.6% | 24.6% | 22.4% | Ranked 1st |
| | 5.8 | 13.6 | 9.3 | 14.4 | 15.9 | 5.4 | 13.8 | Ranked 2nd |
| | 86.1 | 78.0 | 74.1 | 73.3 | 61.4 | 70.1 | 63.8 | Ranked 3rd-6th/not ranked |
| | (173) | (132) | (108) | (326) | (345) | (167) | (174) | Weighted N |
| **High School Only** | 11.8 | 18.7 | 17.3 | 18.4 | 30.7 | 25.9 | 31.2 | Ranked 1st |
| | 14.0 | 19.6 | 20.8 | 16.8 | 14.7 | 16.4 | 19.4 | Ranked 2nd |
| | 74.2 | 61.7 | 62.0 | 64.8 | 54.6 | 57.7 | 49.5 | Ranked 3rd-6th/not ranked |
| | (279) | (230) | (255) | (730) | (797) | (891) | (847) | Weighted N |
| **College Only** | 23.5 | 38.5 | 51.4 | 39.9 | 54.2 | 44.0 | 43.2 | Ranked 1st |
| | 22.7 | 23.8 | 18.1 | 19.7 | 14.6 | 22.7 | 19.6 | Ranked 2nd |
| | 53.8 | 37.8 | 30.6 | 40.4 | 31.1 | 33.3 | 37.2 | Ranked 3rd-6th/not ranked |
| | (119) | (143) | (144) | (386) | (472) | (511) | (723) | Weighted N |

Table 5.74

**Unemployed Respondents**

| | 1958m | 1962k | 1963m | 1965b | 1966a | 1973q | 1974q | |
|---|---|---|---|---|---|---|---|---|
| **Grade School Only** | 14.4% | 18.6% | 12.3% | 11.9% | 37.1% | ** | ** | Ranked 1st |
| | 7.8 | 13.4 | 8.8 | 12.3 | 2.9 | ** | ** | Ranked 2nd |
| | 77.8 | 68.0 | 78.9 | 75.7 | 60.0 | ** | ** | Ranked 3rd-6th/not ranked |
| | (90) | (97) | (114) | (235) | (35) | ** | ** | Weighted N |
| **High School Only** | 13.5 | 23.3 | 19.2 | 16.5 | 24.4 | ** | ** | Ranked 1st |
| | 7.7 | 10.5 | 15.4 | 21.2 | 15.6 | ** | ** | Ranked 2nd |
| | 78.8 | 66.3 | 65.4 | 62.4 | 60.0 | ** | ** | Ranked 3rd-6th/not ranked |
| | (52) | (86) | (78) | (170) | (45) | ** | ** | Weighted N |
| **College Only** | 46.2 | 28.9 | 30.0 | 32.7 | 46.2 | ** | ** | Ranked 1st |
| | 15.4 | 21.1 | 30.0 | 10.2 | 15.4 | ** | ** | Ranked 2nd |
| | 38.5 | 50.0 | 40.0 | 57.1 | 38.5 | ** | ** | Ranked 3rd-6th/not ranked |
| | (26) | (38) | (30) | (98) | (13) | ** | ** | Weighted N |

** Data not available.

Figure 5.10
Work Is Important by Education of Employed R

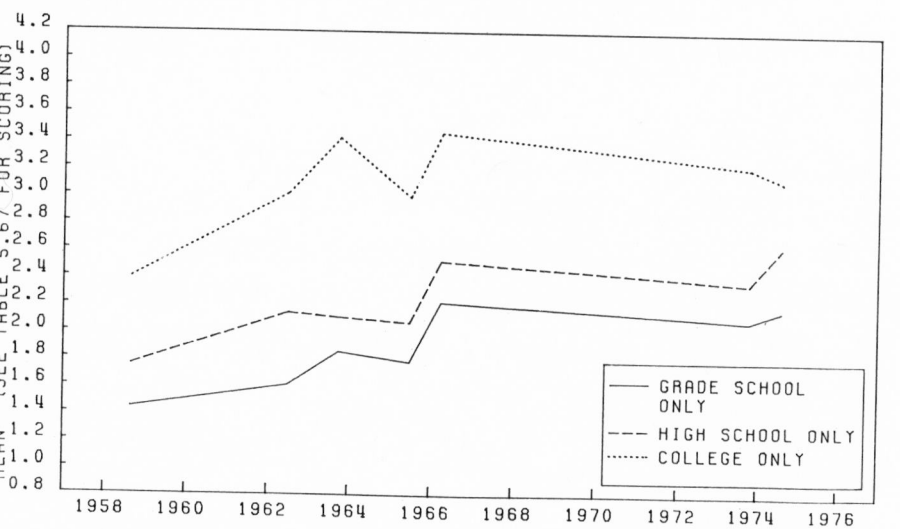

Table 5.75
Preference in a Job: Work Is Important, Gives Feeling of Accomplishment
Age of Respondent

| Employed Respondents | | | | Year | | | | |
|---|---|---|---|---|---|---|---|---|
| | 1958m | 1962k | 1963m | 1965b | 1966a | 1973q | 1974q | |
| 18-24 Only | 20.0% | 23.8% | 32.5% | 16.0% | 40.2% | 28.5% | 35.3% | Ranked 1st |
| | 8.6 | 14.3 | 20.0 | 20.0 | 14.3 | 15.6 | 20.2 | Ranked 2nd |
| | 71.4 | 61.9 | 47.5 | 64.0 | 45.5 | 55.8 | 44.5 | Ranked 3rd-6th/not ranked |
| | (35) | (21) | (40) | (75) | (112) | (326) | (337) | Weighted N |
| | | | | | | | | |
| 25-34 Only | 12.9 | 23.0 | 34.3 | 22.8 | 30.6 | 32.3 | 28.4 | Ranked 1st |
| | 16.9 | 15.1 | 13.0 | 12.2 | 15.7 | 20.2 | 23.1 | Ranked 2nd |
| | 70.2 | 61.9 | 52.8 | 65.0 | 53.7 | 47.6 | 48.5 | Ranked 3rd-6th/not ranked |
| | (124) | (126) | (108) | (303) | (395) | (372) | (468) | Weighted N |
| | | | | | | | | |
| 35-44 Only | 11.7 | 22.8 | 32.2 | 21.3 | 34.5 | 33.0 | 41.3 | Ranked 1st |
| | 12.3 | 16.9 | 17.4 | 18.6 | 12.5 | 17.3 | 15.2 | Ranked 2nd |
| | 76.0 | 60.3 | 50.4 | 60.1 | 53.0 | 49.7 | 43.4 | Ranked 3rd-6th/not ranked |
| | (154) | (136) | (121) | (361) | (423) | (324) | (341) | Weighted N |
| | | | | | | | | |
| 45-54 Only | 14.2 | 20.2 | 19.6 | 25.9 | 38.4 | 30.2 | 35.2 | Ranked 1st |
| | 11.0 | 26.6 | 13.0 | 16.2 | 17.0 | 19.8 | 18.0 | Ranked 2nd |
| | 74.8 | 53.2 | 67.4 | 58.0 | 44.6 | 50.0 | 46.8 | Ranked 3rd-6th/not ranked |
| | (127) | (109) | (138) | (371) | (401) | (328) | (355) | Weighted N |
| | | | | | | | | |
| 55-64 Only | 14.7 | 21.6 | 18.4 | 21.3 | 37.6 | 39.5 | 35.0 | Ranked 1st |
| | 14.7 | 23.9 | 25.3 | 18.3 | 15.2 | 10.0 | 16.8 | Ranked 2nd |
| | 70.5 | 54.5 | 56.3 | 60.4 | 47.2 | 50.5 | 48.2 | Ranked 3rd-6th/not ranked |
| | (95) | (88) | (87) | (268) | (303) | (190) | (226) | Weighted N |
| | | | | | | | | |
| 65-74 Only | 7.9 | 18.8 | 21.4 | 26.8 | 40.4 | 25.8 | 73.7 | Ranked 1st |
| | 13.2 | 0.0 | 21.4 | 30.4 | 10.6 | 9.7 | 0.0 | Ranked 2nd |
| | 78.9 | 81.3 | 57.1 | 42.9 | 48.9 | 64.5 | 26.3 | Ranked 3rd-6th/not ranked |
| | (38) | (16) | (28) | (56) | (47) | (31) | (19) | Weighted N |
| | | | | | | | | |
| 75 And Older Only | ** | 0.0 | 16.7 | 25.0 | 50.0 | 50.0 | 50.0 | Ranked 1st |
| | ** | 20.0 | 16.7 | 12.5 | 16.7 | 0.0 | 0.0 | Ranked 2nd |
| | ** | 80.0 | 66.7 | 62.5 | 33.3 | 50.0 | 50.0 | Ranked 3rd-6th/not ranked |
| | ** | (5) | (6) | (8) | (6) | (2) | (2) | Weighted N |

** Code distinction not made.
Oldest age group coded "65 And Older" in 1958m.

Table 5.76
Preference in a Job: Work Is Important, Gives Feeling of Accomplishment
Age of Respondent

Unemployed Respondents

| | 1958m | 1962k | 1963m | 1965b | 1966a | 1973q | 1974q | |
|---|---|---|---|---|---|---|---|---|
| 18-24 Only | 25.0% | 30.0% | 23.1% | 22.5% | 0.0% | ** | ** | Ranked 1st |
| | 0.0 | 10.0 | 23.1 | 17.5 | 28.6 | ** | ** | Ranked 2nd |
| | 75.0 | 60.0 | 53.8 | 60.0 | 71.4 | ** | ** | Ranked 3rd-6th/not ranked |
| | (4) | (10) | (13) | (40) | (7) | ** | ** | Weighted N |
| 25-34 Only | 29.4 | 33.3 | 13.3 | 31.6 | 38.5 | ** | ** | Ranked 1st |
| | 0.0 | 26.7 | 13.3 | 10.5 | 0.0 | ** | ** | Ranked 2nd |
| | 70.6 | 40.0 | 73.3 | 57.9 | 61.5 | ** | ** | Ranked 3rd-6th/not ranked |
| | (17) | (15) | (15) | (19) | (13) | ** | ** | Weighted N |
| 35-44 Only | 12.5 | 46.7 | 13.3 | 14.3 | 16.7 | ** | ** | Ranked 1st |
| | 0.0 | 6.7 | 20.0 | 17.9 | 16.7 | ** | ** | Ranked 2nd |
| | 87.5 | 46.7 | 66.7 | 67.9 | 66.7 | ** | ** | Ranked 3rd-6th/not ranked |
| | (16) | (15) | (15) | (28) | (12) | ** | ** | Weighted N |
| 45-54 Only | 5.9 | 34.8 | 23.5 | 13.0 | 35.7 | ** | ** | Ranked 1st |
| | 5.9 | 8.7 | 5.9 | 23.9 | 10.7 | ** | ** | Ranked 2nd |
| | 88.2 | 56.5 | 70.6 | 63.0 | 53.6 | ** | ** | Ranked 3rd-6th/not ranked |
| | (17) | (23) | (17) | (46) | (28) | ** | ** | Weighted N |
| 55-64 Only | 38.1 | 14.3 | 13.9 | 22.0 | 21.1 | ** | ** | Ranked 1st |
| | 4.8 | 17.9 | 16.7 | 13.4 | 15.8 | ** | ** | Ranked 2nd |
| | 57.1 | 67.9 | 69.4 | 64.6 | 63.2 | ** | ** | Ranked 3rd-6th/not ranked |
| | (21) | (28) | (36) | (82) | (19) | ** | ** | Weighted N |
| 65-74 Only | 15.6 | 16.5 | 22.7 | 14.1 | 54.5 | ** | ** | Ranked 1st |
| | 13.5 | 11.4 | 12.0 | 15.8 | 9.1 | ** | ** | Ranked 2nd |
| | 70.8 | 72.2 | 65.3 | 70.1 | 36.4 | ** | ** | Ranked 3rd-6th/not ranked |
| | (96) | (79) | (75) | (184) | (11) | ** | ** | Weighted N |
| 75 And Older Only | ** | 15.4 | 16.1 | 17.9 | 66.7 | ** | ** | Ranked 1st |
| | ** | 15.4 | 14.5 | 11.3 | 0.0 | ** | ** | Ranked 2nd |
| | ** | 69.2 | 69.4 | 70.8 | 33.3 | ** | ** | Ranked 3rd-6th/not ranked |
| | ** | (52) | (62) | (106) | (3) | ** | ** | Weighted N |

** Data not available in 1973q and 1974q.
** Code distinction not made in 1958m--oldest age group coded "65 And Older".

Table 5.77
Preference in a Job: Work Is Important, Gives Feeling of Accomplishment
Income of Respondent

| Employed Respondents | 1958m | 1962k | 1963m | 1965b | 1966a | 1973q | 1974q | |
|---|---|---|---|---|---|---|---|---|
| | | | | Year | | | | |
| Income 1 (0-16%) | 14.5% | 8.1% | 16.7% | 13.1% | 27.9% | 26.9% | 31.4% | Ranked 1st |
| | 3.2 | 16.2 | 8.3 | 16.4 | 11.6 | 13.9 | 13.6 | Ranked 2nd |
| | 82.3 | 75.7 | 75.0 | 70.5 | 60.5 | 59.3 | 55.1 | Ranked 3rd-6th/not ranked |
| | (62) | (37) | (24) | (61) | (129) | (108) | (118) | Weighted N |
| Income 2 (17-33%) | 8.8 | 13.3 | 19.2 | 12.3 | 30.1 | 20.7 | 30.4 | Ranked 1st |
| | 8.8 | 17.3 | 12.3 | 16.6 | 15.4 | 18.2 | 16.4 | Ranked 2nd |
| | 82.4 | 69.3 | 68.5 | 71.2 | 54.5 | 61.2 | 53.2 | Ranked 3rd-6th/not ranked |
| | (68) | (75) | (73) | (163) | (292) | (121) | (299) | Weighted N |
| Income 3 (34-67%) | 12.1 | 17.6 | 20.2 | 18.3 | 32.0 | 24.1 | 34.1 | Ranked 1st |
| | 13.4 | 19.4 | 17.1 | 16.0 | 15.3 | 15.5 | 17.9 | Ranked 2nd |
| | 74.5 | 63.1 | 62.7 | 65.7 | 52.7 | 60.4 | 48.0 | Ranked 3rd-6th/not ranked |
| | (231) | (222) | (193) | (536) | (694) | (515) | (625) | Weighted N |
| Income 4 (68-95%) | 13.2 | 30.5 | 34.3 | 27.5 | 41.4 | 36.5 | 42.6 | Ranked 1st |
| | 16.7 | 21.3 | 19.9 | 18.3 | 14.3 | 18.8 | 25.3 | Ranked 2nd |
| | 70.1 | 48.2 | 45.9 | 54.3 | 44.3 | 44.7 | 32.0 | Ranked 3rd-6th/not ranked |
| | (144) | (141) | (181) | (597) | (447) | (611) | (462) | Weighted N |
| Income 5 (96-100%) | 18.5 | 45.8 | 40.5 | 44.7 | 55.6 | 56.8 | 40.9 | Ranked 1st |
| | 22.2 | 20.8 | 21.4 | 16.5 | 17.3 | 13.6 | 6.1 | Ranked 2nd |
| | 59.3 | 33.3 | 38.1 | 38.8 | 27.1 | 29.6 | 53.0 | Ranked 3rd-6th/not ranked |
| | (54) | (24) | (42) | (85) | (133) | (125) | (66) | Weighted N |

Figure 5.11
Work Is Important by Income of Employed R

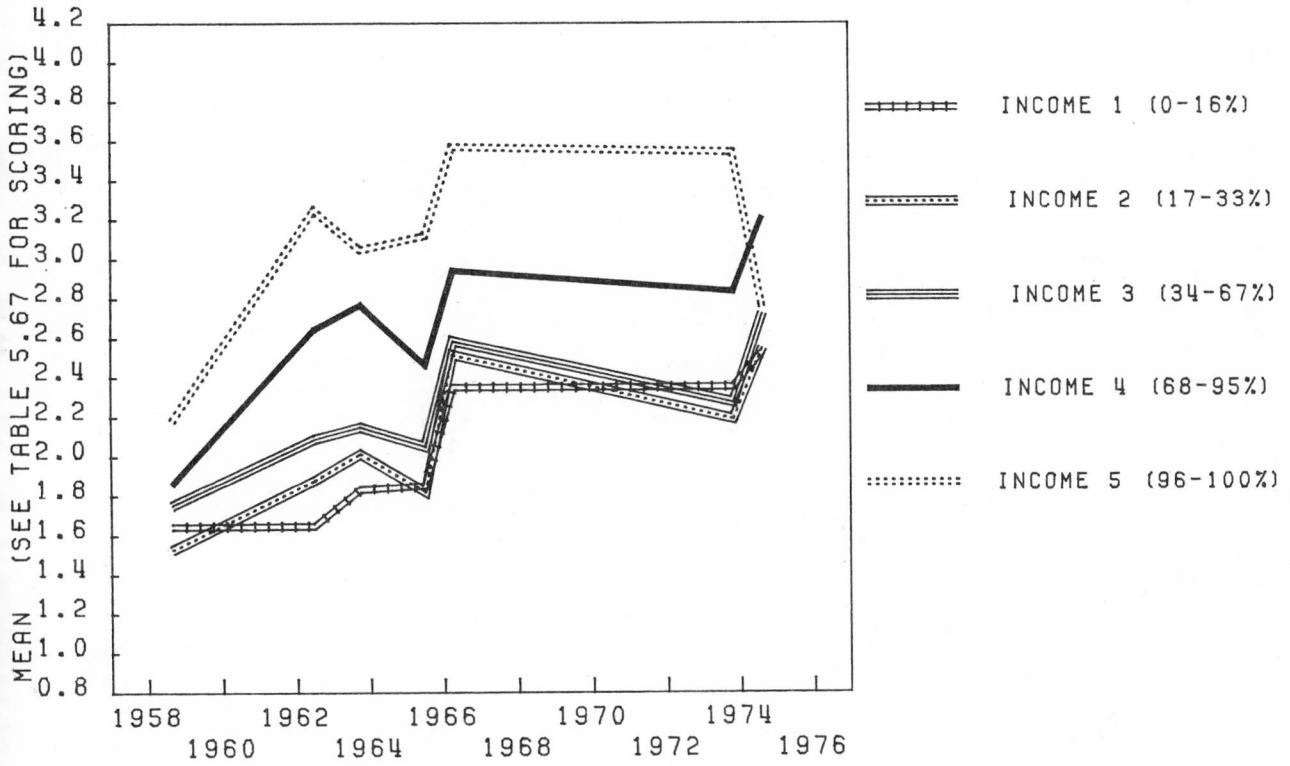

Work And Retirement

Table 5.78
Preference in a Job: Work Is Important, Gives Feeling of Accomplishment
Income of Respondent

Unemployed Respondents

| | Year | | | | | | | |
|---|---|---|---|---|---|---|---|---|
| | 1958m | 1962k | 1963m | 1965b | 1966a | 1973q | 1974q | |
| Income 1 (0-16%) | 14.6% | 21.6% | 12.4% | 17.5% | 27.3% | ** | ** | Ranked 1st |
| | 11.0 | 12.5 | 12.4 | 13.4 | 9.1 | ** | ** | Ranked 2nd |
| | 74.4 | 65.9 | 75.2 | 69.1 | 63.6 | ** | ** | Ranked 3rd-6th/not ranked |
| | (82) | (88) | (105) | (194) | (22) | ** | ** | Weighted N |
| Income 2 (17-33%) | 20.0 | 24.6 | 26.7 | 14.5 | 38.5 | ** | ** | Ranked 1st |
| | 0.0 | 10.1 | 11.7 | 15.9 | 7.7 | ** | ** | Ranked 2nd |
| | 80.0 | 65.2 | 61.7 | 69.6 | 53.8 | ** | ** | Ranked 3rd-6th/not ranked |
| | (30) | (69) | (60) | (138) | (26) | ** | ** | Weighted N |
| Income 3 (34-67%) | 17.6 | 20.5 | 8.3 | 18.8 | 24.2 | ** | ** | Ranked 1st |
| | 14.7 | 15.4 | 16.7 | 17.1 | 18.2 | ** | ** | Ranked 2nd |
| | 67.6 | 64.1 | 75.0 | 64.1 | 57.6 | ** | ** | Ranked 3rd-6th/not ranked |
| | (34) | (39) | (36) | (117) | (33) | ** | ** | Weighted N |
| Income 4 (68-95%) | 41.7 | 10.0 | 33.3 | 23.9 | 33.3 | ** | ** | Ranked 1st |
| | 0.0 | 20.0 | 13.3 | 15.2 | 11.1 | ** | ** | Ranked 2nd |
| | 58.3 | 70.0 | 53.3 | 60.9 | 55.6 | ** | ** | Ranked 3rd-6th/not ranked |
| | (12) | (10) | (15) | (46) | (9) | ** | ** | Weighted N |
| Income 5 (96-100%) | 33.3 | 0.0 | 50.0 | 10.0 | 60.0 | ** | ** | Ranked 1st |
| | 0.0 | 16.7 | 50.0 | 20.0 | 20.0 | ** | ** | Ranked 2nd |
| | 66.7 | 83.3 | 0.0 | 70.0 | 20.0 | ** | ** | Ranked 3rd-6th/not ranked |
| | (3) | (6) | (2) | (10) | (5) | ** | ** | Weighted N |

** Data not available.

Figure 5.12
Preference in a Job: All Responses
Employed Respondents

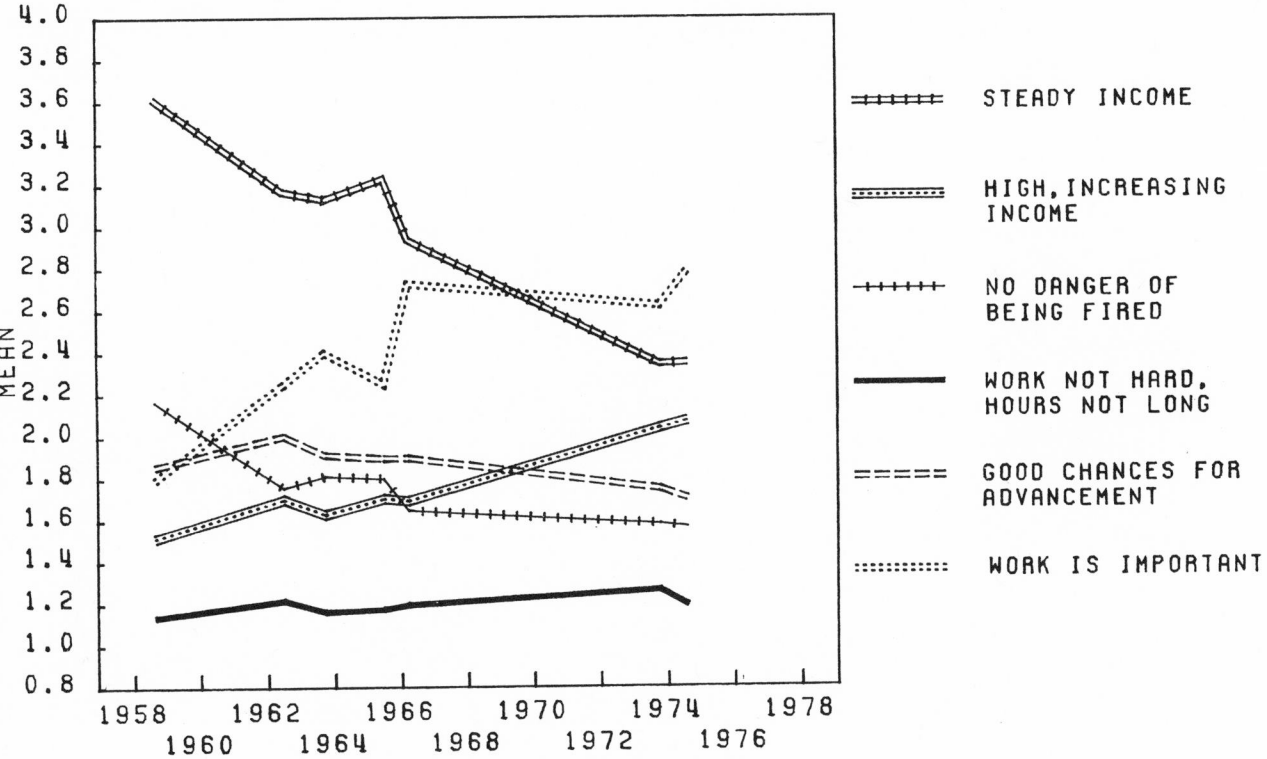

STEADY INCOME

HIGH, INCREASING
INCOME

NO DANGER OF
BEING FIRED

WORK NOT HARD,
HOURS NOT LONG

GOOD CHANCES FOR
ADVANCEMENT

WORK IS IMPORTANT

Table 5.79
Health-Related Work Disability
Total Population

QUESTION: Do you have/have you had an illness,physical condition or nervous condition which limits the type of work or the amount of work you can do? (Do you have any physical or nervous condition that limits the kind of work you can do? Do you have any physical or nervous condition that limits the amount of work you can do?)

| Employed Respondents | Year | | | | | | |
|---|---|---|---|---|---|---|---|
| | 1965b | 1968e | 1969e | 1970e | 1971e | 1972e | 1976e |
| Some disability (1) | 17.9% | 18.5% | 24.4% | 23.4% | 20.9% | 19.4% | 17.8% |
| No disability (5) | 82.1 | 81.5 | 75.6 | 76.6 | 79.1 | 80.6 | 82.2 |
| Total | 100% | 100% | 100% | 100% | 100% | 100% | 100% |
| Weighted N | 2190 | 106003 | 114311 | 123778 | 103614 | 115030 | 240176 |
| Unweighted N | 2190 | 3452 | 3779 | 4153 | 3636 | 4096 | 9289 |
| Mean | 4.28 | 4.26 | 4.03 | 4.06 | 4.16 | 4.22 | 4.29 |
| Standard Deviation | 1.53 | 1.55 | 1.72 | 1.69 | 1.63 | 1.58 | 1.53 |

Figure 5.13
Work Disability--Total Population

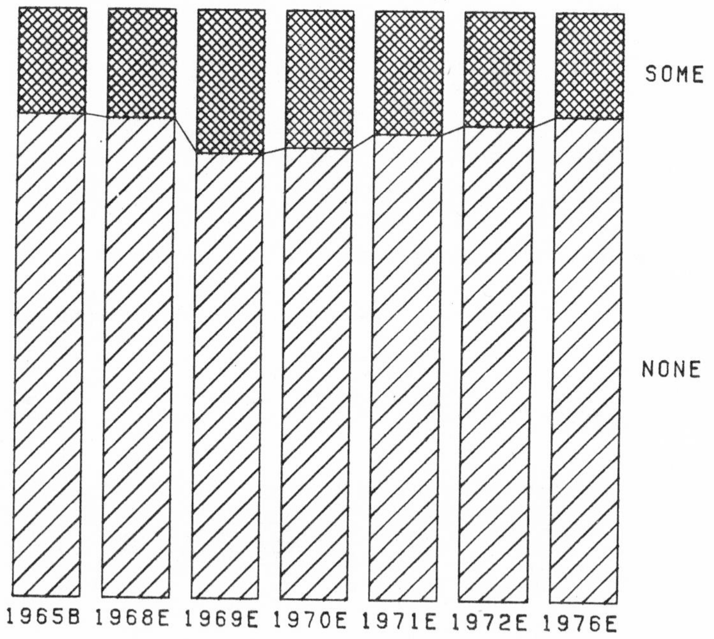


Figure 5.14
Work Disability by Race of R

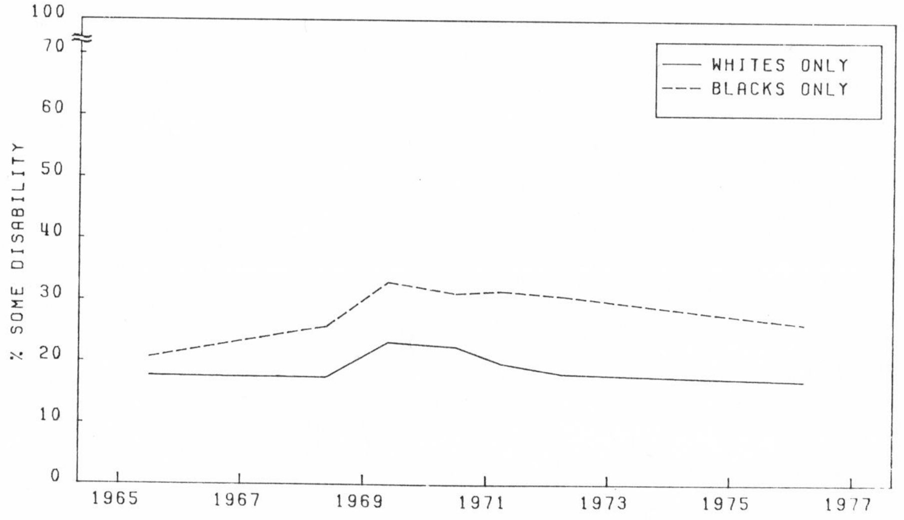

Table 5.80
Health-Related Work Disability
Sex of Respondent

% Some Disability

| | Year | | | | | | | |
|---|---|---|---|---|---|---|---|---|
| | 1965b | 1968e | 1969e | 1970e | 1971e | 1972e | 1976e | |
| Males Only | 15.7 | 16.3 | 21.4 | 20.5 | 17.4 | 16.2 | 16.0 | Some disability |
| | (1620) | (80645) | (85187) | (89808) | (75019) | (82259) | (108990) | Weighted N |
| Females Only | 24.4 | 25.5 | 33.1 | 31.0 | 30.2 | 27.5 | 19.2 | Some disability |
| | (570) | (25358) | (29124) | (33870) | (28544) | (32615) | (131186) | Weighted N |

Sex coded for head of household and wife only in 1968e,1969e,1970e,1971e,and 1972e.

Table 5.81
Race of Respondent

% Some Disability

| | 1965b | 1968e | 1969e | 1970e | 1971e | 1972e | 1976e | |
|---|---|---|---|---|---|---|---|---|
| Whites Only | 17.7 | 17.5 | 23.2 | 22.5 | 19.8 | 18.1 | 17.0 | Some disability |
| | (1953) | (93201) | (99999) | (107168) | (89674) | (99434) | (208675) | Weighted N |
| Blacks Only | 20.7 | 25.8 | 33.0 | 31.2 | 31.6 | 30.8 | 26.3 | Some disability |
| | (208) | (11034) | (12084) | (13420) | (11145) | (12501) | (24494) | Weighted N |

Race coded for head of household and wife only in 1971e.

Table 5.82
Education of Respondent

% Some Disability

| | 1965b | 1968e | 1969e | 1970e | 1971e | 1972e | 1976e | |
|---|---|---|---|---|---|---|---|---|
| Grade School Only | 29.6 | 34.3 | 43.1 | 43.1 | 40.0 | 36.4 | 40.6 | Some disability |
| | (642) | (27078) | (29993) | (30049) | (19033) | (22017) | (35227) | Weighted N |
| High School Only | 13.9 | 15.1 | 19.9 | 18.7 | 18.0 | 16.9 | 15.8 | Some disability |
| | (1014) | (48252) | (51376) | (57440) | (44923) | (54565) | (130854) | Weighted N |
| College Only | 11.4 | 9.9 | 14.2 | 14.3 | 12.2 | 10.8 | 8.7 | Some disability |
| | (525) | (30153) | (32271) | (34570) | (30081) | (34853) | (70149) | Weighted N |

Education coded for head of household only in 1971e  and for head and wife only in 1965b,1968e,1969e,1970e, 1972e,and 1976e.

Table 5.83
Health-Related Work Disability
Age of Respondent

% Some Disability

| | | | | Year | | | | |
|---|---|---|---|---|---|---|---|---|
| | 1965b | 1968e | 1969e | 1970e | 1971e | 1972e | 1976e | |
| 18-24 Only | 6.1 | 8.8 | 11.7 | 12.8 | 10.3 | 7.9 | 6.1 | Some disability |
| | (132) | (8400) | (8957) | (11910) | (10521) | (11822) | (28856) | Weighted N |
| 25-34 Only | 5.0 | 7.0 | 9.4 | 7.7 | 9.6 | 6.0 | 6.7 | Some disability |
| | (363) | (19949) | (21655) | (23558) | (20731) | (23139) | (58258) | Weighted N |
| 35-44 Only | 7.5 | 11.3 | 12.9 | 13.2 | 12.2 | 13.4 | 9.3 | Some disability |
| | (441) | (24200) | (24818) | (25050) | (22475) | (22582) | (39930) | Weighted N |
| 45-54 Only | 15.2 | 16.4 | 20.2 | 19.0 | 19.8 | 17.5 | 16.5 | Some disability |
| | (461) | (20682) | (21816) | (22923) | (19451) | (21334) | (43974) | Weighted N |
| 55-64 Only | 24.7 | 26.5 | 34.9 | 34.6 | 29.4 | 28.4 | 28.6 | Some disability |
| | (385) | (17978) | (19548) | (20141) | (16169) | (17626) | (31728) | Weighted N |
| 65-74 Only | 42.0 | 38.7 | 53.3 | 50.2 | 49.0 | 40.5 | 40.2 | Some disability |
| | (269) | (10472) | (12073) | (13744) | (11027) | (12971) | (24522) | Weighted N |
| 75 And Older Only | 42.0 | 58.9 | 70.9 | 63.9 | 58.0 | 56.9 | 56.9 | Some disability |
| | (131) | (4121) | (5573) | (6288) | (3185) | (5311) | (12503) | Weighted N |

Age coded for head of household and wife only in 1965b,1968e,1969e,1970e,1971e,and 1972e.

Figure 5.15
Work Disability by Education of R

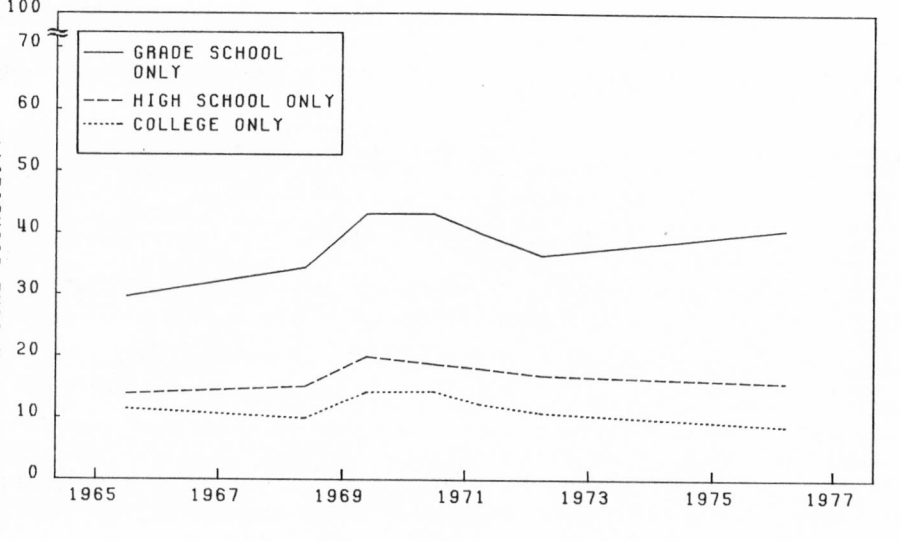

Figure 5.16
Work Disability by Age of R

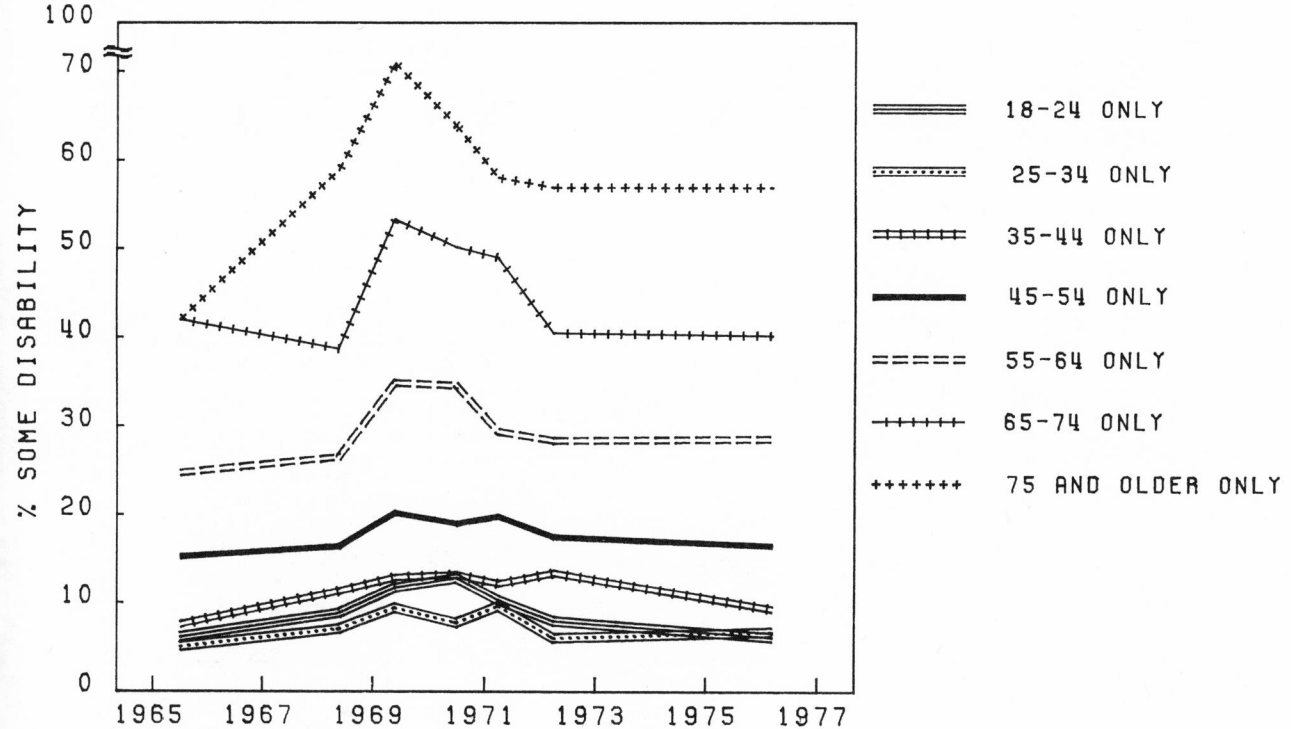

Table 5.84
If R Loses Job, What Are Chances of Getting a New Job that Pays the Same?
Total Population

QUESTION   Suppose that you lose your job for any reason during the next few months, what do you think are the chances
for getting another job that pays about the same?

|  |  | Year | | | | |
|---|---|---|---|---|---|---|
|  |  | 1954m | 1958f | 1958m | 1960d | 1961m |
| Good/confident | (5) | 38.3% | 31.6% | 34.5% | 44.5% | 41.6% |
| Good(qualified) | (4) | 16.9 | 11.1 | 17.4 | 16.7 | 15.3 |
| Pro-con | (3) | 1.7 | 2.2 | 1.5 | 3.5 | 1.1 |
| Bad(qualified) | (2) | 15.0 | 16.0 | 13.9 | 16.0 | 15.7 |
| Bad/impossible | (1) | 24.7 | 36.1 | 29.7 | 16.0 | 22.4 |
| Don't know/depends |  | 3.3 | 3.0 | 3.0 | 3.3 | 3.9 |
| Total |  | 100% | 100% | 100% | 100% | 100% |
| Weighted N |  | 639 | 864 | 656 | 84332 | 536 |
| Unweighted N |  | 639 | 864 | 656 | 1773 | 536 |
| Mean |  | 3.30 | 2.86 | 3.13 | 3.60 | 3.40 |
| Standard Deviation |  | 1.69 | 1.75 | 1.72 | 1.58 | 1.68 |

Question asked of head of household only in 1960d.

Figure 5.17
Chances of a New Job that Pays the Same--Total Population

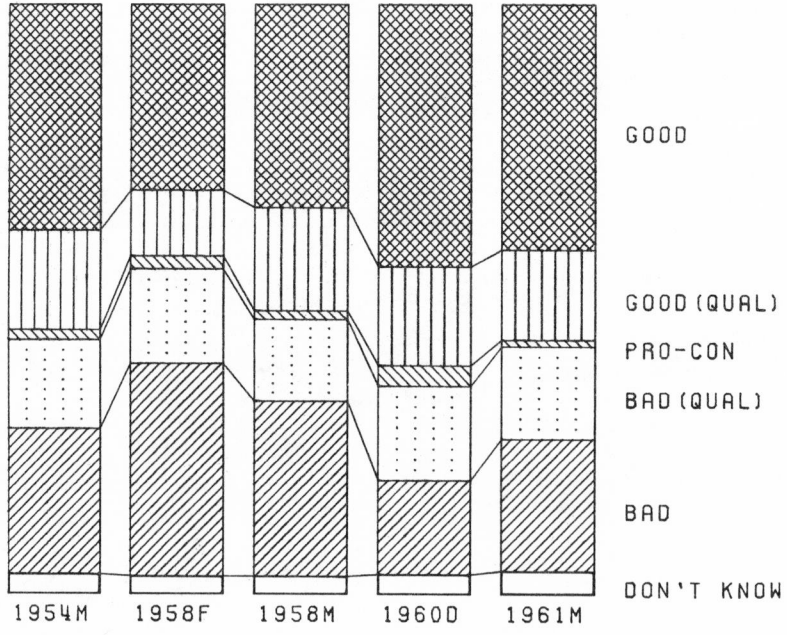

GOOD

GOOD(QUAL)

PRO-CON

BAD(QUAL)

BAD

DON'T KNOW

1954M    1958F    1958M    1960D    1961M

Table 5.85
If R Loses Job  What Are Chances of Getting a New Job that Pays the Same?
Sex of Respondent

|  | | | Year | | | |
|---|---|---|---|---|---|---|
|  | 1954m | 1958f | 1958m | 1960d | 1961m | |
| Males Only | 40.8% | 31.0% | 31.1% | 46.1% | 43.0% | Good/confident |
|  | 17.7 | 9.1 | 16.8 | 16.6 | 15.3 | Good(qualified) |
|  | 3.0 | 3.2 | 2.4 | 3.6 | 1.3 | Pro-con |
|  | 15.7 | 15.7 | 18.9 | 16.8 | 17.0 | Bad(qualified) |
|  | 22.7 | 41.0 | 30.8 | 16.8 | 23.4 | Bad/impossible |
|  | (299) | (407) | (286) | (69043) | (235) | Weighted N |
| Females Only | 38.7 | 34.1 | 39.1 | 45.1 | 43.6 | Good/confident |
|  | 17.3 | 13.7 | 18.9 | 20.9 | 16.4 | Good(qualified) |
|  | 0.6 | 1.4 | 0.9 | 3.8 | 1.1 | Pro-con |
|  | 15.4 | 17.2 | 10.6 | 15.4 | 15.7 | Bad(qualified) |
|  | 28.0 | 33.6 | 30.6 | 14.8 | 23.2 | Bad/impossible |
|  | (318) | (431) | (350) | (12503) | (280) | Weighted N |

Table 5.86
Race of Respondent

|  | 1954m | 1958f | 1958m | 1960d | 1961m | |
|---|---|---|---|---|---|---|
| Whites Only | 40.7% | 34.2% | 35.4% | 46.0% | 44.4% | Good/confident |
|  | 16.3 | 12.0 | 17.9 | 16.9 | 15.3 | Good(qualified) |
|  | 1.5 | 1.6 | 1.7 | 3.8 | 1.3 | Pro-con |
|  | 15.8 | 15.7 | 14.1 | 16.5 | 16.6 | Bad(qualified) |
|  | 25 8 | 36.5 | 30.9 | 16.8 | 22.4 | Bad/impossible |
|  | (546) | (728) | (576) | (73667) | (464) | Weighted N |
| Blacks Only | 27.7 | 22.1 | 34.5 | 45.8 | 33.3 | Good/confident |
|  | 29.2 | 9.5 | 16.4 | 20.4 | 19.4 | Good(qualified) |
|  | 4.6 | 5.3 | 0.0 | 2.0 | 0.0 | Pro-con |
|  | 15.4 | 23.2 | 18.2 | 17.5 | 13.9 | Bad(qualified) |
|  | 23.1 | 40.0 | 30.9 | 14.3 | 33.3 | Bad/impossible |
|  | (65) | (95) | (55) | (7879) | (36) | Weighted N |

Table 5.87

If R Loses Job, What Are Chances of Getting a New Job that Pays the Same?
Education of Respondent

|  | Year | | | | |  |
|---|---|---|---|---|---|---|
|  | 1954m | 1958f | 1958m | 1960d | 1961m |  |
| Grade School Only | 31.1% | 22.9% | 28.4% | 44.2% | 27.0% | Good/confident |
|  | 16.4 | 11.0 | 16.8 | 17.3 | 13.5 | Good(qualified) |
|  | 1.1 | 2.2 | 1.1 | 4.1 | 0.0 | Pro-con |
|  | 19.7 | 13.7 | 14.7 | 17.3 | 17.6 | Bad(qualified) |
|  | 31.7 | 50.2 | 38.9 | 17.0 | 41.9 | Bad/impossible |
|  | (183) | (227) | (95) | (34597) | (74) | Weighted N |
| High School Only | 40.3 | 31.1 | 31.2 | 57.6 | 41.2 | Good/confident |
|  | 17.8 | 11.1 | 18.5 | 17.0 | 19.1 | Good(qualified) |
|  | 1.6 | 2.0 | 1.6 | 2.5 | 0.7 | Pro-con |
|  | 15.2 | 19.6 | 20.6 | 11.1 | 20.6 | Bad(qualified) |
|  | 25.1 | 36.2 | 28.0 | 11.8 | 18.4 | Bad/impossible |
|  | (315) | (450) | (189) | (16338) | (136) | Weighted N |
| College Only | 44.4 | 51.6 | 43.5 | 63.5 | 60.0 | Good/confident |
|  | 18.1 | 13.7 | 16.3 | 15.5 | 18.7 | Good(qualified) |
|  | 4.2 | 3.3 | 3.3 | 4.4 | 2.7 | Pro-con |
|  | 11.1 | 11.1 | 9.8 | 6.8 | 8.0 | Bad(qualified) |
|  | 22.2 | 20.3 | 27.2 | 9.8 | 10.7 | Bad/impossible |
|  | (72) | (153) | (92) | (6224) | (75) | Weighted N |

Education coded for head of household only in 1958m and 1961m.

Figure 5.18

Chances of a New Job that Pays the Same by Education of R

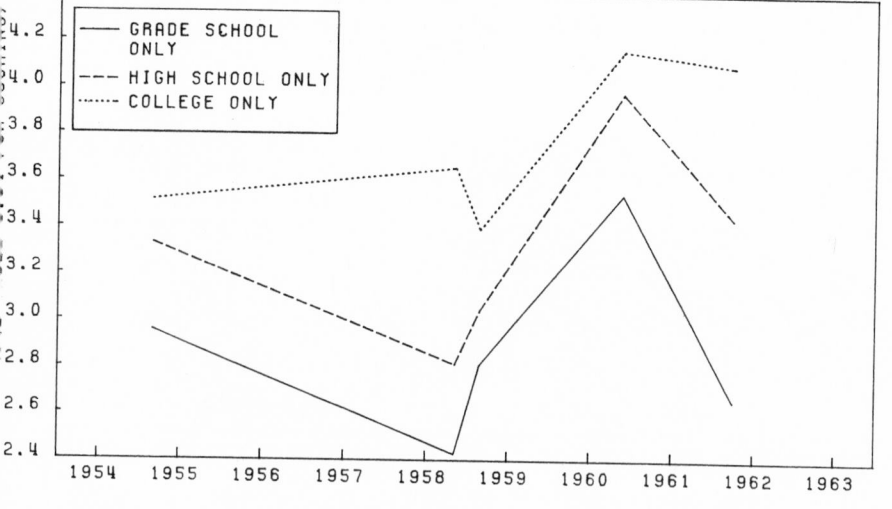

Table 5.88

If R Loses Job. What Are Chances of Getting a New Job that Pays the Same?

Age of Respondent

|  | Year | | | | | |
|---|---|---|---|---|---|---|
|  | 1954m | 1958f | 1958m | 1960d | 1961m | |
| 18-24 Only | 50.0% | 25.0% | 39.1% | 55.6% | 52.6% | Good/confident |
|  | 22.2 | 18.8 | 26.1 | 23.9 | 42.1 | Good(qualified) |
|  | 3.7 | 3.1 | 0.0 | 3.4 | 0.0 | Pro-con |
|  | 13.0 | 26.6 | 13.0 | 10.5 | 5.3 | Bad(qualified) |
|  | 11.1 | 26.6 | 21.7 | 6.6 | 0.0 | Bad/impossible |
|  | (54) | (64) | (23) | (9363) | (19) | Weighted N |
| 25-34 Only | 42.1 | 37.5 | 34.1 | 53.3 | 57.3 | Good/confident |
|  | 16.8 | 15.0 | 20.5 | 18.1 | 21.3 | Good(qualified) |
|  | 3.6 | 1.7 | 2.3 | 3.5 | 1.3 | Pro-con |
|  | 17.8 | 15.4 | 22.7 | 14.3 | 9.3 | Bad(qualified) |
|  | 19.8 | 30.4 | 20.5 | 10.8 | 10.7 | Bad/impossible |
|  | (197) | (240) | (88) | (20730) | (75) | Weighted N |
| 35-44 Only | 43.6 | 37.5 | 37.0 | 49.4 | 35.8 | Good/confident |
|  | 20.5 | 10.5 | 20.4 | 17.9 | 9.4 | Good(qualified) |
|  | 0.0 | 2.3 | 0.9 | 4.6 | 1.9 | Pro-con |
|  | 14.7 | 18.0 | 20.4 | 13.2 | 28.3 | Bad(qualified) |
|  | 21.2 | 31.6 | 21.3 | 14.8 | 24.5 | Bad/impossible |
|  | (156) | (256) | (108) | (21411) | (53) | Weighted N |
| 45-54 Only | 36.2 | 30.5 | 39.0 | 43.3 | 29.6 | Good/confident |
|  | 18.5 | 9.0 | 15.9 | 16.8 | 16.0 | Good(qualified) |
|  | 1.5 | 2.3 | 2.4 | 2.7 | 1.2 | Pro-con |
|  | 12.3 | 14.1 | 8.5 | 20.2 | 23.5 | Bad(qualified) |
|  | 31.5 | 44.1 | 34.1 | 17.1 | 29.6 | Bad/impossible |
|  | (130) | (177) | (82) | (16970) | (81) | Weighted N |
| 55-64 Only | 25.9 | 16.5 | 35.6 | 27.0 | 43.8 | Good/confident |
|  | 8.6 | 2.5 | 16.9 | 9.9 | 16.7 | Good(qualified) |
|  | 0.0 | 2.5 | 1.3 | 4.5 | 0.0 | Pro-con |
|  | 20.7 | 15.2 | 11.6 | 24.5 | 8.3 | Bad(qualified) |
|  | 44.8 | 63.3 | 34.7 | 34.1 | 31.3 | Bad/impossible |
|  | (58) | (79) | (320) | (11442) | (48) | Weighted N |
| 65 and Older Only | 21.1 | 11.1 | 6.7 | 14.1 | 50.0 | Good/confident |
|  | 10.5 | 16.7 | 6.7 | 16.6 | 0.0 | Good(qualified) |
|  | 0.0 | 5.6 | 6.7 | 0.0 | 0.0 | Pro-con |
|  | 10.5 | 5.6 | 13.3 | 30.8 | 10.0 | Bad(qualified) |
|  | 57.9 | 61.1 | 66.7 | 38.5 | 40.0 | Bad/impossible |
|  | (19) | (18) | (15) | (1630) | (10) | Weighted N |

Youngest age group coded "21-24" in 1954m.

Age coded for head of household only in 1958m and 1961m.

Table 5.89

If R Loses Job, What Are Chances of Getting a New Job that Pays the Same?
Income of Respondent

| | | | Year | | | |
|---|---|---|---|---|---|---|
| | 1954m | 1958f | 1958m | 1960d | 1961m | |
| Income 1 (0-16%) | 35.4% | 25.4% | 50.0% | 42.5% | 34.4% | Good/confident |
| | 26.2 | 5.1 | 19.2 | 17.8 | 28.1 | Good(qualified) |
| | 3.1 | 1.7 | 0.0 | 4.6 | 3.1 | Pro-con |
| | 7.7 | 23.7 | 0.0 | 19.3 | 9.4 | Bad(qualified) |
| | 27.7 | 44.1 | 30.8 | 15.8 | 25.0 | Bad/impossible |
| | (65) | (59) | (26) | (5055) | (32) | Weighted N |
| Income 2 (17-33%) | 41.0 | 22.6 | 27.3 | 40.2 | 46.0 | Good/confident |
| | 16.4 | 17.3 | 14.5 | 25.1 | 21.8 | Good(qualified) |
| | 3.3 | 3.0 | 0.0 | 2.4 | 0.0 | Pro-con |
| | 16.4 | 17.3 | 16.4 | 16.7 | 9.2 | Bad(qualified) |
| | 23.0 | 39.9 | 41.8 | 15.5 | 23.0 | Bad/impossible |
| | (61) | (168) | (55) | (10221) | (87) | Weighted N |
| Income 3 (34-67%) | 36.5 | 37.8 | 30.6 | 42.7 | 41.6 | Good/confident |
| | 15.5 | 12.4 | 21.0 | 17.5 | 13.6 | Good(qualified) |
| | 1.7 | 2.1 | 1.8 | 4.0 | 1.2 | Pro-con |
| | 18.9 | 15.5 | 15.3 | 16.7 | 19.2 | Bad(qualified) |
| | 27.5 | 32.2 | 31.3 | 19.1 | 24.4 | Bad/impossible |
| | (233) | (283) | (281) | (32350) | (250) | Weighted N |
| Income 4 (68-95%) | 42.9 | 33.9 | 40.0 | 50.3 | 45.4 | Good/confident |
| | 16.0 | 9.6 | 15.0 | 15.2 | 14.3 | Good(qualified) |
| | 1.4 | 2.5 | 1.5 | 3.5 | 1.7 | Pro-con |
| | 13.7 | 15.1 | 14.0 | 16.4 | 16.8 | Bad(qualified) |
| | 26.0 | 38.9 | 29.5 | 14.7 | 21.8 | Bad/impossible |
| | (219) | (239) | (200) | (30598) | (119) | Weighted N |
| Income 5 (96-100%) | 46.2 | 32.8 | 41.1 | 61.6 | 60.0 | Good/confident |
| | 23.1 | 7.8 | 14.3 | 8.8 | 6.7 | Good(qualified) |
| | 0.0 | 1.6 | 1.8 | 4.3 | 0.0 | Pro-con |
| | 19.2 | 21.9 | 19.6 | 12.3 | 13.3 | Bad(qualified) |
| | 11.5 | 35.9 | 23.2 | 13.0 | 20.0 | Bad/impossible |
| | (26) | (64) | (56) | (3322) | (15) | Weighted N |

Table 5.90
When Does R Plan to Retire?
Total Population

QUESTION  Could you tell me when you think you (Head) will retire from the work you do now—I mean at what age? (At
what age do you think you will retire from the main work you are doing now?)

|  | | | | Year | | |
|---|---|---|---|---|---|---|
|  | | 1960d | 1963k | 1965b | 1968k | 1969k | 1976i |
| 54 or less | (1) | 1.4% | 1.6% | 1.9% | 2.5% | 3.4% | 8.2% |
| 55-59 | (2) | 3.7 | 3.7 | 4.7 | 8.4 | 7.6 | 9.3 |
| 60-64 | (3) | 11.6 | 21.1 | 23.9 | 23.9 | 24.1 | 26.0 |
| 65-69 | (4) | 49.5 | 43.1 | 43.7 | 41.4 | 42.3 | 29.3 |
| 70 or more | (5) | 4.1 | 4.6 | 4.2 | 4.6 | 5.3 | 2.2 |
| Indefinite/never/don't know | | 29.7 | 25.9 | 21.6 | 19.3 | 17.4 | 25.1 |
| Total | | 100% | 100% | 100% | 100% | 100% | 100% |
| Weighted N | | 66601 | 432 | 1055 | 394 | 714 | 940 |
| Unweighted N | | 1442 | 432 | 1055 | 394 | 714 | 444 |
| Mean | | 3.73 | 3.61 | 3.55 | 3.46 | 3.47 | 3.11 |
| Standard Deviation | | 0.73 | 0.77 | 0.79 | 0.87 | 0.90 | 1.03 |

Question asked only of employed head of household at least thirty-five years of age.

Figure 5.19
When Will R Retire?--Total Population

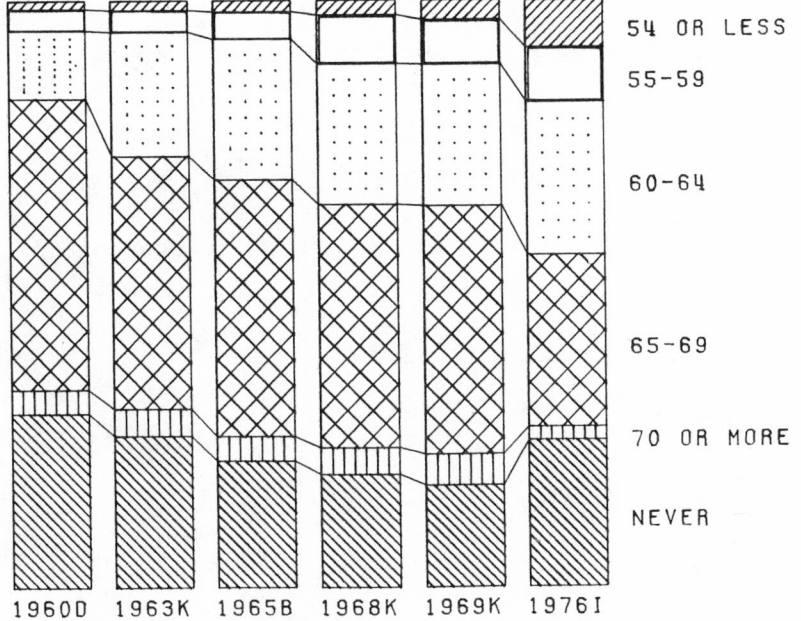

1960D  1963K  1965B  1968K  1969K  1976I

54 OR LESS

55-59

60-64

65-69

70 OR MORE

NEVER

Table 5.91
When Does R Plan to Retire?
Sex of Respondent

|  | Year | | | | | |
|---|---|---|---|---|---|---|
|  | 1960d | 1963k | 1965b | 1968k | 1969k | 1976i |  |
| Males Only | 1.5% | 1.5% | 2.1% | 3.3% | 3.7% | 6.4% | 54 or less |
|  | 3.9 | 4.2 | 5.0 | 11.0 | 8.7 | 9.2 | 55–59 |
|  | 8.7 | 20.4 | 22.6 | 20.3 | 24.8 | 25.7 | 60–64 |
|  | 51.9 | 46.4 | 44.7 | 45.2 | 43.3 | 35.5 | 65–69 |
|  | 4.4 | 4.8 | 4.1 | 3.3 | 4.9 | 3.1 | 70 or more |
|  | 29.6 | 22.8 | 21.5 | 16.9 | 14.6 | 20.0 | Indefinite/never/don't know |
|  | (57715) | (334) | (924) | (301) | (596) | (544) | Weighted N |
| Females Only | 0.3 | 2.0 | 0.8 | 0.0 | 1.7 | 10.6 | 54 or less |
|  | 2.5 | 2.0 | 3.1 | 0.0 | 1.7 | 9.3 | 55–59 |
|  | 30.6 | 23.5 | 32.8 | 35.5 | 20.3 | 26.3 | 60–64 |
|  | 34.3 | 31.6 | 36.6 | 29.0 | 37.3 | 20.7 | 65–69 |
|  | 2.4 | 4.1 | 4.6 | 8.6 | 7.6 | 1.0 | 70 or more |
|  | 29.9 | 36.7 | 22.1 | 26.9 | 31.4 | 32.1 | Indefinite/never/don't know |
|  | (8886) | (98) | (131) | (93) | (118) | (396) | Weighted N |

Table 5.92
Race of Respondent

|  | 1960d | 1963k | 1965b | 1968k | 1969k | 1976i |  |
|---|---|---|---|---|---|---|---|
| Whites Only | 1.4% | 1.6% | 2.0% | 1.7% | 3.1% | 6.5% | 54 or less |
|  | 4.0 | 3.6 | 5.0 | 9.3 | 8.0 | 10.2 | 55–59 |
|  | 11.8 | 20.5 | 24.2 | 23.8 | 24.2 | 26.3 | 60–64 |
|  | 49.9 | 43.9 | 43.5 | 41.2 | 42.8 | 29.3 | 65–69 |
|  | 4.3 | 4.7 | 4.1 | 4.3 | 5.3 | 2.0 | 70 or more |
|  | 28.7 | 25.7 | 21.1 | 19.7 | 16.6 | 25.8 | Indefinite/never/don't know |
|  | (60500) | (385) | (942) | (345) | (640) | (817) | Weighted N |
| Blacks Only | 1.5 | 2.5 | 1.1 | 9.8 | 6.1 | 15.2 | 54 or less |
|  | 0.8 | 5.0 | 2.2 | 0.0 | 3.0 | 0.0 | 55–59 |
|  | 10.0 | 25.0 | 21.7 | 29.3 | 19.7 | 26.1 | 60–64 |
|  | 45.9 | 40.0 | 46.7 | 39.0 | 37.9 | 35.9 | 65–69 |
|  | 2.2 | 5.0 | 3.3 | 7.3 | 6.1 | 0.0 | 70 or more |
|  | 39.7 | 22.5 | 25.0 | 14.6 | 27.3 | 22.8 | Indefinite/never/don't know |
|  | (6101) | (40) | (92) | (41) | (66) | (92) | Weighted N |

Table 5.93
When Does R Plan to Retire?
Education of Respondent

| | | | Year | | | | |
|---|---|---|---|---|---|---|---|
| | 1960d | 1963k | 1965b | 1968k | 1969k | 1976i | |
| Grade School Only | 0.6% | 0.8% | 1.6% | 2.8% | 2.5% | 8.8% | 54 or less |
| | 0.7 | 1.6 | 1.0 | 4.7 | 6.2 | 5.6 | 55-59 |
| | 10.1 | 21.1 | 24.6 | 24.5 | 25.5 | 12.8 | 60-64 |
| | 49.1 | 42.2 | 42.0 | 43.4 | 32.9 | 25.6 | 65-69 |
| | 2.5 | 5.5 | 3.3 | 4.7 | 6.8 | 5.6 | 70 or more |
| | 36.9 | 28.9 | 27.5 | 19.8 | 26.1 | 41.6 | Indefinite/never/don't know |
| | (19339) | (128) | (305) | (106) | (161) | (125) | Weighted N |
| High School Only | 1.2 | 1.5 | 2.2 | 2.2 | 4.0 | 7.8 | 54 or less |
| | 3.8 | 2.6 | 5.8 | 9.3 | 7.1 | 10.1 | 55-59 |
| | 11.6 | 22.2 | 23.3 | 24.7 | 24.5 | 28.1 | 60-64 |
| | 53.5 | 45.4 | 45.7 | 40.7 | 45.3 | 26.0 | 65-69 |
| | 3.3 | 3.1 | 2.6 | 5.5 | 4.8 | 2.1 | 70 or more |
| | 26.6 | 25.3 | 20.5 | 17.6 | 14.2 | 26.0 | Indefinite/never/don't know |
| | (32267) | (194) | (503) | (182) | (351) | (477) | Weighted N |
| College Only | 2.5 | 2.8 | 1.6 | 2.9 | 3.0 | 7.9 | 54 or less |
| | 7.1 | 8.3 | 7.3 | 10.6 | 9.4 | 9.7 | 55-59 |
| | 13.8 | 19.3 | 24.3 | 22.1 | 22.3 | 28.4 | 60-64 |
| | 41.1 | 40.4 | 41.7 | 40.4 | 44.6 | 34.7 | 65-69 |
| | 8.2 | 6.4 | 8.5 | 2.9 | 5.0 | 1.2 | 70 or more |
| | 27.3 | 22.9 | 16.6 | 21.2 | 15.8 | 18.1 | Indefinite/never/don't know |
| | (14458) | (109) | (247) | (104) | (202) | (331) | Weighted N |

Table 5.94
When Does R Plan to Retire?
Age of Respondent

|  | Year | | | | | | |
|---|---|---|---|---|---|---|---|
|  | 1960d | 1963k | 1965b | 1968k | 1969k | 1976i | |
| 35-44 Only | 2.7% | 4.2% | 3.7% | 6.3% | 6.2% | 13.4% | 54 or less |
|  | 5.7 | 4.9 | 7.2 | 9.4 | 12.8 | 10.4 | 55-59 |
|  | 9.6 | 19.6 | 23.6 | 25.0 | 23.3 | 22.3 | 60-64 |
|  | 51.3 | 42.0 | 47.1 | 41.4 | 39.7 | 27.1 | 65-69 |
|  | 3.6 | 2.8 | 2.0 | 0.8 | 3.9 | 0.0 | 70 or more |
|  | 27.2 | 26.6 | 16.4 | 17.2 | 14.0 | 26.8 | Indefinite/never/don't know |
|  | (26583) | (143) | (348) | (128) | (257) | (328) | Weighted N |
| 45-54 Only | 0.9 | 0.6 | 1.4 | 1.5 | 3.2 | 9.0 | 54 or less |
|  | 3.8 | 5.8 | 6.6 | 13.5 | 7.7 | 11.7 | 55-59 |
|  | 14.2 | 24.7 | 22.5 | 27.1 | 27.4 | 25.0 | 60-64 |
|  | 48.5 | 43.5 | 48.4 | 42.9 | 43.1 | 30.4 | 65-69 |
|  | 2.2 | 3.9 | 3.3 | 1.5 | 4.0 | 2.4 | 70 or more |
|  | 30.5 | 21.4 | 17.9 | 13.5 | 14.5 | 21.4 | Indefinite/never/don't know |
|  | (21988) | (154) | (364) | (133) | (248) | (332) | Weighted N |
| 55-64 Only | 0.0 | 0.0 | 0.7 | 0.0 | 0.0 | 0.0 | 54 or less |
|  | 0.7 | 0.0 | 0.4 | 2.8 | 1.2 | 5.2 | 55-59 |
|  | 13.9 | 21.9 | 31.3 | 24.5 | 26.0 | 38.1 | 60-64 |
|  | 53.1 | 49.1 | 39.9 | 42.5 | 50.3 | 33.8 | 65-69 |
|  | 5.3 | 4.4 | 4.6 | 8.5 | 7.1 | 1.3 | 70 or more |
|  | 26.9 | 24.6 | 23.1 | 21.7 | 15.4 | 21.6 | Indefinite/never/don't know |
|  | (15021) | (114) | (281) | (106) | (169) | (231) | Weighted N |
| 65-74 Only | 0.0 | 0.0 | 0.0 | 0.0 | 0.0 | 0.0 | 54 or less |
|  | 0.0 | 0.0 | 0.0 | 0.0 | 0.0 | 0.0 | 55-59 |
|  | 0.0 | 0.0 | 0.0 | 0.0 | 0.0 | 0.0 | 60-64 |
|  | 26.8 | 11.1 | 16.7 | 26.9 | 20.5 | 20.0 | 65-69 |
|  | 17.5 | 27.8 | 18.5 | 23.1 | 15.4 | 22.9 | 70 or more |
|  | 55.7 | 61.1 | 64.8 | 50.0 | 64.1 | 57.1 | Indefinite/never/don't know |
|  | (2661) | (18) | (54) | (26) | (39) | (35) | Weighted N |
| 75 And Older Only | 0.0 | ** | 0.0 | ** | ** | 0.0 | 54 or less |
|  | 0.0 | ** | 0.0 | ** | ** | 0.0 | 55-59 |
|  | 0.0 | ** | 0.0 | ** | ** | 0.0 | 60-64 |
|  | 0.0 | ** | 0.0 | ** | ** | 0.0 | 65-69 |
|  | 15.2 | ** | 25.0 | ** | ** | 28.6 | 70 or more |
|  | 84.8 | ** | 75.0 | ** | ** | 71.4 | Indefinite/never/don't know |
|  | (348) | ** | (8) | ** | ** | (7) | Weighted N |

** Code distinction not made.
Oldest age group coded "65 And Older" in 1963k, 1968k, and 1969k.

Table 5.95
When Does R Plan to Retire?
Income of Respondent

|  | Year | | | | | | |
|---|---|---|---|---|---|---|---|
|  | 1960d | 1963k | 1965b | 1968k | 1969k | 1976i | |
| Income 1 (0-16%) | 0.9% | 1.4% | 0.0% | 0.0% | 0.0% | 7.7% | 54 or less |
|  | 0.0 | 0.0 | 1.7 | 0.0 | 0.0 | 1.5 | 55-59 |
|  | 8.2 | 18.8 | 22.4 | 30.4 | 17.6 | 13.8 | 60-64 |
|  | 36.5 | 29.0 | 20.7 | 28.3 | 31.4 | 12.3 | 65-69 |
|  | 5.6 | 4.3 | 5.2 | 13.0 | 11.8 | 3.1 | 70 or more |
|  | 48.8 | 46.4 | 50.0 | 28.3 | 39.2 | 61.5 | Indefinite/never/don't know |
|  | (5249) | (69) | (58) | (46) | (51) | (65) | Weighted N |
| Income 2 (17-33%) | 0.2 | 1.4 | 1.6 | 0.0 | 1.3 | 4.2 | 54 or less |
|  | 1.6 | 2.9 | 0.0 | 3.4 | 0.0 | 2.1 | 55-59 |
|  | 13.7 | 15.9 | 19.4 | 17.2 | 23.1 | 18.9 | 60-64 |
|  | 36.5 | 49.3 | 42.7 | 50.0 | 39.7 | 42.1 | 65-69 |
|  | 3.2 | 5.8 | 2.4 | 5.2 | 7.7 | 2.1 | 70 or more |
|  | 44.8 | 24.6 | 33.9 | 24.1 | 28.2 | 30.5 | Indefinite/never/don't know |
|  | (9261) | (69) | (124) | (58) | (78) | (95) | Weighted N |
| Income 3 (34-67%) | 1.2 | 0.0 | 2.9 | 2.9 | 3.3 | 8.2 | 54 or less |
|  | 2.8 | 6.1 | 4.4 | 6.5 | 6.5 | 9.4 | 55-59 |
|  | 11.4 | 24.5 | 24.9 | 25.9 | 26.2 | 28.5 | 60-64 |
|  | 52.5 | 46.9 | 46.6 | 41.7 | 42.5 | 31.3 | 65-69 |
|  | 4.4 | 3.1 | 3.2 | 5.0 | 4.0 | 2.0 | 70 or more |
|  | 27.7 | 19.4 | 17.9 | 18.0 | 17.5 | 20.7 | Indefinite/never/don't know |
|  | (21527) | (98) | (341) | (139) | (275) | (256) | Weighted N |
| Income 4 (68-95%) | 1.6 | 3.7 | 1.3 | 4.2 | 5.1 | 9.1 | 54 or less |
|  | 5.2 | 3.0 | 5.9 | 15.8 | 11.7 | 13.0 | 55-59 |
|  | 11.4 | 20.0 | 25.9 | 21.7 | 23.4 | 32.5 | 60-64 |
|  | 57.7 | 46.7 | 45.7 | 45.0 | 46.9 | 27.3 | 65-69 |
|  | 3.1 | 5.2 | 4.6 | 0.8 | 3.9 | 2.3 | 70 or more |
|  | 21.1 | 21.5 | 16.5 | 12.5 | 9.0 | 15.9 | Indefinite/never/don't know |
|  | (25416) | (135) | (455) | (120) | (256) | (308) | Weighted N |
| Income 5 (96-100%) | 3.6 | 0.0 | 2.6 | 0.0 | 0.0 | 14.9 | 54 or less |
|  | 7.5 | 6.7 | 9.1 | 12.5 | 15.8 | 9.5 | 55-59 |
|  | 13.8 | 33.3 | 15.6 | 25.0 | 31.6 | 20.3 | 60-64 |
|  | 33.4 | 35.6 | 37.7 | 25.0 | 31.6 | 25.7 | 65-69 |
|  | 8.1 | 6.7 | 7.8 | 0.0 | 10.5 | 2.7 | 70 or more |
|  | 33.6 | 17.8 | 27.3 | 37.5 | 10.5 | 27.0 | Indefinite/never/don't know |
|  | (5148) | (45) | (77) | (8) | (38) | (74) | Weighted N |

Table 5.96
How Does Retirement Standard of Living Compare with Before?
Total Population

QUESTION: How does your standard of living compare with what you had before you retired, do you live the same way, better, or not quite as well? (Considering income and expenses, are you living about as well as before you retired, not quite as well, or what?)

|  | Year | | | | |
| Retired Respondents | 1960f | 1962f | 1966a | 1968k | 1976i |
|---|---|---|---|---|---|
| Much better (5) | ** | ** | 0.2% | 0.6% | ** |
| Better (4) | 6.6 | 6.4 | 4.2 | 3.4 | 10.0 |
| Same/about as well (3) | 58.6 | 61.7 | 62.4 | 46.9 | 50.7 |
| Worse/not as well (2) | 34.3 | 30.5 | 31.7 | 43.0 | 38.8 |
| Much worse (1) | ** | ** | 1.0 | 6.1 | ** |
| Don't know | 0.6 | 1.4 | 0.5 | ** | 0.5 |
| Total | 100% | 100% | 100% | 100% | 100% |
| Weighted N | 181 | 141 | 407 | 179 | 381 |
| Unweighted N | 181 | 141 | 407 | 179 | 221 |
| Mean | 2.72 | 2.75 | 2.71 | 2.49 | 2.71 |
| Standard Deviation | 0.58 | 0.56 | 0.57 | 0.69 | 0.64 |

** Code distinction not made.

Table 5.97
How Does Retirement Standard of Living Compare With Before?
Sex of Respondent

|  | Year | | | | |  |
|---|---|---|---|---|---|---|
|  | 1960f | 1962f | 1966a | 1968k | 1976i |  |
| Males Only | 6.0% | 5.2% | 4.2% | 6.1% | 11.9% | Much better/better |
|  | 52.2 | 72.4 | 68.0 | 52.4 | 48.2 | Same/about as well |
|  | 41.8 | 22.4 | 27.8 | 41.5 | 39.8 | Worse/much worse |
|  | (67) | (58) | (284) | (82) | (226) | Weighted N |
| Females Only | 6.3 | 7.4 | 5.1 | 2.1 | 5.9 | Much better/better |
|  | 63.1 | 55.6 | 52.1 | 42.7 | 45.4 | Same/about as well |
|  | 30.6 | 37.0 | 42.7 | 55.2 | 48.6 | Worse/much worse |
|  | (111) | (81) | (117) | (96) | (185) | Weighted N |

Sex coded for head of household and wife only in 1962f.


Table 5.98
Race of Respondent

|  | 1960f | 1962f | 1966a | 1968k | 1976i |  |
|---|---|---|---|---|---|---|
| Whites Only | 6.8% | 4.9% | 4.3% | 4.5% | 7.9% | Much better/better |
|  | 58.9 | 65.0 | 65.8 | 50.0 | 53.5 | Same/about as well |
|  | 34.2 | 30.1 | 29.9 | 45.5 | 38.7 | Worse/much worse |
|  | (146) | (123) | (371) | (154) | (318) | Weighted N |
| Blacks Only | 11.1 | 21.4 | 3.6 | 0.0 | 25.0 | Much better/better |
|  | 50.0 | 42.9 | 35.7 | 25.0 | 36.5 | Same/about as well |
|  | 38.9 | 35.7 | 60.7 | 75.0 | 38.5 | Worse/much worse |
|  | (18) | (14) | (28) | (24) | (52) | Weighted N |

Table 5.99
How Does Retirement Standard of Living Compare With Before?
Education of Respondent

|  | Year | | | | | |
|---|---|---|---|---|---|---|
|  | 1960f | 1962f | 1966a | 1968k | 1976i | |
| Grade School Only | 2.4% | 11.5% | 4.3% | 3.0% | 8.8% | Much better/better |
|  | 62.7 | 51.9 | 59.2 | 40.0 | 49.7 | Same/about as well |
|  | 34.9 | 36.5 | 36.5 | 57.0 | 41.5 | Worse/much worse |
|  | (83) | (52) | (211) | (100) | (159) | Weighted N |
| High School Only | 5.9 | 8.3 | 5.6 | 5.7 | 9.3 | Much better/better |
|  | 44.1 | 75.0 | 70.2 | 49.1 | 50.3 | Same/about as well |
|  | 50.0 | 16.7 | 24.2 | 45.3 | 40.4 | Worse/much worse |
|  | (34) | (24) | (124) | (53) | (151) | Weighted N |
| College Only | 13.3 | 8.3 | 3.7 | 3.8 | 14.9 | Much better/better |
|  | 66.7 | 83.3 | 70.4 | 69.2 | 55.2 | Same/about as well |
|  | 20.0 | 8.3 | 25.9 | 26.9 | 29.9 | Worse/much worse |
|  | (15) | (12) | (54) | (26) | (67) | Weighted N |

Education coded for head of household only in 1962f and 1966a, and for head and wife only in 1960f

Table 5.100
Age of Respondent

|  | 1960f | 1962f | 1966a | 1968k | 1976i | |
|---|---|---|---|---|---|---|
| 18-54 Only | 40.0% | 50.0% | 6.1% | 0.0% | 23.1% | Much better/better |
|  | 20.0 | 0.0 | 60.6 | 0.0 | 34.6 | Same/about as well |
|  | 40.0 | 50.0 | 33.3 | 100.0 | 42.3 | Worse/much worse |
|  | (5) | (2) | (33) | (2) | (26) | Weighted N |
| 55-64 Only | 0.0 | 8.3 | 4.9 | 4.8 | 8.2 | Much better/better |
|  | 68.2 | 58.3 | 54.1 | 52.4 | 37.6 | Same/about as well |
|  | 31.8 | 33.3 | 41.0 | 42.9 | 54.1 | Worse/much worse |
|  | (22) | (12) | (61) | (21) | (85) | Weighted N |
| 65 and Older Only | 3.8 | 9.3 | 4.2 | 5.7 | 9.9 | Much better/better |
|  | 58.5 | 64.0 | 65.7 | 49.1 | 57.1 | Same/about as well |
|  | 37.7 | 26.7 | 30.1 | 45.3 | 32.9 | Worse/much worse |
|  | (106) | (75) | (306) | (106) | (252) | Weighted N |

Age coded for head of household only in 1960f, 1962f, and 1968k, and for head and wife only in 1966a.

Table 5.101
How Does Retirement Standard of Living Compare With Before?
Income of Respondent

|                    | Year |  |  |  |  |  |
|--------------------|------|------|------|------|------|---|
|                    | 1960f | 1962f | 1966a | 1968k | 1976i | |
| Income 1 (0-16%)   | 3.7% | 10.2% | 4.5% | 3.2% | 11.9% | Much better/better |
|                    | 46.3 | 39.0 | 48.5 | 33.0 | 45.9 | Same/about as well |
|                    | 50.0 | 50.8 | 47.0 | 63.8 | 42.2 | Worse/much worse |
|                    | (82) | (59) | (198) | (94) | (135) | Weighted N |
| Income 2 (17-33%)  | 0.0 | 2.4 | 3.0 | 0.0 | 4.1 | Much better/better |
|                    | 65.6 | 68.3 | 72.7 | 54.8 | 52.7 | Same/about as well |
|                    | 34.4 | 29.3 | 24.2 | 45.2 | 43.2 | Worse/much worse |
|                    | (32) | (41) | (99) | (42) | (74) | Weighted N |
| Income 3 (34-67%)  | 14.3 | 3.7 | 6.2 | 7.1 | 11.1 | Much better/better |
|                    | 67.9 | 96.3 | 75.4 | 71.4 | 63.9 | Same/about as well |
|                    | 17.9 | 0.0 | 18.5 | 21.4 | 25.0 | Worse/much worse |
|                    | (28) | (27) | (65) | (28) | (72) | Weighted N |
| Income 4 (68-95%)  | 11.1 | 0.0 | 3.8 | 28.6 | 8.3 | Much better/better |
|                    | 77.8 | 100.0 | 92.3 | 71.4 | 54.2 | Same/about as well |
|                    | 11.1 | 0.0 | 3.8 | 0.0 | 37.5 | Worse/much worse |
|                    | (9) | (6) | (26) | (7) | (24) | Weighted N |
| Income 5 (96-100%) | 50.0 | 50.0 | 7.1 | 0.0 | 0.0 | Much better/better |
|                    | 50.0 | 50.0 | 92.9 | 50.0 | 42.9 | Same/about as well |
|                    | 0.0 | 0.0 | 0.0 | 50.0 | 57.1 | Worse/much worse |
|                    | (4) | (2) | (14) | (2) | (7) | Weighted N |

## Chapter 6. Personal Economic Outlook

In the next chapter we review trends in consumer confidence about the state of the national economy. In this chapter we examine reports concerning the financial situation of one's own family or spending unit. Both types of assessment are responsive, naturally enough, to the general state of the economy, although the personal reports are somewhat less sensitive to them in the fine grain.

Two of the central series here involve (1) factual assessments as to the family's current financial situation, relative to the preceding year (tables 6.1-6.18); and (2) expectations as to whether the family's financial situation is likely to be improving or deteriorating in the year or years ahead (tables 6.19-6.48).

The thirty-year series (1947-1978) comparing the present year with last year mirrors handsomely the long upward march of affluence in the United States after World War II. There are minor variations along the way, including some which can be related to events like the 1958 recession, but the upward sweep in proportions reporting annual improvement in their financial situations is truly impressive. Then in 1974, in the wake of the first serious signs of an energy shortage and amid growing recession, the series simply collapses, with reports of annual improvement toppling to the levels of the late 1940s, where the upward sweep began to be monitored.

The cognate data on expectations about future change show something of the same trajectory, but if anything, the collapse in the mid-1970s is even more dramatic. Here three series are presented, reflecting variations in future time frame and question wording. The most complete of these series runs from 1953 to 1978 (tables 6.19-6.36). Although there is a slight upward progression in optimism over the 1950s, reflecting steady gains in prosperity, by 1960 the series is running at a peak which is maintained for more than a decade. When the 1974 collapse occurs, it brings levels of pessimism never registered before, and despite a small rebound in 1975 and 1976, which still fails to return optimism to earlier levels, 1978 dips again to new record lows.

We shall not review the disaggregated data under these trajectories, although they contain numerous interesting features, usually held in common. One that is particularly noteworthy, however, involves the reports from blacks. In the early parts of these series, black responses are extremely distinctive, with assessments of current financial change that are relatively bleak, accompanied by little optimism for the future. Near the ends of the series, their reports have begun to converge with those of the white majority.

The remainder of the chapter addresses reactions to family savings over much of the same period. One item asks whether in the preceding year the family managed to save money, went in the red, or simply lived on its income (tables 6.49-6.60). Despite rising affluence, the incidence of years of saving has declined (although the amounts saved may have increased), just as the incidence of red-ink years had declined: increasing proportions of families report simply living on their current income. Blacks are still less likely to have saving years, but again the contrast with whites has declined over the period. Age patterns appear to have changed as well, with the youngest age category (eighteen to twenty-four) showing among the highest likelihoods of saving years in the 1950s, but after 1964 or so running distinctively the lowest of all age groupings.

While savings years have declined in frequency, a final item addressing the question of satisfaction with family savings does reflect the advances of prosperity over this period. While the proportions expressing satisfaction or dissatisfaction with their savings have remained in more or less the same balance since 1952, the proportion of families ineligible for the question because of lack of savings to evaluate has declined from about 42 percent in 1952 to 25 percent in 1970.

Table 6.1
Is R's Family Better Off Financially than Last Year?
Total Population

QUESTION: Would you say you people/you and your family are better off or worse off financially now
than you were a year ago?

|  |  | Year |  |  |  |  |  |  |  |  |  |
|---|---|---|---|---|---|---|---|---|---|---|---|
|  |  | 1947a | 1948a | 1949a | 1950a | 1951a | 1952k | 1953a | 1954a | 1955a | 1956m |
| Better off | (5) | 32.2% | 29.6% | 33.2% | 32.1% | 32.6% | 26.3% | 38.8% | 36.8% | 38.9% | 32.8% |
| Same/pro-con | (3) | 30.7 | 28.2 | 34.8 | 32.8 | 29.4 | 41.1 | 33.7 | 31.8 | 33.0 | 49.3 |
| Worse off | (1) | 35.1 | 40.4 | 31.4 | 34.3 | 37.4 | 31.8 | 27.1 | 31.2 | 27.6 | 17.3 |
| Don't know |  | 1.9 | 1.9 | 0.6 | 0.8 | 0.5 | 0.9 | 0.4 | 0.2 | 0.4 | 0.6 |
| Total |  | 100% | 100% | 100% | 100% | 100% | 100% | 100% | 100% | 100% | 100% |
| Weighted N |  | 970380 | 878647 | 914300 | 98920 | 98604 | 928 | 90335 | 74274 | 98559 | 1443 |
| Unweighted N |  | 2976 | 3116 | 3210 | 3477 | 3367 | 928 | 2815 | 2208 | 3070 | 1443 |
| Mean |  | 2.94 | 2.78 | 3.04 | 2.96 | 2.90 | 2.89 | 3.23 | 3.11 | 3.23 | 3.31 |
| Standard Deviation |  | 1.66 | 1.67 | 1.61 | 1.64 | 1.68 | 1.53 | 1.61 | 1.65 | 1.62 | 1.38 |

Table 6.2

|  |  | 1957f | 1958a | 1959a | 1960a | 1961a | 1962n | 1963m | 1965a | 1966a | 1967a | 1968a |
|---|---|---|---|---|---|---|---|---|---|---|---|---|
| Better off | (5) | 32.2% | 32.5% | 37.8% | 35.6% | 28.9% | 33.9% | 34.2% | 37.1% | 38.0% | 34.3% | 34.1% |
| Same/pro-con | (3) | 43.4 | 36.0 | 35.0 | 38.1 | 43.8 | 46.0 | 43.9 | 42.7 | 44.0 | 45.2 | 46.2 |
| Worse off | (1) | 23.6 | 31.2 | 26.6 | 25.5 | 26.5 | 18.8 | 20.4 | 19.3 | 17.4 | 19.4 | 18.6 |
| Don't know |  | 0.7 | 0.3 | 0.5 | 0.8 | 0.7 | 1.3 | 1.5 | 1.0 | 0.7 | 1.1 | 1.1 |
| Total |  | 100% | 100% | 100% | 100% | 100% | 100% | 100% | 100% | 100% | 100% | 100% |
| Weighted N |  | 1352 | 99310 | 98655 | 2919 | 49910 | 1296 | 1317 | 1338 | 2409 | 3702 | 15575 |
| Unweighted N |  | 1352 | 3096 | 3059 | 2919 | 1980 | 1296 | 1317 | 1338 | 2409 | 3143 | 2674 |
| Mean |  | 3.17 | 3.03 | 3.23 | 3.20 | 3.05 | 3.30 | 3.28 | 3.36 | 3.42 | 3.30 | 3.31 |
| Standard Deviation |  | 1.49 | 1.60 | 1.59 | 1.56 | 1.49 | 1.43 | 1.46 | 1.47 | 1.43 | 1.44 | 1.43 |

Table 6.3

|  |  | 1969a | 1970a | 1971m | 1972f | 1973c | 1974q | 1975q | 1976m | 1978n |
|---|---|---|---|---|---|---|---|---|---|---|
| Better off | (5) | 36.1% | 33.5% | 31.0% | 46.9% | 35.9% | 29.4% | 32.0% | 34.4% | 34.1% |
| Same/pro-con | (3) | 44.0 | 38.0 | 40.6 | 34.2 | 35.9 | 27.2 | 33.1 | 31.5 | 28.9 |
| Worse off | (1) | 18.6 | 26.8 | 27.3 | 18.2 | 27.2 | 42.0 | 34.0 | 33.1 | 35.8 |
| Don't know |  | 1.3 | 1.7 | 1.2 | 0.7 | 1.0 | 1.3 | 0.9 | 1.0 | 1.2 |
| Total |  | 100% | 100% | 100% | 100% | 100% | 100% | 100% | 100% | 100% |
| Weighted N |  | 11543 | 2552 | 1298 | 1295 | 1344 | 2977 | 2909 | 127173 | 2283 |
| Unweighted N |  | 2296 | 2552 | 1298 | 1295 | 1344 | 1516 | 1514 | 1129 | 2283 |
| Mean |  | 3.35 | 3.14 | 3.07 | 3.58 | 3.18 | 2.74 | 2.96 | 3.03 | 2.96 |
| Standard Deviation |  | 1.45 | 1.56 | 1.53 | 1.51 | 1.59 | 1.68 | 1.63 | 1.65 | 1.68 |

Figure 6.1
Is R Better Off Now?--Total Population

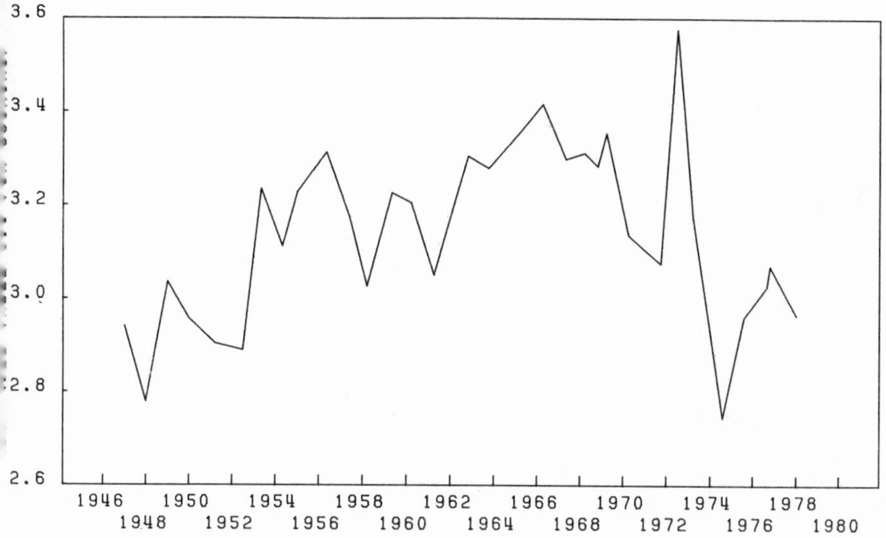

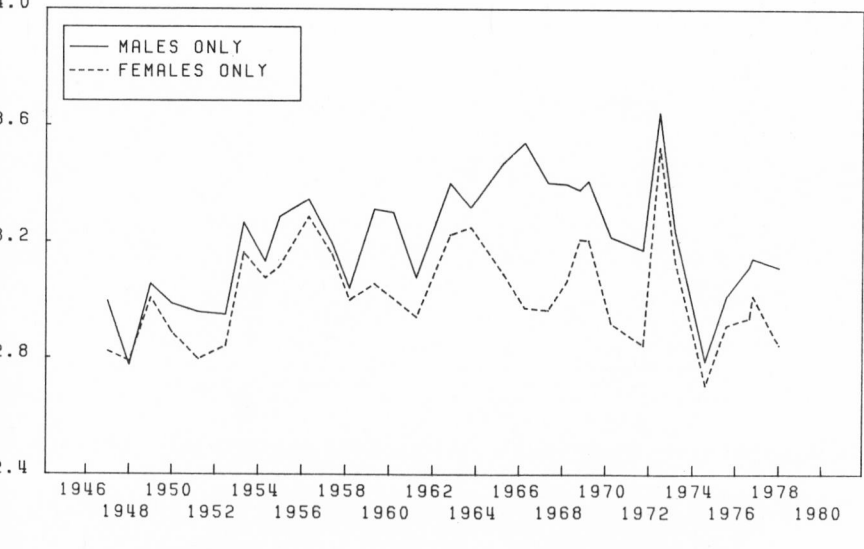

Figure 6.3
Is R Better Off Now? by Race of R

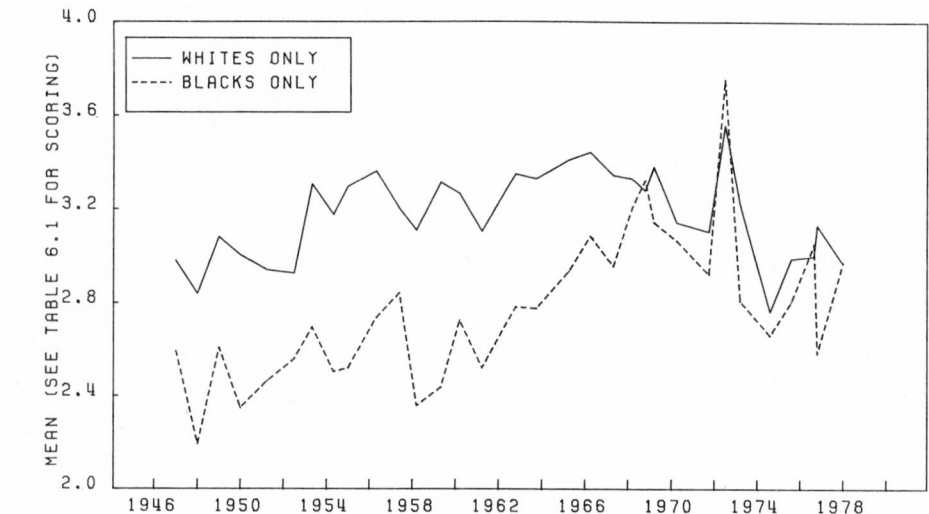

Figure 6.2
Is R Better Off Now? by Sex of R

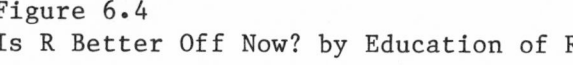

Figure 6.4
Is R Better Off Now? by Education of R

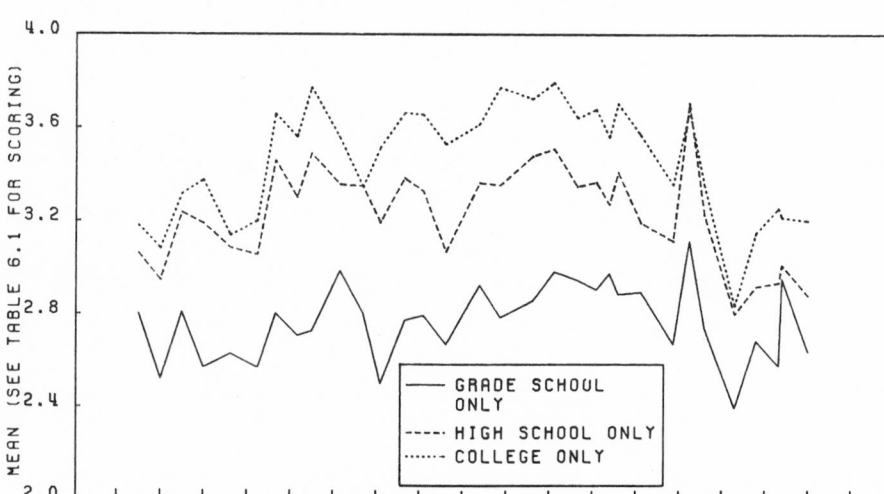

Table 6.4

Is R's Family Better Off Financially than Last Year?

Sex of Respondent

| | | | | | Year | | | | | | |
|---|---|---|---|---|---|---|---|---|---|---|---|
| | 1947a | 1948a | 1949a | 1950a | 1951a | 1952k | 1953a | 1954a | 1955a | 1956m | |
| Males Only | 35.0% | 30.5% | 34.2% | 34.0% | 34.5% | 28.0% | 39.9% | 38.0% | 41.1% | 34.4% | Better |
| | 29.7 | 27.6 | 34.4 | 31.4 | 28.9 | 41.4 | 33.6 | 30.7 | 32.2 | 48.5 | Same |
| | 35.3 | 41.9 | 31.4 | 34.7 | 36.6 | 30.5 | 26.6 | 31.3 | 26.8 | 17.1 | Worse |
| | (636483) | (553284) | (549559) | (67735) | (62582) | (403) | (62567) | (50724) | (64033) | (668) | Weighted N |
| | | | | | | | | | | | |
| Females Only | 28.2 | 29.4 | 32.2 | 28.8 | 29.5 | 25.3 | 36.9 | 34.5 | 35.3 | 31.9 | Better |
| | 34.6 | 30.7 | 35.9 | 36.9 | 30.7 | 41.4 | 34.4 | 34.7 | 35.1 | 50.7 | Same |
| | 37.1 | 39.9 | 31.9 | 34.3 | 39.7 | 33.3 | 28.7 | 30.8 | 29.5 | 17.5 | Worse |
| | (311520) | (308828) | (359454) | (30253) | (32852) | (517) | (27393) | (22531) | (32925) | (766) | Weighted N |

Table 6.5

| | 1957f | 1958a | 1959a | 1960a | 1961a | 1962n | 1963m | 1965a | 1966a | 1967a | 1968a | |
|---|---|---|---|---|---|---|---|---|---|---|---|---|
| Males Only | 31.9% | 34.0% | 40.7% | 39.1% | 29.8% | 37.5% | 36.5% | 41.6% | 42.6% | 38.0% | 37.5% | Better |
| | 46.0 | 34.0 | 34.2 | 36.8 | 44.3 | 45.1 | 42.9 | 40.4 | 41.9 | 44.2 | 44.9 | Same |
| | 22.1 | 32.0 | 25.1 | 24.1 | 25.9 | 17.4 | 20.6 | 18.0 | 15.5 | 17.8 | 17.6 | Worse |
| | (580) | (63990) | (62658) | (1949) | (40385) | (576) | (539) | (933) | (1861) | (2777) | (11257) | Weighted N |
| | | | | | | | | | | | | |
| Females Only | 32.9 | 30.1 | 32.9 | 29.3 | 26.7 | 31.7 | 33.4 | 27.6 | 23.0 | 24.0 | 26.0 | Better |
| | 42.0 | 39.9 | 37.1 | 41.8 | 43.8 | 47.8 | 45.8 | 49.5 | 52.7 | 50.4 | 51.3 | Same |
| | 25.1 | 30.0 | 30.0 | 29.0 | 29.5 | 20.5 | 20.8 | 23.0 | 24.3 | 25.6 | 22.8 | Worse |
| | (762) | (33664) | (33911) | (946) | (9053) | (703) | (758) | (392) | (531) | (885) | (4033) | Weighted N |

Table 6.6

| | 1969a | 1970a | 1971m | 1972f | 1973c | 1974q | 1975q | 1976m | 1978n | |
|---|---|---|---|---|---|---|---|---|---|---|
| Males Only | 38.3% | 36.8% | 34.8% | 49.3% | 38.3% | 31.9% | 33.6% | 37.3% | 39.3% | Better |
| | 43.9 | 37.4 | 39.1 | 33.8 | 35.2 | 25.7 | 33.5 | 31.2 | 27.1 | Same |
| | 17.7 | 25.9 | 26.1 | 17.0 | 26.5 | 42.4 | 32.9 | 31.5 | 33.6 | Worse |
| | (8268) | (1820) | (896) | (542) | (574) | (1317) | (1331) | (50655) | (1000) | Weighted N |
| | | | | | | | | | | |
| Females Only | 32.0 | 27.0 | 23.3 | 45.7 | 34.7 | 28.1 | 31.2 | 32.1 | 30.7 | Better |
| | 46.4 | 42.1 | 45.7 | 34.9 | 37.1 | 29.1 | 33.3 | 32.8 | 31.0 | Same |
| | 21.7 | 30.9 | 31.0 | 19.4 | 28.1 | 42.8 | 35.5 | 35.1 | 38.4 | Worse |
| | (3123) | (689) | (387) | (744) | (757) | (1620) | (1551) | (73790) | (1256) | Weighted N |

Table 6.7

Is R's Family Better Off Financially than Last Year?
Race of Respondent

| | | | | | Year | | | | | | |
|---|---|---|---|---|---|---|---|---|---|---|---|
| | 1947a | 1948a | 1949a | 1950a | 1951a | 1952k | 1953a | 1954a | 1955a | 1956m | |
| Whites Only | 33.8% | 31.3% | 34.2% | 33.4% | 33.3% | 27.2% | 40.5% | 38.0% | 40.9% | 34.3% | Better |
| | 31.3 | 29.4 | 35.6 | 33.4 | 30.3 | 41.8 | 34.4 | 32.9 | 33.1 | 49.6 | Same |
| | 34.9 | 39.3 | 30.2 | 33.2 | 36.3 | 30.9 | 25.1 | 29.1 | 26.0 | 16.1 | Worse |
| | (860085) | (789399) | (831593) | (90429) | (88690) | (815) | (81825) | (66922) | (88131) | (1310) | Weighted N |
| Blacks Only | 24.4 | 18.6 | 24.7 | 19.3 | 26.0 | 21.1 | 28.0 | 26.2 | 20.6 | 17.5 | Better |
| | 30.8 | 22.5 | 31.0 | 28.9 | 21.3 | 35.8 | 28.7 | 22.8 | 34.9 | 51.8 | Same |
| | 44.8 | 58.9 | 44.3 | 51.8 | 52.7 | 43.2 | 43.3 | 51.0 | 44.6 | 30.7 | Worse |
| | (75806) | (79144) | (80451) | (6693) | (7664) | (95) | (9672) | (7185) | (8058) | (114) | Weighted N |

Table 6.8

| | 1957f | 1958a | 1959a | 1960a | 1961a | 1962n | 1963m | 1965a | 1966a | 1967a | 1968a | |
|---|---|---|---|---|---|---|---|---|---|---|---|---|
| Whites Only | 33.3% | 34.3% | 40.1% | 37.5% | 30.4% | 35.6% | 35.8% | 38.4% | 38.7% | 35.6% | 34.9% | Better |
| | 43.6 | 36.9 | 35.4 | 38.2 | 44.4 | 46.2 | 44.9 | 43.6 | 44.8 | 46.1 | 46.8 | Same |
| | 23.1 | 28.8 | 24.5 | 24.2 | 25.2 | 18.1 | 19.3 | 17.9 | 16.5 | 18.3 | 18.3 | Worse |
| | (1188) | (87109) | (87725) | (2589) | (44392) | (1159) | (1146) | (1173) | (2166) | (3216) | (13627) | Weighted N |
| Blacks Only | 23.0 | 19.9 | 19.5 | 22.8 | 16.5 | 19.1 | 21.6 | 28.6 | 32.5 | 28.9 | 30.3 | Better |
| | 46.0 | 28.1 | 32.8 | 40.7 | 43.0 | 50.9 | 45.6 | 39.5 | 39.3 | 39.9 | 49.6 | Same |
| | 30.9 | 52.0 | 47.7 | 36.5 | 40.5 | 30.0 | 32.8 | 31.9 | 28.3 | 31.1 | 20.0 | Worse |
| | (139) | (10524) | (9261) | (312) | (4826) | (110) | (125) | (119) | (191) | (363) | (1428) | Weighted N |

Table 6.9

| | 1969a | 1970a | 1971m | 1972f | 1973c | 1974q | 1975q | 1976m | 1978n | |
|---|---|---|---|---|---|---|---|---|---|---|
| Whites Only | 37.3% | 33.9% | 31.8% | 46.3% | 37.8% | 30.0% | 32.5% | 34.2% | 34.0% | Better |
| | 44.6 | 39.3 | 41.7 | 35.4 | 35.6 | 28.2 | 34.4 | 31.5 | 30.5 | Same |
| | 18.2 | 26.8 | 26.5 | 18.3 | 26.6 | 41.8 | 33.0 | 34.2 | 35.5 | Worse |
| | (10066) | (2209) | (1120) | (1155) | (1109) | (2520) | (2551) | (106282) | (1980) | Weighted N |
| Blacks Only | 31.2 | 34.2 | 28.1 | 56.1 | 28.4 | 29.3 | 32.5 | 35.7 | 38.4 | Better |
| | 44.8 | 34.9 | 39.8 | 25.4 | 33.6 | 24.5 | 25.3 | 31.1 | 21.9 | Same |
| | 24.0 | 30.9 | 32.0 | 18.4 | 37.9 | 46.3 | 42.2 | 33.2 | 39.7 | Worse |
| | (1155) | (272) | (128) | (114) | (116) | (294) | (237) | (11536) | (224) | Weighted N |

ble 6.10
R's Family Better Off Financially than Last Year?
ucation of Respondent

| | | | | | Year | | | | | | |
|---|---|---|---|---|---|---|---|---|---|---|---|
| | 1947a | 1948a | 1949a | 1950a | 1951a | 1952k | 1953a | 1954a | 1955a | 1956m | |
| Grade School Only | 26.9% | 21.8% | 25.7% | 21.7% | 24.6% | 17.1% | 25.2% | 25.1% | 24.3% | 22.7% | Better |
| | 36.4 | 32.4 | 39.0 | 35.2 | 32.4 | 44.4 | 39.8 | 35.4 | 37.9 | 54.0 | Same |
| | 36.7 | 45.8 | 35.3 | 43.1 | 43.0 | 38.6 | 35.0 | 39.6 | 37.8 | 23.3 | Worse |
| | (337500) | (308363) | (299727) | (36232) | (33898) | (363) | (32091) | (25280) | (29367) | (322) | Weighted N |
| High School Only | 38.0 | 35.9 | 38.6 | 39.3 | 38.7 | 32.0 | 45.9 | 43.4 | 47.6 | 34.0 | Better |
| | 27.1 | 25.5 | 34.6 | 30.9 | 26.8 | 38.7 | 31.3 | 28.3 | 29.3 | 49.9 | Same |
| | 34.9 | 38.6 | 26.8 | 29.8 | 34.5 | 29.3 | 22.8 | 28.3 | 23.1 | 16.1 | Worse |
| | (304930) | (274594) | (287982) | (32798) | (30677) | (372) | (31470) | (27042) | (37624) | (341) | Weighted N |
| College Only | 41.1 | 39.0 | 43.8 | 45.1 | 39.8 | 34.6 | 53.1 | 48.9 | 54.2 | 43.2 | Better |
| | 26.8 | 26.1 | 28.3 | 28.6 | 27.2 | 40.8 | 26.8 | 30.1 | 30.2 | 41.4 | Same |
| | 32.1 | 34.9 | 27.9 | 26.3 | 33.0 | 24.6 | 20.1 | 20.9 | 15.6 | 15.4 | Worse |
| | (119292) | (119984) | (125528) | (14060) | (13765) | (179) | (15058) | (11374) | (13709) | (169) | Weighted N |

ble 6.11

| | 1957f | 1958a | 1959a | 1960a | 1961a | 1962n | 1963m | 1965a | 1966a | 1967a | 1968a | |
|---|---|---|---|---|---|---|---|---|---|---|---|---|
| Grade School Only | 16.9% | 16.8% | 23.6% | 22.2% | 15.1% | 19.9% | 16.5% | 19.7% | 23.6% | 21.3% | 18.8% | Better |
| | 56.6 | 41.6 | 41.8 | 45.5 | 53.6 | 56.5 | 56.5 | 53.6 | 52.1 | 54.7 | 57.7 | Same |
| | 26.6 | 41.6 | 34.7 | 32.3 | 31.4 | 23.6 | 27.0 | 26.7 | 24.3 | 23.9 | 23.4 | Worse |
| | (320) | (27226) | (27787) | (807) | (14723) | (356) | (370) | (375) | (675) | (1045) | (4320) | Weighted N |
| High School Only | 37.4 | 37.7 | 42.7 | 40.2 | 31.6 | 37.1 | 37.5 | 40.9 | 40.5 | 36.8 | 35.9 | Better |
| | 42.8 | 34.3 | 33.9 | 36.1 | 40.3 | 44.1 | 42.9 | 42.3 | 44.6 | 44.0 | 46.6 | Same |
| | 19.9 | 28.0 | 23.4 | 23.7 | 28.1 | 18.8 | 19.7 | 16.9 | 14.9 | 19.2 | 17.5 | Worse |
| | (297) | (35309) | (33537) | (1085) | (22171) | (612) | (651) | (629) | (1007) | (1695) | (7071) | Weighted N |
| College Only | 38.9 | 48.9 | 53.1 | 50.6 | 43.1 | 45.6 | 54.0 | 52.6 | 52.8 | 46.8 | 50.2 | Better |
| | 39.6 | 28.0 | 26.9 | 31.6 | 40.2 | 39.7 | 30.8 | 31.1 | 34.2 | 38.5 | 33.6 | Same |
| | 21.5 | 23.1 | 19.9 | 17.8 | 16.6 | 14.8 | 15.2 | 16.3 | 13.0 | 14.7 | 16.2 | Worse |
| | (144) | (17583) | (16391) | (551) | (11947) | (305) | (263) | (312) | (602) | (880) | (3812) | Weighted N |

ucation coded for head of household only in 1947a,1948a,1949a,1950a,1951a,1953a,1954a,1955a,1956m,1957f,1958a,1959a,
1960a,1961a,and 1966a, and for head and wife only in 1963m,1965a,and 1967a.

le 6.12
R's Family Better Off Financially than Last Year?
cation of Respondent

| | | | | | Year | | | | | |
|---|---|---|---|---|---|---|---|---|---|---|
| | 1969a | 1970a | 1971m | 1972f | 1973c | 1974q | 1975q | 1976m | 1978n | |
| Grade School Only | 19.4% | 26.8% | 16.6% | 28.9% | 20.8% | 18.0% | 20.7% | 18.3% | 19.8% | Better |
| | 55.6 | 41.2 | 50.5 | 47.9 | 45.5 | 33.9 | 43.0 | 42.3 | 42.4 | Same |
| | 25.0 | 32.0 | 32.9 | 23.1 | 33.8 | 48.1 | 36.3 | 39.4 | 37.8 | Worse |
| | (2995) | (948) | (319) | (242) | (154) | (484) | (435) | (16774) | (262) | Weighted N |
| | | | | | | | | | | |
| High School Only | 38.2 | 36.5 | 31.8 | 51.4 | 37.8 | 30.5 | 31.8 | 32.1 | 32.0 | Better |
| | 44.2 | 36.7 | 42.3 | 32.7 | 35.9 | 29.0 | 32.4 | 32.6 | 30.1 | Same |
| | 17.6 | 26.8 | 26.0 | 16.0 | 26.3 | 40.5 | 35.8 | 35.3 | 37.9 | Worse |
| | (5076) | (1098) | (570) | (658) | (619) | (1399) | (1505) | (59127) | (1192) | Weighted N |
| | | | | | | | | | | |
| College Only | 50.2 | 45.6 | 43.0 | 52.4 | 43.7 | 34.8 | 38.5 | 43.1 | 43.3 | Better |
| | 34.8 | 37.2 | 31.9 | 29.2 | 30.5 | 22.3 | 30.6 | 26.6 | 23.4 | Same |
| | 15.0 | 17.2 | 25.1 | 18.4 | 25.9 | 42.9 | 30.9 | 30.3 | 33.2 | Worse |
| | (3230) | (401) | (386) | (380) | (394) | (1032) | (941) | (44729) | (794) | Weighted N |

cation coded for head of household only in 1971m, and for head and wife only in 1968a and 1970a.

ble 6.13

R's Family Better Off Financially than Last Year?

e of Respondent

| | Year | | | | | | | | | | |
|---|---|---|---|---|---|---|---|---|---|---|---|
| | 1947a | 1948a | 1949a | 1950a | 1951a | 1952k | 1953a | 1954a | 1955a | 1956m | |
| 18-24 Only | 49.0% | 54.7% | 55.9% | 55.3% | 62.6% | 42.3% | 62.5% | 58.1% | 64.6% | 54.0% | Better |
| | 17.8 | 14.0 | 19.3 | 21.5 | 17.3 | 30.8 | 17.8 | 16.1 | 15.0 | 36.8 | Same |
| | 33.2 | 31.3 | 24.8 | 23.2 | 20.1 | 26.9 | 19.7 | 25.8 | 20.4 | 9.2 | Worse |
| | (79588) | (83270) | (88310) | (9073) | (7680) | (52) | (8260) | (5298) | (7432) | (87) | Weighted N |
| 25-34 Only | 40.0 | 34.9 | 44.0 | 45.7 | 42.4 | 37.8 | 49.0 | 49.2 | 53.1 | 48.3 | Better |
| | 24.4 | 26.3 | 27.3 | 23.2 | 28.3 | 33.9 | 27.8 | 24.2 | 26.2 | 39.6 | Same |
| | 35.5 | 38.8 | 28.7 | 31.1 | 29.3 | 28.3 | 23.3 | 26.6 | 20.6 | 12.1 | Worse |
| | (171132) | (153258) | (149486) | (18855) | (16305) | (230) | (18697) | (13410) | (18062) | (331) | Weighted N |
| 35-44 Only | 29.9 | 26.5 | 32.1 | 30.4 | 35.4 | 29.8 | 41.3 | 37.5 | 42.8 | 35.1 | Better |
| | 29.5 | 28.1 | 36.8 | 33.1 | 27.8 | 41.5 | 29.9 | 30.0 | 31.0 | 48.5 | Same |
| | 40.6 | 45.4 | 31.1 | 36.4 | 36.8 | 28.6 | 28.8 | 32.5 | 26.2 | 16.5 | Worse |
| | (177921) | (151530) | (150633) | (17967) | (17320) | (248) | (16097) | (15110) | (17662) | (328) | Weighted N |
| 45-54 Only | 30.7 | 26.2 | 29.4 | 24.5 | 26.6 | 15.7 | 32.6 | 35.4 | 34.8 | 26.2 | Better |
| | 36.9 | 29.4 | 39.4 | 37.3 | 28.2 | 49.7 | 39.0 | 31.2 | 32.8 | 54.2 | Same |
| | 32.5 | 44.4 | 31.2 | 38.2 | 45.2 | 34.6 | 28.3 | 33.4 | 32.4 | 19.6 | Worse |
| | (249068) | (128570) | (134875) | (15548) | (13597) | (159) | (14378) | (11753) | (13482) | (271) | Weighted N |
| 55-64 Only | ** | 27.4 | 23.5 | 26.2 | 18.4 | 18.6 | 26.6 | 28.5 | 24.4 | 25.4 | Better |
| | ** | 34.5 | 44.7 | 35.3 | 38.9 | 44.2 | 45.5 | 40.4 | 44.0 | 52.1 | Same |
| | ** | 38.2 | 31.8 | 38.5 | 42.6 | 37.2 | 27.9 | 31.1 | 31.6 | 22.5 | Worse |
| | ** | (102279) | (106903) | (11515) | (11927) | (113) | (10567) | (9366) | (12141) | (213) | Weighted N |
| 65 and Older Only | 21.9 | 14.2 | 18.1 | 12.5 | 17.1 | 12.3 | 19.5 | 17.0 | 22.1 | 13.3 | Better |
| | 43.9 | 40.1 | 45.6 | 47.5 | 33.3 | 46.5 | 44.8 | 44.9 | 43.5 | 63.8 | Same |
| | 34.2 | 45.7 | 36.3 | 40.0 | 49.6 | 41.2 | 35.7 | 38.1 | 34.5 | 22.9 | Worse |
| | (89593) | (84034) | (83030) | (9741) | (11321) | (114) | (10620) | (8789) | (10604) | (188) | Weighted N |

Code distinction not made.

e group coded "45-64" in 1947a.

dest age group coded "65 And Older".

e coded for head of household only in 1947a,1948a,1949a,1950a,1951a,1953a,1954a,and 1955a.

Table 6.14

s R's Family Better Off Financially than Last Year?

ge of Respondent

| | 1957f | 1958a | 1959a | 1960a | 1961a | Year 1962n | 1963m | 1965a | 1966a | 1967a | 1968a | |
|---|---|---|---|---|---|---|---|---|---|---|---|---|
| 18-24 Only | 59.0% | 55.8% | 63.0% | 58.7% | 61.8% | 52.7% | 61.3% | 58.3% | 60.2% | 59.6% | 58.8% | Better |
| | 26.5 | 20.2 | 17.6 | 23.4 | 19.9 | 29.7 | 17.2 | 25.0 | 23.4 | 23.7 | 27.8 | Same |
| | 14.5 | 24.0 | 19.3 | 17.9 | 18.3 | 17.6 | 21.5 | 16.7 | 16.4 | 16.7 | 13.3 | Worse |
| | (83) | (8188) | (6990) | (201) | (4556) | (74) | (93) | (120) | (171) | (245) | (967) | Weighted N |
| 25-34 Only | 48.2 | 45.2 | 52.7 | 56.3 | 43.2 | 53.3 | 53.5 | 55.1 | 57.6 | 53.2 | 54.5 | Better |
| | 37.1 | 25.4 | 26.3 | 26.2 | 30.2 | 32.3 | 30.4 | 27.2 | 27.6 | 27.8 | 29.5 | Same |
| | 14.6 | 29.4 | 21.0 | 17.5 | 26.6 | 14.4 | 16.1 | 17.7 | 14.7 | 19.0 | 16.0 | Worse |
| | (280) | (16063) | (14013) | (481) | (10259) | (257) | (230) | (243) | (434) | (658) | (2824) | Weighted N |
| 35-44 Only | 32.6 | 34.2 | 40.4 | 40.4 | 27.1 | 43.5 | 40.1 | 46.9 | 46.0 | 38.8 | 43.2 | Better |
| | 39.9 | 36.2 | 34.5 | 32.8 | 45.5 | 41.0 | 43.4 | 37.7 | 37.9 | 43.0 | 42.1 | Same |
| | 27.5 | 29.6 | 25.1 | 26.8 | 27.4 | 15.5 | 16.5 | 15.4 | 16.2 | 18.2 | 14.7 | Worse |
| | (316) | (17190) | (16899) | (542) | (11121) | (278) | (267) | (273) | (457) | (704) | (2835) | Weighted N |
| 45-54 Only | 29.5 | 28.5 | 34.6 | 31.0 | 24.5 | 29.0 | 32.1 | 32.9 | 36.7 | 33.4 | 34.4 | Better |
| | 45.7 | 37.5 | 33.8 | 39.6 | 48.8 | 48.5 | 46.5 | 46.1 | 45.2 | 47.5 | 46.1 | Same |
| | 24.8 | 34.0 | 31.7 | 29.4 | 26.6 | 22.5 | 21.4 | 21.0 | 18.1 | 19.1 | 19.5 | Worse |
| | (278) | (14596) | (13895) | (487) | (9506) | (262) | (271) | (243) | (469) | (703) | (2880) | Weighted N |
| 55-64 Only | 20.0 | 28.8 | 27.5 | 23.6 | 16.9 | 22.8 | 21.5 | 25.1 | 26.3 | 28.8 | 25.1 | Better |
| | 54.1 | 38.9 | 43.2 | 46.9 | 52.1 | 55.4 | 51.7 | 53.4 | 54.7 | 52.1 | 52.8 | Same |
| | 25.9 | 32.3 | 29.2 | 29.5 | 31.0 | 21.8 | 26.8 | 21.5 | 19.0 | 19.2 | 22.1 | Worse |
| | (185) | (29200) | (12468) | (369) | (7402) | (193) | (205) | (219) | (415) | (584) | (2782) | Weighted N |
| 65-74 Only | 14.2 | 12.3 | 19.4 | 13.4 | 7.8 | 9.4 | 14.7 | 13.1 | 15.8 | 13.0 | 11.1 | Better |
| | 54.8 | 54.8 | 49.8 | 59.4 | 65.0 | 65.9 | 64.7 | 62.6 | 64.5 | 67.5 | 64.0 | Same |
| | 31.0 | 32.9 | 30.8 | 27.3 | 27.2 | 24.6 | 20.6 | 24.3 | 19.7 | 19.5 | 24.9 | Worse |
| | (197) | (12152) | (13009) | (374) | (4339) | (138) | (136) | (222) | (437) | (461) | (1844) | Weighted N |
| 75 And Older Only | ** | ** | ** | ** | 10.0 | 7.1 | 10.6 | ** | ** | 11.9 | 4.5 | Better |
| | ** | ** | ** | ** | 67.7 | 71.4 | 60.0 | ** | ** | 59.4 | 73.9 | Same |
| | ** | ** | ** | ** | 22.3 | 21.4 | 29.4 | ** | ** | 28.7 | 21.6 | Worse |
| | ** | ** | ** | ** | (2121) | (70) | (85) | ** | ** | (286) | (1110) | Weighted N |

* Code distinction not made.

ldest age group coded "65 And Older" in 1957f,1958a,1959a,1960a,1965a,and 1966a.

ge coded for head of household only in 1958a,1959a,1960a,and 1961a, and for head and wife only in 1965a,1966a,and 1967a.

Personal Economic Outlook

Table 6.15

Is R's Family Better Off Financially than Last Year?

Age of Respondent

| | | | | | Year | | | | | |
|---|---|---|---|---|---|---|---|---|---|---|
| | 1969a | 1970a | 1971m | 1972f | 1973c | 1974q | 1975q | 1976m | 1978n | |
| 18-24 Only | 57.9% | 57.1% | 53.1% | 62.3% | 58.7% | 48.9% | 48.6% | 62.0% | 53.4% | Better |
| | 23.0 | 19.7 | 20.4 | 20.3 | 15.3 | 18.3 | 19.4 | 11.3 | 16.2 | Same |
| | 19.1 | 23.2 | 26.5 | 17.4 | 26.0 | 32.8 | 32.0 | 26.7 | 30.4 | Worse |
| | (1032) | (233) | (98) | (207) | (196) | (476) | (444) | (20075) | (339) | Weighted N |
| 25-34 Only | 56.3 | 49.9 | 47.9 | 61.6 | 44.8 | 30.6 | 42.6 | 47.1 | 46.1 | Better |
| | 29.1 | 23.5 | 28.8 | 22.2 | 29.7 | 23.8 | 22.2 | 22.1 | 23.0 | Same |
| | 14.6 | 26.7 | 23.3 | 16.1 | 25.5 | 45.6 | 35.2 | 30.8 | 30.9 | Worse |
| | (2271) | (409) | (240) | (279) | (310) | (669) | (676) | (26627) | (551) | Weighted N |
| 35-44 Only | 39.0 | 40.9 | 36.3 | 56.6 | 40.5 | 30.7 | 33.3 | 32.9 | 31.0 | Better |
| | 42.6 | 34.7 | 36.3 | 30.8 | 32.4 | 27.0 | 30.4 | 38.3 | 26.7 | Same |
| | 18.4 | 24.4 | 27.5 | 12.7 | 27.1 | 42.4 | 36.4 | 28.8 | 42.3 | Worse |
| | (1978) | (435) | (251) | (221) | (210) | (486) | (484) | (17602) | (397) | Weighted N |
| 45-54 Only | 34.3 | 28.0 | 27.9 | 45.8 | 29.6 | 27.9 | 29.9 | 26.2 | 29.0 | Better |
| | 47.2 | 41.4 | 44.6 | 31.6 | 42.9 | 27.1 | 31.8 | 28.8 | 32.6 | Same |
| | 18.4 | 30.6 | 27.5 | 22.6 | 27.6 | 45.0 | 38.3 | 45.0 | 38.4 | Worse |
| | (1948) | (447) | (269) | (190) | (203) | (502) | (415) | (18553) | (331) | Weighted N |
| 55-64 Only | 28.4 | 26.0 | 21.3 | 33.5 | 25.0 | 23.6 | 20.6 | 18.6 | 22.3 | Better |
| | 53.0 | 43.2 | 44.1 | 46.5 | 45.8 | 33.3 | 45.4 | 44.9 | 39.0 | Same |
| | 18.6 | 30.9 | 34.6 | 20.0 | 29.2 | 43.1 | 33.9 | 36.5 | 38.7 | Worse |
| | (1750) | (366) | (211) | (170) | (192) | (436) | (383) | (17033) | (305) | Weighted N |
| 65-74 Only | 15.1 | 13.0 | 13.6 | 17.4 | 12.7 | 12.8 | 13.1 | 15.3 | 17.8 | Better |
| | 63.7 | 60.1 | 57.6 | 59.7 | 56.7 | 38.9 | 54.6 | 51.8 | 42.3 | Same |
| | 21.2 | 26.9 | 28.8 | 22.9 | 30.7 | 48.2 | 32.2 | 32.9 | 39.9 | Worse |
| | (1461) | (253) | (132) | (144) | (150) | (226) | (335) | (14464) | (208) | Weighted N |
| 75 And Older Only | 12.1 | 15.9 | 7.3 | 15.7 | 24.2 | 10.9 | 12.5 | 18.6 | 14.8 | Better |
| | 59.6 | 59.5 | 70.7 | 64.3 | 47.0 | 47.7 | 63.2 | 54.9 | 47.8 | Same |
| | 28.3 | 24.6 | 22.0 | 20.0 | 28.8 | 41.4 | 24.3 | 26.5 | 37.4 | Worse |
| | (891) | (126) | (82) | (70) | (66) | (128) | (136) | (7453) | (115) | Weighted N |

Age coded for head of household only in 1971m, and for head and wife only in 1968a and 1970a.

Personal Economic Outlook

Table 6.16

s R's Family Better Off Financially than Last Year?
ncome of Respondent

|  | Year | | | | | | | | | | |
|---|---|---|---|---|---|---|---|---|---|---|---|
|  | 1947a | 1948a | 1949a | 1950a | 1951a | 1952k | 1953a | 1954a | 1955a | 1956m | |
| Income 1 (0-16%) | 22.9% | 19.2% | 22.2% | 16.8% | 17.2% | 17.6% | 25.5% | 23.9% | 21.5% | 8.1% | Better |
|  | 36.1 | 34.7 | 38.2 | 30.0 | 32.0 | 40.7 | 33.9 | 33.7 | 34.9 | 59.2 | Same |
|  | 40.9 | 46.1 | 39.6 | 53.2 | 50.8 | 41.8 | 40.6 | 42.4 | 43.6 | 32.7 | Worse |
|  | (155142) | (118615) | (139122) | (13820) | (12350) | (91) | (21865) | (16566) | (22705) | (223) | Weighted N |
| Income 2 (17-33%) | 28.8 | 27.7 | 28.7 | 26.7 | 31.1 | 16.7 | 36.8 | 37.3 | 36.7 | 15.4 | Better |
|  | 33.6 | 26.2 | 34.1 | 32.0 | 30.8 | 47.7 | 35.0 | 28.9 | 32.0 | 57.3 | Same |
|  | 37.6 | 46.1 | 37.3 | 41.4 | 38.1 | 35.7 | 28.2 | 33.8 | 31.2 | 27.3 | Worse |
|  | (222594) | (137660) | (133058) | (18332) | (17225) | (258) | (14770) | (10261) | (13624) | (143) | Weighted N |
| Income 3 (34-67%) | 34.9 | 28.2 | 32.6 | 32.6 | 32.2 | 30.9 | 39.1 | 34.0 | 40.9 | 37.9 | Better |
|  | 28.7 | 29.5 | 35.7 | 34.7 | 28.7 | 37.2 | 36.9 | 33.5 | 33.4 | 48.0 | Same |
|  | 36.4 | 42.3 | 31.7 | 32.7 | 39.2 | 31.9 | 24.1 | 32.5 | 25.7 | 14.1 | Worse |
|  | (405829) | (294629) | (338109) | (38642) | (36615) | (298) | (30315) | (23432) | (29951) | (589) | Weighted N |
| Income 4 (68-95%) | 43.7 | 34.3 | 40.2 | 44.2 | 39.0 | 34.8 | 52.7 | 47.3 | 49.9 | 46.5 | Better |
|  | 30.4 | 27.4 | 34.1 | 32.0 | 30.2 | 43.4 | 28.6 | 31.0 | 32.5 | 44.6 | Same |
|  | 25.9 | 38.3 | 25.7 | 23.8 | 30.8 | 21.7 | 18.7 | 21.7 | 17.7 | 8.9 | Worse |
|  | (130638) | (245125) | (257691) | (21151) | (25364) | (198) | (20305) | (19827) | (26689) | (303) | Weighted N |
| Income 5 (96-100%) | 36.9 | 45.6 | 47.2 | 46.9 | 49.6 | 48.8 | 52.9 | 53.8 | 57.4 | 43.3 | Better |
|  | 29.0 | 26.4 | 30.3 | 35.8 | 22.3 | 26.8 | 31.9 | 27.8 | 30.2 | 44.2 | Same |
|  | 34.2 | 28.0 | 22.5 | 17.3 | 28.1 | 24.4 | 15.2 | 18.5 | 12.3 | 12.5 | Worse |
|  | (36541) | (73822) | (48586) | (5031) | (5592) | (41) | (4242) | (4021) | (5151) | (104) | Weighted N |

Personal Economic Outlook

Table 6.17
Is R's Family Better Off Financially than Last Year?
Income of Respondent

| | 1957f | 1958a | 1959a | 1960a | 1961a | Year<br>1962n | 1963m | 1965a | 1966a | 1967a | 1968a | |
|---|---|---|---|---|---|---|---|---|---|---|---|---|
| Income 1 (0-16%) | 11.9% | 18.1% | 21.7% | 17.2% | 20.1% | 7.3% | 12.1% | 17.6% | 19.8% | 16.2% | 13.0% | Better |
| | 54.9 | 39.6 | 38.3 | 43.4 | 50.3 | 64.0 | 50.6 | 47.1 | 51.2 | 54.0 | 58.0 | Same |
| | 33.2 | 42.3 | 40.0 | 39.4 | 29.6 | 28.7 | 37.4 | 35.3 | 29.0 | 29.8 | 28.9 | Worse |
| | (235) | (21398) | (19709) | (548) | (8096) | (164) | (174) | (170) | (465) | (709) | (2560) | Weighted N |
| Income 2 (17-33%) | 29.7 | 26.6 | 31.3 | 30.0 | 23.5 | 18.7 | 21.3 | 23.1 | 27.5 | 26.8 | 20.2 | Better |
| | 43.4 | 38.4 | 35.0 | 41.1 | 43.4 | 55.1 | 51.2 | 52.5 | 49.5 | 51.4 | 54.5 | Same |
| | 26.9 | 35.0 | 33.7 | 28.9 | 33.1 | 26.3 | 27.5 | 24.4 | 23.1 | 21.9 | 25.3 | Worse |
| | (320) | (23195) | (11747) | (609) | (9869) | (198) | (207) | (221) | (477) | (553) | (2557) | Weighted N |
| Income 3 (34-67%) | 38.4 | 37.4 | 36.6 | 39.9 | 30.7 | 39.6 | 35.9 | 37.2 | 45.0 | 35.6 | 38.7 | Better |
| | 40.7 | 33.2 | 37.1 | 36.1 | 42.0 | 44.1 | 44.3 | 43.7 | 41.5 | 41.0 | 44.9 | Same |
| | 20.8 | 29.4 | 26.4 | 23.9 | 27.3 | 16.3 | 19.8 | 19.1 | 13.5 | 23.4 | 16.4 | Worse |
| | (518) | (23711) | (35105) | (1115) | (19318) | (508) | (384) | (419) | (817) | (752) | (5135) | Weighted N |
| Income 4 (68-95%) | 49.7 | 42.6 | 49.0 | 50.4 | 38.4 | 52.5 | 47.9 | 47.8 | 49.8 | 43.1 | 46.8 | Better |
| | 34.7 | 34.7 | 32.8 | 36.1 | 43.1 | 32.0 | 39.4 | 38.3 | 39.3 | 43.0 | 40.1 | Same |
| | 15.5 | 22.7 | 18.1 | 13.6 | 18.5 | 15.5 | 12.8 | 13.9 | 10.9 | 14.0 | 13.2 | Worse |
| | (193) | (28196) | (23175) | (552) | (10684) | (284) | (376) | (418) | (488) | (1340) | (4374) | Weighted N |
| Income 5 (96-100%) | 40.0 | 54.4 | 61.8 | 50.0 | 29.8 | 45.2 | 56.3 | 59.0 | 54.4 | 51.7 | 54.9 | Better |
| | 46.7 | 27.6 | 27.0 | 33.9 | 51.3 | 46.8 | 32.2 | 34.3 | 37.6 | 40.1 | 34.2 | Same |
| | 13.3 | 17.9 | 11.2 | 16.1 | 18.9 | 8.1 | 11.5 | 6.7 | 8.1 | 8.2 | 10.9 | Worse |
| | (30) | (2525) | (8381) | (112) | (1579) | (62) | (87) | (105) | (149) | (319) | (772) | Weighted N |

Personal Economic Outlook

ble 6.18

R's Family Better Off Financially than Last Year?

come of Respondent

|  | | | | | Year | | | | | |
|---|---|---|---|---|---|---|---|---|---|---|
|  | 1969a | 1970a | 1971m | 1972f | 1973c | 1974q | 1975q | 1976m | 1978n | |
| Income 1 (0-16%) | 18.3% | 22.4% | 11.5% | 23.5% | 24.0% | 21.2% | 22.4% | 39.3% | 24.0% | Better |
|  | 53.5 | 42.3 | 49.7 | 50.7 | 38.6 | 28.0 | 38.8 | 26.8 | 28.9 | Same |
|  | 28.2 | 35.3 | 38.7 | 25.8 | 37.4 | 50.8 | 38.8 | 33.8 | 47.1 | Worse |
|  | (2458) | (468) | (191) | (221) | (171) | (396) | (428) | (21976) | (325) | Weighted N |
| Income 2 (17-33%) | 29.5 | 22.8 | 20.6 | 41.8 | 29.2 | 27.0 | 33.0 | 43.0 | 32.1 | Better |
|  | 48.2 | 46.1 | 43.3 | 39.0 | 35.9 | 27.0 | 31.6 | 25.2 | 28.8 | Same |
|  | 22.2 | 31.1 | 36.1 | 19.2 | 34.9 | 46.0 | 35.4 | 31.8 | 39.1 | Worse |
|  | (2200) | (412) | (238) | (146) | (312) | (574) | (491) | (24022) | (358) | Weighted N |
| Income 3 (34-67%) | 40.4 | 36.1 | 36.0 | 48.0 | 35.3 | 32.2 | 34.6 | 37.4 | 35.3 | Better |
|  | 42.6 | 36.2 | 38.0 | 32.6 | 35.6 | 25.8 | 30.6 | 31.1 | 28.0 | Same |
|  | 17.0 | 27.8 | 26.0 | 19.4 | 29.0 | 42.0 | 34.8 | 31.5 | 36.6 | Worse |
|  | (3790) | (871) | (461) | (454) | (365) | (962) | (824) | (14890) | (614) | Weighted N |
| Income 4 (68-95%) | 51.2 | 43.7 | 43.4 | 61.7 | 44.9 | 35.8 | 38.2 | 47.9 | 42.3 | Better |
|  | 36.9 | 35.6 | 38.0 | 25.2 | 35.7 | 30.4 | 32.0 | 23.9 | 27.1 | Same |
|  | 11.8 | 20.7 | 18.5 | 13.1 | 19.4 | 33.9 | 29.8 | 28.2 | 30.6 | Worse |
|  | (2607) | (671) | (297) | (321) | (345) | (593) | (641) | (9285) | (532) | Weighted N |
| Income 5 (96-100%) | 52.9 | 49.5 | 54.7 | 69.2 | 57.0 | 48.4 | 40.4 | 45.2 | 50.7 | Better |
|  | 38.1 | 34.3 | 37.7 | 23.1 | 32.3 | 17.2 | 22.5 | 28.7 | 26.4 | Same |
|  | 9.0 | 16.2 | 7.5 | 7.7 | 10.8 | 34.4 | 37.1 | 26.1 | 22.9 | Worse |
|  | (420) | (105) | (53) | (78) | (93) | (93) | (151) | (8061) | (144) | Weighted N |

gure 6.5

R Better Off Now? by Age of R

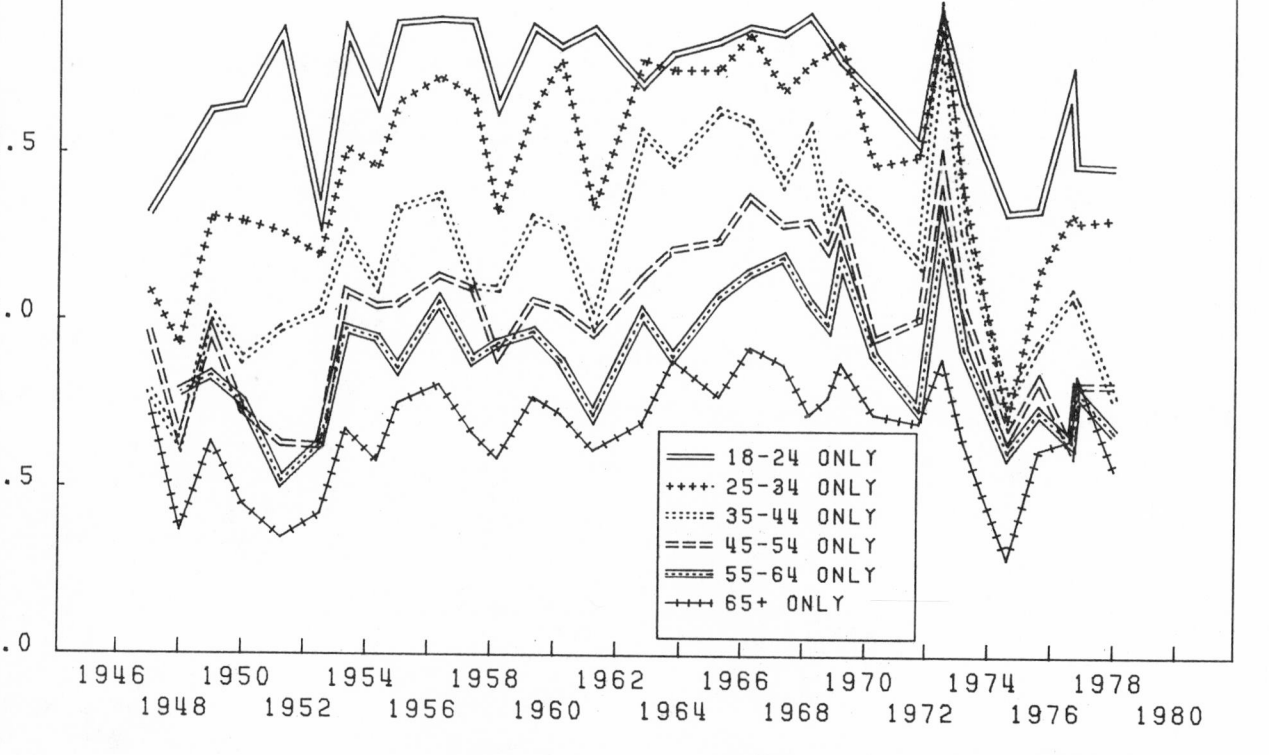

Personal Economic Outlook

Figure 6.6
s R Better Off Now? by Income of R

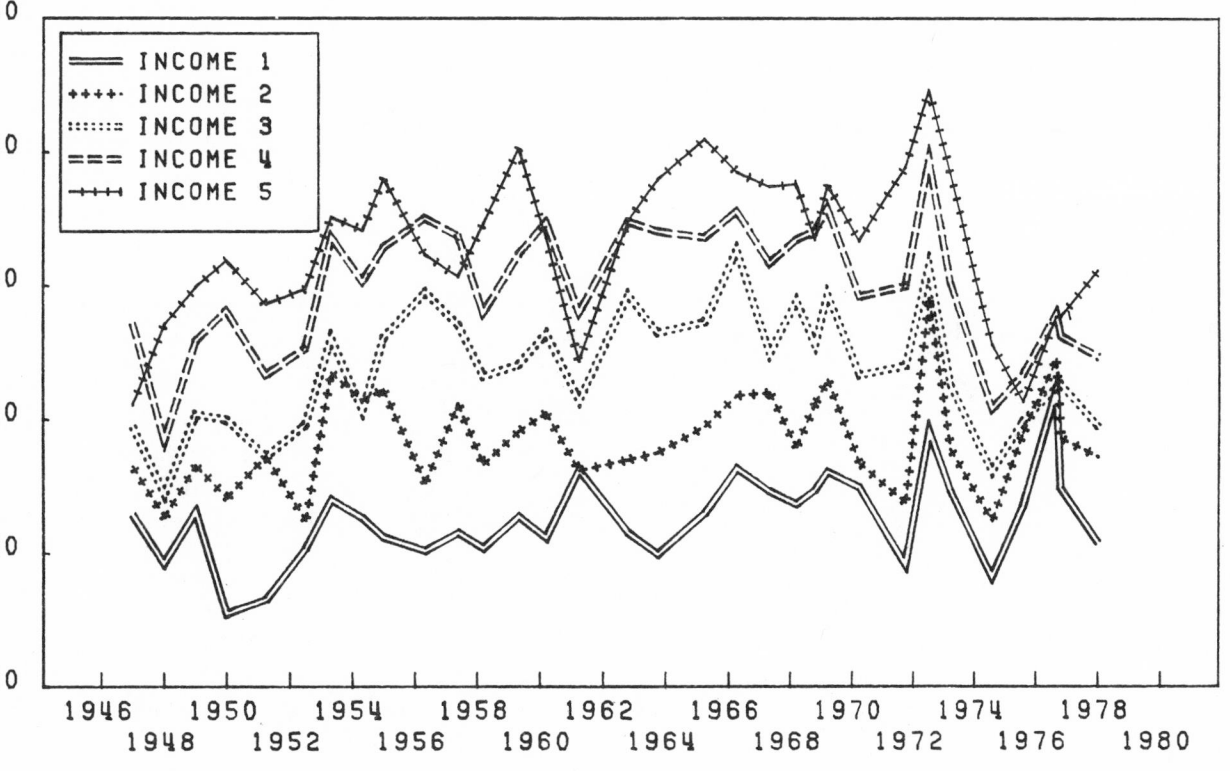

Personal Economic Outlook

Table 6.19
Will R's Family Be Better Off Financially a Year from Now?
Total Population

QUESTION: (Now looking ahead) do you think that a year from now you people (you and your
family) will be better off financially, or worse off, or just about the same as now?

|  |  | Year | | | | | | | | |
|---|---|---|---|---|---|---|---|---|---|---|
|  |  | 1953m | 1954m | 1956m | 1957f | 1958m | 1959f | 1960a | 1961a | 1962n |
| Better off | (5) | 31.0% | 31.1% | 32.6% | 33.1% | 31.8% | 34.5% | 40.9% | 39.1% | 33.6% |
| About the same | (3) | 39.5 | 43.9 | 48.4 | 46.1 | 46.8 | 48.0 | 40.4 | 40.5 | 50.0 |
| Worse off | (1) | 10.5 | 10.8 | 5.5 | 7.9 | 6.9 | 5.4 | 6.6 | 7.0 | 5.2 |
| Don't know/depends |  | 19.1 | 14.2 | 13.5 | 12.9 | 14.6 | 12.1 | 12.1 | 13.3 | 11.2 |
| Total |  | 100% | 100% | 100% | 100% | 100% | 100% | 100% | 100% | 100% |
| Weighted N |  | 1011 | 992 | 1443 | 1348 | 1328 | 1305 | 2908 | 49607 | 1287 |
| Unweighted N |  | 1011 | 992 | 1443 | 1348 | 1328 | 1305 | 2908 | 1966 | 1287 |
| Mean |  | 3.51 | 3.47 | 3.63 | 3.58 | 3.58 | 3.66 | 3.78 | 3.74 | 3.64 |
| Standard Deviation |  | 1.34 | 1.32 | 1.17 | 1.25 | 1.21 | 1.17 | 1.25 | 1.26 | 1.16 |

Table 6.20

|  |  | 1963m | 1964f | 1965a | 1966a | 1967a | 1968a | 1969a | 1970a |
|---|---|---|---|---|---|---|---|---|---|
| Better off | (5) | 32.7% | 37.0% | 38.6% | 38.3% | 35.9% | 37.6% | 37.6% | 33.4% |
| About the same | (3) | 51.1 | 46.5 | 44.4 | 45.8 | 45.8 | 44.7 | 46.8 | 43.0 |
| Worse off | (1) | 5.9 | 6.9 | 6.7 | 7.7 | 7.8 | 8.0 | 6.3 | 12.1 |
| Don't know/depends |  | 10.3 | 9.6 | 10.2 | 8.1 | 10.5 | 9.8 | 9.3 | 11.4 |
| Total |  | 100% | 100% | 100% | 100% | 100% | 100% | 100% | 100% |
| Weighted N |  | 1314 | 1494 | 1330 | 2408 | 3700 | 15556 | 11535 | 2546 |
| Unweighted N |  | 1314 | 1494 | 1330 | 2408 | 3141 | 2673 | 2293 | 2546 |
| Mean |  | 3.60 | 3.67 | 3.71 | 3.67 | 3.63 | 3.66 | 3.69 | 3.48 |
| Standard Deviation |  | 1.17 | 1.22 | 1.23 | 1.25 | 1.25 | 1.26 | 1.21 | 1.35 |

Table 6.21

|  |  | 1971m | 1972f | 1973c | 1974q | 1975q | 1976m | 1978n |
|---|---|---|---|---|---|---|---|---|
| Better off | (5) | 32.1% | 38.1% | 31.5% | 24.0% | 31.8% | 30.8% | 22.7% |
| About the same | (3) | 42.0 | 45.9 | 46.0 | 40.3 | 45.5 | 47.1 | 44.1 |
| Worse off | (1) | 9.7 | 5.9 | 12.9 | 24.2 | 11.7 | 13.1 | 26.2 |
| Don't know/depends |  | 16.2 | 10.1 | 9.7 | 11.5 | 11.1 | 9.0 | 7.0 |
| Total |  | 100% | 100% | 100% | 100% | 100% | 100% | 100% |
| Weighted N |  | 1299 | 1295 | 1344 | 2975 | 2914 | 127083 | 2292 |
| Unweighted N |  | 1299 | 1295 | 1344 | 1514 | 1517 | 1130 | 2292 |
| Mean |  | 3.53 | 3.72 | 3.41 | 2.99 | 3.45 | 3.39 | 2.92 |
| Standard Deviation |  | 1.31 | 1.20 | 1.34 | 1.48 | 1.32 | 1.33 | 1.45 |

Figure 6.7
Will R Be Better Off In a Year?--Total Population

Personal Economic Outlook

Table 6.22

Will R's Family Be Better Off Financially a Year from Now?

Sex of Respondent

|  | Year |  |  |  |  |  |  |  |  |  |
|---|---|---|---|---|---|---|---|---|---|---|
|  | 1953m | 1954m | 1956m | 1957f | 1958m | 1959f | 1960a | 1961a | 1962n |  |
| Males Only | 31.3% | 34.1% | 35.4% | 34.0% | 34.3% | 36.7% | 44.1% | 41.7% | 38.0% | Better |
|  | 37.3 | 41.8 | 44.7 | 45.6 | 44.1 | 46.3 | 37.3 | 38.8 | 47.2 | Same |
|  | 14.9 | 11.4 | 6.9 | 9.2 | 8.4 | 5.8 | 7.1 | 6.9 | 5.2 | Worse |
|  | 16.6 | 12.7 | 13.0 | 11.3 | 13.2 | 11.1 | 11.5 | 12.5 | 9.6 | Don't know |
|  | (451) | (466) | (669) | (577) | (562) | (566) | (1952) | (40480) | (581) | Weighted N |
|  |  |  |  |  |  |  |  |  |  |  |
| Females Only | 30.7 | 28.6 | 30.3 | 32.4 | 29.9 | 32.7 | 34.3 | 27.9 | 30.0 | Better |
|  | 41.3 | 45.6 | 51.5 | 46.4 | 48.7 | 49.4 | 46.8 | 47.9 | 52.3 | Same |
|  | 7.0 | 10.3 | 4.3 | 7.0 | 5.7 | 5.0 | 5.8 | 7.6 | 5.2 | Worse |
|  | 21.1 | 15.5 | 14.0 | 14.1 | 15.7 | 12.9 | 13.2 | 16.6 | 12.5 | Don't know |
|  | (560) | (524) | (773) | (771) | (766) | (737) | (956) | (9019) | (706) | Weighted N |

Table 6.23

|  | 1963m | 1964f | 1965a | 1966a | 1967a | 1968a | 1969a | 1970a |  |
|---|---|---|---|---|---|---|---|---|---|
| Males Only | 39.1% | 42.0% | 43.1% | 42.4% | 39.0% | 40.2% | 40.3% | 35.5% | Better |
|  | 47.2 | 41.5 | 40.9 | 43.1 | 43.4 | 43.2 | 44.7 | 41.4 | Same |
|  | 6.6 | 7.8 | 6.5 | 7.3 | 8.0 | 8.0 | 6.8 | 12.8 | Worse |
|  | 7.1 | 8.7 | 9.6 | 7.2 | 9.7 | 8.6 | 8.2 | 10.3 | Don't know |
|  | (547) | (643) | (942) | (1874) | (2803) | (11371) | (8371) | (1838) | Weighted N |
|  |  |  |  |  |  |  |  |  |  |
| Females Only | 28.2 | 33.3 | 27.8 | 24.2 | 26.2 | 30.9 | 30.5 | 28.0 | Better |
|  | 54.0 | 50.3 | 53.1 | 55.4 | 53.2 | 48.8 | 52.4 | 47.3 | Same |
|  | 5.3 | 6.2 | 7.2 | 9.0 | 7.5 | 8.0 | 4.9 | 10.5 | Worse |
|  | 12.5 | 10.2 | 11.9 | 11.4 | 13.2 | 12.3 | 12.2 | 14.3 | Don't know |
|  | (767) | (851) | (388) | (534) | (897) | (4067) | (3164) | (708) | Weighted N |

Table 6.24

|  | 1971m | 1972f | 1973c | 1974q | 1975q | 1976m | 1978n |  |
|---|---|---|---|---|---|---|---|---|
| Males Only | 36.0% | 39.6% | 36.6% | 27.4% | 33.5% | 36.5% | 26.1% | Better |
|  | 40.3 | 44.1 | 40.3 | 37.9 | 42.9 | 41.1 | 40.2 | Same |
|  | 9.4 | 5.9 | 13.4 | 24.7 | 12.6 | 14.8 | 27.6 | Worse |
|  | 14.3 | 10.4 | 9.7 | 10.0 | 10.9 | 7.6 | 6.1 | Don't know |
|  | (908) | (546) | (576) | (1330) | (1344) | (50609) | (1012) | Weighted N |
|  |  |  |  |  |  |  |  |  |
| Females Only | 23.0 | 37.1 | 27.6 | 21.2 | 30.3 | 27.4 | 20.0 | Better |
|  | 45.8 | 47.1 | 50.3 | 42.2 | 47.7 | 51.5 | 47.2 | Same |
|  | 10.5 | 5.9 | 12.5 | 23.8 | 10.8 | 12.0 | 25.1 | Worse |
|  | 20.7 | 9.9 | 9.6 | 12.8 | 11.1 | 9.2 | 7.7 | Don't know |
|  | (391) | (749) | (768) | (1645) | (1570) | (75061) | (1280) | Weighted N |

Table 6.25

Will R's Family Be Better Off Financially a Year from Now?
Race of Respondent

|  | Year | | | | | | | | |  |
|---|---|---|---|---|---|---|---|---|---|---|
|  | 1953m | 1954m | 1956m | 1957f | 1958m | 1959f | 1960a | 1961a | 1962n |  |
| Whites Only | 31.5% | 31.3% | 32.6% | 33.7% | 32.7% | 35.1% | 41.6% | 39.0% | 34.5% | Better |
|  | 39.5 | 44.4 | 48.9 | 46.0 | 47.0 | 48.5 | 40.8 | 40.6 | 49.8 | Same |
|  | 10.3 | 10.3 | 5.5 | 8.1 | 7.1 | 5.1 | 6.7 | 7.4 | 5.0 | Worse |
|  | 18.7 | 14.0 | 13.0 | 12.2 | 13.2 | 11.3 | 10.9 | 13.0 | 10.7 | Don't know |
|  | (920) | (894) | (1318) | (1194) | (1163) | (1158) | (2602) | (44394) | (1169) | Weighted N |
| Blacks Only | 25.0 | 28.7 | 30.7 | 26.6 | 25.5 | 28.1 | 34.3 | 40.5 | 23.4 | Better |
|  | 40.5 | 39.1 | 44.7 | 48.2 | 43.4 | 43.8 | 37.9 | 38.3 | 53.3 | Same |
|  | 11.9 | 16.1 | 5.3 | 5.8 | 4.8 | 8.6 | 7.1 | 4.4 | 7.5 | Worse |
|  | 22.6 | 16.1 | 19.3 | 19.4 | 26.2 | 19.5 | 20.7 | 16.8 | 15.9 | Don't know |
|  | (84) | (87) | (114) | (139) | (145) | (128) | (309) | (4805) | (107) | Weighted N |

Table 6.26

|  | 1963m | 1964f | 1965a | 1966a | 1967a | 1968a | 1969a | 1970a |  |
|---|---|---|---|---|---|---|---|---|---|
| Whites Only | 33.2% | 37.6% | 40.1% | 38.1% | 36.2% | 37.1% | 37.6% | 33.3% | Better |
|  | 51.5 | 46.9 | 44.0 | 46.9 | 46.1 | 45.8 | 47.5 | 43.2 | Same |
|  | 5.5 | 7.1 | 6.6 | 7.4 | 7.7 | 8.0 | 6.1 | 12.6 | Worse |
|  | 9.8 | 8.4 | 9.3 | 7.6 | 10.0 | 9.1 | 8.8 | 11.0 | Don't know |
|  | (1161) | (1288) | (1177) | (2176) | (3254) | (13755) | (10210) | (2239) | Weighted N |
| Blacks Only | 29.4 | 33.1 | 28.3 | 39.7 | 33.9 | 39.0 | 34.3 | 33.1 | Better |
|  | 49.2 | 43.1 | 45.0 | 36.1 | 42.7 | 37.5 | 43.8 | 41.7 | Same |
|  | 8.7 | 5.6 | 6.7 | 9.3 | 9.9 | 7.2 | 8.0 | 9.0 | Worse |
|  | 12.7 | 18.1 | 20.0 | 14.9 | 13.5 | 16.3 | 13.9 | 16.2 | Don't know |
|  | (126) | (160) | (120) | (194) | (363) | (1433) | (1155) | (278) | Weighted N |

Table 6.27

|  | 1971m | 1972f | 1973c | 1974q | 1975q | 1976m | 1978n |  |
|---|---|---|---|---|---|---|---|---|
| Whites Only | 32.2% | 37.0% | 32.3% | 23.6% | 32.3% | 29.8% | 22.0% | Better |
|  | 43.1 | 47.5 | 46.3 | 41.2 | 46.6 | 48.5 | 44.6 | Same |
|  | 10.1 | 6.0 | 12.9 | 24.7 | 11.4 | 13.3 | 26.6 | Worse |
|  | 14.6 | 9.5 | 8.5 | 10.5 | 9.6 | 8.4 | 6.7 | Don't know |
|  | (1132) | (1163) | (1117) | (2555) | (2581) | (107425) | (2008) | Weighted N |
| Blacks Only | 32.1 | 51.3 | 29.4 | 28.1 | 25.5 | 39.5 | 25.2 | Better |
|  | 33.6 | 29.6 | 39.5 | 31.9 | 38.9 | 43.8 | 42.6 | Same |
|  | 7.6 | 2.6 | 16.0 | 22.7 | 14.2 | 6.3 | 22.2 | Worse |
|  | 26.7 | 16.5 | 15.1 | 17.3 | 21.3 | 10.3 | 10.0 | Don't know |
|  | (131) | (115) | (119) | (295) | (239) | (11618) | (230) | Weighted N |

Table 6.28
Will R's Family Be Better Off Financially a Year from Now?
Education of Respondent

|  | Year | | | | | | | | | |
|---|---|---|---|---|---|---|---|---|---|---|
|  | 1953m | 1954m | 1956m | 1957f | 1958m | 1959f | 1960a | 1961a | 1962n | |
| Grade School Only | 19.2% | 19.8% | 22.4% | 15.7% | 20.0% | 16.4% | 23.6% | 25.4% | 15.4% | Better |
|  | 42.8 | 49.4 | 53.6 | 57.5 | 52.7 | 60.6 | 49.6 | 49.5 | 61.5 | Same |
|  | 13.1 | 11.9 | 6.5 | 11.9 | 9.0 | 8.0 | 8.8 | 9.2 | 7.3 | Worse |
|  | 24.9 | 18.9 | 17.4 | 14.8 | 18.3 | 15.0 | 18.0 | 15.8 | 15.7 | Don't know |
|  | (381) | (354) | (321) | (318) | (300) | (287) | (809) | (14825) | (356) | Weighted N |
| High School Only | 37.9 | 33.9 | 36.7 | 39.1 | 34.9 | 39.4 | 46.0 | 41.6 | 37.8 | Better |
|  | 35.4 | 42.2 | 46.6 | 40.1 | 46.9 | 43.1 | 37.9 | 38.1 | 48.4 | Same |
|  | 9.3 | 11.4 | 5.0 | 9.8 | 5.9 | 5.7 | 6.1 | 6.6 | 4.4 | Worse |
|  | 17.5 | 12.5 | 11.7 | 11.1 | 12.3 | 11.7 | 10.0 | 13.7 | 9.4 | Don't know |
|  | (475) | (457) | (341) | (297) | (341) | (350) | (1081) | (22097) | (616) | Weighted N |
| College Only | 38.9 | 44.0 | 43.6 | 39.6 | 42.7 | 44.8 | 54.7 | 53.0 | 46.3 | Better |
|  | 44.4 | 37.1 | 37.8 | 47.2 | 44.7 | 44.1 | 31.7 | 33.3 | 40.1 | Same |
|  | 6.9 | 6.9 | 9.9 | 3.5 | 5.3 | 2.1 | 6.3 | 5.6 | 4.5 | Worse |
|  | 9.7 | 12.1 | 8.7 | 9.7 | 7.3 | 9.1 | 7.4 | 8.1 | 9.1 | Don't know |
|  | (144) | (116) | (172) | (144) | (150) | (143) | (556) | (11980) | (309) | Weighted N |

Table 6.29

|  | 1963m | 1964f | 1965a | 1966a | 1967a | 1968a | 1969a | 1970a | |
|---|---|---|---|---|---|---|---|---|---|
| Grade School Only | 15.3% | 20.1% | 18.3% | 18.9% | 20.0% | 21.1% | 19.0% | 26.6% | Better |
|  | 58.7 | 57.0 | 54.4 | 56.7 | 56.3 | 54.6 | 58.4 | 48.9 | Same |
|  | 11.3 | 9.2 | 9.8 | 10.4 | 9.0 | 9.7 | 6.5 | 12.0 | Worse |
|  | 14.7 | 13.7 | 17.5 | 14.1 | 14.7 | 14.6 | 16.2 | 12.6 | Don't know |
|  | (373) | (393) | (377) | (676) | (1059) | (4371) | (3013) | (960) | Weighted N |
| High School Only | 37.3 | 40.4 | 44.3 | 43.7 | 39.6 | 41.9 | 39.0 | 36.2 | Better |
|  | 50.2 | 44.4 | 41.3 | 44.3 | 42.8 | 43.1 | 47.3 | 39.7 | Same |
|  | 3.2 | 6.9 | 6.2 | 5.9 | 7.6 | 6.6 | 5.5 | 12.9 | Worse |
|  | 9.4 | 8.3 | 8.3 | 6.0 | 10.0 | 8.4 | 8.1 | 11.2 | Don't know |
|  | (663) | (738) | (630) | (1015) | (1714) | (7124) | (5142) | (1112) | Weighted N |
| College Only | 46.4 | 49.4 | 51.9 | 51.9 | 48.6 | 49.4 | 51.9 | 42.7 | Better |
|  | 41.9 | 39.5 | 39.5 | 36.5 | 38.3 | 36.3 | 35.8 | 39.0 | Same |
|  | 4.9 | 4.4 | 3.5 | 7.7 | 6.4 | 8.2 | 7.2 | 9.5 | Worse |
|  | 6.8 | 6.7 | 5.1 | 3.9 | 6.6 | 6.1 | 5.1 | 8.8 | Don't know |
|  | (265) | (344) | (314) | (609) | (884) | (3851) | (3300) | (410) | Weighted N |

Education coded for head of household only in 1956m,1957f,1958m,1959f,1960a,1961a,and
1966a, and for head and wife only in 1963m,1964f,1965a,1967a,1968a,1969a,and 1970a.

Table 6.30
Will R's Family Be Better Off Financially a Year from Now?
Education of Respondent

|  | | | | Year | | | | |
|---|---|---|---|---|---|---|---|---|
|  | 1971m | 1972f | 1973c | 1974q | 1975q | 1976m | 1978n | |
| Grade School Only | 15.8% | 20.1% | 9.5% | 9.6% | 10.6% | 17.2% | 9.2% | Better |
|  | 46.6 | 50.8 | 51.9 | 43.7 | 49.5 | 47.9 | 45.8 | Same |
|  | 12.4 | 9.8 | 19.6 | 27.3 | 16.5 | 19.9 | 30.4 | Worse |
|  | 25.2 | 19.3 | 19.0 | 19.4 | 23.3 | 15.0 | 14.7 | Don't know |
|  | (322) | (244) | (158) | (490) | (442) | (16821) | (273) | Weighted N |
| High School Only | 32.6 | 41.2 | 34.0 | 23.5 | 31.4 | 29.1 | 21.5 | Better |
|  | 42.2 | 46.9 | 45.5 | 41.6 | 48.1 | 49.3 | 46.0 | Same |
|  | 10.2 | 2.9 | 12.5 | 23.1 | 11.6 | 12.2 | 25.8 | Worse |
|  | 15.0 | 9.0 | 8.0 | 11.8 | 9.0 | 9.5 | 6.6 | Don't know |
|  | (580) | (663) | (624) | (1416) | (1518) | (59826) | (1204) | Weighted N |
| College Only | 45.0 | 45.0 | 39.8 | 31.7 | 42.5 | 39.8 | 29.3 | Better |
|  | 37.8 | 40.6 | 43.1 | 37.4 | 39.7 | 45.4 | 41.2 | Same |
|  | 6.4 | 8.6 | 10.3 | 24.0 | 9.2 | 10.3 | 25.3 | Worse |
|  | 10.8 | 5.8 | 6.8 | 6.9 | 8.6 | 4.6 | 4.2 | Don't know |
|  | (389) | (382) | (397) | (1047) | (949) | (45208) | (806) | Weighted N |

Education coded for head of household only in 1971m.

Table 6.31
Will R's Family Be Better Off Financially a Year from Now?
Age of Respondent

| | 1953m | 1954m | 1956m | 1957f | Year 1958m | 1959f | 1960a | 1961a | 1962n | |
|---|---|---|---|---|---|---|---|---|---|---|
| 18-24 Only | 44.7% | 42.2% | 42.7% | 62.4% | 61.5% | 66.7% | 62.1% | 59.8% | 61.8% | Better |
| | 31.9 | 32.8 | 40.4 | 25.9 | 28.2 | 25.5 | 26.1 | 24.4 | 27.6 | Same |
| | 6.4 | 10.9 | 2.2 | 3.5 | 0.0 | 2.0 | 5.4 | 5.6 | 5.3 | Worse |
| | 17.0 | 14.1 | 14.6 | 8.2 | 10.3 | 5.9 | 6.4 | 10.2 | 5.3 | Don't know |
| | (47) | (64) | (89) | (85) | (39) | (51) | (203) | (4440) | (76) | Weighted N |
| 25-34 Only | 50.0 | 41.5 | 53.0 | 49.6 | 51.0 | 55.4 | 56.8 | 58.3 | 58.0 | Better |
| | 31.5 | 40.7 | 33.4 | 36.8 | 38.5 | 33.1 | 28.1 | 29.0 | 31.1 | Same |
| | 6.5 | 7.8 | 4.2 | 5.0 | 3.5 | 2.9 | 4.3 | 5.0 | 3.9 | Worse |
| | 12.1 | 10.1 | 9.3 | 8.6 | 7.0 | 8.6 | 10.7 | 7.7 | 7.0 | Don't know |
| | (232) | (258) | (332) | (280) | (143) | (139) | (484) | (10437) | (257) | Weighted N |
| 35-44 Only | 32.2 | 36.8 | 34.1 | 38.2 | 37.1 | 39.6 | 47.4 | 45.1 | 41.1 | Better |
| | 33.9 | 40.4 | 51.7 | 42.3 | 43.3 | 39.6 | 34.6 | 33.8 | 48.9 | Same |
| | 12.7 | 8.5 | 3.0 | 7.3 | 6.7 | 5.8 | 5.9 | 6.7 | 2.5 | Worse |
| | 21.2 | 14.3 | 11.2 | 12.3 | 12.9 | 14.9 | 12.1 | 14.4 | 7.5 | Don't know |
| | (245) | (223) | (331) | (317) | (178) | (154) | (544) | (11103) | (280) | Weighted N |
| 45-54 Only | 24.7 | 30.2 | 27.5 | 31.1 | 23.8 | 24.8 | 41.4 | 34.8 | 27.4 | Better |
| | 42.5 | 42.7 | 52.4 | 46.4 | 53.6 | 53.2 | 39.8 | 46.0 | 54.8 | Same |
| | 9.7 | 10.6 | 7.0 | 6.1 | 6.6 | 5.0 | 4.9 | 5.7 | 4.9 | Worse |
| | 23.1 | 16.6 | 13.2 | 16.4 | 15.9 | 17.0 | 13.8 | 13.5 | 12.9 | Don't know |
| | (186) | (199) | (273) | (280) | (151) | (141) | (485) | (9455) | (263) | Weighted N |
| 55-64 Only | 23.1 | 14.2 | 22.6 | 16.7 | 30.9 | 22.3 | 27.0 | 26.9 | 18.4 | Better |
| | 42.5 | 54.9 | 53.3 | 57.0 | 45.1 | 60.1 | 47.6 | 40.3 | 58.7 | Same |
| | 10.4 | 17.7 | 3.3 | 12.9 | 6.6 | 4.7 | 11.1 | 11.2 | 7.1 | Worse |
| | 23.9 | 13.3 | 20.8 | 13.4 | 17.4 | 12.8 | 14.3 | 21.6 | 15.8 | Don't know |
| | (134) | (113) | (212) | (186) | (656) | (148) | (370) | (7352) | (196) | Weighted N |
| 65-74 Only | 11.3 | 11.5 | 9.5 | 6.6 | 12.4 | 8.0 | 9.4 | 7.7 | 8.7 | Better |
| | 56.0 | 53.8 | 60.3 | 63.5 | 62.7 | 69.3 | 66.0 | 68.7 | 68.1 | Same |
| | 15.1 | 15.4 | 13.8 | 13.2 | 13.0 | 12.7 | 12.3 | 9.5 | 5.8 | Worse |
| | 17.6 | 19.2 | 16.4 | 16.8 | 11.8 | 10.0 | 12.3 | 14.2 | 17.4 | Don't know |
| | (159) | (130) | (189) | (197) | (161) | (150) | (374) | (4345) | (138) | Weighted N |
| 75 And Older Only | ** | ** | ** | ** | ** | ** | ** | 3.0 | 1.4 | Better |
| | ** | ** | ** | ** | ** | ** | ** | 79.1 | 67.1 | Same |
| | ** | ** | ** | ** | ** | ** | ** | 9.7 | 15.7 | Worse |
| | ** | ** | ** | ** | ** | ** | ** | 8.2 | 15.7 | Don't know |
| | ** | ** | ** | ** | ** | ** | ** | (2233) | (70) | Weighted N |

** Code distinction not made.
Youngest age group coded "21-24" in 1953m and 1954m.
Oldest age group coded "65 And Older" in 1953m,1954m,1956m,1957f,1958m,1959f,and 1960a.
Age coded for head of household only in 1958m,1959f,1960a,and 1961a.

Table 6.32
Will R's Family Be Better Off Financially a Year from Now?
Age of Respondent

|  | Year | | | | | | | | |
|---|---|---|---|---|---|---|---|---|---|
|  | 1963m | 1964f | 1965a | 1966a | 1967a | 1968a | 1969a | 1970a | |
| 18-24 Only | 64.0% | 66.7% | 62.1% | 66.9% | 67.3% | 70.6% | 65.0% | 62.1% | Better |
|  | 28.0 | 25.4 | 28.2 | 23.8 | 24.3 | 22.4 | 24.3 | 26.7 | Same |
|  | 1.0 | 5.3 | 4.0 | 5.8 | 4.4 | 4.1 | 6.2 | 7.1 | Worse |
|  | 7.0 | 2.6 | 5.6 | 3.5 | 4.0 | 3.0 | 4.5 | 4.2 | Don't know |
|  | (100) | (114) | (124) | (172) | (251) | (982) | (1092) | (240) | Weighted N |
| 25-34 Only | 48.3 | 59.5 | 59.6 | 61.4 | 56.9 | 63.4 | 58.9 | 54.0 | Better |
|  | 40.1 | 31.3 | 32.2 | 29.5 | 31.0 | 26.7 | 31.6 | 31.5 | Same |
|  | 3.4 | 3.9 | 1.2 | 4.8 | 5.6 | 3.8 | 4.1 | 6.1 | Worse |
|  | 8.2 | 5.3 | 6.9 | 4.3 | 6.5 | 6.0 | 5.4 | 8.5 | Don't know |
|  | (232) | (304) | (245) | (438) | (662) | (2868) | (2297) | (413) | Weighted N |
| 35-44 Only | 43.9 | 41.1 | 51.3 | 50.4 | 44.6 | 46.7 | 46.7 | 37.7 | Better |
|  | 45.0 | 45.3 | 34.4 | 39.2 | 38.3 | 39.9 | 40.7 | 39.3 | Same |
|  | 4.1 | 4.2 | 5.5 | 4.3 | 7.0 | 5.4 | 4.6 | 10.8 | Worse |
|  | 7.1 | 9.3 | 8.8 | 6.0 | 10.0 | 8.0 | 8.0 | 12.2 | Don't know |
|  | (269) | (333) | (273) | (464) | (710) | (2850) | (1993) | (435) | Weighted N |
| 45-54 Only | 31.9 | 32.8 | 38.1 | 36.3 | 35.8 | 37.9 | 25.9 | 28.0 | Better |
|  | 49.5 | 49.0 | 43.3 | 46.6 | 47.9 | 45.5 | 45.5 | 44.1 | Same |
|  | 4.8 | 5.9 | 6.9 | 7.4 | 5.9 | 8.0 | 11.4 | 15.6 | Worse |
|  | 13.9 | 12.4 | 11.7 | 9.7 | 10.4 | 8.6 | 17.2 | 12.3 | Don't know |
|  | (273) | (290) | (247) | (474) | (710) | (2890) | (528) | (454) | Weighted N |
| 55-64 Only | 18.0 | 19.9 | 18.1 | 24.8 | 24.2 | 22.8 | 25.5 | 20.3 | Better |
|  | 62.9 | 57.2 | 57.4 | 53.3 | 53.2 | 54.7 | 54.3 | 48.4 | Same |
|  | 9.8 | 9.0 | 9.7 | 10.4 | 10.5 | 10.7 | 5.8 | 17.8 | Worse |
|  | 9.3 | 13.9 | 14.8 | 11.6 | 12.0 | 11.9 | 14.3 | 13.5 | Don't know |
|  | (205) | (201) | (216) | (415) | (590) | (2801) | (1771) | (370) | Weighted N |
| 65-74 Only | 5.1 | 8.3 | 7.3 | 6.2 | 7.7 | 9.3 | 8.5 | 7.1 | Better |
|  | 73.2 | 69.6 | 68.6 | 70.2 | 67.1 | 61.9 | 66.3 | 66.9 | Same |
|  | 9.4 | 14.3 | 12.7 | 12.8 | 11.6 | 12.3 | 10.6 | 15.0 | Worse |
|  | 12.3 | 7.7 | 11.4 | 10.8 | 13.5 | 16.5 | 14.6 | 11.0 | Don't know |
|  | (138) | (168) | (220) | (436) | (465) | (1874) | (1479) | (254) | Weighted N |
| 75 And Older Only | 3.5 | 8.7 | ** | ** | 9.0 | 5.4 | 3.0 | 8.5 | Better |
|  | 69.4 | 59.4 | ** | ** | 61.4 | 66.1 | 75.8 | 61.2 | Same |
|  | 10.6 | 15.9 | ** | ** | 10.3 | 15.2 | 9.1 | 14.7 | Worse |
|  | 16.5 | 15.9 | ** | ** | 19.3 | 13.4 | 12.1 | 15.5 | Don't know |
|  | (85) | (69) | ** | ** | (290) | (1120) | (891) | (129) | Weighted N |

** Code distinction not made.
Oldest age group coded "65 And Older" in 1965a and 1966a.
Age coded for head of household and wife only in 1964f, 1965a, 1966a, 1967a, 1968a, 1969a, and 1970a.

Table 6.33
Will R's Family Be Better Off Financially a Year from Now?
Age of Respondent

|  | | | | Year | | | | |
|---|---|---|---|---|---|---|---|---|
|  | 1971m | 1972f | 1973c | 1974q | 1975q | 1976m | 1978n | |
| 18-24 Only | 52.0% | 59.3% | 52.2% | 37.9% | 51.1% | 52.0% | 39.5% | Better |
|  | 29.0 | 34.9 | 34.3 | 37.7 | 33.6 | 40.2 | 39.5 | Same |
|  | 7.0 | 2.9 | 8.5 | 15.8 | 7.7 | 6.1 | 16.4 | Worse |
|  | 12.0 | 2.9 | 5.0 | 8.6 | 7.5 | 1.7 | 4.5 | Don't know |
|  | (100) | (209) | (201) | (486) | (452) | (20191) | (354) | Weighted N |
| 25-34 Only | 51.8 | 53.6 | 45.5 | 36.7 | 46.5 | 44.7 | 31.8 | Better |
|  | 31.4 | 37.9 | 38.6 | 32.0 | 37.8 | 44.8 | 42.9 | Same |
|  | 3.3 | 3.2 | 9.4 | 21.8 | 7.5 | 6.8 | 21.5 | Worse |
|  | 13.5 | 5.4 | 6.5 | 9.5 | 8.2 | 3.7 | 3.8 | Don't know |
|  | (245) | (280) | (308) | (675) | (680) | (26856) | (550) | Weighted N |
| 35-44 Only | 46.1 | 49.1 | 39.3 | 26.0 | 34.9 | 40.3 | 21.3 | Better |
|  | 38.4 | 38.7 | 40.7 | 42.9 | 44.3 | 43.9 | 42.2 | Same |
|  | 5.4 | 4.5 | 10.3 | 24.7 | 12.4 | 11.8 | 29.5 | Worse |
|  | 10.1 | 7.7 | 9.8 | 6.4 | 8.4 | 4.0 | 6.9 | Don't know |
|  | (258) | (222) | (214) | (503) | (490) | (17693) | (403) | Weighted N |
| 45-54 Only | 26.4 | 33.2 | 25.2 | 15.4 | 26.1 | 24.3 | 16.7 | Better |
|  | 44.0 | 45.8 | 51.0 | 42.0 | 51.3 | 47.0 | 44.9 | Same |
|  | 11.7 | 8.4 | 12.6 | 29.4 | 13.2 | 18.2 | 29.8 | Worse |
|  | 17.9 | 12.6 | 11.2 | 13.2 | 9.4 | 10.5 | 8.6 | Don't know |
|  | (273) | (190) | (206) | (500) | (417) | (18790) | (336) | Weighted N |
| 55-64 Only | 17.1 | 16.3 | 10.9 | 13.5 | 15.3 | 14.9 | 12.3 | Better |
|  | 43.1 | 57.6 | 57.0 | 40.0 | 49.9 | 56.4 | 48.7 | Same |
|  | 16.6 | 7.0 | 19.2 | 30.9 | 15.8 | 18.8 | 31.2 | Worse |
|  | 23.2 | 19.2 | 13.0 | 15.6 | 19.0 | 9.9 | 7.8 | Don't know |
|  | (211) | (172) | (193) | (437) | (385) | (17150) | (308) | Weighted N |
| 65-74 Only | 5.3 | 8.8 | 8.6 | 5.3 | 8.8 | 10.2 | 7.5 | Better |
|  | 61.1 | 66.7 | 61.2 | 51.8 | 58.7 | 48.3 | 44.6 | Same |
|  | 11.5 | 10.9 | 19.1 | 28.1 | 17.1 | 23.5 | 36.6 | Worse |
|  | 22.1 | 13.6 | 11.2 | 14.9 | 15.3 | 18.0 | 11.3 | Don't know |
|  | (131) | (147) | (152) | (228) | (339) | (14793) | (213) | Weighted N |
| 75 And Older Only | 4.9 | 5.7 | 12.1 | 1.5 | 4.3 | 7.0 | 6.8 | Better |
|  | 60.5 | 64.3 | 51.5 | 53.8 | 62.9 | 66.7 | 54.2 | Same |
|  | 18.5 | 8.6 | 18.2 | 17.4 | 13.6 | 8.0 | 24.6 | Worse |
|  | 16.0 | 21.4 | 18.2 | 27.3 | 19.3 | 18.3 | 14.4 | Don't know |
|  | (81) | (70) | (66) | (132) | (140) | (7559) | (118) | Weighted N |

Personal Economic Outlook

ble 6.34

ll R's Family Be Better Off Financially a Year from Now?

come of Respondent

| | 1953m | 1954m | 1956m | 1957f | Year 1958m | 1959f | 1960a | 1961a | 1962n | |
|---|---|---|---|---|---|---|---|---|---|---|
| Income 1 (0-16%) | 14.1% | 18.2% | 15.9% | 13.7% | 15.0% | 16.6% | 21.1% | 24.1% | 12.1% | Better |
| | 44.5 | 45.5 | 58.8 | 59.8 | 52.1 | 60.3 | 52.1 | 52.8 | 62.4 | Same |
| | 12.0 | 16.0 | 7.1 | 10.3 | 10.4 | 10.1 | 11.1 | 6.8 | 8.5 | Worse |
| | 29.3 | 20.3 | 18.1 | 16.2 | 22.5 | 13.1 | 15.7 | 16.4 | 17.0 | Don't know |
| | (191) | (187) | (226) | (234) | (240) | (199) | (549) | (8175) | (165) | Weighted N |
| Income 2 (17-33%) | 28.8 | 21.5 | 14.6 | 30.4 | 23.4 | 22.1 | 35.9 | 34.7 | 20.3 | Better |
| | 37.0 | 47.1 | 55.6 | 45.3 | 58.4 | 55.7 | 43.6 | 40.9 | 61.4 | Same |
| | 11.6 | 13.2 | 8.3 | 9.0 | 5.8 | 7.4 | 5.9 | 7.1 | 5.1 | Worse |
| | 22.6 | 18.2 | 21.5 | 15.2 | 12.3 | 14.8 | 14.6 | 17.2 | 13.2 | Don't know |
| | (146) | (121) | (144) | (322) | (154) | (122) | (615) | (9871) | (197) | Weighted N |
| Income 3 (34-67%) | 33.1 | 30.2 | 36.5 | 41.6 | 33.1 | 40.4 | 46.6 | 43.4 | 38.7 | Better |
| | 41.0 | 46.1 | 46.7 | 40.4 | 46.7 | 42.2 | 36.9 | 35.9 | 47.0 | Same |
| | 10.0 | 10.4 | 4.6 | 8.3 | 5.0 | 5.6 | 5.6 | 7.5 | 4.7 | Worse |
| | 15.8 | 13.3 | 12.2 | 9.7 | 15.2 | 11.8 | 10.9 | 13.2 | 9.6 | Don't know |
| | (329) | (308) | (591) | (517) | (499) | (465) | (1120) | (19456) | (511) | Weighted N |
| Income 4 (68-95%) | 39.8 | 41.9 | 41.3 | 42.6 | 43.3 | 43.9 | 52.0 | 47.0 | 48.4 | Better |
| | 36.8 | 41.2 | 46.9 | 43.7 | 38.4 | 43.7 | 33.5 | 39.2 | 39.6 | Same |
| | 10.2 | 8.3 | 4.9 | 3.6 | 8.1 | 2.7 | 5.6 | 6.3 | 4.6 | Worse |
| | 13.2 | 8.7 | 6.9 | 10.2 | 10.2 | 9.7 | 8.9 | 7.5 | 7.4 | Don't know |
| | (266) | (277) | (305) | (197) | (284) | (371) | (552) | (10542) | (283) | Weighted N |
| Income 5 (96-100%) | 43.6 | 47.0 | 44.2 | 31.0 | 47.0 | 50.0 | 50.4 | 38.9 | 39.7 | Better |
| | 30.8 | 31.8 | 43.3 | 51.7 | 41.0 | 44.7 | 36.3 | 41.1 | 46.0 | Same |
| | 7.7 | 6.1 | 3.8 | 0.0 | 3.0 | 0.0 | 5.3 | 7.4 | 1.6 | Worse |
| | 17.9 | 15.2 | 8.7 | 17.2 | 9.0 | 5.3 | 8.0 | 12.6 | 12.7 | Don't know |
| | (39) | (66) | (104) | (29) | (100) | (38) | (113) | (1563) | (63) | Weighted N |

Table 6.35
Will R's Family Be Better Off Financially a Year from Now?
Income of Respondent

|  | | | | Year | | | | | |
|---|---|---|---|---|---|---|---|---|---|
|  | 1963m | 1964f | 1965a | 1966a | 1967a | 1968a | 1969a | 1970a | |
| Income 1 (0-16%) | 16.6% | 19.9% | 18.2% | 19.7% | 18.2% | 18.4% | 17.0% | 22.6% | Better |
|  | 58.3 | 56.4 | 54.1 | 56.0 | 56.2 | 54.0 | 59.9 | 50.7 | Same |
|  | 12.6 | 11.3 | 10.6 | 10.5 | 8.9 | 11.2 | 7.7 | 12.1 | Worse |
|  | 12.6 | 12.4 | 17.1 | 13.7 | 16.8 | 16.4 | 15.4 | 14.6 | Don't know |
|  | (175) | (266) | (170) | (466) | (721) | (2579) | (2465) | (473) | Weighted N |
| Income 2 (17-33%) | 22.9 | 31.8 | 24.2 | 33.1 | 29.7 | 31.2 | 35.4 | 25.2 | Better |
|  | 58.6 | 46.6 | 52.0 | 51.1 | 50.8 | 49.5 | 45.1 | 51.8 | Same |
|  | 5.2 | 7.5 | 9.0 | 8.7 | 9.3 | 7.7 | 7.5 | 11.3 | Worse |
|  | 13.3 | 14.1 | 14.8 | 7.0 | 10.2 | 11.7 | 12.1 | 11.8 | Don't know |
|  | (210) | (305) | (223) | (483) | (559) | (2587) | (2228) | (417) | Weighted N |
| Income 3 (34-67%) | 34.2 | 40.4 | 41.7 | 44.6 | 41.3 | 42.9 | 42.2 | 37.4 | Better |
|  | 50.9 | 45.7 | 43.9 | 42.3 | 42.0 | 41.9 | 43.8 | 37.4 | Same |
|  | 4.4 | 4.8 | 5.4 | 5.6 | 7.5 | 7.1 | 6.0 | 13.9 | Worse |
|  | 10.5 | 9.1 | 9.0 | 7.6 | 9.2 | 8.0 | 7.9 | 11.4 | Don't know |
|  | (389) | (416) | (424) | (821) | (1418) | (5190) | (3864) | (888) | Weighted N |
| Income 4 (68-95%) | 43.8 | 48.2 | 48.2 | 47.2 | 41.5 | 45.2 | 50.2 | 39.8 | Better |
|  | 44.1 | 41.3 | 38.6 | 40.0 | 42.8 | 40.4 | 40.7 | 39.7 | Same |
|  | 5.8 | 4.8 | 6.2 | 6.7 | 7.8 | 6.9 | 4.8 | 10.8 | Worse |
|  | 6.3 | 5.7 | 7.0 | 6.1 | 7.9 | 7.5 | 4.3 | 9.7 | Don't know |
|  | (381) | (436) | (417) | (492) | (692) | (4413) | (2638) | (678) | Weighted N |
| Income 5 (96-100%) | 44.8 | 35.2 | 55.3 | 48.7 | 50.0 | 44.5 | 45.5 | 38.0 | Better |
|  | 46.0 | 46.5 | 35.0 | 36.7 | 36.6 | 40.4 | 44.1 | 42.6 | Same |
|  | 3.4 | 12.7 | 2.9 | 10.0 | 4.3 | 8.6 | 4.7 | 12.0 | Worse |
|  | 5.7 | 5.6 | 6.8 | 4.7 | 9.0 | 6.4 | 5.7 | 7.4 | Don't know |
|  | (87) | (71) | (103) | (150) | (322) | (777) | (424) | (108) | Weighted N |

Table 6.36

Will R's Family Be Better Off Financially a Year from Now?

Income of Respondent

|  | | | | Year | | | | |
|---|---|---|---|---|---|---|---|---|
|  | 1971m | 1972f | 1973c | 1974q | 1975q | 1976m | 1978n | |
| Income 1 (0-16%) | 16.1% | 25.8% | 18.0% | 18.5% | 18.6% | 40.4% | 20.8% | Better |
|  | 49.0 | 48.0 | 45.9 | 39.0 | 45.6 | 41.0 | 42.0 | Same |
|  | 10.9 | 8.1 | 18.6 | 28.3 | 14.7 | 14.9 | 27.7 | Worse |
|  | 24.0 | 18.1 | 17.4 | 14.3 | 21.1 | 3.7 | 9.5 | Don't know |
|  | (192) | (221) | (172) | (400) | (436) | (22148) | (336) | Weighted N |
| Income 2 (17-33%) | 25.6 | 37.2 | 31.4 | 27.7 | 33.5 | 32.4 | 24.4 | Better |
|  | 42.6 | 46.6 | 44.8 | 40.4 | 45.2 | 49.5 | 42.7 | Same |
|  | 11.2 | 4.7 | 15.2 | 20.0 | 11.7 | 10.6 | 25.5 | Worse |
|  | 20.7 | 11.5 | 8.6 | 11.8 | 9.7 | 7.5 | 7.5 | Don't know |
|  | (242) | (148) | (315) | (584) | (496) | (24303) | (361) | Weighted N |
| Income 3 (34-67%) | 35.0 | 40.7 | 32.0 | 22.4 | 35.7 | 38.6 | 21.7 | Better |
|  | 40.0 | 46.4 | 48.1 | 41.6 | 46.1 | 45.9 | 45.5 | Same |
|  | 10.9 | 4.2 | 10.9 | 23.8 | 10.6 | 10.7 | 27.7 | Worse |
|  | 14.1 | 8.8 | 9.0 | 12.2 | 7.5 | 4.7 | 5.2 | Don't know |
|  | (468) | (457) | (366) | (966) | (828) | (14850) | (618) | Weighted N |
| Income 4 (68-95%) | 42.1 | 42.3 | 38.2 | 29.7 | 38.3 | 38.5 | 24.8 | Better |
|  | 39.8 | 42.0 | 45.1 | 41.2 | 45.9 | 46.0 | 46.1 | Same |
|  | 6.7 | 7.7 | 10.6 | 24.2 | 9.6 | 12.2 | 25.0 | Worse |
|  | 11.4 | 8.0 | 6.0 | 4.9 | 6.2 | 3.3 | 4.1 | Don't know |
|  | (299) | (324) | (348) | (607) | (643) | (9285) | (532) | Weighted N |
| Income 5 (96-100%) | 50.9 | 50.0 | 38.7 | 22.1 | 38.6 | 35.9 | 28.5 | Better |
|  | 39.6 | 44.9 | 45.2 | 45.3 | 41.2 | 42.9 | 45.8 | Same |
|  | 3.8 | 3.8 | 11.8 | 30.5 | 14.4 | 12.1 | 22.9 | Worse |
|  | 5.7 | 1.3 | 4.3 | 2.1 | 5.9 | 9.2 | 2.8 | Don't know |
|  | (53) | (78) | (93) | (95) | (153) | (8337) | (144) | Weighted N |

Table 6.37
Will R's Family Be in a Better Financial Situation in a Few Years?
Total Population

QUESTION: A few years from now, would you think you and your family will have a better (position and) income than you have now or will you be in about the same situation or even in a less satisfactory situation? (Now looking ahead and thinking about the next few years, do you expect your financial situation will stay about the way it is now, get better, or get worse?)

|  |  | Year | | | | | | | | | | | | |
|---|---|---|---|---|---|---|---|---|---|---|---|---|---|---|
|  |  | 1952k | 1956m | 1956n | 1957f | 1958m | 1958n | 1959f | 1960n | 1961f | 1961m | 1962f | 1963m | 1964n |
| Better | (5) | 37.7% | 36.7% | 41.3% | 38.5% | 39.7% | 41.7% | 40.8% | 37.8% | 41.1% | 39.8% | 45.0% | 40.2% | 43.6% |
| Same | (3) | 23.8 | 35.7 | 43.4 | 36.0 | 33.8 | 43.2 | 33.8 | 46.4 | 36.2 | 35.3 | 33.7 | 38.5 | 43.5 |
| Worse | (1) | 7.9 | 7.5 | 9.0 | 8.8 | 7.8 | 12.6 | 10.2 | 9.1 | 9.1 | 9.2 | 10.1 | 10.0 | 9.0 |
| Depends |  | 11.1 | 5.5 | ** | 7.6 | 5.8 | ** | 3.9 | ** | 3.6 | 4.6 | 4.3 | 3.1 | ** |
| R speaks only of hopes or luck |  | 7.2 | 3.5 | ** | 2.5 | 4.1 | ** | 2.5 | ** | 2.0 | 2.6 | 1.2 | 1.3 | ** |
| Don't know |  | 12.3 | 11.0 | 6.4 | 6.7 | 8.8 | 2.6 | 8.7 | 6.7 | 7.9 | 8.5 | 5.7 | 6.8 | 3.9 |
| Total |  | 100% | 100% | 100% | 100% | 100% | 100% | 100% | 100% | 100% | 100% | 100% | 100% | 100% |
| Weighted N |  | 912 | 1419 | 1740 | 1334 | 1329 | 1800 | 1303 | 1899 | 1209 | 937 | 1213 | 1286 | 4601 |
| Unweighted N |  | 912 | 1419 | 1740 | 1334 | 1329 | 1433 | 1303 | 1145 | 1209 | 937 | 1213 | 1286 | 1811 |
| Mean |  | 3.859 | 3.730 | 3.690 | 3.715 | 3.787 | 3.596 | 3.720 | 3.614 | 3.741 | 3.727 | 3.785 | 3.680 | 3.722 |
| Standard Deviation |  | 1.38 | 1.30 | 1.29 | 1.33 | 1.31 | 1.37 | 1.37 | 1.28 | 1.33 | 1.34 | 1.37 | 1.34 | 1.29 |

** Code distinction not made.
1964n includes Black supplement.

Figure 6.8
R's Financial Situation in a Few Years--Total Population

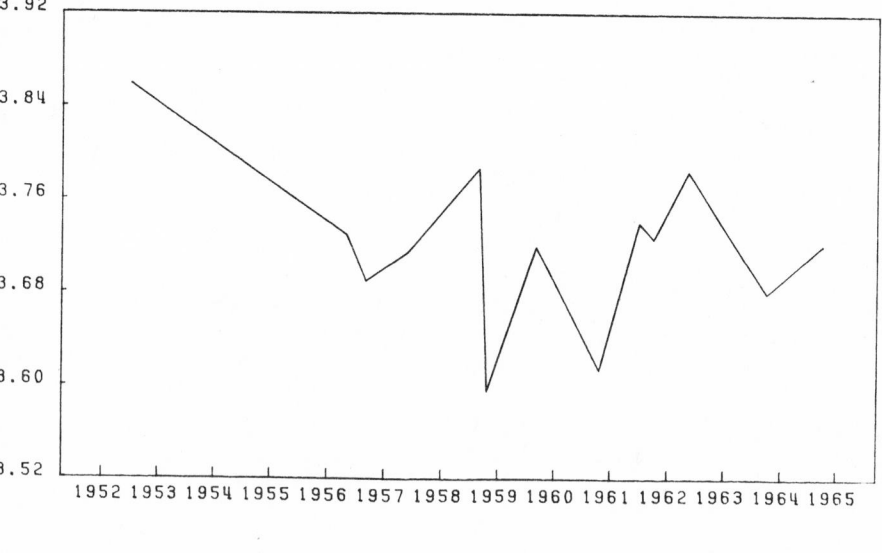

Figure 6.9
R's Financial Situation in a Few Years by Sex of R

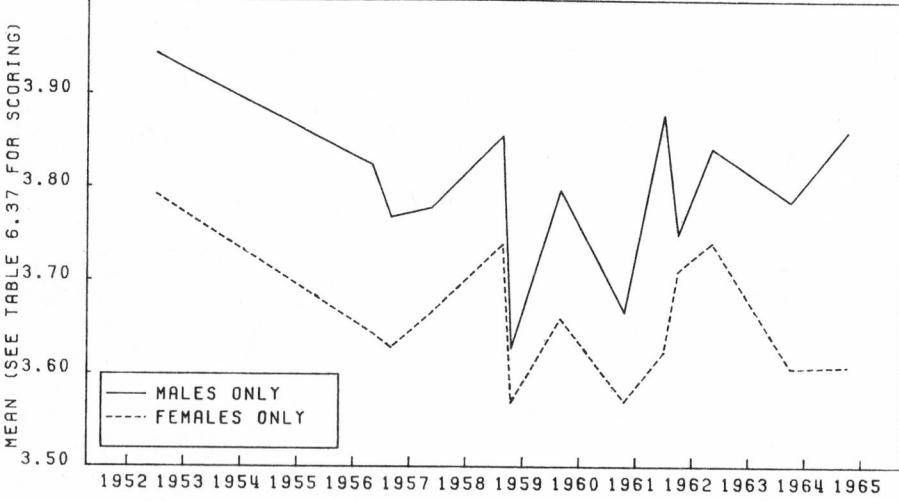

Table 6.38
Will R's Family Be in a Better Financial Situation in a Few Years?
Sex of Respondent

| | | | | | | | Year | | | | | | |
|---|---|---|---|---|---|---|---|---|---|---|---|---|---|---|
| | 1952k | 1956m | 1956n | 1957f | 1958m | 1958n | 1959f | 1960n | 1961f | 1961m | 1962f | 1963m | 1964n | |
| Males Only | 41.3% | 42.0% | 44.4% | 42.2% | 42.2% | 45.4% | 44.2% | 40.3% | 47.2% | 42.9% | 47.6% | 45.0% | 49.9% | Better |
| | 21.9 | 31.9 | 39.7 | 33.3 | 31.0 | 37.8 | 32.0 | 45.8 | 33.8 | 34.6 | 31.8 | 33.8 | 38.2 | Same |
| | 7.8 | 8.2 | 8.7 | 9.2 | 7.7 | 14.7 | 9.9 | 8.7 | 8.1 | 10.1 | 10.0 | 10.1 | 8.4 | Worse |
| | 11.3 | 5.6 | ** | 7.7 | 6.8 | ** | 4.2 | ** | 2.8 | 3.6 | 3.4 | 2.6 | ** | Depends |
| | 7.1 | 3.0 | ** | 2.1 | 3.7 | ** | 2.3 | ** | 1.7 | 1.0 | 0.9 | 1.3 | ** | Hopes/Luck |
| | 10.6 | 9.3 | 7.2 | 5.4 | 8.6 | 2.1 | 7.4 | 5.2 | 6.5 | 7.8 | 6.2 | 7.1 | 3.5 | Don't know |
| | (397) | (659) | (780) | (573) | (561) | (844) | (566) | (862) | (542) | (387) | (531) | (533) | (2076) | Weighted N |
| Females Only | 35.0 | 32.1 | 38.8 | 35.7 | 37.9 | 38.4 | 38.1 | 35.7 | 36.1 | 37.6 | 43.0 | 36.8 | 38.5 | Better |
| | 25.2 | 39.0 | 46.4 | 38.0 | 35.8 | 47.9 | 35.2 | 47.0 | 38.2 | 35.8 | 35.2 | 41.8 | 47.8 | Same |
| | 8.0 | 7.0 | 9.2 | 8.4 | 7.8 | 10.8 | 10.5 | 9.5 | 9.9 | 8.5 | 10.3 | 10.0 | 9.4 | Worse |
| | 10.9 | 5.4 | ** | 7.5 | 5.1 | ** | 3.7 | ** | 4.3 | 5.3 | 5.0 | 3.5 | ** | Depends |
| | 7.4 | 4.0 | ** | 2.8 | 4.4 | ** | 2.7 | ** | 2.2 | 3.6 | 1.3 | 1.3 | ** | Hopes/Luck |
| | 13.6 | 12.5 | 5.7 | 7.6 | 9.0 | 2.9 | 9.8 | 7.9 | 9.1 | 9.1 | 5.3 | 6.6 | 4.3 | Don't know |
| | (515) | (759) | (960) | (761) | (768) | (956) | (735) | (1037) | (667) | (550) | (682) | (753) | (2525) | Weighted N |

** Code distinction not made.
Sex coded for head of household and wife only in 1962f.

Table 6.39
Race of Respondent

| | 1952k | 1956m | 1956n | 1957f | 1958m | 1958n | 1959f | 1960n | 1961f | 1961m | 1962f | 1963m | 1964n | |
|---|---|---|---|---|---|---|---|---|---|---|---|---|---|---|
| Whites Only | 38.3% | 36.8% | 40.4% | 38.9% | 40.3% | 39.8% | 40.9% | 35.9% | 41.6% | 40.4% | 44.6% | 40.5% | 41.6% | Better |
| | 24.1 | 35.9 | 44.4 | 35.8 | 34.8 | 44.6 | 33.9 | 48.1 | 36.5 | 35.2 | 33.9 | 38.4 | 45.0 | Same |
| | 7.4 | 7.6 | 8.9 | 8.7 | 7.8 | 12.9 | 10.6 | 9.4 | 9.1 | 9.2 | 10.7 | 10.6 | 9.4 | Worse |
| | 11.6 | 5.6 | ** | 7.8 | 5.7 | ** | 3.9 | ** | 3.5 | 4.7 | 4.4 | 2.9 | ** | Depends |
| | 7.8 | 3.4 | ** | 2.5 | 3.9 | ** | 2.4 | ** | 1.8 | 2.3 | 1.1 | 1.1 | ** | Hopes/Luck |
| | 10.8 | 10.8 | 6.3 | 6.3 | 7.5 | 2.6 | 8.2 | 6.6 | 7.5 | 8.2 | 5.3 | 6.4 | 4.0 | Don't know |
| | (809) | (1295) | (1590) | (1182) | (1165) | (1622) | (1156) | (1720) | (1037) | (855) | (1060) | (1137) | (4152) | Weighted N |
| Blacks Only | 34.4 | 34.5 | 50.7 | 31.4 | 39.6 | 60.2 | 40.2 | 52.8 | 36.9 | 31.8 | 48.4 | 35.2 | 63.2 | Better |
| | 20.4 | 35.4 | 33.3 | 39.4 | 23.6 | 29.2 | 32.3 | 31.7 | 34.4 | 34.8 | 31.7 | 40.2 | 29.0 | Same |
| | 11.8 | 7.1 | 9.7 | 10.2 | 6.3 | 9.3 | 7.1 | 7.5 | 9.0 | 10.6 | 6.3 | 5.7 | 4.6 | Worse |
| | 6.5 | 3.5 | ** | 6.6 | 6.3 | ** | 3.9 | ** | 4.9 | 4.5 | 4.0 | 4.9 | ** | Depends |
| | 3.2 | 5.3 | ** | 2.2 | 4.9 | ** | 3.1 | ** | 4.1 | 6.1 | 1.6 | 3.3 | ** | Hopes/Luck |
| | 23.7 | 14.2 | 6.3 | 10.2 | 19.4 | 1.2 | 13.4 | 8.1 | 10.7 | 12.1 | 7.9 | 10.7 | 3.2 | Don't know |
| | (93) | (113) | (144) | (137) | (144) | (161) | (127) | (161) | (122) | (66) | (126) | (122) | (410) | Weighted N |

** Code distinction not made.

Table 6.40
Will R's Family Be in a Better Financial Situation in a Few Years?
Education of Respondent

| | 1952k | 1956m | 1956n | 1957f | 1958m | 1958n | Year 1959f | 1960n | 1961f | 1961m | 1962f | 1963m | 1964n | |
|---|---|---|---|---|---|---|---|---|---|---|---|---|---|---|
| Grade School | 25.0% | 25.2% | 28.9% | 21.0% | 21.3% | 31.2% | 18.6% | 26.4% | 20.4% | 18.8% | 20.0% | 16.8% | 26.7% | Better |
| | 28.1 | 38.2 | 49.4 | 42.9 | 44.7 | 50.0 | 50.9 | 52.5 | 46.8 | 48.2 | 47.5 | 53.4 | 53.6 | Same |
| | 12.1 | 12.6 | 12.5 | 14.5 | 9.3 | 14.8 | 15.1 | 11.9 | 13.4 | 15.7 | 16.5 | 15.4 | 14.5 | Worse |
| | 12.9 | 7.6 | ** | 9.0 | 6.7 | ** | 3.9 | ** | 4.2 | 5.1 | 6.3 | 4.2 | ** | Depends |
| | 6.2 | 2.5 | ** | 3.2 | 4.7 | ** | 1.8 | ** | 2.8 | 1.0 | 0.0 | 1.1 | ** | Hopes/Luck |
| | 15.7 | 13.9 | 9.1 | 9.4 | 13.3 | 4.1 | 9.8 | 9.1 | 12.3 | 11.2 | 9.8 | 9.2 | 5.2 | Don't know |
| | (356) | (317) | (536) | (310) | (300) | (542) | (285) | (571) | (357) | (197) | (255) | (358) | (1148) | Weighted N |
| High School | 42.3 | 41.0 | 43.8 | 44.3 | 42.9 | 43.9 | 47.7 | 40.0 | 44.8 | 37.9 | 49.7 | 45.6 | 46.3 | Better |
| | 23.7 | 33.6 | 42.9 | 34.5 | 31.5 | 40.6 | 28.9 | 46.2 | 35.5 | 37.0 | 31.4 | 36.1 | 42.4 | Same |
| | 4.9 | 5.9 | 7.6 | 7.4 | 7.1 | 13.4 | 5.1 | 7.8 | 8.1 | 11.0 | 8.7 | 7.4 | 7.5 | Worse |
| | 8.9 | 5.3 | ** | 6.8 | 6.2 | ** | 3.7 | ** | 3.4 | 4.1 | 3.6 | 3.2 | ** | Depends |
| | 8.9 | 3.5 | ** | 2.0 | 3.5 | ** | 3.7 | ** | 2.0 | 0.9 | 1.7 | 1.4 | ** | Hopes/Luck |
| | 11.3 | 10.6 | 5.7 | 5.1 | 8.8 | 2.2 | 10.9 | 5.9 | 6.3 | 9.1 | 5.0 | 6.3 | 3.8 | Don't know |
| | (371) | (339) | (870) | (296) | (340) | (882) | (350) | (909) | (558) | (219) | (759) | (653) | (2338) | Weighted N |
| College | 54.4 | 58.5 | 55.2 | 59.3 | 55.3 | 52.5 | 56.3 | 48.3 | 60.6 | 65.3 | 59.6 | 59.9 | 56.0 | Better |
| | 15.6 | 24.4 | 34.7 | 24.8 | 25.3 | 38.5 | 22.9 | 38.5 | 24.7 | 24.2 | 25.4 | 23.3 | 34.8 | Same |
| | 5.6 | 6.1 | 7.1 | 6.2 | 7.3 | 7.5 | 7.6 | 8.1 | 5.6 | 4.0 | 7.3 | 9.5 | 6.5 | Worse |
| | 12.2 | 4.9 | ** | 5.5 | 5.3 | ** | 4.9 | ** | 3.5 | 1.6 | 4.1 | 1.1 | ** | Depends |
| | 6.1 | 2.4 | ** | 0.7 | 2.7 | ** | 2.1 | ** | 1.0 | 0.0 | 0.5 | 1.1 | ** | Hopes/Luck |
| | 6.1 | 3.7 | 3.1 | 3.4 | 4.0 | 1.4 | 6.3 | 5.0 | 4.5 | 4.8 | 3.1 | 5.0 | 2.8 | Don't know |
| | (180) | (164) | (326) | (145) | (150) | (358) | (144) | (418) | (287) | (124) | (193) | (262) | (1083) | Weighted N |

** Code distinction not made.
Education coded for head of household only in 1956m,1957f,1958m,1959f,and 1961m, and for head and wife only in 1962f and 1963m.

Personal Economic Outlook

Table 6.41

Will R's Family Be in a Better Financial Situation in a Few Years?

Age of Respondent

| | 1952k | 1956m | 1956n | 1957f | 1958m | 1958n | 1959f | 1960n | 1961f | 1961m | 1962f | 1963m | 1964n | |
|---|---|---|---|---|---|---|---|---|---|---|---|---|---|---|
| 18-24 | 50.0% | 62.9% | 56.8% | 71.8% | 71.8% | 69.7% | 72.5% | 72.4% | 73.5% | 88.2% | 79.6% | 69.7% | 74.7% | Better |
| | 13.5 | 14.6 | 28.8 | 16.5 | 15.4 | 15.7 | 9.8 | 24.1 | 14.7 | 5.9 | 10.8 | 16.2 | 14.5 | Same |
| | 0.0 | 6.7 | 8.1 | 1.2 | 0.0 | 12.4 | 2.0 | 0.0 | 1.0 | 0.0 | 3.2 | 3.0 | 7.5 | Worse |
| | 15.4 | 4.5 | ** | 5.9 | 5.1 | ** | 2.0 | ** | 3.9 | 0.0 | 0.0 | 3.0 | ** | Depends |
| | 11.5 | 2.2 | ** | 0.0 | 2.6 | ** | 5.9 | ** | 2.9 | 0.0 | 2.2 | 3.0 | ** | Hopes/Luck |
| | 9.6 | 9.0 | 6.3 | 4.7 | 5.1 | 2.2 | 7.8 | 3.4 | 3.9 | 5.9 | 4.3 | 5.1 | 3.3 | Don't know |
| | (52) | (89) | (111) | (85) | (39) | (89) | (51) | (58) | (102) | (34) | (93) | (99) | (359) | Weighted N |
| 25-34 | 54.6 | 54.7 | 58.7 | 56.9 | 60.4 | 57.9 | 63.6 | 61.5 | 65.4 | 63.4 | 68.6 | 70.9 | 64.7 | Better |
| | 15.7 | 28.1 | 35.1 | 28.3 | 19.4 | 29.7 | 22.1 | 27.9 | 20.3 | 24.8 | 20.8 | 18.3 | 29.5 | Same |
| | 3.9 | 2.4 | 4.5 | 4.0 | 2.8 | 10.0 | 1.4 | 4.4 | 4.1 | 2.0 | 1.8 | 2.2 | 3.1 | Worse |
| | 10.0 | 4.9 | ** | 3.6 | 4.9 | ** | 2.1 | ** | 3.0 | 4.0 | 2.2 | 2.2 | ** | Depends |
| | 8.7 | 3.1 | ** | 3.6 | 3.5 | ** | 3.6 | ** | 1.9 | 0.0 | 1.8 | 1.7 | ** | Hopes/Luck |
| | 7.0 | 6.7 | 1.7 | 3.6 | 9.0 | 2.5 | 7.1 | 6.2 | 5.3 | 5.9 | 4.9 | 4.8 | 2.7 | Don't know |
| | (229) | (327) | (419) | (276) | (144) | (401) | (140) | (405) | (266) | (101) | (226) | (230) | (946) | Weighted N |
| 35-44 | 45.9 | 40.9 | 45.7 | 45.9 | 52.2 | 49.9 | 54.8 | 44.9 | 51.0 | 45.6 | 63.9 | 50.4 | 51.0 | Better |
| | 19.9 | 34.8 | 39.2 | 32.1 | 23.0 | 39.9 | 20.6 | 42.4 | 30.4 | 34.2 | 24.7 | 36.2 | 39.7 | Same |
| | 2.8 | 3.3 | 8.1 | 5.3 | 2.8 | 8.1 | 5.2 | 4.9 | 5.5 | 7.6 | 4.1 | 2.6 | 5.7 | Worse |
| | 9.3 | 4.2 | ** | 6.9 | 9.0 | ** | 2.6 | ** | 2.8 | 0.0 | 2.6 | 1.5 | ** | Depends |
| | 9.8 | 5.5 | ** | 4.1 | 3.9 | ** | 4.5 | ** | 2.8 | 1.3 | 1.0 | 1.5 | ** | Hopes/Luck |
| | 12.2 | 11.2 | 7.0 | 5.7 | 9.0 | 2.2 | 12.3 | 7.8 | 7.5 | 11.4 | 3.6 | 7.8 | 3.6 | Don't know |
| | (246) | (330) | (444) | (318) | (178) | (459) | (155) | (472) | (253) | (79) | (194) | (268) | (1011) | Weighted N |
| 45-54 | 34.2 | 29.5 | 35.9 | 38.6 | 18.7 | 38.3 | 37.9 | 31.7 | 32.8 | 42.1 | 40.6 | 39.4 | 39.4 | Better |
| | 27.8 | 42.5 | 46.9 | 36.8 | 45.5 | 49.1 | 37.1 | 53.7 | 36.5 | 31.0 | 37.4 | 37.2 | 50.1 | Same |
| | 8.2 | 7.1 | 8.6 | 6.5 | 16.3 | 11.1 | 11.4 | 10.1 | 7.9 | 10.3 | 10.3 | 9.7 | 6.3 | Worse |
| | 12.7 | 5.6 | ** | 9.4 | 4.9 | ** | 3.6 | ** | 5.4 | 6.3 | 5.2 | 3.7 | ** | Depends |
| | 4.4 | 3.0 | ** | 2.5 | 3.3 | ** | 1.4 | ** | 5.8 | 0.0 | 0.6 | 0.7 | ** | Hopes/Luck |
| | 12.7 | 12.3 | 8.6 | 6.1 | 11.4 | 1.4 | 8.6 | 4.5 | 11.6 | 10.3 | 5.8 | 9.3 | 4.3 | Don't know |
| | (158) | (268) | (326) | (277) | (123) | (350) | (140) | (378) | (241) | (126) | (155) | (269) | (894) | Weighted N |
| 55-64 | 14.0 | 25.8 | 26.8 | 17.2 | 18.7 | 23.4 | 21.9 | 20.5 | 18.8 | 14.6 | 30.1 | 15.2 | 29.1 | Better |
| | 35.1 | 36.8 | 52.2 | 41.9 | 45.5 | 50.6 | 41.8 | 55.3 | 46.3 | 43.8 | 38.6 | 48.5 | 47.7 | Same |
| | 19.3 | 14.4 | 11.6 | 23.1 | 16.3 | 21.5 | 17.1 | 16.4 | 20.0 | 23.6 | 16.1 | 26.3 | 17.0 | Worse |
| | 14.0 | 8.6 | ** | 8.6 | 4.9 | ** | 7.5 | ** | 4.4 | 4.5 | 7.0 | 4.5 | ** | Depends |
| | 5.3 | 2.4 | ** | 1.1 | 3.3 | ** | 2.7 | ** | 1.3 | 2.2 | 1.3 | 1.0 | ** | Hopes/Luck |
| | 12.3 | 12.0 | 9.4 | 8.1 | 11.4 | 4.6 | 8.9 | 7.8 | 9.4 | 11.2 | 7.0 | 4.5 | 6.3 | Don't know |
| | (114) | (209) | (224) | (186) | (123) | (261) | (146) | (293) | (160) | (89) | (386) | (198) | (671) | Weighted N |
| 65-74 | 8.3 | 8.3 | 11.9 | 5.3 | 8.7 | 13.8 | 4.0 | 10.8 | 5.2 | 4.4 | 5.9 | 5.1 | 9.3 | Better |
| | 35.8 | 49.4 | 61.9 | 55.6 | 58.4 | 63.8 | 66.0 | 62.6 | 66.5 | 64.9 | 59.4 | 66.2 | 67.5 | Same |
| | 18.3 | 17.8 | 18.7 | 14.3 | 14.9 | 18.8 | 13.3 | 18.2 | 17.0 | 16.7 | 22.8 | 16.9 | 19.6 | Worse |
| | 10.1 | 5.0 | ** | 11.6 | 5.6 | ** | 4.7 | ** | 2.6 | 4.4 | 5.9 | 3.7 | ** | Depends |
| | 2.8 | 3.9 | ** | 0.5 | 1.9 | ** | 0.0 | ** | 1.0 | 1.8 | 0.0 | 0.0 | ** | Hopes/Luck |
| | 24.8 | 15.6 | 7.5 | 12.7 | 10.6 | 3.8 | 12.0 | 8.4 | 7.7 | 7.9 | 5.9 | 8.1 | 3.7 | Don't know |
| | (109) | (180) | (134) | (189) | (161) | (160) | (150) | (203) | (194) | (114) | (101) | (136) | (464) | Weighted N |
| 75 and Older | ** | ** | 11.3 | ** | ** | 12.5 | ** | 14.0 | ** | ** | 7.8 | 4.1 | 6.3 | Better |
| | ** | ** | 62.9 | ** | ** | 68.8 | ** | 68.6 | ** | ** | 68.6 | 66.2 | 74.2 | Same |
| | ** | ** | 17.7 | ** | ** | 17.5 | ** | 10.5 | ** | ** | 13.7 | 14.9 | 15.4 | Worse |
| | ** | ** | ** | ** | ** | ** | ** | ** | ** | ** | 2.0 | 5.4 | ** | Depends |
| | ** | ** | ** | ** | ** | ** | ** | ** | ** | ** | 0.0 | 2.7 | ** | Hopes/Luck |
| | ** | ** | 8.1 | ** | ** | 1.3 | ** | 7.0 | ** | ** | 7.8 | 6.8 | 4.2 | Don't know |
| | ** | ** | (62) | ** | ** | (80) | ** | (86) | ** | ** | (51) | (74) | (240) | Weighted N |

** Code distinction not made.

Oldest age group coded "65 And Older" in 1952k,1956m,1957f,1958m,1959f,1961f,and 1961m.

Age coded for head of household only in 1958m,1959f,and 1961m, and for head and wife only in 1962f.

Personal Economic Outlook

Table 6.42
Will R's Family Be in a Better Financial Situation in a Few Years?
Income of Respondent

| | 1952k | 1956m | 1956n | 1957f | 1958m | 1958n | 1959f | 1960n | 1961f | 1961m | 1962f | 1963m | 1964n | |
|---|---|---|---|---|---|---|---|---|---|---|---|---|---|---|
| **Income 1** | 12.6% | 18.0% | 27.6% | 18.0% | 18.8% | 28.3% | 19.5% | 21.8% | 18.8% | 19.6% | 26.4% | 21.2% | 20.8% | Better |
| | 31.0 | 45.6 | 49.6 | 45.2 | 44.8 | 48.2 | 51.0 | 53.6 | 51.7 | 48.4 | 44.4 | 50.6 | 55.9 | Same |
| | 18.4 | 12.4 | 15.7 | 15.4 | 10.0 | 19.2 | 11.5 | 16.4 | 13.1 | 12.4 | 13.5 | 15.3 | 18.4 | Worse |
| | 6.9 | 6.9 | ** | 5.3 | 7.1 | ** | 4.5 | ** | 2.8 | 4.6 | 3.9 | 4.1 | ** | Depends |
| | 4.6 | 4.1 | ** | 5.3 | 5.9 | ** | 2.0 | '** | 2.8 | 3.9 | 2.2 | 1.2 | ** | Hopes/Luck |
| | 26.4 | 12.9 | 7.1 | 11.0 | 13.4 | 4.3 | 11.5 | 8.2 | 10.8 | 11.1 | 9.6 | 7.6 | 4.9 | Don't know |
| | (87) | (217) | (268) | (228) | (239) | (276) | (200) | (280) | (176) | (153) | (178) | (170) | (852) | Weighted N |
| **Income 2** | 33.2 | 23.4 | 36.4 | 33.8 | 35.1 | 38.5 | 28.9 | 32.6 | 32.9 | 32.6 | 34.6 | 29.9 | 38.5 | Better |
| | 25.0 | 35.5 | 44.4 | 38.5 | 38.3 | 43.9 | 36.4 | 47.3 | 42.0 | 38.1 | 43.6 | 47.1 | 50.8 | Same |
| | 9.0 | 10.6 | 8.8 | 6.9 | 11.0 | 14.3 | 13.2 | 12.0 | 10.7 | 14.4 | 9.5 | 8.3 | 7.3 | Worse |
| | 12.1 | 7.8 | ** | 10.7 | 3.2 | ** | 3.3 | ** | 2.9 | 2.8 | 3.3 | 5.4 | ** | Depends |
| | 6.6 | 2.1 | ** | 1.9 | 1.3 | ** | 5.0 | ** | 2.1 | 2.8 | 1.4 | 2.9 | ** | Hopes/Luck |
| | 14.1 | 20.6 | 10.4 | 8.2 | 11.0 | 3.2 | 13.2 | 8.1 | 9.5 | 9.4 | 7.6 | 6.4 | 3.4 | Don't know |
| | (256) | (141) | (376) | (317) | (154) | (371) | (121) | (334) | (243) | (181) | (211) | (204) | (813) | Weighted N |
| **Income 3** | 42.6 | 40.0 | 45.9 | 46.4 | 41.2 | 46.5 | 44.9 | 36.2 | 49.4 | 49.0 | 48.5 | 42.9 | 53.5 | Better |
| | 24.2 | 36.2 | 42.8 | 33.8 | 35.1 | 39.6 | 33.5 | 49.0 | 31.5 | 30.3 | 32.3 | 36.8 | 36.8 | Same |
| | 5.4 | 6.3 | 7.3 | 6.8 | 4.6 | 12.4 | 9.2 | 8.3 | 7.5 | 7.1 | 10.2 | 8.9 | 6.4 | Worse |
| | 10.4 | 3.9 | ** | 5.8 | 5.2 | ** | 4.1 | ** | 4.2 | 4.5 | 4.6 | 2.9 | ** | Depends |
| | 9.1 | 3.2 | ** | 1.7 | 4.8 | ** | 2.4 | ** | 1.6 | 1.7 | 0.9 | 1.1 | ** | Hopes/Luck |
| | 8.4 | 10.3 | 4.0 | 5.4 | 9.0 | 1.4 | 5.8 | 6.6 | 5.8 | 7.4 | 3.5 | 7.4 | 3.3 | Don't know |
| | (298) | (585) | (521) | (515) | (498) | (490) | (465) | (531) | (429) | (353) | (431) | (380) | (1157) | Weighted N |
| **Income 4** | 46.5 | 48.5 | 46.9 | 51.5 | 56.7 | 47.9 | 55.3 | 45.5 | 52.8 | 50.6 | 58.3 | 54.5 | 53.5 | Better |
| | 20.7 | 31.6 | 41.4 | 28.6 | 22.5 | 42.9 | 25.6 | 42.9 | 29.0 | 30.1 | 24.0 | 27.9 | 36.7 | Same |
| | 5.6 | 5.6 | 7.6 | 8.2 | 8.5 | 8.1 | 7.8 | 6.2 | 7.3 | 6.3 | 7.7 | 9.6 | 6.2 | Worse |
| | 12.6 | 5.3 | ** | 6.6 | 6.7 | ** | 3.0 | ** | 2.8 | 5.7 | 4.3 | 2.7 | ** | Depends |
| | 7.6 | 3.7 | ** | 2.6 | 2.1 | ** | 1.9 | ** | 1.6 | 4.0 | 0.7 | 0.8 | ** | Hopes/Luck |
| | 7.1 | 5.3 | 4.2 | 2.6 | 3.5 | 1.1 | 6.5 | 5.4 | 6.5 | 3.4 | 5.0 | 4.5 | 3.5 | Don't know |
| | (198) | (301) | (382) | (196) | (284) | (534) | (371) | (648) | (248) | (176) | (300) | (376) | (1285) | Weighted N |
| **Income 5** | 56.1 | 44.7 | 55.6 | 43.3 | 50.0 | 54.5 | 50.0 | 55.4 | 47.4 | 53.1 | 60.4 | 42.4 | 48.9 | Better |
| | 19.5 | 28.2 | 32.3 | 33.3 | 30.0 | 30.9 | 23.7 | 38.6 | 26.3 | 28.1 | 20.8 | 35.3 | 39.6 | Same |
| | 7.3 | 5.8 | 7.5 | 10.0 | 9.0 | 14.5 | 15.8 | 3.6 | 10.5 | 9.4 | 13.2 | 12.9 | 6.7 | Worse |
| | 9.8 | 7.8 | ** | 10.0 | 5.0 | ** | 5.3 | ** | 3.5 | 0.0 | 5.7 | 1.2 | ** | Depends |
| | 0.0 | 3.9 | ** | 0.0 | 3.0 | ** | 2.6 | ** | 3.5 | 0.0 | 0.0 | 1.2 | ** | Hopes/Luck |
| | 7.3 | 9.7 | 4.5 | 3.3 | 3.0 | 0.0 | 2.6 | 2.4 | 8.8 | 9.4 | 0.0 | 7.1 | 4.8 | Don't know |
| | (41) | (103) | (133) | (30) | (100) | (55) | (38) | (83) | (57) | (32) | (53) | (85) | (313) | Weighted N |

* Code distinction not made.

Personal Economic Outlook

Figure 6.10
R's Financial Situation in a Few Years by Race of R

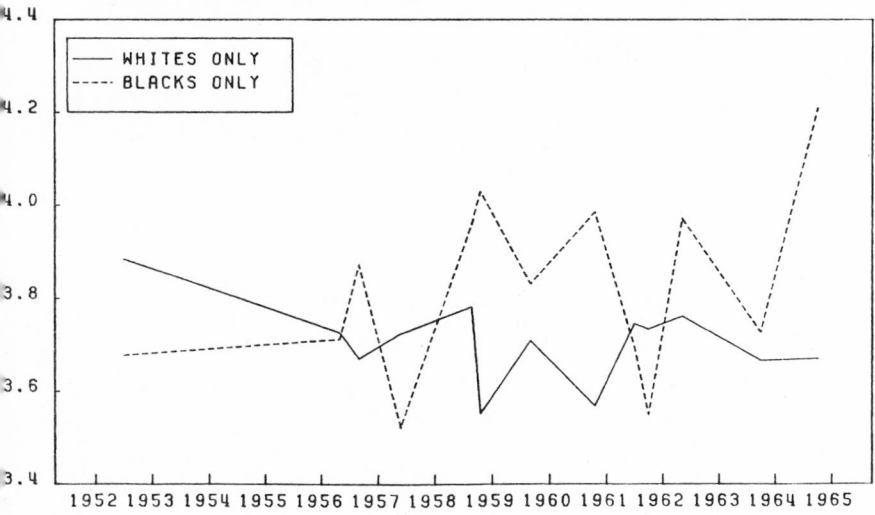

Figure 6.11
R's Financial Situation in a Few Years by Education of R

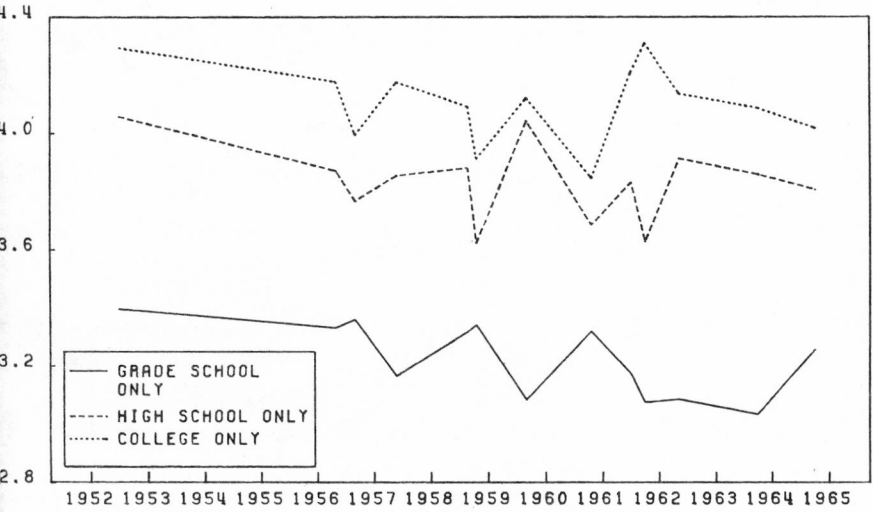

Figure 6.12

's Financial Situation in a Few Years by Age of R

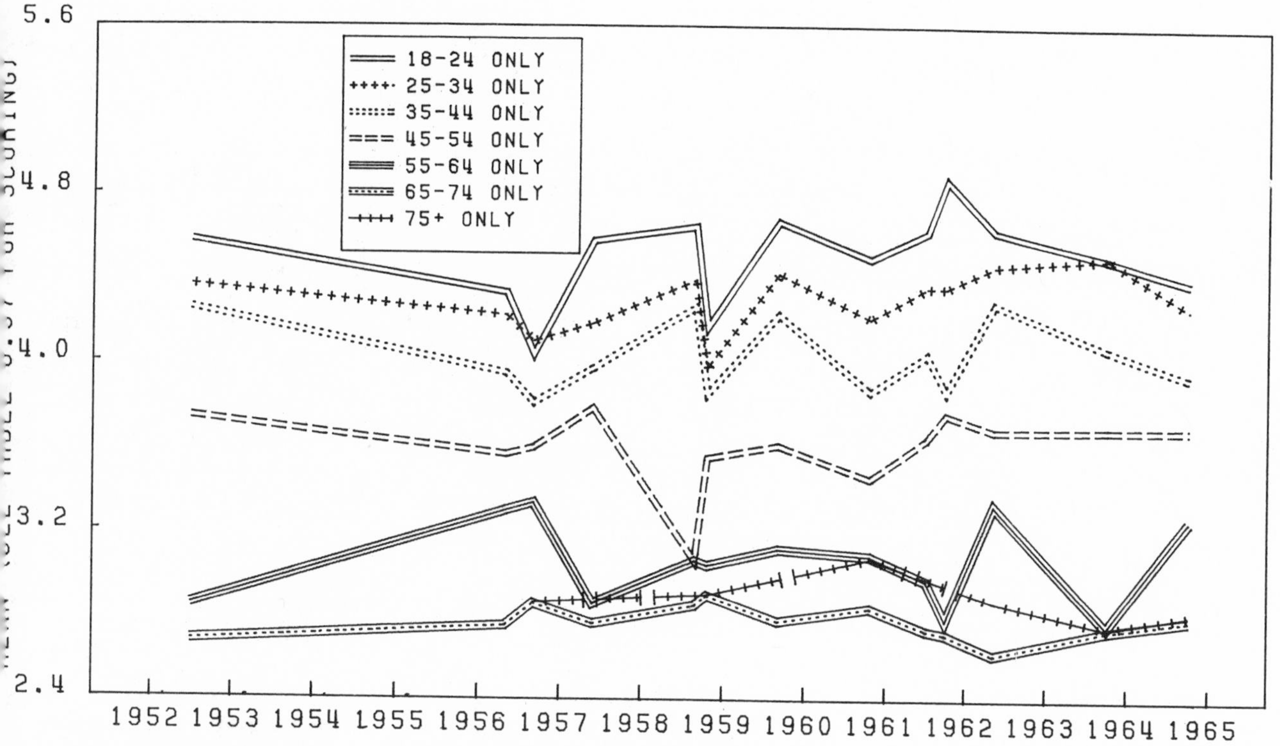

Figure 6.13

's Financial Situation in a Few Years by Income of R

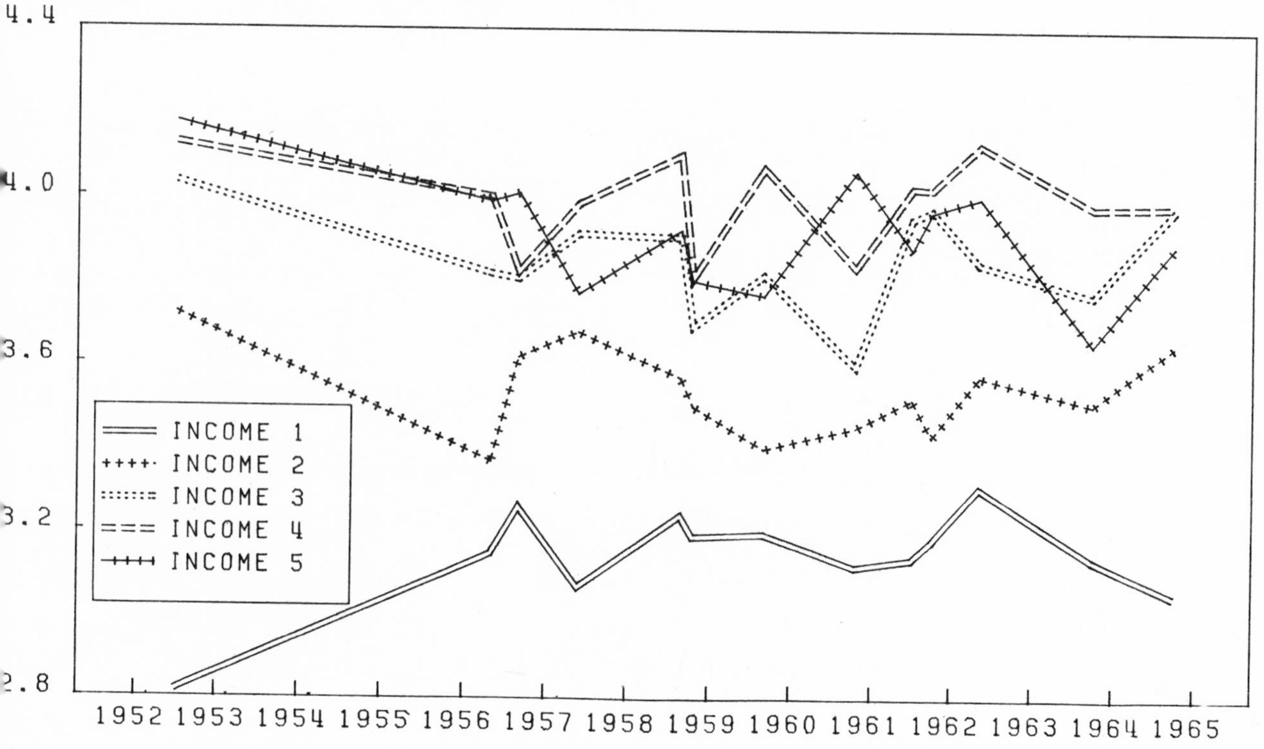

Personal Economic Outlook

Table 6.43
Will R's Family Be Better or Worse Off in the Next Few Years?
Total Population

QUESTION: What about the next few years--do you think that you (and
your family) will be better off or worse off or what?

|  |  | Year | | | |
|  |  | 1969e | 1970e | 1971e | 1975e |
| Better off | (5) | 58.1% | 54.6% | 56.9% | 54.8% |
| No difference/same | (3) | 21.9 | 15.8 | 17.7 | 20.1 |
| Worse off | (1) | 9.8 | 10.0 | 8.8 | 14.9 |
| Don't know |  | 10.2 | 19.6 | 16.6 | 10.2 |
| Total |  | 100% | 100% | 100% | 100% |
| Weighted N |  | 111672 | 122255 | 105350 | 136704 |
| Unweighted N |  | 3679 | 4096 | 3667 | 5277 |
| Mean |  | 4.07 | 4.11 | 4.15 | 3.89 |
| Standard Deviation |  | 1.37 | 1.41 | 1.35 | 1.52 |

Figure 6.14
Will R Be Better Off in the Next Few Years?--Total Population

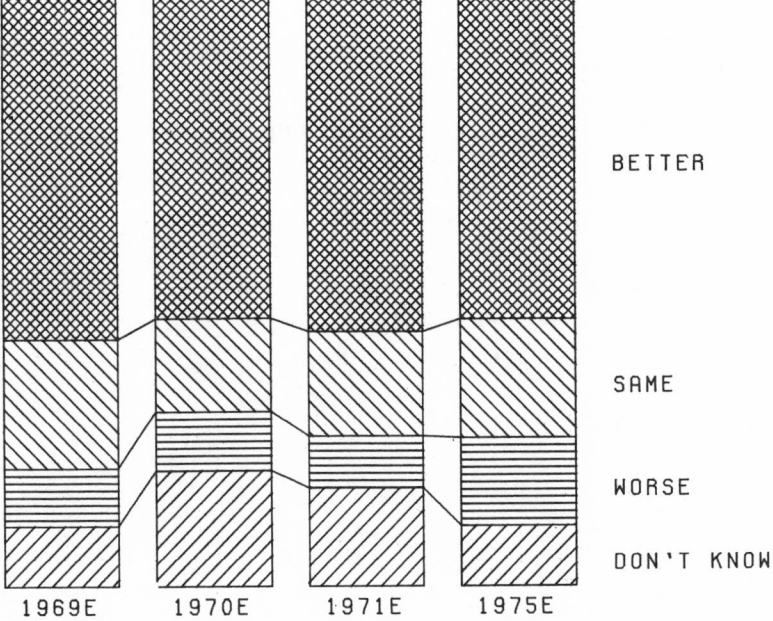

Personal Economic Outlook

Table 6.44
Will R's Family Be Better or Worse Off in the Next Few Years?
Sex of Respondent

|  | | Year | | | |
| --- | --- | --- | --- | --- | --- |
|  | 1969e | 1970e | 1971e | 1975e | |
| Males Only | 62.4% | 58.9% | 62.5% | 59.4% | Better off |
|  | 20.1 | 15.0 | 16.6 | 19.0 | No difference/same |
|  | 8.8 | 9.8 | 7.9 | 14.3 | Worse off |
|  | (83532) | (88799) | (76280) | (88958) | Weighted N |
| Females Only | 45.3 | 43.1 | 42.5 | 46.3 | Better off |
|  | 27.3 | 17.9 | 20.6 | 22.4 | No difference/same |
|  | 12.9 | 10.4 | 11.2 | 16.1 | Worse off |
|  | (28140) | (33456) | (29070) | (47109) | Weighted N |

Sex coded for head of household and wife only in 1969e,1970e,and 1971e.

Table 6.45
Race of Respondent

|  | 1969e | 1970e | 1971e | 1975e | |
| --- | --- | --- | --- | --- | --- |
| Whites Only | 57.2% | 54.7% | 57.1% | 54.7% | Better off |
|  | 22.9 | 17.0 | 19.3 | 21.7 | No difference/same |
|  | 10.1 | 10.2 | 9.0 | 14.6 | Worse off |
|  | (97740) | (105933) | (91355) | (117328) | Weighted N |
| Blacks Only | 61.9 | 54.0 | 57.6 | 55.5 | Better off |
|  | 14.3 | 7.7 | 4.9 | 9.2 | No difference/same |
|  | 9.1 | 10.2 | 8.6 | 16.6 | Worse off |
|  | (11736) | (13262) | (11119) | (15431) | Weighted N |

Race coded for head of household and wife only in 1971e.

Table 6.46
Will R's Family Be Better or Worse Off in the Next Few Years?
Education of Respondent

|  | Year | | | | |
|---|---|---|---|---|---|
|  | 1969e | 1970e | 1971e | 1975e | |
| Grade School Only | 38.7% | 29.6% | 34.4% | 31.8% | Better off |
|  | 31.1 | 19.9 | 25.1 | 25.4 | No difference/same |
|  | 15.5 | 15.4 | 10.7 | 24.4 | Worse off |
|  | (29317) | (29652) | (19919) | (22707) | Weighted N |
| High School Only | 63.8 | 60.6 | 61.5 | 56.3 | Better off |
|  | 18.9 | 14.1 | 16.3 | 20.0 | No difference/same |
|  | 8.1 | 8.1 | 7.6 | 13.8 | Worse off |
|  | (50005) | (56731) | (45412) | (67114) | Weighted N |
| College Only | 67.0 | 66.3 | 65.9 | 66.2 | Better off |
|  | 18.2 | 15.2 | 16.7 | 17.7 | No difference/same |
|  | 7.6 | 8.7 | 9.5 | 10.7 | Worse off |
|  | (31683) | (34273) | (30460) | (43609) | Weighted N |

Education coded for head of household only in 1971e, and for head and wife only
  in 1969e and 1970e.

Table 6.47
Will R's Family Be Better or Worse Off in the Next Few Years?
Age of Respondent

|  | Year | | | | |
|---|---|---|---|---|---|
|  | 1969e | 1970e | 1971e | 1975e | |
| 18-24 Only | 85.2% | 79.8% | 83.1% | 80.6% | Better off |
|  | 5.1 | 8.1 | 4.3 | 6.5 | No difference/same |
|  | 2.5 | 4.4 | 3.8 | 7.0 | Worse off |
|  | (8788) | (11840) | (10616) | (15279) | Weighted N |
| 25-34 Only | 85.5 | 78.1 | 79.2 | 75.2 | Better off |
|  | 7.5 | 6.3 | 7.1 | 10.5 | No difference/same |
|  | 3.5 | 4.5 | 4.4 | 7.0 | Worse off |
|  | (21442) | (23297) | (20721) | (30767) | Weighted N |
| 35-44 Only | 70.9 | 68.0 | 67.9 | 68.0 | Better off |
|  | 15.0 | 10.2 | 13.2 | 12.0 | No difference/same |
|  | 6.4 | 6.9 | 6.5 | 11.7 | Worse off |
|  | (24421) | (24922) | (22440) | (21902) | Weighted N |
| 45-54 Only | 58.6 | 57.6 | 53.2 | 51.8 | Better off |
|  | 20.6 | 15.3 | 17.8 | 17.5 | No difference/same |
|  | 9.5 | 7.0 | 9.3 | 17.9 | Worse off |
|  | (21240) | (22517) | (19630) | (25313) | Weighted N |
| 55-64 Only | 37.6 | 32.6 | 36.0 | 37.1 | Better off |
|  | 33.6 | 22.9 | 26.1 | 29.5 | No difference/same |
|  | 15.4 | 16.5 | 14.8 | 22.1 | Worse off |
|  | (18824) | (19865) | (16351) | (18361) | Weighted N |
| 65-74 Only | 14.8 | 15.6 | 23.7 | 20.7 | Better off |
|  | 45.8 | 28.8 | 35.5 | 44.4 | No difference/same |
|  | 21.6 | 20.7 | 16.3 | 22.8 | Worse off |
|  | (11737) | (13510) | (11576) | (15412) | Weighted N |
| 75 And Older Only | 10.3 | 8.6 | 10.9 | 12.5 | Better off |
|  | 51.3 | 39.3 | 46.5 | 43.3 | No difference/same |
|  | 17.0 | 20.2 | 9.1 | 26.1 | Worse off |
|  | (5310) | (6247) | (4007) | (8976) | Weighted N |

Age coded for head of household and wife only in 1969e,1970e,and 1971e.

Personal Economic Outlook

ble 6.48
11 R's Family Be Better or Worse Off in the Next Few Years?
come of Respondent

| | | Year | | | |
|---|---|---|---|---|---|
| | 1969e | 1970e | 1971e | 1975e | |
| Income 1 (0-16%) | 35.5% | 30.2% | 35.4% | 37.9% | Better off |
| | 32.7 | 19.3 | 23.5 | 23.9 | No difference/same |
| | 15.9 | 16.7 | 10.4 | 20.8 | Worse off |
| | (20327) | (22460) | (17409) | (22749) | Weighted N |
| Income 2 (17-33%) | 50.4 | 48.9 | 52.3 | 50.0 | Better off |
| | 24.8 | 16.7 | 16.3 | 20.8 | No difference/same |
| | 10.0 | 10.5 | 9.4 | 16.3 | Worse off |
| | (19360) | (21059) | (17772) | (23027) | Weighted N |
| Income 3 (34-67%) | 65.4 | 60.8 | 61.6 | 59.1 | Better off |
| | 18.6 | 15.1 | 15.9 | 19.4 | No difference/same |
| | 8.2 | 8.0 | 8.1 | 12.9 | Worse off |
| | (37652) | (41618) | (34913) | (45200) | Weighted N |
| Income 4 (68-95%) | 67.9 | 65.9 | 65.7 | 61.2 | Better off |
| | 16.5 | 13.1 | 16.3 | 18.6 | No difference/same |
| | 7.9 | 7.6 | 8.5 | 12.8 | Worse off |
| | (29328) | (31871) | (29977) | (39127) | Weighted N |
| Income 5 (96-100%) | 65.2 | 63.8 | 63.2 | 62.3 | Better off |
| | 23.4 | 17.9 | 22.9 | 19.1 | No difference/same |
| | 7.7 | 9.2 | 8.0 | 14.7 | Worse off |
| | (5286) | (5546) | (5279) | (6601) | Weighted N |

Personal Economic Outlook

Table 6.49

Did R Save Money in the Last Twelve Months?

Total Population

QUESTION: Would you say that you people saved money in the last twelve months, or did you decrease your savings or did you just break even?

| | | Year | | | | | | | |
|---|---|---|---|---|---|---|---|---|---|
| | | 1947a | 1952k | 1954a | 1955a | 1957f | 1958m | 1959a | 1960f |
| Increased savings | (5) | 35.2% | 38.8% | 35.6% | 37.3% | 36.9% | 31.2% | 40.9% | 32.1% |
| No change | (3) | 27.2 | 34.5 | 35.0 | 31.5 | 43.0 | 48.7 | 29.9 | 46.3 |
| Decreased savings | (1) | 37.6 | 25.4 | 29.2 | 31.2 | 19.9 | 19.6 | 29.3 | 21.1 |
| Don't know | | ** | 1.3 | 0.3 | ** | 0.2 | 0.5 | ** | 0.5 |
| Total | | 100% | 100% | 100% | 100% | 100% | 100% | 100% | 100% |
| Weighted N | | 451034 | 528 | 54750 | 50200 | 1328 | 1334 | 48975 | 1343 |
| Unweighted N | | 1461 | 528 | 1761 | 1718 | 1328 | 1334 | 1514 | 1343 |
| Mean | | 2.95 | 3.27 | 3.13 | 3.12 | 3.34 | 3.23 | 3.23 | 3.22 |
| Standard Deviation | | 1.71 | 1.59 | 1.61 | 1.65 | 1.47 | 1.41 | 1.66 | 1.45 |

Table 6.50

| | | 1961a | 1961m | 1962k | 1963f | 1964a | 1965a | 1971m | 1973i |
|---|---|---|---|---|---|---|---|---|---|
| Increased savings | (5) | 33.3% | 32.9% | 29.5% | 33.0% | 31.4% | 36.6% | 27.1% | 32.1% |
| No change | (3) | 34.5 | 48.6 | 48.4 | 47.8 | 49.1 | 41.7 | 51.5 | 44.9 |
| Decreased savings | (1) | 32.2 | 18.5 | 21.9 | 18.9 | 19.5 | 21.7 | 21.4 | 22.7 |
| Don't know | | ** | ** | 0.2 | 0.3 | 0.1 | ** | 0.1 | 0.3 |
| Total | | 100% | 100% | 100% | 100% | 100% | 100% | 100% | 100% |
| Weighted N | | 30276 | 914 | 1278 | 1278 | 1478 | 1157 | 1302 | 2719 |
| Unweighted N | | 1211 | 914 | 1278 | 1278 | 1478 | 1157 | 1302 | 1390 |
| Mean | | 3.02 | 3.29 | 3.15 | 3.28 | 3.24 | 3.30 | 3.11 | 3.19 |
| Standard Deviation | | 1.62 | 1.41 | 1.43 | 1.41 | 1.41 | 1.50 | 1.39 | 1.47 |

** Code distinction not made.

Figure 6.15

R's Savings--Total Population

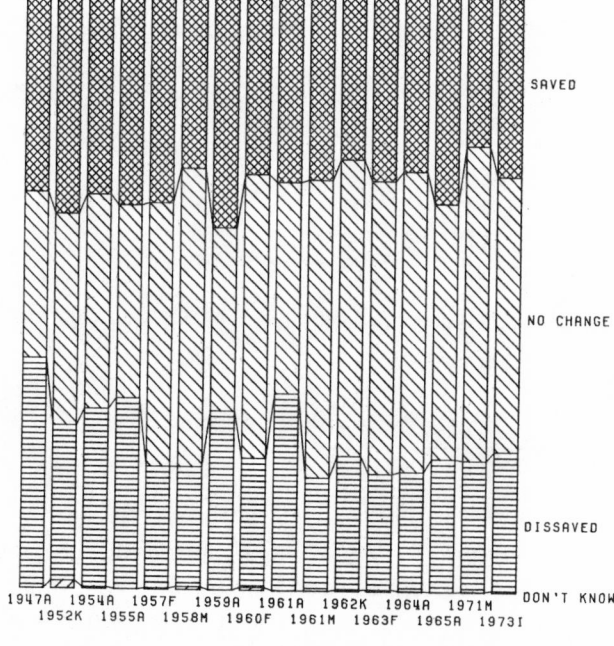

Personal Economic Outlook

ble 6.51
d R Save Money in the Last Twelve Months?
x of Respondent

|  | Year | | | | | | | | |
|---|---|---|---|---|---|---|---|---|---|
|  | 1947a | 1952k | 1954a | 1955a | 1957f | 1958m | 1959a | 1960f | |
| Males Only | 34.4% | 45.0% | 34.2% | 37.3% | 41.6% | 31.6% | 39.1% | 33.6% | Saved |
|  | 27.6 | 32.0 | 36.1 | 32.4 | 39.9 | 48.6 | 29.5 | 46.7 | No change |
|  | 38.1 | 23.0 | 29.7 | 30.3 | 18.5 | 19.8 | 31.5 | 19.7 | Dissaved |
|  | (296794) | (222) | (37316) | (31562) | (572) | (560) | (31917) | (574) | Weighted N |
| Females Only | 36.4 | 35.1 | 38.8 | 36.9 | 33.5 | 31.2 | 44.5 | 31.3 | Saved |
|  | 26.7 | 37.1 | 32.6 | 30.4 | 45.6 | 49.3 | 30.5 | 46.5 | No change |
|  | 36.9 | 27.8 | 28.5 | 32.7 | 21.0 | 19.6 | 24.9 | 22.2 | Dissaved |
|  | (152267) | (299) | (17296) | (17907) | (753) | (767) | (16393) | (761) | Weighted N |

ble 6.52

|  | 1961a | 1961m | 1962k | 1963f | 1964a | 1965a | 1971m | 1973i | |
|---|---|---|---|---|---|---|---|---|---|
| Males Only | 33.2% | 33.1% | 30.0% | 33.3% | 31.9% | 38.9% | 30.7% | 34.6% | Saved |
|  | 34.5 | 48.1 | 48.3 | 48.0 | 48.7 | 39.4 | 47.5 | 43.0 | No change |
|  | 32.3 | 18.9 | 21.8 | 18.6 | 19.4 | 21.7 | 21.8 | 22.4 | Dissaved |
|  | (25155) | (387) | (524) | (531) | (1116) | (840) | (908) | (1201) | Weighted N |
| Females Only | 33.7 | 32.8 | 29.3 | 33.0 | 29.7 | 30.3 | 18.8 | 30.2 | Saved |
|  | 34.6 | 49.0 | 48.6 | 47.9 | 50.4 | 47.9 | 60.8 | 23.1 | No change |
|  | 31.7 | 18.2 | 22.1 | 19.1 | 19.9 | 21.8 | 20.4 | 46.7 | Dissaved |
|  | (5096) | (527) | (751) | (743) | (357) | (317) | (393) | (1511) | Weighted N |

Personal Economic Outlook

Table 6.53
Did R Save Money in the Last Twelve Months?
Race of Respondent

|  | Year | | | | | | | |
|---|---|---|---|---|---|---|---|---|
|  | 1947a | 1952k | 1954a | 1955a | 1957f | 1958m | 1959a | 1960f |
| Whites Only | 35.4% | 40.2% | 36.3% | 38.1% | 39.5% | 33.9% | 41.7% | 33.7% Saved |
|  | 27.3 | 34.7 | 35.2 | 31.1 | 40.5 | 46.7 | 29.7 | 45.5 No change |
|  | 37.4 | 25.1 | 28.6 | 30.8 | 19.9 | 19.4 | 28.6 | 20.8 Dissaved |
|  | (427061) | (498) | (52710) | (47515) | (1179) | (1162) | (45960) | (1066) Weighted N |
| Blacks Only | 27.1 | 22.7 | 28.3 | 16.0 | 12.8 | 11.7 | 22.1 | 8.8 Saved |
|  | 25.4 | 36.4 | 26.0 | 40.4 | 66.9 | 67.6 | 33.3 | 66.7 No change |
|  | 47.5 | 40.9 | 45.7 | 43.6 | 20.3 | 20.7 | 44.6 | 24.6 Dissaved |
|  | (16662) | (22) | (2666) | (2052) | (133) | (145) | (2334) | (114) Weighted N |

Table 6.54

|  | 1961a | 1961m | 1962k | 1963f | 1964a | 1965a | 1971m | 1973i |
|---|---|---|---|---|---|---|---|---|
| Whites Only | 33.4% | 34.7% | 31.2% | 34.4% | 33.3% | 38.0% | 28.8% | 34.8% Saved |
|  | 34.7 | 46.9 | 46.9 | 46.0 | 46.9 | 39.7 | 49.3 | 43.5 No change |
|  | 32.0 | 18.4 | 22.0 | 19.5 | 19.8 | 22.3 | 21.9 | 21.7 Dissaved |
|  | (28976) | (832) | (1152) | (1147) | (1303) | (1042) | (1134) | (2375) Weighted N |
| Blacks Only | 29.1 | 6.3 | 13.0 | 19.1 | 12.1 | 20.2 | 13.7 | 10.1 Saved |
|  | 33.9 | 75.0 | 65.7 | 68.2 | 68.9 | 66.7 | 69.5 | 60.8 No change |
|  | 37.0 | 18.8 | 21.3 | 12.7 | 18.9 | 13.1 | 16.8 | 29.1 Dissaved |
|  | (1067) | (64) | (108) | (110) | (132) | (84) | (131) | (227) Weighted N |

Figure 6.16
R's Savings by Race of R

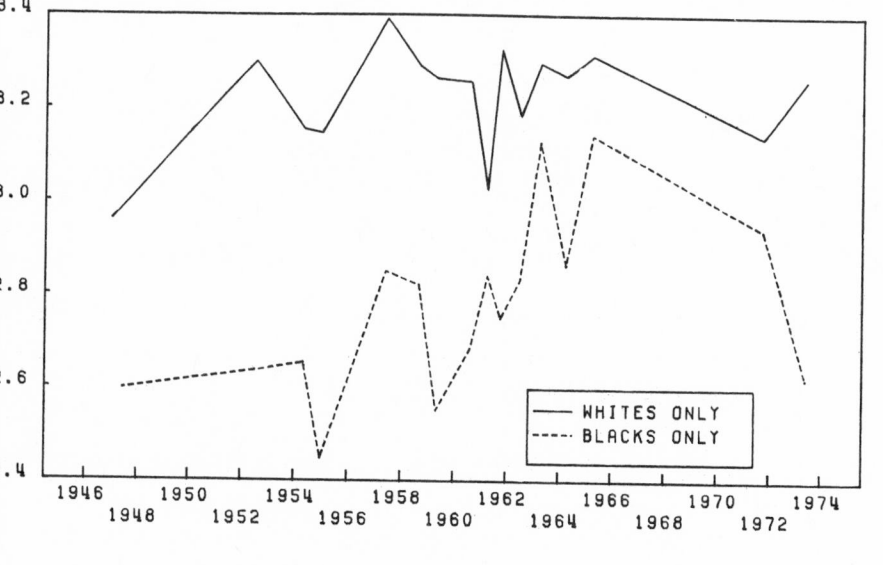

Figure 6.17
R's Savings by Education of R

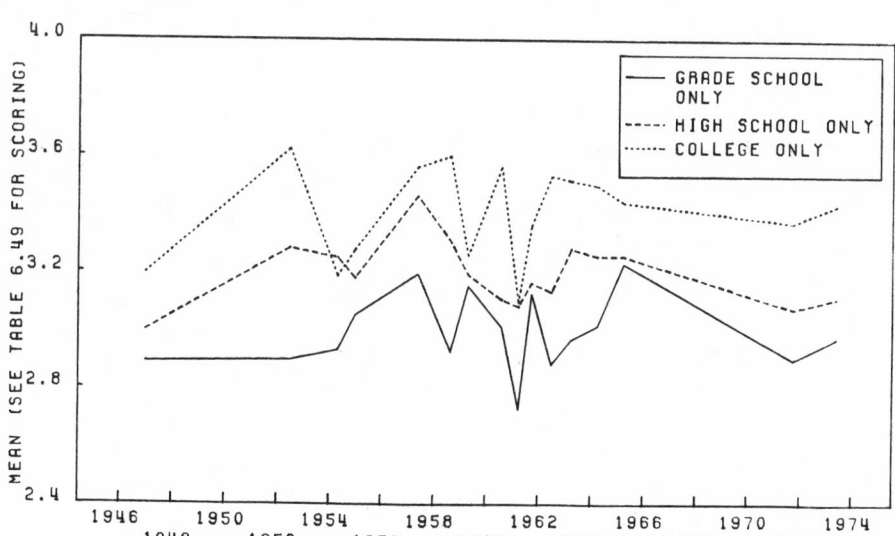

Table 6.55
Did R Save Money in the Last Twelve Months?
Education of Respondent

|                   |        |        |        |        | Year   |        |        |        |           |
|-------------------|--------|--------|--------|--------|--------|--------|--------|--------|-----------|
|                   | 1947a  | 1952k  | 1954a  | 1955a  | 1957f  | 1958m  | 1959a  | 1960f  |           |
| Grade School Only | 32.0%  | 29.0%  | 31.6%  | 34.3%  | 27.7%  | 18.4%  | 36.2%  | 21.8%  | Saved     |
|                   | 30.6   | 37.0   | 33.5   | 34.1   | 54.4   | 59.7   | 35.4   | 57.2   | No change |
|                   | 37.4   | 34.1   | 34.9   | 31.6   | 17.9   | 22.0   | 28.5   | 21.0   | Dissaved  |
|                   | (115215)| (138) | (15022)| (10298)| (307)  | (305)  | (9652) | (271)  | Weighted N|
| High School Only  | 37.4   | 39.0   | 38.1   | 39.5   | 42.3   | 34.5   | 39.8   | 28.7   | Saved     |
|                   | 25.2   | 36.1   | 36.2   | 29.9   | 38.6   | 46.4   | 30.0   | 48.0   | No change |
|                   | 37.4   | 24.9   | 25.6   | 30.5   | 19.1   | 19.0   | 30.2   | 23.3   | Dissaved  |
|                   | (166799)| (241) | (21098)| (21070)| (293)  | (336)  | (18499)| (352)  | Weighted N|
| College Only      | 41.5   | 50.4   | 35.8   | 41.9   | 52.8   | 46.0   | 43.6   | 45.7   | Saved     |
|                   | 26.7   | 30.5   | 37.7   | 30.0   | 22.5   | 38.0   | 25.7   | 37.0   | No change |
|                   | 31.8   | 19.1   | 26.5   | 28.1   | 24.6   | 16.0   | 30.7   | 17.4   | Dissaved  |
|                   | (70215)| (141)  | (10849)| (8974) | (142)  | (150)  | (11057)| (138)  | Weighted N|

Table 6.56

|                   | 1961a  | 1961m  | 1962k  | 1963f  | 1964a  | 1965a  | 1971m  | 1973i  |           |
|-------------------|--------|--------|--------|--------|--------|--------|--------|--------|-----------|
| Grade School Only | 22.3%  | 19.1%  | 16.7%  | 19.5%  | 19.7%  | 28.1%  | 12.4%  | 17.9%  | Saved     |
|                   | 41.9   | 68.1   | 60.9   | 59.6   | 61.5   | 55.4   | 70.2   | 63.0   | No change |
|                   | 35.8   | 12.8   | 22.4   | 21.0   | 18.8   | 16.5   | 17.4   | 19.1   | Dissaved  |
|                   | (6387) | (188)  | (366)  | (267)  | (462)  | (303)  | (322)  | (481)  | Weighted N|
| High School Only  | 36.3   | 31.2   | 29.8   | 32.6   | 33.0   | 35.4   | 26.4   | 30.4   | Saved     |
|                   | 31.6   | 45.9   | 47.2   | 48.9   | 46.7   | 42.1   | 51.0   | 44.9   | No change |
|                   | 32.1   | 22.9   | 23.0   | 18.5   | 20.3   | 22.6   | 22.6   | 24.7   | Dissaved  |
|                   | (13740)| (218)  | (625)  | (319)  | (636)  | (554)  | (580)  | (1379) | Weighted N|
| College Only      | 35.7   | 42.1   | 46.7   | 43.1   | 44.0   | 47.6   | 40.9   | 43.6   | Saved     |
|                   | 33.4   | 34.1   | 33.3   | 39.7   | 37.1   | 26.9   | 36.8   | 34.5   | No change |
|                   | 30.9   | 23.8   | 20.0   | 17.2   | 19.0   | 25.5   | 22.3   | 21.9   | Dissaved  |
|                   | (9722) | (126)  | (270)  | (174)  | (364)  | (294)  | (391)  | (844)  | Weighted N|

Education coded for head of household only in 1947a,1954a,1955a,1957f,1958m,1959a,1961a,1961m,
and 1971m, and for head and wife only in 1960f,1962f,1963f,1964a,and 1965a.

Table 6.57
Did R Save Money in the Last Twelve Months?
Age of Respondent

|  | Year | | | | | | | | |
|---|---|---|---|---|---|---|---|---|---|
|  | 1947a | 1952k | 1954a | 1955a | 1957f | 1958m | 1959a | 1960f | |
| 18-24 Only | 48.5% | 48.0% | 50.8% | 54.1% | 43.4% | 33.3% | 42.5% | 45.2% | Saved |
|  | 10.6 | 20.0 | 26.7 | 11.9 | 41.0 | 51.3 | 27.1 | 41.9 | No change |
|  | 40.9 | 32.0 | 22.5 | 34.0 | 15.7 | 15.4 | 30.4 | 12.9 | Dissaved |
|  | (41155) | (25) | (3433) | (3758) | (83) | (39) | (3422) | (31) | Weighted N |
| 25-34 Only | 32.8 | 42.2 | 38.4 | 41.5 | 36.9 | 38.0 | 37.0 | 31.5 | Saved |
|  | 19.2 | 29.9 | 35.6 | 21.1 | 45.4 | 37.3 | 27.7 | 52.4 | No change |
|  | 48.0 | 27.9 | 26.0 | 37.4 | 17.7 | 24.6 | 35.3 | 16.1 | Dissaved |
|  | (89092) | (147) | (9679) | (9285) | (271) | (142) | (7521) | (143) | Weighted N |
| 35-44 Only | 34.3 | 45.9 | 31.8 | 33.8 | 38.7 | 28.2 | 42.4 | 30.0 | Saved |
|  | 29.1 | 32.6 | 34.8 | 36.1 | 39.6 | 52.0 | 26.1 | 45.0 | No change |
|  | 36.6 | 21.5 | 33.4 | 30.1 | 21.7 | 19.8 | 31.5 | 25.0 | Dissaved |
|  | (79588) | (135) | (11533) | (9165) | (318) | (177) | (8983) | (160) | Weighted N |
| 45-54 Only | 38.1 | 40.0 | 37.6 | 37.1 | 43.7 | 26.4 | 45.4 | 31.4 | Saved |
|  | 32.6 | 35.3 | 37.1 | 38.2 | 39.7 | 54.7 | 28.2 | 44.4 | No change |
|  | 29.3 | 24.7 | 25.3 | 24.7 | 16.6 | 18.9 | 26.5 | 24.2 | Dissaved |
|  | (113765) | (85) | (9090) | (6571) | (277) | (148) | (7513) | (153) | Weighted N |
| 55-64 Only | ** | 29.7 | 34.1 | 39.8 | 34.8 | 33.8 | 39.8 | 29.2 | Saved |
|  | ** | 47.3 | 39.4 | 35.6 | 39.7 | 47.6 | 29.3 | 50.0 | No change |
|  | ** | 23.0 | 26.5 | 24.6 | 25.5 | 18.6 | 30.9 | 20.8 | Dissaved |
|  | ** | (74) | (7422) | (5900) | (184) | (656) | (6284) | (130) | Weighted N |
| 65 and Older Only | 30.6 | 22.2 | 27.3 | 29.1 | 23.8 | 23.0 | 30.3 | 20.4 | Saved |
|  | 49.9 | 44.4 | 36.5 | 41.2 | 55.0 | 55.8 | 46.4 | 57.8 | No change |
|  | 19.5 | 33.3 | 36.2 | 29.6 | 21.2 | 21.2 | 23.3 | 21.8 | Dissaved |
|  | (30707) | (54) | (5842) | (4985) | (189) | (165) | (5359) | (147) | Weighted N |

* Code distinction not made.
ge group coded "45-64" in 1947a.
ldest age group coded "65 And Older".
ge coded for head of household only in 1947a,1954a,1955a,1957f,1958m,1959a,and 1960f.

Table 6.58

d R Save Money in the Last Twelve Months?

ge of Respondent

|  |  | | | | Year | | | | |
|---|---|---|---|---|---|---|---|---|---|
|  |  | 1961a | 1961m | 1962k | 1963f | 1964a | 1965a | 1971m | 1973i |  |
| 18-24 Only | | 30.1% | 35.1% | 37.7% | 28.0% | 31.4% | 34.0% | 24.0% | 31.6% | Saved |
| | | 32.5 | 37.8 | 45.5 | 52.7 | 49.5 | 35.1 | 47.0 | 37.3 | No change |
| | | 37.3 | 27.0 | 16.9 | 19.4 | 19.0 | 30.9 | 29.0 | 31.1 | Dissaved |
| | | (2670) | (37) | (77) | (93) | (105) | (97) | (100) | (434) | Weighted N |
| 25-34 Only | | 34.8 | 32.4 | 31.6 | 38.5 | 31.2 | 36.8 | 35.9 | 33.2 | Saved |
| | | 30.0 | 50.0 | 47.6 | 45.6 | 45.1 | 38.2 | 41.2 | 42.0 | No change |
| | | 35.2 | 17.6 | 20.7 | 15.9 | 23.7 | 25.0 | 22.9 | 24.8 | Dissaved |
| | | (6455) | (102) | (275) | (226) | (253) | (220) | (245) | (576) | Weighted N |
| 35-44 Only | | 39.2 | 44.3 | 36.8 | 36.7 | 33.8 | 39.4 | 27.5 | 31.0 | Saved |
| | | 31.9 | 39.2 | 42.9 | 43.2 | 48.9 | 47.2 | 48.8 | 45.3 | No change |
| | | 28.9 | 16.5 | 20.3 | 20.1 | 17.4 | 13.4 | 23.6 | 23.7 | Dissaved |
| | | (6742) | (79) | (266) | (294) | (311) | (246) | (258) | (503) | Weighted N |
| 45-54 Only | | 34.2 | 26.8 | 25.3 | 35.0 | 32.5 | 38.7 | 28.3 | 34.4 | Saved |
| | | 30.3 | 51.2 | 50.2 | 44.9 | 48.5 | 33.8 | 48.5 | 45.8 | No change |
| | | 35.5 | 22.0 | 24.4 | 20.1 | 19.0 | 27.6 | 23.2 | 19.8 | Dissaved |
| | | (6067) | (123) | (225) | (234) | (305) | (225) | (272) | (474) | Weighted N |
| 55-64 Only | | 37.9 | 34.9 | 33.5 | 30.2 | 33.6 | 36.5 | 23.8 | 37.5 | Saved |
| | | 37.6 | 48.8 | 45.2 | 52.3 | 48.5 | 43.6 | 57.1 | 43.4 | No change |
| | | 24.5 | 16.3 | 21.3 | 17.6 | 17.9 | 19.9 | 19.0 | 19.0 | Dissaved |
| | | (4202) | (86) | (188) | (199) | (235) | (181) | (210) | (373) | Weighted N |
| 65-74 Only | | 16.3 | 13.8 | 15.2 | 25.6 | 28.5 | 31.9 | 18.7 | 27.7 | Saved |
| | | 57.6 | 65.1 | 55.2 | 54.4 | 52.5 | 49.2 | 67.9 | 59.4 | No change |
| | | 26.2 | 21.1 | 29.7 | 20.0 | 19.0 | 18.9 | 13.4 | 12.9 | Dissaved |
| | | (2680) | (109) | (145) | (215) | (179) | (185) | (134) | (249) | Weighted N |
| 75 And Older Only | | 17.5 | ** | 19.5 | ** | 18.8 | ** | 22.0 | 17.0 | Saved |
| | | 37.3 | ** | 62.2 | ** | 58.8 | ** | 64.6 | 60.0 | No change |
| | | 45.3 | ** | 18.3 | ** | 22.4 | ** | 13.4 | 23.0 | Dissaved |
| | | (1317) | ** | (82) | ** | (85) | ** | (82) | (100) | Weighted N |

Code distinction not made.

dest age group coded "65 And Older" in 1961m, 1963f, and 1965a.

e coded for head of household only in 1961a and 1961m, and for head and wife only in
1962k, 1964a, and 1965a.

ble 6.59
d R Save Money in the Last Twelve Months?
come of Respondent

|  | Year | | | | | | | | |
|---|---|---|---|---|---|---|---|---|---|
|  | 1947a | 1952k | 1954a | 1955a | 1957f | 1958m | 1959a | 1960f | |
| Income 1 (0-16%) | 27.3% | 5.9% | 25.0% | 26.6% | 8.9% | 10.3% | 34.1% | 12.4% | Saved |
|  | 30.2 | 29.4 | 39.4 | 37.5 | 60.3 | 65.4 | 36.5 | 60.5 | No change |
|  | 42.4 | 64.7 | 35.6 | 35.9 | 30.8 | 24.3 | 29.4 | 27.1 | Dissaved |
|  | (43193) | (17) | (7856) | (5994) | (224) | (243) | (5765) | (210) | Weighted N |
| Income 2 (17-33%) | 35.0 | 22.6 | 33.1 | 40.5 | 25.9 | 19.4 | 30.0 | 15.8 | Saved |
|  | 29.1 | 45.3 | 38.0 | 32.3 | 56.0 | 55.5 | 34.8 | 61.2 | No change |
|  | 36.0 | 32.1 | 28.9 | 27.2 | 18.0 | 25.2 | 35.2 | 23.0 | Dissaved |
|  | (83294) | (106) | (6809) | (5972) | (316) | (155) | (4222) | (196) | Weighted N |
| Income 3 (34-67%) | 34.9 | 41.3 | 36.0 | 38.7 | 44.5 | 29.4 | 39.6 | 29.4 | Saved |
|  | 24.5 | 28.8 | 35.2 | 29.7 | 37.1 | 51.2 | 33.5 | 45.5 | No change |
|  | 40.5 | 29.9 | 28.8 | 31.6 | 18.4 | 19.4 | 26.9 | 25.1 | Dissaved |
|  | (220082) | (184) | (18314) | (15616) | (515) | (500) | (17624) | (402) | Weighted N |
| Income 4 (68-95%) | 38.8 | 46.5 | 41.0 | 38.2 | 63.3 | 50.5 | 46.1 | 44.4 | Saved |
|  | 28.8 | 35.2 | 31.2 | 29.6 | 21.9 | 33.6 | 22.7 | 40.1 | No change |
|  | 32.4 | 18.2 | 27.8 | 32.2 | 14.8 | 15.9 | 31.2 | 15.6 | Dissaved |
|  | (80986) | (159) | (18423) | (18660) | (196) | (283) | (15343) | (302) | Weighted N |
| Income 5 (96-100%) | 39.9 | 65.0 | 37.5 | 39.1 | 65.5 | 60.6 | 45.7 | 73.7 | Saved |
|  | 34.2 | 30.0 | 34.3 | 36.9 | 17.2 | 28.3 | 28.0 | 17.9 | No change |
|  | 25.8 | 5.0 | 28.1 | 24.1 | 17.2 | 11.1 | 26.3 | 8.4 | Dissaved |
|  | (22970) | (40) | (3974) | (3958) | (29) | (99) | (5989) | (95) | Weighted N |

Table 6.60
Did R Save Money in the Last Twelve Months?
Income of Respondent

|  | Year | | | | | | | | |
|---|---|---|---|---|---|---|---|---|---|
|  | 1961a | 1961m | 1962k | 1963f | 1964a | 1965a | 1971m | 1973i |  |
| Income 1 (0-16%) | 22.3% | 8.9% | 7.7% | 7.7% | 9.8% | 16.9% | 7.3% | 11.1% | Saved |
|  | 35.8 | 69.2 | 65.2 | 69.6 | 69.2 | 58.5 | 76.2 | 59.2 | No change |
|  | 41.9 | 21.9 | 27.1 | 22.7 | 21.0 | 24.6 | 16.6 | 29.7 | Dissaved |
|  | (2827) | (146) | (181) | (207) | (214) | (118) | (193) | (377) | Weighted N |
| Income 2 (17-33%) | 23.0 | 18.4 | 13.1 | 20.2 | 15.6 | 24.7 | 16.0 | 22.0 | Saved |
|  | 41.5 | 62.6 | 55.9 | 53.4 | 58.2 | 57.7 | 60.1 | 53.6 | No change |
|  | 35.5 | 19.0 | 31.1 | 26.5 | 26.2 | 17.6 | 23.9 | 24.4 | Dissaved |
|  | (4757) | (174) | (222) | (223) | (237) | (182) | (243) | (431) | Weighted N |
| Income 3 (34-67%) | .33.6 | 35.4 | 31.6 | 33.2 | 30.5 | 31.4 | 27.9 | 29.2 | Saved |
|  | 33.0 | 45.0 | 49.2 | 48.2 | 51.2 | 46.5 | 48.2 | 48.4 | No change |
|  | 33.5 | 19.6 | 19.3 | 18.7 | 18.2 | 22.2 | 23.9 | 22.5 | Dissaved |
|  | (12635) | (347) | (488) | (407) | (521) | (370) | (469) | (761) | Weighted N |
| Income 4 (68-95%) | 39.6 | 56.6 | 50.2 | 49.8 | 47.3 | 46.4 | 44.3 | 45.2 | Saved |
|  | 32.9 | 30.9 | 32.7 | 37.6 | 35.3 | 28.9 | 34.2 | 34.3 | No change |
|  | 27.5 | 12.6 | 17.1 | 12.5 | 17.4 | 24.6 | 21.5 | 20.4 | Dissaved |
|  | (8699) | (175) | (281) | (327) | (431) | (394) | (298) | (842) | Weighted N |
| Income 5 (96-100%) | 48.7 | 59.4 | 51.7 | 69.7 | 58.1 | 60.6 | 60.4 | 54.2 | Saved |
|  | 32.5 | 25.0 | 28.3 | 19.7 | 27.0 | 26.3 | 30.2 | 28.4 | No change |
|  | 18.8 | 15.6 | 20.0 | 10.5 | 14.9 | 13.1 | 9.4 | 17.4 | Dissaved |
|  | (1358) | (32) | (60) | (76) | (74) | (99) | (53) | (201) | Weighted N |

able 6.61
 the Amount of R's Savings Satisfactory?
tal Population

JESTION: How do you feel about the amount of money you now have saved up--is it far too little,fairly
tisfactory, fully adequate,or what? (We have discussed various forms of savings and reserve funds, money in
nks, bonds and stocks. How do you feel about the total amount of savings and assets you have accumulated--
 it less than adequate, adequate, fully adequate, or what?) (Are you satisfied or dissatisfied with the
esent amount of your savings and reserve funds?)

|                      | Year |       |       |       |       |       |       |
|----------------------|------|-------|-------|-------|-------|-------|-------|
|                      | 1952k | 1960f | 1961a | 1962f | 1965m | 1969a | 1970a |
| Satisfactory (5)     | 23.8% | 26.2% | 20.5% | 33.3% | 30.2% | 33.4% | 35.2% |
| Pro-con (3)          | 3.0   | 0.7   | 0.4   | 0.8   | 2.2   | **    | **    |
| Not satisfactory (1) | 30.9  | 34.8  | 28.9  | 36.2  | 30.3  | 47.7  | 38.3  |
| No savings           | 41.7  | 38.0  | 50.2  | 29.2  | 36.7  | 18.5  | 24.6  |
| Don't know           | 0.6   | 0.4   | **    | 0.4   | 0.6   | 0.3   | 1.9   |
| Total                | 100%  | 100%  | 100%  | 100%  | 100%  | 100%  | 100%  |
| Weighted N           | 903   | 1356  | 35939 | 1269  | 1570  | 11291 | 2560  |
| Unweighted N         | 903   | 1356  | 1574  | 1269  | 1570  | 2241  | 2560  |
| Mean                 | 2.75  | 2.72  | 2.66  | 2.92  | 3.00  | 2.65  | 2.91  |
| Standard Deviation   | 1.93  | 1.97  | 1.96  | 1.99  | 1.96  | 1.97  | 2.00  |

 Code distinction not made.

gure 6.18
tisfaction With Savings--Total Population

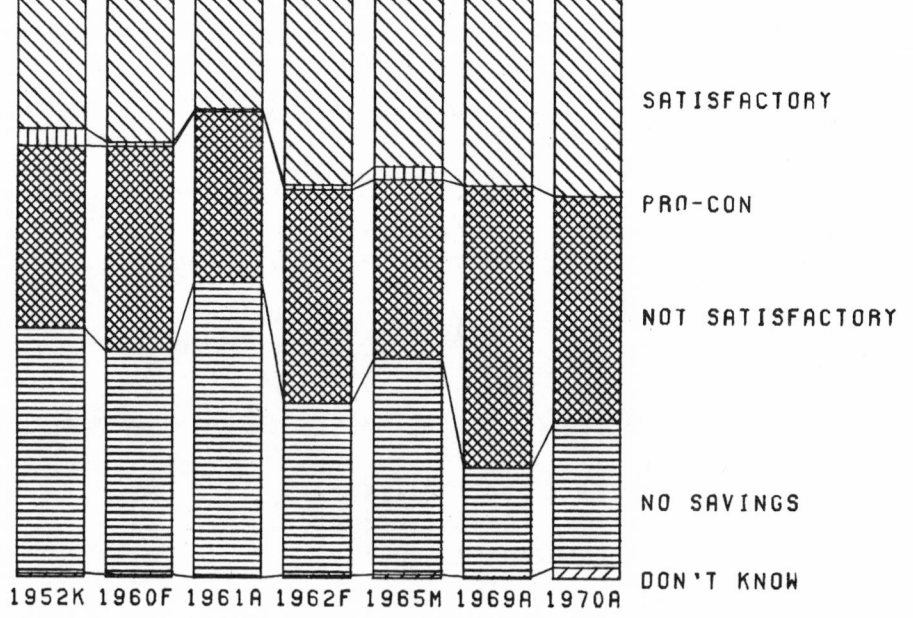

SATISFACTORY

PRO-CON

NOT SATISFACTORY

NO SAVINGS

DON'T KNOW

1952K 1960F 1961A 1962F 1965M 1969A 1970A

Personal Economic Outlook

ble 6.62
the Amount of R's Savings Satisfactory?
x of Respondent

|  | | 1952k | 1960f | 1961a | Year 1962f | 1965m | 1969a | 1970a | |
|---|---|---|---|---|---|---|---|---|---|
| Males Only | | 25.1% | 24.9% | 20.8% | 32.2% | 32.9% | 34.2% | 35.5% | Satisfactory |
| | | 2.5 | 0.4 | 0.3 | 1.0 | 2.3 | ** | ** | Pro-con |
| | | 28.9 | 35.6 | 30.5 | 39.1 | 31.3 | 50.6 | 39.9 | Not satisfactory |
| | | 43.4 | 38.6 | 48.3 | 27.8 | 33.0 | 15.0 | 22.7 | No savings |
| | | 0.0 | 0.6 | ** | 0.0 | 0.6 | 0.3 | 1.9 | Don't know |
| | | (394) | (531) | (29136) | (594) | (1132) | (8129) | (1814) | Weighted N |
| Females Only | | 22.8 | 27.3 | 19.1 | 34.4 | 23.3 | 31.8 | 32.8 | Satisfactory |
| | | 3.3 | 0.8 | 0.8 | 0.6 | 2.1 | ** | ** | Pro-con |
| | | 32.4 | 33.4 | 22.4 | 33.8 | 27.7 | 39.8 | 35.0 | Not satisfactory |
| | | 40.5 | 38.4 | 57.7 | 30.5 | 46.2 | 27.9 | 30.2 | No savings |
| | | 1.0 | 0.1 | ** | 0.7 | 0.7 | 0.5 | 2.0 | Don't know |
| | | (509) | (730) | (6695) | (675) | (437) | (3078) | (708) | Weighted N |

Code distinction not made.
x coded for head of household and wife only in 1962f and 1965m.

ble 6.63
ce of Respondent

|  | | 1952k | 1960f | 1961a | 1962f | 1965m | 1969a | 1970a | |
|---|---|---|---|---|---|---|---|---|---|
| Whites Only | | 26.2% | 28.6% | 22.9% | 35.8% | 33.1% | 36.6% | 37.7% | Satisfactory |
| | | 3.2 | 0.7 | 0.4 | 0.9 | 2.4 | ** | ** | Pro-con |
| | | 32.5 | 36.7 | 31.7 | 37.0 | 32.3 | 49.9 | 39.2 | Not satisfactory |
| | | 37.4 | 33.7 | 45.0 | 25.9 | 31.5 | 13.1 | 21.2 | No savings |
| | | 0.6 | 0.3 | ** | 0.5 | 0.7 | 0.4 | 2.0 | Don't know |
| | | (804) | (1074) | (31338) | (1109) | (1351) | (9908) | (2236) | Weighted N |
| Blacks Only | | 4.4 | 6.3 | 4.8 | 14.3 | 12.8 | 11.1 | 16.6 | Satisfactory |
| | | 1.1 | 0.0 | 0.0 | 0.0 | 1.1 | ** | ** | Pro-con |
| | | 18.7 | 18.3 | 8.6 | 30.1 | 17.6 | 31.5 | 31.8 | Not satisfactory |
| | | 75.8 | 74.6 | 86.6 | 55.6 | 67.9 | 57.5 | 50.2 | No savings |
| | | 0.0 | 0.8 | ** | 0.0 | 0.5 | 0.0 | 1.4 | Don't know |
| | | (91) | (126) | (4349) | (133) | (187) | (1122) | (277) | Weighted N |

Code distinction not made.

Personal Economic Outlook

Table 6.64

Is the Amount of R's Savings Satisfactory?

Education of Respondent

|  | Year | | | | | | | |
|---|---|---|---|---|---|---|---|---|
|  | 1952k | 1960f | 1961a | 1962f | 1965m | 1969a | 1970a | |
| Grade School Only | 16.4% | 19.0% | 15.3% | 20.8% | 19.0% | 28.7% | 33.1% | Satisfactory |
|  | 2.5 | 0.5 | 0.0 | 1.9 | 1.4 | ** | ** | Pro-con |
|  | 19.8 | 21.1 | 17.8 | 29.0 | 19.0 | 34.2 | 21.7 | Not satisfactory |
|  | 60.3 | 59.1 | 66.9 | 47.6 | 60.1 | 36.6 | 42.8 | No savings |
|  | 0.8 | 0.3 | ** | 0.7 | 0.5 | 0.4 | 2.5 | Don't know |
|  | (353) | (384) | (12200) | (269) | (421) | (2929) | (568) | Weighted N |
| High School Only | 24.9 | 25.8 | 19.1 | 35.2 | 31.5 | 32.8 | 33.4 | Satisfactory |
|  | 3.8 | 0.8 | 0.5 | 0.5 | 2.5 | ** | ** | Pro-con |
|  | 37.0 | 39.2 | 31.0 | 37.5 | 31.8 | 49.8 | 41.9 | Not satisfactory |
|  | 33.8 | 33.9 | 49.4 | 26.4 | 33.1 | 17.0 | 23.3 | No savings |
|  | 0.5 | 0.3 | ** | 0.4 | 1.2 | 0.4 | 1.5 | Don't know |
|  | (370) | (623) | (15687) | (779) | (607) | (4976) | (1211) | Weighted N |
| College Only | 36.9 | 39.9 | 31.6 | 41.6 | 40.1 | 40.0 | 39.9 | Satisfactory |
|  | 2.3 | 0.4 | 0.8 | 0.5 | 2.9 | ** | ** | Pro-con |
|  | 40.9 | 43.0 | 43.2 | 41.1 | 40.4 | 55.7 | 44.9 | Not satisfactory |
|  | 19.9 | 16.2 | 24.4 | 16.8 | 16.6 | 4.4 | 13.2 | No savings |
|  | 0.0 | 0.4 | ** | 0.0 | 0.0 | 0.0 | 2.0 | Don't know |
|  | (176) | (228) | (7620) | (214) | (379) | (2733) | (740) | Weighted N |

** Code distinction not made.

Education coded for head of household only in 1952k, 1961a, and 1965m, and for head and wife only in 1960f, 1962f, 1969a, and 1970a.

able 6.65

s the Amount of R's Savings Satisfactory?

ge of Respondent

|  | 1952k | 1960f | 1961a | 1962f | 1965m | 1969a | 1970a |  |
|---|---|---|---|---|---|---|---|---|
| 18-24 Only | 5.7% | 22.2% | 8.2% | 27.7% | 19.5% | 24.9% | 25.8% | Satisfactory |
|  | 5.7 | 0.0 | 0.0 | 1.0 | 3.3 | ** | ** | Pro-con |
|  | 34.0 | 37.0 | 16.5 | 24.8 | 32.5 | 56.6 | 43.8 | Not satisfactory |
|  | 52.8 | 40.7 | 75.4 | 46.5 | 44.7 | 18.6 | 29.2 | No savings |
|  | 1.9 | 0.0 | ** | 0.0 | 0.0 | 0.0 | 1.2 | Don't know |
|  | (53) | (27) | (2230) | (101) | (123) | (1061) | (260) | Weighted N |
| 25-34 Only | 16.7 | 25.0 | 15.3 | 33.9 | 29.0 | 29.9 | 27.7 | Satisfactory |
|  | 1.8 | 0.0 | 0.3 | 0.4 | 2.0 | ** | ** | Pro-con |
|  | 45.4 | 30.9 | 32.4 | 37.7 | 34.8 | 54.6 | 45.5 | Not satisfactory |
|  | 36.1 | 44.1 | 52.0 | 27.6 | 33.4 | 15.3 | 26.2 | No savings |
|  | 0.0 | 0.0 | ** | 0.4 | 0.7 | 0.2 | 0.6 | Don't know |
|  | (227) | (136) | (6469) | (239) | (293) | (2233) | (470) | Weighted N |
| 35-44 Only | 23.2 | 20.4 | 19.2 | 29.8 | 29.6 | 30.8 | 28.9 | Satisfactory |
|  | 3.3 | 0.0 | 0.3 | 0.9 | 1.9 | ** | ** | Pro-con |
|  | 29.5 | 36.2 | 32.6 | 41.4 | 38.1 | 52.0 | 43.9 | Not satisfactory |
|  | 43.6 | 42.8 | 47.9 | 27.9 | 30.5 | 17.2 | 26.2 | No savings |
|  | 0.4 | 0.7 | ** | 0.0 | 0.0 | 0.0 | 1.0 | Don't know |
|  | (241) | (152) | (8529) | (215) | (318) | (1929) | (485) | Weighted N |
| 45-54 Only | 28.8 | 19.4 | 19.1 | 21.6 | 34.2 | 29.3 | 32.5 | Satisfactory |
|  | 2.6 | 0.0 | 0.6 | 0.6 | 2.9 | ** | ** | Pro-con |
|  | 23.1 | 41.7 | 33.9 | 45.7 | 28.7 | 51.8 | 42.8 | Not satisfactory |
|  | 44.9 | 38.9 | 46.4 | 32.1 | 33.9 | 18.4 | 22.8 | No savings |
|  | 0.6 | 0.0 | ** | 0.0 | 0.3 | 0.4 | 2.0 | Don't know |
|  | (156) | (144) | (7170) | (162) | (310) | (1892) | (505) | Weighted N |
| 55-64 Only | 33.6 | 23.2 | 25.9 | 38.4 | 39.1 | 38.0 | 42.5 | Satisfactory |
|  | 3.5 | 1.6 | 0.4 | 0.8 | 2.5 | ** | ** | Pro-con |
|  | 29.2 | 32.0 | 23.2 | 36.8 | 24.4 | 41.4 | 34.1 | Not satisfactory |
|  | 32.7 | 43.2 | 50.5 | 23.3 | 32.8 | 20.4 | 21.6 | No savings |
|  | 0.9 | 0.0 | ** | 0.8 | 1.3 | 0.2 | 1.7 | Don't know |
|  | (113) | (125) | (5850) | (391) | (238) | (1716) | (402) | Weighted N |
| 65-74 Only | 32.1 | 38.3 | 28.4 | 42.7 | 24.9 | 40.3 | 52.8 | Satisfactory |
|  | 3.7 | 0.0 | 0.7 | 1.0 | 1.4 | ** | ** | Pro-con |
|  | 15.6 | 20.6 | 23.5 | 26.2 | 22.5 | 37.9 | 18.7 | Not satisfactory |
|  | 47.7 | 39.7 | 47.3 | 30.1 | 49.8 | 21.2 | 24.7 | No savings |
|  | 0.9 | 1.4 | ** | 0.0 | 1.4 | 0.6 | 3.7 | Don't know |
|  | (109) | (141) | (3523) | (103) | (285) | (1461) | (267) | Weighted N |
| 75 And Older Only | ** | ** | 30.8 | 36.0 | ** | 49.0 | 54.8 | Satisfactory |
|  | ** | ** | 0.0 | 2.0 | ** | ** | ** | Pro-con |
|  | ** | ** | 24.1 | 18.0 | ** | 28.1 | 14.8 | Not satisfactory |
|  | ** | ** | 45.1 | 42.0 | ** | 21.9 | 23.7 | No savings |
|  | ** | ** | ** | 2.0 | ** | 1.0 | 6.7 | Don't know |
|  | ** | ** | (1942) | (50) | ** | (864) | (135) | Weighted N |

Code distinction not made.

ungest age group coded "Less Than 25" in 1965m.

lest age group coded "65 And Older" in 1952k,1960f,and 1965m.

 coded for head of household only in 1952k,1960f,and 1961a, and for head and wife only in 1962f,1969a,and 1970a.

Personal Economic Outlook

Table 6.66

Is the Amount of R's Savings Satisfactory?

Income of Respondent

| | 1952k | 1960f | 1961a | 1962f | 1965m | 1969a | 1970a | |
|---|---|---|---|---|---|---|---|---|
| | | | | Year | | | | |
| Income 1 (0-16%) | 5.7% | 14.9% | 10.8% | 19.0% | 9.2% | 26.5% | 30.2% | Satisfactory |
| | 3.4 | 0.5 | 0.0 | 2.2 | 2.7 | ** | ** | Pro-con |
| | 9.1 | 16.2 | 11.7 | 17.9 | 13.0 | 29.7 | 22.8 | Not satisfactory |
| | 80.7 | 67.6 | 77.5 | 59.8 | 74.3 | 43.2 | 44.0 | No savings |
| | 1.1 | 0.9 | ** | 1.1 | 0.8 | 0.7 | 3.0 | Don't know |
| | (88) | (222) | (6854) | (184) | (261) | (2412) | (470) | Weighted N |
| Income 2 (17-33%) | 15.5 | 16.6 | 13.3 | 25.4 | 16.4 | 29.7 | 29.7 | Satisfactory |
| | 1.6 | 0.0 | 0.7 | 0.9 | 1.6 | ** | ** | Pro-con |
| | 24.2 | 26.1 | 21.0 | 31.3 | 24.4 | 46.0 | 29.4 | Not satisfactory |
| | 58.3 | 57.3 | 65.1 | 42.4 | 57.6 | 24.0 | 38.8 | No savings |
| | 0.4 | 0.0 | ** | 0.0 | 0.0 | 0.4 | 2.2 | Don't know |
| | (252) | (199) | (7548) | (224) | (250) | (2141) | (418) | Weighted N |
| Income 3 (34-67%) | 20.7 | 23.1 | 18.6 | 33.4 | 28.0 | 31.5 | 32.9 | Satisfactory |
| | 3.4 | 1.0 | 0.3 | 0.7 | 1.7 | ** | ** | Pro-con |
| | 37.3 | 37.7 | 32.9 | 38.7 | 38.2 | 56.2 | 41.0 | Not satisfactory |
| | 38.0 | 38.0 | 48.2 | 27.0 | 31.2 | 12.2 | 24.5 | No savings |
| | 0.7 | 0.2 | ** | 0.2 | 0.9 | 0.1 | 1.6 | Don't know |
| | (295) | (403) | (12823) | (452) | (468) | (3720) | (885) | Weighted N |
| Income 4 (68-95%) | 37.2 | 33.3 | 35.8 | 40.3 | 46.8 | 43.0 | 41.8 | Satisfactory |
| | 4.6 | 0.0 | 0.6 | 0.3 | 3.2 | ** | ** | Pro-con |
| | 40.8 | 48.0 | 44.3 | 51.1 | 36.4 | 53.3 | 50.0 | Not satisfactory |
| | 17.3 | 18.3 | 19.3 | 8.3 | 13.2 | 3.3 | 6.5 | No savings |
| | 0.0 | 0.3 | ** | 0.0 | 0.4 | 0.3 | 1.8 | Don't know |
| | (196) | (306) | (7443) | (315) | (506) | (2582) | (680) | Weighted N |
| Income 5 (96-100%) | 63.4 | 54.1 | 45.6 | 70.9 | 78.1 | 50.2 | 55.1 | Satisfactory |
| | 0.0 | 3.1 | 0.0 | 0.0 | 0.0 | ** | ** | Pro-con |
| | 34.1 | 36.7 | 39.7 | 23.6 | 15.6 | 49.8 | 44.9 | Not satisfactory |
| | 2.4 | 6.1 | 14.6 | 3.6 | 6.3 | 0.0 | 0.0 | No savings |
| | 0.0 | 0.0 | ** | 1.8 | 0.0 | 0.0 | 0.0 | Don't know |
| | (41) | (98) | (1271) | (55) | (32) | (412) | (107) | Weighted N |

** Code distinction not made.

Chapter 7. National Economic Outlook

One of the longest and most publicized series to arise from the national sample surveys carried out by the Survey Research Center is the Index of Consumer Sentiment, based on a combination of responses to five questions predictive of changes in discretionary consumer expenditures. Two components of the Index, involving assessments of change in the family financial situation during the previous year and likely changes in the year to come, were presented in the preceding chapter. The remaining items in the Index shift the context from the somewhat idiosyncratic family situation evaluations of the broader national economic climate, the object of this chapter.

We begin with three items dealing with assessments of recent and future business conditions. The first of these items, asking whether the respondent expects good times or bad financially for the nation as a whole in the next twelve months, has been measured since 1947 and is also a component of the summary Index. The trajectory shown by this item over the past thirty years bears some rough resemblance to those for the two Index items of the preceding chapter, in that there is an upward march in consumer confidence through the 1950s, marred chiefly by a major trough associated with the recession of 1958, and a gloom of stunning proportions in the 1970s. However, in this series the peak of optimism is reached by the middle of the 1960s, and confidence is plummeting by 1970.

The other two series about business conditions—one "actual", dealing with change in the past year, and the other asking for expectations as to changes that will have been consummated by a year hence—also show higher peaks toward the middle of the series, although the finer timing is not necessarily the same. For the comparison of current business conditions with those of the preceding year, the highest segment is again the middle 1960s, but the greatest sustained optimism about the state of business occurred in the wake of the 1958 recession and had nearly dissipated by 1966.

The next trio of measurements test consumer estimates as to whether the current time is a good one to make major purchases, such as a house, a car, or large household durable goods. The latter item also figures as another component of the Index of Consumer Sentiment. All three of these series show peaks for the total time span achieved about 1964 or 1965, but the general cast of results after that time varies somewhat. In both car and house series, caution is generally more marked in the 1970s than in the 1950s, consonant with earlier data concerning personal financial situations. The household durable series in the 1970s is less obviously restrained relative to the 1950s, although part of this impression flows from the existence of earlier and hence lower observations for the durables question.

Apart from a major spike of concern about inflation at the outset of the Korean War, the item asking whether the respondent expects prices to rise or decline in the coming year shows a steady upward march over the first twenty years of the series, with gloom about more price increases continuing with little respite after the mid-1960s.

Because of the nature of all of these items and their focus on a common "objective" economic climate, the responses from different social groupings generally move in tandem. However, where business conditions and the timing of prospective purchases are concerned, women, blacks, and the less well educated are usually less optimistic than contrasting segments. These modest differences largely disappear where judgments as to likely inflation are concerned; indeed, in recent years the well-educated have been more apprehensive about price changes.

We close the chapter with a graphic display of the behavior of the Index of Consumer Sentiment over the total period for which it has been calculated. For technical reasons associated with data retrieval problems, the full series has a density of observations which goes beyond what we have been able to present here for its components. For a discussion of the construction of the full Index, see Richard T. Curtin, "Index Construction: An Appraisal of the Index of Consumer Sentiment," in L. Mandell, G. Katona, J. Morgan, and J. Schmiedeskamp, Surveys of Consumers 1971-72: Contributions to Behavioral Economics (Ann Arbor: Institute for Social Research, 1973).

Table 7.1
Does R Expect Good Times or Bad Times in the Next Twelve Months?
Total Population

QUESTION: Considering the country as a whole, do you think we will have good times or bad times or what during the next twelve months?

| | | Year | | | | | | | | | |
|---|---|---|---|---|---|---|---|---|---|---|---|
| | | 1947a | 1948a | 1949a | 1952k | 1953m | 1954a | 1955a | 1956m | 1957f | 1958a |
| Good | (5) | 51.0% | 39.2% | 23.8% | 25.9% | 30.1% | 31.9% | 55.6% | 57.9% | 49.9% | 22.1% |
| Good(qualified) | (4) | 10.6 | 12.4 | 25.8 | 16.8 | 18.0 | 19.4 | 15.2 | 16.7 | 16.8 | 12.8 |
| Pro-con | (3) | 13.8 | 6.6 | 14.1 | 7.4 | 10.6 | 10.4 | 6.1 | 5.0 | 5.5 | 9.9 |
| Bad(qualified) | (2) | 5.4 | ** | 17.0 | 5.4 | 8.9 | 11.8 | 6.0 | 2.1 | 4.6 | 17.9 |
| Bad | (1) | 19.3 | 28.0 | 9.3 | 10.6 | 10.2 | 18.7 | 8.2 | 3.3 | 6.3 | 27.2 |
| Don't know/depends | | ** | 13.8 | 10.0 | 33.9 | 22.1 | 7.7 | 8.8 | 14.9 | 16.9 | 10.0 |
| Total | | 100% | 100% | 100% | 100% | 100% | 100% | 100% | 100% | 100% | 100% |
| Weighted N | | 814676 | 878647 | 914210 | 919 | 1005 | 73422 | 83189 | 1426 | 1335 | 90079 |
| Unweighted N | | 2497 | 3116 | 3210 | 919 | 1005 | 2208 | 2606 | 1426 | 1335 | 2812 |
| Mean | | 3.69 | 3.40 | 3.42 | 3.64 | 3.63 | 3.37 | 4.14 | 4.46 | 4.20 | 2.83 |
| Standard Deviation | | 1.58 | 1.76 | 1.33 | 1.46 | 1.42 | 1.55 | 1.32 | 0.99 | 1.24 | 1.58 |

Table 7.2

| | | 1959a | 1960a | 1961a | 1962n | 1963m | 1964a | 1965a | 1966a | 1967a | 1968a |
|---|---|---|---|---|---|---|---|---|---|---|---|
| Good | (5) | 47.2% | 64.6% | 34.1% | 47.9% | 51.7% | 57.5% | 63.9% | 67.4% | 51.9% | 44.9% |
| Good(qualified) | (4) | 14.2 | 12.3 | 20.5 | 16.5 | 14.4 | 15.0 | 11.8 | 7.8 | 11.4 | 12.0 |
| Pro-con | (3) | 8.9 | 4.7 | 8.7 | 6.5 | 5.7 | 5.2 | 3.3 | 2.2 | 4.9 | 6.5 |
| Bad(qualified) | (2) | 7.6 | 2.3 | 7.1 | 3.8 | 3.6 | 2.9 | 2.4 | 2.0 | 4.8 | 4.7 |
| Bad | (1) | 11.5 | 5.3 | 12.1 | 5.9 | 5.3 | 7.2 | 4.9 | 8.2 | 11.6 | 13.3 |
| Don't know/depends | | 10.6 | 10.7 | 17.5 | 19.3 | 19.3 | 12.3 | 13.7 | 12.3 | 15.4 | 18.6 |
| Total | | 100% | 100% | 100% | 100% | 100% | 100% | 100% | 100% | 100% | 100% |
| Weighted N | | 87713 | 2875 | 48960 | 1281 | 1309 | 1525 | 1337 | 2219 | 3661 | 15491 |
| Unweighted N | | 2724 | 2875 | 1937 | 1281 | 1309 | 1525 | 1337 | 2219 | 3112 | 2663 |
| Mean | | 3.87 | 4.44 | 3.70 | 4.20 | 4.28 | 4.28 | 4.48 | 4.42 | 4.03 | 3.87 |
| Standard Deviation | | 1.45 | 1.10 | 1.44 | 1.22 | 1.19 | 1.23 | 1.08 | 1.25 | 1.46 | 1.52 |

Table 7.3

| | | 1969a | 1970a | 1971m | 1972f | 1973c | 1974q | 1975q | 1976m |
|---|---|---|---|---|---|---|---|---|---|
| Good | (5) | 52.8% | 23.5% | 25.5% | 31.8% | 28.0% | 6.6% | 18.4% | 35.3% |
| Good(qualified) | (4) | 10.9 | 13.7 | 14.5 | 12.8 | 8.1 | 6.7 | 16.9 | 12.3 |
| Pro-con | (3) | 5.5 | 8.2 | 8.0 | 9.1 | 9.1 | 8.0 | 12.6 | 11.5 |
| Bad(qualified) | (2) | 2.3 | 7.2 | 5.3 | 5.0 | 6.9 | 8.4 | 8.8 | 4.4 |
| Bad | (1) | 11.1 | 31.6 | 24.8 | 21.7 | 29.8 | 59.2 | 32.4 | 22.7 |
| Don't know/depends | | 17.4 | 15.8 | 21.9 | 19.5 | 18.1 | 11.1 | 10.9 | 13.8 |
| Total | | 100% | 100% | 100% | 100% | 100% | 100% | 100% | 100% |
| Weighted N | | 11423 | 2526 | 1272 | 1279 | 1329 | 2940 | 2860 | 123970 |
| Unweighted N | | 2274 | 2526 | 1272 | 1279 | 1329 | 1496 | 1488 | 1104 |
| Mean | | 4.11 | 2.88 | 3.13 | 3.35 | 2.97 | 1.80 | 2.77 | 3.39 |
| Standard Deviation | | 1.42 | 1.69 | 1.68 | 1.66 | 1.73 | 1.30 | 1.59 | 1.65 |

National Economic Outlook

Figure 7.1
od Times or Bad Times--Total Population

National Economic Outlook

Table 7.4

Does R Expect Good Times or Bad Times in the Next Twelve Months?

Sex of Respondent

|  | Year | | | | | | | | | | |
|---|---|---|---|---|---|---|---|---|---|---|---|
|  | 1947a | 1948a | 1949a | 1952k | 1953m | 1954a | 1955a | 1956m | 1957f | 1958a | |
| Males Only | 54.4% | 44.4% | 26.7% | 31.1% | 31.9% | 32.1% | 57.6% | 61.6% | 55.0% | 24.0% | Good |
|  | 10.9 | 13.2 | 27.5 | 16.9 | 20.5 | 20.0 | 15.0 | 16.6 | 19.6 | 13.9 | Good(qualified) |
|  | 12.1 | 6.7 | 14.4 | 9.7 | 12.7 | 10.7 | 6.8 | 5.2 | 5.2 | 11.0 | Pro-con |
|  | 5.0 | ** | 16.3 | 5.7 | 9.2 | 11.9 | 5.9 | 2.3 | 4.0 | 18.6 | Bad(qualified) |
|  | 17.7 | 24.4 | 7.7 | 9.7 | 10.7 | 18.4 | 7.8 | 2.9 | 5.6 | 25.8 | Bad |
|  | ** | 11.3 | 7.5 | 26.9 | 15.0 | 6.9 | 6.9 | 11.6 | 10.6 | 6.8 | Don't know/depends |
|  | (552903) | (562634) | (553096) | (402) | (448) | (50859) | (54379) | (658) | (576) | (57784) | Weighted N |
| Females Only | 43.9 | 30.0 | 19.4 | 21.9 | 28.7 | 31.6 | 51.8 | 54.8 | 46.0 | 18.6 | Good |
|  | 9.9 | 10.9 | 23.3 | 16.6 | 16.0 | 18.2 | 15.7 | 16.8 | 14.6 | 10.7 | Good(qualified) |
|  | 17.3 | 6.4 | 13.7 | 5.6 | 9.0 | 9.6 | 4.9 | 5.0 | 5.7 | 8.4 | Pro-con |
|  | 6.2 | ** | 18.0 | 5.2 | 8.6 | 11.5 | 6.1 | 2.0 | 5.1 | 16.9 | Bad(qualified) |
|  | 22.7 | 34.5 | 11.7 | 11.2 | 9.9 | 19.5 | 9.2 | 3.7 | 6.9 | 30.1 | Bad |
|  | ** | 18.2 | 13.8 | 39.5 | 27.8 | 9.7 | 12.3 | 17.9 | 21.7 | 15.3 | Don't know/depends |
|  | (261413) | (316013) | (361204) | (517) | (557) | (22563) | (27807) | (767) | (759) | (30999) | Weighted N |

Table 7.5

|  | 1959a | 1960a | 1961a | 1962n | 1963m | 1964a | 1965a | 1966a | 1967a | 1968a | |
|---|---|---|---|---|---|---|---|---|---|---|---|
| Males Only | 50.5% | 68.8% | 35.2% | 54.5% | 58.5% | 59.6% | 66.0% | 72.3% | 56.5% | 49.7% | Good |
|  | 15.1 | 12.1 | 21.6 | 17.6 | 14.5 | 15.5 | 13.3 | 8.3 | 11.8 | 12.5 | Good(qualified) |
|  | 9.7 | 4.3 | 8.8 | 6.6 | 6.1 | 5.4 | 2.6 | 2.3 | 4.9 | 6.3 | Pro-con |
|  | 6.6 | 2.4 | 7.7 | 3.7 | 3.7 | 2.8 | 2.1 | 1.5 | 4.4 | 4.6 | Bad(qualified) |
|  | 10.9 | 4.1 | 11.1 | 5.2 | 5.0 | 6.6 | 4.3 | 6.9 | 10.7 | 12.2 | Bad |
|  | 7.2 | 8.3 | 15.6 | 12.4 | 12.3 | 10.3 | 11.5 | 8.7 | 11.6 | 14.7 | Don't know/depends |
|  | (56122) | (1933) | (39955) | (573) | (545) | (1157) | (945) | (1739) | (2773) | (11301) | Weighted N |
| Females Only | 41.0 | 56.2 | 29.1 | 42.7 | 46.9 | 50.8 | 58.9 | 49.6 | 37.4 | 32.2 | Good |
|  | 12.0 | 12.8 | 15.9 | 15.7 | 14.3 | 13.5 | 8.2 | 6.0 | 10.0 | 10.4 | Good(qualified) |
|  | 7.6 | 5.5 | 8.6 | 6.4 | 5.4 | 4.4 | 4.8 | 1.9 | 4.8 | 7.3 | Pro-con |
|  | 9.3 | 2.2 | 4.7 | 4.0 | 3.5 | 3.3 | 3.1 | 3.8 | 6.0 | 4.6 | Bad(qualified) |
|  | 13.1 | 7.6 | 15.4 | 6.5 | 5.6 | 9.3 | 6.1 | 13.1 | 14.4 | 16.7 | Bad |
|  | 17.1 | 15.6 | 26.2 | 24.9 | 24.3 | 18.7 | 18.9 | 25.6 | 27.4 | 28.8 | Don't know/depends |
|  | (30178) | (942) | (8897) | (708) | (764) | (364) | (392) | (480) | (888) | (4072) | Weighted N |

**Code distinction not made.

National Economic Outlook

Table 7.6

Does R Expect Good Times or Bad Times in the Next Twelve Months?

Sex of Respondent

|  | Year | | | | | | | | |
|---|---|---|---|---|---|---|---|---|---|
|  | 1969a | 1970a | 1971m | 1972f | 1973c | 1974q | 1975q | 1976m | |
| Males Only | 56.5% | 25.7% | 29.3% | 37.4% | 35.1% | 8.6% | 22.0% | 40.7% | Good |
|  | 11.8 | 14.8 | 15.0 | 13.3 | 10.2 | 9.3 | 18.6 | 12.9 | Good(qualified) |
|  | 5.5 | 8.8 | 8.6 | 9.6 | 9.1 | 9.5 | 14.1 | 13.3 | Pro-con |
|  | 2.4 | 7.7 | 5.5 | 4.6 | 5.8 | 9.1 | 9.4 | 4.2 | Bad(qualified) |
|  | 10.0 | 30.4 | 22.9 | 19.4 | 26.7 | 55.2 | 27.8 | 22.1 | Bad |
|  | 13.8 | 12.5 | 18.7 | 15.6 | 13.2 | 8.3 | 8.1 | 6.8 | Don't know/depends |
|  | (8304) | (1828) | (884) | (540) | (570) | (1318) | (1315) | (48640) | Weighted N |
| Females Only | 42.9 | 17.6 | 16.8 | 27.7 | 22.7 | 4.9 | 15.3 | 31.9 | Good |
|  | 8.4 | 10.9 | 13.1 | 12.4 | 6.5 | 4.6 | 15.4 | 12.1 | Good(qualified) |
|  | 5.4 | 6.4 | 6.7 | 8.7 | 9.1 | 6.8 | 11.3 | 10.5 | Pro-con |
|  | 2.2 | 5.9 | 4.9 | 5.3 | 7.8 | 7.8 | 8.3 | 4.7 | Bad(qualified) |
|  | 14.0 | 34.8 | 29.4 | 23.4 | 32.1 | 62.5 | 36.4 | 22.9 | Bad |
|  | 27.1 | 24.4 | 29.1 | 22.5 | 21.9 | 13.3 | 13.3 | 17.8 | Don't know/depends |
|  | (3119) | (698) | (388) | (739) | (759) | (1622) | (1545) | (73917) | Weighted N |

* Code distinction not made.

National Economic Outlook

Table 7.7

Does R Expect Good Times or Bad Times in the Next Twelve Months?
Race of Respondent

|  | Year | | | | | | | | | |  |
|  | 1947a | 1948a | 1949a | 1952k | 1953m | 1954a | 1955a | 1956m | 1957f | 1958a |  |
|---|---|---|---|---|---|---|---|---|---|---|---|
| Whites Only | 52.3% | 40.5% | 24.0% | 26.7% | 30.3% | 32.5% | 56.7% | 59.9% | 51.8% | 23.0% | Good |
|  | 10.9 | 12.3 | 26.3 | 17.1 | 19.2 | 20.9 | 15.4 | 17.0 | 16.7 | 13.0 | Good(qualified) |
|  | 13.3 | 6.9 | 14.4 | 8.2 | 11.0 | 11.0 | 6.4 | 5.0 | 5.7 | 10.3 | Pro-con |
|  | 5.3 | ** | 17.4 | 5.6 | 9.0 | 12.0 | 6.2 | 2.0 | 4.9 | 18.5 | Bad(qualified) |
|  | 18.2 | 27.0 | 8.9 | 9.8 | 9.5 | 16.5 | 6.9 | 3.0 | 5.6 | 26.7 | Bad |
|  | ** | 13.3 | 9.0 | 32.5 | 21.0 | 7.1 | 8.4 | 13.1 | 15.3 | 8.5 | Don't know/depends |
|  | (749935) | (804038) | (837114) | (815) | (916) | (67058) | (74939) | (1303) | (1186) | (79317) | Weighted N |
| Blacks Only | 35.2 | 27.0 | 21.3 | 19.1 | 28.9 | 26.5 | 43.8 | 32.1 | 32.4 | 14.4 | Good |
|  | 7.7 | 11.9 | 21.7 | 12.8 | 6.0 | 7.0 | 13.3 | 14.3 | 18.4 | 10.7 | Good(qualified) |
|  | 19.3 | 4.5 | 10.5 | 1.1 | 6.0 | 4.7 | 4.9 | 6.3 | 2.9 | 7.7 | Pro-con |
|  | 6.1 | ** | 14.3 | 4.3 | 7.2 | 9.0 | 4.3 | 3.6 | 2.9 | 12.7 | Bad(qualified) |
|  | 31.7 | 37.8 | 12.7 | 17.0 | 18.1 | 39.2 | 21.6 | 6.3 | 12.5 | 33.6 | Bad |
|  | ** | 18.7 | 19.5 | 45.7 | 33.7 | 13.7 | 12.2 | 37.5 | 30.9 | 20.9 | Don't know/depends |
|  | (62972) | (81157) | (80451) | (94) | (83) | (7216) | (6615) | (112) | (136) | (9424) | Weighted N |

Table 7.8

|  | 1959a | 1960a | 1961a | 1962n | 1963m | 1964a | 1965a | 1966a | 1967a | 1968a |  |
|---|---|---|---|---|---|---|---|---|---|---|---|
| Whites Only | 48.5% | 67.2% | 33.7% | 49.5% | 53.7% | 59.3% | 65.5% | 69.7% | 53.2% | 45.4% | Good |
|  | 14.6 | 12.0 | 21.6 | 16.6 | 14.2 | 14.7 | 11.3 | 8.2 | 11.7 | 12.5 | Good(qualified) |
|  | 9.4 | 4.6 | 9.0 | 6.1 | 5.8 | 4.8 | 3.0 | 1.9 | 5.0 | 6.7 | Pro-con |
|  | 7.4 | 2.2 | 7.6 | 4.1 | 3.5 | 2.8 | 2.4 | 2.0 | 4.9 | 5.0 | Bad(qualified) |
|  | 10.6 | 4.6 | 12.1 | 5.4 | 4.8 | 6.9 | 4.6 | 7.4 | 11.1 | 12.7 | Bad |
|  | 9.5 | 9.5 | 16.1 | 18.4 | 18.1 | 11.5 | 13.2 | 10.9 | 14.0 | 17.7 | Don't know/depends |
|  | (78584) | (2577) | (43842) | (1160) | (1156) | (1342) | (1185) | (2017) | (3218) | (13690) | Weighted N |
| Blacks Only | 35.8 | 43.4 | 36.4 | 34.5 | 36.5 | 44.1 | 47.9 | 44.4 | 40.9 | 44.2 | Good |
|  | 10.8 | 15.6 | 10.8 | 16.4 | 16.7 | 16.9 | 14.3 | 5.9 | 8.8 | 8.2 | Good(qualified) |
|  | 5.1 | 4.6 | 6.1 | 10.0 | 5.6 | 6.6 | 5.0 | 6.5 | 5.2 | 4.5 | Pro-con |
|  | 9.1 | 3.3 | 3.0 | 1.8 | 4.8 | 3.7 | 2.5 | 1.8 | 4.4 | 1.7 | Bad(qualified) |
|  | 19.4 | 11.9 | 11.6 | 10.9 | 10.3 | 10.3 | 7.6 | 16.6 | 14.4 | 16.5 | Bad |
|  | 19.8 | 21.2 | 32.1 | 26.4 | 26.2 | 18.4 | 22.7 | 24.9 | 26.2 | 24.8 | Don't know/depends |
|  | (8098) | (302) | (4735) | (110) | (126) | (136) | (119) | (169) | (362) | (1433) | Weighted N |

National Economic Outlook

Table 7.9
Does R Expect Good Times or Bad Times in the Next Twelve Months?
Race of Respondent

|  | Year | | | | | | | | |
|---|---|---|---|---|---|---|---|---|---|
|  | 1969a | 1970a | 1971m | 1972f | 1973c | 1974q | 1975q | 1976m | |
| Whites Only | 54.9% | 24.6% | 26.1% | 33.4% | 30.7% | 6.2% | 18.9% | 35.0% | Good |
|  | 11.2 | 14.2 | 15.1 | 13.0 | 8.6 | 7.0 | 17.7 | 12.5 | Good(qualified) |
|  | 5.5 | 8.5 | 7.9 | 8.8 | 9.7 | 8.7 | 12.9 | 11.9 | Pro-con |
|  | 2.4 | 7.4 | 5.9 | 5.1 | 7.4 | 8.7 | 9.3 | 4.6 | Bad(qualified) |
|  | 10.1 | 31.2 | 24.1 | 21.1 | 28.9 | 59.4 | 31.5 | 23.0 | Bad |
|  | 15.8 | 14.2 | 20.9 | 18.6 | 14.7 | 10.0 | 9.6 | 12.9 | Don't know/depends |
|  | (10135) | (2224) | (1111) | (1147) | (1102) | (2522) | (2529) | (104945) | Weighted N |
| Blacks Only | 35.7 | 16.8 | 19.7 | 18.3 | 11.9 | 7.8 | 13.9 | 39.6 | Good |
|  | 7.5 | 10.3 | 10.2 | 12.2 | 7.6 | 5.1 | 8.9 | 13.8 | Good(qualified) |
|  | 5.7 | 5.1 | 10.2 | 11.3 | 5.9 | 4.7 | 12.7 | 7.0 | Pro-con |
|  | 1.5 | 6.6 | 2.4 | 2.6 | 4.2 | 7.5 | 3.0 | 3.4 | Bad(qualified) |
|  | 20.6 | 33.3 | 26.8 | 26.1 | 39.8 | 55.3 | 40.9 | 23.7 | Bad |
|  | 29.0 | 27.8 | 30.7 | 29.6 | 30.5 | 19.7 | 20.7 | 12.4 | Don't know/depends |
|  | (1118) | (273) | (127) | (115) | (118) | (295) | (237) | (11099) | Weighted N |

Figure 7.2
Good Times or Bad Times by Race of R

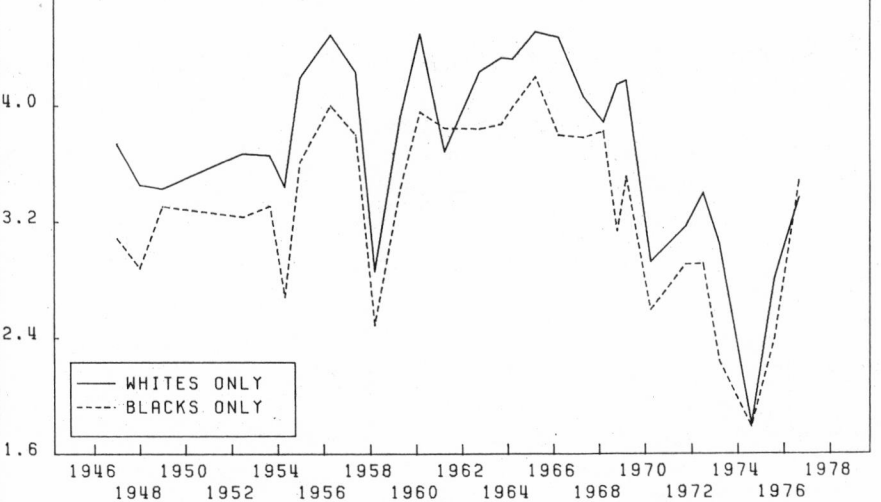

National Economic Outlook

Table 7.10
Does R Expect Good Times or Bad Times in the Next Twelve Months?
Education of Respondent

| | | | | | Year | | | | | | |
|---|---|---|---|---|---|---|---|---|---|---|---|
| | 1947a | 1948a | 1949a | 1952k | 1953m | 1954a | 1955a | 1956m | 1957f | 1958a | |
| Grade School Only | 45.5% | 39.0% | 20.8% | 22.0% | 23.0% | 26.3% | 45.1% | 46.2% | 44.5% | 17.3% | Good |
| | 11.5 | 12.3 | 25.6 | 13.2 | 14.9 | 16.6 | 14.6 | 18.7 | 15.5 | 11.2 | Good(qualified) |
| | 16.3 | 5.5 | 15.0 | 6.9 | 12.8 | 8.2 | 6.0 | 5.7 | 6.6 | 8.2 | Pro-con |
| | 3.8 | ** | 16.4 | 5.8 | 9.2 | 12.4 | 7.7 | 2.5 | 5.0 | 16.9 | Bad(qualified) |
| | 22.9 | 27.5 | 9.1 | 13.2 | 11.8 | 25.0 | 13.7 | 4.7 | 7.6 | 30.5 | Bad |
| | ** | 15.7 | 13.0 | 39.0 | 28.3 | 11.4 | 12.9 | 22.2 | 20.8 | 15.9 | Don't know/depends |
| | (292432) | (314837) | (301159) | (364) | (382) | (25399) | (24502) | (316) | (317) | (24322) | Weighted N |
| High School Only | 54.6 | 40.2 | 26.7 | 25.6 | 31.1 | 34.0 | 59.4 | 59.7 | 55.3 | 24.3 | Good |
| | 10.1 | 12.8 | 28.2 | 18.6 | 19.6 | 19.7 | 15.2 | 19.1 | 19.2 | 12.6 | Good(qualified) |
| | 12.9 | 8.1 | 14.2 | 8.1 | 9.8 | 11.7 | 6.3 | 6.9 | 3.4 | 10.1 | Pro-con |
| | 6.2 | ** | 15.7 | 5.4 | 8.7 | 13.0 | 6.1 | 3.0 | 4.1 | 19.1 | Bad(qualified) |
| | 16.2 | 26.9 | 8.6 | 9.4 | 11.5 | 15.8 | 6.3 | 2.4 | 6.2 | 27.3 | Bad |
| | ** | 12.0 | 6.6 | 32.9 | 19.4 | 5.8 | 6.8 | 9.0 | 11.7 | 6.6 | Don't know/depends |
| | (273575) | (279062) | (289402) | (371) | (470) | (27042) | (32276) | (335) | (291) | (32551) | Weighted N |
| College Only | 62.1 | 47.6 | 31.3 | 34.3 | 46.1 | 38.5 | 74.9 | 78.2 | 61.5 | 28.9 | Good |
| | 8.3 | 12.7 | 25.9 | 20.8 | 22.7 | 24.1 | 13.6 | 13.5 | 18.9 | 17.8 | Good(qualified) |
| | 7.5 | 6.1 | 13.6 | 7.3 | 7.1 | 12.4 | 4.2 | 3.5 | 4.2 | 11.8 | Pro-con |
| | 6.6 | ** | 17.4 | 5.1 | 7.8 | 9.7 | 1.8 | 0.6 | 3.5 | 17.7 | Bad(qualified) |
| | 15.6 | 24.1 | 7.2 | 7.9 | 2.1 | 11.6 | 2.0 | 0.6 | 5.6 | 19.0 | Bad |
| | ** | 9.5 | 4.6 | 24.7 | 14.2 | 3.7 | 3.6 | 3.5 | 6.3 | 4.9 | Don't know/depends |
| | (105187) | (122093) | (127050) | (178) | (141) | (11390) | (11886) | (170) | (143) | (15717) | Weighted N |

** Code distinction not made.
Education coded for head of household only in 1947a,1949a,1954a,1955a,1956m,1957f,and 1958a.

National Economic Outlook

ble 7.11
es R Expect Good Times or Bad Times in the Next Twelve Months?
ucation of Respondent

| | | | | | Year | | | | | | |
|---|---|---|---|---|---|---|---|---|---|---|---|
| | 1959a | 1960a | 1961a | 1962n | 1963m | 1964a | 1965a | 1966a | 1967a | 1968a | |
| Grade School Only | 36.2% | 56.1% | 35.1% | 36.7% | 43.8% | 45.5% | 52.9% | 53.8% | 42.7% | 40.8% | Good |
| | 12.7 | 12.3 | 17.4 | 15.8 | 10.8 | 14.3 | 12.7 | 7.1 | 9.9 | 9.3 | Good(qualified) |
| | 10.1 | 4.0 | 7.9 | 5.9 | 6.5 | 6.4 | 4.0 | 2.6 | 5.2 | 6.9 | Pro-con |
| | 8.1 | 2.9 | 4.1 | 4.2 | 3.2 | 2.9 | 2.9 | 2.4 | 5.6 | 4.4 | Bad(qualified) |
| | 17.8 | 8.8 | 10.6 | 7.1 | 9.2 | 10.8 | 7.4 | 12.8 | 12.4 | 12.5 | Bad |
| | 15.1 | 15.8 | 24.9 | 30.2 | 26.5 | 20.0 | 20.1 | 21.2 | 24.4 | 26.1 | Don't know/depends |
| | (25087) | (795) | (14517) | (354) | (370) | (481) | (378) | (617) | (1043) | (4330) | Weighted N |
| High School Only | 51.1 | 69.3 | 33.1 | 50.0 | 51.2 | 59.8 | 65.8 | 71.7 | 54.4 | 46.6 | Good |
| | 14.7 | 11.3 | 20.9 | 16.7 | 15.6 | 16.2 | 10.7 | 7.7 | 10.9 | 11.3 | Good(qualified) |
| | 10.6 | 4.6 | 8.7 | 6.1 | 5.3 | 4.9 | 3.6 | 2.1 | 4.8 | 7.0 | Pro-con |
| | 7.2 | 1.8 | 8.4 | 3.4 | 4.4 | 2.6 | 2.2 | 1.8 | 4.5 | 4.2 | Bad(qualified) |
| | 8.8 | 3.8 | 13.3 | 6.5 | 4.4 | 7.2 | 4.3 | 6.7 | 12.3 | 13.9 | Bad |
| | 7.7 | 9.2 | 15.6 | 17.3 | 19.2 | 9.3 | 13.4 | 9.9 | 13.0 | 17.1 | Don't know/depends |
| | (29679) | (1072) | (21858) | (618) | (662) | (654) | (635) | (938) | (1699) | (7109) | Weighted N |
| College Only | 63.2 | 73.2 | 35.2 | 56.8 | 64.4 | 69.1 | 73.3 | 77.3 | 58.9 | 47.2 | Good |
| | 16.0 | 13.3 | 24.5 | 17.5 | 16.7 | 13.9 | 13.0 | 9.2 | 13.5 | 16.1 | Good(qualified) |
| | 6.2 | 3.6 | 10.0 | 7.9 | 5.3 | 3.7 | 1.9 | 2.1 | 4.5 | 5.6 | Pro-con |
| | 3.7 | 2.9 | 8.5 | 4.3 | 2.3 | 3.5 | 2.2 | 1.4 | 4.6 | 5.7 | Bad(qualified) |
| | 5.0 | 2.5 | 10.6 | 3.3 | 2.7 | 2.7 | 3.2 | 4.1 | 9.5 | 13.4 | Bad |
| | 5.8 | 4.5 | 11.2 | 10.2 | 8.7 | 7.2 | 6.3 | 5.9 | 9.1 | 12.0 | Don't know/depends |
| | (14897) | (555) | (11906) | (303) | (264) | (375) | (315) | (563) | (876) | (3842) | Weighted N |

Code distinction not made.
ucation coded for head of household only in 1959a,1960a,and 1961a, and for head and wife only in 1963m,1964a,1965a,
1966a,1967a,1968a.

Table 7-12

Does R Expect Good Times or Bad Times in the Next Twelve Months?
Education of Respondent

|  | Year | | | | | | | | |
|---|---|---|---|---|---|---|---|---|---|
|  | 1969a | 1970a | 1971m | 1972f | 1973c | 1974q | 1975q | 1976m | |
| Grade School Only | 42.4% | 20.5% | 21.6% | 25.1% | 19.2% | 5.2% | 13.7% | 29.9% | Good |
|  | 9.9 | 12.8 | 11.9 | 12.1 | 9.0 | 6.2 | 11.9 | 13.4 | Good(qualified) |
|  | 5.6 | 7.0 | 6.3 | 3.8 | 7.7 | 7.2 | 13.3 | 3.7 | Pro-con |
|  | 2.0 | 7.2 | 4.1 | 5.4 | 5.8 | 12.0 | 9.8 | 5.6 | Bad(qualified) |
|  | 12.2 | 31.0 | 27.5 | 21.3 | 24.4 | 47.4 | 30.9 | 24.2 | Bad |
|  | 27.9 | 21.6 | 28.8 | 32.2 | 34.0 | 22.1 | 20.4 | 23.2 | Don't know/depends |
|  | (2982) | (948) | (320) | (239) | (156) | (485) | (437) | (16031) | Weighted N |
| High School Only | 54.6 | 24.6 | 25.0 | 31.4 | 28.7 | 7.8 | 16.0 | 39.2 | Good |
|  | 9.7 | 12.6 | 12.9 | 11.7 | 5.7 | 6.5 | 16.1 | 11.4 | Good(qualified) |
|  | 5.6 | 9.1 | 10.2 | 9.8 | 8.8 | 8.8 | 12.0 | 13.1 | Pro-con |
|  | 2.7 | 6.5 | 4.6 | 4.4 | 9.2 | 5.7 | 9.4 | 3.4 | Bad(qualified) |
|  | 11.7 | 34.4 | 25.4 | 24.1 | 31.9 | 59.4 | 35.5 | 20.5 | Bad |
|  | 15.7 | 12.8 | 21.9 | 18.6 | 15.7 | 11.8 | 11.1 | 12.4 | Don't know/depends |
|  | (5094) | (1104) | (567) | (656) | (617) | (1406) | (1495) | (58331) | Weighted N |
| College Only | 60.0 | 26.5 | 29.4 | 37.3 | 32.2 | 5.4 | 24.5 | 33.4 | Good |
|  | 13.7 | 19.2 | 19.1 | 15.1 | 12.8 | 7.2 | 20.2 | 13.0 | Good(qualified) |
|  | 5.2 | 8.3 | 6.4 | 11.4 | 11.0 | 7.5 | 13.2 | 11.6 | Pro-con |
|  | 2.0 | 9.5 | 7.4 | 5.8 | 5.4 | 10.6 | 7.6 | 5.6 | Bad(qualified) |
|  | 9.1 | 26.3 | 21.8 | 17.5 | 28.6 | 64.5 | 28.5 | 26.4 | Bad |
|  | 10.0 | 10.2 | 15.9 | 13.0 | 10.0 | 4.9 | 6.1 | 9.9 | Don't know/depends |
|  | (3270) | (411) | (377) | (378) | (391) | (1027) | (923) | (44380) | Weighted N |

Code distinction not made.

Education coded for head of household only in 1971m, and for head and wife only in 1969a, and 1970a.

Figure 7.3

Good Times or Bad Times by Education of R

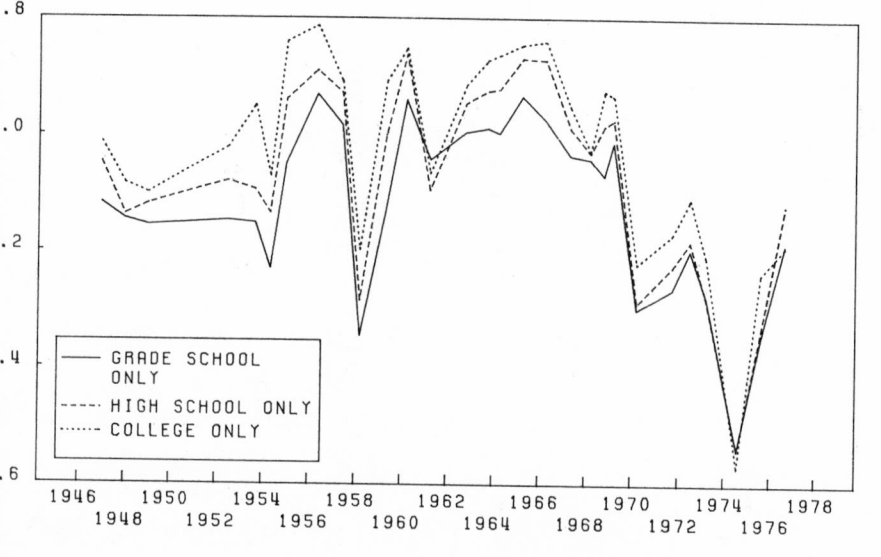

National Economic Outlook

ble 7.13

es R Expect Good Times or Bad Times in the Next Twelve Months?

e of Respondent

|  | 1947a | 1948a | 1949a | 1952k | 1953m | 1954a | 1955a | 1956m | 1957f | 1958a |  |
|---|---|---|---|---|---|---|---|---|---|---|---|
| 18-24 Only | 56.2% | 43.4% | 31.8% | 23.1% | 45.8% | 41.5% | 52.5% | 51.7% | 51.2% | 30.8% | Good |
|  | 8.1 | 10.8 | 25.6 | 19.2 | 4.2 | 16.2 | 15.4 | 17.2 | 14.3 | 15.1 | Good(qualified) |
|  | 14.4 | 5.5 | 12.4 | 3.8 | 10.4 | 8.5 | 4.5 | 3.4 | 7.1 | 8.4 | Pro-con |
|  | 4.8 | ** | 10.7 | 5.8 | 10.4 | 8.0 | 4.3 | 6.9 | 3.6 | 15.0 | Bad(qualified) |
|  | 16.4 | 25.8 | 10.1 | 15.4 | 8.3 | 15.3 | 14.3 | 5.7 | 6.0 | 24.5 | Bad |
|  | ** | 14.5 | 9.4 | 32.7 | 20.8 | 10.5 | 9.0 | 14.9 | 17.9 | 6.1 | Don't know/depends |
|  | (73561) | (85690) | (88986) | (52) | (48) | (5298) | (6490) | (87) | (84) | (7754) | Weighted N |
| 25-34 Only | 55.6 | 45.0 | 31.5 | 26.8 | 36.4 | 34.9 | 62.4 | 62.3 | 57.2 | 25.5 | Good |
|  | 9.5 | 13.3 | 27.6 | 14.7 | 19.9 | 19.6 | 14.9 | 14.6 | 15.5 | 13.7 | Good(qualified) |
|  | 10.1 | 7.6 | 13.8 | 11.3 | 11.7 | 11.7 | 5.7 | 6.7 | 3.6 | 13.0 | Pro-con |
|  | 5.3 | ** | 15.3 | 3.9 | 5.6 | 9.7 | 4.7 | 1.5 | 3.2 | 17.5 | Bad(qualified) |
|  | 19.4 | 24.9 | 6.6 | 12.1 | 8.7 | 19.1 | 6.1 | 3.0 | 4.7 | 25.1 | Bad |
|  | ** | 9.2 | 5.2 | 31.2 | 17.7 | 5.2 | 6.2 | 11.9 | 15.8 | 5.2 | Don't know/depends |
|  | (151874) | (155781) | (150514) | (231) | (231) | (13410) | (16256) | (329) | (278) | (14617) | Weighted N |
| 35-44 Only | 54.8 | 42.0 | 23.1 | 29.0 | 28.8 | 31.8 | 57.6 | 62.0 | 49.7 | 20.8 | Good |
|  | 11.0 | 13.5 | 28.4 | 20.0 | 19.8 | 18.0 | 17.9 | 16.6 | 17.2 | 14.0 | Good(qualified) |
|  | 11.6 | 6.9 | 14.9 | 8.6 | 12.3 | 11.8 | 5.4 | 3.1 | 6.9 | 9.0 | Pro-con |
|  | 5.4 | ** | 17.2 | 7.3 | 8.6 | 13.4 | 6.6 | 2.5 | 3.8 | 18.9 | Bad(qualified) |
|  | 17.2 | 27.6 | 9.2 | 6.9 | 9.5 | 18.5 | 7.7 | 2.1 | 7.5 | 29.5 | Bad |
|  | ** | 10.0 | 7.2 | 28.2 | 21.0 | 6.4 | 4.9 | 13.8 | 15.0 | 7.7 | Don't know/depends |
|  | (156201) | (155213) | (151051) | (245) | (243) | (15154) | (14717) | (326) | (320) | (15616) | Weighted N |
| 45-54 Only | 47.9 | 38.8 | 21.5 | 25.2 | 31.9 | 31.6 | 57.0 | 61.6 | 48.2 | 22.8 | Good |
|  | 12.0 | 11.4 | 26.1 | 20.1 | 16.8 | 20.0 | 14.1 | 14.0 | 19.9 | 11.3 | Good(qualified) |
|  | 15.2 | 7.3 | 16.1 | 7.5 | 5.9 | 9.4 | 6.7 | 3.7 | 4.8 | 13.0 | Pro-con |
|  | 4.9 | ** | 16.9 | 3.8 | 10.8 | 15.5 | 7.1 | 1.5 | 6.3 | 16.7 | Bad(qualified) |
|  | 19.9 | 28.0 | 8.4 | 14.5 | 13.0 | 17.2 | 7.1 | 3.7 | 5.1 | 25.6 | Bad |
|  | ** | 14.4 | 11.0 | 28.9 | 21.6 | 6.3 | 8.0 | 15.5 | 15.8 | 10.6 | Don't know/depends |
|  | (215308) | (129437) | (135962) | (159) | (185) | (11753) | (11147) | (271) | (272) | (12788) | Weighted N |
| 55-64 Only | ** | 40.2 | 19.9 | 22.4 | 28.8 | 26.3 | 54.3 | 54.5 | 53.0 | 19.3 | Good |
|  | ** | 12.7 | 26.8 | 13.8 | 16.7 | 23.9 | 14.0 | 17.5 | 17.5 | 11.2 | Good(qualified) |
|  | ** | 7.1 | 15.6 | 3.4 | 12.1 | 10.1 | 6.6 | 7.1 | 4.9 | 9.8 | Pro-con |
|  | ** | ** | 19.5 | 6.0 | 12.1 | 14.2 | 7.6 | 0.9 | 4.4 | 18.3 | Bad(qualified) |
|  | ** | 22.5 | 8.7 | 8.6 | 6.1 | 17.6 | 8.0 | 1.9 | 4.9 | 28.1 | Bad |
|  | ** | 17.5 | 9.4 | 45.7 | 24.2 | 7.9 | 9.5 | 18.0 | 15.3 | 13.3 | Don't know/depends |
|  | ** | (104404) | (107281) | (116) | (132) | (9398) | (9996) | (211) | (183) | (26904) | Weighted N |
| 65 and Older Only | 43.9 | 33.2 | 21.9 | 22.3 | 18.4 | 27.0 | 49.5 | 44.3 | 38.5 | 19.1 | Good |
|  | 8.9 | 13.0 | 24.3 | 11.6 | 19.0 | 17.0 | 12.1 | 23.8 | 13.3 | 13.4 | Good(qualified) |
|  | 19.4 | 3.9 | 12.9 | 2.7 | 11.4 | 9.4 | 5.5 | 5.9 | 6.7 | 5.5 | Pro-con |
|  | 5.5 | ** | 17.3 | 6.3 | 8.9 | 9.8 | 5.1 | 2.7 | 6.7 | 19.6 | Bad(qualified) |
|  | 22.3 | 32.2 | 9.2 | 9.8 | 14.6 | 23.3 | 10.1 | 4.9 | 9.7 | 28.4 | Bad |
|  | ** | 17.7 | 14.4 | 47.3 | 27.8 | 13.5 | 17.6 | 18.4 | 25.1 | 13.9 | Don't know/depends |
|  | (76078) | (85467) | (83817) | (112) | (158) | (8848) | (8932) | (185) | (195) | (10943) | Weighted N |

* Code distinction not made.

ge coded for head of household only in 1947a,1949a,1954a,1955a,and 1958a.

ɔungest age group coded "21-24" in 1953m.

ge group coded "45-64" in 1947a.

ldest age group coded "65 And Older" in 1959a,1960a,1965a, and 1966a.

National Economic Outlook

Table 7.14

Does R Expect Good Times or Bad Times in the Next Twelve Months?

Age of Respondent

| | 1959a | 1960a | 1961a | 1962n | 1963m | 1964a | 1965a | 1966a | 1967a | 1968a | |
|---|---|---|---|---|---|---|---|---|---|---|---|
| 18-24 Only | 52.6% | 70.1% | 35.0% | 53.9% | 44.4% | 63.0% | 64.0% | 58.8% | 52.8% | 44.7% | Good |
| | 11.2 | 8.5 | 15.0 | 10.5 | 9.1 | 11.1 | 12.8 | 9.8 | 8.0 | 9.2 | Good(qualified) |
| | 11.0 | 2.5 | 6.7 | 6.6 | 10.1 | 6.5 | 2.4 | 5.2 | 2.4 | 5.2 | Pro-con |
| | 4.9 | 2.5 | 11.4 | 3.9 | 5.1 | 3.7 | 0.8 | 1.3 | 5.6 | 4.3 | Bad(qualified) |
| | 9.6 | 5.0 | 13.5 | 10.5 | 8.1 | 5.6 | 7.2 | 12.4 | 22.0 | 22.6 | Bad |
| | 10.8 | 11.4 | 18.4 | 14.5 | 23.2 | 10.2 | 12.8 | 12.4 | 9.2 | 13.9 | Don't know/depends |
| | (6236) | (201) | (4550) | (76) | (99) | (108) | (125) | (153) | (250) | (977) | Weighted N |
| 25-34 Only | 51.6 | 71.6 | 36.3 | 51.7 | 57.6 | 62.4 | 65.6 | 73.6 | 50.2 | 48.0 | Good |
| | 13.8 | 10.8 | 21.1 | 15.1 | 17.3 | 15.5 | 12.7 | 6.4 | 10.6 | 13.0 | Good(qualified) |
| | 11.6 | 4.8 | 9.6 | 5.8 | 3.9 | 3.1 | 4.1 | 1.2 | 5.8 | 4.9 | Pro-con |
| | 8.0 | 1.9 | 5.5 | 3.9 | 3.0 | 3.5 | 2.5 | 1.7 | 4.9 | 5.7 | Bad(qualified) |
| | 9.3 | 3.1 | 13.6 | 5.8 | 3.9 | 7.0 | 4.1 | 7.2 | 15.6 | 17.5 | Bad |
| | 5.6 | 7.9 | 13.9 | 17.8 | 14.3 | 8.5 | 11.1 | 9.9 | 12.9 | 10.8 | Don't know/depends |
| | (12444) | (482) | (10357) | (259) | (231) | (258) | (244) | (405) | (659) | (2863) | Weighted N |
| 35-44 Only | 50.9 | 67.0 | 35.2 | 53.7 | 57.8 | 59.0 | 67.3 | 73.0 | 60.0 | 53.3 | Good |
| | 16.1 | 12.7 | 23.8 | 16.7 | 15.2 | 17.0 | 10.9 | 9.2 | 10.7 | 11.4 | Good(qualified) |
| | 9.4 | 3.9 | 8.0 | 6.0 | 4.4 | 4.3 | 2.5 | 2.5 | 3.4 | 6.6 | Pro-con |
| | 5.7 | 2.8 | 8.2 | 2.8 | 2.6 | 2.4 | 1.8 | 2.5 | 3.7 | 3.6 | Bad(qualified) |
| | 9.7 | 5.0 | 11.2 | 5.7 | 4.1 | 7.3 | 4.7 | 6.7 | 10.6 | 10.4 | Bad |
| | 8.1 | 8.6 | 13.7 | 14.9 | 15.9 | 10.0 | 12.7 | 6.0 | 11.6 | 14.7 | Don't know/depends |
| | (15537) | (536) | (10860) | (281) | (270) | (329) | (275) | (434) | (707) | (2840) | Weighted N |
| 45-54 Only | 48.7 | 67.5 | 35.1 | 43.3 | 49.6 | 61.5 | 67.9 | 73.1 | 56.3 | 49.7 | Good |
| | 14.8 | 13.3 | 20.9 | 23.0 | 15.7 | 13.4 | 12.2 | 6.8 | 11.1 | 13.6 | Good(qualified) |
| | 10.2 | 3.3 | 10.5 | 9.2 | 6.6 | 4.8 | 2.4 | 1.6 | 5.4 | 6.8 | Pro-con |
| | 6.6 | 2.5 | 10.3 | 4.2 | 4.4 | 2.2 | 3.7 | 1.1 | 4.7 | 4.3 | Bad(qualified) |
| | 11.3 | 5.2 | 10.4 | 3.8 | 5.5 | 7.6 | 2.4 | 6.6 | 8.6 | 10.5 | Bad |
| | 8.5 | 8.3 | 12.8 | 16.5 | 18.2 | 10.5 | 11.4 | 10.7 | 13.8 | 15.1 | Don't know/depends |
| | (12189) | (483) | (9302) | (261) | (274) | (314) | (246) | (438) | (701) | (2880) | Weighted N |
| 55-64 Only | 43.4 | 60.7 | 29.1 | 43.4 | 52.0 | 54.3 | 61.4 | 66.8 | 52.7 | 42.3 | Good |
| | 14.7 | 14.0 | 20.8 | 13.8 | 14.2 | 18.4 | 12.3 | 8.4 | 13.0 | 12.1 | Good(qualified) |
| | 8.4 | 5.8 | 8.4 | 6.1 | 5.4 | 6.9 | 5.0 | 2.1 | 6.3 | 6.3 | Pro-con |
| | 9.5 | 1.9 | 3.3 | 3.1 | 4.9 | 1.6 | 2.7 | 1.6 | 4.8 | 5.7 | Bad(qualified) |
| | 13.0 | 4.9 | 14.6 | 9.7 | 4.4 | 6.5 | 4.5 | 7.1 | 9.4 | 11.9 | Bad |
| | 11.0 | 12.6 | 23.8 | 24.0 | 19.1 | 12.2 | 14.1 | 14.1 | 13.7 | 21.7 | Don't know/depends |
| | (11190) | (364) | (7284) | (196) | (204) | (245) | (220) | (382) | (583) | (2796) | Weighted N |
| 65-74 Only | 43.0 | 55.9 | 29.3 | 50.0 | 44.4 | 46.4 | 55.4 | 52.4 | 40.7 | 34.4 | Good |
| | 13.2 | 12.3 | 20.9 | 15.7 | 12.0 | 14.2 | 10.8 | 7.5 | 12.9 | 10.3 | Good(qualified) |
| | 7.4 | 4.4 | 8.8 | 4.5 | 6.8 | 4.9 | 3.2 | 2.5 | 4.4 | 11.9 | Pro-con |
| | 5.3 | 2.7 | 4.9 | 6.0 | 2.3 | 4.9 | 2.3 | 3.3 | 6.6 | 4.9 | Bad(qualified) |
| | 13.8 | 8.2 | 9.7 | 0.7 | 7.5 | 8.7 | 7.7 | 12.3 | 11.4 | 13.6 | Bad |
| | 17.3 | 16.6 | 26.3 | 23.1 | 27.1 | 20.8 | 20.7 | 22.1 | 24.1 | 24.9 | Don't know/depends |
| | (11691) | (367) | (4148) | (134) | (133) | (183) | (222) | (399) | (457) | (1844) | Weighted N |
| 75 And Older Only | ** | ** | 36.1 | 31.3 | 40.7 | 47.6 | ** | ** | 41.8 | 29.5 | Good |
| | ** | ** | 10.3 | 13.4 | 11.6 | 8.3 | ** | ** | 12.1 | 10.7 | Good(qualified) |
| | ** | ** | 6.6 | 4.5 | 5.8 | 9.5 | ** | ** | 4.3 | 3.6 | Pro-con |
| | ** | ** | 4.1 | 4.5 | 2.3 | 3.6 | ** | ** | 4.3 | 2.7 | Bad(qualified) |
| | ** | ** | 6.9 | 9.0 | 8.1 | 7.1 | ** | ** | 7.8 | 13.4 | Bad |
| | ** | ** | 36.0 | 37.3 | 31.4 | 23.8 | ** | ** | 29.8 | 40.2 | Don't know/depends |
| | ** | ** | (2217) | (67) | (86) | (84) | ** | ** | (282) | (1120) | Weighted N |

* Code distinction not made.

e coded for head of household only in 1959a,1960a,and 1961a,and for head and wife only in 1964a,1965a,1966a,1967a,and 1968a.

dest age group coded "65 And Older" in 1959a,1960a,1965a, and 1966a.

National Economic Outlook

Table 7.15

Does R Expect Good Times or Bad Times in the Next Twelve Months?

Age of Respondent

|  | Year | | | | | | | | |
|---|---|---|---|---|---|---|---|---|---|
|  | 1969a | 1970a | 1971m | 1972f | 1973c | 1974q | 1975q | 1976m | |
| 18-24 Only | 51.7% | 31.4% | 21.4% | 32.9% | 21.9% | 6.7% | 23.2% | 49.4% | Good |
|  | 6.8 | 13.4 | 14.3 | 13.5 | 4.5 | 6.1 | 15.3 | 4.8 | Good(qualified) |
|  | 3.5 | 6.3 | 5.1 | 8.2 | 5.5 | 9.6 | 6.3 | 9.7 | Pro-con |
|  | 4.5 | 7.5 | 6.1 | 4.3 | 8.5 | 6.9 | 7.0 | 1.6 | Bad(qualified) |
|  | 20.1 | 27.6 | 34.7 | 26.1 | 41.8 | 60.5 | 40.1 | 22.2 | Bad |
|  | 13.4 | 13.8 | 18.4 | 15.0 | 17.9 | 10.2 | 8.1 | 12.4 | Don't know/depends |
|  | (1075) | (239) | (98) | (207) | (201) | (479) | (444) | (19961) | Weighted N |
| 25-34 Only | 53.6 | 24.2 | 25.7 | 31.6 | 28.6 | 5.6 | 18.8 | 38.7 | Good |
|  | 11.1 | 13.4 | 13.1 | 12.4 | 8.2 | 5.7 | 17.0 | 12.8 | Good(qualified) |
|  | 5.5 | 8.1 | 9.7 | 8.7 | 8.2 | 5.0 | 9.5 | 11.3 | Pro-con |
|  | 1.1 | 6.8 | 5.5 | 5.1 | 7.2 | 5.3 | 6.7 | 4.2 | Bad(qualified) |
|  | 15.7 | 33.3 | 25.3 | 25.8 | 37.8 | 70.9 | 37.4 | 24.7 | Bad |
|  | 13.0 | 14.2 | 20.7 | 16.4 | 9.9 | 7.5 | 10.6 | 8.3 | Don't know/depends |
|  | (2293) | (409) | (237) | (275) | (304) | (663) | (671) | (26494) | Weighted N |
| 35-44 Only | 53.7 | 24.8 | 30.0 | 36.7 | 33.3 | 7.6 | 18.9 | 38.0 | Good |
|  | 11.7 | 14.8 | 15.6 | 9.0 | 7.1 | 6.0 | 17.0 | 17.0 | Good(qualified) |
|  | 5.8 | 8.6 | 8.0 | 13.6 | 10.0 | 8.5 | 13.0 | 14.9 | Pro-con |
|  | 2.6 | 5.8 | 5.6 | 5.0 | 7.6 | 7.6 | 7.1 | 3.1 | Bad(qualified) |
|  | 11.0 | 33.3 | 22.0 | 20.8 | 23.8 | 60.0 | 33.3 | 20.2 | Bad |
|  | 15.2 | 12.7 | 18.8 | 14.9 | 18.1 | 10.3 | 10.7 | 6.8 | Don't know/depends |
|  | (1985) | (432) | (250) | (221) | (210) | (497) | (477) | (17386) | Weighted N |
| 45-54 Only | 60.6 | 23.2 | 28.6 | 33.5 | 30.7 | 6.8 | 15.5 | 34.9 | Good |
|  | 8.8 | 15.3 | 15.8 | 11.7 | 9.8 | 8.8 | 16.9 | 6.7 | Good(qualified) |
|  | 5.7 | 6.9 | 7.5 | 5.9 | 13.7 | 9.4 | 14.8 | 11.5 | Pro-con |
|  | 2.2 | 8.8 | 5.6 | 5.9 | 3.9 | 10.6 | 10.4 | 5.7 | Bad(qualified) |
|  | 6.6 | 29.6 | 21.8 | 24.5 | 23.9 | 54.6 | 32.7 | 29.9 | Bad |
|  | 15.9 | 16.2 | 20.7 | 18.6 | 18.0 | 9.6 | 9.7 | 11.3 | Don't know/depends |
|  | (1925) | (452) | (266) | (188) | (205) | (498) | (413) | (18651) | Weighted N |
| 55-64 Only | 49.9 | 24.0 | 25.5 | 32.4 | 31.2 | 7.9 | 18.0 | 29.5 | Good |
|  | 13.2 | 13.1 | 13.0 | 16.5 | 10.1 | 10.2 | 21.0 | 13.1 | Good(qualified) |
|  | 8.4 | 10.6 | 6.3 | 9.4 | 8.5 | 9.0 | 19.1 | 15.8 | Pro-con |
|  | 2.4 | 9.0 | 3.4 | 3.5 | 5.3 | 9.7 | 8.2 | 9.7 | Bad(qualified) |
|  | 7.5 | 29.4 | 30.3 | 13.5 | 28.0 | 50.9 | 24.4 | 20.0 | Bad |
|  | 18.6 | 13.9 | 21.6 | 24.7 | 16.9 | 12.3 | 9.3 | 11.8 | Don't know/depends |
|  | (1755) | (367) | (208) | (170) | (189) | (432) | (377) | (16094) | Weighted N |
| 65-74 Only | 46.7 | 21.3 | 18.3 | 26.9 | 25.2 | 4.9 | 13.9 | 25.6 | Good |
|  | 13.0 | 15.4 | 15.3 | 17.2 | 9.9 | 1.3 | 16.3 | 23.2 | Good(qualified) |
|  | 3.1 | 7.5 | 9.9 | 9.7 | 8.6 | 8.8 | 15.4 | 8.6 | Pro-con |
|  | 3.1 | 7.1 | 8.4 | 6.2 | 6.6 | 11.1 | 12.7 | 4.2 | Bad(qualified) |
|  | 8.1 | 30.0 | 22.9 | 13.8 | 22.5 | 55.8 | 27.8 | 20.8 | Bad |
|  | 26.0 | 18.6 | 25.2 | 26.2 | 27.2 | 18.1 | 13.9 | 17.6 | Don't know/depends |
|  | (1452) | (253) | (131) | (145) | (151) | (226) | (331) | (13893) | Weighted N |
| 75 And Older Only | 49.5 | 18.3 | 17.1 | 17.6 | 16.9 | 6.1 | 16.9 | 23.7 | Good |
|  | 10.1 | 7.1 | 13.4 | 10.3 | 4.6 | 6.1 | 11.8 | 12.7 | Good(qualified) |
|  | 4.0 | 9.5 | 9.8 | 5.9 | 10.8 | 6.9 | 15.4 | 7.5 | Pro-con |
|  | 1.0 | 5.6 | 2.4 | 4.4 | 13.8 | 14.5 | 18.4 | 4.1 | Bad(qualified) |
|  | 11.1 | 28.6 | 19.5 | 25.0 | 13.8 | 42.0 | 14.0 | 20.9 | Bad |
|  | 24.2 | 31.0 | 37.8 | 36.8 | 40.0 | 24.4 | 23.5 | 31.2 | Don't know/depends |
|  | (891) | (126) | (82) | (68) | (65) | (131) | (136) | (7553) | Weighted N |

* Code distinction not made.

Age coded for head and wife only in 1969a, and 1970a.

Table 7.16

Does R Expect Good Times or Bad Times in the Next Twelve Months?

Income of Respondent

| | | | | | Year | | | | | | |
|---|---|---|---|---|---|---|---|---|---|---|---|
| | 1947a | 1948a | 1949a | 1952k | 1953m | 1954a | 1955a | 1956m | 1957f | 1958a | |
| Income 1 (0-16%) | 38.0% | 32.3% | 21.3% | 15.6% | 18.1% | 29.5% | 43.1% | 39.0% | 37.6% | 18.0% | Good |
| | 9.9 | 10.0 | 20.1 | 14.4 | 13.3 | 14.0 | 14.1 | 17.0 | 14.8 | 9.5 | Good(qualified) |
| | 21.4 | 4.7 | 12.4 | 3.3 | 10.1 | 7.6 | 7.0 | 5.4 | 7.4 | 6.8 | Pro-con |
| | 3.4 | ** | 17.7 | 4.4 | 11.7 | 10.5 | 8.2 | 3.6 | 3.5 | 18.5 | Bad(qualified) |
| | 27.4 | 34.3 | 11.7 | 15.6 | 17.0 | 25.5 | 12.4 | 7.2 | 9.2 | 28.2 | Bad |
| | ** | 18.8 | 16.8 | 46.7 | 29.8 | 12.9 | 15.1 | 27.8 | 27.5 | 18.9 | Don't know/depends |
| | (132211) | (120703) | (139909) | (90) | (188) | (16653) | (18635) | (223) | (229) | (19439) | Weighted N |
| Income 2 (17-33%) | 48.2 | 35.7 | 22.6 | 23.7 | 25.2 | 30.5 | 48.6 | 39.7 | 40.9 | 21.9 | Good |
| | 8.8 | 10.2 | 23.1 | 14.0 | 17.0 | 17.6 | 15.5 | 22.0 | 17.2 | 13.3 | Good(qualified) |
| | 17.0 | 7.7 | 11.3 | 5.8 | 10.9 | 6.8 | 4.6 | 5.0 | 5.6 | 9.5 | Pro-con |
| | 6.3 | ** | 17.8 | 3.5 | 7.5 | 12.1 | 6.6 | 5.7 | 7.5 | 14.1 | Bad(qualified) |
| | 19.6 | 32.0 | 12.8 | 12.8 | 10.9 | 22.0 | 12.4 | 5.7 | 8.1 | 29.9 | Bad |
| | ** | 14.4 | 12.4 | 40.1 | 28.6 | 11.0 | 12.2 | 22.0 | 20.6 | 11.3 | Don't know/depends |
| | (124743) | (140706) | (133500) | (257) | (147) | (10261) | (11332) | (141) | (320) | (20907) | Weighted N |
| Income 3 (34-67%) | 51.9 | 36.8 | 21.6 | 28.4 | 31.9 | 30.8 | 53.6 | 60.2 | 56.1 | 21.8 | Good |
| | 12.0 | 13.4 | 28.4 | 20.4 | 22.2 | 20.3 | 17.3 | 16.5 | 18.6 | 13.4 | Good(qualified) |
| | 12.1 | 7.7 | 15.8 | 11.4 | 12.8 | 11.1 | 6.5 | 5.2 | 4.1 | 8.4 | Pro-con |
| | 4.9 | ** | 16.0 | 6.0 | 7.0 | 10.8 | 6.2 | 1.7 | 3.9 | 19.0 | Bad(qualified) |
| | 19.0 | 27.3 | 8.8 | 9.4 | 7.9 | 20.7 | 8.3 | 2.9 | 5.0 | 29.3 | Bad |
| | ** | 14.9 | 9.4 | 24.4 | 18.2 | 6.3 | 8.0 | 13.4 | 12.2 | 8.1 | Don't know/depends |
| | (276635) | (300889) | (340539) | (299) | (329) | (23496) | (25423) | (581) | (515) | (22226) | Weighted N |
| Income 4 (68-95%) | 58.2 | 45.9 | 28.1 | 28.6 | 38.6 | 34.6 | 66.9 | 71.9 | 64.8 | 25.1 | Good |
| | 9.6 | 12.7 | 26.3 | 17.6 | 17.4 | 22.3 | 14.0 | 14.9 | 15.5 | 13.8 | Good(qualified) |
| | 10.8 | 6.5 | 13.6 | 5.5 | 10.2 | 12.9 | 6.7 | 5.0 | 5.2 | 13.8 | Pro-con |
| | 6.0 | ** | 18.1 | 8.0 | 9.8 | 14.1 | 4.2 | 0.7 | 2.1 | 19.6 | Bad(qualified) |
| | 15.3 | 24.6 | 7.1 | 7.5 | 8.3 | 11.4 | 4.0 | 1.7 | 2.1 | 23.6 | Bad |
| | ** | 10.3 | 6.8 | 32.7 | 15.5 | 4.7 | 4.1 | 5.9 | 10.4 | 4.2 | Don't know/depends |
| | (235892) | (249101) | (259345) | (199) | (264) | (19843) | (23351) | (303) | (193) | (25282) | Weighted N |
| Income 5 (96-100%) | 53.3 | 45.4 | 25.1 | 39.0 | 40.5 | 38.3 | 77.5 | 78.1 | 70.0 | 29.5 | Good |
| | 13.7 | 14.1 | 30.5 | 14.6 | 16.2 | 30.4 | 13.3 | 10.5 | 10.0 | 21.2 | Good(qualified) |
| | 8.5 | 4.8 | 16.6 | 12.2 | 2.7 | 14.6 | 1.4 | 3.8 | 6.7 | 12.8 | Pro-con |
| | 8.0 | ** | 15.2 | 2.4 | 10.8 | 9.1 | 4.1 | 1.9 | 6.7 | 18.7 | Bad(qualified) |
| | 16.5 | 24.3 | 8.7 | 7.3 | 5.4 | 6.1 | 1.1 | 1.0 | 6.7 | 14.2 | Bad |
| | ** | 11.5 | 3.9 | 24.4 | 24.3 | 1.5 | 2.6 | 4.8 | 0.0 | 3.6 | Don't know/depends |
| | (45195) | (75104) | (48794) | (41) | (37) | (4021) | (4448) | (105) | (30) | (2225) | Weighted N |

Code distinction not made.

National Economic Outlook

Table 7.17

Does R Expect Good Times or Bad Times in the Next Twelve Months?

Income of Respondent

|  | Year | | | | | | | | | | |
|---|---|---|---|---|---|---|---|---|---|---|---|
|  | 1959a | 1960a | 1961a | 1962n | 1963m | 1964a | 1965a | 1966a | 1967a | 1968a | |
| Income 1 (0-16%) | 33.3% | 49.8% | 33.3% | 31.9% | 40.8% | 46.4% | 50.0% | 45.6% | 39.9% | 32.7% | Good |
|  | 13.8 | 12.0 | 11.9 | 12.9 | 8.6 | 10.5 | 8.2 | 7.1 | 8.9 | 8.9 | Good(qualified) |
|  | 8.9 | 3.9 | 6.5 | 2.5 | 5.2 | 5.9 | 5.9 | 3.1 | 3.5 | 6.0 | Pro-con |
|  | 7.3 | 2.6 | 4.4 | 4.9 | 3.4 | 2.3 | 2.4 | 3.1 | 4.4 | 3.3 | Bad(qualified) |
|  | 18.7 | 9.9 | 14.2 | 10.4 | 9.2 | 10.5 | 6.5 | 12.6 | 13.0 | 17.0 | Bad |
|  | 18.1 | 21.7 | 29.7 | 37.4 | 32.8 | 24.5 | 27.1 | 28.5 | 30.2 | 32.0 | Don't know/depends |
|  | (17585) | (534) | (7870) | (163) | (174) | (220) | (170) | (421) | (706) | (2559) | Weighted N |
| Income 2 (17-33%) | 38.4 | 57.9 | 34.3 | 41.1 | 44.5 | 46.4 | 56.3 | 58.8 | 44.5 | 37.6 | Good |
|  | 13.4 | 14.6 | 19.3 | 12.7 | 14.4 | 14.1 | 13.4 | 7.6 | 8.3 | 10.5 | Good(qualified) |
|  | 7.9 | 4.6 | 6.9 | 9.6 | 6.7 | 5.6 | 3.1 | 4.6 | 6.3 | 8.1 | Pro-con |
|  | 7.2 | 2.0 | 5.5 | 4.6 | 4.3 | 3.6 | 2.2 | 2.5 | 4.7 | 5.1 | Bad(qualified) |
|  | 16.1 | 6.5 | 12.0 | 8.1 | 8.1 | 11.7 | 8.9 | 12.7 | 15.2 | 16.3 | Bad |
|  | 16.9 | 14.4 | 22.0 | 23.9 | 22.0 | 18.5 | 16.1 | 13.8 | 21.0 | 22.4 | Don't know/depends |
|  | (10718) | (603) | (9759) | (197) | (209) | (248) | (224) | (434) | (553) | (2577) | Weighted N |
| Income 3 (34-67%) | 45.6 | 69.0 | 34.4 | 53.6 | 51.3 | 57.9 | 64.1 | 75.5 | 54.7 | 48.1 | Good |
|  | 14.2 | 12.1 | 22.3 | 17.3 | 16.3 | 16.1 | 11.3 | 7.7 | 11.0 | 11.8 | Good(qualified) |
|  | 9.6 | 5.2 | 10.2 | 4.7 | 5.7 | 6.0 | 3.1 | 1.2 | 4.7 | 6.7 | Pro-con |
|  | 9.8 | 2.4 | 8.3 | 3.3 | 3.9 | 2.8 | 2.1 | 1.8 | 5.2 | 4.3 | Bad(qualified) |
|  | 10.7 | 4.0 | 10.7 | 6.3 | 4.7 | 7.1 | 4.7 | 6.8 | 12.4 | 13.0 | Bad |
|  | 10.1 | 7.3 | 14.1 | 14.7 | 18.1 | 10.1 | 14.8 | 6.9 | 12.0 | 16.1 | Don't know/depends |
|  | (31248) | (1115) | (19286) | (509) | (386) | (535) | (426) | (763) | (1407) | (5165) | Weighted N |
| Income 4 (68-95%) | 56.9 | 75.2 | 32.1 | 53.1 | 59.6 | 65.3 | 69.8 | 77.4 | 58.7 | 51.4 | Good |
|  | 16.1 | 10.3 | 22.9 | 19.6 | 16.0 | 16.8 | 13.1 | 9.5 | 15.2 | 14.2 | Good(qualified) |
|  | 9.4 | 4.7 | 10.2 | 9.4 | 5.2 | 4.0 | 3.1 | 1.1 | 5.4 | 6.0 | Pro-con |
|  | 6.1 | 2.5 | 8.7 | 3.5 | 4.5 | 2.9 | 2.6 | 0.7 | 4.8 | 5.8 | Bad(qualified) |
|  | 6.9 | 2.5 | 13.9 | 1.7 | 3.7 | 4.0 | 3.1 | 4.1 | 9.5 | 9.9 | Bad |
|  | 4.7 | 4.7 | 12.2 | 12.6 | 11.0 | 6.9 | 8.3 | 7.2 | 6.4 | 12.7 | Don't know/depends |
|  | (20644) | (552) | (10561) | (286) | (381) | (447) | (420) | (461) | (686) | (4403) | Weighted N |
| Income 5 (96-100%) | 73.3 | 72.3 | 45.2 | 56.7 | 70.1 | 77.3 | 78.1 | 80.6 | 63.2 | 52.3 | Good |
|  | 10.7 | 14.3 | 34.6 | 15.0 | 14.9 | 12.0 | 11.4 | 6.3 | 15.3 | 15.2 | Good(qualified) |
|  | 5.9 | 2.7 | 3.6 | 8.3 | 2.3 | 2.7 | 1.0 | 1.4 | 5.3 | 4.5 | Pro-con |
|  | 3.5 | 0.9 | 5.5 | 5.0 | 0.0 | 2.7 | 2.9 | 2.8 | 4.0 | 5.1 | Bad(qualified) |
|  | 4.2 | 3.6 | 6.2 | 5.0 | 1.1 | 2.7 | 1.0 | 3.5 | 4.0 | 12.1 | Bad |
|  | 2.5 | 6.3 | 4.9 | 10.0 | 11.5 | 2.7 | 5.7 | 5.6 | 8.1 | 10.8 | Don't know/depends |
|  | (7486) | (112) | (1484) | (60) | (87) | (75) | (105) | (144) | (321) | (777) | Weighted N |

National Economic Outlook

Table 7-18

Does R Expect Good Times or Bad Times in the Next Twelve Months?

Income of Respondent

| | 1969a | 1970a | 1971m | 1972f | 1973c | 1974q | 1975q | 1976m | |
|---|---|---|---|---|---|---|---|---|---|
| Income 1 (0-16%) | 39.1% | 23.1% | 14.7% | 22.1% | 17.8% | 5.8% | 11.8% | 35.2% | Good |
| | 8.1 | 10.7 | 9.5 | 11.5 | 5.9 | 7.6 | 9.3 | 12.9 | Good(qualified) |
| | 6.1 | 4.7 | 4.2 | 7.8 | 2.4 | 5.3 | 12.1 | 11.6 | Pro-con |
| | 2.3 | 5.6 | 3.2 | 5.1 | 5.9 | 7.3 | 10.4 | 3.9 | Bad(qualified) |
| | 15.4 | 30.2 | 33.2 | 22.1 | 31.4 | 55.1 | 34.3 | 24.0 | Bad |
| | 29.1 | 25.7 | 35.3 | 31.3 | 36.7 | 18.9 | 22.0 | 12.3 | Don't know/depends |
| | (2443) | (467) | (190) | (217) | (169) | (396) | (431) | (21879) | Weighted N |
| Income 2 (17-33%) | 50.0 | 21.7 | 19.0 | 24.8 | 20.4 | 8.0 | 15.2 | 38.9 | Good |
| | 8.3 | 16.2 | 14.0 | 16.6 | 5.1 | 4.7 | 16.8 | 11.0 | Good(qualified) |
| | 3.7 | 9.9 | 8.3 | 9.0 | 9.9 | 6.6 | 13.9 | 13.1 | Pro-con |
| | 2.7 | 8.0 | 4.5 | 3.4 | 9.6 | 6.6 | 11.1 | 3.9 | Bad(qualified) |
| | 14.1 | 26.8 | 30.6 | 25.5 | 32.9 | 57.7 | 31.8 | 24.5 | Bad |
| | 21.2 | 17.4 | 23.6 | 20.7 | 22.0 | 16.5 | 11.3 | 8.7 | Don't know/depends |
| | (2193) | (414) | (242) | (145) | (313) | (577) | (488) | (23841) | Weighted N |
| Income 3 (34-67%) | 54.7 | 23.6 | 27.5 | 30.2 | 28.6 | 5.5 | 21.9 | 37.0 | Good |
| | 13.6 | 12.6 | 14.6 | 13.5 | 11.3 | 7.2 | 16.5 | 12.3 | Good(qualified) |
| | 6.1 | 8.0 | 8.4 | 7.5 | 9.5 | 8.1 | 13.1 | 11.7 | Pro-con |
| | 2.3 | 6.5 | 6.2 | 5.7 | 0.9 | 8.3 | 8.4 | 3.7 | Bad(qualified) |
| | 10.3 | 35.3 | 23.9 | 22.5 | 32.4 | 62.4 | 31.4 | 23.5 | Bad |
| | 12.9 | 14.0 | 19.3 | 20.5 | 17.3 | 8.4 | 8.7 | 11.8 | Don't know/depends |
| | (3848) | (883) | (451) | (453) | (336) | (959) | (818) | (14085) | Weighted N |
| Income 4 (68-95%) | 62.1 | 23.8 | 31.8 | 39.8 | 36.7 | 8.4 | 20.7 | 44.2 | Good |
| | 11.4 | 15.6 | 17.8 | 13.8 | 9.4 | 9.5 | 19.8 | 16.0 | Good(qualified) |
| | 5.3 | 9.8 | 9.6 | 9.7 | 10.3 | 10.9 | 12.5 | 13.4 | Pro-con |
| | 2.3 | 8.0 | 5.8 | 6.0 | 5.0 | 8.9 | 7.4 | 5.6 | Bad(qualified) |
| | 7.0 | 31.4 | 18.5 | 19.1 | 28.4 | 58.0 | 35.8 | 15.6 | Bad |
| | 11.9 | 11.3 | 16.4 | 11.6 | 10.3 | 4.3 | 3.8 | 5.3 | Don't know/depends |
| | (2603) | (672) | (292) | (319) | (341) | (598) | (632) | (9285) | Weighted N |
| Income 5 (96-100%) | 67.1 | 29.6 | 42.3 | 45.5 | 51.6 | 4.3 | 22.2 | 36.3 | Good |
| | 12.6 | 16.7 | 17.3 | 6.5 | 7.5 | 5.4 | 33.3 | 13.3 | Good(qualified) |
| | 6.0 | 5.6 | 5.8 | 16.9 | 10.8 | 4.3 | 11.8 | 11.0 | Pro-con |
| | 1.0 | 13.0 | 7.7 | 2.6 | 4.3 | 18.3 | 4.9 | 5.4 | Bad(qualified) |
| | 3.8 | 25.9 | 11.5 | 19.5 | 22.6 | 61.3 | 25.7 | 28.3 | Bad |
| | 9.5 | 9.3 | 15.4 | 9.1 | 3.2 | 6.5 | 2.1 | 5.7 | Don't know/depends |
| | (420) | (108) | (52) | (77) | (93) | (93) | (144) | (8034) | Weighted N |

National Economic Outlook

Table 7.19
Are Current Business Conditions Better than Last Year's?
Total Population

QUESTION  Would you say that at present business conditions are better or worse than they were a year ago?

|  | | Year | | | | | | | |
|---|---|---|---|---|---|---|---|---|---|
|  | | 1954m | 1956m | 1957f | 1958m | 1959f | 1960a | 1961a | 1962n |
| Better | (5) | 21.2% | 28.2% | 21.3% | 35.3% | 48.5% | 43.9% | 13.1% | 40.0% |
| Same | (3) | 35.4 | 53.7 | 50.0 | 33.4 | 33.1 | 36.1 | 28.9 | 39.2 |
| Worse | (1) | 40.6 | 13.6 | 25.5 | 28.6 | 13.9 | 17.7 | 55.9 | 16.3 |
| Don't know | | 2.7 | 4.5 | 3.2 | 2.8 | 4.5 | 2.3 | 2.0 | 4.6 |
| Total | | 100% | 100% | 100% | 100% | 100% | 100% | 100% | 100% |
| Weighted N | | 982 | 1431 | 1340 | 1327 | 1300 | 2889 | 49454 | 1289 |
| Unweighted N | | 982 | 1431 | 1340 | 1327 | 1300 | 2889 | 1962 | 1289 |
| Mean | | 2.60 | 3.31 | 2.91 | 3.14 | 3.72 | 3.53 | 2.13 | 3.50 |
| Standard Deviation | | 1.54 | 1.29 | 1.39 | 1.61 | 1.45 | 1.49 | 1.43 | 1.45 |

Table 7.20

|  | | 1963m | 1964a | 1965a | 1966a | 1967a | 1968a | 1968n | 1969a |
|---|---|---|---|---|---|---|---|---|---|
| Better | (5) | 40.4% | 42.2% | 43.9% | 57.8% | 34.4% | 36.6% | 36.2% | 35.3% |
| Same | (3) | 42.9 | 41.0 | 40.7 | 30.1 | 38.3 | 40.0 | 49.5 | 50.6 |
| Worse | (1) | 13.7 | 13.6 | 11.7 | 7.7 | 23.4 | 20.8 | 10.0 | 11.3 |
| Don't know | | 3.1 | 3.2 | 3.7 | 4.5 | 3.9 | 2.6 | 4.3 | 2.8 |
| Total | | 100% | 100% | 100% | 100% | 100% | 100% | 100% | 100% |
| Weighted N | | 1311 | 1524 | 1334 | 2396 | 3682 | 15426 | 2623 | 11502 |
| Unweighted N | | 1311 | 1524 | 1334 | 2396 | 3126 | 2655 | 1414 | 2287 |
| Mean | | 3.55 | 3.59 | 3.67 | 4.05 | 3.23 | 3.32 | 3.55 | 3.49 |
| Standard Deviation | | 1.39 | 1.40 | 1.36 | 1.28 | 1.53 | 1.50 | 1.28 | 1.29 |

Table 7.21

|  | | 1970a | 1971m | 1972f | 1973c | 1975q | 1976m | 1978n |
|---|---|---|---|---|---|---|---|---|
| Better | (5) | 18.7% | 26.6% | 40.1% | 40.2% | 34.5% | 46.9% | 35.0% |
| Same | (3) | 27.9 | 29.5 | 30.1 | 29.7 | 16.0 | 17.1 | 18.4 |
| Worse | (1) | 50.4 | 39.9 | 27.4 | 25.2 | 45.9 | 32.3 | 37.1 |
| Don't know | | 3.0 | 3.9 | 2.4 | 4.9 | 3.6 | 3.7 | 9.5 |
| Total | | 100% | 100% | 100% | 100% | 100% | 100% | 100% |
| Weighted N | | 2537 | 1293 | 1294 | 1339 | 2883 | 126865 | 2289 |
| Unweighted N | | 2537 | 1293 | 1294 | 1339 | 1499 | 1127 | 2289 |
| Mean | | 2.35 | 2.72 | 3.26 | 3.32 | 2.76 | 3.30 | 2.95 |
| Standard Deviation | | 1.56 | 1.64 | 1.64 | 1.63 | 1.81 | 1.79 | 1.78 |

1968n includes Black supplement.

National Economic Outlook

Figure 7.4
Current Business Conditions--Total Population

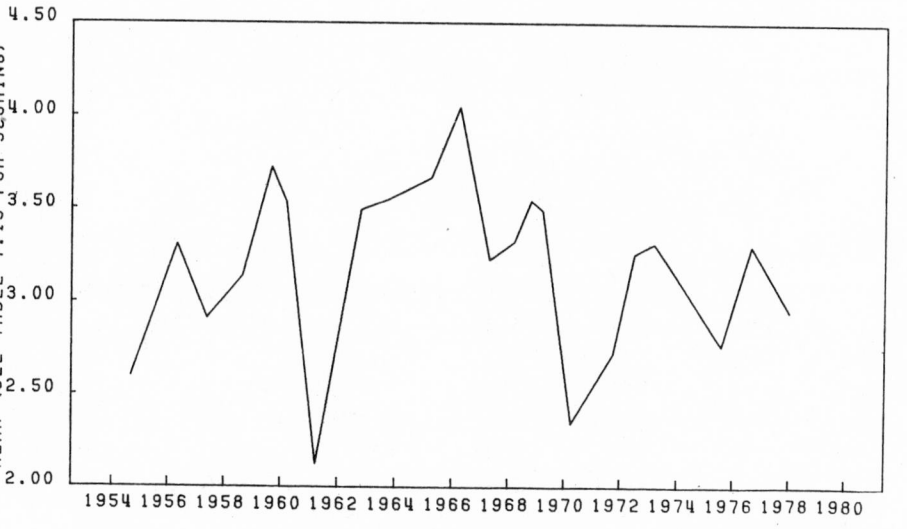

National Economic Outlook

Table 7.22
Are Current Business Conditions Better than Last Year's?
Sex of Respondent

Year

|  | 1954m | 1956m | 1957f | 1958m | 1959f | 1960a | 1961a | 1962n | |
|---|---|---|---|---|---|---|---|---|---|
| Males Only | 22.7% | 31.9% | 22.0% | 37.8% | 55.4% | 46.9% | 13.7% | 44.7% | Better |
|  | 31.2 | 50.0 | 51.0 | 31.7 | 28.6 | 34.0 | 28.0 | 35.9 | Same |
|  | 44.9 | 16.5 | 25.3 | 28.5 | 13.7 | 17.4 | 57.0 | 17.0 | Worse |
|  | 1.3 | 1.7 | 1.7 | 2.0 | 2.3 | 1.6 | 1.3 | 2.4 | Don't know |
|  | (459) | (662) | (577) | (558) | (563) | (1945) | (40443) | (582) | Weighted N |
| Females Only | 20.0 | 25.1 | 20.7 | 33.4 | 43.0 | 37.5 | 10.7 | 36.1 | Better |
|  | 39.2 | 56.8 | 49.3 | 34.6 | 36.6 | 40.5 | 32.4 | 41.9 | Same |
|  | 36.9 | 11.1 | 25.7 | 28.6 | 14.1 | 18.3 | 51.6 | 15.7 | Worse |
|  | 4.0 | 7.0 | 4.3 | 3.4 | 6.3 | 3.7 | 5.3 | 6.4 | Don't know |
|  | (521) | (768) | (763) | (769) | (735) | (944) | (8903) | (707) | Weighted N |

Table 7.23

|  | 1963m | 1964a | 1965a | 1966a | 1967a | 1968a | 1968n | 1969a | |
|---|---|---|---|---|---|---|---|---|---|
| Males Only | 46.4% | 45.3% | 46.9% | 62.2% | 35.9% | 39.4% | 41.8% | 38.2% | Better |
|  | 39.0 | 38.6 | 39.5 | 28.6 | 37.3 | 38.1 | 46.2 | 48.8 | Same |
|  | 13.6 | 13.6 | 11.5 | 6.6 | 24.7 | 21.0 | 10.0 | 11.3 | Worse |
|  | 0.9 | 2.5 | 2.0 | 2.6 | 2.2 | 1.5 | 1.9 | 1.7 | Don't know |
|  | (543) | (1155) | (944) | (1872) | (2794) | (11281) | (1136) | (8355) | Weighted N |
| Females Only | 36.1 | 32.1 | 36.7 | 42.0 | 29.6 | 28.9 | 31.9 | 27.5 | Better |
|  | 45.7 | 48.8 | 43.6 | 35.1 | 41.7 | 45.2 | 52.1 | 55.2 | Same |
|  | 13.7 | 13.7 | 12.1 | 11.6 | 19.3 | 20.5 | 10.0 | 11.5 | Worse |
|  | 4.6 | 5.5 | 7.7 | 11.3 | 9.5 | 5.4 | 6.1 | 5.8 | Don't know |
|  | (768) | (365) | (390) | (524) | (888) | (4032) | (1487) | (3147) | Weighted N |

Table 7.24

|  | 1970a | 1971m | 1972f | 1973c | 1975q | 1976m | 1978n | |
|---|---|---|---|---|---|---|---|---|
| Males Only | 18.6% | 28.8% | 46.7% | 47.1% | 37.6% | 54.1% | 42.6% | Better |
|  | 26.6 | 27.9 | 27.5 | 27.0 | 17.1 | 16.3 | 18.8 | Same |
|  | 53.0 | 40.3 | 24.9 | 23.1 | 43.0 | 28.0 | 33.4 | Worse |
|  | 1.7 | 3.0 | 0.9 | 2.8 | 2.3 | 1.6 | 5.2 | Don't know |
|  | (1835) | (906) | (546) | (575) | (1330) | (50307) | (1010) | Weighted N |
| Females Only | 18.9 | 21.4 | 35.3 | 34.9 | 31.9 | 42.6 | 29.0 | Better |
|  | 31.5 | 33.3 | 32.1 | 31.8 | 15.1 | 17.9 | 18.1 | Same |
|  | 43.4 | 39.0 | 29.1 | 26.7 | 48.3 | 34.3 | 40.0 | Worse |
|  | 6.1 | 6.2 | 3.5 | 6.5 | 4.7 | 5.2 | 12.9 | Don't know |
|  | (702) | (387) | (748) | (764) | (1553) | (75145) | (1279) | Weighted N |

Table 7.25
Are Current Business Conditions Better than Last Year's?
Race of Respondent

|              | Year |  |  |  |  |  |  |  |  |
|--------------|-------|-------|-------|-------|-------|-------|-------|-------|---|
|              | 1954m | 1956m | 1957f | 1958m | 1959f | 1960a | 1961a | 1962n |   |
| Whites Only  | 22.3% | 28.4% | 21.4% | 37.6% | 50.3% | 45.2% | 12.9% | 39.7% | Better |
|              | 36.3  | 53.9  | 50.0  | 33.6  | 32.8  | 36.3  | 27.8  | 39.8  | Same |
|              | 38.9  | 13.5  | 25.8  | 26.9  | 12.2  | 16.3  | 57.7  | 15.8  | Worse |
|              | 2.4   | 4.2   | 2.9   | 1.9   | 4.7   | 2.2   | 1.6   | 4.6   | Don't know |
|              | (886) | (1305)| (1188)| (1162)| (1155)| (2590)| (44243)| (1168)| Weighted N |
|              |       |       |       |       |       |       |       |       |   |
| Blacks Only  | 10.6  | 21.7  | 19.6  | 17.9  | 31.7  | 34.8  | 15.6  | 40.9  | Better |
|              | 23.5  | 53.9  | 50.7  | 31.0  | 34.9  | 33.4  | 38.3  | 33.6  | Same |
|              | 60.0  | 15.7  | 25.4  | 42.8  | 29.4  | 29.2  | 41.5  | 21.8  | Worse |
|              | 5.9   | 8.7   | 4.3   | 8.3   | 4.0   | 2.6   | 4.7   | 3.6   | Don't know |
|              | (85)  | (115) | (138) | (145) | (126) | (305) | (4828)| (110) | Weighted N |

Table 7.26

|              | 1963m | 1964a | 1965a | 1966a | 1967a | 1968a | 1968n | 1969a |   |
|--------------|-------|-------|-------|-------|-------|-------|-------|-------|---|
| Whites Only  | 40.1% | 43.2% | 45.1% | 59.0% | 33.8% | 36.2% | 36.5% | 36.0% | Better |
|              | 43.1  | 40.5  | 40.0  | 30.0  | 38.7  | 40.2  | 49.1  | 49.9  | Same |
|              | 13.7  | 13.2  | 11.0  | 7.0   | 24.3  | 21.2  | 10.3  | 11.5  | Worse |
|              | 3.1   | 3.1   | 3.9   | 4.0   | 3.2   | 2.4   | 4.1   | 2.6   | Don't know |
|              | (1158)| (1341)| (1182)| (2167)| (3235)| (13630)| (2346)| (10166)| Weighted N |
|              |       |       |       |       |       |       |       |       |   |
| Blacks Only  | 38.1  | 34.3  | 37.8  | 42.2  | 38.1  | 38.6  | 33.6  | 30.8  | Better |
|              | 45.2  | 45.3  | 42.9  | 34.9  | 35.6  | 41.9  | 52.7  | 55.2  | Same |
|              | 14.3  | 18.2  | 16.8  | 14.6  | 16.2  | 16.0  | 8.3   | 10.7  | Worse |
|              | 2.4   | 2.2   | 2.5   | 8.3   | 10.1  | 3.4   | 5.4   | 3.3   | Don't know |
|              | (126) | (137) | (119) | (192) | (365) | (1428)| (241) | (1159)| Weighted N |

Table 7.27

|              | 1970a | 1971m | 1972f | 1973c | 1975q | 1976m | 1978n |   |
|--------------|-------|-------|-------|-------|-------|-------|-------|---|
| Whites Only  | 18.5% | 26.4% | 40.7% | 42.1% | 36.7% | 48.6% | 35.9% | Better |
|              | 27.3  | 29.4  | 29.8  | 29.0  | 15.5  | 16.6  | 18.6  | Same |
|              | 51.3  | 40.4  | 27.1  | 24.1  | 44.5  | 31.0  | 36.3  | Worse |
|              | 2.9   | 3.9   | 2.4   | 4.8   | 3.3   | 3.8   | 9.2   | Don't know |
|              | (2232)| (1130)| (1163)| (1115)| (2550)| (107355)| (2004)| Weighted N |
|              |       |       |       |       |       |       |       |   |
| Blacks Only  | 20.5  | 27.3  | 32.5  | 34.2  | 16.3  | 30.8  | 30.3  | Better |
|              | 34.2  | 32.8  | 32.5  | 25.6  | 19.7  | 24.1  | 17.7  | Same |
|              | 42.1  | 36.7  | 32.5  | 34.2  | 58.2  | 42.4  | 39.4  | Worse |
|              | 3.2   | 3.1   | 2.6   | 6.0   | 5.9   | 2.7   | 12.6  | Don't know |
|              | (278) | (128) | (114) | (117) | (239) | (11618)| (231) | Weighted N |

Table 7.28
Are Current Business Conditions Better than Last Year's?
Education of Respondent

| | 1954m | 1956m | 1957f | 1958m | 1959f | 1960a | 1961a | 1962n | |
|---|---|---|---|---|---|---|---|---|---|
| Grade School Only | 16.8% | 23.4% | 19.6% | 24.8% | 33.1% | 33.5% | 10.5% | 32.1% | Better |
| | 36.9 | 54.5 | 53.2 | 38.1 | 40.8 | 41.3 | 34.4 | 44.5 | Same |
| | 42.0 | 17.1 | 22.8 | 32.8 | 20.2 | 22.9 | 52.6 | 15.5 | Worse |
| | 4.3 | 5.0 | 4.4 | 4.3 | 5.9 | 2.4 | 2.5 | 7.9 | Don't know |
| | (352) | (321) | (316) | (302) | (287) | (800) | (14727) | (355) | Weighted N |
| | | | | | | | | | |
| High School Only | 20.2 | 31.6 | 24.1 | 43.8 | 53.4 | 47.2 | 13.3 | 41.7 | Better |
| | 35.7 | 51.0 | 44.7 | 30.4 | 31.3 | 35.3 | 26.9 | 38.6 | Same |
| | 41.9 | 15.5 | 30.2 | 24.1 | 13.2 | 15.5 | 57.7 | 16.5 | Worse |
| | 2.2 | 1.8 | 1.0 | 1.8 | 2.0 | 2.0 | 2.0 | 3.2 | Don't know |
| | (451) | (335) | (295) | (336) | (348) | (1075) | (22070) | (619) | Weighted N |
| | | | | | | | | | |
| College Only | 32.8 | 40.8 | 21.7 | 41.7 | 66.9 | 55.8 | 15.9 | 46.0 | Better |
| | 28.4 | 46.7 | 55.9 | 31.1 | 17.2 | 27.0 | 24.7 | 34.0 | Same |
| | 37.9 | 9.5 | 21.0 | 25.8 | 9.7 | 14.7 | 57.8 | 16.8 | Worse |
| | 0.9 | 3.0 | 1.4 | 1.3 | 6.2 | 2.5 | 1.6 | 3.2 | Don't know |
| | (116) | (169) | (143) | (151) | (145) | (556) | (12008) | (309) | Weighted N |

Table 7.29

| | 1963m | 1964a | 1965a | 1966a | 1967a | 1968a | 1968n | 1969a | |
|---|---|---|---|---|---|---|---|---|---|
| Grade School Only | 31.3% | 34.4% | 34.5% | 46.0% | 31.7% | 29.8% | 21.3% | 26.3% | Better |
| | 50.0 | 44.5 | 46.7 | 37.0 | 42.6 | 48.2 | 59.3 | 56.7 | Same |
| | 16.0 | 17.1 | 12.7 | 10.4 | 18.9 | 18.2 | 13.6 | 11.9 | Worse |
| | 2.7 | 3.9 | 6.1 | 6.6 | 6.7 | 3.8 | 5.9 | 5.2 | Don't know |
| | (368) | (485) | (377) | (670) | (1052) | (4325) | (597) | (3017) | Weighted N |
| | | | | | | | | | |
| High School Only | 41.7 | 42.8 | 46.0 | 61.8 | 36.9 | 39.1 | 38.2 | 38.3 | Better |
| | 41.5 | 41.6 | 37.8 | 27.7 | 37.3 | 38.7 | 49.6 | 49.8 | Same |
| | 14.2 | 13.2 | 13.1 | 7.0 | 22.7 | 20.0 | 8.8 | 10.4 | Worse |
| | 2.6 | 2.5 | 3.0 | 3.5 | 3.1 | 2.2 | 3.3 | 1.5 | Don't know |
| | (662) | (652) | (632) | (1014) | (1705) | (7060) | (1289) | (5124) | Weighted N |
| | | | | | | | | | |
| College Only | 49.3 | 51.6 | 50.9 | 65.5 | 33.3 | 40.1 | 44.8 | 39.3 | Better |
| | 36.9 | 36.0 | 38.9 | 26.4 | 34.7 | 33.2 | 41.7 | 46.3 | Same |
| | 9.3 | 9.7 | 7.9 | 5.3 | 30.0 | 25.0 | 9.0 | 12.1 | Worse |
| | 4.5 | 2.7 | 2.2 | 2.8 | 1.9 | 1.7 | 4.5 | 2.3 | Don't know |
| | (268) | (372) | (316) | (606) | (882) | (3826) | (734) | (3271) | Weighted N |

Education coded for head of household only in 1956m,1957f,1958m,1960a,1961a, and 1966a, and for head and wife only in 1959f,1963m,1964a,1965a,1968a,and 1969a.

Table 7.30
Are Current Business Conditions Better than Last Year's?
Education of Respondent

|  | Year | | | | | | | |
|---|---|---|---|---|---|---|---|---|
|  | 1970a | 1971m | 1972f | 1973c | 1975q | 1976m | 1978n | |
| Grade School Only | 19.3% | 22.2% | 27.0% | 32.3% | 22.2% | 33.2% | 30.3% | Better |
|  | 32.9 | 38.4 | 41.0 | 35.5 | 19.7 | 25.8 | 21.8 | Same |
|  | 43.0 | 34.1 | 28.3 | 27.7 | 50.6 | 35.4 | 33.2 | Worse |
|  | 4.8 | 5.3 | 3.7 | 4.5 | 7.6 | 5.7 | 14.8 | Don't know |
|  | (958) | (320) | (244) | (155) | (437) | (16694) | (271) | Weighted N |
| High School Only | 18.6 | 26.8 | 38.8 | 40.2 | 32.8 | 44.3 | 36.8 | Better |
|  | 25.1 | 29.4 | 31.2 | 30.3 | 16.3 | 17.2 | 18.0 | Same |
|  | 54.3 | 40.1 | 27.9 | 24.8 | 47.7 | 33.7 | 36.0 | Worse |
|  | 2.1 | 3.6 | 2.1 | 4.6 | 3.2 | 4.8 | 9.1 | Don't know |
|  | (1105) | (578) | (663) | (624) | (1504) | (59775) | (1203) | Weighted N |
| College Only | 16.3 | 29.7 | 51.4 | 47.2 | 43.2 | 55.4 | 33.7 | Better |
|  | 23.7 | 22.2 | 21.0 | 25.4 | 14.0 | 15.0 | 17.8 | Same |
|  | 59.0 | 44.7 | 25.5 | 22.6 | 40.4 | 28.1 | 40.3 | Worse |
|  | 1.0 | 3.4 | 2.1 | 4.8 | 2.3 | 1.6 | 8.2 | Don't know |
|  | (410) | (387) | (381) | (398) | (937) | (45168) | (807) | Weighted N |

Education coded for head of household only in 1971m.

National Economic Outlook

ble 7.31
e Current Business Conditions Better than Last Year's?
e of Respondent

| | | | | Year | | | | | |
|---|---|---|---|---|---|---|---|---|---|
| | 1954m | 1956m | 1957f | 1958m | 1959f | 1960a | 1961a | 1962n | |
| 18-24 Only | 39.7% | 36.4% | 27.4% | 46.2% | 58.0% | 55.0% | 22.1% | 52.6% | Better |
| | 33.3 | 45.5 | 39.3 | 28.2 | 26.0 | 29.5 | 27.1 | 28.9 | Same |
| | 23.8 | 10.2 | 27.4 | 23.1 | 14.0 | 11.5 | 45.8 | 13.2 | Worse |
| | 3.2 | 8.0 | 6.0 | 2.6 | 2.0 | 4.0 | 4.9 | 5.3 | Don't know |
| | (63) | (88) | (84) | (39) | (50) | (200) | (4575) | (76) | Weighted N |
| 25-34 Only | 18.5 | 32.0 | 28.1 | 45.5 | 58.7 | 54.2 | 19.3 | 53.5 | Better |
| | 35.0 | 52.7 | 48.2 | 30.1 | 24.6 | 26.5 | 27.3 | 31.5 | Same |
| | 42.9 | 10.7 | 21.6 | 23.8 | 13.0 | 17.2 | 50.9 | 10.0 | Worse |
| | 3.5 | 4.6 | 2.2 | 0.7 | 3.6 | 2.1 | 2.5 | 5.0 | Don't know |
| | (254) | (328) | (278) | (143) | (138) | (483) | (10352) | (260) | Weighted N |
| 35-44 Only | 18.3 | 32.8 | 20.8 | 35.8 | 56.5 | 46.7 | 11.8 | 45.6 | Better |
| | 36.1 | 50.9 | 50.6 | 31.3 | 29.2 | 31.4 | 28.3 | 32.9 | Same |
| | 43.8 | 12.6 | 27.0 | 30.1 | 13.0 | 20.2 | 58.4 | 19.1 | Worse |
| | 1.8 | 3.7 | 1.6 | 2.8 | 1.3 | 1.7 | 1.4 | 2.5 | Don't know |
| | (219) | (326) | (318) | (176) | (154) | (544) | (11062) | (283) | Weighted N |
| 45-54 Only | 19.8 | 24.3 | 19.0 | 32.0 | 54.9 | 41.2 | 9.3 | 36.4 | Better |
| | 35.0 | 54.4 | 49.8 | 34.7 | 25.4 | 37.7 | 23.7 | 45.5 | Same |
| | 43.7 | 16.9 | 28.7 | 29.9 | 17.6 | 19.4 | 65.8 | 15.9 | Worse |
| | 1.5 | 4.4 | 2.5 | 3.4 | 2.1 | 1.6 | 1.1 | 2.3 | Don't know |
| | (197) | (272) | (279) | (147) | (142) | (485) | (9454) | (264) | Weighted N |
| 55-64 Only | 24.3 | 24.1 | 17.5 | 34.8 | 40.3 | 37.9 | 9.5 | 29.7 | Better |
| | 29.7 | 59.4 | 55.2 | 32.8 | 36.9 | 42.6 | 27.9 | 44.1 | Same |
| | 44.1 | 14.2 | 25.7 | 29.3 | 18.1 | 17.9 | 61.6 | 20.5 | Worse |
| | 1.8 | 2.4 | 1.6 | 3.0 | 4.7 | 1.6 | 1.0 | 5.6 | Don't know |
| | (111) | (212) | (183) | (658) | (149) | (364) | (7328) | (195) | Weighted N |
| 65-74 Only | 21.1 | 20.2 | 16.4 | 28.0 | 30.7 | 33.7 | 10.8 | 23.5 | Better |
| | 42.1 | 54.8 | 52.8 | 40.9 | 44.7 | 45.9 | 38.7 | 52.2 | Same |
| | 31.6 | 17.6 | 22.6 | 28.0 | 14.7 | 16.3 | 47.7 | 16.9 | Worse |
| | 5.3 | 7.4 | 8.2 | 3.0 | 10.0 | 4.1 | 2.7 | 7.4 | Don't know |
| | (133) | (188) | (195) | (164) | (150) | (368) | (4233) | (136) | Weighted N |
| 75 And Older Only | ** | ** | ** | ** | ** | ** | 5.7 | 26.1 | Better |
| | ** | ** | ** | ** | ** | ** | 47.0 | 42.0 | Same |
| | ** | ** | ** | ** | ** | ** | 43.8 | 21.7 | Worse |
| | ** | ** | ** | ** | ** | ** | 3.5 | 10.1 | Don't know |
| | ** | ** | ** | ** | ** | ** | (2208) | (69) | Weighted N |

** Code distinction not made.
Oldest age group coded "65 And Older" in 1954m, 1956m, 1957f, 1958m, 1959f, and 1960a.
Age coded for head of household only in 1958m, 1959f, 1960a, and 1961a.

Table 7.32
Are Current Business Conditions Better than Last Year's?
Age of Respondent

| | 1963m | 1964a | 1965a | 1966a | 1967a | 1968a | 1968n | 1969a | |
|---|---|---|---|---|---|---|---|---|---|
| **18-24 Only** | 50.5% | 56.5% | 56.0% | 62.2% | 43.4% | 47.2% | 46.7% | 47.2% | Better |
| | 30.3 | 36.1 | 34.4 | 27.3 | 26.5 | 27.4 | 37.7 | 36.7 | Same |
| | 15.2 | 6.5 | 5.6 | 5.8 | 28.1 | 25.4 | 6.0 | 12.1 | Worse |
| | 4.0 | 0.9 | 4.0 | 4.7 | 2.0 | 0.0 | 9.5 | 4.0 | Don't know |
| | (99) | (108) | (125) | (172) | (249) | (978) | (199) | (1079) | Weighted N |
| **25-34 Only** | 46.2 | 49.2 | 55.1 | 65.2 | 42.3 | 45.3 | 46.8 | 43.9 | Better |
| | 40.2 | 32.4 | 33.5 | 23.3 | 26.5 | 33.7 | 39.0 | 42.2 | Same |
| | 9.8 | 12.9 | 9.8 | 6.9 | 27.7 | 18.6 | 8.0 | 12.3 | Worse |
| | 3.8 | 5.5 | 1.6 | 4.6 | 3.5 | 2.4 | 6.2 | 1.6 | Don't know |
| | (234) | (256) | (245) | (434) | (664) | (2853) | (513) | (2308) | Weighted N |
| **35-44 Only** | 44.4 | 48.3 | 38.9 | 59.1 | 37.2 | 42.1 | 39.6 | 38.2 | Better |
| | 39.2 | 36.2 | 42.9 | 29.7 | 37.2 | 37.2 | 47.2 | 46.4 | Same |
| | 14.9 | 13.4 | 16.0 | 8.8 | 23.9 | 19.4 | 10.9 | 13.4 | Worse |
| | 1.5 | 2.1 | 2.2 | 2.4 | 1.7 | 1.4 | 2.3 | 2.0 | Don't know |
| | (268) | (329) | (275) | (464) | (712) | (2850) | (568) | (1982) | Weighted N |
| **45-54 Only** | 43.1 | 39.9 | 49.0 | 61.6 | 34.0 | 36.4 | 33.7 | 35.0 | Better |
| | 40.1 | 44.7 | 38.4 | 26.8 | 41.0 | 40.8 | 54.1 | 53.6 | Same |
| | 13.9 | 13.1 | 9.8 | 8.9 | 22.0 | 20.4 | 10.7 | 10.1 | Worse |
| | 2.9 | 2.2 | 2.9 | 2.8 | 3.0 | 2.4 | 1.6 | 1.2 | Don't know |
| | (274) | (313) | (245) | (471) | (708) | (2874) | (516) | (1944) | Weighted N |
| **55-64 Only** | 34.5 | 36.5 | 38.1 | 54.0 | 30.4 | 31.2 | 32.6 | 27.9 | Better |
| | 47.8 | 44.4 | 40.4 | 32.7 | 45.4 | 43.1 | 54.6 | 59.6 | Same |
| | 13.8 | 16.2 | 15.6 | 8.5 | 20.4 | 22.7 | 11.1 | 10.3 | Worse |
| | 3.9 | 2.9 | 6.0 | 4.8 | 3.7 | 2.9 | 1.6 | 2.2 | Don't know |
| | (203) | (241) | (218) | (413) | (588) | (2761) | (377) | (1759) | Weighted N |
| **65-74 Only** | 27.2 | 31.4 | 30.8 | 46.2 | 26.7 | 23.7 | 24.8 | 26.4 | Better |
| | 56.6 | 50.3 | 52.5 | 39.7 | 45.7 | 49.1 | 59.4 | 60.2 | Same |
| | 14.0 | 16.2 | 10.4 | 6.2 | 24.1 | 24.5 | 9.9 | 8.5 | Worse |
| | 2.2 | 2.2 | 6.3 | 7.9 | 3.5 | 2.7 | 5.9 | 4.9 | Don't know |
| | (136) | (185) | (221) | (433) | (457) | (1834) | (303) | (1479) | Weighted N |
| **75 And Older Only** | 25.9 | 26.1 | ** | ** | 24.1 | 27.0 | 12.3 | 23.2 | Better |
| | 54.1 | 48.9 | ** | ** | 44.0 | 49.5 | 63.0 | 57.6 | Same |
| | 15.3 | 14.8 | ** | ** | 16.3 | 16.2 | 14.5 | 13.1 | Worse |
| | 4.7 | 10.2 | ** | ** | 15.6 | 7.2 | 10.1 | 6.1 | Don't know |
| | (85) | (88) | ** | ** | (282) | (1110) | (138) | (891) | Weighted N |

*Code distinction not made.

.dest age group coded "65 And Older" in 1965a and 1966a.

.e coded for head of household and wife only in 1964a,1965a,1966a,1968a,and 1969a.

Table 7.33
Are Current Business Conditions Better than Last Year's?
Age of Respondent

|  | Year | | | | | | | |
|---|---|---|---|---|---|---|---|---|
|  | 1970a | 1971m | 1972f | 1973c | 1975q | 1976m | 1978n | |
| 18-24 Only | 32.6% | 32.0% | 40.0% | 38.9% | 28.1% | 53.5% | 43.1% | Better |
|  | 29.3 | 27.0 | 30.5 | 28.8 | 12.9 | 12.1 | 14.4 | Same |
|  | 36.0 | 35.0 | 27.1 | 23.2 | 55.7 | 32.4 | 31.8 | Worse |
|  | 2.1 | 6.0 | 2.4 | 9.1 | 3.3 | 2.0 | 10.7 | Don't know |
|  | (239) | (100) | (210) | (198) | (449) | (20191) | (355) | Weighted N |
| 25-34 Only | 21.4 | 31.4 | 48.4 | 46.8 | 40.0 | 56.4 | 35.6 | Better |
|  | 24.0 | 22.0 | 24.4 | 24.8 | 12.0 | 12.9 | 14.6 | Same |
|  | 52.2 | 42.0 | 24.7 | 25.2 | 45.8 | 29.0 | 43.2 | Worse |
|  | 2.4 | 4.5 | 2.5 | 3.2 | 2.2 | 1.7 | 6.6 | Don't know |
|  | (412) | (245) | (279) | (310) | (677) | (26856) | (548) | Weighted N |
| 35-44 Only | 19.3 | 29.8 | 46.2 | 44.4 | 38.5 | 53.7 | 35.3 | Better |
|  | 22.2 | 28.2 | 26.2 | 31.8 | 13.0 | 19.0 | 19.4 | Same |
|  | 56.7 | 38.4 | 26.7 | 20.1 | 44.4 | 23.5 | 35.6 | Worse |
|  | 1.8 | 3.5 | 0.9 | 3.7 | 4.1 | 3.8 | 9.7 | Don't know |
|  | (436) | (255) | (221) | (214) | (486) | (17649) | (402) | Weighted N |
| 45-54 Only | 16.2 | 31.4 | 43.7 | 44.7 | 34.5 | 48.4 | 36.4 | Better |
|  | 26.1 | 25.1 | 22.6 | 30.1 | 16.8 | 11.9 | 18.6 | Same |
|  | 56.0 | 41.3 | 32.1 | 21.8 | 47.0 | 35.5 | 37.6 | Worse |
|  | 1.8 | 2.2 | 1.6 | 3.4 | 1.7 | 4.2 | 7.4 | Don't know |
|  | (452) | (271) | (190) | (206) | (411) | (18985) | (338) | Weighted N |
| 55-64 Only | 14.1 | 20.2 | 33.1 | 37.7 | 34.8 | 40.2 | 32.1 | Better |
|  | 30.8 | 33.7 | 39.5 | 29.8 | 18.2 | 18.7 | 23.1 | Same |
|  | 52.4 | 42.8 | 25.0 | 29.3 | 43.5 | 39.2 | 34.1 | Worse |
|  | 2.7 | 3.4 | 2.3 | 3.1 | 3.4 | 2.0 | 10.7 | Don't know |
|  | (370) | (208) | (172) | (191) | (379) | (16781) | (308) | Weighted N |
| 65-74 Only | 13.0 | 16.7 | 29.9 | 27.8 | 27.2 | 31.6 | 29.9 | Better |
|  | 35.0 | 43.9 | 41.5 | 32.5 | 25.7 | 27.1 | 20.9 | Same |
|  | 47.2 | 36.4 | 25.9 | 33.1 | 43.1 | 36.9 | 39.8 | Worse |
|  | 4.7 | 3.0 | 2.7 | 6.6 | 3.9 | 4.4 | 9.5 | Don't know |
|  | (254) | (132) | (147) | (151) | (334) | (14793) | (211) | Weighted N |
| 75 And Older Only | 17.1 | 12.2 | 18.6 | 20.3 | 30.1 | 34.6 | 20.3 | Better |
|  | 34.1 | 40.2 | 37.1 | 42.2 | 26.5 | 27.3 | 26.3 | Same |
|  | 40.3 | 37.8 | 35.7 | 28.1 | 30.1 | 22.5 | 31.4 | Worse |
|  | 8.5 | 9.8 | 8.6 | 9.4 | 13.2 | 15.7 | 22.0 | Don't know |
|  | (129) | (82) | (70) | (64) | (136) | (7559) | (118) | Weighted N |

Age coded for head of household and wife only in 1970a.

National Economic Outlook

Table 7.34
Are Current Business Conditions Better than Last Year's?
Income of Respondent

| | Year | | | | | | | | |
|---|---|---|---|---|---|---|---|---|---|
| | 1954m | 1956m | 1957f | 1958m | 1959f | 1960a | 1961a | 1962n | |
| Income 1 (0-16%) | 14.3% | 18.3% | 19.0% | 22.1% | 31.3% | 31.8% | 11.9% | 25.6% | Better |
| | 37.6 | 56.3 | 54.1 | 38.5 | 42.3 | 41.5 | 36.2 | 48.8 | Same |
| | 42.9 | 17.0 | 20.8 | 32.8 | 19.4 | 22.0 | 46.8 | 15.9 | Worse |
| | 5.3 | 8.5 | 6.1 | 6.6 | 7.0 | 4.7 | 5.1 | 9.8 | Don't know |
| | (189) | (224) | (231) | (244) | (201) | (537) | (7950) | (164) | Weighted N |
| Income 2 (17-33%) | 22.7 | 23.6 | 18.4 | 27.5 | 40.2 | 38.4 | 14.0 | 32.7 | Better |
| | 35.3 | 53.5 | 49.1 | 43.8 | 41.0 | 40.0 | 31.8 | 43.7 | Same |
| | 39.5 | 18.8 | 28.4 | 27.5 | 15.6 | 19.1 | 52.7 | 17.1 | Worse |
| | 2.5 | 4.2 | 4.1 | 1.3 | 3.3 | 2.5 | 1.6 | 6.5 | Don't know |
| | (119) | (144) | (320) | (153) | (122) | (607) | (9827) | (199) | Weighted N |
| Income 3 (34-67%) | 19.2 | 27.7 | 22.8 | 35.5 | 48.6 | 46.7 | 14.6 | 45.7 | Better |
| | 36.4 | 56.0 | 50.3 | 32.1 | 34.1 | 35.7 | 26.9 | 35.7 | Same |
| | 42.7 | 12.5 | 25.1 | 30.7 | 13.4 | 16.1 | 56.5 | 14.3 | Worse |
| | 1.7 | 3.8 | 1.7 | 1.8 | 3.9 | 1.5 | 2.0 | 4.3 | Don't know |
| | (302) | (582) | (517) | (499) | (461) | (1122) | (19432) | (512) | Weighted N |
| Income 4 (68-95%) | 26.4 | 37.7 | 24.7 | 45.7 | 64.1 | 52.6 | 10.7 | 48.1 | Better |
| | 33.3 | 49.0 | 47.4 | 29.3 | 24.1 | 29.8 | 25.4 | 34.8 | Same |
| | 37.7 | 11.3 | 26.8 | 23.9 | 10.5 | 15.6 | 63.3 | 15.7 | Worse |
| | 2.6 | 2.0 | 1.0 | 1.1 | 1.4 | 2.0 | 0.6 | 1.4 | Don't know |
| | (273) | (302) | (194) | (280) | (370) | (553) | (10684) | (287) | Weighted N |
| Income 5 (96-100%) | 26.2 | 33.3 | 36.7 | 44.9 | 73.7 | 59.8 | 11.7 | 41.3 | Better |
| | 32.3 | 50.5 | 50.0 | 26.5 | 23.7 | 21.4 | 23.1 | 38.1 | Same |
| | 40.0 | 14.3 | 13.3 | 26.5 | 2.6 | 18.8 | 65.2 | 20.6 | Worse |
| | 1.5 | 1.9 | 0.0 | 2.0 | 0.0 | 0.0 | 0.0 | 0.0 | Don't know |
| | (65) | (105) | (30) | (98) | (38) | (112) | (1561) | (63) | Weighted N |

National Economic Outlook

Table 7.35
Are Current Business Conditions Better than Last Year's?
Income of Respondent

|  | Year | | | | | | | |  |
|---|---|---|---|---|---|---|---|---|---|
|  | 1963m | 1964a | 1965a | 1966a | 1967a | 1968a | 1968n | 1969a |  |
| Income 1 (0-16%) | 28.7% | 27.6% | 28.8% | 38.6% | 27.7% | 24.6% | 21.1% | 20.4% | Better |
|  | 50.0 | 48.9 | 42.9 | 40.7 | 40.9 | 49.0 | 58.5 | 59.6 | Same |
|  | 16.7 | 17.8 | 15.9 | 10.6 | 19.7 | 20.6 | 14.1 | 13.2 | Worse |
|  | 4.6 | 5.8 | 12.4 | 10.1 | 11.6 | 5.9 | 6.3 | 6.9 | Don't know |
|  | (174) | (225) | (170) | (464) | (714) | (2530) | (412) | (2456) | Weighted N |
| Income 2 (17-33%) | 38.9 | 31.2 | 37.8 | 53.1 | 32.0 | 29.4 | 29.8 | 35.5 | Better |
|  | 47.1 | 45.6 | 46.8 | 33.7 | 46.8 | 44.7 | 52.6 | 50.6 | Same |
|  | 12.0 | 16.8 | 12.2 | 8.6 | 17.7 | 21.0 | 10.7 | 10.6 | Worse |
|  | 1.9 | 6.4 | 3.2 | 4.6 | 3.4 | 5.0 | 6.9 | 3.4 | Don't know |
|  | (208) | (250) | (222) | (478) | (553) | (2587) | (346) | (2243) | Weighted N |
| Income 3 (34-67%) | 37.8 | 44.4 | 42.8 | 63.2 | 38.7 | 39.9 | 39.1 | 40.4 | Better |
|  | 44.7 | 40.5 | 42.6 | 26.7 | 35.3 | 39.0 | 48.4 | 48.6 | Same |
|  | 15.2 | 12.8 | 11.8 | 7.1 | 23.5 | 19.8 | 9.3 | 10.2 | Worse |
|  | 2.3 | 2.3 | 2.8 | 3.0 | 2.5 | 1.2 | 3.2 | 0.8 | Don't know |
|  | (389) | (531) | (425) | (821) | (1412) | (5164) | (1006) | (3844) | Weighted N |
| Income 4 (68-95%) | 48.3 | 51.4 | 49.6 | 66.6 | 35.7 | 43.6 | 42.1 | 41.8 | Better |
|  | 35.7 | 35.8 | 37.5 | 26.0 | 36.5 | 34.3 | 46.6 | 44.8 | Same |
|  | 13.4 | 11.3 | 11.0 | 5.1 | 26.9 | 21.4 | 8.5 | 12.0 | Worse |
|  | 2.6 | 1.6 | 1.9 | 2.3 | 0.9 | 0.8 | 2.8 | 1.3 | Don't know |
|  | (381) | (444) | (419) | (488) | (691) | (4383) | (672) | (2623) | Weighted N |
| Income 5 (96-100%) | 52.9 | 52.7 | 62.3 | 71.8 | 30.7 | 38.2 | 48.9 | 37.1 | Better |
|  | 36.8 | 36.5 | 29.2 | 18.1 | 35.0 | 34.0 | 35.9 | 48.8 | Same |
|  | 9.2 | 9.5 | 5.7 | 8.7 | 33.7 | 25.1 | 10.7 | 11.4 | Worse |
|  | 1.1 | 1.4 | 2.8 | 1.3 | 0.6 | 2.7 | 4.6 | 2.6 | Don't know |
|  | (87) | (74) | (106) | (149) | (323) | (752) | (131) | (420) | Weighted N |

Table 7.36
Are Current Business Conditions Better than Last Year's?
Income of Respondent

| | | | | Year | | | | |
|---|---|---|---|---|---|---|---|---|
| | 1970a | 1971m | 1972f | 1973c | 1975q | 1976m | 1978n | |
| Income 1 (0-16%) | 20.6% | 13.1% | 25.8% | 24.9% | 22.9% | 43.8% | 30.7% | Better |
| | 36.2 | 39.8 | 41.6 | 37.3 | 19.7 | 15.6 | 18.2 | Same |
| | 36.8 | 39.3 | 28.5 | 30.2 | 50.2 | 35.7 | 34.6 | Worse |
| | 6.3 | 7.9 | 4.1 | 7.7 | 7.2 | 5.0 | 16.4 | Don't know |
| | (475) | (191) | (221) | (169) | (432) | (22071) | (335) | Weighted N |
| Income 2 (17-33%) | 18.3 | 19.5 | 32.7 | 36.3 | 31.1 | 53.2 | 35.1 | Better |
| | 37.3 | 35.7 | 39.5 | 31.5 | 20.2 | 11.7 | 14.2 | Same |
| | 40.2 | 39.8 | 22.4 | 28.3 | 44.2 | 32.8 | 40.1 | Worse |
| | 4.1 | 5.0 | 5.4 | 3.8 | 4.4 | 2.3 | 10.6 | Don't know |
| | (415) | (241) | (147) | (314) | (495) | (24320) | (359) | Weighted N |
| Income 3 (34-67%) | 20.7 | 30.3 | 43.5 | 40.9 | 36.7 | 53.5 | 37.6 | Better |
| | 25.6 | 26.0 | 29.3 | 28.6 | 16.8 | 15.6 | 19.7 | Same |
| | 51.9 | 40.9 | 24.9 | 25.3 | 45.0 | 28.4 | 35.1 | Worse |
| | 1.8 | 2.8 | 2.2 | 5.2 | 1.5 | 2.5 | 7.6 | Don't know |
| | (888) | (465) | (457) | (364) | (822) | (14521) | (615) | Weighted N |
| Income 4 (68-95%) | 16.4 | 34.8 | 45.2 | 50.0 | 39.9 | 60.5 | 37.5 | Better |
| | 20.2 | 22.7 | 22.9 | 23.9 | 9.8 | 15.0 | 17.8 | Same |
| | 61.7 | 40.5 | 31.3 | 23.3 | 48.6 | 22.6 | 37.9 | Worse |
| | 1.6 | 2.0 | 0.6 | 2.9 | 1.7 | 1.9 | 6.8 | Don't know |
| | (669) | (299) | (323) | (348) | (632) | (9285) | (533) | Weighted N |
| Income 5 (96-100%) | 9.3 | 26.9 | 65.4 | 49.5 | 44.3 | 57.8 | 34.9 | Better |
| | 24.1 | 32.7 | 10.3 | 33.3 | 16.1 | 16.5 | 19.9 | Same |
| | 65.7 | 34.6 | 24.4 | 14.0 | 38.3 | 25.7 | 40.4 | Worse |
| | 0.9 | 5.8 | 0.0 | 3.2 | 1.3 | 0.0 | 4.8 | Don't know |
| | (108) | (52) | (78) | (93) | (149) | (8337) | (146) | Weighted N |

Table 7-37
Will Business Conditions Be Better a Year from Now?
Total Population

QUESTION: And how about a year from now, do you expect that in the country as a whole business conditions will be better or worse?

|  | | Year | | | | | | | |
|---|---|---|---|---|---|---|---|---|---|
|  | | 1954m | 1956m | 1957f | 1958m | 1959f | 1960a | 1961a | 1962n |
| Better | (5) | 19.1% | 15.7% | 13.0% | 32.2% | 27.5% | 34.1% | 51.3% | 24.7% |
| Same | (3) | 62.1 | 73.1 | 71.5 | 56.5 | 62.8 | 54.1 | 37.0 | 61.1 |
| Worse | (1) | 11.5 | 4.4 | 8.8 | 4.9 | 4.8 | 6.5 | 6.2 | 5.1 |
| Don't Know | | 7.3 | 6.8 | 6.7 | 6.4 | 4.9 | 5.3 | 5.6 | 9.1 |
| Total | | 100% | 100% | 100% | 100% | 100% | 100% | 100% | 100% |
| Weighted N | | 990 | 1429 | 1334 | 1330 | 1295 | 2867 | 49471 | 1287 |
| Unweighted N | | 990 | 1429 | 1334 | 1330 | 1295 | 2867 | 1960 | 1287 |
| Mean | | 3.16 | 3.24 | 3.09 | 3.58 | 3.48 | 3.58 | 3.95 | 3.43 |
| Standard Deviation | | 1.14 | 0.90 | 0.96 | 1.12 | 1.06 | 1.17 | 1.23 | 1.06 |

Table 7-38

|  | | 1963m | 1964a | 1965m | 1966a | 1967a | 1968a | 1969a | 1970a |
|---|---|---|---|---|---|---|---|---|---|
| Better | (5) | 24.0% | 30.9% | 36.1% | 29.5% | 21.7% | 20.6% | 21.7% | 20.3% |
| Same | (3) | 62.8 | 56.0 | 53.2 | 54.9 | 60.2 | 57.9 | 61.8 | 49.7 |
| Worse | (1) | 6.6 | 8.0 | 5.9 | 8.4 | 11.7 | 15.1 | 11.8 | 25.7 |
| Don't Know | | 6.6 | 5.1 | 4.8 | 7.2 | 6.3 | 6.4 | 4.7 | 4.3 |
| Total | | 100% | 100% | 100% | 100% | 100% | 100% | 100% | 100% |
| Weighted N | | 1309 | 1529 | 1641 | 2371 | 3644 | 15318 | 11470 | 2538 |
| Unweighted N | | 1309 | 1529 | 1641 | 2371 | 3094 | 2630 | 2283 | 2538 |
| Mean | | 3.37 | 3.48 | 3.63 | 3.45 | 3.21 | 3.12 | 3.21 | 2.89 |
| Standard Deviation | | 1.08 | 1.19 | 1.17 | 1.19 | 1.18 | 1.23 | 1.17 | 1.38 |

Table 7-39

|  | | 1971m | 1972f | 1973c | 1974q | 1975q | 1976m | 1978n |
|---|---|---|---|---|---|---|---|---|
| Better | (5) | 33.4% | 31.1% | 25.1% | 18.3% | 30.1% | 39.9% | 14.9% |
| Same | (3) | 47.3 | 51.9 | 47.5 | 39.1 | 47.5 | 46.8 | 39.7 |
| Worse | (1) | 13.7 | 12.0 | 22.1 | 36.5 | 17.1 | 9.2 | 35.7 |
| Don't Know | | 5.6 | 4.9 | 5.2 | 6.1 | 5.2 | 4.1 | 9.7 |
| Total | | 100% | 100% | 100% | 100% | 100% | 100% | 100% |
| Weighted N | | 1295 | 1288 | 1341 | 2960 | 2897 | 126288 | 2292 |
| Unweighted N | | 1295 | 1288 | 1341 | 1507 | 1507 | 1127 | 2292 |
| Mean | | 3.42 | 3.40 | 3.06 | 2.61 | 3.27 | 3.64 | 2.54 |
| Standard Deviation | | 1.35 | 1.29 | 1.41 | 1.48 | 1.38 | 1.28 | 1.42 |

National Economic Outlook

Figure 7.5
Business Conditions in a Year--Total Population

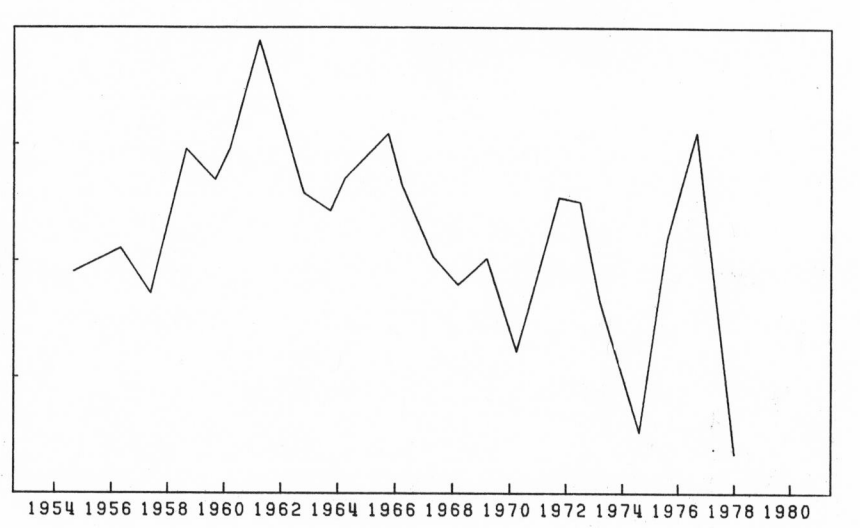

National Economic Outlook

Table 7.40
Will Business Conditions Be Better a Year from Now?
Sex of Respondent

Year

|  | 1954m | 1956m | 1957f | 1958m | 1959f | 1960a | 1961a | 1962n |  |
|---|---|---|---|---|---|---|---|---|---|
| Males Only | 21.7% | 20.2% | 15.4% | 38.6% | 32.3% | 36.8% | 53.9% | 29.2% | Better |
|  | 60.2 | 69.6 | 70.5 | 52.0 | 59.1 | 52.1 | 35.6 | 58.9 | Same |
|  | 12.5 | 5.9 | 8.6 | 4.6 | 5.2 | 7.0 | 6.6 | 6.0 | Worse |
|  | 5.6 | 4.4 | 5.4 | 4.8 | 3.4 | 4.1 | 3.9 | 5.9 | Don't know |
|  | (465) | (665) | (570) | (560) | (563) | (1928) | (40409) | (579) | Weighted N |
| Females Only | 16.6 | 11.9 | 11.1 | 27.5 | 23.6 | 28.6 | 40.0 | 21.0 | Better |
|  | 64.1 | 76.0 | 72.3 | 59.9 | 65.8 | 58.1 | 42.2 | 62.9 | Same |
|  | 10.7 | 3.1 | 9.0 | 5.1 | 4.5 | 5.4 | 4.7 | 4.4 | Worse |
|  | 8.6 | 8.9 | 7.5 | 7.5 | 6.2 | 7.8 | 13.2 | 11.7 | Don't know |
|  | (523) | (763) | (763) | (770) | (730) | (939) | (8954) | (708) | Weighted N |

Table 7.41

|  | 1963m | 1964a | 1965m | 1966a | 1967a | 1968a | 1969a | 1970a |  |
|---|---|---|---|---|---|---|---|---|---|
| Males Only | 27.9% | 33.3% | 39.5% | 32.1% | 23.9% | 22.7% | 22.2% | 21.8% | Better |
|  | 62.1 | 54.6 | 51.5 | 53.8 | 59.9 | 57.0 | 62.1 | 48.0 | Same |
|  | 6.5 | 8.3 | 5.5 | 8.1 | 11.2 | 14.7 | 12.2 | 26.6 | Worse |
|  | 3.5 | 3.9 | 3.5 | 6.0 | 5.0 | 5.5 | 3.5 | 3.6 | Don't know |
|  | (538) | (1160) | (1172) | (1846) | (2762) | (11147) | (8298) | (1834) | Weighted N |
| Females Only | 21.3 | 23.0 | 27.8 | 20.6 | 14.9 | 15.1 | 20.5 | 16.5 | Better |
|  | 63.3 | 60.8 | 57.5 | 58.7 | 61.3 | 59.7 | 60.8 | 54.0 | Same |
|  | 6.7 | 7.1 | 6.8 | 9.3 | 13.3 | 16.3 | 10.9 | 23.4 | Worse |
|  | 8.7 | 9.0 | 7.9 | 11.4 | 10.5 | 8.9 | 7.7 | 6.1 | Don't know |
|  | (771) | (365) | (468) | (525) | (882) | (4058) | (3172) | (704) | Weighted N |

Table 7.42

|  | 1971m | 1972f | 1973c | 1974q | 1975q | 1976m | 1978n |  |
|---|---|---|---|---|---|---|---|---|
| Males Only | 36.0% | 35.2% | 30.4% | 20.8% | 36.2% | 45.8% | 17.7% | Better |
|  | 46.7 | 48.4 | 43.7 | 37.6 | 41.7 | 41.6 | 36.3 | Same |
|  | 12.9 | 12.7 | 22.3 | 37.5 | 17.2 | 10.6 | 39.1 | Worse |
|  | 4.3 | 3.7 | 3.7 | 4.1 | 4.9 | 2.0 | 7.0 | Don't know |
|  | (905) | (545) | (575) | (1329) | (1336) | (50005) | (1014) | Weighted N |
| Females Only | 27.2 | 28.1 | 21.1 | 16.3 | 25.0 | 36.8 | 12.7 | Better |
|  | 48.7 | 54.5 | 50.4 | 40.2 | 52.5 | 50.5 | 42.3 | Same |
|  | 15.4 | 11.6 | 22.1 | 35.7 | 17.0 | 8.1 | 33.1 | Worse |
|  | 8.7 | 5.8 | 6.4 | 7.7 | 5.5 | 4.6 | 11.9 | Don't know |
|  | (390) | (743) | (766) | (1631) | (1561) | (74870) | (1278) | Weighted N |

Sex coded for head of household and wife only in 1965m.

National Economic Outlook

Table 7.43
Will Business Conditions Be Better a Year from Now?
Race of Respondent

|  | Year | | | | | | | | |
|---|---|---|---|---|---|---|---|---|---|
|  | 1954m | 1956m | 1957f | 1958m | 1959f | 1960a | 1961a | 1962n | |
| Whites Only | 18.1% | 15.6% | 13.0% | 33.7% | 27.6% | 34.5% | 51.4% | 23.8% | Better |
|  | 64.1 | 73.2 | 72.3 | 56.0 | 62.9 | 54.7 | 36.6 | 62.2 | Same |
|  | 11.0 | 4.6 | 8.3 | 5.2 | 4.9 | 6.0 | 6.6 | 5.1 | Worse |
|  | 6.8 | 6.6 | 6.4 | 5.1 | 4.6 | 4.9 | 5.4 | 8.9 | Don't know |
|  | (891) | (1304) | (1183) | (1167) | (1151) | (2565) | (44221) | (1167) | Weighted N |
| Blacks Only | 30.7 | 16.7 | 11.8 | 22.4 | 25.4 | 31.5 | 50.3 | 34.9 | Better |
|  | 40.9 | 71.1 | 66.9 | 58.7 | 62.7 | 50.6 | 39.1 | 50.5 | Same |
|  | 17.0 | 2.6 | 13.2 | 2.8 | 4.0 | 9.7 | 2.9 | 6.4 | Worse |
|  | 11.4 | 9.6 | 8.1 | 16.1 | 7.9 | 8.1 | 7.6 | 8.3 | Don't know |
|  | (88) | (114) | (136) | (143) | (126) | (308) | (4842) | (109) | Weighted N |

Table 7.44

|  | 1963m | 1964a | 1965m | 1966a | 1967a | 1968a | 1969a | 1970a | |
|---|---|---|---|---|---|---|---|---|---|
| Whites Only | 24.1% | 30.8% | 35.7% | 28.9% | 21.0% | 20.2% | 21.6% | 20.9% | Better |
|  | 63.6 | 56.9 | 53.5 | 56.0 | 60.9 | 58.0 | 62.3 | 49.2 | Same |
|  | 6.0 | 7.6 | 6.0 | 8.4 | 12.2 | 15.5 | 11.3 | 25.4 | Worse |
|  | 6.4 | 4.7 | 4.8 | 6.7 | 5.9 | 6.3 | 4.9 | 4.5 | Don't know |
|  | (1158) | (1346) | (1420) | (2143) | (3203) | (13555) | (10140) | (2230) | Weighted N |
| Blacks Only | 23.4 | 33.8 | 39.5 | 34.9 | 26.9 | 24.9 | 23.0 | 17.6 | Better |
|  | 56.5 | 48.5 | 51.1 | 44.3 | 55.3 | 59.4 | 57.5 | 52.3 | Same |
|  | 13.7 | 11.0 | 5.3 | 10.4 | 7.2 | 9.8 | 16.2 | 27.2 | Worse |
|  | 6.5 | 6.6 | 4.2 | 10.4 | 10.6 | 5.9 | 3.3 | 2.9 | Don't know |
|  | (124) | (136) | (190) | (192) | (360) | (1414) | (1153) | (279) | Weighted N |

Table 7.45

|  | 1971m | 1972f | 1973c | 1974q | 1975q | 1976m | 1978n | |
|---|---|---|---|---|---|---|---|---|
| Whites Only | 34.3% | 31.3% | 26.7% | 18.4% | 31.0% | 39.1% | 14.3% | Better |
|  | 47.0 | 52.3 | 47.0 | 39.5 | 48.6 | 47.8 | 39.5 | Same |
|  | 12.9 | 11.5 | 21.5 | 36.4 | 15.8 | 9.9 | 37.1 | Worse |
|  | 5.8 | 4.8 | 4.8 | 5.8 | 4.6 | 3.2 | 9.2 | Don't know |
|  | (1130) | (1158) | (1114) | (2539) | (2566) | (106778) | (2007) | Weighted N |
| Blacks Only | 26.2 | 29.2 | 15.3 | 14.2 | 20.1 | 46.5 | 19.5 | Better |
|  | 50.8 | 49.6 | 52.5 | 43.9 | 42.7 | 41.9 | 43.3 | Same |
|  | 18.5 | 15.9 | 28.8 | 37.5 | 28.5 | 3.9 | 23.4 | Worse |
|  | 4.6 | 5.3 | 3.4 | 4.4 | 8.8 | 7.7 | 13.9 | Don't know |
|  | (130) | (113) | (118) | (296) | (239) | (11470) | (231) | Weighted N |

Table 7-46
Will Business Conditions Be Better a Year from Now?
Education of Respondent

|  | Year | | | | | | | |  |
|---|---|---|---|---|---|---|---|---|---|
|  | 1954m | 1956m | 1957f | 1958m | 1959f | 1960a | 1961a | 1962n |  |
| Grade School Only | 14.4% | 13.8% | 11.1% | 22.3% | 18.5% | 28.0% | 43.3% | 18.5% | Better |
|  | 60.2 | 69.8 | 70.1 | 62.3 | 66.4 | 55.9 | 42.9 | 62.9 | Same |
|  | 13.8 | 6.0 | 8.0 | 5.0 | 7.7 | 8.7 | 6.6 | 5.9 | Worse |
|  | 11.6 | 10.4 | 10.8 | 10.3 | 7.3 | 7.4 | 7.2 | 12.6 | Don't know |
|  | (354) | (318) | (314) | (300) | (286) | (789) | (14652) | (356) | Weighted N |
| High School Only | 20.7 | 18.1 | 13.7 | 36.1 | 32.0 | 35.3 | 52.5 | 25.8 | Better |
|  | 63.3 | 74.8 | 69.4 | 54.5 | 60.8 | 54.5 | 36.5 | 62.6 | Same |
|  | 11.1 | 3.0 | 11.3 | 4.7 | 4.6 | 6.0 | 6.1 | 3.7 | Worse |
|  | 4.8 | 4.2 | 5.5 | 4.7 | 2.6 | 4.3 | 4.9 | 7.9 | Don't know |
|  | (458) | (337) | (291) | (341) | (347) | (1075) | (22053) | (617) | Weighted N |
| College Only | 23.7 | 25.6 | 19.4 | 48.7 | 42.0 | 41.1 | 59.4 | 29.9 | Better |
|  | 62.3 | 65.1 | 66.7 | 43.3 | 50.3 | 48.2 | 31.1 | 55.8 | Same |
|  | 9.6 | 7.0 | 9.0 | 3.3 | 4.2 | 6.4 | 5.7 | 6.8 | Worse |
|  | 4.4 | 2.3 | 4.9 | 4.7 | 3.5 | 4.4 | 3.9 | 7.5 | Don't know |
|  | (114) | (172) | (144) | (150) | (143) | (550) | (12061) | (308) | Weighted N |

Table 7-47

|  | 1963m | 1964a | 1965m | 1966a | 1967a | 1968a | 1969a | 1970a |  |
|---|---|---|---|---|---|---|---|---|---|
| Grade School Only | 17.5% | 20.7% | 21.4% | 22.8% | 14.7% | 15.3% | 18.9% | 17.1% | Better |
|  | 67.7 | 64.7 | 62.4 | 58.3 | 63.6 | 62.1 | 64.7 | 50.1 | Same |
|  | 7.5 | 8.2 | 7.8 | 10.3 | 10.5 | 14.0 | 10.1 | 27.2 | Worse |
|  | 7.3 | 6.4 | 8.5 | 8.5 | 11.3 | 8.5 | 6.3 | 5.7 | Don't know |
|  | (371) | (487) | (425) | (667) | (1040) | (4317) | (2990) | (953) | Weighted N |
| High School Only | 24.6 | 31.5 | 40.3 | 30.0 | 21.7 | 21.2 | 19.5 | 20.7 | Better |
|  | 62.2 | 54.7 | 51.1 | 55.6 | 62.5 | 58.1 | 64.8 | 50.5 | Same |
|  | 6.3 | 9.2 | 5.5 | 7.5 | 11.3 | 14.5 | 12.1 | 25.7 | Worse |
|  | 6.8 | 4.6 | 3.1 | 6.9 | 4.5 | 6.1 | 3.6 | 3.1 | Don't know |
|  | (662) | (654) | (640) | (1001) | (1681) | (7018) | (5107) | (1113) | Weighted N |
| College Only | 31.8 | 43.4 | 48.0 | 36.7 | 30.5 | 25.9 | 27.7 | 27.4 | Better |
|  | 57.6 | 47.7 | 43.5 | 50.3 | 52.4 | 52.2 | 54.8 | 46.2 | Same |
|  | 6.1 | 5.1 | 5.3 | 7.9 | 13.5 | 17.1 | 12.8 | 22.0 | Worse |
|  | 4.5 | 3.8 | 3.3 | 5.1 | 3.6 | 4.7 | 4.8 | 4.4 | Don't know |
|  | (264) | (373) | (400) | (594) | (880) | (3778) | (3283) | (409) | Weighted N |

Education coded for head of household only in 1956m,1957f,1958m,1959f,1960a,1961a,1965m,and 1966a, and for head and wife only in 1963m,1964a,1967a,1968a,1969a,and 1970a.

Table 7.48
Will Business Conditions Be Better a Year from Now?
Education of Respondent

|                    | Year |  |  |  |  |  |  | |
|--------------------|-------|-------|-------|-------|-------|-------|-------|---------------|
|                    | 1971m | 1972f | 1973c | 1974q | 1975q | 1976m | 1978n | |
| Grade School Only  | 21.5% | 21.9% | 12.1% | 11.1% | 18.6% | 36.3% | 13.2% | Better |
|                    | 53.0  | 55.4  | 57.3  | 42.6  | 50.2  | 44.0  | 41.0  | Same |
|                    | 18.1  | 14.0  | 25.5  | 35.6  | 20.2  | 11.7  | 28.2  | Worse |
|                    | 7.5   | 8.7   | 5.1   | 10.7  | 10.9  | 8.0   | 17.6  | Don't know |
|                    | (321) | (242) | (157) | (486) | (440) | (16570) | (273) | Weighted N |
|                    |       |       |       |       |       |       |       | |
| High School Only   | 32.9  | 29.4  | 24.8  | 17.9  | 27.6  | 39.9  | 14.1  | Better |
|                    | 49.2  | 53.3  | 48.3  | 40.8  | 52.0  | 48.8  | 43.6  | Same |
|                    | 11.8  | 12.7  | 21.7  | 35.4  | 16.3  | 7.9   | 32.8  | Worse |
|                    | 6.1   | 4.5   | 5.2   | 5.8   | 4.0   | 3.4   | 9.6   | Don't know |
|                    | (575) | (660) | (621) | (1408)| (1511)| (59582)| (1203)| Weighted N |
|                    |       |       |       |       |       |       |       | |
| College Only       | 44.2  | 40.5  | 31.5  | 22.2  | 39.3  | 41.7  | 16.6  | Better |
|                    | 39.9  | 47.6  | 43.6  | 35.7  | 39.3  | 46.2  | 33.7  | Same |
|                    | 12.3  | 8.9   | 20.9  | 38.3  | 16.8  | 9.7   | 42.9  | Worse |
|                    | 3.6   | 2.9   | 4.0   | 3.8   | 4.6   | 2.5   | 6.8   | Don't know |
|                    | (391) | (380) | (397) | (1045)| (941) | (44908)| (807) | Weighted N |

Education coded for head of household only in 1971m.

Table 7-49

Will Business Conditions Be Better a Year from Now?

Age of Respondent

|  | Year | | | | | | | |  |
|---|---|---|---|---|---|---|---|---|---|
|  | 1954m | 1956m | 1957f | 1958m | 1959f | 1960a | 1961a | 1962n |  |
| 18-24 Only | 18.8% | 14.6% | 14.5% | 46.2% | 30.8% | 39.8% | 46.0% | 22.4% | Better |
|  | 67.2 | 74.2 | 73.5 | 46.2 | 63.5 | 51.2 | 40.5 | 60.5 | Same |
|  | 10.9 | 2.2 | 8.4 | 2.6 | 3.8 | 3.0 | 7.0 | 6.6 | Worse |
|  | 3.1 | 9.0 | 3.6 | 5.1 | 1.9 | 6.0 | 6.5 | 10.5 | Don't know |
|  | (64) | (89) | (83) | (39) | (52) | (201) | (4551) | (76) | Weighted N |
| 25-34 Only | 17.2 | 18.6 | 18.0 | 46.9 | 33.8 | 40.2 | 55.4 | 32.0 | Better |
|  | 65.6 | 74.4 | 71.2 | 46.9 | 57.6 | 53.1 | 36.6 | 57.9 | Same |
|  | 10.9 | 3.7 | 7.9 | 4.2 | 2.9 | 4.4 | 4.3 | 3.5 | Worse |
|  | 6.3 | 3.4 | 2.9 | 2.1 | 5.8 | 2.3 | 3.7 | 6.6 | Don't know |
|  | (256) | (328) | (278) | (143) | (139) | (480) | (10449) | (259) | Weighted N |
| 35-44 Only | 21.0 | 17.7 | 12.4 | 34.5 | 35.3 | 35.8 | 52.9 | 26.9 | Better |
|  | 58.5 | 75.6 | 73.2 | 55.9 | 54.9 | 53.2 | 36.4 | 61.8 | Same |
|  | 12.1 | 2.7 | 8.6 | 3.4 | 6.5 | 7.4 | 6.7 | 6.0 | Worse |
|  | 8.5 | 4.0 | 5.7 | 6.2 | 3.3 | 3.5 | 4.0 | 5.3 | Don't know |
|  | (224) | (328) | (314) | (177) | (153) | (539) | (11075) | (283) | Weighted N |
| 45-54 Only | 18.9 | 15.9 | 10.8 | 30.0 | 34.1 | 34.6 | 54.1 | 22.3 | Better |
|  | 64.2 | 73.1 | 73.4 | 59.3 | 59.4 | 52.8 | 34.8 | 66.5 | Same |
|  | 10.4 | 4.8 | 9.7 | 4.0 | 3.6 | 6.8 | 6.7 | 4.6 | Worse |
|  | 6.5 | 6.3 | 6.1 | 6.7 | 2.9 | 5.8 | 4.4 | 6.5 | Don't know |
|  | (201) | (271) | (278) | (150) | (138) | (483) | (9388) | (260) | Weighted N |
| 55-64 Only | 18.8 | 16.2 | 9.8 | 30.2 | 23.6 | 26.1 | 52.0 | 21.4 | Better |
|  | 65.2 | 70.5 | 77.2 | 58.1 | 64.9 | 58.8 | 35.6 | 62.2 | Same |
|  | 12.5 | 4.8 | 8.2 | 5.3 | 8.1 | 9.0 | 4.0 | 4.1 | Worse |
|  | 3.6 | 8.6 | 4.9 | 6.4 | 3.4 | 6.2 | 8.4 | 12.2 | Don't know |
|  | (112) | (210) | (184) | (658) | (148) | (357) | (7291) | (196) | Weighted N |
| 65-74 Only | 19.5 | 8.6 | 12.4 | 23.3 | 18.0 | 27.9 | 45.9 | 21.7 | Better |
|  | 53.9 | 69.4 | 60.6 | 59.5 | 66.7 | 51.6 | 37.5 | 57.2 | Same |
|  | 13.3 | 8.1 | 10.4 | 6.7 | 7.3 | 10.4 | 11.2 | 3.6 | Worse |
|  | 13.3 | 14.0 | 16.6 | 10.4 | 8.0 | 10.1 | 5.4 | 17.4 | Don't know |
|  | (128) | (186) | (193) | (163) | (150) | (366) | (4258) | (138) | Weighted N |
| 75 And Older Only | ** | ** | ** | ** | ** | ** | 32.7 | 14.7 | Better |
|  | ** | ** | ** | ** | ** | ** | 43.0 | 55.9 | Same |
|  | ** | ** | ** | ** | ** | ** | 7.1 | 14.7 | Worse |
|  | ** | ** | ** | ** | ** | ** | 17.1 | 14.7 | Don't know |
|  | ** | ** | ** | ** | ** | ** | (2217) | (68) | Weighted N |

** Code distinction not made.

Youngest age group coded "21-24" in 1954m.

Oldest age group coded "65 And Older" in 1954m,1956m,1957f,1958m,1959f,and 1960a.

Age coded for head of household only in 1958m,1959f,1960a,and 1961a.

Table 7-50

Will Business Conditions Be Better a Year from Now?

Age of Respondent

|  | Year | | | | | | | | |
|---|---|---|---|---|---|---|---|---|---|
|  | 1963m | 1964a | 1965m | 1966a | 1967a | 1968a | 1969a | 1970a | |
| 18-24 Only | 34.0% | 41.1% | 45.7% | 36.5% | 30.0% | 26.7% | 31.1% | 31.0% | Better |
|  | 57.0 | 48.6 | 44.1 | 48.2 | 53.8 | 52.2 | 52.7 | 46.4 | Same |
|  | 4.0 | 7.5 | 7.1 | 12.4 | 13.4 | 16.6 | 11.4 | 20.1 | Worse |
|  | 5.0 | 2.8 | 3.1 | 2.9 | 2.8 | 4.5 | 4.7 | 2.5 | Don't know |
|  | (100) | (107) | (127) | (170) | (247) | (968) | (1092) | (239) | Weighted N |
| 25-34 Only | 25.3 | 37.4 | 44.7 | 32.7 | 27.1 | 27.9 | 25.6 | 25.9 | Better |
|  | 60.9 | 52.3 | 48.0 | 50.9 | 55.9 | 53.2 | 57.0 | 49.3 | Same |
|  | 6.9 | 6.5 | 4.0 | 9.2 | 12.6 | 13.3 | 14.0 | 20.2 | Worse |
|  | 6.9 | 3.8 | 3.3 | 7.1 | 4.4 | 5.6 | 3.4 | 4.6 | Don't know |
|  | (233) | (262) | (302) | (434) | (658) | (2840) | (2305) | (410) | Weighted N |
| 35-44 Only | 28.4 | 31.3 | 40.8 | 38.3 | 27.6 | 25.4 | 24.2 | 24.0 | Better |
|  | 59.3 | 56.4 | 50.8 | 50.9 | 58.8 | 56.8 | 58.8 | 49.1 | Same |
|  | 8.2 | 7.4 | 6.3 | 6.4 | 10.9 | 11.7 | 12.3 | 24.2 | Worse |
|  | 4.1 | 4.9 | 2.1 | 4.4 | 2.7 | 6.1 | 4.7 | 2.8 | Don't know |
|  | (268) | (326) | (331) | (454) | (704) | (2820) | (1975) | (434) | Weighted N |
| 45-54 Only | 25.7 | 34.1 | 38.5 | 29.6 | 22.7 | 22.7 | 18.1 | 18.2 | Better |
|  | 60.3 | 52.9 | 54.1 | 57.9 | 61.1 | 60.5 | 69.5 | 50.1 | Same |
|  | 7.0 | 7.6 | 3.7 | 5.8 | 10.5 | 12.2 | 8.5 | 27.7 | Worse |
|  | 7.0 | 5.4 | 3.7 | 6.7 | 5.7 | 4.6 | 3.9 | 4.0 | Don't know |
|  | (272) | (314) | (327) | (466) | (696) | (2814) | (1945) | (455) | Weighted N |
| 55-64 Only | 19.7 | 28.0 | 35.5 | 23.2 | 17.4 | 15.7 | 16.6 | 16.5 | Better |
|  | 69.0 | 57.2 | 54.6 | 58.5 | 64.4 | 61.6 | 66.1 | 47.4 | Same |
|  | 5.4 | 8.6 | 6.4 | 8.8 | 10.3 | 15.6 | 12.0 | 32.0 | Worse |
|  | 5.9 | 6.2 | 3.6 | 9.5 | 7.9 | 7.2 | 5.3 | 4.1 | Don't know |
|  | (203) | (243) | (251) | (410) | (582) | (2756) | (1768) | (369) | Weighted N |
| 65-74 Only | 16.9 | 21.1 | 16.4 | 20.1 | 10.9 | 12.8 | 20.0 | 11.4 | Better |
|  | 71.3 | 63.8 | 62.5 | 59.1 | 66.5 | 58.7 | 61.3 | 54.3 | Same |
|  | 5.1 | 10.3 | 9.0 | 10.7 | 14.4 | 21.4 | 13.1 | 28.7 | Worse |
|  | 6.6 | 4.9 | 12.0 | 10.0 | 8.1 | 7.1 | 5.6 | 5.5 | Don't know |
|  | (136) | (185) | (299) | (428) | (457) | (1824) | (1443) | (254) | Weighted N |
| 75 And Older Only | 12.9 | 13.6 | ** | ** | 12.2 | 6.2 | 14.3 | 14.0 | Better |
|  | 63.5 | 67.0 | ** | ** | 59.0 | 58.4 | 69.4 | 47.3 | Same |
|  | 8.2 | 10.2 | ** | ** | 10.8 | 23.0 | 9.2 | 27.1 | Worse |
|  | 15.3 | 9.1 | ** | ** | 18.0 | 12.4 | 7.1 | 11.6 | Don't know |
|  | (85) | (88) | ** | ** | (278) | (1130) | (882) | (129) | Weighted N |

** Code distinction not made.

Youngest age group coded "Under 25" in 1965m.

Oldest age group coded "65 And Older" in 1965m and 1966a.

Age coded for head of household and wife only in 1964a,1966a,1967a,1968a,1969a and 1970a.

ble 7.51

ll Business Conditions Be Better a Year from Now?

e of Respondent

|  | Year | | | | | | | |
|---|---|---|---|---|---|---|---|---|
|  | 1971m | 1972f | 1973c | 1974q | 1975q | 1976m | 1978n | |
| 18-24 Only | 29.3% | 34.9% | 28.4% | 18.8% | 28.7% | 43.9% | 18.3% | Better |
|  | 49.5 | 55.0 | 45.8 | 40.0 | 45.3 | 47.1 | 44.2 | Same |
|  | 17.2 | 9.6 | 21.4 | 36.9 | 23.8 | 5.6 | 29.9 | Worse |
|  | 4.0 | 0.5 | 4.5 | 4.3 | 2.2 | 3.4 | 7.6 | Don't know |
|  | (99) | (209) | (201) | (485) | (450) | (19971) | (355) | Weighted N |
| 25-34 Only | 37.6 | 31.2 | 27.9 | 17.2 | 31.5 | 40.5 | 15.3 | Better |
|  | 47.8 | 55.9 | 45.1 | 40.7 | 47.0 | 48.7 | 41.5 | Same |
|  | 10.6 | 10.4 | 24.0 | 38.0 | 15.9 | 8.3 | 38.1 | Worse |
|  | 4.1 | 2.5 | 2.9 | 4.0 | 5.6 | 2.5 | 5.1 | Don't know |
|  | (245) | (279) | (308) | (673) | (679) | (26815) | (549) | Weighted N |
| 35-44 Only | 38.9 | 32.9 | 28.5 | 22.1 | 34.9 | 35.1 | 14.2 | Better |
|  | 45.9 | 47.7 | 45.8 | 41.6 | 46.1 | 54.6 | 35.6 | Same |
|  | 8.9 | 14.0 | 22.4 | 31.8 | 13.2 | 8.3 | 40.5 | Worse |
|  | 6.2 | 5.4 | 3.3 | 4.6 | 5.8 | 2.0 | 9.7 | Don't know |
|  | (257) | (222) | (214) | (503) | (484) | (17693) | (402) | Weighted N |
| 45-54 Only | 36.0 | 33.9 | 23.8 | 16.3 | 27.3 | 38.5 | 14.8 | Better |
|  | 46.7 | 46.0 | 46.6 | 37.1 | 49.9 | 43.0 | 38.2 | Same |
|  | 13.6 | 12.2 | 24.3 | 41.3 | 19.7 | 13.0 | 37.3 | Worse |
|  | 3.7 | 7.9 | 5.3 | 5.4 | 3.1 | 5.4 | 9.8 | Don't know |
|  | (272) | (189) | (206) | (504) | (417) | (18685) | (338) | Weighted N |
| 55-64 Only | 28.1 | 24.9 | 19.3 | 19.5 | 30.9 | 47.4 | 14.9 | Better |
|  | 49.0 | 56.8 | 50.5 | 35.3 | 48.1 | 41.2 | 37.7 | Same |
|  | 18.6 | 12.4 | 20.8 | 35.3 | 15.1 | 7.8 | 35.1 | Worse |
|  | 4.3 | 5.9 | 9.4 | 9.8 | 6.0 | 3.6 | 12.3 | Don't know |
|  | (210) | (169) | (192) | (430) | (385) | (16721) | (308) | Weighted N |
| 65-74 Only | 22.9 | 33.6 | 24.0 | 19.0 | 26.3 | 41.1 | 11.8 | Better |
|  | 49.6 | 46.6 | 52.7 | 33.0 | 48.4 | 42.6 | 38.2 | Same |
|  | 17.6 | 12.3 | 18.7 | 37.1 | 18.5 | 12.5 | 37.7 | Worse |
|  | 9.9 | 7.5 | 4.7 | 10.9 | 6.9 | 3.8 | 12.3 | Don't know |
|  | (131) | (146) | (150) | (221) | (335) | (14793) | (212) | Weighted N |
| 75 And Older Only | 29.6 | 15.9 | 15.2 | 10.0 | 27.9 | 36.3 | 11.9 | Better |
|  | 42.0 | 56.5 | 51.5 | 46.9 | 49.3 | 47.2 | 43.2 | Same |
|  | 14.8 | 17.4 | 21.2 | 31.5 | 10.3 | 13.5 | 19.5 | Worse |
|  | 13.6 | 10.1 | 12.1 | 11.5 | 12.5 | 3.0 | 25.4 | Don't know |
|  | (81) | (69) | (66) | (130) | (136) | (7559) | (118) | Weighted N |

Table 7-52
Will Business Conditions Be Better a Year from Now?
Income of Respondent

| | | | | Year | | | | | |
|---|---|---|---|---|---|---|---|---|---|
| | 1954m | 1956m | 1957f | 1958m | 1959f | 1960a | 1961a | 1962n | |
| Income 1 (0-16%) | 16.9% | 11.2% | 11.4% | 19.3% | 20.4% | 23.0% | 40.1% | 14.6% | Better |
| | 52.9 | 70.0 | 68.6 | 60.1 | 62.2 | 57.4 | 43.4 | 65.2 | Same |
| | 17.5 | 4.9 | 7.9 | 6.6 | 8.5 | 9.2 | 6.6 | 4.9 | Worse |
| | 12.7 | 13.9 | 12.2 | 14.0 | 9.0 | 10.5 | 9.9 | 15.2 | Don't know |
| | (189) | (223) | (229) | (243) | (201) | (535) | (8101) | (164) | Weighted N |
| Income 2 (17-33%) | 13.1 | 9.2 | 10.7 | 23.0 | 25.4 | 29.3 | 44.7 | 26.3 | Better |
| | 69.7 | 77.3 | 70.2 | 66.4 | 63.9 | 58.2 | 41.8 | 58.1 | Same |
| | 11.5 | 6.4 | 11.0 | 3.9 | 5.7 | 6.0 | 5.3 | 7.6 | Worse |
| | 5.7 | 7.1 | 8.2 | 6.6 | 4.9 | 6.5 | 8.1 | 8.1 | Don't know |
| | (122) | (141) | (319) | (152) | (122) | (598) | (9802) | (198) | Weighted N |
| Income 3 (34-67%) | 21.8 | 16.8 | 14.8 | 29.0 | 27.2 | 37.9 | 53.5 | 25.1 | Better |
| | 60.3 | 74.0 | 72.8 | 61.6 | 64.9 | 53.7 | 36.0 | 59.9 | Same |
| | 11.4 | 5.3 | 8.3 | 6.0 | 5.2 | 5.1 | 6.5 | 5.0 | Worse |
| | 6.5 | 3.9 | 4.1 | 3.4 | 2.6 | 3.3 | 4.0 | 10.0 | Don't know |
| | (307) | (584) | (515) | (497) | (459) | (1114) | (19430) | (521) | Weighted N |
| Income 4 (68-95%) | 19.4 | 18.8 | 16.6 | 45.2 | 33.1 | 40.2 | 58.2 | 29.9 | Better |
| | 66.7 | 74.7 | 75.1 | 47.7 | 60.2 | 50.2 | 32.0 | 60.9 | Same |
| | 8.8 | 2.6 | 5.7 | 2.8 | 3.8 | 6.5 | 6.4 | 2.5 | Worse |
| | 5.1 | 3.9 | 2.6 | 4.2 | 3.0 | 3.1 | 3.3 | 6.7 | Don't know |
| | (273) | (304) | (193) | (283) | (369) | (550) | (10559) | (284) | Weighted N |
| Income 5 (96-100%) | 24.2 | 21.0 | 13.3 | 56.4 | 56.8 | 43.8 | 76.1 | 31.7 | Better |
| | 68.2 | 72.4 | 76.7 | 37.6 | 43.2 | 42.0 | 17.3 | 60.3 | Same |
| | 6.1 | 1.9 | 6.7 | 3.0 | 0.0 | 8.9 | 5.1 | 7.9 | Worse |
| | 1.5 | 4.8 | 3.3 | 3.0 | 0.0 | 5.4 | 1.5 | 0.0 | Don't know |
| | (66) | (105) | (30) | (101) | (37) | (112) | (1579) | (63) | Weighted N |

Table 7-53
Will Business Conditions Be Better a Year from Now?
Income of Respondent

| | | | | Year | | | | | |
|---|---|---|---|---|---|---|---|---|---|
| | 1963m | 1964a | 1965m | 1966a | 1967a | 1968a | 1969a | 1970a | |
| Income 1 (0-16%) | 18.2% | 20.5% | 27.9% | 22.0% | 15.3% | 14.1% | 19.8% | 17.6% | Better |
| | 64.8 | 62.1 | 53.3 | 56.2 | 59.2 | 58.3 | 60.8 | 48.1 | Same |
| | 8.0 | 11.2 | 9.6 | 10.7 | 12.0 | 18.5 | 13.0 | 26.9 | Worse |
| | 9.1 | 6.3 | 9.2 | 11.1 | 13.6 | 9.1 | 6.4 | 7.4 | Don't know |
| | (176) | (224) | (272) | (459) | (708) | (2555) | (2451) | (472) | Weighted N |
| Income 2 (17-33%) | 18.8 | 26.1 | 24.5 | 22.5 | 17.1 | 17.3 | 22.7 | 15.2 | Better |
| | 68.8 | 59.7 | 63.6 | 59.1 | 66.4 | 61.2 | 57.1 | 55.7 | Same |
| | 8.2 | 6.7 | 6.3 | 12.1 | 11.2 | 15.1 | 13.9 | 25.3 | Worse |
| | 4.3 | 7.5 | 5.5 | 6.3 | 5.3 | 6.4 | 6.3 | 3.9 | Don't know |
| | (208) | (253) | (253) | (479) | (545) | (2553) | (2221) | (415) | Weighted N |
| Income 3 (34-67%) | 24.0 | 33.3 | 37.9 | 33.3 | 23.4 | 22.7 | 20.5 | 19.3 | Better |
| | 63.0 | 55.2 | 54.9 | 53.5 | 60.7 | 56.7 | 65.9 | 51.2 | Same |
| | 5.7 | 6.9 | 4.5 | 6.2 | 11.2 | 15.0 | 9.9 | 26.2 | Worse |
| | 7.2 | 4.5 | 2.7 | 7.0 | 4.7 | 5.6 | 3.7 | 3.3 | Don't know |
| | (387) | (534) | (488) | (810) | (1393) | (5118) | (3857) | (885) | Weighted N |
| Income 4 (68-95%) | 28.9 | 34.8 | 44.8 | 36.1 | 24.7 | 22.7 | 23.5 | 25.6 | Better |
| | 60.4 | 53.0 | 48.1 | 52.2 | 59.2 | 58.9 | 62.1 | 46.5 | Same |
| | 7.8 | 8.6 | 4.5 | 6.3 | 12.6 | 12.8 | 11.2 | 24.0 | Worse |
| | 2.9 | 3.6 | 2.6 | 5.4 | 3.5 | 5.6 | 3.1 | 3.9 | Don't know |
| | (384) | (443) | (536) | (479) | (688) | (4350) | (2610) | (675) | Weighted N |
| Income 5 (96-100%) | 38.1 | 37.3 | 41.2 | 32.4 | 30.1 | 28.4 | 26.0 | 29.4 | Better |
| | 51.2 | 49.3 | 38.2 | 53.4 | 52.2 | 46.7 | 52.5 | 38.5 | Same |
| | 3.6 | 6.7 | 11.8 | 10.1 | 12.4 | 18.2 | 16.6 | 27.5 | Worse |
| | 7.1 | 6.7 | 8.8 | 4.1 | 5.3 | 6.7 | 4.8 | 4.6 | Don't know |
| | (84) | (75) | (34) | (148) | (322) | (732) | (415) | (109) | Weighted N |

National Economic Outlook

Table 7.54
Will Business Conditions Be Better a Year from Now?
Income of Respondent

|  | Year | | | | | | | |
|---|---|---|---|---|---|---|---|---|
|  | 1971m | 1972f | 1973c | 1974q | 1975q | 1976m | 1978n |  |
| Income 1 (0-16%) | 18.4% | 23.4% | 18.2% | 12.5% | 13.9% | 35.0% | 14.3% | Better |
|  | 50.0 | 54.1 | 54.7 | 39.3 | 51.5 | 48.7 | 41.1 | Same |
|  | 23.2 | 17.9 | 20.6 | 39.8 | 24.4 | 9.6 | 25.6 | Worse |
|  | 8.4 | 4.6 | 6.5 | 8.3 | 10.2 | 6.8 | 19.0 | Don't know |
|  | (190) | (218) | (170) | (399) | (431) | (22000) | (336) | Weighted N |
| Income 2 (17-33%) | 25.3 | 30.1 | 19.3 | 15.6 | 29.9 | 38.3 | 16.4 | Better |
|  | 52.3 | 52.7 | 49.7 | 38.8 | 50.5 | 53.0 | 37.9 | Same |
|  | 16.6 | 13.7 | 26.9 | 38.1 | 13.5 | 7.2 | 37.0 | Worse |
|  | 5.8 | 3.4 | 4.1 | 7.5 | 6.1 | 1.5 | 8.6 | Don't know |
|  | (241) | (146) | (316) | (577) | (495) | (24243) | (359) | Weighted N |
| Income 3 (34-67%) | 32.7 | 28.6 | 23.1 | 20.1 | 28.5 | 41.0 | 15.2 | Better |
|  | 50.4 | 54.5 | 48.4 | 40.7 | 50.8 | 47.3 | 42.2 | Same |
|  | 12.2 | 10.1 | 23.1 | 34.7 | 16.1 | 9.2 | 35.3 | Worse |
|  | 4.7 | 6.8 | 5.5 | 4.5 | 4.6 | 2.5 | 7.3 | Don't know |
|  | (468) | (455) | (364) | (963) | (827) | (14745) | (618) | Weighted N |
| Income 4 (68-95%) | 48.8 | 36.1 | 32.8 | 22.1 | 39.8 | 48.1 | 13.9 | Better |
|  | 37.0 | 50.3 | 43.4 | 38.6 | 41.7 | 42.8 | 41.7 | Same |
|  | 10.1 | 10.5 | 20.1 | 34.9 | 16.5 | 8.1 | 39.8 | Worse |
|  | 4.0 | 3.1 | 3.7 | 4.4 | 2.0 | 1.0 | 4.7 | Don't know |
|  | (297) | (324) | (348) | (607) | (636) | (9285) | (533) | Weighted N |
| Income 5 (96-100%) | 49.1 | 51.3 | 34.8 | 26.3 | 37.9 | 42.3 | 15.9 | Better |
|  | 41.5 | 35.9 | 42.4 | 33.7 | 45.8 | 46.5 | 30.3 | Same |
|  | 5.7 | 11.5 | 17.4 | 36.8 | 15.0 | 9.9 | 49.7 | Worse |
|  | 3.8 | 1.3 | 5.4 | 3.2 | 1.3 | 1.3 | 4.1 | Don't know |
|  | (53) | (78) | (92) | (95) | (153) | (8232) | (145) | Weighted N |

Table 7.55
Does R Think Now is a Good Time or a Bad Time to Buy a House?
Total Population

QUESTION: Generally speaking, do you think now is a good time or a bad time to buy a house?

|  | | Year | | | | | | | |
|---|---|---|---|---|---|---|---|---|---|
|  | | 1956m | 1957f | 1958m | 1959f | 1960a | 1961a | 1962m | 1963m |
| Good | (5) | 40.0% | 32.5% | 37.4% | 43.2% | 51.9% | 46.7% | 43.9% | 53.1% |
| Pro-con | (3) | 8.4 | 9.0 | 9.7 | 10.3 | 8.5 | 6.5 | 8.4 | 10.0 |
| Bad | (1) | 30.4 | 38.4 | 32.2 | 25.8 | 29.0 | 34.3 | 26.8 | 15.3 |
| Don't know/uncertain | | 21.3 | 20.0 | 20.7 | 20.7 | 10.5 | 12.5 | 20.9 | 21.5 |
| Total | | 100% | 100% | 100% | 100% | 100% | 100% | 100% | 100% |
| Weighted N | | 1410 | 1318 | 1309 | 1282 | 2775 | 47643 | 1336 | 1305 |
| Unweighted N | | 1410 | 1318 | 1309 | 1282 | 2775 | 1900 | 1336 | 1305 |
| Mean | | 3.24 | 2.85 | 3.13 | 3.44 | 3.51 | 3.28 | 3.43 | 3.96 |
| Standard Deviation | | 1.88 | 1.88 | 1.87 | 1.81 | 1.83 | 1.90 | 1.84 | 1.60 |

Table 7.56

|  | | 1964a | 1965a | 1966k | 1967m | 1968a | 1969a | 1970a | 1971m |
|---|---|---|---|---|---|---|---|---|---|
| Good | (5) | 55.0% | 55.1% | 37.2% | 48.7% | 47.8% | 38.9% | 19.4% | 40.6% |
| Pro-con | (3) | 9.5 | 7.0 | 7.2 | 8.2 | 9.0 | 9.1 | 8.8 | 8.2 |
| Bad | (1) | 21.2 | 20.5 | 39.4 | 27.2 | 29.9 | 39.6 | 65.3 | 40.2 |
| Don't know/uncertain | | 14.3 | 17.4 | 16.3 | 15.9 | 13.4 | 12.4 | 6.5 | 10.9 |
| Total | | 100% | 100% | 100% | 100% | 100% | 100% | 100% | 100% |
| Weighted N | | 1521 | 1324 | 1216 | 1325 | 15517 | 11492 | 2538 | 1292 |
| Unweighted N | | 1521 | 1324 | 1216 | 1325 | 2663 | 2285 | 2538 | 1292 |
| Mean | | 3.79 | 3.83 | 2.95 | 3.51 | 3.41 | 2.98 | 2.02 | 3.01 |
| Standard Deviation | | 1.71 | 1.72 | 1.91 | 1.83 | 1.85 | 1.89 | 1.63 | 1.91 |

Table 7.57

|  | | 1972f | 1973c | 1974q | 1975q | 1976m |
|---|---|---|---|---|---|---|
| Good | (5) | 44.8% | 43.7% | 15.3% | 35.4% | 44.2% |
| Pro-con | (3) | 8.2 | 9.4 | 8.6 | 8.7 | 7.2 |
| Bad | (1) | 36.7 | 35.8 | 71.2 | 49.6 | 44.1 |
| Don't know/uncertain | | 10.4 | 11.2 | 5.0 | 6.3 | 4.5 |
| Total | | 100% | 100% | 100% | 100% | 100% |
| Weighted N | | 1284 | 1331 | 2960 | 2899 | 127488 |
| Unweighted N | | 1284 | 1331 | 1507 | 1509 | 1134 |
| Mean | | 3.18 | 3.18 | 1.82 | 2.70 | 3.00 |
| Standard Deviation | | 1.90 | 1.88 | 1.50 | 1.88 | 1.92 |

Figure 7.6
Good or Bad Time to Buy a House--Total Population

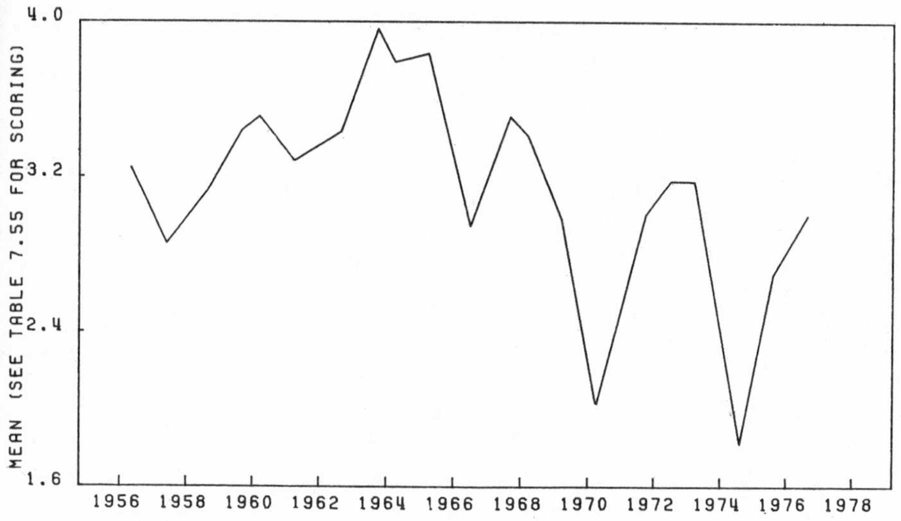

Figure 7.8
Good or Bad Time to Buy a House by Race of R

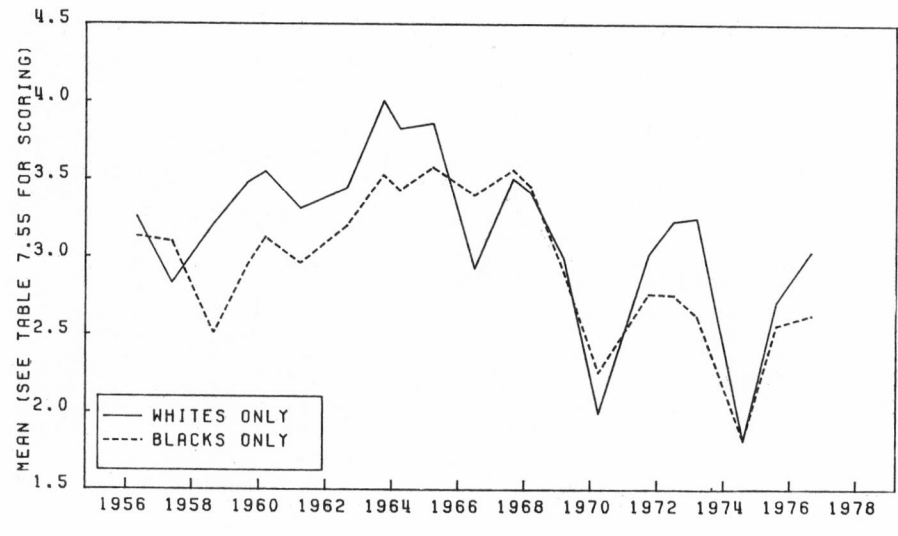

Figure 7.7
Good or Bad Time to Buy a House by Sex of R

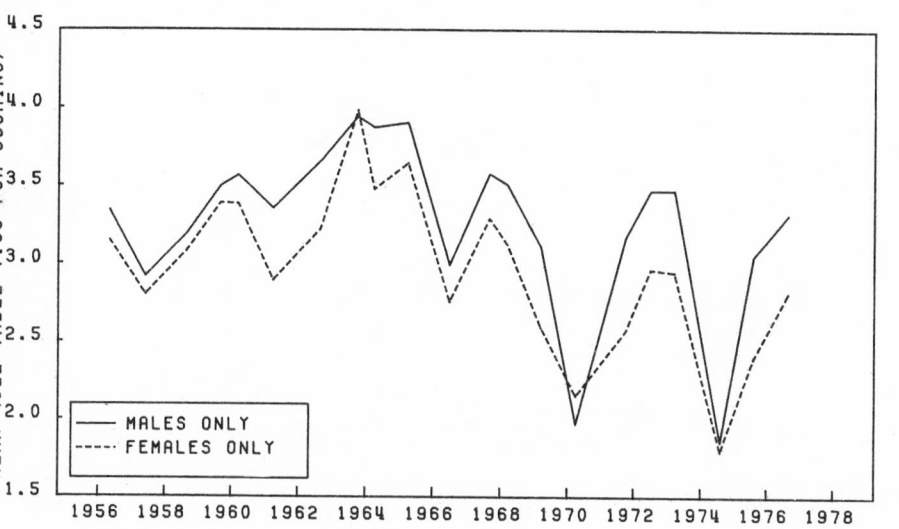

National Economic Outlook

Table 7.58
Does R Think Now is a Good Time or a Bad Time to Buy a House?
Sex of Respondent

| | | | | Year | | | | | |
|---|---|---|---|---|---|---|---|---|---|
| | 1956m | 1957f | 1958m | 1959f | 1960a | 1961a | 1962m | 1963m | |
| Males Only | 46.0% | 36.4% | 41.2% | 48.3% | 54.1% | 49.1% | 52.8% | 56.1% | Good |
| | 9.0 | 10.7 | 10.8 | 10.1 | 8.9 | 6.7 | 9.5 | 11.4 | Pro-con |
| | 31.3 | 40.1 | 33.1 | 27.0 | 28.2 | 33.4 | 24.4 | 16.5 | Bad |
| | 13.8 | 12.8 | 14.8 | 14.6 | 8.8 | 10.8 | 13.4 | 16.0 | Don't know |
| | (659) | (569) | (553) | (555) | (1887) | (39464) | (599) | (544) | Weighted N |
| | | | | | | | | | |
| Females Only | 34.8 | 29.7 | 34.5 | 39.3 | 47.2 | 34.9 | 36.8 | 51.0 | Good |
| | 7.9 | 7.8 | 8.9 | 10.5 | 7.9 | 5.7 | 7.5 | 9.1 | Pro-con |
| | 29.5 | 37.2 | 31.6 | 24.8 | 30.7 | 39.4 | 28.8 | 14.5 | Bad |
| | 27.9 | 25.4 | 25.0 | 25.4 | 14.2 | 20.0 | 27.0 | 25.5 | Don't know |
| | (750) | (748) | (756) | (725) | (888) | (8071) | (737) | (761) | Weighted N |

Table 7.59

| | 1964a | 1965a | 1966k | 1967m | 1968a | 1969a | 1970a | 1971m | |
|---|---|---|---|---|---|---|---|---|---|
| Males Only | 58.6% | 59.0% | 40.2% | 52.4% | 52.0% | 42.9% | 18.8% | 46.0% | Good |
| | 10.0 | 7.6 | 8.1 | 8.3 | 9.4 | 10.0 | 8.9 | 8.8 | Pro-con |
| | 20.0 | 20.0 | 40.6 | 27.0 | 29.1 | 37.8 | 68.0 | 38.1 | Bad |
| | 11.4 | 13.4 | 11.1 | 12.2 | 9.5 | 9.2 | 4.3 | 7.1 | Don't know |
| | (1155) | (937) | (923) | (973) | (11331) | (8353) | (1831) | (904) | Weighted N |
| | | | | | | | | | |
| Females Only | 43.4 | 45.5 | 27.6 | 38.4 | 36.6 | 28.2 | 21.1 | 28.1 | Good |
| | 8.3 | 5.7 | 4.1 | 8.0 | 7.5 | 6.6 | 8.5 | 6.7 | Pro-con |
| | 25.1 | 22.0 | 35.9 | 27.6 | 31.8 | 44.2 | 58.3 | 45.4 | Bad |
| | 23.2 | 26.9 | 32.4 | 26.1 | 24.1 | 21.0 | 12.2 | 19.8 | Don't know |
| | (362) | (387) | (290) | (352) | (4068) | (3139) | (707) | (388) | Weighted N |

Table 7.60

| | 1972f | 1973c | 1974q | 1975q | 1976m | |
|---|---|---|---|---|---|---|
| Males Only | 51.8% | 51.3% | 16.3% | 44.0% | 52.0% | Good |
| | 8.7 | 10.3 | 8.6 | 8.5 | 7.5 | Pro-con |
| | 30.4 | 29.8 | 71.2 | 41.8 | 36.7 | Bad |
| | 9.0 | 8.6 | 4.0 | 5.8 | 3.8 | Don't know |
| | (542) | (571) | (1329) | (1336) | (50755) | Weighted N |
| | | | | | | |
| Females Only | 39.6 | 37.9 | 14.5 | 28.0 | 39.6 | Good |
| | 7.8 | 8.7 | 8.6 | 9.0 | 7.0 | Pro-con |
| | 41.2 | 40.3 | 71.2 | 56.2 | 48.5 | Bad |
| | 11.3 | 13.2 | 5.8 | 6.8 | 4.8 | Don't know |
| | (742) | (760) | (1631) | (1563) | (75320) | Weighted N |

Table 7.61

Does R Think Now is a Good Time or a Bad Time to Buy a House?

Race of Respondent

|  | Year | | | | | | | | |
|---|---|---|---|---|---|---|---|---|---|
|  | 1956m | 1957f | 1958m | 1959f | 1960a | 1961a | 1962m | 1963m | |
| Whites Only | 40.6% | 32.3% | 38.8% | 44.4% | 52.9% | 47.3% | 44.4% | 54.8% | Good |
|  | 8.6 | 9.4 | 10.2 | 10.9 | 8.5 | 6.9 | 8.6 | 9.9 | Pro-con |
|  | 30.3 | 39.2 | 30.4 | 25.1 | 28.2 | 33.6 | 26.6 | 14.8 | Bad |
|  | 20.5 | 19.1 | 20.6 | 19.6 | 10.4 | 12.3 | 20.3 | 20.5 | Don't know |
|  | (1289) | (1167) | (1152) | (1141) | (2496) | (42903) | (1209) | (1155) | Weighted N |
| Blacks Only | 33.6 | 36.3 | 27.5 | 31.1 | 42.5 | 40.6 | 36.7 | 36.6 | Good |
|  | 5.5 | 5.9 | 5.1 | 4.9 | 8.4 | 3.7 | 6.4 | 12.2 | Pro-con |
|  | 29.1 | 32.6 | 47.1 | 32.8 | 36.9 | 42.4 | 29.4 | 18.7 | Bad |
|  | 31.8 | 25.2 | 20.3 | 31.1 | 12.2 | 13.3 | 27.5 | 32.5 | Don't know |
|  | (110) | (135) | (138) | (122) | (287) | (4365) | (109) | (123) | Weighted N |

Table 7.62

|  | 1964a | 1965a | 1966k | 1967m | 1968a | 1969a | 1970a | 1971m | |
|---|---|---|---|---|---|---|---|---|---|
| Whites Only | 55.9% | 55.8% | 37.4% | 48.7% | 48.1% | 39.5% | 19.0% | 41.5% | Good |
|  | 9.2 | 7.2 | 7.6 | 8.8 | 9.3 | 9.6 | 8.7 | 8.6 | Pro-con |
|  | 20.5 | 20.0 | 40.4 | 27.2 | 29.8 | 39.6 | 66.2 | 40.5 | Bad |
|  | 14.3 | 17.0 | 14.6 | 15.3 | 12.8 | 11.3 | 6.0 | 9.5 | Don't know |
|  | (1339) | (1171) | (1106) | (1175) | (13741) | (10172) | (2234) | (1129) | Weighted N |
| Blacks Only | 46.7 | 50.4 | 37.2 | 48.8 | 47.6 | 35.8 | 23.6 | 32.8 | Good |
|  | 11.1 | 7.6 | 2.3 | 4.1 | 7.8 | 6.2 | 9.5 | 5.5 | Pro-con |
|  | 28.1 | 26.1 | 24.4 | 26.4 | 28.5 | 39.5 | 57.1 | 42.2 | Bad |
|  | 14.1 | 16.0 | 36.0 | 20.7 | 16.1 | 18.5 | 9.8 | 19.5 | Don't know |
|  | (135) | (119) | (86) | (121) | (1413) | (1143) | (275) | (128) | Weighted N |

Table 7.63

|  | 1972f | 1973c | 1974q | 1975q | 1976m | |
|---|---|---|---|---|---|---|
| Whites Only | 45.8% | 45.9% | 14.9% | 35.7% | 45.1% | Good |
|  | 8.7 | 10.1 | 9.2 | 9.4 | 7.7 | Pro-con |
|  | 35.4 | 34.4 | 71.3 | 49.1 | 43.2 | Bad |
|  | 10.1 | 9.6 | 4.6 | 5.9 | 3.9 | Don't know |
|  | (1154) | (1107) | (2542) | (2566) | (107999) | Weighted N |
| Blacks Only | 36.0 | 29.9 | 16.6 | 33.9 | 37.0 | Good |
|  | 4.4 | 6.8 | 4.4 | 4.2 | 2.8 | Pro-con |
|  | 46.5 | 45.3 | 70.5 | 54.0 | 54.4 | Bad |
|  | 13.2 | 17.9 | 8.5 | 7.9 | 5.7 | Don't know |
|  | (114) | (117) | (295) | (239) | (11449) | Weighted N |

National Economic Outlook

Table 7.64

Does R Think Now is a Good Time or a Bad Time to Buy a House?

Education of Respondent

| | 1956m | 1957f | 1958m | 1959f | 1960a | 1961a | 1962m | 1963m | |
|---|---|---|---|---|---|---|---|---|---|
| | | | | | Year | | | | |
| **Grade School Only** | 36.6% | 27.7% | 28.1% | 34.2% | 47.4% | 36.2% | 32.7% | 47.8% | Good |
| | 5.7 | 6.2 | 9.2 | 7.2 | 7.4 | 7.0 | 9.1 | 8.7 | Pro-con |
| | 34.1 | 41.4 | 40.0 | 34.2 | 32.7 | 41.2 | 29.5 | 16.6 | Bad |
| | 23.7 | 24.8 | 22.7 | 24.5 | 12.5 | 15.6 | 28.7 | 26.9 | Don't know |
| | (317) | (307) | (295) | (278) | (758) | (14206) | (254) | (368) | Weighted N |
| **High School Only** | 44.6 | 34.5 | 37.4 | 45.7 | 54.0 | 44.1 | 51.3 | 53.2 | Good |
| | 9.0 | 10.1 | 11.1 | 10.1 | 8.6 | 6.4 | 8.5 | 10.1 | Pro-con |
| | 31.4 | 40.9 | 34.4 | 25.1 | 27.3 | 37.2 | 23.6 | 15.3 | Bad |
| | 15.0 | 14.5 | 17.1 | 19.1 | 10.1 | 12.3 | 16.6 | 21.5 | Don't know |
| | (334) | (296) | (334) | (346) | (1037) | (21124) | (343) | (662) | Weighted N |
| **College Only** | 52.4 | 42.3 | 51.0 | 55.2 | 56.2 | 64.1 | 59.4 | 61.6 | Good |
| | 8.4 | 14.1 | 7.3 | 10.5 | 11.5 | 6.0 | 8.5 | 11.8 | Pro-con |
| | 25.3 | 35.2 | 20.5 | 19.6 | 23.1 | 21.9 | 19.8 | 12.9 | Bad |
| | 13.9 | 8.5 | 21.2 | 14.7 | 9.2 | 8.0 | 12.3 | 13.7 | Don't know |
| | (166) | (142) | (151) | (143) | (541) | (11664) | (212) | (263) | Weighted N |

Table 7.65

| | 1964a | 1965a | 1966k | 1967m | 1968a | 1969a | 1970a | 1971m | |
|---|---|---|---|---|---|---|---|---|---|
| **Grade School Only** | 47.0% | 44.7% | 34.1% | ** | 38.0% | 33.2% | 21.2% | 28.8% | Good |
| | 10.6 | 7.5 | 4.7 | ** | 8.7 | 7.5 | 7.7 | 9.0 | Pro-con |
| | 25.5 | 23.5 | 36.8 | ** | 30.3 | 36.8 | 59.2 | 46.4 | Bad |
| | 17.0 | 24.3 | 24.4 | ** | 23.0 | 22.5 | 11.9 | 15.8 | Don't know |
| | (483) | (374) | (361) | ** | (4340) | (2982) | (954) | (323) | Weighted N |
| **High School Only** | 59.2 | 57.2 | 42.8 | ** | 52.2 | 41.6 | 18.1 | 40.2 | Good |
| | 8.7 | 7.1 | 7.4 | ** | 9.3 | 9.4 | 8.2 | 7.5 | Pro-con |
| | 20.8 | 20.8 | 35.9 | ** | 28.8 | 40.1 | 70.2 | 40.9 | Bad |
| | 11.3 | 14.9 | 13.9 | ** | 9.6 | 8.9 | 3.5 | 11.3 | Don't know |
| | (654) | (631) | (512) | ** | (7124) | (5132) | (1110) | (574) | Weighted N |
| **College Only** | 58.5 | 64.2 | 32.8 | ** | 51.3 | 40.0 | 18.3 | 51.4 | Good |
| | 10.0 | 6.5 | 10.9 | ** | 8.6 | 10.3 | 13.2 | 8.8 | Pro-con |
| | 16.5 | 16.5 | 48.9 | ** | 31.0 | 41.3 | 66.8 | 33.9 | Bad |
| | 14.9 | 12.9 | 7.3 | ** | 9.1 | 8.5 | 1.7 | 5.9 | Don't know |
| | (369) | (310) | (274) | ** | (3833) | (3297) | (410) | (387) | Weighted N |

** Data not available--education not coded in 1967m.

Education coded for head of household only in 1956m,1957f,1958m,1959f,1960a,1961a,1962m,1966k,and 1971m, and for head and wife only in 1963m,1964a,1965a,and 1970a.

Table 7.66
Does R Think Now is a Good Time or a Bad Time to Buy a House?
Education of Respondent

| | | Year | | | | |
|---|---|---|---|---|---|---|
| | 1972f | 1973c | 1974q | 1975q | 1976m | |
| Grade School Only | 33.7% | 36.5% | 13.2% | 21.6% | 27.8% | Good |
| | 9.5 | 10.9 | 9.3 | 7.5 | 7.1 | Pro-con |
| | 39.1 | 33.3 | 65.8 | 58.4 | 55.8 | Bad |
| | 17.7 | 19.2 | 11.7 | 12.5 | 9.3 | Don't know |
| | (243) | (156) | (486) | (440) | (16925) | Weighted N |
| High School Only | 44.7 | 41.8 | 14.3 | 30.3 | 39.6 | Good |
| | 7.2 | 7.6 | 7.5 | 7.8 | 8.0 | Pro-con |
| | 37.9 | 41.2 | 74.1 | 55.7 | 48.6 | Bad |
| | 10.2 | 9.4 | 4.0 | 6.2 | 3.9 | Don't know |
| | (657) | (617) | (1410) | (1507) | (60127) | Weighted N |
| College Only | 52.4 | 50.9 | 17.8 | 49.8 | 56.6 | Good |
| | 9.3 | 11.6 | 9.7 | 10.8 | 6.5 | Pro-con |
| | 32.3 | 28.6 | 69.3 | 35.8 | 33.7 | Bad |
| | 6.1 | 8.9 | 3.2 | 3.6 | 3.2 | Don't know |
| | (378) | (395) | (1044) | (946) | (45208) | Weighted N |

Figure 7.9
Good or Bad Time to Buy a House by Education of R

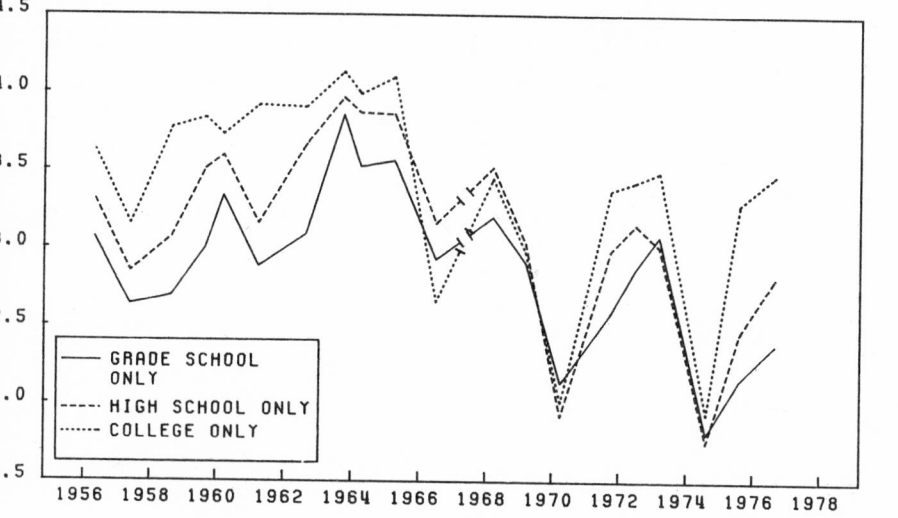

Table 7.67
Does R Think Now is a Good Time or a Bad Time to Buy a House?
Age of Respondent

| | | | | Year | | | | | |
|---|---|---|---|---|---|---|---|---|---|
| | 1956m | 1957f | 1958m | 1959f | 1960a | 1961a | 1962m | 1963m | |
| 18-24 Only | 43.4% | 31.7% | 41.0% | 50.0% | 61.4% | 46.0% | 67.2% | 51.5% | Good |
| | 2.4 | 9.8 | 7.7 | 5.8 | 4.2 | 3.2 | 4.9 | 9.1 | Pro-con |
| | 27.7 | 30.5 | 25.6 | 21.2 | 20.6 | 32.5 | 9.8 | 8.1 | Bad |
| | 26.5 | 28.0 | 25.6 | 23.1 | 13.8 | 18.2 | 18.0 | 31.3 | Don't know |
| | (83) | (82) | (39) | (52) | (189) | (4163) | (61) | (99) | Weighted N |
| 25-34 Only | 43.4 | 39.3 | 45.8 | 51.9 | 55.7 | 53.3 | 50.7 | 53.4 | Good |
| | 11.9 | 10.7 | 5.6 | 8.1 | 8.6 | 5.5 | 6.7 | 12.5 | Pro-con |
| | 26.9 | 35.3 | 32.4 | 23.7 | 27.4 | 32.6 | 26.9 | 12.1 | Bad |
| | 17.7 | 14.7 | 16.2 | 16.3 | 8.3 | 8.7 | 15.7 | 22.0 | Don't know |
| | (327) | (272) | (142) | (135) | (456) | (10141) | (134) | (232) | Weighted N |
| 35-44 Only | 38.7 | 34.2 | 36.4 | 46.4 | 53.3 | 49.6 | 50.0 | 59.3 | Good |
| | 8.4 | 8.3 | 12.1 | 12.4 | 6.9 | 6.1 | 11.5 | 7.1 | Pro-con |
| | 34.1 | 38.7 | 34.7 | 28.8 | 29.3 | 33.4 | 23.7 | 16.0 | Bad |
| | 18.9 | 18.8 | 16.8 | 12.4 | 10.5 | 11.0 | 14.7 | 17.5 | Don't know |
| | (323) | (313) | (173) | (153) | (522) | (10766) | (156) | (268) | Weighted N |
| 45-54 Only | 40.9 | 30.8 | 43.8 | 46.8 | 51.5 | 48.6 | 53.9 | 55.2 | Good |
| | 7.4 | 11.0 | 12.5 | 6.5 | 10.5 | 6.5 | 10.8 | 11.1 | Pro-con |
| | 32.3 | 41.8 | 31.3 | 27.3 | 29.4 | 34.0 | 21.6 | 18.5 | Bad |
| | 19.3 | 16.5 | 12.5 | 19.4 | 8.6 | 10.9 | 13.8 | 15.2 | Don't know |
| | (269) | (273) | (144) | (139) | (466) | (9139) | (167) | (270) | Weighted N |
| 55-64 Only | 39.5 | 33.0 | 37.1 | 41.7 | 49.4 | 40.5 | 37.5 | 51.2 | Good |
| | 9.0 | 8.8 | 10.5 | 9.0 | 9.5 | 6.2 | 7.8 | 12.8 | Pro-con |
| | 27.1 | 36.3 | 30.5 | 26.4 | 29.1 | 41.5 | 35.2 | 16.7 | Bad |
| | 24.3 | 22.0 | 21.9 | 22.9 | 12.0 | 11.9 | 19.5 | 19.2 | Don't know |
| | (210) | (182) | (649) | (144) | (358) | (6892) | (128) | (203) | Weighted N |
| 65-74 Only | 33.7 | 22.9 | 25.3 | 26.5 | 46.2 | 39.6 | 37.0 | 50.0 | Good |
| | 5.5 | 5.2 | 5.6 | 10.2 | 11.3 | 10.8 | 6.7 | 8.1 | Pro-con |
| | 31.5 | 43.2 | 38.9 | 32.7 | 28.5 | 33.2 | 23.0 | 15.4 | Bad |
| | 29.3 | 28.6 | 30.2 | 30.6 | 14.1 | 16.4 | 33.3 | 26.5 | Don't know |
| | (181) | (192) | (162) | (147) | (355) | (4218) | (165) | (136) | Weighted N |
| 75 And Older Only | ** | ** | ** | ** | ** | 31.0 | ** | 37.6 | Good |
| | ** | ** | ** | ** | ** | 13.3 | ** | 7.1 | Pro-con |
| | ** | ** | ** | ** | ** | 33.9 | ** | 17.6 | Bad |
| | ** | ** | ** | ** | ** | 21.9 | ** | 37.6 | Don't know |
| | ** | ** | ** | ** | ** | (2082) | ** | (85) | Weighted N |

* Code distinction not made.
Oldest age group coded "65 And Older" in 1956m,1957f,1958m,1959f,1960a,and 1962m.
Age coded for head of household only in 1958m,1959f,1960a,1961a and 1962m.

Table 7.68

Does R Think Now is a Good Time or a Bad Time to Buy a House?

Age of Respondent

| | | | | Year | | | | | |
|---|---|---|---|---|---|---|---|---|---|
| | 1964a | 1965a | 1966k | 1967m | 1968a | 1969a | 1970a | 1971m | |
| 18-24 Only | 51.4% | 53.6% | 36.6% | 45.2% | 47.2% | 38.2% | 27.7% | 44.9% | Good |
| | 5.7 | 4.8 | 6.1 | 6.5 | 5.8 | 7.4 | 5.0 | 7.1 | Pro-con |
| | 19.0 | 18.4 | 35.4 | 26.9 | 33.3 | 40.0 | 59.7 | 32.7 | Bad |
| | 23.8 | 23.2 | 22.0 | 21.5 | 13.6 | 14.3 | 7.6 | 15.3 | Don't know |
| | (105) | (125) | (82) | (93) | (978) | (1088) | (238) | (98) | Weighted N |
| 25-34 Only | 62.7 | 62.9 | 34.9 | 50.8 | 54.2 | 42.7 | 20.8 | 51.2 | Good |
| | 5.0 | 6.7 | 6.7 | 4.2 | 5.8 | 8.4 | 8.5 | 9.5 | Pro-con |
| | 23.5 | 14.2 | 45.0 | 30 1 | 31.2 | 40.2 | 67.6 | 31.4 | Bad |
| | 8.8 | 16.3 | 13.4 | 14.8 | 8.8 | 8.7 | 3.1 | 7.9 | Don't know |
| | (260) | (240) | (209) | (236) | (2868) | (2305) | (414) | (242) | Weighted N |
| 35-44 Only | 58.2 | 62.6 | 41.7 | 49.6 | 52.8 | 40.3 | 15.8 | 46.7 | Good |
| | 10.2 | 7.7 | 7.5 | 11.5 | 9.5 | 9.2 | 9.2 | 7.8 | Pro-con |
| | 20.3 | 17.2 | 40.8 | 30.2 | 29.6 | 42.3 | 70.9 | 39.2 | Bad |
| | 11.4 | 12.5 | 10.1 | 8.7 | 8.1 | 8.2 | 4.1 | 6.3 | Don't know |
| | (325) | (273) | (228) | (252) | (2830) | (1993) | (436) | (255) | Weighted N |
| 45-54 Only | 56.5 | 56.6 | 40.8 | 51.1 | 52.9 | 41.2 | 17.1 | 39.6 | Good |
| | 10.9 | 7.4 | 9.0 | 8.7 | 9.0 | 10.8 | 9.3 | 7.7 | Pro-con |
| | 19.8 | 21.7 | 39.0 | 24.3 | 29.5 | 40.2 | 69.0 | 45.4 | Bad |
| | 12.8 | 14.3 | 11.2 | 15.9 | 8.6 | 7.8 | 4.7 | 7.3 | Don't know |
| | (313) | (244) | (267) | (276) | (2880) | (1948) | (451) | (273) | Weighted N |
| 55-64 Only | 53.7 | 50.7 | 39.3 | 51.7 | 44.3 | 35.3 | 19.2 | 34.8 | Good |
| | 9.8 | 7.9 | 6.3 | 7.3 | 9.1 | 7.6 | 8.4 | 8.1 | Pro-con |
| | 23.0 | 24.2 | 36.4 | 25.4 | 30.8 | 42.3 | 65.0 | 44.3 | Bad |
| | 13.5 | 17.2 | 18.0 | 15.6 | 15.8 | 14.9 | 7.3 | 12.9 | Don't know |
| | (244) | (215) | (206) | (205) | (2786) | (1764) | (369) | (210) | Weighted N |
| 65-74 Only | 43.7 | 41.4 | 29.7 | 41.9 | 36.2 | 36.5 | 19.8 | 25.8 | Good |
| | 14.8 | 6.8 | 7.1 | 9.8 | 13.4 | 10.5 | 10.3 | 10.6 | Pro-con |
| | 23.0 | 27.9 | 43.2 | 26.0 | 31.1 | 36.6 | 57.9 | 45.5 | Bad |
| | 18.6 | 23.9 | 20.0 | 22.4 | 19.3 | 16.4 | 11.9 | 18.2 | Don't know |
| | (183) | (222) | (155) | (246) | (1864) | (1452) | (252) | (132) | Weighted N |
| 75 And Older Only | 46.0 | ** | 25.4 | ** | 36.0 | 32.7 | 19.5 | 28.0 | Good |
| | 9.2 | ** | 4.5 | ** | 10.5 | 10.2 | 9.4 | 4.9 | Pro-con |
| | 17.2 | ** | 23.9 | ** | 19.3 | 29.6 | 53.9 | 42.7 | Bad |
| | 27.6 | ** | 46.3 | ** | 34.2 | 27.6 | 17.2 | 24.4 | Don't know |
| | (87) | ** | (67) | ** | (1140) | (882) | (128) | (82) | Weighted N |

* Code distinction not made.

Oldest age group coded "65 And Older" in 1965a and 1967m.

Age coded for head of household and wife only in 1964a, 1965a, 1966k, 1968a, 1969a, and 1970a.

Table 7.69
Does R Think Now is a Good Time or a Bad Time to Buy a House?
Age of Respondent

|  | Year | | | | | |
|---|---|---|---|---|---|---|
|  | 1972f | 1973c | 1974q | 1975q | 1976m | |
| 18-24 Only | 50.5% | 47.0% | 20.9% | 48.1% | 52.7% | Good |
|  | 8.8 | 6.1 | 5.4 | 2.6 | 2.3 | Pro-con |
|  | 29.9 | 29.3 | 66.9 | 43.7 | 39.7 | Bad |
|  | 10.8 | 17.7 | 6.8 | 5.5 | 5.3 | Don't know |
|  | (204) | (198) | (484) | (453) | (20191) | Weighted N |
| 25-34 Only | 52.5 | 48.7 | 12.9 | 42.2 | 54.4 | Good |
|  | 8.3 | 8.2 | 9.1 | 10.8 | 6.7 | Pro-con |
|  | 33.5 | 36.3 | 74.7 | 43.6 | 35.4 | Bad |
|  | 5.8 | 6.9 | 3.3 | 3.4 | 3.5 | Don't know |
|  | (278) | (306) | (668) | (676) | (26896) | Weighted N |
| 35-44 Only | 45.2 | 46.5 | 14.9 | 37.1 | 46.1 | Good |
|  | 6.8 | 8.9 | 10.0 | 7.7 | 7.0 | Pro-con |
|  | 39.8 | 35.2 | 70.5 | 48.8 | 46.0 | Bad |
|  | 8.1 | 9.4 | 4.6 | 6.4 | 0.8 | Don't know |
|  | (221) | (213) | (498) | (482) | (17820) | Weighted N |
| 45-54 Only | 43.4 | 40.4 | 14.1 | 26.3 | 38.3 | Good |
|  | 6.3 | 10.8 | 10.9 | 10.8 | 7.6 | Pro-con |
|  | 41.8 | 38.9 | 71.0 | 59.3 | 50.4 | Bad |
|  | 8.5 | 9.9 | 4.0 | 3.6 | 3.8 | Don't know |
|  | (189) | (203) | (504) | (415) | (18985) | Weighted N |
| 55-64 Only | 38.0 | 41.7 | 15.9 | 27.3 | 47.1 | Good |
|  | 9.4 | 11.5 | 9.4 | 7.5 | 8.9 | Pro-con |
|  | 39.8 | 37.5 | 71.4 | 57.9 | 41.5 | Bad |
|  | 12.9 | 9.4 | 3.2 | 7.3 | 2.5 | Don't know |
|  | (171) | (192) | (434) | (385) | (17264) | Weighted N |
| 65-74 Only | 41.5 | 35.5 | 15.4 | 25.5 | 29.2 | Good |
|  | 8.8 | 10.5 | 5.7 | 11.0 | 10.0 | Pro-con |
|  | 34.7 | 40.8 | 72.2 | 52.8 | 53.9 | Bad |
|  | 15.0 | 13.2 | 6.6 | 10.7 | 6.9 | Don't know |
|  | (147) | (152) | (227) | (337) | (14553) | Weighted N |
| 75 And Older Only | 21.7 | 36.5 | 9.2 | 30.0 | 29.9 | Good |
|  | 10.1 | 14.3 | 4.6 | 11.4 | 7.1 | Pro-con |
|  | 44.9 | 28.6 | 71.0 | 40.7 | 44.1 | Bad |
|  | 23.2 | 20.6 | 15.3 | 17.9 | 19.0 | Don't know |
|  | (69) | (63) | (131) | (140) | (7728) | Weighted N |

Table 7.70
Does R Think Now is a Good Time or a Bad Time to Buy a House?
Income of Respondent

|                    |        |        |        | Year   |        |         |        |        |             |
|--------------------|--------|--------|--------|--------|--------|---------|--------|--------|-------------|
|                    | 1956m  | 1957f  | 1958m  | 1959f  | 1960a  | 1961a   | 1962m  | 1963m  |             |
| Income 1 (0-16%)   | 32.4%  | 27.0%  | 21.3%  | 32.1%  | 45.8%  | 34.7%   | 33.9%  | 42.0%  | Good        |
|                    | 4.1    | 4.4    | 6.8    | 5.6    | 7.0    | 6.0     | 6.3    | 6.3    | Pro-con     |
|                    | 31.5   | 39.8   | 40.0   | 30.6   | 31.3   | 41.1    | 23.6   | 14.4   | Bad         |
|                    | 32.0   | 28.8   | 31.9   | 31.6   | 15.9   | 18.2    | 36.2   | 37.4   | Don't know  |
|                    | (219)  | (226)  | (235)  | (196)  | (498)  | (7373)  | (174)  | (174)  | Weighted N  |
| Income 2 (17-33%)  | 32.4   | 26.8   | 33.8   | 30.0   | 47.4   | 41.2    | 40.6   | 50.0   | Good        |
|                    | 5.0    | 7.0    | 9.3    | 14.2   | 8.5    | 6.2     | 4.7    | 11.0   | Pro-con     |
|                    | 31.7   | 39.3   | 36.4   | 30.8   | 32.5   | 38.0    | 30.7   | 15.2   | Bad         |
|                    | 30.9   | 26.8   | 20.5   | 25.0   | 11.6   | 14.5    | 24.1   | 23.8   | Don't know  |
|                    | (139)  | (313)  | (151)  | (120)  | (578)  | (9156)  | (212)  | (210)  | Weighted N  |
| Income 3 (34-67%)  | 41.2   | 33.9   | 37.1   | 45.3   | 53.8   | 45.3    | 43.2   | 52.1   | Good        |
|                    | 9.1    | 10.5   | 9.4    | 9.2    | 8.3    | 7.3     | 9.8    | 11.1   | Pro-con     |
|                    | 29.8   | 40.0   | 34.2   | 27.2   | 28.7   | 35.7    | 27.0   | 16.5   | Bad         |
|                    | 19.8   | 15.6   | 19.3   | 18.3   | 9.2    | 11.7    | 20.0   | 20.4   | Don't know  |
|                    | (580)  | (507)  | (491)  | (459)  | (1090) | (19166) | (530)  | (388)  | Weighted N  |
| Income 4 (68-95%)  | 47.0   | 38.9   | 48.2   | 52.6   | 55.6   | 58.7    | 50.0   | 61.9   | Good        |
|                    | 9.6    | 14.5   | 11.4   | 12.2   | 10.6   | 5.5     | 10.9   | 9.8    | Pro-con     |
|                    | 32.8   | 37.3   | 25.4   | 21.9   | 25.6   | 26.5    | 28.9   | 15.3   | Bad         |
|                    | 10.6   | 9.3    | 15.0   | 13.3   | 8.3    | 9.3     | 10.2   | 13.0   | Don't know  |
|                    | (302)  | (193)  | (280)  | (361)  | (540)  | (10387) | (284)  | (378)  | Weighted N  |
| Income 5 (96-100%) | 48.0   | 63.3   | 57.0   | 78.4   | 64.5   | 72.5    | 63.1   | 67.4   | Good        |
|                    | 14.0   | 13.3   | 10.0   | 5.4    | 7.3    | 7.9     | 6.2    | 9.3    | Pro-con     |
|                    | 26.0   | 23.3   | 19.0   | 10.8   | 23.6   | 15.9    | 18.5   | 16.3   | Bad         |
|                    | 12.0   | 0.0    | 14.0   | 5.4    | 4.5    | 3.7     | 12.3   | 7.0    | Don't know  |
|                    | (100)  | (30)   | (100)  | (37)   | (110)  | (1561)  | (65)   | (86)   | Weighted N  |

National Economic Outlook

le 7.71
s R Think Now is a Good Time or a Bad Time to Buy a House?
ome of Respondent

|  | Year | | | | | | | |  |
|---|---|---|---|---|---|---|---|---|---|
|  | 1964a | 1965a | 1966k | 1967m | 1968a | 1969a | 1970a | 1971m |  |
| Income 1 (0-16%) | 39.8% | 39.5% | 28.4% | 38.8% | 31.7% | 28.6% | 23.2% | 18.2% | Good |
|  | 9.0 | 5.8 | 5.5 | 8.7 | 9.4 | 7.7 | 6.6 | 8.3 | Pro-con |
|  | 24.4 | 26.7 | 30.9 | 26.6 | 26.7 | 35.9 | 55.7 | 43.8 | Bad |
|  | 26.7 | 27.9 | 35.2 | 25.9 | 32.3 | 27.9 | 14.5 | 29.7 | Don't know |
|  | (221) | (172) | (236) | (263) | (2584) | (2440) | (470) | (192) | Weighted N |
| Income 2 (17-33%) | 47.4 | 43.6 | 32.6 | 44.5 | 44.6 | 39.1 | 22.4 | 33.8 | Good |
|  | 9.6 | 7.7 | 5.3 | 7.9 | 9.1 | 8.1 | 9.4 | 10.4 | Pro-con |
|  | 20.5 | 22.7 | 43.2 | 24.6 | 31.8 | 39.5 | 57.5 | 41.3 | Bad |
|  | 22.5 | 25.9 | 18.9 | 23.0 | 14.6 | 13.3 | 10.8 | 14.6 | Don't know |
|  | (249) | (220) | (95) | (191) | (2572) | (2230) | (416) | (240) | Weighted N |
| Income 3 (34-67%) | 57.3 | 56.3 | 39.9 | 51.7 | 51.5 | 41.3 | 16.0 | 41.2 | Good |
|  | 10.3 | 6.2 | 7.2 | 6.4 | 8.2 | 9.2 | 8.1 | 7.8 | Pro-con |
|  | 21.8 | 18.9 | 37.2 | 29.4 | 29.5 | 41.1 | 71.4 | 44.0 | Bad |
|  | 10.5 | 18.6 | 15.7 | 12.5 | 10.8 | 8.4 | 4.5 | 7.1 | Don't know |
|  | (532) | (419) | (363) | (487) | (5184) | (3856) | (887) | (464) | Weighted N |
| Income 4 (68-95%) | 61.7 | 63.0 | 38.5 | 55.9 | 53.6 | 43.1 | 19.6 | 54.7 | Good |
|  | 9.0 | 7.2 | 8.7 | 9.8 | 8.9 | 10.5 | 10.7 | 7.0 | Pro-con |
|  | 20.0 | 19.7 | 46.8 | 25.5 | 31.1 | 41.4 | 68.1 | 34.8 | Bad |
|  | 9.2 | 10.1 | 6.0 | 8.8 | 6.4 | 5.0 | 1.6 | 3.5 | Don't know |
|  | (444) | (416) | (436) | (306) | (4390) | (2635) | (675) | (287) | Weighted N |
| ncome 5 (96-100%) | 69.3 | 70.2 | 54.8 | 53.3 | 54.3 | 48.0 | 21.3 | 66.0 | Good |
|  | 8.0 | 9.6 | 9.7 | 16.7 | 11.6 | 12.0 | 11.1 | 9.4 | Pro-con |
|  | 16.0 | 14.4 | 32.3 | 30.0 | 30.4 | 39.0 | 65.7 | 20.8 | Bad |
|  | 6.7 | 5.8 | 3.2 | 0.0 | 3.7 | 1.0 | 1.9 | 3.8 | Don't know |
|  | (75) | (104) | (31) | (30) | (777) | (415) | (108) | (53) | Weighted N |

Table 7·72

Does R Think Now is a Good Time or a Bad Time to Buy a House?

Income of Respondent

| | | | Year | | | |
|---|---|---|---|---|---|---|
| | 1972f | 1973c | 1974q | 1975q | 1976m | |
| Income 1 (0-16%) | 32.9% | 33.1% | 13.5% | 23.6% | 40.4% | Good |
| | 10.0 | 7.0 | 7.5 | 5.5 | 7.2 | Pro-con |
| | 34.2 | 39.5 | 67.1 | 59.2 | 48.8 | Bad |
| | 22.8 | 20.3 | 12.0 | 11.7 | 3.5 | Don't know |
| | (219) | (172) | (401) | (436) | (21973) | Weighted N |
| Income 2 (17-33%) | 42.1 | 36.4 | 14.1 | 33.1 | 47.1 | Good |
| | 6.9 | 8.6 | 10.9 | 10.8 | 4.7 | Pro-con |
| | 39.3 | 42.5 | 70.3 | 46.4 | 43.8 | Bad |
| | 11.7 | 12.5 | 4.7 | 9.6 | 4.4 | Don't know |
| | (145) | (313) | (576) | (489) | (24417) | Weighted N |
| Income 3 (34-67%) | 45.7 | 43.6 | 15.9 | 36.0 | 53.3 | Good |
| | 8.6 | 9.9 | 8.0 | 7.4 | 7.0 | Pro-con |
| | 36.6 | 36.2 | 73.2 | 53.2 | 37.4 | Bad |
| | 9.1 | 10.2 | 2.9 | 3.4 | 2.4 | Don't know |
| | (453) | (362) | (962) | (824) | (14846) | Weighted N |
| Income 4 (68-95%) | 49.5 | 50.7 | 16.1 | 43.1 | 65.4 | Good |
| | 6.8 | 10.0 | 9.8 | 11.8 | 9.9 | Pro-con |
| | 38.1 | 31.4 | 70.4 | 43.3 | 23.5 | Bad |
| | 5.6 | 7.9 | 3.8 | 1.9 | 1.1 | Don't know |
| | (323) | (341) | (604) | (638) | (9285) | Weighted N |
| Income 5 (96-100%) | 60.3 | 64.5 | 23.2 | 43.8 | 60.7 | Good |
| | 7.7 | 14.0 | 8.4 | 13.1 | 6.6 | Pro-con |
| | 30.8 | 18.3 | 68.4 | 41.2 | 30.7 | Bad |
| | 1.3 | 3.2 | 0.0 | 2.0 | 1.9 | Don't know |
| | (78) | (93) | (95) | (153) | (8337) | Weighted N |

Table 7.73
Does R Think Now Is a Good Time or a Bad Time to Buy a Car?
Total Population

QUESTION: Speaking now of the automobile market--do you think the next twelve months or so will be a good time or a bad time for people to buy a car?

|  | | Year | | | | | | | |
|---|---|---|---|---|---|---|---|---|---|
|  | | 1954m | 1956m | 1957f | 1958m | 1959f | 1960a | 1961a | 1962m |
| Good | (5) | 48.4% | 36.8% | 38.2% | 32.8% | 33.6% | 49.8% | 51.7% | 49.1% |
| Pro-con/depends | (3) | 8.0 | 9.6 | 10.5 | 10.8 | 12.0 | 9.6 | 10.0 | 11.2 |
| Bad | (1) | 32.0 | 23.3 | 25.2 | 31.0 | 26.3 | 20.3 | 18.4 | 14.6 |
| Don't know | | 11.7 | 30.3 | 26.1 | 25.3 | 28.1 | 20.2 | 19.9 | 25.0 |
| Total | | 100% | 100% | 100% | 100% | 100% | 100% | 100% | 100% |
| Weighted N | | 943 | 1414 | 1319 | 1306 | 1275 | 2841 | 48492 | 1326 |
| Unweighted N | | 943 | 1414 | 1319 | 1306 | 1275 | 2841 | 1932 | 1326 |
| Mean | | 3.37 | 3.39 | 3.35 | 3.05 | 3.20 | 3.74 | 3.83 | 3.92 |
| Standard Deviation | | 1.87 | 1.82 | 1.82 | 1.85 | 1.81 | 1.72 | 1.68 | 1.60 |

Table 7.74

|  | | 1963m | 1964a | 1965a | 1966k | 1967m | 1968a | 1969a | 1970a |
|---|---|---|---|---|---|---|---|---|---|
| Good | (5) | 47.4% | 52.4% | 51.5% | 43.5% | 39.8% | 46.4% | 44.7% | 35.5% |
| Pro-con/depends | (3) | 10.0 | 12.6 | 12.5 | 11.3 | 9.9 | 11.2 | 11.3 | 11.1 |
| Bad | (1) | 13.6 | 12.3 | 12.2 | 21.4 | 30.3 | 19.9 | 20.5 | 35.5 |
| Don't know | | 29.0 | 22.7 | 23.8 | 23.9 | 19.9 | 22.6 | 23.5 | 18.0 |
| Total | | 100% | 100% | 100% | 100% | 100% | 100% | 100% | 100% |
| Weighted N | | 1305 | 1522 | 1316 | 1199 | 1325 | 15461 | 11404 | 2530 |
| Unweighted N | | 1305 | 1522 | 1316 | 1199 | 1325 | 2653 | 2271 | 2530 |
| Mean | | 3.95 | 4.04 | 4.03 | 3.58 | 3.24 | 3.68 | 3.63 | 3.00 |
| Standard Deviation | | 1.59 | 1.51 | 1.51 | 1.75 | 1.86 | 1.72 | 1.73 | 1.86 |

Table 7.75

|  | | 1971m | 1972f | 1973c | 1974q | 1975q | 1976m |
|---|---|---|---|---|---|---|---|
| Good | (5) | 45.1% | 41.8% | 36.8% | 14.6% | 33.5% | 40.1% |
| Pro-con/depends | (3) | 11.2 | 9.9 | 12.7 | 9.6 | 10.2 | 7.8 |
| Bad | (1) | 24.8 | 24.6 | 29.4 | 63.0 | 41.6 | 37.6 |
| Don't know | | 19.0 | 23.7 | 21.1 | 12.8 | 14.6 | 14.4 |
| Total | | 100% | 100% | 100% | 100% | 100% | 100% |
| Weighted N | | 1287 | 1288 | 1329 | 2949 | 2879 | 126445 |
| Unweighted N | | 1287 | 1288 | 1329 | 1504 | 1497 | 1121 |
| Mean | | 3.50 | 3.45 | 3.19 | 1.89 | 2.81 | 3.06 |
| Standard Deviation | | 1.79 | 1.81 | 1.82 | 1.52 | 1.87 | 1.90 |

National Economic Outlook

Figure 7.10
Good or Bad Time to Buy a Car--Total Population

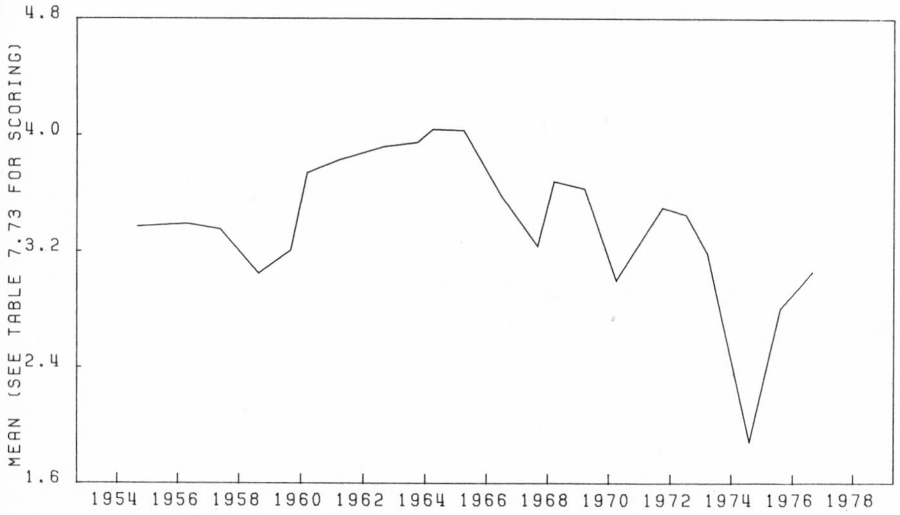

Figure 7.12
Good or Bad Time to Buy a Car by Race of R

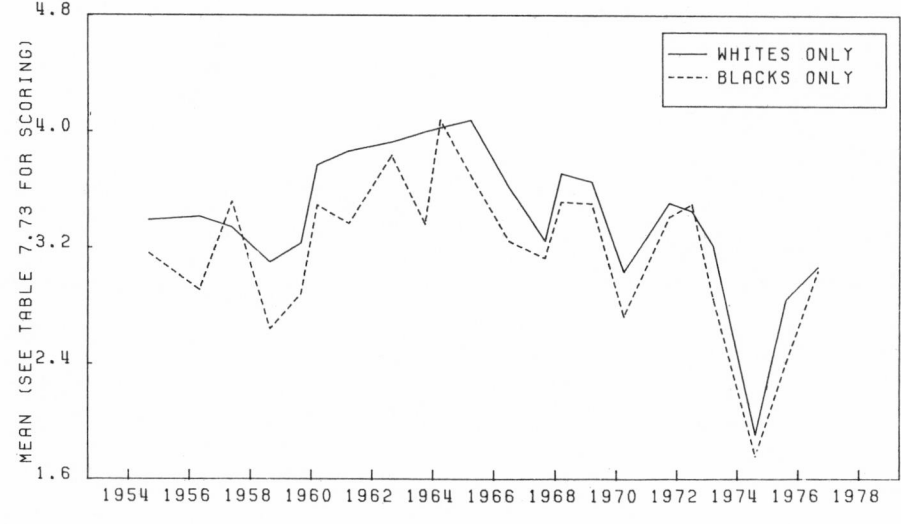

Figure 7.11
Good or Bad Time to Buy a Car by Sex of R

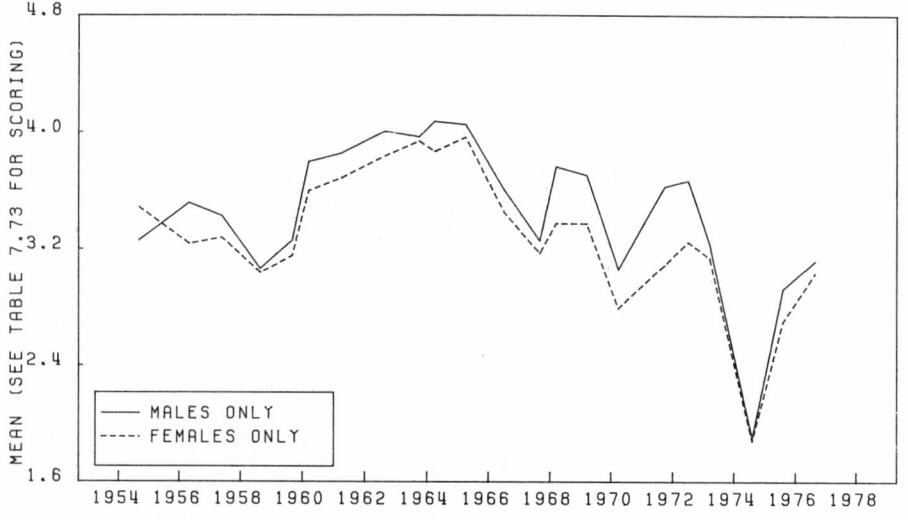

National Economic Outlook

Table 7.76
Does R Think Now Is a Good Time or a Bad Time to Buy a Car?
Sex of Respondent

|  | Year | | | | | | | |  |
|---|---|---|---|---|---|---|---|---|---|
|  | 1954m | 1956m | 1957f | 1958m | 1959f | 1960a | 1961a | 1962m |  |
| Males Only | 49.3% | 45.1% | 44.9% | 37.6% | 40.7% | 54.8% | 55.9% | 57.2% | Good |
|  | 8.2 | 12.0 | 13.3 | 14.0 | 13.7 | 10.7 | 10.8 | 12.2 | Pro-con |
|  | 37.2 | 24.2 | 26.8 | 34.9 | 29.9 | 20.6 | 19.2 | 14.9 | Bad |
|  | 5.3 | 18.6 | 14.9 | 13.5 | 15.7 | 14.0 | 14.1 | 15.7 | Don't know |
|  | (452) | (656) | (570) | (550) | (555) | (1912) | (39642) | (591) | Weighted N |
|  |  |  |  |  |  |  |  |  |  |
| Females Only | 47.3 | 29.5 | 33.2 | 29.4 | 28.1 | 39.6 | 32.9 | 42.6 | Good |
|  | 7.8 | 7.5 | 8.3 | 8.5 | 10.7 | 7.5 | 6.7 | 10.5 | Pro-con |
|  | 27.3 | 22.5 | 24.1 | 28.2 | 23.4 | 19.7 | 14.4 | 14.4 | Bad |
|  | 17.6 | 40.6 | 34.5 | 34.0 | 37.7 | 33.2 | 46.0 | 32.5 | Don't know |
|  | (490) | (757) | (748) | (756) | (718) | (929) | (8742) | (735) | Weighted N |

Table 7.77

|  | 1963m | 1964a | 1965a | 1966k | 1967m | 1968a | 1969a | 1970a |  |
|---|---|---|---|---|---|---|---|---|---|
| Males Only | 53.2% | 57.3% | 56.4% | 46.9% | 43.0% | 52.1% | 49.4% | 39.6% | Good |
|  | 10.5 | 13.8 | 12.9 | 12.6 | 11.1 | 12.8 | 12.9 | 11.7 | Pro-con |
|  | 15.2 | 12.5 | 13.0 | 22.1 | 32.0 | 19.8 | 20.3 | 37.0 | Bad |
|  | 21.1 | 16.4 | 17.7 | 18.4 | 14.0 | 15.2 | 17.3 | 11.6 | Don't know |
|  | (541) | (1156) | (928) | (913) | (973) | (11295) | (8301) | (1826) | Weighted N |
|  |  |  |  |  |  |  |  |  |  |
| Females Only | 43.2 | 36.7 | 39.9 | 32.9 | 31.3 | 30.6 | 32.0 | 24.6 | Good |
|  | 9.7 | 8.8 | 11.3 | 7.1 | 6.5 | 6.4 | 7.2 | 9.5 | Pro-con |
|  | 12.6 | 11.9 | 10.3 | 19.4 | 25.9 | 20.0 | 20.8 | 31.4 | Bad |
|  | 34.6 | 42.5 | 38.4 | 40.6 | 36.4 | 43.0 | 40.0 | 34.5 | Don't know |
|  | (764) | (362) | (388) | (283) | (352) | (4053) | (3103) | (704) | Weighted N |

Table 7.78

|  | 1971m | 1972f | 1973c | 1974q | 1975q | 1976m |  |
|---|---|---|---|---|---|---|---|
| Males Only | 52.0% | 52.4% | 42.8% | 15.3% | 38.2% | 43.3% | Good |
|  | 12.6 | 11.9 | 13.8 | 11.1 | 10.5 | 9.9 | Pro-con |
|  | 24.2 | 23.2 | 32.3 | 66.3 | 41.5 | 38.0 | Bad |
|  | 11.2 | 12.5 | 11.0 | 7.3 | 9.8 | 8.7 | Don't know |
|  | (900) | (544) | (572) | (1314) | (1331) | (50480) | Weighted N |
|  |  |  |  |  |  |  |  |
| Females Only | 28.9 | 34.1 | 32.2 | 14.0 | 29.5 | 38.7 | Good |
|  | 8.0 | 8.3 | 11.9 | 8.4 | 10.0 | 6.6 | Pro-con |
|  | 26.1 | 25.7 | 27.2 | 60.4 | 41.7 | 37.5 | Bad |
|  | 37.0 | 31.9 | 28.7 | 17.2 | 18.8 | 17.2 | Don't know |
|  | (387) | (744) | (757) | (1635) | (1548) | (74552) | Weighted N |

Table 7.79
Does R Think Now Is a Good Time or a Bad Time to Buy a Car?
Race of Respondent

|              |       |       |       | Year  |       |        |         |        |            |
|--------------|-------|-------|-------|-------|-------|--------|---------|--------|------------|
|              | 1954m | 1956m | 1957f | 1958m | 1959f | 1960a  | 1961a   | 1962m  |            |
| Whites Only  | 48.6% | 37.6% | 39.0% | 34.3% | 35.2% | 50.8%  | 53.2%   | 50.5%  | Good       |
|              | 8.6   | 9.9   | 10.5  | 11.4  | 11.9  | 10.1   | 10.6    | 11.2   | Pro-con    |
|              | 31.3  | 22.9  | 26.0  | 30.4  | 26.6  | 19.7   | 17.8    | 14.9   | Bad        |
|              | 11.5  | 29.5  | 24.5  | 23.9  | 26.3  | 19.4   | 18.4    | 23.4   | Don't know |
|              | (851) | (1290)| (1170)| (1153)| (1131)| (2541) | (43556) | (1199) | Weighted N |
| Blacks Only  | 46.4  | 25.7  | 34.3  | 22.6  | 20.8  | 42.5   | 36.3    | 36.9   | Good       |
|              | 1.2   | 7.1   | 7.5   | 5.1   | 10.4  | 5.9    | 5.1     | 11.7   | Pro-con    |
|              | 39.3  | 28.3  | 18.7  | 33.6  | 24.0  | 24.5   | 24.2    | 11.7   | Bad        |
|              | 13.1  | 38.9  | 39.6  | 38.7  | 44.8  | 27.1   | 34.4    | 39.6   | Don't know |
|              | (84)  | (113) | (134) | (137) | (125) | (306)  | (4528)  | (111)  | Weighted N |

Table 7.80

|              | 1963m | 1964a | 1965a | 1966k | 1967m | 1968a   | 1969a   | 1970a  |            |
|--------------|-------|-------|-------|-------|-------|---------|---------|--------|------------|
| Whites Only  | 48.8% | 52.8% | 53.1% | 44.8% | 40.3% | 47.5%   | 45.6%   | 36.6%  | Good       |
|              | 10.6  | 13.3  | 12.3  | 11.6  | 10.4  | 11.6    | 12.1    | 11.9   | Pro-con    |
|              | 12.7  | 12.4  | 11.6  | 20.9  | 30.1  | 19.4    | 20.1    | 35.1   | Bad        |
|              | 27.9  | 21.5  | 23.1  | 22.6  | 19.2  | 21.5    | 22.3    | 16.4   | Don't know |
|              | (1154)| (1343)| (1166)| (1091)| (1175)| (13684) | (10085) | (2226) | Weighted N |
| Blacks Only  | 33.1  | 47.0  | 43.2  | 34.1  | 38.0  | 38.7    | 40.1    | 27.2   | Good       |
|              | 7.3   | 8.2   | 11.9  | 7.1   | 5.0   | 8.5     | 6.8     | 6.2    | Pro-con    |
|              | 21.8  | 11.2  | 17.8  | 25.9  | 33.1  | 21.1    | 22.6    | 36.6   | Bad        |
|              | 37.9  | 33.6  | 27.1  | 32.9  | 24.0  | 31.8    | 30.4    | 30.1   | Don't know |
|              | (124) | (134) | (118) | (85)  | (121) | (1414)  | (1141)  | (276)  | Weighted N |

Table 7.81

|              | 1971m | 1972f | 1973c | 1974q | 1975q | 1976m    |            |
|--------------|-------|-------|-------|-------|-------|----------|------------|
| Whites Only  | 46.2% | 42.1% | 38.0% | 15.0% | 34.1% | 41.1%    | Good       |
|              | 11.6  | 10.1  | 12.8  | 10.1  | 10.7  | 8.0      | Pro-con    |
|              | 25.0  | 24.7  | 29.3  | 62.8  | 40.7  | 38.1     | Bad        |
|              | 17.2  | 23.1  | 19.9  | 12.1  | 14.4  | 12.8     | Don't know |
|              | (1122)| (1156)| (1107)| (2538)| (2548)| (107034) | Weighted N |
| Blacks Only  | 38.8  | 40.9  | 27.4  | 11.9  | 26.4  | 39.9     | Good       |
|              | 8.5   | 5.2   | 10.3  | 6.3   | 5.4   | 7.4      | Pro-con    |
|              | 24.0  | 23.5  | 32.5  | 60.5  | 51.0  | 38.2     | Bad        |
|              | 28.7  | 30.4  | 29.9  | 21.3  | 17.2  | 14.5     | Don't know |
|              | (129) | (115) | (117) | (286) | (239) | (11525)  | Weighted N |

Table 7.82
Does R Think Now Is a Good Time or a Bad Time to Buy a Car?
Education of Respondent

| | | | | Year | | | | | |
|---|---|---|---|---|---|---|---|---|---|
| | 1954m | 1956m | 1957f | 1958m | 1959f | 1960a | 1961a | 1962m | |
| Grade School Only | 37.9% | 34.8% | 28.6% | 24.7% | 28.7% | 42.9% | 41.7% | 39.0% | Good |
| | 5.7 | 6.1 | 11.3 | 10.5 | 12.1 | 7.8 | 6.4 | 11.2 | Pro-con |
| | 35.2 | 22.7 | 25.7 | 34.2 | 29.1 | 22.6 | 22.4 | 16.5 | Bad |
| | 21.2 | 36.4 | 34.4 | 30.5 | 30.1 | 26.7 | 29.5 | 33.3 | Don't know |
| | (335) | (313) | (311) | (295) | (282) | (791) | (14423) | (249) | Weighted N |
| High School Only | 52.0 | 40.5 | 41.4 | 39.2 | 38.0 | 53.2 | 51.2 | 55.2 | Good |
| | 9.2 | 13.4 | 12.3 | 12.6 | 14.2 | 10.5 | 12.8 | 11.6 | Pro-con |
| | 31.0 | 25.0 | 25.7 | 29.9 | 25.2 | 19.7 | 19.6 | 12.5 | Bad |
| | 7.8 | 21.1 | 20.5 | 18.3 | 22.6 | 16.6 | 16.3 | 20.6 | Don't know |
| | (435) | (336) | (292) | (334) | (345) | (1059) | (21578) | (344) | Weighted N |
| College Only | 56.3 | 52.7 | 58.7 | 34.0 | 41.4 | 56.9 | 65.7 | 59.1 | Good |
| | 10.7 | 14.4 | 9.8 | 17.7 | 12.9 | 9.6 | 9.5 | 15.9 | Pro-con |
| | 30.4 | 16.8 | 22.4 | 26.5 | 27.1 | 18.0 | 11.1 | 13.5 | Bad |
| | 2.7 | 16.2 | 9.1 | 21.8 | 18.6 | 15.5 | 13.7 | 11.5 | Don't know |
| | (112) | (167) | (143) | (147) | (140) | (543) | (11870) | (208) | Weighted N |

Table 7.83

| | 1963m | 1964a | 1965a | 1966k | 1967m | 1968a | 1969a | 1970a | |
|---|---|---|---|---|---|---|---|---|---|
| Grade School Only | 35.3% | 40.4% | 40.1% | 34.1% | ** | 36.7% | 33.2% | 27.3% | Good |
| | 7.3 | 10.1 | 13.3 | 9.6 | ** | 9.8 | 13.1 | 9.2 | Pro-con |
| | 20.2 | 16.1 | 15.2 | 21.7 | ** | 20.5 | 20.8 | 35.4 | Bad |
| | 37.2 | 33.3 | 31.4 | 34.6 | ** | 33.1 | 33.0 | 28.2 | Don't know |
| | (371) | (483) | (369) | (355) | ** | (4365) | (2973) | (950) | Weighted N |
| High School Only | 50.2 | 58.3 | 54.0 | 48.4 | ** | 49.7 | 49.0 | 38.7 | Good |
| | 10.0 | 11.8 | 11.5 | 11.4 | ** | 11.0 | 10.5 | 12.7 | Pro-con |
| | 11.4 | 11.0 | 12.6 | 21.3 | ** | 19.0 | 19.4 | 37.6 | Bad |
| | 28.5 | 18.9 | 22.0 | 18.9 | ** | 20.3 | 21.1 | 11.0 | Don't know |
| | (660) | (652) | (628) | (508) | ** | (7055) | (5107) | (1107) | Weighted N |
| College Only | 56.9 | 58.3 | 60.1 | 48.3 | ** | 52.4 | 49.3 | 47.3 | Good |
| | 14.1 | 17.5 | 13.5 | 14.1 | ** | 12.8 | 11.3 | 11.0 | Pro-con |
| | 10.3 | 9.9 | 8.0 | 21.6 | ** | 20.2 | 21.9 | 27.8 | Bad |
| | 18.7 | 14.2 | 18.3 | 16.0 | ** | 14.6 | 17.5 | 13.9 | Don't know |
| | (262) | (372) | (311) | (269) | ** | (3826) | (3243) | (410) | Weighted N |

** Data not available--education not coded in 1967m.
Education coded for head of household only in 1956m,1958m,1959f,1960a,1961a,1962m,and 1966k, and for head and wife only in 1963m,1964a,1965a,1968a,1969a,and 1970a.

Table 7.84
Does R Think Now Is a Good Time or a Bad Time to Buy a Car?
Education of Respondent

|  | Year | | | | | | |
|---|---|---|---|---|---|---|---|
|  | 1971m | 1972f | 1973c | 1974q | 1975q | 1976m | |
| Grade School Only | 31.0% | 28.0% | 28.8% | 11.7% | 24.2% | 31.3% | Good |
|  | 9.4 | 8.6 | 8.3 | 7.9 | 10.4 | 6.2 | Pro-con |
|  | 27.6 | 22.6 | 30.1 | 56.0 | 40.1 | 31.0 | Bad |
|  | 32.0 | 40.7 | 32.7 | 24.4 | 25.3 | 31.4 | Don't know |
|  | (319) | (243) | (156) | (480) | (434) | (16854) | Weighted N |
| High School Only | 49.0 | 42.0 | 36.4 | 14.1 | 31.6 | 40.1 | Good |
|  | 10.3 | 10.6 | 9.9 | 8.6 | 10.6 | 7.7 | Pro-con |
|  | 22.6 | 25.8 | 32.0 | 64.7 | 44.3 | 40.6 | Bad |
|  | 18.1 | 21.5 | 21.7 | 12.6 | 13.4 | 11.5 | Don't know |
|  | (574) | (659) | (618) | (1412) | (1504) | (59692) | Weighted N |
| College Only | 51.4 | 50.8 | 41.3 | 16.9 | 40.6 | 44.1 | Good |
|  | 14.2 | 9.5 | 19.4 | 11.8 | 9.6 | 9.5 | Pro-con |
|  | 25.3 | 23.9 | 25.0 | 64.3 | 38.0 | 38.7 | Bad |
|  | 9.0 | 15.8 | 14.3 | 7.1 | 11.8 | 7.8 | Don't know |
|  | (387) | (380) | (392) | (1035) | (936) | (44825) | Weighted N |

Education coded for head of houshold only in 1971m.

Figure 7.13
Good or Bad Time to Buy a Car by Education of R

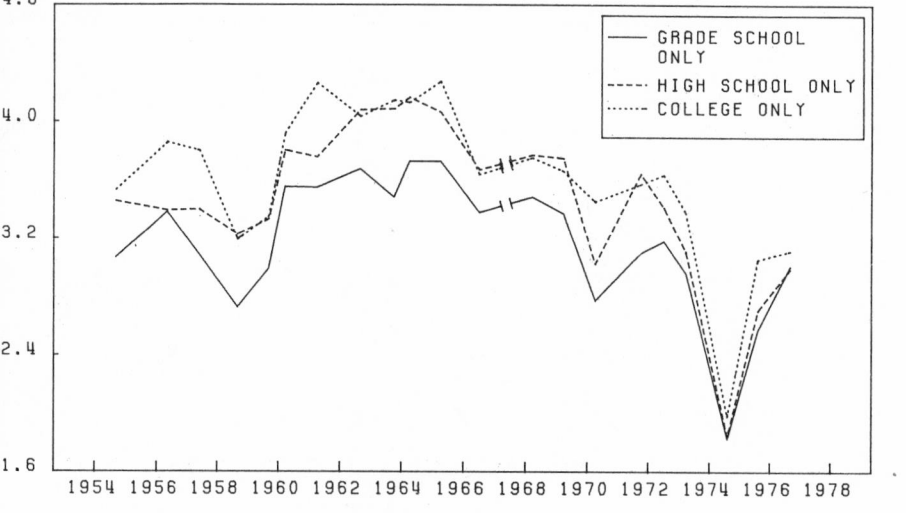

Table 7.85
Does R Think Now Is a Good Time or a Bad Time to Buy a Car?
Age of Respondent

| | | | | Year | | | | | |
|---|---|---|---|---|---|---|---|---|---|
| | 1954m | 1956m | 1957f | 1958m | 1959f | 1960a | 1961a | 1962m | |
| 18-24 Only | 60.7% | 37.5% | 53.2% | 46.2% | 42.3% | 61.2% | 55.4% | 71.4% | Good |
| | 8.2 | 6.8 | 5.1 | 10.3 | 13.5 | 6.0 | 11.5 | 4.8 | Pro-con |
| | 23.0 | 23.9 | 15.2 | 20.5 | 30.8 | 18.9 | 15.6 | 9.5 | Bad |
| | 8.2 | 31.8 | 26.6 | 23.1 | 13.5 | 13.9 | 17.5 | 14.3 | Don't know |
| | (61) | (88) | (79) | (39) | (52) | (201) | (4379) | (63) | Weighted N |
| 25-34 Only | 51.6 | 39.5 | 41.5 | 41.3 | 38.8 | 53.4 | 58.4 | 49.6 | Good |
| | 7.8 | 9.6 | 10.9 | 11.2 | 11.9 | 8.4 | 8.3 | 17.6 | Pro-con |
| | 35.2 | 24.7 | 24.4 | 35.7 | 29.9 | 23.1 | 19.7 | 14.5 | Bad |
| | 5.3 | 26.2 | 23.3 | 11.9 | 19.4 | 15.1 | 13.6 | 18.3 | Don't know |
| | (244) | (324) | (275) | (143) | (134) | (476) | (10167) | (131) | Weighted N |
| 35-44 Only | 47.9 | 39.8 | 41.0 | 34.3 | 37.3 | 50.4 | 56.2 | 50.0 | Good |
| | 11.3 | 11.8 | 9.1 | 15.1 | 11.8 | 11.4 | 7.5 | 14.1 | Pro-con |
| | 30.5 | 20.8 | 28.7 | 30.2 | 30.1 | 19.9 | 21.1 | 17.3 | Bad |
| | 10.3 | 27.6 | 21.1 | 20.3 | 20.9 | 18.4 | 15.2 | 18.6 | Don't know |
| | (213) | (322) | (317) | (172) | (153) | (528) | (10941) | (156) | Weighted N |
| 45-54 Only | 51.3 | 37.2 | 39.9 | 35.2 | 39.1 | 52.9 | 53.8 | 59.4 | Good |
| | 6.3 | 11.2 | 11.1 | 11.0 | 17.4 | 9.8 | 13.8 | 10.0 | Pro-con |
| | 32.3 | 25.7 | 27.7 | 31.7 | 25.4 | 20.3 | 16.0 | 11.9 | Bad |
| | 10.1 | 26.0 | 21.4 | 22.1 | 18.1 | 16.9 | 16.4 | 18.8 | Don't know |
| | (189) | (269) | (271) | (145) | (138) | (478) | (9248) | (160) | Weighted N |
| 55-64 Only | 42.2 | 35.5 | 33.0 | 31.4 | 29.7 | 46.7 | 44.1 | 48.4 | Good |
| | 4.9 | 8.1 | 13.2 | 9.4 | 18.6 | 11.3 | 11.4 | 13.5 | Pro-con |
| | 32.4 | 19.0 | 23.6 | 31.6 | 22.8 | 21.2 | 17.4 | 15.9 | Bad |
| | 20.6 | 37.4 | 30.2 | 27.6 | 29.0 | 20.9 | 27.1 | 22.2 | Don't know |
| | (102) | (211) | (182) | (649) | (145) | (364) | (7022) | (126) | Weighted N |
| 65-74 Only | 37.2 | 27.9 | 25.1 | 24.1 | 28.4 | 40.9 | 41.6 | 40.7 | Good |
| | 7.8 | 6.6 | 11.0 | 11.4 | 6.8 | 7.0 | 10.6 | 10.2 | Pro-con |
| | 31.8 | 26.8 | 23.6 | 27.2 | 25.0 | 17.5 | 16.7 | 12.6 | Bad |
| | 23.3 | 38.8 | 40.3 | 37.3 | 39.9 | 34.5 | 31.1 | 36.5 | Don't know |
| | (129) | (183) | (191) | (158) | (148) | (359) | (4287) | (167) | Weighted N |
| 75 And Older Only | ** | ** | ** | ** | ** | ** | 29.1 | ** | Good |
| | ** | ** | ** | ** | ** | ** | 7.4 | ** | Pro-con |
| | ** | ** | ** | ** | ** | ** | 18.8 | ** | Bad |
| | ** | ** | ** | ** | ** | ** | 44.7 | ** | Don't know |
| | ** | ** | ** | ** | ** | ** | (2206) | ** | Weighted N |

** Code distinction not made.
Youngest age group coded "21-24" in 1954m.
Oldest age group coded "65 And Older" in 1954m,1956m,1957f,1958m,1959f,1960a,and 1962m.
Age coded for head of household only in 1958m,1959f,1960a,1961a,1962m.

Table 7.86
Does R Think Now Is a Good Time or a Bad Time to Buy a Car?
Age of Respondent

|  | Year | | | | | | | | |
|---|---|---|---|---|---|---|---|---|---|
|  | 1963m | 1964a | 1965a | 1966k | 1967m | 1968a | 1969a | 1970a | |
| 18-24 Only | 50.0% | 64.5% | 58.2% | 48.8% | 34.4% | 43.5% | 45.3% | 43.5% | Good |
|  | 7.0 | 9.3 | 12.3 | 11.0 | 11.8 | 13.6 | 8.7 | 7.1 | Pro-con |
|  | 11.0 | 9.3 | 14.8 | 22.0 | 40.9 | 27.6 | 30.2 | 41.0 | Bad |
|  | 32.0 | 16.8 | 14.8 | 18.3 | 12.9 | 15.3 | 15.8 | 8.4 | Don't know |
|  | (100) | (107) | (122) | (82) | (93) | (977) | (1066) | (239) | Weighted N |
| 25-34 Only | 49.3 | 60.9 | 60.0 | 49.3 | 38.4 | 50.9 | 53.0 | 38.5 | Good |
|  | 12.7 | 11.9 | 12.9 | 8.7 | 10.5 | 13.0 | 11.1 | 12.0 | Pro-con |
|  | 17.5 | 14.6 | 11.7 | 25.1 | 34.6 | 21.9 | 20.7 | 33.4 | Bad |
|  | 20.5 | 12.6 | 15.4 | 16.9 | 16.5 | 14.1 | 15.3 | 16.1 | Don't know |
|  | (229) | (261) | (240) | (207) | (237) | (2843) | (2280) | (410) | Weighted N |
| 35-44 Only | 53.0 | 55.4 | 55.1 | 47.7 | 45.5 | 54.0 | 50.4 | 40.6 | Good |
|  | 7.5 | 14.7 | 12.4 | 12.6 | 9.5 | 10.1 | 11.9 | 11.8 | Pro-con |
|  | 13.5 | 12.2 | 11.2 | 22.5 | 30.4 | 19.2 | 17.1 | 34.6 | Bad |
|  | 25.9 | 17.7 | 21.3 | 17.1 | 14.6 | 16.6 | 20.5 | 13.1 | Don't know |
|  | (266) | (327) | (267) | (222) | (253) | (2831) | (1977) | (434) | Weighted N |
| 45-54 Only | 46.9 | 53.2 | 51.6 | 43.8 | 42.0 | 48.3 | 46.9 | 36.9 | Good |
|  | 13.2 | 12.5 | 13.5 | 13.6 | 10.5 | 12.8 | 12.6 | 14.4 | Pro-con |
|  | 14.3 | 13.1 | 13.9 | 20.4 | 28.6 | 19.9 | 20.1 | 36.7 | Bad |
|  | 25.6 | 21.2 | 20.9 | 22.3 | 18.8 | 18.9 | 20.3 | 11.9 | Don't know |
|  | (273) | (312) | (244) | (265) | (276) | (2859) | (1937) | (452) | Weighted N |
| 55-64 Only | 49.5 | 53.1 | 48.1 | 46.6 | 44.8 | 47.0 | 43.9 | 33.2 | Good |
|  | 11.3 | 12.4 | 13.4 | 10.8 | 9.4 | 11.2 | 10.1 | 11.2 | Pro-con |
|  | 11.3 | 12.4 | 9.7 | 16.7 | 27.1 | 15.9 | 17.3 | 36.5 | Bad |
|  | 27.9 | 22.0 | 28.7 | 26.0 | 18.7 | 26.0 | 28.7 | 19.1 | Don't know |
|  | (204) | (241) | (216) | (204) | (203) | (2771) | (1759) | (367) | Weighted N |
| 65-74 Only | 42.2 | 36.1 | 37.8 | 30.9 | 31.3 | 36.5 | 35.7 | 30.0 | Good |
|  | 8.1 | 14.2 | 10.4 | 11.2 | 9.3 | 9.1 | 14.8 | 10.8 | Pro-con |
|  | 11.9 | 8.7 | 13.1 | 24.3 | 26.0 | 20.8 | 24.3 | 32.8 | Bad |
|  | 37.8 | 41.0 | 38.7 | 33.6 | 33.3 | 33.6 | 25.3 | 26.4 | Don't know |
|  | (135) | (183) | (222) | (152) | (246) | (1874) | (1461) | (250) | Weighted N |
| 75 And Older Only | 24.4 | 29.9 | ** | 23.1 | ** | 30.7 | 22.9 | 20.3 | Good |
|  | 5.8 | 9.2 | ** | 7.7 | ** | 5.3 | 8.3 | 3.9 | Pro-con |
|  | 14.0 | 13.8 | ** | 16.9 | ** | 16.7 | 16.7 | 30.5 | Bad |
|  | 55.8 | 47.1 | ** | 52.3 | ** | 47.4 | 52.1 | 45.3 | Don't know |
|  | (86) | (87) | ** | (65) | ** | (1140) | (864) | (128) | Weighted N |

** Code distinction not made.
Oldest age group coded "65 And Older" in 1965a and 1967m.
Age coded for head of household and wife only in 1964a,1965a,1966k,1968a,1969a,and 1970a.

National Economic Outlook

Table 7.87
Does R Think Now Is a Good Time or a Bad Time to Buy a Car?
Age of Respondent

| | Year | | | | | | |
|---|---|---|---|---|---|---|---|
| | 1971m | 1972f | 1973c | 1974q | 1975q | 1976m | |
| 18-24 Only | 53.5% | 52.4% | 42.1% | 22.0% | 41.9% | 51.0% | Good |
| | 9.1 | 6.3 | 11.7 | 10.3 | 5.1 | 3.9 | Pro-con |
| | 28.3 | 25.0 | 33.0 | 54.4 | 43.3 | 35.3 | Bad |
| | 9.1 | 16.3 | 13.2 | 13.4 | 9.7 | 9.7 | Don't know |
| | (99) | (208) | (197) | (478) | (453) | (20037) | Weighted N |
| 25-34 Only | 51.4 | 49.5 | 38.7 | 14.2 | 36.4 | 44.8 | Good |
| | 11.5 | 10.0 | 12.8 | 11.5 | 8.5 | 6.5 | Pro-con |
| | 23.5 | 24.7 | 28.9 | 65.4 | 44.0 | 42.3 | Bad |
| | 13.6 | 15.8 | 19.7 | 8.8 | 11.2 | 6.4 | Don't know |
| | (243) | (279) | (305) | (668) | (671) | (26630) | Weighted N |
| 35-44 Only | 48.6 | 43.8 | 40.3 | 16.1 | 32.0 | 40.7 | Good |
| | 10.9 | 11.9 | 18.0 | 5.4 | 12.1 | 12.0 | Pro-con |
| | 28.4 | 23.3 | 24.2 | 68.8 | 40.0 | 37.2 | Bad |
| | 12.1 | 21.0 | 17.5 | 9.7 | 15.8 | 10.1 | Don't know |
| | (257) | (219) | (211) | (497) | (487) | (17693) | Weighted N |
| 45-54 Only | 49.1 | 39.7 | 34.6 | 11.8 | 33.1 | 37.3 | Good |
| | 10.8 | 12.2 | 12.7 | 10.6 | 12.6 | 8.3 | Pro-con |
| | 25.3 | 29.1 | 34.1 | 66.1 | 42.2 | 38.8 | Bad |
| | 14.9 | 19.0 | 18.5 | 11.4 | 12.1 | 15.6 | Don't know |
| | (269) | (189) | (205) | (499) | (405) | (18854) | Weighted N |
| 55-64 Only | 38.0 | 33.9 | 32.6 | 12.7 | 24.9 | 38.1 | Good |
| | 12.0 | 10.5 | 11.1 | 11.1 | 11.1 | 7.8 | Pro-con |
| | 21.6 | 31.0 | 29.5 | 64.9 | 45.8 | 37.6 | Bad |
| | 28.4 | 24.6 | 26.8 | 11.3 | 18.3 | 16.5 | Don't know |
| | (208) | (171) | (190) | (433) | (378) | (16873) | Weighted N |
| 65-74 Only | 33.3 | 32.0 | 34.9 | 11.4 | 32.2 | 37.7 | Good |
| | 12.9 | 8.8 | 11.8 | 8.8 | 11.6 | 10.6 | Pro-con |
| | 22.0 | 15.0 | 31.6 | 61.0 | 38.5 | 37.8 | Bad |
| | 31.8 | 44.2 | 21.7 | 18.9 | 17.6 | 13.8 | Don't know |
| | (132) | (147) | (152) | (228) | (335) | (14579) | Weighted N |
| 75 And Older Only | 27.8 | 20.0 | 24.6 | 7.6 | 26.6 | 18.5 | Good |
| | 10.1 | 8.6 | 3.1 | 6.8 | 15.8 | 6.7 | Pro-con |
| | 24.1 | 20.0 | 18.5 | 43.9 | 23.0 | 32.4 | Bad |
| | 38.0 | 51.4 | 53.8 | 41.7 | 34.5 | 42.4 | Don't know |
| | (79) | (70) | (65) | (132) | (139) | (7728) | Weighted N |

Table 7.88
Does R Think Now Is a Good Time or a Bad Time to Buy a Car?
Income of Respondent

|  | Year | | | | | | | | |
|---|---|---|---|---|---|---|---|---|---|
|  | 1954m | 1956m | 1957f | 1958m | 1959f | 1960a | 1961a | 1962m | |
| Income 1 (0–16%) | 38.8% | 27.7% | 23.9% | 16.9% | 20.6% | 39.2% | 32.0% | 30.8% | Good |
|  | 4.4 | 5.5 | 8.1 | 7.6 | 7.2 | 5.3 | 6.3 | 12.2 | Pro-con |
|  | 37.2 | 23.2 | 24.8 | 28.3 | 27.8 | 20.8 | 20.5 | 16.9 | Bad |
|  | 19.7 | 43.6 | 43.2 | 47.3 | 44.3 | 34.7 | 41.2 | 40.1 | Don't know |
|  | (183) | (220) | (222) | (237) | (194) | (533) | (7834) | (172) | Weighted N |
| Income 2 (17–33%) | 36.8 | 31.0 | 36.3 | 29.3 | 33.3 | 44.9 | 46.5 | 48.8 | Good |
|  | 14.0 | 5.6 | 8.3 | 9.3 | 12.5 | 8.3 | 9.2 | 8.0 | Pro-con |
|  | 36.8 | 25.4 | 24.8 | 33.3 | 24.2 | 23.1 | 17.8 | 15.5 | Bad |
|  | 12.3 | 38.0 | 30.6 | 28.0 | 30.0 | 23.8 | 26.5 | 27.7 | Don't know |
|  | (114) | (142) | (314) | (150) | (120) | (602) | (9557) | (213) | Weighted N |
| Income 3 (34–67%) | 49.3 | 39.0 | 40.0 | 35.0 | 37.0 | 53.1 | 52.8 | 51.3 | Good |
|  | 8.0 | 9.1 | 12.3 | 9.0 | 11.3 | 11.2 | 12.7 | 10.9 | Pro-con |
|  | 31.9 | 25.2 | 27.7 | 33.9 | 27.5 | 20.3 | 20.8 | 14.7 | Bad |
|  | 10.8 | 26.7 | 20.1 | 22.1 | 24.2 | 15.3 | 13.7 | 23.1 | Don't know |
|  | (288) | (580) | (513) | (489) | (451) | (1097) | (19152) | (524) | Weighted N |
| Income 4 (68–95%) | 56.1 | 40.9 | 51.6 | 43.5 | 38.0 | 55.7 | 65.7 | 56.9 | Good |
|  | 6.1 | 13.5 | 11.6 | 16.2 | 14.8 | 13.0 | 8.9 | 11.7 | Pro-con |
|  | 30.7 | 22.3 | 21.6 | 27.7 | 26.0 | 17.4 | 14.2 | 13.5 | Bad |
|  | 7.2 | 23.3 | 15.3 | 12.6 | 21.3 | 13.9 | 11.1 | 17.8 | Don't know |
|  | (264) | (296) | (190) | (278) | (366) | (539) | (10370) | (281) | Weighted N |
| Income 5 (96–100%) | 64.1 | 49.5 | 70.0 | 35.4 | 43.2 | 64.2 | 74.3 | 58.5 | Good |
|  | 17.2 | 17.5 | 10.0 | 15.2 | 21.6 | 6.4 | 8.3 | 20.0 | Pro-con |
|  | 14.1 | 11.7 | 16.7 | 32.3 | 16.2 | 18.3 | 11.4 | 12.3 | Bad |
|  | 4.7 | 21.4 | 3.3 | 17.2 | 18.9 | 11.0 | 6.0 | 9.2 | Don't know |
|  | (64) | (103) | (30) | (99) | (37) | (109) | (1579) | (65) | Weighted N |

National Economic Outlook

Table 7.89
Does R Think Now Is a Good Time or a Bad Time to Buy a Car?
Income of Respondent

|  | Year | | | | | | | | |
|---|---|---|---|---|---|---|---|---|---|
|  | 1963m | 1964a | 1965a | 1966k | 1967m | 1968a | 1969a | 1970a | |
| Income 1 (0-16%) | 32.8% | 35.3% | 33.7% | 30.0% | 28.2% | 25.3% | 28.3% | 25.4% | Good |
|  | 5.7 | 5.4 | 10.7 | 7.7 | 8.8 | 6.8 | 7.3 | 7.0 | Pro-con |
|  | 14.9 | 14.0 | 13.0 | 21.5 | 25.6 | 20.2 | 22.1 | 33.3 | Bad |
|  | 46.6 | 45.2 | 42.6 | 40.8 | 37.4 | 47.8 | 42.2 | 34.3 | Don't know |
|  | (174) | (221) | (169) | (233) | (262) | (2584) | (2398) | (472) | Weighted N |
| Income 2 (17-33%) | 44.8 | 47.6 | 43.4 | 43.6 | 42.9 | 44.3 | 38.3 | 27.7 | Good |
|  | 7.6 | 10.4 | 12.3 | 6.4 | 6.8 | 8.4 | 13.4 | 10.5 | Pro-con |
|  | 13.8 | 12.4 | 15.5 | 23.4 | 29.3 | 19.0 | 23.7 | 40.7 | Bad |
|  | 33.8 | 29.6 | 28.8 | 26.6 | 20.9 | 28.4 | 24.6 | 21.1 | Don't know |
|  | (210) | (250) | (219) | (94) | (191) | (2587) | (2230) | (408) | Weighted N |
| Income 3 (34-67%) | 45.7 | 52.6 | 53.9 | 46.5 | 40.6 | 48.6 | 52.5 | 33.2 | Good |
|  | 11.4 | 15.5 | 13.0 | 12.5 | 10.9 | 12.2 | 10.4 | 10.9 | Pro-con |
|  | 14.5 | 13.7 | 12.3 | 23.3 | 34.8 | 22.9 | 19.0 | 41.2 | Bad |
|  | 28.4 | 18.2 | 20.8 | 17.7 | 13.7 | 16.2 | 18.0 | 14.7 | Don't know |
|  | (387) | (534) | (423) | (361) | (488) | (5140) | (3840) | (882) | Weighted N |
| Income 4 (68-95%) | 57.2 | 62.9 | 58.3 | 48.9 | 45.8 | 54.0 | 52.8 | 47.0 | Good |
|  | 10.8 | 12.7 | 11.8 | 13.3 | 11.4 | 13.8 | 13.6 | 14.2 | Pro-con |
|  | 13.1 | 10.0 | 10.8 | 20.8 | 30.4 | 18.9 | 19.8 | 28.5 | Bad |
|  | 18.9 | 14.5 | 19.1 | 16.9 | 12.4 | 13.2 | 13.8 | 10.3 | Don't know |
|  | (381) | (442) | (408) | (427) | (306) | (4368) | (2610) | (677) | Weighted N |
| Income 5 (96-100%) | 56.0 | 56.0 | 60.6 | 41.4 | 63.3 | 66.1 | 48.1 | 54.1 | Good |
|  | 17.9 | 20.0 | 15.4 | 13.8 | 6.7 | 11.7 | 20.0 | 12.8 | Pro-con |
|  | 9.5 | 10.7 | 10.6 | 13.8 | 16.7 | 8.4 | 14.2 | 23.9 | Bad |
|  | 16.7 | 13.3 | 13.5 | 31.0 | 13.3 | 13.9 | 17.7 | 9.2 | Don't know |
|  | (84) | (75) | (104) | (29) | (30) | (772) | (401) | (109) | Weighted N |

National Economic Outlook

Table 7.90
Does R Think Now Is a Good Time or a Bad Time to Buy a Car?
Income of Respondent

|                      | Year   |        |        |        |        |         |            |
|----------------------|--------|--------|--------|--------|--------|---------|------------|
|                      | 1971m  | 1972f  | 1973c  | 1974q  | 1975q  | 1976m   |            |
| Income 1 (0-16%)     | 28.0%  | 27.6%  | 24.9%  | 12.2%  | 22.4%  | 38.1%   | Good       |
|                      | 7.4    | 10.4   | 7.7    | 8.4    | 7.2    | 8.7     | Pro-con    |
|                      | 22.2   | 18.6   | 30.2   | 53.8   | 47.3   | 39.0    | Bad        |
|                      | 42.3   | 43.4   | 37.3   | 25.6   | 23.1   | 14.2    | Don't know |
|                      | (189)  | (221)  | (169)  | (394)  | (433)  | (22035) | Weighted N |
|                      |        |        |        |        |        |         |            |
| Income 2 (17-33%)    | 39.2   | 35.6   | 34.3   | 16.0   | 24.4   | 43.7    | Good       |
|                      | 12.9   | 8.9    | 9.3    | 8.7    | 8.8    | 5.7     | Pro-con    |
|                      | 24.6   | 26.0   | 30.1   | 60.2   | 48.6   | 39.1    | Bad        |
|                      | 23.3   | 29.5   | 26.3   | 15.1   | 18.2   | 11.5    | Don't know |
|                      | (240)  | (146)  | (312)  | (583)  | (488)  | (24138) | Weighted N |
|                      |        |        |        |        |        |         |            |
| Income 3 (34-67%)    | 46.3   | 41.0   | 37.8   | 15.5   | 36.9   | 43.3    | Good       |
|                      | 11.1   | 10.2   | 14.4   | 9.3    | 10.4   | 7.2     | Pro-con    |
|                      | 28.7   | 28.2   | 30.7   | 65.0   | 40.6   | 41.5    | Bad        |
|                      | 13.9   | 20.6   | 17.1   | 10.2   | 12.1   | 8.0     | Don't know |
|                      | (467)  | (451)  | (362)  | (960)  | (818)  | (14833) | Weighted N |
|                      |        |        |        |        |        |         |            |
| Income 4 (68-95%)    | 58.0   | 53.4   | 43.6   | 15.4   | 38.8   | 45.4    | Good       |
|                      | 12.2   | 11.4   | 13.9   | 9.4    | 13.4   | 8.9     | Pro-con    |
|                      | 22.0   | 23.1   | 28.6   | 68.1   | 39.5   | 41.1    | Bad        |
|                      | 7.8    | 12.0   | 13.9   | 7.0    | 8.3    | 4.6     | Don't know |
|                      | (295)  | (324)  | (346)  | (596)  | (640)  | (9196)  | Weighted N |
|                      |        |        |        |        |        |         |            |
| Income 5 (96-100%)   | 63.5   | 53.8   | 44.0   | 17.9   | 50.0   | 46.9    | Good       |
|                      | 13.5   | 7.7    | 19.8   | 16.8   | 10.3   | 13.0    | Pro-con    |
|                      | 15.4   | 25.6   | 22.0   | 58.9   | 30.8   | 30.2    | Bad        |
|                      | 7.7    | 12.8   | 14.3   | 6.3    | 8.9    | 9.9     | Don't know |
|                      | (52)   | (78)   | (91)   | (95)   | (146)  | (8249)  | Weighted N |

National Economic Outlook

Table 7.91
Does R Think Now Is a Good Time or a Bad Time to Buy Household Durables?
Total Population

QUESTION: About the big things people buy for their homes—such as furniture,refrigerators,stoves,televisions and
things like that. Generally speaking, do you think now is a good time or a bad time for people to buy major household
items?

|  |  | Year | | | | | | | | | |
|---|---|---|---|---|---|---|---|---|---|---|---|
|  |  | 1951m | 1952k | 1953m | 1954m | 1956m | 1957f | 1958m | 1959f | 1960a | 1961a |
| Good | (5) | 28.5% | 34.0% | 36.7% | 54.8% | 52.4% | 48.9% | 46.7% | 49.6% | 60.7% | 56.7% |
| Pro-con | (3) | 17.5 | 14.0 | 13.7 | 3.7 | 12.1 | 14.6 | 15.2 | 17.0 | 12.9 | 11.4 |
| Bad | (1) | 43.9 | 41.6 | 39.0 | 33.3 | 17.7 | 20.2 | 20.9 | 15.1 | 12.5 | 18.0 |
| Don't know |  | 10.0 | 10.5 | 10.5 | 8.2 | 17.8 | 16.3 | 17.2 | 18.3 | 13.8 | 13.8 |
| Total |  | 100% | 100% | 100% | 100% | 100% | 100% | 100% | 100% | 100% | 100% |
| Weighted N |  | 918 | 909 | 997 | 946 | 1406 | 1312 | 1294 | 1273 | 2790 | 47410 |
| Unweighted N |  | 918 | 909 | 997 | 946 | 1406 | 1312 | 1294 | 1273 | 2790 | 1877 |
| Mean |  | 2.66 | 2.83 | 2.95 | 3.47 | 3.84 | 3.68 | 3.62 | 3.84 | 4.12 | 3.90 |
| Standard Deviation |  | 1.76 | 1.83 | 1.84 | 1.90 | 1.64 | 1.68 | 1.70 | 1.57 | 1.47 | 1.63 |

Table 7.92

|  |  | 1962m | 1963m | 1964a | 1965a | 1966a | 1967a | 1968a | 1969a | 1970a |
|---|---|---|---|---|---|---|---|---|---|---|
| Good | (5) | 46.7% | 55.0% | 58.2% | 57.7% | 57.4% | 45.2% | 58.4% | 51.9% | 38.3% |
| Pro-con | (3) | 14.5 | 16.4 | 15.1 | 13.8 | 13.4 | 14.1 | 15.4 | 14.7 | 17.6 |
| Bad | (1) | 17.1 | 10.2 | 8.7 | 8.9 | 12.7 | 24.1 | 11.6 | 14.5 | 28.7 |
| Don't know |  | 21.7 | 18.5 | 18.0 | 19.6 | 16.5 | 16.6 | 14.6 | 18.9 | 15.3 |
| Total |  | 100% | 100% | 100% | 100% | 100% | 100% | 100% | 100% | 100% |
| Weighted N |  | 1316 | 1290 | 1507 | 1308 | 2374 | 3089 | 15452 | 11441 | 2522 |
| Unweighted N |  | 1316 | 1290 | 1507 | 1308 | 2374 | 3089 | 2654 | 2276 | 2522 |
| Mean |  | 3.76 | 4.10 | 4.21 | 4.22 | 4.07 | 3.51 | 4.09 | 3.92 | 3.23 |
| Standard Deviation |  | 1.64 | 1.41 | 1.34 | 1.36 | 1.49 | 1.75 | 1.44 | 1.56 | 1.76 |

Table 7.93

|  |  | 1971m | 1972f | 1973c | 1974q | 1975q | 1976m |
|---|---|---|---|---|---|---|---|
| Good | (5) | 53.8% | 49.7% | 51.1% | 32.5% | 43.9% | 50.0% |
| Pro-con | (3) | 14.8 | 15.5 | 17.5 | 19.5 | 18.5 | 15.7 |
| Bad | (1) | 20.2 | 17.6 | 14.7 | 34.0 | 23.8 | 22.7 |
| Don't know |  | 11.2 | 17.1 | 16.7 | 14.1 | 13.9 | 11.7 |
| Total |  | 100% | 100% | 100% | 100% | 100% | 100% |
| Weighted N |  | 1281 | 1287 | 1320 | 2946 | 2871 | 126669 |
| Unweighted N |  | 1281 | 1287 | 1320 | 1496 | 1491 | 1123 |
| Mean |  | 3.76 | 3.77 | 3 87 | 2.96 | 3.47 | 3.62 |
| Standard Deviation |  | 1.66 | 1.63 | 1.55 | 1.76 | 1.71 | 1.70 |

Figure 7.14
Good or Bad Time to Buy Durables--Total Population

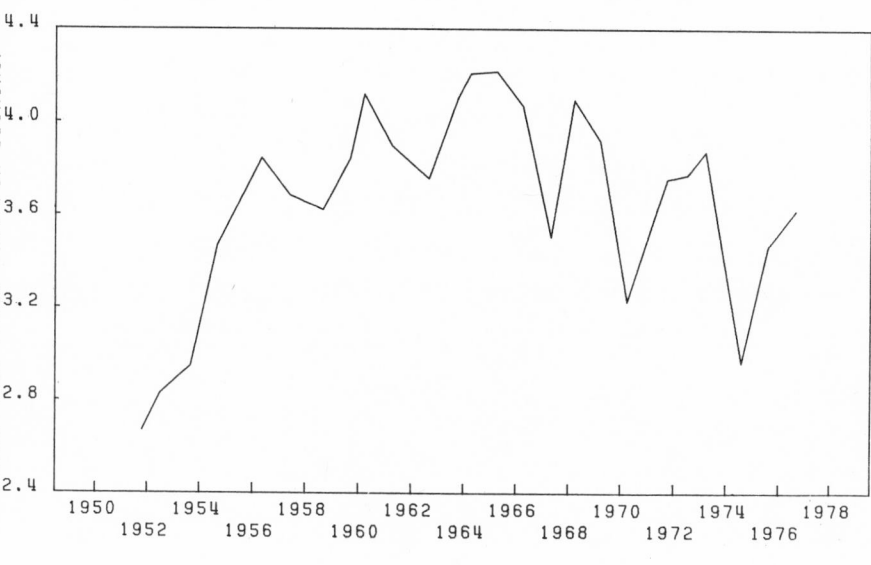

Figure 7.15
Good or Bad Time to Buy Durables by Race of R

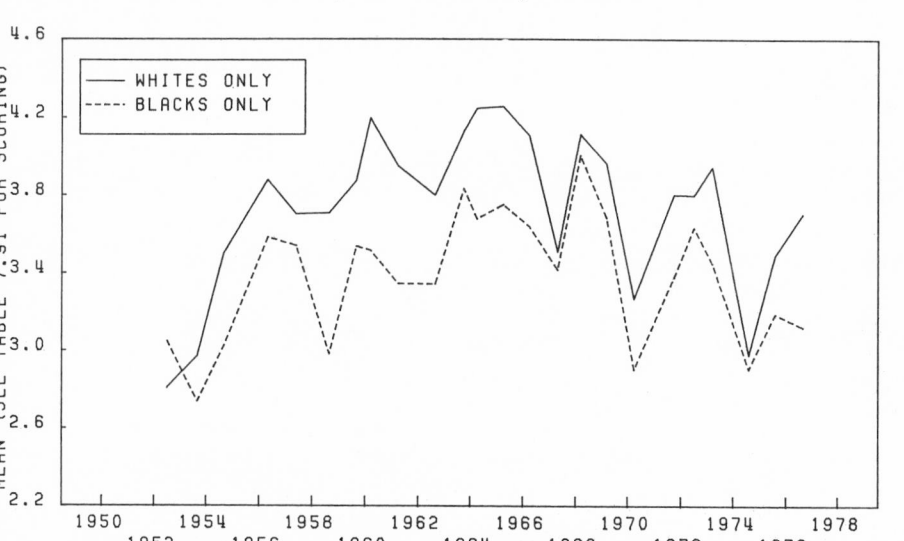

Table 7.94
Does R Think Now Is a Good Time or a Bad Time to Buy Household Durables?
Sex of Respondent

| | 1951m | 1952k | 1953m | 1954m | 1956m | 1957f | 1958m | 1959f | 1960a | 1961a | |
|---|---|---|---|---|---|---|---|---|---|---|---|
| Males Only | 27.3% | 37.6% | 33.7% | 51.9% | 56.5% | 50.4% | 51.9% | 54.1% | 62.2% | 60.2% | Good |
| | 20.7 | 15.8 | 14.3 | 3.5 | 13.2 | 19.1 | 14.4 | 15.0 | 12.5 | 11.3 | Pro-con |
| | 43.3 | 38.3 | 42.0 | 38.8 | 19.1 | 18.4 | 19.2 | 14.5 | 11.5 | 16.5 | Bad |
| | 8.8 | 8.3 | 10.0 | 5.8 | 11.1 | 12.0 | 14.5 | 16.5 | 13.8 | 12.0 | Don't know |
| | (411) | (399) | (448) | (451) | (658) | (565) | (557) | (553) | (1882) | (38825) | Weighted N |
| Females Only | 29.4 | 31.2 | 39.2 | 57.2 | 48.7 | 47.7 | 42.7 | 46.1 | 57.6 | 40.6 | Good |
| | 15.1 | 12.5 | 13.3 | 3.9 | 11.1 | 11.2 | 15.9 | 18.7 | 13.8 | 12.0 | Pro-con |
| | 44.3 | 44.1 | 36.6 | 28.4 | 16.5 | 21.6 | 22.3 | 15.5 | 14.8 | 25.3 | Bad |
| | 11.1 | 12.2 | 10.9 | 10.5 | 23.7 | 19.5 | 19.1 | 19.8 | 13.9 | 22.0 | Don't know |
| | (503) | (510) | (549) | (493) | (747) | (747) | (737) | (718) | (908) | (8502) | Weighted N |

Table 7.95

| | 1962m | 1963m | 1964a | 1965a | 1966a | 1967a | 1968a | 1969a | 1970a | |
|---|---|---|---|---|---|---|---|---|---|---|
| Males Only | 51.7% | 55.4% | 59.9% | 60.2% | 60.3% | 46.3% | 61.1% | 56.3% | 39.9% | Good |
| | 13.0 | 16.8 | 15.4 | 14.4 | 13.3 | 14.4 | 15.6 | 14.9 | 18.1 | Pro-con |
| | 18.9 | 10.1 | 8.1 | 7.6 | 12.3 | 24.0 | 9.9 | 12.5 | 28.3 | Bad |
| | 16.4 | 17.7 | 16.6 | 17.8 | 14.1 | 15.3 | 13.4 | 16.2 | 13.7 | Don't know |
| | (592) | (536) | (1142) | (925) | (1848) | (2751) | (11292) | (8317) | (1816) | Weighted N |
| Females Only | 42.7 | 54.6 | 52.9 | 51.7 | 47.1 | 37.3 | 51.3 | 40.0 | 34.3 | Good |
| | 15.7 | 16.0 | 13.9 | 12.3 | 13.7 | 13.7 | 14.6 | 14.1 | 16.4 | Pro-con |
| | 15.6 | 10.2 | 10.8 | 12.0 | 14.1 | 24.3 | 16.6 | 19.8 | 29.6 | Bad |
| | 26.0 | 19.1 | 22.4 | 24.0 | 25.1 | 24.7 | 17.5 | 26.0 | 19.7 | Don't know |
| | (724) | (754) | (361) | (383) | (526) | (888) | (4042) | (3124) | (706) | Weighted N |

Table 7.96

| | 1971m | 1972f | 1973c | 1974q | 1975q | 1976m | |
|---|---|---|---|---|---|---|---|
| Males Only | 58.9% | 54.7% | 53.3% | 34.3% | 47.9% | 51.0% | Good |
| | 15.6 | 15.0 | 16.7 | 20.1 | 15.3 | 14.4 | Pro-con |
| | 16.8 | 13.9 | 13.7 | 31.9 | 22.0 | 21.5 | Bad |
| | 8.7 | 16.5 | 16.3 | 13.7 | 14.8 | 13.1 | Don't know |
| | (895) | (541) | (570) | (1323) | (1331) | (50703) | Weighted N |
| Females Only | 42.0 | 46.1 | 49.3 | 31.0 | 40.4 | 49.5 | Good |
| | 12.7 | 16.0 | 18.1 | 18.9 | 21.3 | 16.7 | Pro-con |
| | 28.2 | 20.4 | 15.5 | 35.7 | 25.3 | 22.9 | Bad |
| | 17.1 | 17.6 | 17.1 | 14.4 | 13.1 | 10.9 | Don't know |
| | (386) | (746) | (750) | (1623) | (1540) | (74553) | Weighted N |

National Economic Outlook

Table 7.97

Does R Think Now Is a Good Time or a Bad Time to Buy Household Durables?

Race of Respondent

|  | | | | | | Year | | | | | |
|---|---|---|---|---|---|---|---|---|---|---|---|
|  | 1951m | 1952k | 1953m | 1954m | 1956m | 1957f | 1958m | 1959f | 1960a | 1961a | |
| Whites Only | ** | 33.2% | 37.1% | 55.2% | 53.0% | 49.2% | 47.9% | 49.9% | 62.3% | 57.8% | Good |
|  | ** | 15.1 | 14.4 | 4.0 | 12.6 | 15.5 | 16.1 | 17.7 | 13.1 | 12.0 | Pro-con |
|  | ** | 41.8 | 38.3 | 32.2 | 16.7 | 19.5 | 18.6 | 14.2 | 10.7 | 16.7 | Bad |
|  | ** | 9.9 | 10.2 | 8.7 | 17.7 | 15.8 | 17.5 | 18.2 | 13.9 | 13.5 | Don't know |
|  | ** | (807) | (911) | (852) | (1284) | (1165) | (1140) | (1130) | (2504) | (42530) | Weighted N |
| Blacks Only | ** | 42.4 | 33.8 | 47.6 | 48.6 | 47.7 | 39.0 | 47.2 | 48.5 | 45.6 | Good |
|  | ** | 4.3 | 7.5 | 1.2 | 6.3 | 7.6 | 7.4 | 13.0 | 10.0 | 7.0 | Pro-con |
|  | ** | 40.2 | 45.0 | 46.4 | 25.2 | 25.8 | 39.7 | 24.4 | 26.5 | 31.1 | Bad |
|  | ** | 13.0 | 13.8 | 4.8 | 19.8 | 18.9 | 14.0 | 15.4 | 15.1 | 16.4 | Don't know |
|  | ** | (92) | (80) | (84) | (111) | (132) | (136) | (123) | (291) | (4499) | Weighted N |

Table 7.98

|  | 1962m | 1963m | 1964a | 1965a | 1966a | 1967a | 1968a | 1969a | 1970a | |
|---|---|---|---|---|---|---|---|---|---|---|
| Whites Only | 47.4% | 55.0% | 59.5% | 58.6% | 58.0% | 44.3% | 58.7% | 52.7% | 38.7% | Good |
|  | 14.9 | 17.1 | 15.4 | 14.0 | 13.9 | 14.7 | 15.7 | 15.5 | 18.8 | Pro-con |
|  | 16.0 | 9.1 | 7.9 | 7.9 | 11.6 | 23.3 | 11.0 | 13.3 | 27.3 | Bad |
|  | 21.6 | 18.8 | 17.2 | 19.5 | 16.6 | 17.7 | 14.6 | 18.5 | 15.2 | Don't know |
|  | (1192) | (1141) | (1332) | (1159) | (2150) | (3203) | (13681) | (10118) | (2214) | Weighted N |
| Blacks Only | 41.7 | 54.1 | 44.3 | 50.0 | 51.1 | 45.8 | 58.1 | 48.0 | 34.8 | Good |
|  | 11.1 | 11.5 | 13.7 | 10.3 | 8.4 | 11.5 | 14.1 | 10.6 | 10.4 | Pro-con |
|  | 27.8 | 18.9 | 18.3 | 19.8 | 24.2 | 27.9 | 14.5 | 20.8 | 38.7 | Bad |
|  | 19.4 | 15.6 | 23.7 | 19.8 | 16.3 | 14.8 | 13.3 | 20.7 | 16.1 | Don't know |
|  | (108) | (122) | (131) | (116) | (190) | (358) | (1408) | (1146) | (279) | Weighted N |

Table 7.99

|  | 1971m | 1972f | 1973c | 1974q | 1975q | 1976m | |
|---|---|---|---|---|---|---|---|
| Whites Only | 54.9% | 50.0% | 53.0% | 32.7% | 43.7% | 50.7% | Good |
|  | 14.7 | 15.3 | 18.4 | 20.0 | 19.6 | 15.9 | Pro-con |
|  | 19.2 | 17.0 | 13.0 | 33.5 | 22.6 | 20.2 | Bad |
|  | 11.2 | 17.6 | 15.6 | 13.8 | 14.1 | 13.3 | Don't know |
|  | (1115) | (1156) | (1098) | (2530) | (2542) | (107186) | Weighted N |
| Blacks Only | 45.8 | 50.0 | 42.2 | 32.0 | 43.7 | 44.8 | Good |
|  | 13.7 | 16.7 | 13.8 | 14.8 | 10.1 | 12.1 | Pro-con |
|  | 29.0 | 21.9 | 24.1 | 35.7 | 35.3 | 38.9 | Bad |
|  | 11.5 | 11.4 | 19.8 | 17.5 | 10.9 | 4.3 | Don't know |
|  | (131) | (114) | (116) | (291) | (238) | (11443) | Weighted N |

** Data not available--race not coded in 1951m.

Table 7.100

Does R Think Now Is a Good Time or a Bad Time to Buy Household Durables?

Education of Respondent

| | | | | | Year | | | | | | |
|---|---|---|---|---|---|---|---|---|---|---|---|
| | 1951m | 1952k | 1953m | 1954m | 1956m | 1957f | 1958m | 1959f | 1960a | 1961a | |
| Grade School Only | 27.4% | 27.7% | 31.8% | 43.9% | 45.2% | 39.7% | 37.2% | 39.6% | 53.6% | 46.2% | Good |
| | 12.1 | 9.2 | 11.1 | 2.7 | 12.4 | 17.3 | 16.2 | 17.1 | 12.0 | 9.2 | Pro-con |
| | 47.2 | 51.3 | 42.4 | 40.6 | 23.9 | 24.4 | 26.7 | 22.9 | 19.2 | 26.3 | Bad |
| | 13.3 | 11.8 | 14.6 | 12.8 | 18.5 | 18.6 | 19.9 | 20.4 | 15.2 | 18.3 | Don't know |
| | (339) | (357) | (377) | (335) | (314) | (307) | (296) | (280) | (765) | (13875) | Weighted N |
| High School Only | 29.5 | 37.4 | 38.3 | 58.9 | 55.8 | 49.7 | 47.0 | 53.8 | 64.7 | 59.1 | Good |
| | 19.3 | 17.3 | 14.8 | 3.9 | 12.4 | 15.1 | 16.9 | 17.1 | 11.9 | 12.2 | Pro-con |
| | 41.4 | 35.8 | 38.7 | 31.6 | 19.4 | 19.5 | 20.8 | 12.9 | 10.0 | 18.0 | Bad |
| | 9.8 | 9.5 | 8.2 | 5.7 | 12.4 | 15.8 | 15.4 | 16.2 | 13.4 | 10.7 | Don't know |
| | (440) | (369) | (465) | (440) | (330) | (292) | (332) | (340) | (1046) | (21429) | Weighted N |
| College Only | 27.3 | 40.4 | 46.5 | 65.1 | 63.1 | 61.4 | 57.7 | 53.6 | 62.1 | 65.9 | Good |
| | 26.5 | 16.3 | 16.9 | 5.5 | 13.1 | 20.0 | 11.4 | 16.4 | 14.9 | 12.5 | Pro-con |
| | 43.2 | 33.1 | 30.3 | 22.9 | 11.9 | 10.7 | 9.4 | 10.0 | 7.8 | 8.7 | Bad |
| | 3.0 | 10.1 | 6.3 | 6.4 | 11.9 | 7.9 | 21.5 | 20.0 | 15.2 | 12.9 | Don't know |
| | (132) | (178) | (142) | (109) | (168) | (140) | (149) | (140) | (538) | (11443) | Weighted N |

Table 7 101

| | 1962m | 1963m | 1964a | 1965a | 1966a | 1967a | 1968a | 1969a | 1970a | |
|---|---|---|---|---|---|---|---|---|---|---|
| Grade School Only | 32.8% | 47.6% | 48.3% | 52.5% | 48.3% | 37.3% | 50.2% | 42.4% | 33.7% | Good |
| | 11.7 | 16.2 | 15.6 | 14.2 | 11.1 | 13.9 | 17.1 | 18.1 | 15.5 | Pro-con |
| | 30.8 | 15.3 | 13.1 | 12.0 | 20.2 | 25.9 | 14.7 | 17.3 | 32.8 | Bad |
| | 24.7 | 20.9 | 22.9 | 21.3 | 20.5 | 22.8 | 18.0 | 22.2 | 17.9 | Don't know |
| | (247) | (359) | (480) | (366) | (660) | (1029) | (4345) | (2991) | (953) | Weighted N |
| High School Only | 52.0 | 56.8 | 64.9 | 58.7 | 61.8 | 44.6 | 61.8 | 55.4 | 41.0 | Good |
| | 14.0 | 16.9 | 13.7 | 13.8 | 13.2 | 14.7 | 14.8 | 13.1 | 18.5 | Pro-con |
| | 16.4 | 8.8 | 6.9 | 9.6 | 10.5 | 24.9 | 10.4 | 13.2 | 27.4 | Bad |
| | 17.5 | 17.5 | 14.5 | 17.8 | 14.5 | 15.8 | 13.0 | 18.3 | 13.1 | Don't know |
| | (342) | (658) | (649) | (623) | (1004) | (1692) | (7080) | (5088) | (1101) | Weighted N |
| College Only | 55.9 | 60.2 | 60.6 | 62.6 | 60.6 | 52.2 | 62.9 | 55.3 | 41.6 | Good |
| | 15.2 | 15.3 | 16.5 | 12.9 | 17.1 | 13.8 | 13.5 | 14.4 | 20.3 | Pro-con |
| | 9.5 | 6.5 | 6.1 | 3.9 | 7.3 | 19.5 | 10.6 | 13.8 | 23.5 | Bad |
| | 19.4 | 18.0 | 16.8 | 20.6 | 15.0 | 14.4 | 13.0 | 16.5 | 14.6 | Don't know |
| | (211) | (261) | (363) | (310) | (601) | (875) | (3817) | (3272) | (404) | Weighted N |

Education coded for head of household only in 1956m,1957f,1958m,1959f,1960a,1961a,1962m and 1966a, and for head and wife only in 1964a,1965a,1966a,1967a,1968a,1969a,and 1970a.

Table 7.102
Does R Think Now Is a Good Time or a Bad Time to Buy Household Durables?
Education of Respondent

|  | 1971m | 1972f | 1973c | 1974q | 1975q | 1976m | |
|---|---|---|---|---|---|---|---|
| Grade School Only | 39.0% | 43.0% | 47.0% | 23.3% | 34.6% | 37.4% | Good |
|  | 16.0 | 16.5 | 13.9 | 15.5 | 17.5 | 14.6 | Pro-con |
|  | 30.2 | 19.8 | 19.9 | 42.1 | 31.6 | 30.8 | Bad |
|  | 14.8 | 20.7 | 19.2 | 19.2 | 16.4 | 17.2 | Don't know |
|  | (318) | (242) | (151) | (485) | (434) | (16681) | Weighted N |
| High School Only | 57.8 | 51.4 | 52.3 | 33.7 | 42.3 | 50.7 | Good |
|  | 14.9 | 16.0 | 16.9 | 19.2 | 18.9 | 16.2 | Pro-con |
|  | 18.4 | 17.2 | 14.8 | 32.9 | 24.2 | 20.9 | Bad |
|  | 8.9 | 15.3 | 16.1 | 14.2 | 14.7 | 12.2 | Don't know |
|  | (571) | (661) | (616) | (1403) | (1494) | (59761) | Weighted N |
| College Only | 60.4 | 51.1 | 52.9 | 35.7 | 51.0 | 53.7 | Good |
|  | 13.5 | 14.3 | 20.2 | 21.2 | 18.0 | 14.7 | Pro-con |
|  | 14.6 | 16.7 | 11.5 | 31.6 | 19.4 | 21.5 | Bad |
|  | 11.5 | 18.0 | 15.3 | 11.5 | 11.5 | 10.2 | Don't know |
|  | (384) | (378) | (391) | (1038) | (937) | (44999) | Weighted N |

Education coded for head of household only in 1971m.

Figure 7.16
Good or Bad Time to Buy Durables by Education of R

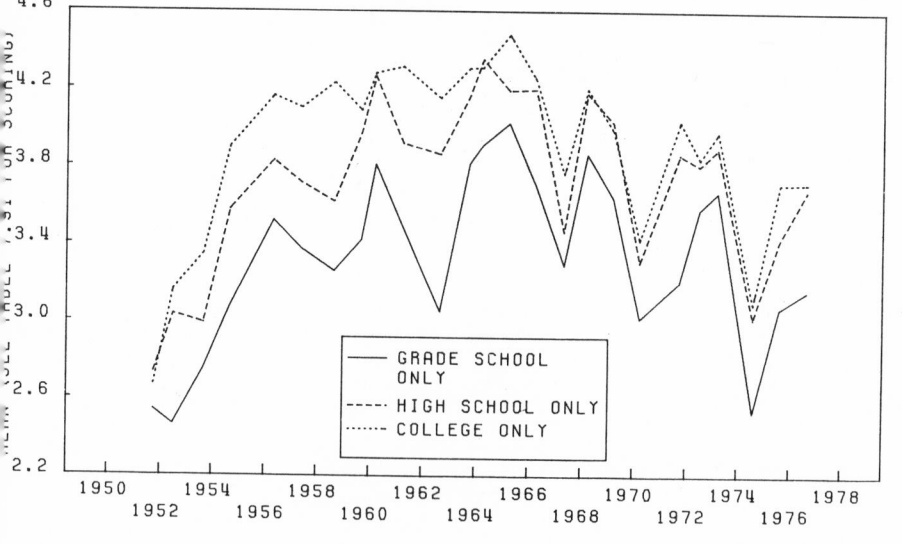

National Economic Outlook

Table 7.103
Does R Think Now Is a Good Time or a Bad Time to Buy Household Durables?
Age of Respondent

|  | Year | | | | | | | | | |  |
|---|---|---|---|---|---|---|---|---|---|---|---|
|  | 1951m | 1952k | 1953m | 1954m | 1956m | 1957f | 1958m | 1959f | 1960a | 1961a |  |
| 18-24 Only | 33.9% | 27.5% | 63.8% | 65.6% | 65.9% | 58.8% | 53.8% | 61.2% | 60.8% | 54.3% | Good |
|  | 22.6 | 13.7 | 6.4 | 3.3 | 6.8 | 13.8 | 5.1 | 8.2 | 9.8 | 9.3 | Pro-con |
|  | 30.6 | 47.1 | 27.7 | 23.0 | 12.5 | 15.0 | 17.9 | 14.3 | 9.3 | 14.6 | Bad |
|  | 12.9 | 11.8 | 2.1 | 8.2 | 14.8 | 12.5 | 23.1 | 16.3 | 20.1 | 21.8 | Don't know |
|  | (62) | (51) | (47) | (61) | (88) | (80) | (39) | (49) | (194) | (4339) | Weighted N |
| 25-34 Only | 35.8 | 44.3 | 45.0 | 58.6 | 61.0 | 56.9 | 54.9 | 56.2 | 64.3 | 61.6 | Good |
|  | 17.5 | 13.6 | 14.7 | 4.0 | 11.3 | 13.9 | 13.2 | 15.3 | 12.0 | 11.6 | Pro-con |
|  | 41.0 | 31.6 | 34.2 | 30.7 | 15.6 | 15.0 | 18.1 | 10.2 | 9.9 | 15.8 | Bad |
|  | 5.7 | 10.5 | 6.1 | 6.8 | 12.0 | 14.2 | 13.9 | 18.2 | 13.8 | 10.9 | Don't know |
|  | (229) | (228) | (231) | (251) | (326) | (274) | (144) | (137) | (465) | (9954) | Weighted N |
| 35-44 Only | 31.4 | 35.0 | 34.9 | 57.5 | 51.4 | 53.2 | 41.3 | 48.4 | 63.2 | 59.3 | Good |
|  | 20.9 | 15.9 | 13.4 | 5.1 | 11.8 | 12.4 | 15.1 | 16.3 | 11.3 | 13.1 | Pro-con |
|  | 42.3 | 38.2 | 42.4 | 28.5 | 19.2 | 20.4 | 25.6 | 17.6 | 13.0 | 16.7 | Bad |
|  | 5.5 | 11.0 | 9.2 | 8.9 | 17.6 | 14.0 | 18.0 | 17.6 | 12.6 | 10.8 | Don't know |
|  | (220) | (246) | (238) | (214) | (323) | (314) | (172) | (153) | (524) | (10723) | Weighted N |
| 45-54 Only | 22.9 | 31.2 | 34.1 | 57.5 | 50.6 | 48.4 | 51.0 | 56.8 | 62.9 | 56.4 | Good |
|  | 17.9 | 13.6 | 12.4 | 5.1 | 13.7 | 15.6 | 16.3 | 15.1 | 13.6 | 12.3 | Pro-con |
|  | 47.5 | 49.4 | 44.3 | 28.5 | 20.5 | 21.5 | 19.7 | 14.4 | 11.4 | 20.5 | Bad |
|  | 11.8 | 5.8 | 9.2 | 8.9 | 15.2 | 14.5 | 12.9 | 13.7 | 12.1 | 10.8 | Don't know |
|  | (280) | (154) | (185) | (214) | (263) | (275) | (147) | (139) | (472) | (9160) | Weighted N |
| 55-64 Only | ** | 32.2 | 37.2 | 47.1 | 50.2 | 44.9 | 48.3 | 38.1 | 55.0 | 54.8 | Good |
|  | ** | 13.9 | 16.3 | 2.9 | 14.6 | 19.1 | 15.5 | 27.3 | 12.5 | 10.2 | Pro-con |
|  | ** | 41.7 | 31.8 | 37.5 | 12.7 | 20.8 | 20.3 | 17.3 | 15.0 | 21.6 | Bad |
|  | ** | 12.2 | 14.7 | 12.5 | 22.4 | 15.2 | 16.0 | 17.3 | 17.6 | 13.5 | Don't know |
|  | ** | (115) | (129) | (104) | (205) | (178) | (632) | (139) | (353) | (6988) | Weighted N |
| 65-74 Only | 18.9 | 18.0 | 22.6 | 37.4 | 38.0 | 29.9 | 33.1 | 38.4 | 53.1 | 50.8 | Good |
|  | 9.0 | 11.7 | 14.5 | 0.8 | 12.0 | 14.4 | 17.5 | 13.7 | 15.5 | 11.5 | Pro-con |
|  | 51.6 | 57.7 | 44.0 | 50.4 | 22.8 | 27.3 | 23.1 | 20.5 | 16.7 | 18.2 | Bad |
|  | 20.5 | 12.6 | 18.9 | 11.4 | 27.2 | 28.3 | 26.3 | 27.4 | 14.7 | 19.6 | Don't know |
|  | (122) | (111) | (159) | (123) | (184) | (187) | (160) | (146) | (354) | (3983) | Weighted N |
| 75 And Older Only | ** | ** | ** | ** | ** | ** | ** | ** | ** | 42.0 | Good |
|  | ** | ** | ** | ** | ** | ** | ** | ** | ** | 8.0 | Pro-con |
|  | ** | ** | ** | ** | ** | ** | ** | ** | ** | 21.8 | Bad |
|  | ** | ** | ** | ** | ** | ** | ** | ** | ** | 28.2 | Don't know |
|  | ** | ** | ** | ** | ** | ** | ** | ** | ** | (2046) | Weighted N |

** Code distinction not made.
Youngest age group coded "21-24" in 1953m.
Age group coded "45-54" in 1951m.
Oldest age group coded "65 And Older" in 1951m,1952k,1953m,1954m,1956m,1957f,1958m,1959f,and 1960a.
Age coded for head of household only in 1958m,1959f,1960a,and 1961a.

Table 7.104
Does R Think Now Is a Good Time or a Bad Time to Buy Household Durables?
Age of Respondent

|  | 1962m | 1963m | 1964a | 1965a | 1966a | 1967a | 1968a | 1969a | 1970a |  |
|---|---|---|---|---|---|---|---|---|---|---|
| 18-24 Only | 58.7% | 63.6% | 58.7% | 56.9% | 60.0% | 47.2% | 57.8% | 54.3% | 44.5% | Good |
|  | 12.7 | 11.1 | 13.5 | 13.8 | 10.0 | 12.1 | 15.1 | 11.3 | 13.9 | Pro-con |
|  | 14.3 | 9.1 | 8.7 | 8.9 | 13.5 | 25.8 | 11.2 | 13.1 | 26.5 | Bad |
|  | 14.3 | 16.2 | 19.2 | 20.3 | 16.5 | 14.9 | 15.8 | 21.3 | 15.1 | Don't know |
|  | (63) | (99) | (104) | (123) | (170) | (248) | (972) | (1092) | (238) | Weighted N |
| 25-34 Only | 52.6 | 52.2 | 68.6 | 60.4 | 59.6 | 45.1 | 63.6 | 57.0 | 39.9 | Good |
|  | 12.0 | 18.4 | 13.7 | 15.8 | 11.8 | 12.7 | 13.0 | 14.9 | 20.8 | Pro-con |
|  | 16.5 | 7.9 | 6.7 | 7.9 | 13.9 | 28.4 | 10.0 | 13.1 | 27.6 | Bad |
|  | 18.8 | 21.5 | 11.0 | 15.8 | 14.8 | 13.9 | 13.4 | 15.0 | 11.7 | Don't know |
|  | (133) | (228) | (255) | (240) | (433) | (648) | (2850) | (2273) | (409) | Weighted N |
| 35-44 Only | 53.2 | 57.5 | 63.3 | 63.7 | 60.6 | 48.7 | 64.4 | 53.7 | 41.7 | Good |
|  | 15.4 | 15.7 | 15.0 | 13.9 | 15.9 | 13.9 | 14.5 | 14.7 | 19.3 | Pro-con |
|  | 16.7 | 10.4 | 6.3 | 6.4 | 11.3 | 22.7 | 10.2 | 14.9 | 26.1 | Bad |
|  | 14.7 | 16.4 | 15.4 | 16.1 | 12.2 | 14.7 | 10.8 | 16.8 | 12.8 | Don't know |
|  | (156) | (268) | (319) | (267) | (459) | (700) | (2815) | (1985) | (429) | Weighted N |
| 45-54 Only | 48.2 | 56.7 | 56.6 | 63.2 | 60.5 | 48.4 | 64.3 | 54.5 | 39.4 | Good |
|  | 15.9 | 16.3 | 18.6 | 15.3 | 12.7 | 15.4 | 14.1 | 16.7 | 16.8 | Pro-con |
|  | 20.1 | 11.5 | 8.0 | 7.0 | 11.8 | 21.0 | 8.9 | 13.8 | 27.9 | Bad |
|  | 15.9 | 15.6 | 16.7 | 14.5 | 15.0 | 15.3 | 12.7 | 15.0 | 15.9 | Don't know |
|  | (164) | (270) | (311) | (242) | (466) | (701) | (2884) | (1926) | (452) | Weighted N |
| 55-64 Only | 41.3 | 53.8 | 58.6 | 55.7 | 59.2 | 43.9 | 57.6 | 52.9 | 37.8 | Good |
|  | 16.7 | 18.3 | 12.3 | 9.9 | 14.2 | 13.8 | 16.1 | 12.4 | 17.1 | Pro-con |
|  | 23.0 | 10.7 | 11.1 | 10.4 | 12.0 | 22.5 | 11.4 | 12.6 | 30.2 | Bad |
|  | 19.0 | 17.3 | 18.0 | 24.1 | 14.7 | 19.9 | 14.9 | 22.0 | 14.9 | Don't know |
|  | (126) | (197) | (244) | (212) | (409) | (579) | (2786) | (1771) | (368) | Weighted N |
| 65-74 Only | 35.0 | 46.6 | 46.2 | 44.3 | 45.6 | 38.6 | 46.3 | 43.4 | 30.0 | Good |
|  | 9.4 | 20.3 | 16.7 | 13.7 | 13.8 | 16.5 | 18.4 | 19.1 | 18.4 | Pro-con |
|  | 21.3 | 9.0 | 10.2 | 13.7 | 14.5 | 23.9 | 17.9 | 17.2 | 33.6 | Bad |
|  | 34.4 | 24.1 | 26.9 | 28.3 | 26.2 | 21.0 | 17.4 | 20.3 | 18.0 | Don't know |
|  | (160) | (133) | (186) | (219) | (428) | (461) | (1844) | (1461) | (250) | Weighted N |
| 75 And Older Only | ** | 51.8 | 38.1 | ** | ** | 28.6 | 40.7 | 37.1 | 26.2 | Good |
|  | ** | 10.8 | 11.9 | ** | ** | 15.0 | 16.8 | 12.4 | 13.5 | Pro-con |
|  | ** | 12.0 | 16.7 | ** | ** | 26.4 | 17.7 | 19.6 | 34.1 | Bad |
|  | ** | 25.3 | 33.3 | ** | ** | 30.0 | 24.8 | 30.9 | 26.2 | Don't know |
|  | ** | (83) | (84) | ** | ** | (280) | (1130) | (873) | (126) | Weighted N |

** Code distinction not made.
Oldest age group coded "65 And Older" in 1962m, 1965a and 1966a.
Age coded for head of household only in 1962m, and for head and wife only in 1964a,1965a,1966a,1967a,1968a,1969a,and
1970a.

Table 7.105
Does R Think Now Is a Good Time or a Bad Time to Buy Household Durables?
Age of Respondent

| | | | Year | | | | |
|---|---|---|---|---|---|---|---|
| | 1971m | 1972f | 1973c | 1974q | 1975q | 1976m | |
| 18-24 Only | 60.6% | 52.2% | 55.8% | 37.5% | 51.6% | 58.7% | Good |
| | 14.1 | 12.1 | 8.1 | 17.9 | 13.8 | 9.6 | Pro-con |
| | 18.2 | 20.3 | 13.7 | 25.0 | 17.6 | 16.1 | Bad |
| | 7.1 | 15.5 | 22.3 | 19.6 | 17.0 | 15.6 | Don't know |
| | (99) | (207) | (197) | (480) | (448) | (20191) | Weighted N |
| 25-34 Only | 62.0 | 56.0 | 57.3 | 33.5 | 51.3 | 52.0 | Good |
| | 12.0 | 15.2 | 14.0 | 17.1 | 15.1 | 16.2 | Pro-con |
| | 15.7 | 13.7 | 12.7 | 35.6 | 24.1 | 23.6 | Bad |
| | 10.3 | 15.2 | 16.0 | 13.8 | 9.4 | 8.2 | Don't know |
| | (242) | (277) | (300) | (668) | (667) | (26486) | Weighted N |
| 35-44 Only | 57.3 | 50.2 | 51.4 | 35.3 | 37.9 | 53.1 | Good |
| | 15.8 | 14.0 | 21.2 | 16.8 | 20.7 | 14.0 | Pro-con |
| | 18.6 | 15.8 | 12.3 | 38.5 | 25.3 | 24.3 | Bad |
| | 8.3 | 19.9 | 15.1 | 9.4 | 16.1 | 8.6 | Don't know |
| | (253) | (221) | (212) | (499) | (478) | (17743) | Weighted N |
| 45-54 Only | 58.5 | 42.6 | 47.5 | 34.3 | 49.8 | 50.3 | Good |
| | 15.2 | 19.5 | 20.8 | 22.8 | 18.0 | 14.0 | Pro-con |
| | 17.4 | 22.1 | 14.9 | 30.3 | 21.4 | 27.1 | Bad |
| | 8.9 | 15.8 | 16.8 | 12.6 | 10.9 | 8.6 | Don't know |
| | (270) | (190) | (202) | (492) | (412) | (18929) | Weighted N |
| 55-64 Only | 45.9 | 51.2 | 49.2 | 29.4 | 38.3 | 54.5 | Good |
| | 16.1 | 15.9 | 22.0 | 23.7 | 24.4 | 20.1 | Pro-con |
| | 25.4 | 15.3 | 15.2 | 38.2 | 24.7 | 18.9 | Bad |
| | 12.7 | 17.6 | 13.6 | 8.7 | 12.6 | 6.6 | Don't know |
| | (205) | (170) | (191) | (435) | (381) | (17020) | Weighted N |
| 65-74 Only | 40.5 | 44.9 | 43.0 | 21.6 | 34.1 | 42.4 | Good |
| | 14.5 | 20.4 | 23.8 | 23.8 | 20.7 | 17.8 | Pro-con |
| | 24.4 | 19.0 | 20.5 | 36.1 | 29.6 | 27.6 | Bad |
| | 20.6 | 15.6 | 12.6 | 18.5 | 15.6 | 12.2 | Don't know |
| | (131) | (147) | (151) | (227) | (334) | (14752) | Weighted N |
| 75 And Older Only | 35.8 | 41.4 | 41.3 | 19.8 | 24.3 | 26.1 | Good |
| | 16.0 | 10.0 | 7.9 | 13.7 | 20.7 | 25.0 | Pro-con |
| | 30.9 | 22.9 | 22.2 | 36.6 | 28.6 | 24.0 | Bad |
| | 17.3 | 25.7 | 28.6 | 29.8 | 26.4 | 24.9 | Don't know |
| | (81) | (70) | (63) | (131) | (140) | (7553) | Weighted N |

Table 7-106
Does R Think Now Is a Good Time or a Bad Time to Buy Household Durables?
Income of Respondent

|  | | | | | | Year | | | | | |
|---|---|---|---|---|---|---|---|---|---|---|---|
|  | 1951m | 1952k | 1953m | 1954m | 1956m | 1957f | 1958m | 1959f | 1960a | 1961a | |
| Income 1 (0-16%) | 20.9% | 22.5% | 26.7% | 41.0% | 36.1% | 35.4% | 28.3% | 38.7% | 52.3% | 39.1% | Good |
|  | 8.1 | 9.0 | 7.5 | 1.1 | 9.1 | 9.9 | 12.6 | 16.2 | 8.8 | 8.3 | Pro-con |
|  | 54.7 | 52.8 | 49.7 | 44.9 | 24.2 | 30.5 | 31.3 | 23.6 | 21.0 | 29.4 | Bad |
|  | 16.3 | 15.7 | 16.0 | 12.9 | 30.6 | 24.2 | 27.8 | 21.5 | 17.9 | 23.2 | Don't know |
|  | (86) | (89) | (187) | (178) | (219) | (223) | (230) | (191) | (514) | (7472) | Weighted N |
| Income 2 (17-33%) | 23.9 | 30.4 | 35.2 | 38.5 | 52.6 | 45.3 | 43.1 | 40.3 | 56.0 | 50.5 | Good |
|  | 17.2 | 13.0 | 10.3 | 6.8 | 8.1 | 14.5 | 14.4 | 15.1 | 11.7 | 11.8 | Pro-con |
|  | 47.8 | 45.5 | 41.4 | 43.6 | 22.2 | 20.9 | 28.8 | 23.5 | 16.2 | 22.0 | Bad |
|  | 11.1 | 11.1 | 13.1 | 11.1 | 17.0 | 19.3 | 13.7 | 21.0 | 16.2 | 15.7 | Don't know |
|  | (297) | (253) | (145) | (117) | (135) | (311) | (153) | (119) | (588) | (9377) | Weighted N |
| Income 3 (34-67%) | 31.9 | 39.1 | 37.7 | 56.2 | 54.4 | 50.7 | 49.6 | 50.4 | 64.1 | 58.7 | Good |
|  | 16.4 | 14.5 | 16.4 | 4.1 | 14.0 | 15.5 | 16.1 | 18.6 | 13.5 | 12.8 | Pro-con |
|  | 44.4 | 37.4 | 38.9 | 34.5 | 17.0 | 20.2 | 19.6 | 14.0 | 10.1 | 17.8 | Bad |
|  | 7.2 | 9.1 | 7.1 | 5.2 | 14.6 | 13.7 | 14.7 | 16.9 | 12.3 | 10.7 | Don't know |
|  | (207) | (297) | (324) | (290) | (577) | (511) | (484) | (456) | (1085) | (18754) | Weighted N |
| Income 4 (68-95%) | 31.3 | 38.6 | 44.5 | 66.2 | 62.7 | 63.9 | 56.5 | 59.7 | 65.7 | 68.5 | Good |
|  | 23.2 | 17.3 | 13.3 | 4.1 | 11.7 | 17.5 | 15.5 | 15.7 | 16.1 | 11.1 | Pro-con |
|  | 38.6 | 38.1 | 33.1 | 21.9 | 15.7 | 8.8 | 13.3 | 8.8 | 6.5 | 8.6 | Bad |
|  | 6.9 | 6.1 | 9.1 | 7.8 | 10.0 | 9.8 | 14.7 | 15.7 | 11.7 | 11.8 | Don't know |
|  | (233) | (197) | (263) | (269) | (300) | (194) | (278) | (362) | (539) | (10228) | Weighted N |
| Income 5 (96-100%) | 38.0 | 41.5 | 26.3 | 72.6 | 52.4 | 65.5 | 58.6 | 73.0 | 66.3 | 77.1 | Good |
|  | 24.0 | 14.6 | 34.2 | 1.6 | 12.6 | 20.7 | 15.2 | 10.8 | 16.3 | 10.5 | Pro-con |
|  | 32.0 | 29.3 | 36.8 | 22.6 | 10.7 | 13.8 | 12.1 | 0.0 | 5.8 | 4.2 | Bad |
|  | 6.0 | 14.6 | 2.6 | 3.2 | 24.3 | 0.0 | 14.1 | 16.2 | 11.5 | 8.2 | Don't know |
|  | (50) | (41) | (38) | (62) | (103) | (29) | (99) | (37) | (104) | (1579) | Weighted N |

National Economic Outlook

Table 7.107
Does R Think Now Is a Good Time or a Bad Time to Buy Household Durables?
Income of Respondent

| | 1962m | 1963m | 1964a | 1965a | Year 1966a | 1967a | 1968a | 1969a | 1970a | |
|---|---|---|---|---|---|---|---|---|---|---|
| Income 1 (0-16%) | 31.6% | 49.7% | 40.2% | 45.1% | 43.2% | 35.9% | 45.3% | 36.0% | 32.0% | Good |
| | 11.7 | 9.9 | 11.9 | 9.1 | 11.7 | 11.2 | 17.5 | 12.7 | 14.9 | Pro-con |
| | 24.6 | 17.5 | 17.8 | 17.7 | 20.9 | 27.1 | 16.0 | 22.2 | 34.3 | Bad |
| | 32.2 | 22.8 | 30.1 | 28.0 | 24.2 | 25.8 | 21.3 | 29.1 | 18.8 | Don't know |
| | (171) | (171) | (219) | (164) | (454) | (708) | (2559) | (2443) | (469) | Weighted N |
| Income 2 (17-33%) | 43.6 | 55.5 | 51.4 | 53.0 | 58.2 | 38.5 | 49.7 | 50.2 | 35.7 | Good |
| | 9.5 | 17.7 | 15.7 | 12.3 | 10.5 | 17.9 | 18.3 | 13.8 | 16.3 | Pro-con |
| | 25.1 | 11.0 | 9.6 | 10.0 | 15.4 | 26.4 | 14.0 | 15.8 | 30.3 | Bad |
| | 21.8 | 15.8 | 23.3 | 24.7 | 15.8 | 17.2 | 18.0 | 20.2 | 17.7 | Don't know |
| | (211) | (209) | (249) | (219) | (474) | (553) | (2582) | (2228) | (412) | Weighted N |
| Income 3 (34-67%) | 51.2 | 53.1 | 61.0 | 52.8 | 59.9 | 45.3 | 60.0 | 57.9 | 39.5 | Good |
| | 14.9 | 17.5 | 15.2 | 17.3 | 13.7 | 12.6 | 14.0 | 16.4 | 17.0 | Pro-con |
| | 15.8 | 9.7 | 7.8 | 9.8 | 10.7 | 25.8 | 11.6 | 10.9 | 29.6 | Bad |
| | 18.1 | 19.6 | 16.0 | 20.1 | 15.8 | 16.3 | 14.4 | 14.8 | 13.9 | Don't know |
| | (518) | (382) | (526) | (417) | (812) | (1393) | (5164) | (3832) | (882) | Weighted N |
| Income 4 (68-95%) | 51.2 | 59.5 | 67.3 | 67.2 | 62.9 | 48.2 | 68.0 | 58.9 | 41.2 | Good |
| | 18.7 | 16.3 | 15.5 | 13.3 | 16.6 | 16.7 | 14.0 | 14.3 | 20.9 | Pro-con |
| | 11.0 | 6.8 | 5.5 | 5.3 | 8.2 | 19.5 | 8.3 | 12.0 | 23.3 | Bad |
| | 19.1 | 17.4 | 11.8 | 14.1 | 12.3 | 15.5 | 9.6 | 14.7 | 14.6 | Don't know |
| | (283) | (380) | (440) | (412) | (488) | (676) | (4379) | (2618) | (670) | Weighted N |
| Income 5 (96-100%) | 55.4 | 63.1 | 60.3 | 68.9 | 64.7 | 58.3 | 66.4 | 53.7 | 49.5 | Good |
| | 16.9 | 17.9 | 20.5 | 13.6 | 15.3 | 16.5 | 15.2 | 18.3 | 19.6 | Pro-con |
| | 10.8 | 8.3 | 4.1 | 1.9 | 6.7 | 15.0 | 8.6 | 11.6 | 23.4 | Bad |
| | 16.9 | 10.7 | 15.1 | 15.5 | 13.3 | 10.3 | 9.9 | 16.3 | 7.5 | Don't know |
| | (65) | (84) | (73) | (103) | (150) | (321) | (758) | (404) | (107) | Weighted N |

National Economic Outlook

Table 7.108
Does R Think Now Is a Good Time or a Bad Time to Buy Household Durables?
Income of Respondent

| | Year | | | | | | |
|---|---|---|---|---|---|---|---|
| | 1971m | 1972f | 1973c | 1974q | 1975q | 1976m | |
| Income 1 (0-16%) | 34.0% | 38.6% | 39.1% | 25.5% | 31.6% | 49.5% | Good |
| | 14.4 | 18.2 | 13.6 | 13.4 | 18.4 | 12.5 | Pro-con |
| | 28.7 | 22.7 | 26.0 | 38.4 | 32.3 | 24.5 | Bad |
| | 22.9 | 20.5 | 21.3 | 22.7 | 17.7 | 13.6 | Don't know |
| | (188) | (220) | (169) | (396) | (434) | (22067) | Weighted N |
| Income 2 (17-33%) | 45.9 | 43.8 | 44.7 | 24.6 | 38.6 | 50.7 | Good |
| | 18.2 | 12.3 | 17.8 | 22.9 | 18.0 | 14.3 | Pro-con |
| | 25.2 | 19.9 | 19.4 | 36.3 | 26.7 | 25.7 | Bad |
| | 10.7 | 24.0 | 18.1 | 16.2 | 16.7 | 9.3 | Don't know |
| | (242) | (146) | (309) | (581) | (490) | (24152) | Weighted N |
| Income 3 (34-67%) | 56.5 | 50.9 | 55.6 | 36.4 | 52.0 | 51.4 | Good |
| | 14.6 | 17.0 | 17.8 | 17.4 | 16.1 | 16.6 | Pro-con |
| | 20.7 | 16.6 | 11.1 | 34.7 | 19.7 | 21.6 | Bad |
| | 8.3 | 15.5 | 15.6 | 11.4 | 12.1 | 10.4 | Don't know |
| | (460) | (452) | (360) | (953) | (807) | (14890) | Weighted N |
| Income 4 (68-95%) | 67.7 | 57.0 | 58.2 | 37.3 | 46.6 | 70.7 | Good |
| | 12.2 | 15.8 | 17.0 | 21.1 | 16.5 | 12.8 | Pro-con |
| | 10.9 | 15.2 | 10.2 | 30.0 | 23.7 | 12.8 | Bad |
| | 9.2 | 12.1 | 14.6 | 11.6 | 13.2 | 3.7 | Don't know |
| | (294) | (323) | (342) | (603) | (637) | (9133) | Weighted N |
| Income 5 (96-100%) | 73.1 | 62.8 | 60.9 | 53.8 | 58.7 | 58.0 | Good |
| | 15.4 | 5.1 | 20.7 | 24.7 | 28.0 | 12.9 | Pro-con |
| | 7.7 | 11.5 | 4.3 | 16.1 | 7.3 | 14.6 | Bad |
| | 3.8 | 20.5 | 14.1 | 5.4 | 6.0 | 14.5 | Don't know |
| | (52) | (78) | (92) | (93) | (150) | (8337) | Weighted N |

Table 7.109
Does R Expect Prices to Go Up or Down in the Next Twelve Months?
Total Population

QUESTION   During the next twelve months, do you think that prices in general will go up, or go down or stay where they are now?

| | | Year | | | | | | | | | |
|---|---|---|---|---|---|---|---|---|---|---|---|
| | | 1947a | 1948a | 1949a | 1950a | 1951a | 1952a | 1953a | 1954a | 1958a | 1959a |
| Prices will go up | (5) | 12.6% | 34.4% | 7.7% | 14.8% | 76.7% | 52.5% | 16.4% | 15.4% | 47.1% | 61.8% |
| Prices will stay the same | (3) | 32.2 | 28.4 | 31.2 | 36.4 | 16.9 | 33.4 | 45.6 | 43.3 | 31.8 | 26.0 |
| Prices will go down | (1) | 47.3 | 29.1 | 55.9 | 42.1 | 3.4 | 6.7 | 31.2 | 36.0 | 12.6 | 6.7 |
| Don't know | | 7.8 | 8.1 | 5.2 | 6.7 | 3.0 | 7.5 | 6.8 | 5.4 | 8.4 | 5.5 |
| Total | | 100% | 100% | 100% | 100% | 100% | 100% | 100% | 100% | 100% | 100% |
| Weighted N | | 884420 | 878647 | 914300 | 98380 | 98819 | 97345 | 90360 | 73392 | 97992 | 98238 |
| Unweighted N | | 2711 | 3116 | 3210 | 3460 | 3374 | 2736 | 2815 | 2207 | 3055 | 3046 |
| Mean | | 2.25 | 3.12 | 1.98 | 2.42 | 4.51 | 3.99 | 2.68 | 2.56 | 3.75 | 4.17 |
| Standard Deviation | | 1.43 | 1.66 | 1.29 | 1.45 | 1.01 | 1.26 | 1.39 | 1.41 | 1.43 | 1.24 |

Table 7.110

| | | 1960a | 1961a | 1962n | 1963m | 1964a | 1965a | 1966a | 1967a | 1968n | 1969a |
|---|---|---|---|---|---|---|---|---|---|---|---|
| Prices will go up | (5) | 73.7% | 61.4% | 57.7% | 62.8% | 69.0% | 73.1% | 87.2% | 82.6% | 76.8% | 82.7% |
| Prices will stay the same | (3) | 17.7 | 25.0 | 26.8 | 28.6 | 21.9 | 18.1 | 8.8 | 13.2 | 18.0 | 13.1 |
| Prices will go down | (1) | 3.7 | 7.4 | 4.2 | 1.8 | 3.3 | 1.8 | 0.8 | 2.4 | 2.5 | 2.6 |
| Don't know | | 5.0 | 6.2 | 11.3 | 6.8 | 5.8 | 7.0 | 3.2 | 1.7 | 2.6 | 1.5 |
| Total | | 100% | 100% | 100% | 100% | 100% | 100% | 100% | 100% | 100% | 100% |
| Weighted N | | 2876 | 49549 | 1280 | 1306 | 1508 | 1317 | 2390 | 3700 | 2651 | 11562 |
| Unweighted N | | 2876 | 1965 | 1280 | 1306 | 1508 | 1317 | 2390 | 3144 | 1429 | 2299 |
| Mean | | 4.47 | 4.15 | 4.21 | 4.31 | 4.39 | 4.53 | 4.78 | 4.63 | 4.53 | 4.63 |
| Standard Deviation | | 1.04 | 1.27 | 1.16 | 1.03 | 1.06 | 0.93 | 0.67 | 0.89 | 0.96 | 0.91 |

Table 7.111

| | | 1970a | 1971m | 1972f | 1973c | 1974q | 1975q | 1976m |
|---|---|---|---|---|---|---|---|---|
| Prices will go up | (5) | 78.1% | 59.9% | 58.1% | 80.3% | 81.5% | 75.9% | 66.1% |
| Prices will stay the same | (3) | 11.6 | 26.6 | 30.6 | 11.4 | 12.3 | 17.6 | 23.3 |
| Prices will go down | (1) | 3.3 | 4.0 | 7.6 | 4.3 | 3.7 | 4.1 | 6.6 |
| Don't know | | 7.0 | 9.4 | 3.6 | 4.0 | 2.5 | 2.5 | 4.0 |
| Total | | 100% | 100% | 100% | 100% | 100% | 100% | 100% |
| Weighted N | | 2552 | 1293 | 1295 | 1346 | 2969 | 2911 | 127186 |
| Unweighted N | | 2552 | 1293 | 1295 | 1346 | 1512 | 1516 | 1131 |
| Mean | | 4.61 | 4.23 | 4.05 | 4.58 | 4.60 | 4.47 | 4.24 |
| Standard Deviation | | 0.95 | 1.14 | 1.28 | 1.01 | 0.97 | 1.05 | 1.22 |

1968n includes Black supplement.

Figure 7.17
Will Prices Go Up or Down?--Total Population

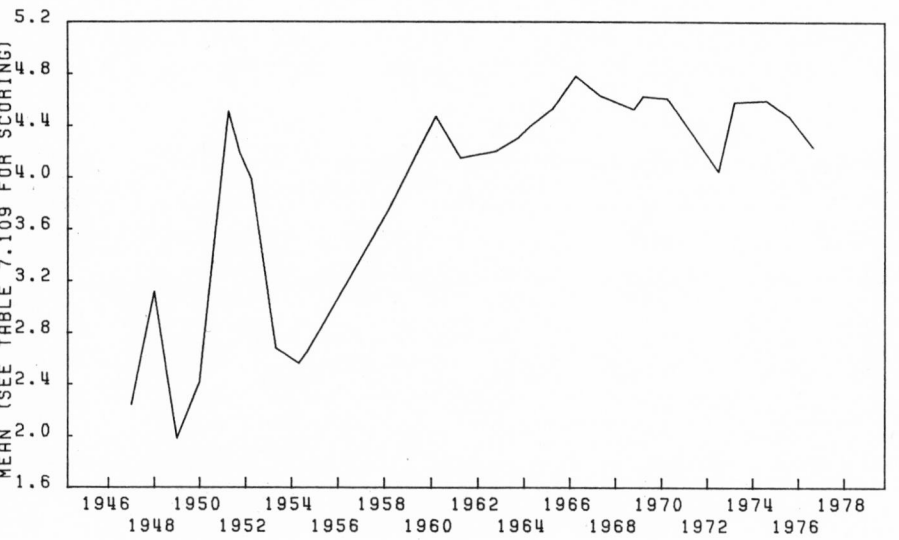

National Economic Outlook

Table 7.112
Does R Expect Prices to Go Up or Down in the Next Twelve Months?
Sex of Respondent

| | | | | | Year | | | | | | |
|---|---|---|---|---|---|---|---|---|---|---|---|
| | 1947a | 1948a | 1949a | 1950a | 1951a | 1952a | 1953a | 1954a | 1958a | 1959a | |
| Males Only | 12.1% | 35.2% | 7.8% | 14.9% | 76.9% | 55.0% | 17.0% | 13.9% | 47.3% | 64.8% | Up |
| | 33.3 | 28.6 | 31.7 | 36.8 | 17.8 | 32.8 | 45.1 | 43.7 | 33.8 | 25.2 | Same |
| | 47.5 | 29.2 | 56.6 | 42.5 | 3.3 | 5.9 | 32.5 | 37.6 | 12.2 | 6.2 | Down |
| | 7.1 | 7.1 | 3.9 | 5.8 | 2.1 | 6.2 | 5.4 | 4.8 | 6.7 | 3.7 | Don't know |
| | (596685) | (562634) | (553096) | (67793) | (62803) | (66786) | (62772) | (50829) | (63484) | (62552) | Weighted N |
| Females Only | 13.7 | 33.1 | 7.7 | 14.6 | 76.3 | 46.8 | 15.1 | 18.7 | 46.2 | 56.3 | Up |
| | 29.8 | 28.1 | 30.4 | 35.5 | 15.2 | 34.2 | 46.6 | 42.4 | 28.6 | 27.3 | Same |
| | 47.1 | 28.9 | 54.8 | 41.2 | 3.6 | 8.5 | 28.3 | 32.4 | 13.3 | 7.6 | Down |
| | 9.4 | 9.9 | 7.1 | 8.6 | 4.9 | 10.6 | 10.0 | 6.6 | 11.8 | 8.8 | Don't know |
| | (287735) | (316013) | (361204) | (30452) | (33399) | (29246) | (27588) | (22563) | (33214) | (34075) | Weighted N |

Table 7.113

| | 1960a | 1961a | 1962n | 1963m | 1964a | 1965a | 1966a | 1967a | 1968n | 1969a | |
|---|---|---|---|---|---|---|---|---|---|---|---|
| Males Only | 76.0% | 62.3% | 60.2% | 66.8% | 70.8% | 75.6% | 88.7% | 84.3% | 80.4% | 84.4% | Up |
| | 17.3 | 25.3 | 29.2 | 27.2 | 21.1 | 17.3 | 8.4 | 11.8 | 15.9 | 11.7 | Same |
| | 3.5 | 7.7 | 4.2 | 1.1 | 3.4 | 1.9 | 0.8 | 2.6 | 1.7 | 2.9 | Down |
| | 3.3 | 4.8 | 6.4 | 5.0 | 4.7 | 5.1 | 2.2 | 1.4 | 2.0 | 1.0 | Don't know |
| | (1942) | (40422) | (578) | (545) | (1146) | (934) | (1863) | (2804) | (1150) | (8390) | Weighted N |
| Females Only | 68.8 | 57.8 | 55.7 | 59.9 | 63.1 | 67.1 | 81.8 | 77.5 | 74.1 | 78.3 | Up |
| | 18.5 | 23.8 | 24.8 | 29.6 | 24.6 | 19.8 | 10.2 | 17.6 | 19.6 | 16.8 | Same |
| | 4.2 | 5.5 | 4.3 | 2.4 | 3.1 | 1.6 | 1.1 | 2.0 | 3.2 | 2.0 | Down |
| | 8.5 | 12.9 | 15.2 | 8.1 | 9.2 | 11.5 | 6.8 | 2.9 | 3.1 | 2.9 | Don't know |
| | (934) | (9019) | (702) | (761) | (358) | (383) | (527) | (896) | (1501) | (3172) | Weighted N |

Table 7.114

| | 1970a | 1971m | 1972f | 1973c | 1974q | 1975q | 1976m | |
|---|---|---|---|---|---|---|---|---|
| Males Only | 80.9% | 63.0% | 62.3% | 83.7% | 80.1% | 79.4% | 75.2% | Up |
| | 11.9 | 26.1 | 27.7 | 8.8 | 13.6 | 15.5 | 16.0 | Same |
| | 3.1 | 3.2 | 6.0 | 5.0 | 4.9 | 3.3 | 5.5 | Down |
| | 4.1 | 7.7 | 4.0 | 2.4 | 1.4 | 1.7 | 3.2 | Don't know |
| | (1845) | (901) | (546) | (578) | (1327) | (1345) | (50621) | Weighted N |
| Females Only | 71.0 | 52.8 | 55.1 | 77.7 | 82.7 | 72.9 | 60.2 | Up |
| | 10.9 | 27.8 | 32.7 | 13.3 | 11.3 | 19.3 | 28.6 | Same |
| | 3.5 | 5.9 | 8.8 | 3.8 | 2.7 | 4.7 | 7.4 | Down |
| | 14.6 | 13.5 | 3.3 | 5.2 | 3.3 | 3.1 | 3.7 | Don't know |
| | (707) | (392) | (749) | (768) | (1642) | (1566) | (75152) | Weighted N |

National Economic Outlook

Table 7.115
Does R Expect Prices to Go Up or Down in the Next Twelve Months?
Race of Respondent

|  | | | | | Year | | | | | | |
|---|---|---|---|---|---|---|---|---|---|---|---|
|  | 1947a | 1948a | 1949a | 1950a | 1951a | 1952a | 1953a | 1954a | 1958a | 1959a | |
| Whites Only | 11.6% | 33.3% | 6.9% | 14.1% | 76.3% | 52.7% | 16.0% | 14.5% | 47.0% | 62.5% | Up |
|  | 33.1 | 29.1 | 31.5 | 36.6 | 17.6 | 33.9 | 46.3 | 43.3 | 32.5 | 26.1 | Same |
|  | 47.9 | 30.1 | 56.8 | 43.0 | 3.3 | 6.6 | 31.0 | 36.9 | 12.9 | 6.3 | Down |
|  | 7.5 | 7.5 | 4.7 | 6.3 | 2.7 | 6.8 | 6.7 | 5.2 | 7.6 | 5.1 | Don't know |
|  | (812748) | (804038) | (837114) | (90623) | (89305) | (86319) | (82145) | (67028) | (86435) | (87841) | Weighted N |
| Blacks Only | 23.5 | 45.4 | 16.2 | 25.4 | 77.8 | 51.5 | 19.7 | 23.3 | 46.9 | 54.2 | Up |
|  | 21.0 | 21.8 | 30.1 | 34.2 | 11.5 | 31.2 | 40.5 | 41.0 | 27.3 | 27.3 | Same |
|  | 42.8 | 18.6 | 44.0 | 29.2 | 4.9 | 6.7 | 32.5 | 28.8 | 10.4 | 9.8 | Down |
|  | 12.7 | 14.2 | 9.7 | 11.2 | 5.8 | 10.6 | 7.2 | 6.9 | 15.4 | 8.7 | Don't know |
|  | (69410) | (81157) | (80451) | (6756) | (7738) | (9362) | (9752) | (7216) | (10165) | (9200) | Weighted N |

Table 7.116

|  | 1960a | 1961a | 1962n | 1963m | 1964a | 1965a | 1966a | 1967a | 1968n | 1969a | |
|---|---|---|---|---|---|---|---|---|---|---|---|
| Whites Only | 74.7% | 62.3% | 57.1% | 63.6% | 69.6% | 74.1% | 87.8% | 83.6% | 77.2% | 82.9% | Up |
|  | 18.0 | 24.6 | 27.6 | 28.7 | 21.8 | 17.8 | 8.5 | 13.0 | 18.2 | 13.1 | Same |
|  | 3.3 | 7.4 | 4.3 | 1.3 | 2.9 | 1.9 | 0.8 | 2.0 | 2.1 | 2.3 | Down |
|  | 4.0 | 5.7 | 11.0 | 6.4 | 5.6 | 6.2 | 2.9 | 1.4 | 2.4 | 1.7 | Don't know |
|  | (2575) | (44349) | (1159) | (1154) | (1329) | (1170) | (2161) | (3253) | (2370) | (10226) | Weighted N |
| Blacks Only | 65.1 | 53.8 | 62.7 | 57.6 | 66.2 | 68.1 | 80.3 | 75.4 | 73.9 | 80.1 | Up |
|  | 14.5 | 27.9 | 19.1 | 28.0 | 19.5 | 19.0 | 12.4 | 15.6 | 15.9 | 14.4 | Same |
|  | 7.2 | 6.6 | 3.6 | 5.6 | 7.5 | 1.7 | 1.0 | 5.7 | 6.9 | 5.5 | Down |
|  | 13.2 | 11.8 | 14.5 | 8.8 | 6.8 | 11.2 | 6.2 | 3.3 | 3.3 | 0.0 | Don't know |
|  | (304) | (4792) | (110) | (125) | (133) | (116) | (193) | (366) | (245) | (1159) | Weighted N |

Table 7.117

|  | 1970a | 1971m | 1972f | 1973c | 1974q | 1975q | 1976m | |
|---|---|---|---|---|---|---|---|---|
| Whites Only | 78.0% | 59.9% | 58.6% | 81.4% | 82.0% | 75.6% | 69.2% | Up |
|  | 12.2 | 27.5 | 30.7 | 11.4 | 12.3 | 18.4 | 23.3 | Same |
|  | 3.3 | 4.0 | 7.1 | 3.9 | 3.4 | 4.0 | 4.8 | Down |
|  | 6.4 | 8.5 | 3.7 | 3.2 | 2.3 | 2.1 | 2.8 | Don't know |
|  | (2245) | (1126) | (1163) | (1118) | (2551) | (2578) | (107528) | Weighted N |
| Blacks Only | 78.4 | 58.8 | 53.0 | 73.9 | 76.8 | 76.2 | 49.9 | Up |
|  | 7.6 | 22.1 | 30.4 | 10.9 | 12.6 | 12.1 | 21.7 | Same |
|  | 2.5 | 3.1 | 13.0 | 8.4 | 5.8 | 5.0 | 22.5 | Down |
|  | 11.5 | 16.0 | 3.5 | 6.7 | 4.8 | 6.7 | 5.9 | Don't know |
|  | (278) | (131) | (115) | (119) | (293) | (239) | (11618) | Weighted N |

National Economic Outlook

Table 7.118
Does R Expect Prices to Go Up or Down in the Next Twelve Months?
Education of Respondent

| | | | | | Year | | | | | | |
|---|---|---|---|---|---|---|---|---|---|---|---|
| | 1947a | 1948a | 1949a | 1950a | 1951a | 1952a | 1953a | 1954a | 1958a | 1959a | |
| Grade School Only | 13.7% | 37.2% | 10.5% | 18.7% | 76.3% | 50.7% | 15.7% | 18.2% | 46.4% | 56.2% | Up |
| | 33.9 | 28.1 | 34.9 | 38.7 | 16.4 | 33.7 | 44.3 | 41.0 | 31.2 | 26.9 | Same |
| | 42.9 | 25.0 | 47.7 | 33.3 | 3.7 | 5.1 | 30.8 | 33.0 | 10.6 | 8.2 | Down |
| | 9.5 | 9.6 | 6.8 | 9.3 | 3.7 | 10.5 | 9.3 | 7.9 | 11.7 | 8.7 | Don't know |
| | (322640) | (314837) | (301159) | (36253) | (33901) | (36556) | (32250) | (25399) | (26751) | (27852) | Weighted N |
| High School Only | 11.7 | 32.0 | 5.4 | 13.6 | 77.1 | 56.0 | 17.4 | 13.2 | 46.9 | 64.6 | Up |
| | 31.8 | 29.8 | 32.2 | 34.5 | 18.0 | 32.1 | 46.2 | 46.7 | 35.2 | 26.0 | Same |
| | 49.9 | 31.7 | 59.1 | 46.9 | 3.1 | 7.8 | 31.0 | 35.5 | 12.4 | 6.3 | Down |
| | 6.5 | 6.5 | 3.3 | 5.1 | 1.9 | 4.0 | 5.4 | 4.6 | 5.5 | 3.1 | Don't know |
| | (290662) | (279062) | (289402) | (33051) | (30975) | (31989) | (31634) | (27012) | (35184) | (33306) | Weighted N |
| College Only | 6.3 | 33.9 | 5.2 | 10.1 | 80.0 | 55.0 | 18.1 | 12.4 | 48.1 | 73.9 | Up |
| | 32.4 | 27.1 | 23.6 | 33.9 | 14.1 | 31.7 | 44.8 | 38.4 | 31.4 | 20.2 | Same |
| | 58.1 | 32.3 | 69.4 | 53.4 | 3.2 | 6.0 | 33.4 | 46.7 | 14.2 | 3.6 | Down |
| | 3.2 | 6.7 | 1.7 | 2.6 | 2.7 | 7.3 | 3.7 | 2.5 | 6.2 | 2.3 | Don't know |
| | (113179) | (122093) | (127050) | (14113) | (13750) | (13647) | (15058) | (11390) | (17500) | (16610) | Weighted N |

Table 7.119

| | 1960a | 1961a | 1962n | 1963m | 1964a | 1965a | 1966a | 1967a | 1968n | 1969a | |
|---|---|---|---|---|---|---|---|---|---|---|---|
| Grade School Only | 67.6% | 54.1% | 53.9% | 64.4% | 66.6% | 69.1% | 83.5% | 78.0% | 62.9% | 77.5% | Up |
| | 17.8 | 26.2 | 22.5 | 24.5 | 20.8 | 17.2 | 9.3 | 15.2 | 25.9 | 16.3 | Same |
| | 5.7 | 7.2 | 4.8 | 3.0 | 3.2 | 1.6 | 0.7 | 2.9 | 6.9 | 3.9 | Down |
| | 8.8 | 12.5 | 18.8 | 8.2 | 9.5 | 12.0 | 6.4 | 3.9 | 4.3 | 2.3 | Don't know |
| | (791) | (14774) | (356) | (368) | (476) | (366) | (668) | (1054) | (606) | (3021) | Weighted N |
| High School Only | 76.2 | 62.1 | 58.5 | 59.1 | 69.0 | 75.5 | 88.3 | 83.9 | 79.6 | 84.8 | Up |
| | 17.9 | 25.7 | 28.6 | 32.1 | 23.0 | 17.7 | 8.4 | 12.8 | 16.4 | 12.2 | Same |
| | 2.4 | 8.2 | 4.2 | 1.8 | 3.4 | 2.1 | 0.8 | 2.2 | 1.8 | 1.7 | Down |
| | 3.5 | 4.0 | 8.7 | 7.0 | 4.6 | 4.8 | 2.5 | 1.2 | 2.2 | 1.2 | Don't know |
| | (1072) | (21994) | (612) | (660) | (649) | (628) | (1011) | (1716) | (1302) | (5143) | Weighted N |
| College Only | 80.3 | 70.3 | 60.6 | 69.4 | 71.8 | 72.9 | 89.2 | 85.9 | 83.2 | 84.3 | Up |
| | 14.7 | 22.1 | 28.0 | 25.7 | 21.7 | 20.4 | 8.6 | 11.6 | 14.3 | 11.9 | Same |
| | 2.3 | 4.9 | 3.6 | 0.4 | 3.5 | 1.3 | 1.0 | 2.1 | 0.3 | 2.5 | Down |
| | 2.7 | 2.6 | 7.8 | 4.5 | 3.0 | 5.4 | 1.2 | 0.3 | 2.2 | 1.3 | Don't know |
| | (558) | (12094) | (307) | (265) | (369) | (314) | (604) | (887) | (740) | (3308) | Weighted N |

Education coded for head of household only in 1947a,1948a,1949a,1950a,1951a,1952a,1953a,1954a,1958a,1959a,1960a,1961a, and 1966a, and for head and wife only in 1963m,1964a,1965a,1967a,and 1969a.

Table 7.120
Does R Expect Prices to Go Up or Down in the Next Twelve Months?
Education of Respondent

|  | | | | Year | | | | |
|---|---|---|---|---|---|---|---|---|
|  | 1970a | 1971m | 1972f | 1973c | 1974q | 1975q | 1976m | |
| Grade School Only | 73.3% | 53.8% | 48.4% | 65.8% | 64.5% | 65.6% | 52.7% | Up |
|  | 11.7 | 25.9 | 29.9 | 13.3 | 20.6 | 21.3 | 21.8 | Same |
|  | 3.4 | 6.9 | 12.3 | 12.7 | 8.4 | 6.1 | 17.5 | Down |
|  | 11.6 | 13.4 | 9.4 | 8.2 | 6.5 | 7.0 | 8.0 | Don't know |
|  | (959) | (320) | (244) | (158) | (490) | (442) | (16788) | Weighted N |
| High School Only | 80.9 | 59.7 | 60.8 | 81.6 | 84.5 | 76.3 | 66.1 | Up |
|  | 12.1 | 29.0 | 29.0 | 12.2 | 10.5 | 16.9 | 25.6 | Same |
|  | 2.8 | 3.0 | 7.5 | 3.2 | 3.3 | 4.7 | 4.9 | Down |
|  | 4.2 | 8.3 | 2.7 | 3.0 | 1.7 | 2.1 | 3.4 | Don't know |
|  | (1118) | (576) | (663) | (625) | (1415) | (1517) | (59962) | Weighted N |
| College Only | 81.8 | 65.8 | 59.4 | 85.6 | 86.0 | 80.0 | 73.6 | Up |
|  | 10.5 | 23.9 | 34.0 | 9.3 | 10.5 | 17.1 | 21.4 | Same |
|  | 4.6 | 3.3 | 5.0 | 2.0 | 2.0 | 2.0 | 3.7 | Down |
|  | 3.2 | 6.9 | 1.6 | 3.0 | 1.5 | 0.8 | 1.4 | Don't know |
|  | (411) | (389) | (382) | (397) | (1042) | (946) | (45208) | Weighted N |

Education coded for head of household only in 1971m, and for head and wife only in 1970a.

Table 7.121
Does R Expect Prices to Go Up or Down in the Next Twelve Months?
Age of Respondent

| | | | | | Year | | | | | | |
|---|---|---|---|---|---|---|---|---|---|---|---|
| | 1947a | 1948a | 1949a | 1950a | 1951a | 1952a | 1953a | 1954a | 1958a | 1959a | |
| 18-24 Only | 11.4% | 38.7% | 11.9% | 13.7% | 79.4% | 48.8% | 19.1% | 16.6% | 54.0% | 64.9% | Up |
| | 32.4 | 34.4 | 29.7 | 32.4 | 16.3 | 40.6 | 48.4 | 55.1 | 32.9 | 29.4 | Same |
| | 49.2 | 23.2 | 54.9 | 51.8 | 2.0 | 3.8 | 28.0 | 25.7 | 8.5 | 2.9 | Down |
| | 7.0 | 3.7 | 3.4 | 2.2 | 2.3 | 6.9 | 4.5 | 2.5 | 4.6 | 2.8 | Don't know |
| | (80551) | (85690) | (88986) | (9261) | (7654) | (7543) | (8260) | (5298) | (8265) | (7120) | Weighted N |
| 25-34 Only | 14.5 | 33.7 | 6.6 | 12.0 | 79.9 | 57.2 | 19.0 | 16.4 | 48.4 | 69.1 | Up |
| | 32.2 | 25.5 | 27.8 | 37.9 | 15.1 | 31.9 | 45.4 | 44.0 | 34.1 | 23.2 | Same |
| | 49.7 | 32.4 | 61.8 | 45.8 | 3.3 | 5.8 | 31.2 | 35.3 | 11.5 | 5.2 | Down |
| | 3.6 | 8.4 | 3.7 | 4.3 | 1.7 | 5.1 | 4.3 | 4.3 | 6.1 | 2.5 | Don't know |
| | (166535) | (155781) | (150514) | (19016) | (16403) | (18776) | (18776) | (13410) | (15877) | (14071) | Weighted N |
| 35-44 Only | 11.2 | 38.5 | 5.8 | 16.7 | 72.7 | 58.4 | 18.8 | 12.4 | 50.6 | 66.8 | Up |
| | 35.6 | 27.5 | 37.6 | 35.1 | 20.9 | 28.9 | 45.9 | 46.0 | 33.1 | 24.2 | Same |
| | 47.4 | 26.3 | 53.0 | 43.0 | 4.7 | 7.5 | 29.1 | 36.9 | 12.7 | 5.8 | Down |
| | 5.8 | 7.7 | 3.6 | 5.1 | 1.7 | 5.2 | 6.1 | 4.7 | 3.6 | 3.2 | Don't know |
| | (167518) | (155213) | (151051) | (17898) | (17314) | (17594) | (16109) | (15154) | (17081) | (16767) | Weighted N |
| 45-54 Only | 10.5 | 34.0 | 7.7 | 15.2 | 76.8 | 51.8 | 12.9 | 13.1 | 44.0 | 70.1 | Up |
| | 30.5 | 28.4 | 29.6 | 36.4 | 16.6 | 33.5 | 42.3 | 39.7 | 33.9 | 19.1 | Same |
| | 49.2 | 30.6 | 57.5 | 40.9 | 3.9 | 7.5 | 38.2 | 42.9 | 14.8 | 6.4 | Down |
| | 9.8 | 6.9 | 5.2 | 7.6 | 2.7 | 7.3 | 6.6 | 4.4 | 7.4 | 4.3 | Don't know |
| | (231295) | (129437) | (135962) | (15587) | (13820) | (15684) | (14454) | (11723) | (14392) | (14052) | Weighted N |
| 55-64 Only | ** | 30.6 | 7.0 | 17.2 | 78.6 | 50.4 | 17.3 | 17.1 | 45.6 | 55.5 | Up |
| | ** | 29.0 | 29.4 | 41.2 | 16.6 | 34.3 | 45.7 | 36.8 | 28.6 | 30.4 | Same |
| | ** | 29.0 | 59.2 | 34.4 | 2.1 | 4.8 | 30.7 | 38.3 | 14.0 | 7.1 | Down |
| | ** | 11.4 | 4.4 | 7.3 | 2.7 | 10.4 | 6.4 | 7.8 | 11.7 | 7.0 | Don't know |
| | ** | (104404) | (107281) | (11515) | (11965) | (10521) | (10665) | (9398) | (28670) | (12529) | Weighted N |
| 65 and Older Only | 11.4 | 31.1 | 7.9 | 17.6 | 78.2 | 47.0 | 12.9 | 16.8 | 43.1 | 53.5 | Up |
| | 36.6 | 30.4 | 37.5 | 33.9 | 12.7 | 32.9 | 44.2 | 39.9 | 30.0 | 26.9 | Same |
| | 42.2 | 29.8 | 47.0 | 34.3 | 2.7 | 6.9 | 29.3 | 33.8 | 12.0 | 9.6 | Down |
| | 9.7 | 8.8 | 7.6 | 14.2 | 6.5 | 13.2 | 13.6 | 9.5 | 14.9 | 10.0 | Don't know |
| | (79990) | (85467) | (83817) | (9749) | (11280) | (11073) | (10678) | (8848) | (12071) | (12821) | Weighted N |

** Code distinction not made.
Youngest age group coded "21-24" in 1954m.
Age group coded "45-64" in 1947a.
Oldest age group coded "65 And Older" in 1947a,1948a,1949a,1950a,1951a,1952a,1953a,1954a,1958a,and 1959a.
Age coded for head of household only in 1947a,1948a,1949a,1950a,1951a,1953a,1954a,1958a,and 1959a.

Table 7.122
Does R Expect Prices to Go Up or Down in the Next Twelve Months?
Age of Respondent

| | | | | | | Year | | | | | |
|---|---|---|---|---|---|---|---|---|---|---|---|
| | 1960a | 1961a | 1962n | 1963m | 1964a | 1965a | 1966a | 1967a | 1968n | 1969a | |
| 18-24 Only | 74.4% | 60.4% | 59.2% | 70.7% | 66.7% | 72.8% | 80.8% | 86.8% | 85.6% | 86.6% | Up |
| | 16.7 | 27.0 | 27.6 | 25.3 | 27.8 | 21.6 | 15.1 | 10.0 | 13.4 | 10.8 | Same |
| | 3.4 | 8.4 | 6.6 | 0.0 | 2.8 | 1.6 | 2.3 | 2.8 | 0.0 | 1.9 | Down |
| | 5.4 | 4.3 | 6.6 | 4.0 | 2.8 | 4.0 | 1.7 | 0.4 | 1.0 | 0.6 | Don't know |
| | (203) | (4550) | (76) | (99) | (108) | (125) | (172) | (250) | (201) | (1092) | Weighted N |
| 25-34 Only | 80.2 | 67.3 | 62.3 | 66.5 | 74.0 | 76.0 | 88.7 | 86.7 | 85.6 | 87.3 | Up |
| | 14.9 | 22.6 | 26.8 | 27.0 | 21.3 | 18.6 | 8.8 | 10.4 | 10.9 | 11.3 | Same |
| | 2.9 | 6.2 | 3.9 | 1.7 | 1.6 | 1.7 | 0.9 | 2.4 | 0.6 | 1.1 | Down |
| | 2.1 | 3.9 | 7.0 | 4.7 | 3.1 | 3.7 | 1.6 | 0.5 | 2.9 | 0.3 | Don't know |
| | (484) | (10449) | (257) | (233) | (258) | (242) | (434) | (664) | (521) | (2312) | Weighted N |
| 35-44 Only | 76.6 | 64.7 | 58.9 | 62.6 | 72.9 | 74.7 | 89.6 | 86.8 | 82.7 | 86.0 | Up |
| | 14.8 | 24.4 | 30.7 | 31.1 | 19.5 | 19.8 | 7.8 | 11.6 | 15.1 | 11.3 | Same |
| | 3.3 | 6.1 | 2.9 | 3.0 | 3.4 | 0.7 | 0.6 | 1.3 | 1.2 | 2.2 | Down |
| | 5.2 | 4.8 | 7.5 | 3.3 | 4.3 | 4.8 | 1.9 | 0.3 | 1.1 | 0.6 | Don't know |
| | (539) | (11053) | (280) | (270) | (328) | (273) | (462) | (714) | (571) | (1997) | Weighted N |
| 45-54 Only | 75.6 | 56.5 | 59.5 | 58.3 | 64.4 | 72.3 | 88.5 | 83.9 | 76.8 | 85.8 | Up |
| | 16.9 | 30.7 | 25.6 | 33.2 | 26.7 | 17.4 | 7.6 | 12.4 | 17.1 | 11.8 | Same |
| | 3.3 | 7.2 | 3.4 | 1.1 | 3.6 | 3.3 | 0.8 | 2.0 | 4.4 | 1.6 | Down |
| | 4.1 | 5.6 | 11.5 | 7.4 | 5.3 | 7.0 | 3.0 | 1.7 | 1.7 | 0.8 | Don't know |
| | (484) | (9372) | (262) | (271) | (303) | (242) | (471) | (709) | (526) | (1956) | Weighted N |
| 55-64 Only | 71.2 | 62.1 | 55.7 | 61.0 | 68.4 | 64.8 | 86.3 | 81.6 | 70.4 | 79.6 | Up |
| | 19.9 | 22.6 | 23.2 | 28.5 | 18.1 | 21.6 | 8.8 | 14.1 | 22.8 | 15.4 | Same |
| | 3.6 | 9.5 | 4.6 | 2.0 | 5.5 | 2.3 | 0.5 | 2.9 | 2.6 | 3.6 | Down |
| | 5.3 | 5.8 | 16.5 | 8.5 | 8.0 | 11.3 | 4.4 | 1.4 | 4.2 | 1.4 | Don't know |
| | (361) | (7336) | (194) | (200) | (237) | (213) | (410) | (588) | (378) | (1775) | Weighted N |
| 65-74 Only | 63.7 | 55.6 | 48.9 | 61.8 | 66.1 | 77.4 | 85.2 | 74.5 | 62.9 | 76.0 | Up |
| | 22.0 | 23.6 | 28.1 | 25.0 | 20.8 | 11.1 | 8.3 | 19.0 | 26.1 | 16.7 | Same |
| | 4.9 | 6.9 | 6.7 | 3.7 | 2.7 | 0.9 | 0.7 | 2.6 | 5.9 | 3.0 | Down |
| | 9.3 | 13.9 | 16.3 | 9.6 | 10.4 | 10.6 | 5.8 | 3.9 | 5.2 | 4.3 | Don't know |
| | (364) | (4314) | (135) | (136) | (183) | (217) | (432) | (463) | (307) | (1479) | Weighted N |
| 75 And Older Only | ** | 50.6 | 50.7 | 64.7 | 65.5 | ** | ** | 72.4 | 58.0 | 69.7 | Up |
| | ** | 22.7 | 21.7 | 17.6 | 21.8 | ** | ** | 16.6 | 33.3 | 18.2 | Same |
| | ** | 9.2 | 5.8 | 0.0 | 3.4 | ** | ** | 4.1 | 4.3 | 7.1 | Down |
| | ** | 17.6 | 21.7 | 17.6 | 9.2 | ** | ** | 6.9 | 4.3 | 5.1 | Don't know |
| | ** | (2233) | (69) | (85) | (87) | ** | ** | (290) | (138) | (891) | Weighted N |

** Code distinction not made.
Oldest age group coded "65 And Older" in 1960a,1965a,and 1966a.
Age coded for head of household only in 1960a,1961a,and 1966a, and for head and wife only in 1964a,1965a,1966a,1967a, and 1969a.

Table 7.123
Does R Expect Prices to Go Up or Down in the Next Twelve Months?
Age of Respondent

|  | Year | | | | | | | |
|---|---|---|---|---|---|---|---|---|
|  | 1970a | 1971m | 1972f | 1973c | 1974q | 1975q | 1976m | |
| 18-24 Only | 87.9% | 76.0% | 62.2% | 86.6% | 89.7% | 83.6% | 67.9% | Up |
|  | 7.1 | 16.0 | 28.7 | 9.5 | 7.4 | 12.2 | 26.6 | Same |
|  | 2.9 | 2.0 | 6.7 | 2.0 | 2.7 | 3.3 | 4.3 | Down |
|  | 2.1 | 6.0 | 2.4 | 2.0 | 0.2 | 0.9 | 1.1 | Don't know |
|  | (240) | (100) | (209) | (201) | (486) | (450) | (20191) | Weighted N |
| 25-34 Only | 83.9 | 67.1 | 64.6 | 92.6 | 87.6 | 80.7 | 75.0 | Up |
|  | 8.9 | 24.7 | 29.6 | 5.5 | 9.5 | 16.2 | 21.7 | Same |
|  | 3.4 | 1.2 | 4.3 | 0.6 | 2.4 | 2.5 | 3.2 | Down |
|  | 3.9 | 7.0 | 1.4 | 1.3 | 0.6 | 0.6 | 0.1 | Don't know |
|  | (415) | (243) | (280) | (310) | (676) | (678) | (26856) | Weighted N |
| 35-44 Only | 87.2 | 67.7 | 59.9 | 82.7 | 84.5 | 81.2 | 72.5 | Up |
|  | 8.0 | 23.7 | 29.7 | 11.7 | 12.5 | 13.7 | 21.6 | Same |
|  | 1.6 | 2.3 | 8.1 | 2.8 | 3.0 | 3.9 | 3.3 | Down |
|  | 3.2 | 6.2 | 2.3 | 2.8 | 0.0 | 1.2 | 2.6 | Don't know |
|  | (437) | (257) | (222) | (214) | (502) | (490) | (17820) | Weighted N |
| 45-54 Only | 75.7 | 64.6 | 64.7 | 78.3 | 81.5 | 74.2 | 63.4 | Up |
|  | 13.8 | 23.2 | 25.3 | 13.5 | 11.1 | 21.3 | 28.4 | Same |
|  | 4.2 | 4.4 | 8.4 | 5.8 | 4.6 | 2.6 | 5.5 | Down |
|  | 6.3 | 7.7 | 1.6 | 2.4 | 2.8 | 1.9 | 2.7 | Don't know |
|  | (457) | (271) | (190) | (207) | (497) | (418) | (18854) | Weighted N |
| 55-64 Only | 72.6 | 44.3 | 57.0 | 75.0 | 76.9 | 72.5 | 59.4 | Up |
|  | 16.3 | 35.7 | 29.7 | 11.5 | 16.4 | 18.4 | 23.3 | Same |
|  | 4.3 | 8.6 | 9.9 | 7.8 | 3.9 | 5.5 | 10.4 | Down |
|  | 6.8 | 11.4 | 3.5 | 5.7 | 2.7 | 3.6 | 6.8 | Don't know |
|  | (369) | (210) | (172) | (192) | (438) | (385) | (17264) | Weighted N |
| 65-74 Only | 72.4 | 51.5 | 41.5 | 62.5 | 66.1 | 63.6 | 63.9 | Up |
|  | 11.0 | 27.3 | 38.8 | 18.4 | 16.5 | 23.7 | 18.5 | Same |
|  | 3.5 | 4.5 | 10.2 | 9.2 | 7.1 | 6.8 | 10.9 | Down |
|  | 13.0 | 16.7 | 9.5 | 9.9 | 10.3 | 5.9 | 6.7 | Don't know |
|  | (254) | (132) | (147) | (152) | (224) | (338) | (14422) | Weighted N |
| 75 And Older Only | 56.6 | 32.5 | 35.7 | 59.1 | 52.3 | 53.9 | 47.7 | Up |
|  | 20.2 | 41.3 | 41.4 | 19.7 | 28.0 | 26.2 | 25.2 | Same |
|  | 3.1 | 6.3 | 8.6 | 7.6 | 6.8 | 8.5 | 13.5 | Down |
|  | 20.2 | 20.0 | 14.3 | 13.6 | 12.9 | 11.3 | 13.6 | Don't know |
|  | (129) | (80) | (70) | (66) | (132) | (141) | (7728) | Weighted N |

Age coded for head of household only in 1971m, and for head and wife only in 1970a.

Table 7.124
Does R Expect Prices to Go Up or Down in the Next Twelve Months?
Income of Respondent

|  | Year | | | | | | | | | | |
|---|---|---|---|---|---|---|---|---|---|---|---|
|  | 1947a | 1948a | 1949a | 1950a | 1951a | 1952a | 1953a | 1954a | 1958a | 1959a | |
| Income 1 (0-16%) | 14.0% | 33.6% | 10.4% | 20.8% | 76.9% | 48.2% | 14.9% | 19.3% | 45.6% | 55.7% | Up |
|  | 30.6 | 26.3 | 35.5 | 38.3 | 13.1 | 32.0 | 44.8 | 37.5 | 29.1 | 25.7 | Same |
|  | 43.3 | 28.9 | 44.0 | 29.9 | 3.3 | 4.4 | 29.0 | 32.9 | 11.4 | 7.8 | Down |
|  | 12.0 | 11.3 | 10.0 | 11.0 | 6.8 | 15.5 | 11.3 | 10.3 | 14.0 | 10.8 | Don't know |
|  | (145471) | (120703) | (139909) | (13933) | (12315) | (14942) | (21999) | (16653) | (21117) | (19679) | Weighted N |
| Income 2 (17-33%) | 20.3 | 35.8 | 10.4 | 16.5 | 77.2 | 51.2 | 17.9 | 18.5 | 49.4 | 55.4 | Up |
|  | 52.3 | 29.5 | 27.6 | 34.6 | 17.0 | 33.4 | 46.2 | 47.5 | 31.0 | 29.6 | Same |
|  | 14.1 | 24.6 | 55.4 | 41.3 | 2.7 | 7.2 | 27.4 | 29.0 | 9.5 | 8.5 | Down |
|  | 13.2 | 10.1 | 6.6 | 7.6 | 3.1 | 8.2 | 8.5 | 4.9 | 10.1 | 6.6 | Don't know |
|  | (93943) | (140706) | (133500) | (18580) | (17150) | (13826) | (14799) | (10261) | (23041) | (11901) | Weighted N |
| Income 3 (34-67%) | 12.4 | 36.0 | 7.9 | 12.8 | 76.6 | 54.5 | 17.8 | 15.7 | 51.5 | 60.8 | Up |
|  | 33.0 | 28.7 | 32.0 | 38.2 | 17.4 | 33.5 | 44.0 | 44.3 | 29.9 | 27.8 | Same |
|  | 47.7 | 26.7 | 55.7 | 42.4 | 3.5 | 7.1 | 32.5 | 36.2 | 12.7 | 7.2 | Down |
|  | 6.9 | 8.6 | 4.4 | 6.6 | 2.5 | 5.0 | 5.7 | 3.7 | 5.9 | 4.3 | Don't know |
|  | (304612) | (300889) | (340539) | (38557) | (37068) | (34518) | (30464) | (23496) | (23509) | (34814) | Weighted N |
| Income 4 (68-95%) | 11.9 | 33.3 | 5.7 | 14.6 | 75.9 | 53.5 | 15.5 | 11.5 | 43.2 | 67.1 | Up |
|  | 30.5 | 29.1 | 30.6 | 32.9 | 18.3 | 32.3 | 50.0 | 44.4 | 35.7 | 24.4 | Same |
|  | 51.7 | 31.9 | 60.5 | 49.0 | 3.8 | 7.3 | 31.7 | 39.8 | 15.6 | 4.9 | Down |
|  | 6.0 | 5.7 | 3.3 | 3.5 | 2.0 | 7.0 | 2.9 | 4.3 | 5.5 | 3.7 | Don't know |
|  | (252819) | (249101) | (259345) | (21091) | (25803) | (19961) | (20381) | (19813) | (27891) | (23337) | Weighted N |
| Income 5 (96-100%) | 9.3 | 30.6 | 2.5 | 8.8 | 78.3 | 58.1 | 12.8 | 8.2 | 41.7 | 74.8 | Up |
|  | 28.9 | 27.2 | 28.3 | 36.6 | 16.2 | 31.1 | 39.4 | 41.8 | 37.8 | 18.8 | Same |
|  | 54.8 | 37.3 | 66.5 | 49.3 | 4.2 | 6.8 | 44.1 | 48.9 | 18.5 | 4.5 | Down |
|  | 6.9 | 4.9 | 2.7 | 5.3 | 1.3 | 4.0 | 3.7 | 1.1 | 2.1 | 1.9 | Don't know |
|  | (46875) | (75104) | (48794) | (5050) | (5557) | (5041) | (4254) | (4021) | (2434) | (8475) | Weighted N |

Table 7.125

Does R Expect Prices to Go Up or Down in the Next Twelve Months?

Income of Respondent

| | | | | | Year | | | | | | |
|---|---|---|---|---|---|---|---|---|---|---|---|
| | 1960a | 1961a | 1962n | 1963m | 1964a | 1965a | 1966a | 1967a | 1968n | 1969a | |
| Income 1 (0–16%) | 63.2% | 54.5% | 50.9% | 55.7% | 66.2% | 68.3% | 81.8% | 74.2% | 63.8% | 72.4% | Up |
| | 19.1 | 27.4 | 23.0 | 26.1 | 21.0 | 18.6 | 9.3 | 17.6 | 26.6 | 19.8 | Same |
| | 6.4 | 5.1 | 5.0 | 4.5 | 3.2 | 0.6 | 1.1 | 3.5 | 5.6 | 4.6 | Down |
| | 11.4 | 13.1 | 21.1 | 13.6 | 9.6 | 12.6 | 7.8 | 4.7 | 4.0 | 3.2 | Don't know |
| | (535) | (8158) | (161) | (176) | (219) | (167) | (462) | (721) | (621) | (2469) | Weighted N |
| Income 2 (17–33%) | 69.7 | 57.8 | 55.6 | 65.0 | 68.4 | 68.8 | 84.5 | 80.1 | 77.8 | 82.4 | Up |
| | 20.6 | 25.6 | 27.8 | 27.6 | 20.1 | 18.1 | 11.1 | 15.4 | 17.3 | 12.6 | Same |
| | 4.1 | 7.9 | 3.5 | 1.0 | 4.9 | 1.8 | 1.3 | 2.3 | 2.0 | 2.5 | Down |
| | 5.6 | 8.7 | 13.1 | 6.4 | 6.6 | 11.3 | 3.1 | 2.2 | 2.9 | 2.5 | Don't know |
| | (607) | (9877) | (198) | (203) | (244) | (221) | (477) | (557) | (347) | (2243) | Weighted N |
| Income 3 (34–67%) | 77.7 | 63.3 | 61.4 | 62.0 | 68.7 | 73.6 | 88.5 | 84.1 | 83.4 | 84.5 | Up |
| | 16.1 | 24.1 | 24.4 | 29.8 | 22.5 | 18.2 | 8.8 | 12.3 | 14.0 | 12.6 | Same |
| | 2.2 | 7.7 | 5.1 | 1.8 | 3.0 | 1.9 | 0.9 | 2.5 | 1.1 | 2.2 | Down |
| | 4.0 | 4.9 | 9.1 | 6.4 | 5.8 | 6.2 | 1.8 | 1.2 | 1.5 | 0.7 | Don't know |
| | (1112) | (19305) | (505) | (389) | (530) | (417) | (817) | (1417) | (819) | (3868) | Weighted N |
| Income 4 (68–95%) | 80.2 | 66.0 | 59.6 | 67.7 | 70.7 | 76.1 | 91.2 | 88.6 | 82.6 | 88.0 | Up |
| | 15.5 | 24.5 | 30.9 | 27.8 | 23.4 | 18.8 | 7.0 | 9.2 | 13.9 | 9.7 | Same |
| | 3.5 | 7.8 | 2.1 | 1.6 | 2.7 | 2.2 | 0.2 | 2.0 | 1.9 | 1.8 | Down |
| | 0.9 | 1.7 | 7.4 | 2.9 | 3.2 | 2.9 | 1.6 | 0.1 | 1.5 | 0.5 | Don't know |
| | (550) | (10630) | (285) | (381) | (441) | (415) | (488) | (694) | (674) | (2642) | Weighted N |
| Income 5 (96–100%) | 76.1 | 65.4 | 57.1 | 61.6 | 71.6 | 76.2 | 92.0 | 86.4 | 79.4 | 94.6 | Up |
| | 18.6 | 23.2 | 38.1 | 30.2 | 17.6 | 14.3 | 5.3 | 12.7 | 15.3 | 4.5 | Same |
| | 4.4 | 9.1 | 3.2 | 0.0 | 4.1 | 1.9 | 0.7 | 0.9 | 0.0 | 0.9 | Down |
| | 0.9 | 2.3 | 1.6 | 8.1 | 6.8 | 7.6 | 2.0 | 0.0 | 5.3 | 0.0 | Don't know |
| | (113) | (1579) | (63) | (86) | (74) | (105) | (150) | (323) | (131) | (424) | Weighted N |

National Economic Outlook

Table 7.126

Does R Expect Prices to Go Up or Down in the Next Twelve Months?
Income of Respondent

|  | | | | Year | | | | |
|---|---|---|---|---|---|---|---|---|
|  | 1970a | 1971m | 1972f | 1973c | 1974q | 1975q | 1976m | |
| Income 1 (0-16%) | 71.2% | 50.3% | 48.0% | 70.2% | 73.7% | 68.1% | 63.0% | Up |
|  | 12.1 | 27.0 | 30.8 | 16.4 | 15.4 | 17.2 | 27.0 | Same |
|  | 3.8 | 6.3 | 13.1 | 2.3 | 5.5 | 7.1 | 7.9 | Down |
|  | 12.9 | 16.4 | 8.1 | 11.1 | 5.5 | 7.6 | 2.1 | Don't know |
|  | (472) | (189) | (221) | (171) | (403) | (436) | (22148) | Weighted N |
| Income 2 (17-33%) | 74.9 | 51.0 | 62.2 | 80.1 | 82.5 | 74.8 | 68.7 | Up |
|  | 11.7 | 32.8 | 24.3 | 12.0 | 11.3 | 17.9 | 23.9 | Same |
|  | 3.6 | 3.7 | 8.1 | 5.4 | 4.5 | 4.6 | 5.5 | Down |
|  | 9.8 | 12.4 | 5.4 | 2.5 | 1.7 | 2.6 | 1.8 | Don't know |
|  | (418) | (241) | (148) | (316) | (582) | (497) | (24417) | Weighted N |
| Income 3 (34-67%) | 80.2 | 63.8 | 58.9 | 81.1 | 81.6 | 82.0 | 76.9 | Up |
|  | 11.8 | 26.3 | 31.4 | 9.0 | 12.2 | 14.0 | 18.6 | Same |
|  | 2.6 | 3.4 | 7.7 | 5.2 | 4.5 | 2.9 | 3.5 | Down |
|  | 5.5 | 6.4 | 2.0 | 4.6 | 1.8 | 1.1 | 1.0 | Don't know |
|  | (892) | (467) | (455) | (366) | (966) | (826) | (14850) | Weighted N |
| Income 4 (68-95%) | 81.6 | 66.7 | 60.9 | 82.8 | 86.6 | 75.4 | 76.0 | Up |
|  | 10.7 | 22.6 | 32.0 | 12.0 | 11.4 | 20.7 | 19.9 | Same |
|  | 3.7 | 3.7 | 4.9 | 3.7 | 1.7 | 2.5 | 2.1 | Down |
|  | 4.0 | 7.1 | 2.2 | 1.4 | 0.3 | 1.4 | 2.0 | Don't know |
|  | (681) | (297) | (325) | (349) | (603) | (643) | (9285) | Weighted N |
| Income 5 (96-100%) | 82.2 | 66.0 | 65.4 | 89.2 | 78.5 | 78.7 | 84.9 | Up |
|  | 14.0 | 24.5 | 32.1 | 8.6 | 18.3 | 17.3 | 9.6 | Same |
|  | 2.8 | 3.8 | 2.6 | 1.1 | 0.0 | 2.7 | 2.0 | Down |
|  | 0.9 | 5.7 | 0.0 | 1.1 | 3.2 | 1.3 | 3.5 | Don't know |
|  | (107) | (53) | (78) | (93) | (93) | (150) | (8249) | Weighted N |

Figure 7.18
Index of Consumer Sentiment

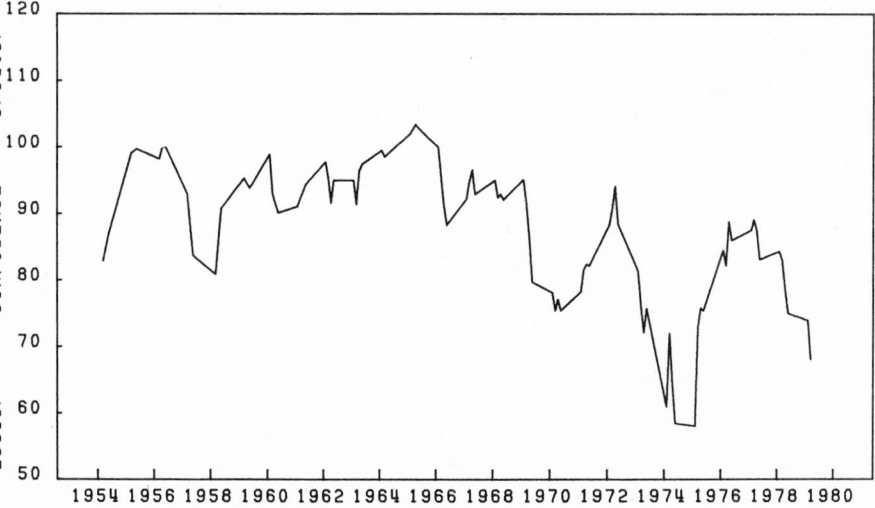

National Economic Outlook

## Chapter 8. Government Spending

We close this volume with two brief chapters that are essentially political in their focus. There is no reason why they might not equally well have been placed in the companion sourcebook on political trends, save for the fact that they involve items outside the ambit of the National Election Study sequence. While the series involved are relatively limited in scope for both chapters, enough changes of generic interest were registered that the items survived several editorial winnowings.

From one point of view, the current chapter focuses on a single item, and one which, with only three observation years, forms a rather sparse series at that. Actually, the "single" item is a battery of questions, posed across a span from 1961 to 1973, evoking reactions to a variety of possible allocations of the federal budget. In each case, the root question asks whether the government should be spending more money, less money, or about the same amount in the area designated. The majority of these allocation targets have shown major shifts in levels of popular reaction to them.

Popular support for most areas of expenditure declined over the 1961-73 period. Indeed, since it is currently assumed that there is substantial public resistance to increased government expenditure, the amount of enthusiasm for more spending in a number of areas in 1961 is quite impressive. The biggest drops in support by 1973 had occurred for welfare and defense expenditures. Welfare allocations, which showed close to the highest levels of support over all areas tested in 1961, showed a progressive drop so precipitous that by 1973 it had become one of the less favored programs. The decline was severe in all segments of the population we have isolated, although it was less marked for blacks and women than for whites and males, and especially for those of high school education.

Defense expenditures lost nearly as much support, with almost all of the decline taking place between 1961 and 1969. This decline was extremely general across all population groups, although perhaps slightly sharper among the college educated. Another program which was a major loser, albeit one which had only feeble support as of 1961, involved expenditures for space exploration. The least popular allocation in all three years was for foreign aid, and this item managed to lose significant ground as well.

Few programs held their own or gained ground in the interim. Support for agricultural expenditures actually advanced, although their popularity was very limited at the outset in 1961. Two of the areas which received the most enthusiastic support in 1961--expenditures for education and for medical care--continued to maintain this support, and by 1973 they stood out sharply against the field. Despite the massive drop in support for welfare over this period, along with well-publicized difficulties of government housing programs through the Department of Housing and Urban Development, allocations for low-cost housing, while losing a small margin of support, still seemed to generate considerable enthusiasm as a target for increased government spending.

Table 8.1
How Much Should the Government Spend on Defense?
Total Population

QUESTION  The government spends money on a variety of things.  I
want to ask briefly about some areas of government spending. How
about defense?  Do you think the government should be spending
more money, less money, or about the same amount on defense as it
does now?

|  |  | Year | | |
|  |  | 1961m | 1969m | 1973c |
| More | (5) | 47.6% | 13.8% | 14.3% |
| Same as now | (3) | 34.4 | 49.6 | 43.4 |
| Less | (1) | 6.2 | 36.7 | 40.0 |
| Don't know/no opinion |  | 11.8 | ** | 2.3 |
| Total |  | 100% | 100% | 100% |
| Weighted N |  | 939 | 1410 | 1327 |
| Unweighted N |  | 939 | 1410 | 1327 |
| Mean |  | 3.94 | 2.54 | 2.47 |
| Standard Deviation |  | 1.25 | 1.34 | 1.40 |

** Code distinction not made.
"No opinion" was explicitly offered as a response in 1961m.

Figure 8.1
Defense Expenditures--Total Population

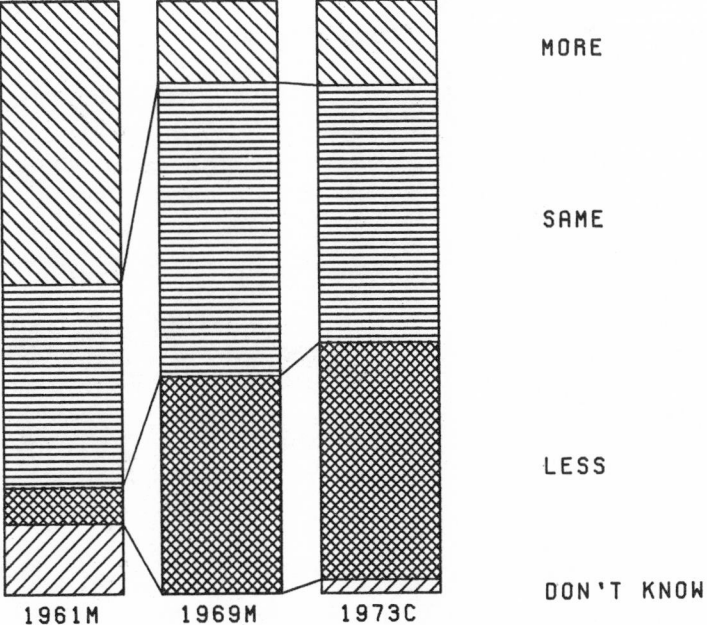

Government Spending

Table 8.2
How Much Should the Government Spend on Defense?
Sex of Respondent

|  | Year | | | |
|---|---|---|---|---|
|  | 1961m | 1969m | 1973c | |
| Males Only | 47.4% | 14.9% | 15.6% | More |
|  | 33.8 | 50.0 | 42.4 | Same as now |
|  | 10.1 | 35.1 | 40.8 | Less |
|  | 8.8 | ** | 1.2 | Don't know/no opinion |
|  | (388) | (1044) | (569) | Weighted N |
| Females Only | 47.7 | 10.4 | 13.3 | More |
|  | 34.8 | 48.2 | 44.2 | Same as now |
|  | 3.4 | 41.4 | 39.4 | Less |
|  | 14.0 | ** | 3.0 | Don't know/no opinion |
|  | (551) | (365) | (758) | Weighted N |

Table 8.3
Race of Respondent

|  | 1961m | 1969m | 1973c | |
|---|---|---|---|---|
| Whites Only | 47.9% | 14.0% | 14.9% | More |
|  | 34.9 | 50.1 | 43.3 | Same as now |
|  | 6.2 | 36.0 | 40.3 | Less |
|  | 11.0 | ** | 1.4 | Don't know/no opinion |
|  | (854) | (1246) | (1106) | Weighted N |
| Blacks Only | 37.3 | 12.8 | 9.5 | More |
|  | 32.8 | 45.9 | 43.1 | Same as now |
|  | 7.5 | 41.2 | 44.8 | Less |
|  | 22.4 | ** | 2.6 | Don't know/no opinion |
|  | (67) | (148) | (116) | Weighted N |

* Code distinction not made.

Table 8.4
How Much Should the Government Spend on Defense?
Education of Respondent

|  | Year | | | |
|---|---|---|---|---|
|  | 1961m | 1969m | 1973c | |
| Grade School Only | 42.1% | 12.9% | 13.5% | More |
|  | 33.5 | 48.7 | 50.3 | Same as now |
|  | 4.1 | 38.4 | 29.7 | Less |
|  | 20.3 | ** | 6.5 | Don't know/no opinion |
|  | (197) | (310) | (155) | Weighted N |
|  |  |  |  |  |
| High School Only | 50.4 | 15.8 | 15.7 | More |
|  | 31.3 | 49.4 | 46.1 | Same as now |
|  | 9.4 | 34.8 | 36.9 | Less |
|  | 8.9 | ** | 1.3 | Don't know/no opinion |
|  | (224) | (563) | (616) | Weighted N |
|  |  |  |  |  |
| College Only | 49.2 | 10.2 | 11.9 | More |
|  | 33.6 | 51.1 | 35.1 | Same as now |
|  | 12.3 | 38.7 | 52.8 | Less |
|  | 4.9 | ** | 0.3 | Don't know/no opinion |
|  | (122) | (372) | (396) | Weighted N |

** Code distinction not made.
Education coded for head of household only in 1961m and 1969m.

Table 8.5
How Much Should the Government Spend on Defense?
Age of Respondent

|  | Year | | | |
|---|---|---|---|---|
|  | 1961m | 1969m | 1973c | |
| 18-24 Only | 43.2% | 11.0% | 13.9% | More |
|  | 32.4 | 57.8 | 40.3 | Same as now |
|  | 13.5 | 31.2 | 44.8 | Less |
|  | 10.8 | ** | 1.0 | Don't know/no opinion |
|  | (37) | (109) | (201) | Weighted N |
|  |  |  |  |  |
| 25-34 Only | 46.0 | 12.8 | 12.7 | More |
|  | 31.0 | 49.6 | 41.8 | Same as now |
|  | 15.0 | 37.6 | 45.1 | Less |
|  | 8.0 | ** | 0.3 | Don't know/no opinion |
|  | (100) | (250) | (306) | Weighted N |
|  |  |  |  |  |
| 35-44 Only | 57.5 | 16.0 | 12.8 | More |
|  | 27.5 | 52.1 | 46.4 | Same as now |
|  | 5.0 | 31.9 | 38.4 | Less |
|  | 10.0 | ** | 2.4 | Don't know/no opinion |
|  | (80) | (257) | (211) | Weighted N |
|  |  |  |  |  |
| 45-54 Only | 52.8 | 16.4 | 16.5 | More |
|  | 33.9 | 43.4 | 45.1 | Same as now |
|  | 5.5 | 40.2 | 36.9 | Less |
|  | 7.9 | ** | 1.5 | Don't know/no opinion |
|  | (127) | (256) | (206) | Weighted N |
|  |  |  |  |  |
| 55-64 Only | 43.8 | 18.0 | 17.6 | More |
|  | 38.2 | 46.1 | 40.4 | Same as now |
|  | 6.7 | 36.0 | 37.8 | Less |
|  | 11.2 | ** | 4.3 | Don't know/no opinion |
|  | (89) | (228) | (188) | Weighted N |
|  |  |  |  |  |
| 65 and older | 38.6 | 8.0 | 14.2 | More |
|  | 32.5 | 51.7 | 46.4 | Same as now |
|  | 6.1 | 40.3 | 34.1 | Less |
|  | 22.8 | ** | 5.2 | Don't know/no opinion |
|  | (114) | (201) | (211) | Weighted N |

* Code distinction not made.
Youngest age group coded "Under 25" in 1969m.
Age coded for head of household only in 1961m and 1969m.

Table 8.6
How Much Should the Government Spend on Foreign Aid?
Total Population

QUESTION: How about foreign aid?  Do you think the government
should be spending more money, less money, or about the same
amount on foreign aid as it does now?

|  |  | Year | | |
|---|---|---|---|---|
|  |  | 1961m | 1969m | 1973c |
| More | (5) | 7.0% | 3.8% | 3.4% |
| Same as now | (3) | 28.8 | 21.3 | 20.4 |
| Less | (1) | 53.7 | 74.9 | 74.1 |
| Don't know/no opinion |  | 10.4 | ** | 2.2 |
| Total |  | 100% | 100% | 100% |
| Weighted N |  | 940 | 1421 | 1342 |
| Unweighted N |  | 940 | 1421 | 1342 |
| Mean |  | 1.96 | 1.58 | 1.55 |
| Standard Deviation |  | 1.28 | 1.06 | 1.04 |

* Code distinction not made.
"No opinion" was explicitly offered as a response in 1961m.

Figure 8.2
Foreign Aid Expenditures--Total Population

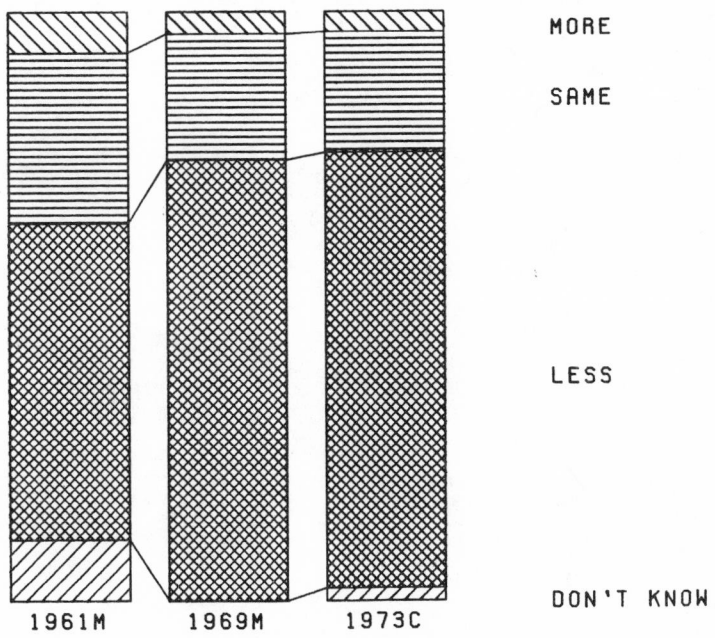

Government Spending

Table 8.7
How Much Should the Government Spend on Foreign Aid?
Sex of Respondent

|  | Year | | | |
|---|---|---|---|---|
|  | 1961m | 1969m | 1973c | |
| Males Only | 7.8% | 3.6% | 2.6% | More |
|  | 25.2 | 19.9 | 17.9 | Same as now |
|  | 58.4 | 76.5 | 77.8 | Less |
|  | 8.6 | ** | 1.7 | Don't know/no opinion |
|  | (385) | (1045) | (577) | Weighted N |
| Females Only | 6.5 | 4.3 | 3.9 | More |
|  | 31.4 | 25.1 | 22.4 | Same as now |
|  | 50.5 | 70.7 | 71.2 | Less |
|  | 11.7 | ** | 2.5 | Don't know/no opinion |
|  | (555) | (375) | (765) | Weighted N |

Table 8.8
Race of Respondent

|  | 1961m | 1969m | 1973c | |
|---|---|---|---|---|
| Whites Only | 7.4% | 3.0% | 2.7% | More |
|  | 29.4 | 20.9 | 19.9 | Same as now |
|  | 54.2 | 76.1 | 76.0 | Less |
|  | 9.0 | ** | 1.4 | Don't know/no opinion |
|  | (854) | (1254) | (1117) | Weighted N |
| Blacks Only | 4.4 | 9.9 | 6.8 | More |
|  | 17.6 | 25.0 | 21.2 | Same as now |
|  | 54.4 | 65.1 | 66.9 | Less |
|  | 23.5 | ** | 5.1 | Don't know/no opinion |
|  | (68) | (152) | (118) | Weighted N |

** Code distinction not made.

Table 8.9
How Much Should the Government Spend on Foreign Aid?
Education of Respondent

|  | Year | | | |
|---|---|---|---|---|
|  | 1961m | 1969m | 1973c | |
| Grade School Only | 6.8% | 4.5% | 3.2% | More |
|  | 24.0 | 23.9 | 24.4 | Same as now |
|  | 50.0 | 71.7 | 64.7 | Less |
|  | 19.3 | ** | 7.7 | Don't know/no opinion |
|  | (192) | (314) | (156) | Weighted N |
| High School Only | 5.9 | 1.9 | 3.7 | More |
|  | 27.5 | 17.3 | 17.0 | Same as now |
|  | 60.8 | 80.7 | 77.9 | Less |
|  | 5.9 | ** | 1.4 | Don't know/no opinion |
|  | (222) | (566) | (624) | Weighted N |
| College Only | 13.6 | 5.9 | 2.8 | More |
|  | 29.6 | 22.2 | 25.4 | Same as now |
|  | 52.0 | 71.9 | 71.6 | Less |
|  | 4.8 | ** | 0.3 | Don't know/no opinion |
|  | (125) | (374) | (398) | Weighted N |

** Code distinction not made.
Education coded for head of household only in 1961m and 1969m.

Table 8.10
How Much Should the Government Spend on Foreign Aid?
Age of Respondent

|  | Year | | | |
|---|---|---|---|---|
|  | 1961m | 1969m | 1973c | |
| 18-24 Only | 10.8% | 3.6% | 9.0% | More |
|  | 35.1 | 28.8 | 26.9 | Same as now |
|  | 51.4 | 67.6 | 62.7 | Less |
|  | 2.7 | ** | 1.5 | Don't know/no opinion |
|  | (37) | (111) | (201) | Weighted N |
| 25-34 Only | 6.9 | 2.8 | 2.9 | More |
|  | 35.3 | 19.3 | 21.9 | Same as now |
|  | 52.9 | 78.0 | 74.2 | Less |
|  | 4.9 | ** | 1.0 | Don't know/no opinion |
|  | (102) | (254) | (310) | Weighted N |
| 35-44 Only | 10.1 | 4.3 | 1.9 | More |
|  | 26.6 | 23.3 | 22.0 | Same as now |
|  | 55.7 | 72.5 | 74.8 | Less |
|  | 7.6 | ** | 1.4 | Don't know/no opinion |
|  | (79) | (258) | (214) | Weighted N |
| 45-54 Only | 8.9 | 3.5 | 2.9 | More |
|  | 21.0 | 20.0 | 18.8 | Same as now |
|  | 58.9 | 76.5 | 74.9 | Less |
|  | 11.3 | ** | 3.4 | Don't know/no opinion |
|  | (124) | (255) | (207) | Weighted N |
| 55-64 Only | 6.7 | 4.8 | 2.1 | More |
|  | 28.1 | 19.2 | 14.5 | Same as now |
|  | 57.3 | 76.0 | 80.3 | Less |
|  | 7.9 | ** | 3.1 | Don't know/no opinion |
|  | (89) | (229) | (193) | Weighted N |
| 65 and older | 6.3 | 3.4 | 1.9 | More |
|  | 21.4 | 16.7 | 17.8 | Same as now |
|  | 51.8 | 79.9 | 77.0 | Less |
|  | 20.5 | ** | 3.3 | Don't know/no opinion |
|  | (112) | (204) | (213) | Weighted N |

* Code distinction not made.
Youngest age group coded "Under 25" in 1969m.
Age coded for head of household only in 1961m and 1969m.

Table 8.11
How Much Should the Government Spend on Education?
Total Population

QUESTION: How about education?  Do you think the government should
be spending more money, less money, or about the same amount on
education as it does now?

|  |  | Year | | | |
|---|---|---|---|---|---|
|  |  | 1961f | 1961m | 1969m | 1973c |
| More | (5) | 60.3% | 60.0% | 63.1% | 57.5% |
| Same as now | (3) | 25.4 | 24.7 | 27.7 | 33.2 |
| Less | (1) | 6.5 | 7.1 | 9.2 | 7.7 |
| Don't know/no opinion |  | 7.9 | 8.2 | ** | 1.6 |
| Total |  | 100% | 100% | 100% | 100% |
| Weighted N |  | 1218 | 947 | 1440 | 1342 |
| Unweighted N |  | 1218 | 947 | 1440 | 1342 |
| Mean |  | 4.17 | 4.15 | 4.08 | 4.01 |
| Standard Deviation |  | 1.24 | 1.26 | 1.32 | 1.28 |

* Code distinction not made.
"No opinion" was explicitly offered as a response in 1961f and 1961m.

Figure 8.3
Education Expenditures--Total Population

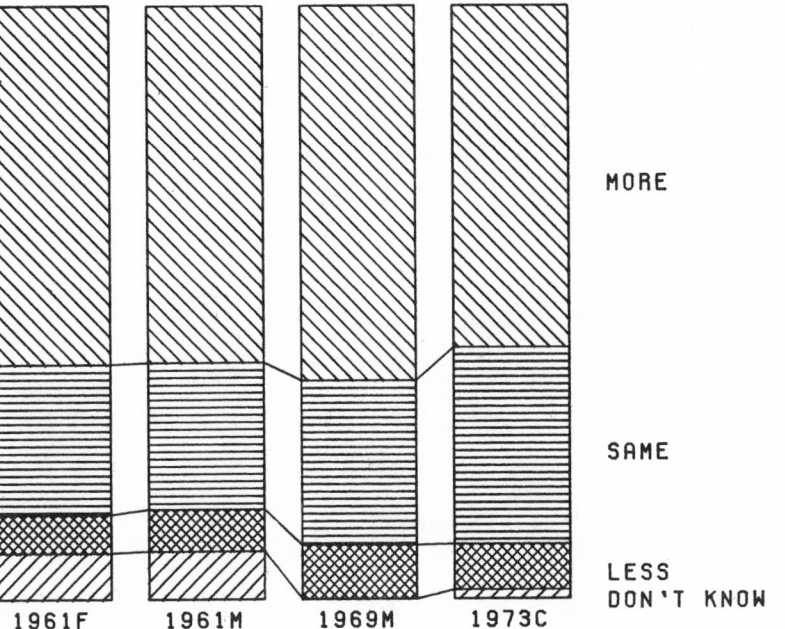

Government Spending

Table 8.12
How Much Should the Government Spend on Education?
Sex of Respondent

|  | Year | | | |  |
|---|---|---|---|---|---|
|  | 1961f | 1961m | 1969m | 1973c |  |
| Males Only | 63.5% | 62.8% | 62.5% | 57.1% | More |
|  | 22.2 | 21.5 | 27.5 | 31.3 | Same as now |
|  | 8.3 | 10.6 | 10.0 | 10.8 | Less |
|  | 6.1 | 5.1 | ** | 0.9 | Don't know/no opinion |
|  | (545) | (395) | (1056) | (576) | Weighted N |
| Females Only | 57.7 | 58.0 | 64.5 | 57.7 | More |
|  | 27.9 | 27.0 | 28.5 | 34.6 | Same as now |
|  | 5.1 | 4.5 | 7.0 | 5.5 | Less |
|  | 9.4 | 10.5 | ** | 2.2 | Don't know/no opinion |
|  | (673) | (552) | (383) | (766) | Weighted N |

Table 8.13
Race of Respondent

|  | 1961f | 1961m | 1969m | 1973c |  |
|---|---|---|---|---|---|
| Whites Only | 59.5% | 60.4% | 60.8% | 56.8% | More |
|  | 26.1 | 23.6 | 29.0 | 33.6 | Same as now |
|  | 7.3 | 7.7 | 10.2 | 8.4 | Less |
|  | 7.1 | 8.4 | ** | 1.2 | Don't know/no opinion |
|  | (1043) | (861) | (1271) | (1117) | Weighted N |
| Blacks Only | 63.7 | 57.4 | 81.0 | 72.0 | More |
|  | 22.6 | 35.3 | 17.0 | 23.7 | Same as now |
|  | 0.8 | 1.5 | 2.0 | 1.7 | Less |
|  | 12.9 | 5.9 | ** | 2.5 | Don't know/no opinion |
|  | (124) | (68) | (153) | (118) | Weighted N |

** Code distinction not made.

Table 8.14
How Much Should the Government Spend on Education?
Education of Respondent

|  | Year | | | | |
|---|---|---|---|---|---|
|  | 1961f | 1961m | 1969m | 1973c | |
| Grade School Only | 54.3% | 52.0% | 56.5% | 39.5% | More |
|  | 28.7 | 25.3 | 31.6 | 43.3 | Same as now |
|  | 4.7 | 9.6 | 11.9 | 12.7 | Less |
|  | 12.4 | 13.1 | ** | 4.5 | Don't know/no opinion |
|  | (363) | (198) | (345) | (157) | Weighted N |
| High School Only | 60.4 | 61.8 | 63.8 | 56.8 | More |
|  | 26.2 | 24.9 | 27.5 | 36.3 | Same as now |
|  | 5.7 | 6.2 | 8.7 | 6.1 | Less |
|  | 7.7 | 7.1 | ** | 0.8 | Don't know/no opinion |
|  | (558) | (225) | (687) | (623) | Weighted N |
| College Only | 67.4 | 65.1 | 67.3 | 68.8 | More |
|  | 19.6 | 18.3 | 24.9 | 22.6 | Same as now |
|  | 10.3 | 15.1 | 7.8 | 7.8 | Less |
|  | 2.7 | 1.6 | ** | 0.8 | Don't know/no opinion |
|  | (291) | (126) | (397) | (398) | Weighted N |

** Code distinction not made.
Education coded for head of household only in 1961m and 1969m.

Table 8.15
How Much Should the Government Spend on Education?
Age of Respondent

|              | Year |       |       |       |                        |
|--------------|------|-------|-------|-------|------------------------|
|              | 1961f | 1961m | 1969m | 1973c |                        |
| 18-24 Only   | 72.7% | 81.1% | 80.2% | 67.2% | More                   |
|              | 21.2  | 10.8  | 17.1  | 30.3  | Same as now            |
|              | 3.0   | 2.7   | 2.7   | 1.0   | Less                   |
|              | 3.0   | 5.4   | **    | 1.5   | Don't know/no opinion  |
|              | (99)  | (37)  | (111) | (201) | Weighted N             |
| 25-34 Only   | 65.0  | 69.6  | 70.2  | 68.2  | More                   |
|              | 22.2  | 23.5  | 23.9  | 26.6  | Same as now            |
|              | 5.3   | 3.9   | 5.9   | 5.2   | Less                   |
|              | 7.5   | 2.9   | **    | 0.0   | Don't know/no opinion  |
|              | (266) | (102) | (255) | (308) | Weighted N             |
| 35-44 Only   | 64.7  | 61.7  | 68.6  | 61.2  | More                   |
|              | 24.0  | 22.2  | 25.3  | 30.8  | Same as now            |
|              | 4.7   | 9.9   | 6.1   | 6.1   | Less                   |
|              | 6.6   | 6.2   | **    | 1.9   | Don't know/no opinion  |
|              | (258) | (81)  | (261) | (214) | Weighted N             |
| 45-54 Only   | 57.4  | 66.9  | 62.9  | 53.6  | More                   |
|              | 27.8  | 16.5  | 23.9  | 34.3  | Same as now            |
|              | 9.6   | 9.4   | 13.1  | 12.1  | Less                   |
|              | 5.2   | 7.1   | **    | 0.0   | Don't know/no opinion  |
|              | (230) | (127) | (259) | (207) | Weighted N             |
| 55-64 Only   | 56.3  | 48.4  | 58.8  | 49.7  | More                   |
|              | 26.3  | 35.2  | 30.9  | 35.8  | Same as now            |
|              | 6.0   | 11.0  | 10.3  | 9.3   | Less                   |
|              | 11.4  | 5.5   | **    | 5.2   | Don't know/no opinion  |
|              | (167) | (91)  | (233) | (193) | Weighted N             |
| 65 and older | 49.0  | 40.9  | 42.9  | 39.1  | More                   |
|              | 29.6  | 27.0  | 42.9  | 44.7  | Same as now            |
|              | 8.7   | 14.8  | 14.3  | 14.0  | Less                   |
|              | 12.8  | 17.4  | **    | 2.3   | Don't know/no opinion  |
|              | (196) | (115) | (210) | (215) | Weighted N             |

** Code distinction not made.
Youngest age group coded "Under 25" in 1969m.
Age coded for head of household only in 1961m and 1969m.

Table 8.16
How Much Should the Government Spend on Welfare?
Total Population

QUESTION: How about welfare?  Do you think the government should be
spending more money, less money, or about the same amount on welfare as
it does now?

|  | | Year | | |
|---|---|---|---|---|
|  | 1961f | 1961m | 1969m | 1973c |
| More          (5) | 64.1% | 52.1% | 37.5% | 22.6% |
| Same as now   (3) | 25.0 | 34.1 | 32.2 | 26.1 |
| Less          (1) | 7.1 | 8.4 | 30.3 | 49.1 |
| Don't know/no opinion | 3.8 | 5.4 | ** | 2.3 |
| Total | 100% | 100% | 100% | 100% |
| Weighted N | 1213 | 941 | 1411 | 1333 |
| Unweighted N | 1213 | 941 | 1411 | 1333 |
| Mean | 4.19 | 3.92 | 3.14 | 2.46 |
| Standard Deviation | 1.25 | 1.31 | 1.64 | 1.63 |

** Code distinction not made.
"No opinion" was explicitly offered as a response in 1961f and 1961m.

Figure 8.4
Welfare Expenditures--Total Population

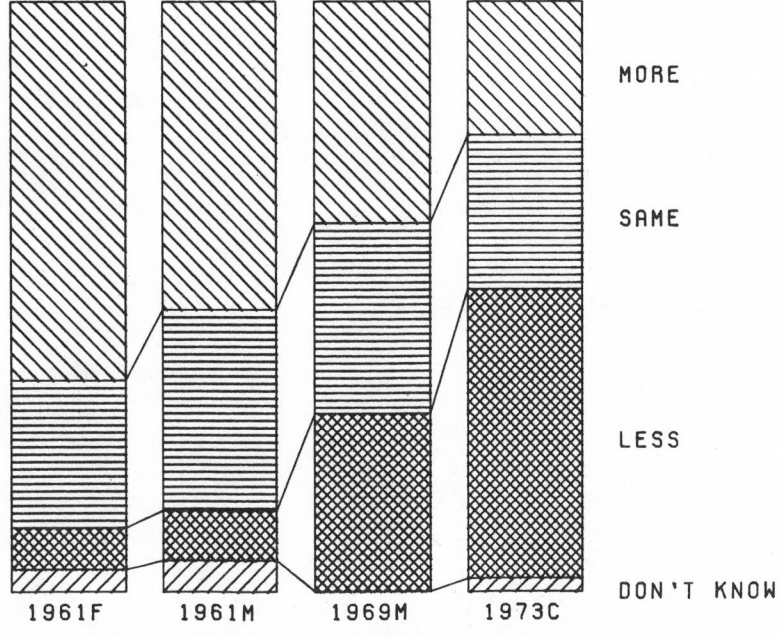

Figure 8.5
Welfare Expenditures by Race of R

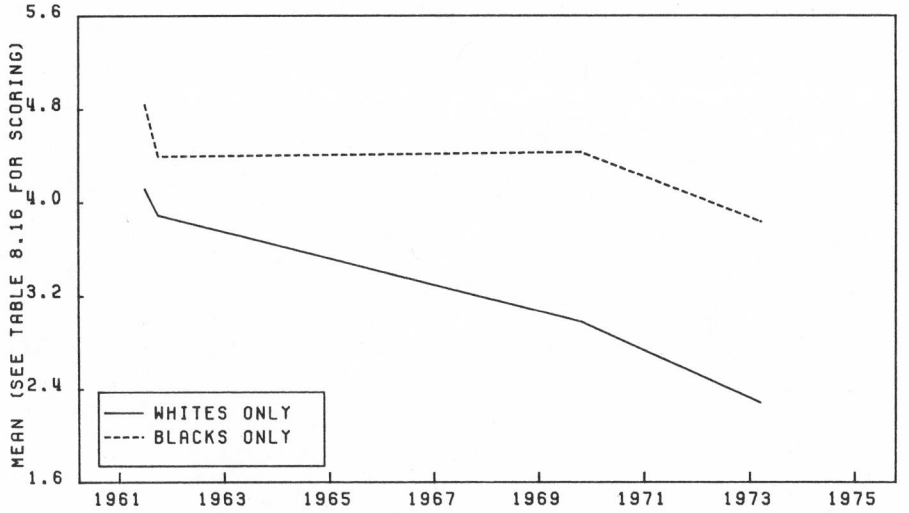

Table 8.17
How Much Should the Government Spend on Welfare?
Sex of Respondent

|  | Year | | | | |
|---|---|---|---|---|---|
|  | 1961f | 1961m | 1969m | 1973c | |
| Males Only | 64.0% | 52.7% | 36.8% | 21.2% | More |
|  | 23.7 | 33.0 | 31.4 | 24.1 | Same as now |
|  | 8.3 | 10.1 | 31.7 | 53.0 | Less |
|  | 4.1 | 4.2 | ** | 1.7 | Don't know/no opinion |
|  | (541) | (385) | (1040) | (572) | Weighted N |
|  |  |  |  |  |  |
| Females Only | 64.3 | 51.6 | 39.4 | 23.7 | More |
|  | 26.0 | 34.9 | 34.5 | 27.6 | Same as now |
|  | 6.1 | 7.2 | 26.1 | 46.1 | Less |
|  | 3.6 | 6.3 | ** | 2.6 | Don't know/no opinion |
|  | (672) | (556) | (371) | (761) | Weighted N |

Table 8.18
Race of Respondent

|  | 1961f | 1961m | 1969m | 1973c | |
|---|---|---|---|---|---|
| Whites Only | 61.1% | 50.9% | 32.4% | 18.4% | More |
|  | 26.9 | 34.7 | 34.1 | 26.1 | Same as now |
|  | 7.8 | 8.9 | 33.5 | 53.4 | Less |
|  | 4.1 | 5.5 | ** | 2.1 | Don't know/no opinion |
|  | (1039) | (855) | (1245) | (1108) | Weighted N |
|  |  |  |  |  |  |
| Blacks Only | 90.2 | 69.1 | 78.1 | 56.8 | More |
|  | 8.1 | 26.5 | 15.2 | 24.6 | Same as now |
|  | 0.0 | 1.5 | 6.6 | 16.1 | Less |
|  | 1.6 | 2.9 | ** | 2.5 | Don't know/no opinion |
|  | (123) | (68) | (151) | (118) | Weighted N |

** Code distinction not made.

Table 8.19
How Much Should the Government Spend on Welfare?
Education of Respondent

|  | Year | | | |  |
| --- | --- | --- | --- | --- | --- |
|  | 1961f | 1961m | 1969m | 1973c |  |
| Grade School Only | 73.2% | 62.4% | 48.7% | 32.1% | More |
|  | 19.6 | 27.8 | 28.6 | 30.1 | Same as now |
|  | 2.5 | 3.6 | 22.6 | 34.0 | Less |
|  | 4.7 | 6.2 | ** | 3.8 | Don't know/no opinion |
|  | (362) | (194) | (318) | (156) | Weighted N |
|  |  |  |  |  |  |
| High School Only | 63.6 | 52.7 | 38.3 | 21.7 | More |
|  | 25.8 | 34.2 | 30.8 | 23.8 | Same as now |
|  | 7.2 | 8.1 | 31.0 | 52.6 | Less |
|  | 3.4 | 5.0 | ** | 1.9 | Don't know/no opinion |
|  | (555) | (222) | (562) | (622) | Weighted N |
|  |  |  |  |  |  |
| College Only | 53.4 | 37.9 | 29.2 | 22.4 | More |
|  | 30.7 | 40.3 | 36.9 | 27.0 | Same as now |
|  | 12.8 | 19.4 | 33.9 | 48.5 | Less |
|  | 3.1 | 2.4 | ** | 2.0 | Don't know/no opinion |
|  | (290) | (124) | (366) | (392) | Weighted N |

** Code distinction not made.
Education coded for head of household only in 1961m and 1969m.

Table 8.20
How Much Should the Government Spend on Welfare?
Age of Respondent

|  | Year | | | | |
|---|---|---|---|---|---|
|  | 1961f | 1961m | 1969m | 1973c | |
| 18-24 Only | 63.0% | 63.9% | 30.6% | 23.9% | More |
|  | 29.0 | 27.8 | 34.3 | 28.4 | Same as now |
|  | 6.0 | 2.8 | 35.2 | 45.8 | Less |
|  | 2.0 | 5.6 | ** | 2.0 | Don't know/no opinion |
|  | (100) | (36) | (108) | (201) | Weighted N |
| 25-34 Only | 60.5 | 44.1 | 35.1 | 22.5 | More |
|  | 27.4 | 35.3 | 28.3 | 27.4 | Same as now |
|  | 7.9 | 14.7 | 36.7 | 49.5 | Less |
|  | 4.1 | 5.9 | ** | 0.7 | Don't know/no opinion |
|  | (266) | (102) | (251) | (307) | Weighted N |
| 35-44 Only | 62.7 | 47.5 | 38.4 | 23.4 | More |
|  | 27.8 | 36.3 | 34.1 | 18.2 | Same as now |
|  | 7.1 | 13.8 | 27.5 | 56.0 | Less |
|  | 2.4 | 2.5 | ** | 2.4 | Don't know/no opinion |
|  | (255) | (80) | (255) | (209) | Weighted N |
| 45-54 Only | 62.6 | 57.6 | 40.9 | 22.3 | More |
|  | 25.7 | 28.8 | 29.0 | 23.8 | Same as now |
|  | 7.8 | 8.8 | 30.2 | 52.4 | Less |
|  | 3.9 | 4.8 | ** | 1.5 | Don't know/no opinion |
|  | (230) | (125) | (252) | (206) | Weighted N |
| 55-64 Only | 70.1 | 48.9 | 43.2 | 22.5 | More |
|  | 20.1 | 40.0 | 30.6 | 27.2 | Same as now |
|  | 6.1 | 5.6 | 26.2 | 46.1 | Less |
|  | 3.7 | 5.6 | ** | 4.2 | Don't know/no opinion |
|  | (164) | (90) | (229) | (191) | Weighted N |
| 65 and older | 68.4 | 58.6 | 37.0 | 21.4 | More |
|  | 19.4 | 30.6 | 38.5 | 30.7 | Same as now |
|  | 6.1 | 6.3 | 24.5 | 44.7 | Less |
|  | 6.1 | 4.5 | ** | 3.3 | Don't know/no opinion |
|  | (196) | (111) | (208) | (215) | Weighted N |

** Code distinction not made.
Youngest age group coded "Under 25" in 1969m.
Age coded for head of household only in 1961m and 1969m.

Table 8.21
How Much Should the Government Spend on Low-Cost Housing?
Total Population

QUESTION: How about low-cost housing?  Do you think the government
should be spending more money, less money, or about the same
amount on low-cost housing as it does now?

|  | | Year | | |
|---|---|---|---|---|
|  | | 1961f | 1969m | 1973c |
| More | (5) | 55.4% | 53.9% | 50.0% |
| Same as now | (3) | 23.4 | 30.3 | 29.4 |
| Less | (1) | 9.4 | 15.7 | 18.0 |
| Don't know/no opinion | | 11.8 | ** | 2.6 |
| Total | | 100% | 100% | 100% |
| Weighted N | | 1216 | 1430 | 1326 |
| Unweighted N | | 1216 | 1430 | 1326 |
| Mean | | 4.04 | 3.76 | 3.66 |
| Standard Deviation | | 1.36 | 1.48 | 1.54 |

** Code distinction not made.
"No opinion" was explicitly offered as a response in 1961f.

Figure 8.6
Low-Cost Housing Expenditures--Total Population

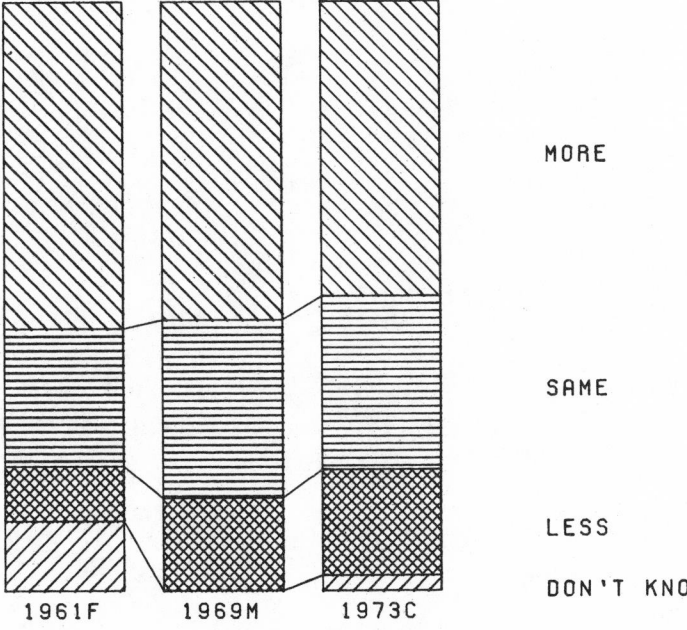

Figure 8.7
Low-Cost Housing Expenditures by Race of R

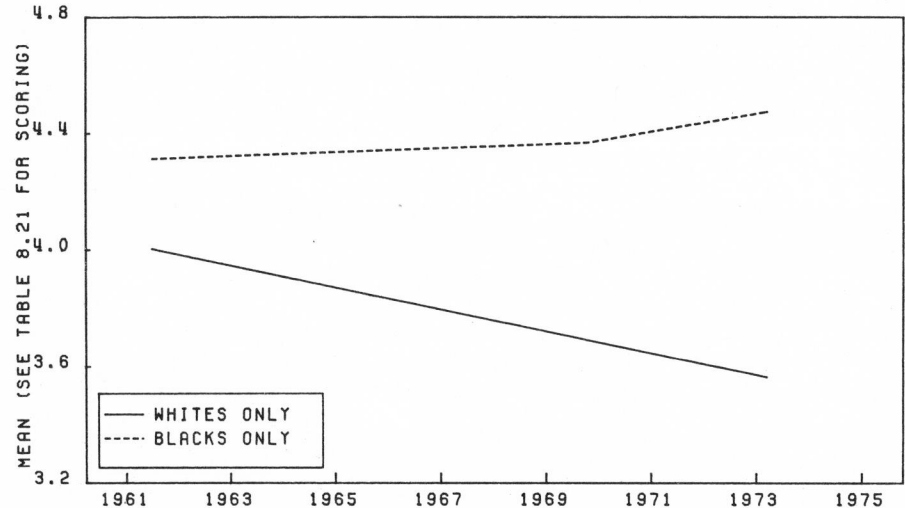

Table 8.22
How Much Should the Government Spend on Low-Cost Housing?
Sex of Respondent

|  | Year | | |
|---|---|---|---|
|  | 1961f | 1969m | 1973c |
| Males Only | 55.9% | 54.2% | 50.7% More |
|  | 23.4 | 30.0 | 26.8 Same as now |
|  | 10.8 | 15.8 | 21.0 Less |
|  | 9.9 | ** | 1.6 Don't know/no opinion |
|  | (547) | (1056) | (568) Weighted N |
| Females Only | 55.0 | 53.4 | 49.5 More |
|  | 23.3 | 31.1 | 31.4 Same as now |
|  | 8.2 | 15.5 | 15.8 Less |
|  | 13.5 | ** | 3.3 Don't know/no opinion |
|  | (669) | (373) | (758) Weighted N |

Table 8.23
Race of Respondent

|  | 1961f | 1969m | 1973c |
|---|---|---|---|
| Whites Only | 54.9% | 50.8% | 47.6% More |
|  | 23.8 | 32.9 | 30.1 Same as now |
|  | 10.3 | 16.3 | 20.1 Less |
|  | 11.0 | ** | 2.2 Don't know/no opinion |
|  | (1042) | (1259) | (1102) Weighted N |
| Blacks Only | 56.1 | 78.1 | 75.2 More |
|  | 21.1 | 12.3 | 18.8 Same as now |
|  | 3.3 | 9.7 | 3.4 Less |
|  | 19.5 | ** | 2.6 Don't know/no opinion |
|  | (123) | (155) | (117) Weighted N |

** Code distinction not made.

Table 8.24
How Much Should the Government Spend on Low-Cost Housing?
Education of Respondent

|                    | Year |  |  | |
| --- | --- | --- | --- | --- |
|                    | 1961f | 1969m | 1973c | |
| Grade School Only  | 51.9% | 50.2% | 46.2% | More |
|                    | 20.8  | 32.5  | 34.0  | Same as now |
|                    | 5.3   | 17.3  | 13.5  | Less |
|                    | 21.9  | **    | 6.4   | Don't know/no opinion |
|                    | (360) | (323) | (156) | Weighted N |
|                    |       |       |       | |
| High School Only   | 56.4  | 57.2  | 50.1  | More |
|                    | 24.9  | 27.5  | 29.0  | Same as now |
|                    | 9.8   | 15.3  | 19.3  | Less |
|                    | 8.9   | **    | 1.6   | Don't know/no opinion |
|                    | (559) | (570) | (617) | Weighted N |
|                    |       |       |       | |
| College Only       | 57.7  | 55.1  | 52.9  | More |
|                    | 24.1  | 29.7  | 28.1  | Same as now |
|                    | 13.7  | 15.1  | 17.4  | Less |
|                    | 4.5   | **    | 1.5   | Don't know/no opinion |
|                    | (291) | (370) | (391) | Weighted N |

** Code distinction not made.
Education coded for head of household only in 1969m.

Table 8.25
How Much Should the Government Spend on Low-Cost Housing?
Age of Respondent

|  | Year | | | |
| --- | --- | --- | --- | --- |
|  | 1961f | 1969m | 1973c | |
| 18-24 Only | 67.0% | 52.3% | 62.5% | More |
|  | 23.0 | 33.3 | 27.5 | Same as now |
|  | 3.0 | 14.4 | 8.0 | Less |
|  | 7.0 | ** | 2.0 | Don't know/no opinion |
|  | (100) | (111) | (200) | Weighted N |
| 25-34 Only | 55.6 | 53.7 | 49.0 | More |
|  | 27.1 | 27.8 | 26.8 | Same as now |
|  | 10.5 | 18.4 | 23.5 | Less |
|  | 6.8 | ** | 0.7 | Don't know/no opinion |
|  | (266) | (255) | (306) | Weighted N |
| 35-44 Only | 56.5 | 56.0 | 52.1 | More |
|  | 25.5 | 30.1 | 27.5 | Same as now |
|  | 8.2 | 13.9 | 18.5 | Less |
|  | 9.8 | ** | 1.9 | Don't know/no opinion |
|  | (255) | (259) | (211) | Weighted N |
| 45-54 Only | 58.4 | 55.6 | 49.3 | More |
|  | 18.6 | 28.8 | 31.5 | Same as now |
|  | 11.7 | 15.6 | 18.2 | Less |
|  | 11.3 | ** | 1.0 | Don't know/no opinion |
|  | (231) | (257) | (203) | Weighted N |
| 55-64 Only | 54.8 | 57.5 | 44.4 | More |
|  | 19.3 | 30.0 | 32.3 | Same as now |
|  | 12.0 | 12.4 | 16.9 | Less |
|  | 13.9 | ** | 6.3 | Don't know/no opinion |
|  | (166) | (233) | (189) | Weighted N |
| 65 and older | 45.4 | 52.2 | 42.7 | More |
|  | 24.5 | 30.0 | 32.4 | Same as now |
|  | 7.7 | 17.9 | 20.2 | Less |
|  | 22.4 | ** | 4.7 | Don't know/no opinion |
|  | (196) | (207) | (213) | Weighted N |

** Code distinction not made.
Youngest age group coded "Under 25" in 1969m.
Age coded for head of household only in 1969m.

Table 8.26
How Much Should the Government Spend on Hospitals and Medical Care?
Total Population

QUESTION: How about hospitals and medical care?  Do you think the
government should be spending more money, less money, or about the same
amount on hospitals and medical care as it does now?

|  | | Year | |
| --- | --- | --- | --- |
|  | 1961f | 1961m | 1973c |
| More (5) | 56.3% | 49.5% | 58.6% |
| Same as now (3) | 26.0 | 31.6 | 32.0 |
| Less (1) | 8.6 | 8.7 | 7.3 |
| Don't know/no opinion | 9.2 | 10.1 | 2.0 |
| Total | 100% | 100% | 100% |
| Weighted N | 1216 | 939 | 1336 |
| Unweighted N | 1216 | 939 | 1336 |
| Mean | 4.05 | 3.91 | 4.05 |
| Standard Deviation | 1.32 | 1.33 | 1.26 |

"No opinion" was explicitly offered as a response in 1961f and 1961m.

Figure 8.8
Hospitals and Medical Care Expenditures--Total Population

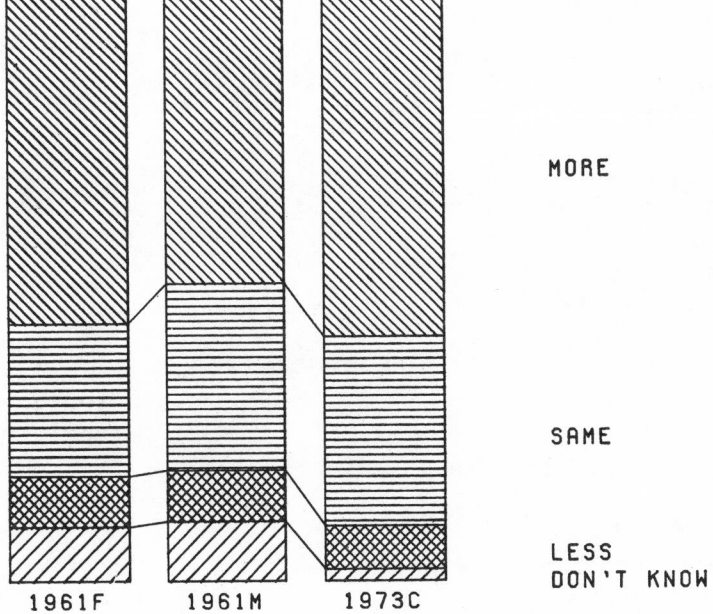

Figure 8.9
Hospitals and Medical Care Expenditures by Education of R

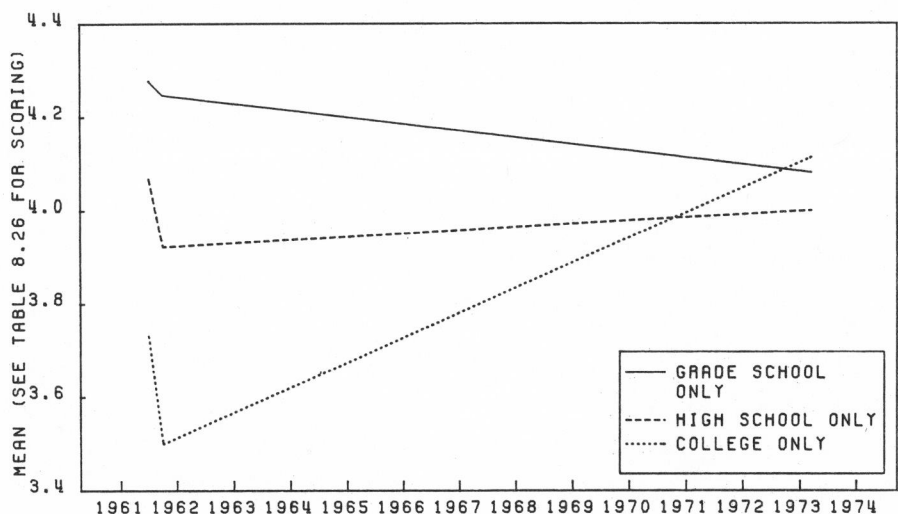

Table 8.27
How Much Should the Government Spend on Hospitals and Medical Care?
Sex of Respondent

|  | Year | | |  |
|---|---|---|---|---|
|  | 1961f | 1961m | 1973c |  |
| Males Only | 58.6% | 48.3% | 61.8% | More |
|  | 23.6 | 30.7 | 28.6 | Same as now |
|  | 10.9 | 11.9 | 7.9 | Less |
|  | 7.0 | 9.0 | 1.7 | Don't know/no opinion |
|  | (543) | (387) | (573) | Weighted N |
|  |  |  |  |  |
| Females Only | 54.4 | 50.4 | 56.2 | More |
|  | 27.9 | 32.2 | 34.6 | Same as now |
|  | 6.7 | 6.5 | 6.9 | Less |
|  | 11.0 | 10.9 | 2.2 | Don't know/no opinion |
|  | (673) | (552) | (763) | Weighted N |

Table 8.28
Race of Respondent

|  | 1961f | 1961m | 1973c |  |
|---|---|---|---|---|
| Whites Only | 53.4% | 47.7% | 56.9% | More |
|  | 27.8 | 32.5 | 33.8 | Same as now |
|  | 9.5 | 9.2 | 7.7 | Less |
|  | 9.3 | 10.5 | 1.6 | Don't know/no opinion |
|  | (1041) | (855) | (1113) | Weighted N |
|  |  |  |  |  |
| Blacks Only | 77.4 | 75.8 | 75.4 | More |
|  | 11.3 | 18.2 | 20.3 | Same as now |
|  | 1.6 | 1.5 | 2.5 | Less |
|  | 9.7 | 4.5 | 1.7 | Don't know/no opinion |
|  | (124) | (66) | (118) | Weighted N |

Table 8.29
How Much Should the Government Spend on Hospitals and Medical Care?
Education of Respondent

|  | Year | | | |
|---|---|---|---|---|
|  | 1961f | 1961m | 1973c | |
| Grade School Only | 61.2% | 57.8% | 55.8% | More |
|  | 21.2 | 25.5 | 34.6 | Same as now |
|  | 5.2 | 3.6 | 4.5 | Less |
|  | 12.4 | 13.0 | 5.1 | Don't know/no opinion |
|  | (363) | (192) | (156) | Weighted N |
| High School Only | 56.7 | 52.5 | 56.6 | More |
|  | 28.2 | 30.0 | 35.4 | Same as now |
|  | 7.4 | 9.9 | 7.1 | Less |
|  | 7.7 | 7.6 | 1.0 | Don't know/no opinion |
|  | (556) | (223) | (624) | Weighted N |
| College Only | 48.8 | 42.4 | 63.7 | More |
|  | 28.2 | 31.2 | 25.9 | Same as now |
|  | 15.1 | 19.2 | 8.9 | Less |
|  | 7.9 | 7.2 | 1.5 | Don't know/no opinion |
|  | (291) | (125) | (394) | Weighted N |

Education coded for head of household only in 1961m.

Table 8.30
How Much Should the Government Spend on Hospitals and Medical Care?
Age of Respondent

|  | Year | | | |
|---|---|---|---|---|
|  | 1961f | 1961m | 1973c | |
| 18-24 Only | 57.0% | 62.2% | 61.7% | More |
|  | 35.0 | 24.3 | 35.3 | Same as now |
|  | 4.0 | 8.1 | 2.5 | Less |
|  | 4.0 | 5.4 | 0.5 | Don't know/no opinion |
|  | (100) | (37) | (201) | Weighted N |
| 25-34 Only | 52.1 | 38.0 | 62.6 | More |
|  | 30.2 | 43.0 | 28.4 | Same as now |
|  | 9.1 | 10.0 | 7.7 | Less |
|  | 8.7 | 9.0 | 1.3 | Don't know/no opinion |
|  | (265) | (100) | (310) | Weighted N |
| 35-44 Only | 57.2 | 50.0 | 59.2 | More |
|  | 27.2 | 30.0 | 29.9 | Same as now |
|  | 7.4 | 15.0 | 7.6 | Less |
|  | 8.2 | 5.0 | 3.3 | Don't know/no opinion |
|  | (257) | (80) | (211) | Weighted N |
| 45-54 Only | 57.6 | 57.9 | 63.7 | More |
|  | 22.3 | 21.4 | 29.4 | Same as now |
|  | 11.8 | 10.3 | 5.9 | Less |
|  | 8.3 | 10.3 | 1.0 | Don't know/no opinion |
|  | (229) | (126) | (204) | Weighted N |
| 55-64 Only | 60.5 | 51.1 | 54.4 | More |
|  | 22.2 | 30.7 | 33.2 | Same as now |
|  | 7.2 | 11.4 | 8.3 | Less |
|  | 10.2 | 6.8 | 4.1 | Don't know/no opinion |
|  | (167) | (88) | (193) | Weighted N |
| 65 and older | 55.1 | 55.8 | 49.3 | More |
|  | 21.9 | 23.0 | 37.1 | Same as now |
|  | 8.7 | 6.2 | 11.7 | Less |
|  | 14.3 | 15.0 | 1.9 | Don't know/no opinion |
|  | (196) | (113) | (213) | Weighted N |

Age coded for head of household only in 1961m.

Table 8.31
How Much Should the Government Spend on Highway Construction?
Total Population

QUESTION: How about highway construction?  Do you think the government
should be spending more money, less money, or about the same amount on
highway construction as it does now?

|  | | Year | | | |
|---|---|---|---|---|---|
|  | | 1961f | 1961m | 1969m | 1973c |
| More | (5) | 36.9% | 33.3% | 36.7% | 32.4% |
| Same as now | (3) | 45.0 | 46.6 | 48.1 | 44.8 |
| Less | (1) | 10.6 | 11.3 | 15.2 | 20.8 |
| Don't know/no opinion | | 7.5 | 8.9 | ** | 2.0 |
| Total | | 100% | 100% | 100% | 100% |
| Weighted N | | 1220 | 947 | 1429 | 1342 |
| Unweighted N | | 1220 | 947 | 1429 | 1342 |
| Mean | | 3.57 | 3.48 | 3.43 | 3.24 |
| Standard Deviation | | 1.32 | 1.31 | 1.38 | 1.45 |

* Code distinction not made.
"No opinion" was explicitly offered as a response in 1961f and 1961m.


Figure 8.10
Highway Construction Expenditures--Total Population

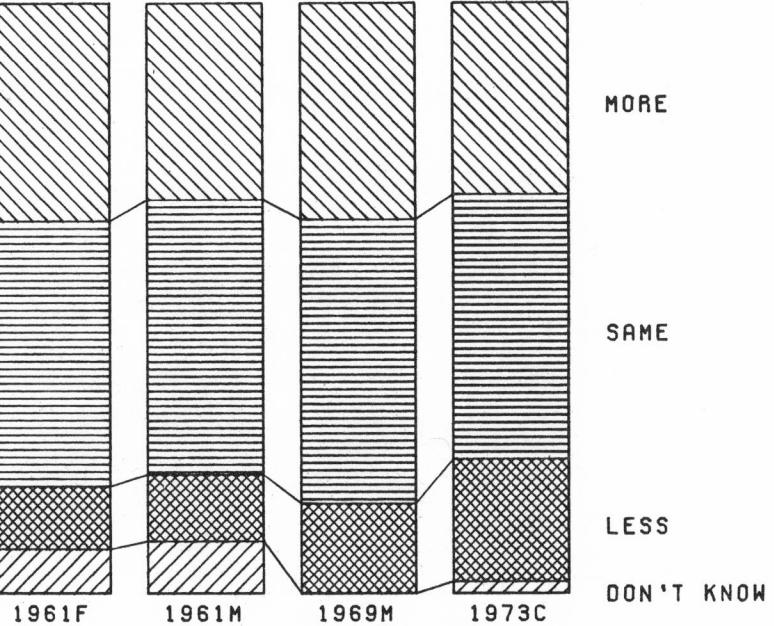

Table 8.32
How Much Should the Government Spend on Highway Construction?
Sex of Respondent

|  | Year | | | |  |
|---|---|---|---|---|---|
|  | 1961f | 1961m | 1969m | 1973c |  |
| Males Only | 45.3% | 40.7% | 38.4% | 35.7% | More |
|  | 39.1 | 43.5 | 47.7 | 41.2 | Same as now |
|  | 11.3 | 10.7 | 13.9 | 21.7 | Less |
|  | 4.2 | 5.1 | ** | 1.4 | Don't know/no opinion |
|  | (547) | (393) | (1058) | (575) | Weighted N |
| Females Only | 30.0 | 28.0 | 32.1 | 30.0 | More |
|  | 49.8 | 48.7 | 49.1 | 47.5 | Same as now |
|  | 10.0 | 11.7 | 18.9 | 20.1 | Less |
|  | 10.3 | 11.6 | ** | 2.5 | Don't know/no opinion |
|  | (673) | (554) | (371) | (767) | Weighted N |

Table 8.33
Race of Respondent

|  | 1961f | 1961m | 1969m | 1973c |  |
|---|---|---|---|---|---|
| Whites Only | 37.1% | 33.8% | 36.1% | 33.0% | More |
|  | 46.2 | 47.9 | 48.9 | 44.7 | Same as now |
|  | 10.3 | 10.2 | 15.0 | 20.9 | Less |
|  | 6.4 | 8.1 | ** | 1.4 | Don't know/no opinion |
|  | (1046) | (861) | (1263) | (1117) | Weighted N |
| Blacks Only | 33.1 | 22.1 | 40.4 | 30.5 | More |
|  | 37.1 | 35.3 | 43.0 | 43.2 | Same as now |
|  | 14.5 | 26.5 | 16.6 | 22.9 | Less |
|  | 15.3 | 16.2 | ** | 3.4 | Don't know/no opinion |
|  | (124) | (68) | (151) | (118) | Weighted N |

** Code distinction not made.

Table 8.34
How Much Should the Government Spend on Highway Construction?
Education of Respondent

|  | Year | | | |  |
|---|---|---|---|---|---|
|  | 1961f | 1961m | 1969m | 1973c |  |
| Grade School Only | 37.2% | 29.3% | 40.6% | 39.7% | More |
|  | 37.5 | 41.4 | 41.5 | 39.7 | Same as now |
|  | 12.1 | 14.1 | 17.9 | 14.7 | Less |
|  | 13.2 | 15.2 | ** | 5.8 | Don't know/no opinion |
|  | (363) | (198) | (318) | (156) | Weighted N |
|  |  |  |  |  |  |
| High School Only | 37.0 | 44.6 | 37.8 | 34.9 | More |
|  | 46.5 | 40.6 | 50.7 | 44.8 | Same as now |
|  | 10.4 | 7.6 | 11.5 | 19.2 | Less |
|  | 6.1 | 7.1 | ** | 1.1 | Don't know/no opinion |
|  | (559) | (224) | (572) | (625) | Weighted N |
|  |  |  |  |  |  |
| College Only | 36.3 | 34.9 | 31.8 | 24.9 | More |
|  | 51.4 | 48.4 | 50.5 | 47.6 | Same as now |
|  | 9.2 | 13.5 | 17.6 | 27.0 | Less |
|  | 3.1 | 3.2 | ** | 0.5 | Don't know/no opinion |
|  | (292) | (126) | (374) | (397) | Weighted N |

** Code distinction not made.
Education coded for head of household only in 1961m and 1969m.

Table 8.35
How Much Should the Government Spend on Highway Construction?
Age of Respondent

|  |  | Year |  |  |  |
|---|---|---|---|---|---|
|  | 1961f | 1961m | 1969m | 1973c |  |
| 18-24 Only | 30.0% | 32.4% | 32.4% | 27.9% | More |
|  | 55.0 | 54.1 | 53.2 | 44.8 | Same as now |
|  | 8.0 | 10.8 | 14.4 | 26.9 | Less |
|  | 7.0 | 2.7 | ** | 0.5 | Don't know/no opinion |
|  | (100) | (37) | (111) | (201) | Weighted N |
| 25-34 Only | 34.1 | 45.1 | 33.7 | 31.3 | More |
|  | 50.6 | 43.1 | 52.2 | 47.4 | Same as now |
|  | 9.0 | 7.8 | 14.1 | 20.6 | Less |
|  | 6.4 | 3.9 | ** | 0.6 | Don't know/no opinion |
|  | (267) | (102) | (255) | (310) | Weighted N |
| 35-44 Only | 38.8 | 41.3 | 37.0 | 39.7 | More |
|  | 45.3 | 45.0 | 46.2 | 42.5 | Same as now |
|  | 9.7 | 11.3 | 16.8 | 17.3 | Less |
|  | 6.2 | 2.5 | ** | 0.5 | Don't know/no opinion |
|  | (258) | (80) | (262) | (214) | Weighted N |
| 45-54 Only | 42.0 | 47.2 | 43.2 | 33.5 | More |
|  | 42.4 | 36.2 | 42.1 | 46.1 | Same as now |
|  | 9.5 | 10.2 | 14.7 | 19.4 | Less |
|  | 6.1 | 6.3 | ** | 1.0 | Don't know/no opinion |
|  | (231) | (127) | (259) | (206) | Weighted N |
| 55-64 Only | 40.1 | 27.5 | 41.2 | 36.3 | More |
|  | 40.7 | 51.6 | 49.4 | 40.9 | Same as now |
|  | 12.0 | 13.2 | 9.4 | 19.7 | Less |
|  | 7.2 | 7.7 | ** | 3.1 | Don't know/no opinion |
|  | (167) | (91) | (233) | (193) | Weighted N |
| 65 and older | 33.3 | 24.3 | 31.0 | 27.6 | More |
|  | 39.0 | 38.3 | 47.8 | 45.3 | Same as now |
|  | 14.4 | 13.9 | 21.2 | 20.1 | Less |
|  | 13.3 | 23.5 | ** | 7.0 | Don't know/no opinion |
|  | (195) | (115) | (203) | (214) | Weighted N |

** Code distinction not made.
Youngest age group coded "Under 25" in 1969m.
Age coded for head of household only in 1961m and 1969m.

Table 8.36
How Much Should the Government Spend on Agriculture?
Total Population

QUESTION: How about agriculture?  Do you think the government should be
spending more money, less money, or about the same amount on agriculture
as it does now?

|  |  | Year | | | |
|---|---|---|---|---|---|
|  |  | 1961f | 1961m | 1969m | 1973c |
| More | (5) | 22.5% | 18.3% | 32.1% | 37.6% |
| Same as now | (3) | 32.7 | 35.2 | 36.7 | 36.6 |
| Less | (1) | 25.9 | 27.3 | 31.2 | 22.0 |
| Don't know/no opinion |  | 18.8 | 19.2 | ** | 3.8 |
| Total |  | 100% | 100% | 100% | 100% |
| Weighted N |  | 1216 | 942 | 1396 | 1338 |
| Unweighted N |  | 1216 | 942 | 1396 | 1338 |
| Mean |  | 2.92 | 2.78 | 3.02 | 3.32 |
| Standard Deviation |  | 1.54 | 1.49 | 1.59 | 1.54 |

** Code distinction not made.
"No opinion" was explicitly offered as a response in 1961f and 1961m.

Figure 8.11
Agriculture Expenditures--Total Population

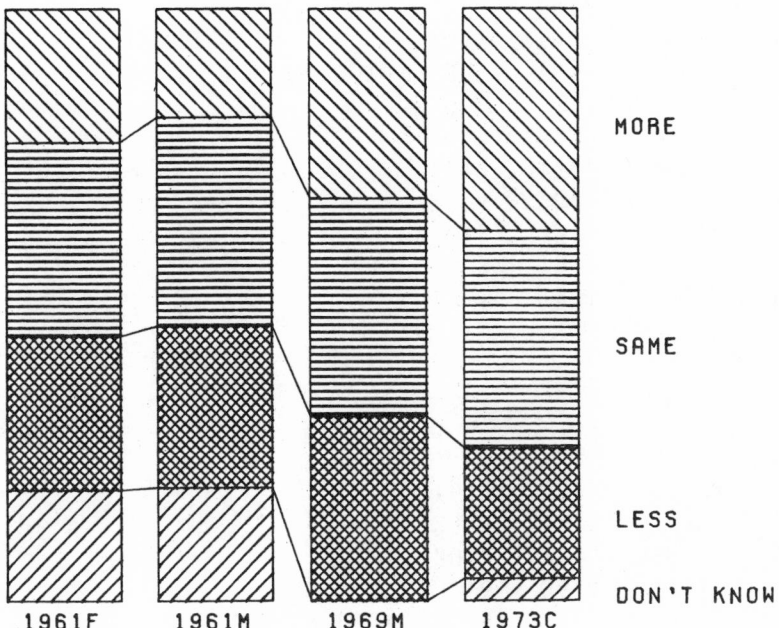

Table 8.37
How Much Should the Government Spend on Agriculture?
Sex of Respondent

|  | Year | | | |  |
| --- | --- | --- | --- | --- | --- |
|  | 1961f | 1961m | 1969m | 1973c |  |
| Males Only | 23.3% | 19.9% | 32.5% | 36.8% | More |
|  | 32.9 | 33.7 | 34.6 | 33.1 | Same as now |
|  | 32.9 | 34.2 | 32.9 | 28.0 | Less |
|  | 10.8 | 12.2 | ** | 2.1 | Don't know/no opinion |
|  | (544) | (392) | (1039) | (574) | Weighted N |
|  |  |  |  |  |  |
| Females Only | 21.9 | 17.1 | 30.8 | 38.2 | More |
|  | 32.6 | 36.4 | 43.1 | 39.3 | Same as now |
|  | 20.2 | 22.4 | 26.1 | 17.4 | Less |
|  | 25.3 | 24.2 | ** | 5.1 | Don't know/no opinion |
|  | (672) | (550) | (357) | (764) | Weighted N |

Table 8.38
Race of Respondent

|  | 1961f | 1961m | 1969m | 1973c |  |
| --- | --- | --- | --- | --- | --- |
| Whites Only | 20.3% | 18.3% | 29.2% | 36.2% | More |
|  | 34.1 | 35.5 | 37.4 | 37.9 | Same as now |
|  | 28.4 | 28.5 | 33.3 | 22.4 | Less |
|  | 17.2 | 17.7 | ** | 3.5 | Don't know/no opinion |
|  | (1043) | (857) | (1231) | (1114) | Weighted N |
|  |  |  |  |  |  |
| Blacks Only | 43.4 | 16.2 | 53.6 | 52.1 | More |
|  | 20.5 | 36.8 | 32.5 | 31.6 | Same as now |
|  | 6.6 | 14.7 | 13.9 | 13.7 | Less |
|  | 29.5 | 32.4 | ** | 2.6 | Don't know/no opinion |
|  | (122) | (68) | (151) | (117) | Weighted N |

** Code distinction not made.

Table 8.39
How Much Should the Government Spend on Agriculture?
Education of Respondent

|  | Year | | | | |
|---|---|---|---|---|---|
|  | 1961f | 1961m | 1969m | 1973c | |
| Grade School Only | 26.9% | 23.5% | 40.3% | 37.9% | More |
|  | 31.3 | 34.7 | 36.8 | 41.8 | Same as now |
|  | 17.7 | 17.9 | 22.9 | 13.1 | Less |
|  | 24.1 | 24.0 | ** | 7.2 | Don't know/no opinion |
|  | (361) | (196) | (310) | (153) | Weighted N |
| High School Only | 23.1 | 18.8 | 33.5 | 40.8 | More |
|  | 35.3 | 33.9 | 38.0 | 35.5 | Same as now |
|  | 23.1 | 27.7 | 28.5 | 20.2 | Less |
|  | 18.5 | 19.6 | ** | 3.5 | Don't know/no opinion |
|  | (558) | (224) | (555) | (623) | Weighted N |
| College Only | 15.5 | 15.2 | 20.3 | 34.7 | More |
|  | 29.6 | 30.4 | 35.9 | 36.9 | Same as now |
|  | 41.9 | 49.6 | 43.8 | 26.4 | Less |
|  | 13.1 | 4.8 | ** | 2.0 | Don't know/no opinion |
|  | (291) | (125) | (370) | (398) | Weighted N |

** Code distinction not made.
Education coded for head of household only in 1961m and 1969m.

Table 8.40
How Much Should the Government Spend on Agriculture?
Age of Respondent

|  | Year | | | |  |
|---|---|---|---|---|---|
|  | 1961f | 1961m | 1969m | 1973c |  |
| 18-24 Only | 26.3% | 27.0% | 40.7% | 47.3% | More |
|  | 43.4 | 32.4 | 42.6 | 38.8 | Same as now |
|  | 13.1 | 32.4 | 16.7 | 12.4 | Less |
|  | 17.2 | 8.1 | ** | 1.5 | Don't know/no opinion |
|  | (99) | (37) | (108) | (201) | Weighted N |
| 25-34 Only | 22.1 | 18.6 | 30.9 | 42.3 | More |
|  | 34.8 | 41.2 | 44.2 | 38.7 | Same as now |
|  | 28.1 | 26.5 | 24.9 | 15.8 | Less |
|  | 15.0 | 13.7 | ** | 3.2 | Don't know/no opinion |
|  | (267) | (102) | (249) | (310) | Weighted N |
| 35-44 Only | 23.4 | 18.5 | 29.7 | 37.1 | More |
|  | 33.2 | 37.0 | 34.7 | 35.7 | Same as now |
|  | 25.8 | 30.9 | 35.5 | 23.9 | Less |
|  | 17.6 | 13.6 | ** | 3.3 | Don't know/no opinion |
|  | (256) | (81) | (259) | (213) | Weighted N |
| 45-54 Only | 23.6 | 24.6 | 30.0 | 32.2 | More |
|  | 34.9 | 29.4 | 32.0 | 35.6 | Same as now |
|  | 27.5 | 30.2 | 37.9 | 27.8 | Less |
|  | 14.0 | 15.9 | ** | 4.4 | Don't know/no opinion |
|  | (229) | (126) | (253) | (205) | Weighted N |
| 55-64 Only | 21.7 | 15.6 | 35.0 | 36.8 | More |
|  | 29.5 | 32.2 | 35.0 | 26.8 | Same as now |
|  | 27.7 | 37.8 | 30.1 | 33.2 | Less |
|  | 21.1 | 14.4 | ** | 3.2 | Don't know/no opinion |
|  | (166) | (90) | (226) | (190) | Weighted N |
| 65 and older | 19.8 | 16.8 | 31.0 | 28.4 | More |
|  | 24.4 | 29.2 | 32.0 | 41.9 | Same as now |
|  | 25.4 | 23.0 | 37.1 | 22.3 | Less |
|  | 30.5 | 31.0 | ** | 7.4 | Don't know/no opinion |
|  | (197) | (113) | (197) | (215) | Weighted N |

** Code distinction not made.
Youngest age group coded "Under 25" in 1969m.
Age coded for head of household only in 1961m and 1969m.

Table 8.41
How Much Should the Government Spend on Space Exploration?
Total Population

QUESTION: How about space exploration?  Do you think the government should
be spending more money, less money, or about the same amount on space
exploration as it does now?

|  |  | Year | | |
|---|---|---|---|---|
|  |  | 1961m | 1969m | 1973c |
| More | (5) | 26.5% | 8.5% | 8.9% |
| Same as now | (3) | 28.0 | 32.4 | 25.6 |
| Less | (1) | 32.1 | 59.1 | 63.8 |
| Don't know/no opinion |  | 13.4 | ** | 1.8 |
| Total |  | 100% | 100% | 100% |
| Weighted N |  | 943 | 1433 | 1344 |
| Unweighted N |  | 943 | 1433 | 1344 |
| Mean |  | 2.87 | 1.99 | 1.88 |
| Standard Deviation |  | 1.64 | 1.30 | 1.31 |

** Code distinction not made.
"No opinion" was explicitly offered as a response in 1961m.

Figure 8.12
Space Exploration Expenditures--Total Population

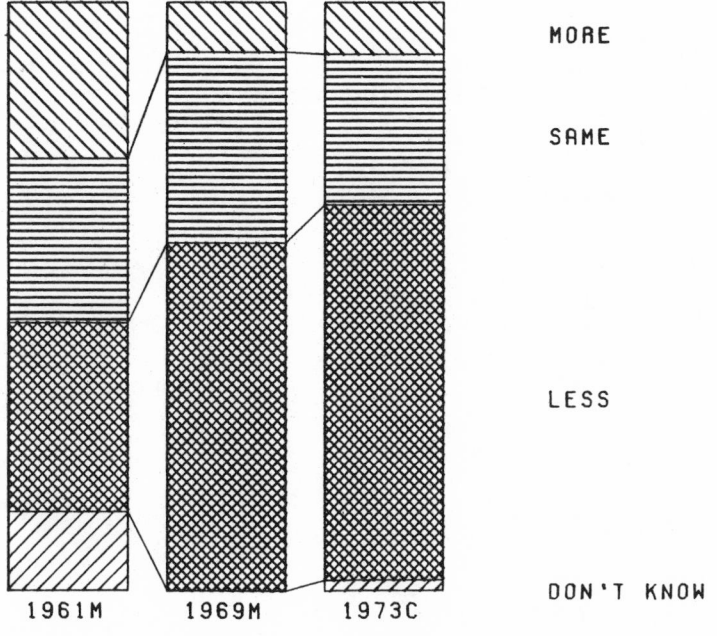

MORE

SAME

LESS

DON'T KNOW

1961M     1969M     1973C

Figure 8.13
Space Exploration Expenditures by Race of R

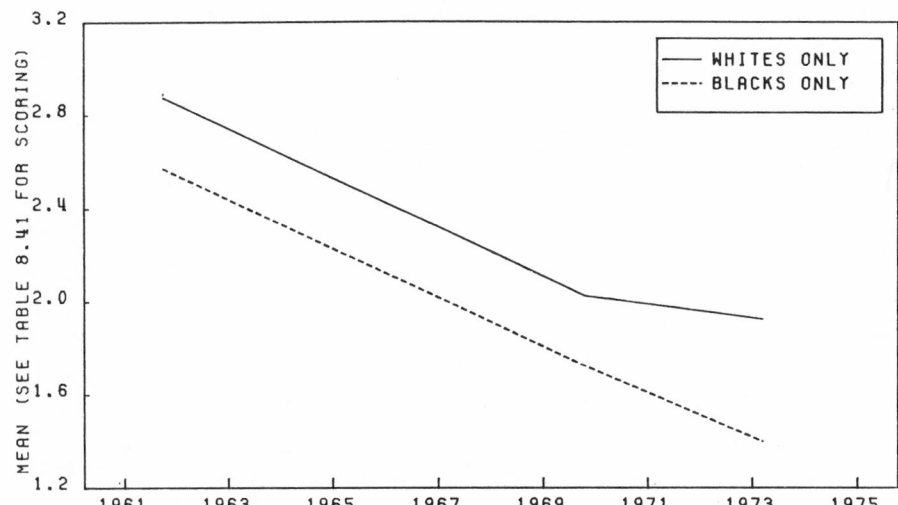

Table 8.42
How Much Should the Government Spend on Space Exploration?
Sex of Respondent

|            | Year |      |       |                         |
|------------|------|------|-------|-------------------------|
|            | 1961m | 1969m | 1973c |                        |
| Males Only | 32.0% | 9.5% | 13.0% | More                   |
|            | 27.1 | 33.9 | 28.4 | Same as now             |
|            | 30.4 | 56.6 | 57.2 | Less                    |
|            | 10.5 | ** | 1.4 | Don't know/no opinion      |
|            | (391) | (1046) | (577) | Weighted N             |
| Females Only | 22.6 | 6.0 | 5.7 | More                   |
|            | 28.6 | 28.2 | 23.5 | Same as now             |
|            | 33.3 | 65.8 | 68.7 | Less                    |
|            | 15.4 | ** | 2.1 | Don't know/no opinion      |
|            | (552) | (386) | (767) | Weighted N             |

Table 8.43
Race of Respondent

|            | 1961m | 1969m | 1973c |                        |
|------------|------|------|-------|-------------------------|
| Whites Only | 27.3% | 8.6% | 9.1% | More                   |
|            | 28.7 | 34.0 | 27.4 | Same as now             |
|            | 32.8 | 57.4 | 62.1 | Less                    |
|            | 11.3 | ** | 1.3 | Don't know/no opinion      |
|            | (858) | (1265) | (1119) | Weighted N            |
| Blacks Only | 16.4 | 8.6 | 5.9 | More                   |
|            | 16.4 | 19.1 | 7.6 | Same as now             |
|            | 29.9 | 72.4 | 83.9 | Less                    |
|            | 37.3 | ** | 2.5 | Don't know/no opinion      |
|            | (67) | (152) | (118) | Weighted N             |

* Code distinction not made.

Table 8.44
How Much Should the Government Spend on Space Exploration?
Education of Respondent

|  | Year | | | |
|---|---|---|---|---|
|  | 1961m | 1969m | 1973c | |
| Grade School Only | 18.9% | 5.0% | 5.7% | More |
|  | 19.9 | 22.6 | 18.5 | Same as now |
|  | 38.3 | 72.4 | 68.2 | Less |
|  | 23.0 | ** | 7.6 | Don't know/no opinion |
|  | (196) | (319) | (157) | Weighted N |
|  |  |  |  |  |
| High School Only | 34.7 | 9.5 | 6.9 | More |
|  | 26.2 | 30.5 | 22.1 | Same as now |
|  | 27.6 | 60.0 | 70.1 | Less |
|  | 11.6 | ** | 1.0 | Don't know/no opinion |
|  | (225) | (568) | (625) | Weighted N |
|  |  |  |  |  |
| College Only | 38.4 | 11.2 | 14.1 | More |
|  | 29.6 | 44.5 | 33.7 | Same as now |
|  | 25.6 | 44.3 | 52.0 | Less |
|  | 6.4 | ** | 0.3 | Don't know/no opinion |
|  | (125) | (375) | (398) | Weighted N |

** Code distinction not made.
Education coded for head of household only in 1961m and 1969m.

Figure 8.14
Space Exploration Expenditures by Education of R

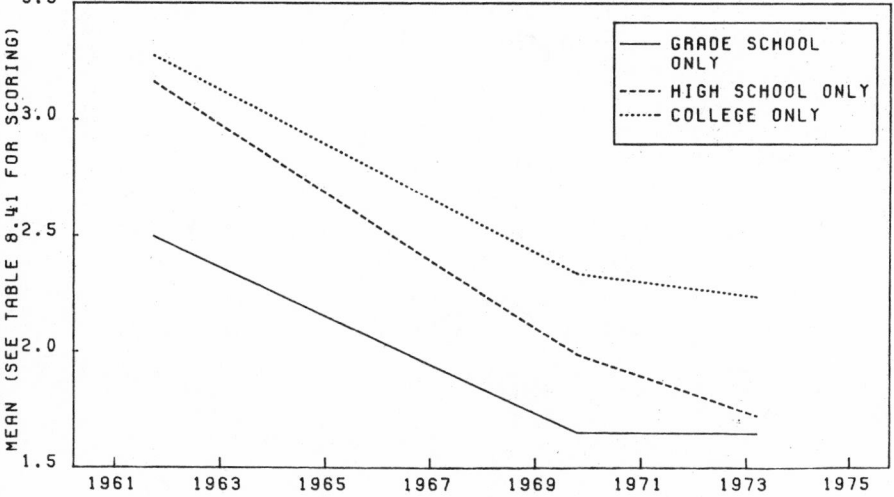

Table 8.45
How Much Should the Government Spend on Space Exploration?
Age of Respondent

|  | Year | | | |
|---|---|---|---|---|
|  | 1961m | 1969m | 1973c | |
| 18-24 Only | 43.2% | 14.4% | 10.9% | More |
|  | 32.4 | 43.2 | 31.3 | Same as now |
|  | 18.9 | 42.3 | 57.2 | Less |
|  | 5.4 | ** | 0.5 | Don't know/no opinion |
|  | (37) | (111) | (201) | Weighted N |
| 25-34 Only | 43.1 | 11.8 | 12.9 | More |
|  | 24.5 | 37.0 | 31.3 | Same as now |
|  | 25.5 | 51.2 | 55.5 | Less |
|  | 6.9 | ** | 0.3 | Don't know/no opinion |
|  | (102) | (254) | (310) | Weighted N |
| 35-44 Only | 32.1 | 8.5 | 9.3 | More |
|  | 25.9 | 38.1 | 26.6 | Same as now |
|  | 27.2 | 53.5 | 62.1 | Less |
|  | 14.8 | ** | 1.9 | Don't know/no opinion |
|  | (81) | (260) | (214) | Weighted N |
| 45-54 Only | 34.9 | 10.1 | 7.7 | More |
|  | 20.6 | 33.1 | 28.0 | Same as now |
|  | 35.7 | 56.8 | 62.3 | Less |
|  | 8.7 | ** | 1.9 | Don't know/no opinion |
|  | (126) | (257) | (207) | Weighted N |
| 55-64 Only | 20.0 | 6.1 | 5.7 | More |
|  | 35.6 | 24.0 | 18.7 | Same as now |
|  | 31.1 | 69.9 | 73.6 | Less |
|  | 13.3 | ** | 2.1 | Don't know/no opinion |
|  | (90) | (229) | (193) | Weighted N |
| 65 and older | 13.3 | 4.8 | 4.2 | More |
|  | 17.7 | 22.6 | 15.3 | Same as now |
|  | 37.2 | 72.6 | 75.8 | Less |
|  | 31.9 | ** | 4.7 | Don't know/no opinion |
|  | (113) | (208) | (215) | Weighted N |

** Code distinction not made.
Youngest age group coded "Under 25" in 1969m.
Age coded for head of household only in 1961m and 1969m.

## Chapter 9. War And Peace

We close with a collation of items dealing with the reactions of the American public to postures of the country concerning war and peace. The series tend to be somewhat fragmented by the changing reality of the foreign involvements of the United States. In periods when we are participating in a foreign war, as in Korea or Vietnam, interest turns to questions of public judgment as to the wisdom of the specific involvement. In periods of peace, items are posed about the chances of avoiding another war.

The first item evaluating our participation in Korea is the shortest series in the volume, involving only two applications a mere year apart. We include it, however, because exactly the same question was later applied to our Vietnam involvement, generating a somewhat longer series, and hence levels of support can be compared across the two wars. Declining public enthusiasm, or what may reasonably be seen as "war-weariness," comes through very clearly in the Vietnam series. This decline in support is progressive over the series, but the major downturn occurs in 1968, after the Tet offensive of that spring, launched by the enemy, showed surprising strength. Public support for the Korean involvement looks somewhat shakier at a comparable point a year or two into the conflict, but both measurements occurred after the public had been stunned by the vigor of the Yalu River offensive in the fall of 1950.

The next several items (tables 9.11-9.20) deal with the public's estimate during periods of peace as to the likelihood of the outbreak of war involving the country or, in the Vietnam period, the chances of the nation's getting into a "bigger" war. These items show a marked sensitivity to major changes in the international climate. Thus, for example, in 1960, after the discovery of the U-2 reconnaissance flights over the Soviet Union, expressions of worry about the United States getting into another war increased considerably, and judgments as to the likelihood of the country avoiding war plummeted, relative to assessments in 1956 or 1964. Perceived changes in the likelihood of the spread of the Vietnam conflict to a larger war were generally for the worse throughout the later 1960s and only abated in 1972. Nonetheless, more optimism about the chances of avoiding war were expressed in 1956--near the peak of the "Cold War"--than even in 1972. Throughout these series, there are signs that the young are more apprehensive about the possibility of war than are older people, and women consistently express slightly more concern than men.

The final series deals less with war per se than with perceptions of recent changes in the strength of the United States' position on the world scene. The series runs only from 1958 to 1968 and is reasonably constant over much of this period despite a slight increase in feelings of loss of national strength associated with the crises and confrontations of 1960. A major collapse is registered in the final reading of the series in 1968, however, and it seems likely that this dismay at the deterioration of the American position was integrally bound up with the unexpected reverses of the Vietnam War.

Table 9.1
Were We Right to Fight in Korea?
Total Population

QUESTION: Do you think we did the right thing in getting
into the fighting in Korea or should we have stayed out?

|  | | Year | |
|---|---|---|---|
|  | | 1951f | 1952n |
| Yes,did the right thing | (1) | 43.5% | 40.6% |
| Pro-con | (3) | 3.4 | 5.5 |
| No,should have stayed out | (5) | 41.9 | 42.5 |
| Don't know | | 11.2 | 11.4 |
| Total | | 100% | 100% |
| Weighted N | | 967 | 1738 |
| Unweighted N | | 967 | 1738 |
| Mean | | 2.96 | 3.04 |
| Standard Deviation | | 1.96 | 1.94 |

Figure 9.1
Korean Involvement--Total Population

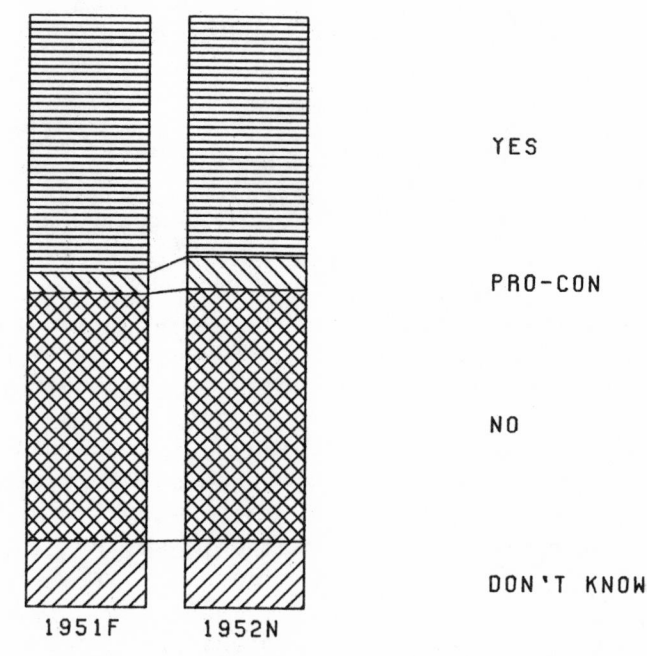

YES

PRO-CON

NO

DON'T KNOW

1951F     1952N

Table 9.2
Were We Right to Fight in Korea?
Sex of Respondent

|  | Year 1951f | 1952n |  |
|---|---|---|---|
| Males Only | 48.3% | 49.6% | Yes,did the right thing |
|  | 3.4 | 4.8 | Pro-con |
|  | 38.7 | 38.1 | No,should have stayed out |
|  | 9.7 | 7.5 | Don't know |
|  | (445) | (789) | Weighted N |
| Females Only | 39.5 | 33.1 | Yes,did the right thing |
|  | 3.4 | 6.1 | Pro-con |
|  | 44.6 | 46.2 | No,should have stayed out |
|  | 12.5 | 14.6 | Don't know |
|  | (522) | (949) | Weighted N |

Table 9.3
Race of Respondent

|  | 1951f | 1952n |  |
|---|---|---|---|
| Whites Only | 44.6% | 41.2% | Yes,did the right thing |
|  | 3.5 | 5.9 | Pro-con |
|  | 42.0 | 42.5 | No,should have stayed out |
|  | 9.8 | 10.4 | Don't know |
|  | (885) | (1566) | Weighted N |
| Blacks Only | 30.6 | 33.9 | Yes,did the right thing |
|  | 1.4 | 2.4 | Pro-con |
|  | 38.9 | 43.6 | No,should have stayed out |
|  | 29.2 | 20.0 | Don't know |
|  | (72) | (165) | Weighted N |

Table 9.4
Were We Right to Fight in Korea?
Education of Respondent

|  | Year | | |
|---|---|---|---|
|  | 1951f | 1952n |  |
| Grade School Only | 36.7% | 30.7% | Yes,did the right thing |
|  | 1.9 | 4.7 | Pro-con |
|  | 45.5 | 50.6 | No,should have stayed out |
|  | 15.9 | 13.9 | Don't know |
|  | (365) | (717) | Weighted N |
| High School Only | 45.1 | 44.8 | Yes,did the right thing |
|  | 4.8 | 5.1 | Pro-con |
|  | 41.2 | 39.2 | No,should have stayed out |
|  | 8.9 | 10.9 | Don't know |
|  | (437) | (763) | Weighted N |
| College Only | 54.4 | 56.0 | Yes,did the right thing |
|  | 3.2 | 9.1 | Pro-con |
|  | 35.4 | 29.4 | No,should have stayed out |
|  | 7.0 | 5.6 | Don't know |
|  | (158) | (252) | Weighted N |

War And Peace

Table 9.5
Were We Right to Fight in Korea?
Age of Respondent

|  | Year | | |
| --- | --- | --- | --- |
|  | 1951f | 1952n | |
| 18-24 Only | 55.0% | 52.6% | Yes, did the right thing |
|  | 0.0 | 6.0 | Pro-con |
|  | 30.0 | 31.0 | No, should have stayed out |
|  | 15.0 | 10.3 | Don't know |
|  | (60) | (116) | Weighted N |
| 25-34 Only | 45.9 | 49.0 | Yes, did the right thing |
|  | 5.0 | 5.3 | Pro-con |
|  | 37.6 | 36.1 | No, should have stayed out |
|  | 11.6 | 9.6 | Don't know |
|  | (242) | (416) | Weighted N |
| 35-44 Only | 46.3 | 43.1 | Yes, did the right thing |
|  | 4.8 | 6.5 | Pro-con |
|  | 41.0 | 38.8 | No, should have stayed out |
|  | 7.9 | 11.6 | Don't know |
|  | (227) | (415) | Weighted N |
| 45-54 Only | 39.6 | 39.0 | Yes, did the right thing |
|  | 2.6 | 4.3 | Pro-con |
|  | 44.9 | 47.3 | No, should have stayed out |
|  | 12.9 | 9.3 | Don't know |
|  | (303) | (300) | Weighted N |
| 55-64 Only | ** | 30.7 | Yes, did the right thing |
|  | ** | 5.4 | Pro-con |
|  | ** | 51.0 | No, should have stayed out |
|  | ** | 12.9 | Don't know |
|  | ** | (241) | Weighted N |
| 65 and older only | 38.9 | 27.9 | Yes, did the right thing |
|  | 1.5 | 4.9 | Pro-con |
|  | 49.6 | 51.3 | No, should have stayed out |
|  | 9.9 | 15.9 | Don't know |
|  | (131) | (226) | Weighted N |

** Code distinction not made.
Age group coded "45-64" in 1951f.

Table 9.6
Were We Right to Fight in Vietnam?
Total Population

QUESTION: Do you think we did the right thing in getting into the fighting in
Vietnam or should we have stayed out?

|  | | Year | | | | |
|---|---|---|---|---|---|---|
|  | | 1964n | 1966n | 1968n | 1970n | 1972n |
| Yes, did the right thing | (5) | 47.9% | 47.6% | 30.6% | 31.2% | 28.8% |
| It depends | (3) | 1.1 | 0.8 | 1.2 | 1.0 | 5.6 |
| No, should have stayed out | (1) | 29.9 | 31.1 | 51.8 | 49.5 | 57.0 |
| Don't know | | 21.1 | 20.5 | 16.4 | 18.3 | 8.6 |
| Total | | 100% | 100% | 100% | 100% | 100% |
| Weighted N | | 3467 | 1188 | 3079 | 1859 | 2699 |
| Unweighted N | | 1342 | 1188 | 1661 | 1680 | 2699 |
| Mean | | 3.46 | 3.41 | 2.49 | 2.55 | 2.38 |
| Standard Deviation | | 1.93 | 1.95 | 1.92 | 1.94 | 1.84 |

1964n, 1968n, and 1970n include Black supplement.
1964n and 1966n include only those respondents answering "Yes" to the question
  "Have you been paying any attention to what is going on in Vietnam?".

Figure 9.2
Vietnam Involvement--Total Population

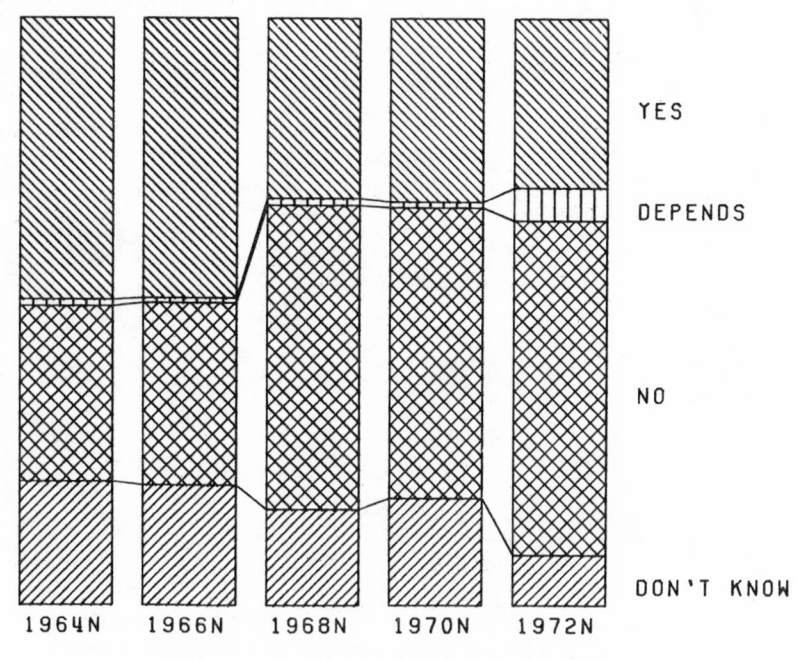

Table 9.7
Were We Right to Fight in Vietnam?
Sex of Respondent

|            |        |        | Year   |        |        |                            |
|------------|--------|--------|--------|--------|--------|----------------------------|
|            | 1964n  | 1966n  | 1968n  | 1970n  | 1972n  |                            |
| Males Only | 54.4%  | 55.7%  | 37.7%  | 35.3%  | 32.0%  | Yes, did the right thing   |
|            | 1.4    | 0.6    | 1.5    | 1.3    | 6.6    | It depends                 |
|            | 27.5   | 30.0   | 48.7   | 50.5   | 56.0   | No, should have stayed out |
|            | 16.8   | 13.8   | 12.1   | 12.8   | 5.4    | Don't know                 |
|            | (1613) | (537)  | (1347) | (809)  | (1165) | Weighted N                 |
| Females Only | 42.2 | 40.9   | 25.0   | 28.0   | 26.3   | Yes, did the right thing   |
|            | 0.9    | 0.9    | 1.0    | 0.7    | 4.9    | It depends                 |
|            | 32.0   | 32.1   | 54.3   | 48.8   | 57.8   | No, should have stayed out |
|            | 24.9   | 26.1   | 19.7   | 22.6   | 11.0   | Don't know                 |
|            | (1854) | (651)  | (1732) | (1051) | (1534) | Weighted N                 |

Table 9.8
Race of Respondent

|             |        |        |        |        |        |                            |
|-------------|--------|--------|--------|--------|--------|----------------------------|
|             | 1964n  | 1966n  | 1968n  | 1970n  | 1972n  |                            |
| Whites Only | 48.3%  | 48.3%  | 31.2%  | 32.6%  | 30.2%  | Yes, did the right thing   |
|             | 1.1    | 0.8    | 1.4    | 1.1    | 5.8    | It depends                 |
|             | 29.4   | 30.8   | 51.5   | 48.2   | 55.3   | No, should have stayed out |
|             | 21.1   | 20.2   | 15.9   | 18.1   | 8.7    | Don't know                 |
|             | (3210) | (1062) | (2760) | (1663) | (2391) | Weighted N                 |
| Blacks Only | 43.2   | 38.4   | 23.3   | 17.2   | 16.9   | Yes, did the right thing   |
|             | 1.3    | 0.9    | 0.0    | 0.0    | 4.1    | It depends                 |
|             | 34.7   | 35.7   | 55.2   | 63.4   | 71.5   | No, should have stayed out |
|             | 20.8   | 25.0   | 21.5   | 19.4   | 7.5    | Don't know                 |
|             | (236)  | (112)  | (279)  | (167)  | (267)  | Weighted N                 |

Figure 9.3
Vietnam Involvement by Sex of R

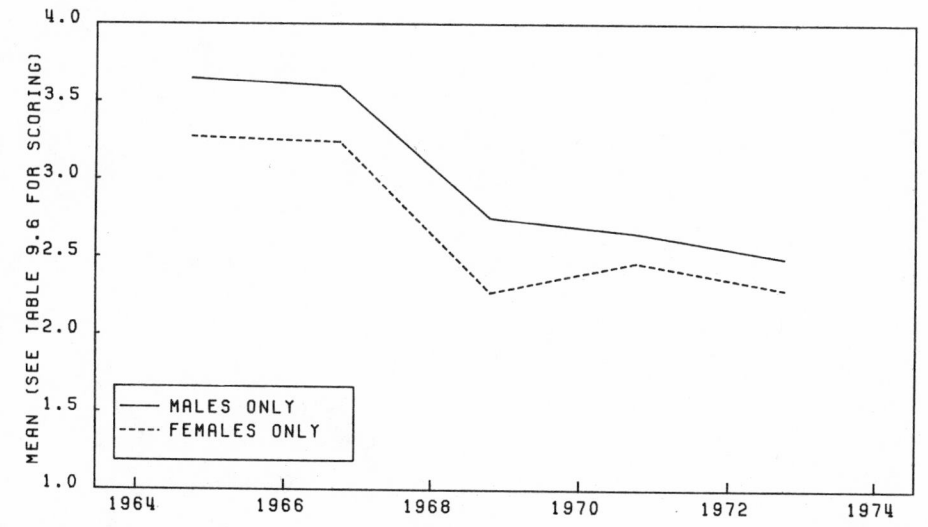

Figure 9.4
Vietnam Involvement by Race of R

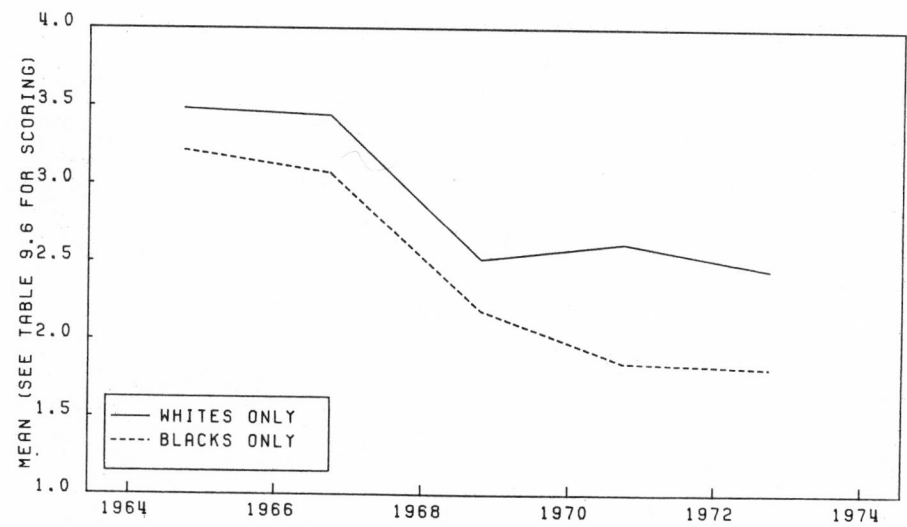

War And Peace

Table 9.9
Were We Right to Fight in Vietnam?
Education of Respondent

|  | Year | | | | | |
|---|---|---|---|---|---|---|
|  | 1964n | 1966n | 1968n | 1970n | 1972n | |
| Grade School Only | 33.4% | 32.2% | 19.0% | 18.7% | 18.7% | Yes,did the right thing |
|  | 0.0 | 1.4 | 0.6 | 0.6 | 6.5 | It depends |
|  | 43.1 | 38.5 | 56.9 | 56.2 | 62.9 | No,should have stayed out |
|  | 23.5 | 28.0 | 23.6 | 24.5 | 11.9 | Don't know |
|  | (652) | (286) | (696) | (433) | (539) | Weighted N |
| High School Only | 48.2 | 49.9 | 32.6 | 33.5 | 29.9 | Yes,did the right thing |
|  | 1.1 | 0.3 | 0.9 | 1.0 | 5.1 | It depends |
|  | 27.8 | 29.7 | 50.0 | 46.2 | 56.3 | No,should have stayed out |
|  | 22.8 | 20.0 | 16.4 | 19.2 | 8.7 | Don't know |
|  | (1858) | (609) | (1538) | (943) | (1370) | Weighted N |
| College Only | 57.2 | 58.3 | 36.6 | 37.8 | 33.7 | Yes,did the right thing |
|  | 1.9 | 1.0 | 2.4 | 1.3 | 6.0 | It depends |
|  | 24.9 | 26.2 | 51.1 | 49.7 | 54.4 | No,should have stayed out |
|  | 16.0 | 14.5 | 9.9 | 11.2 | 6.0 | Don't know |
|  | (939) | (290) | (838) | (478) | (787) | Weighted N |

Figure 9.5
Vietnam Involvement by Education of R

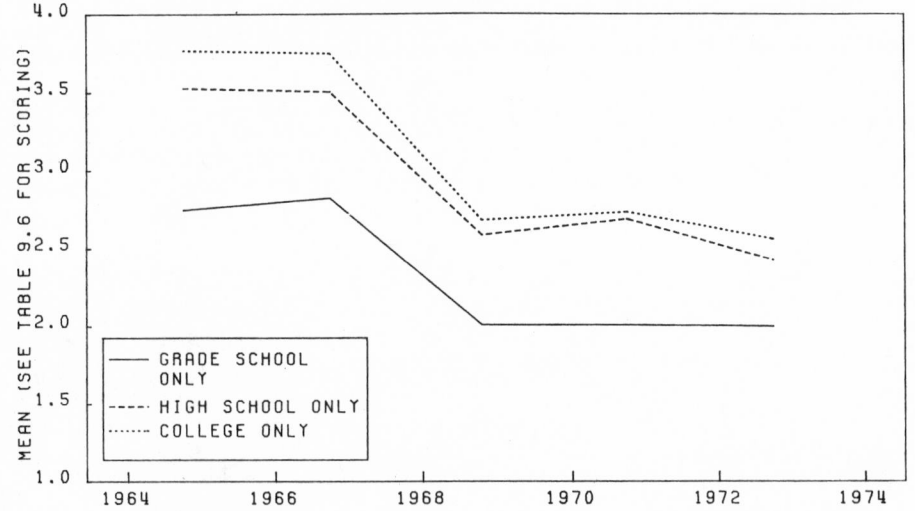

Figure 9.6
Vietnam Involvement by Age of R

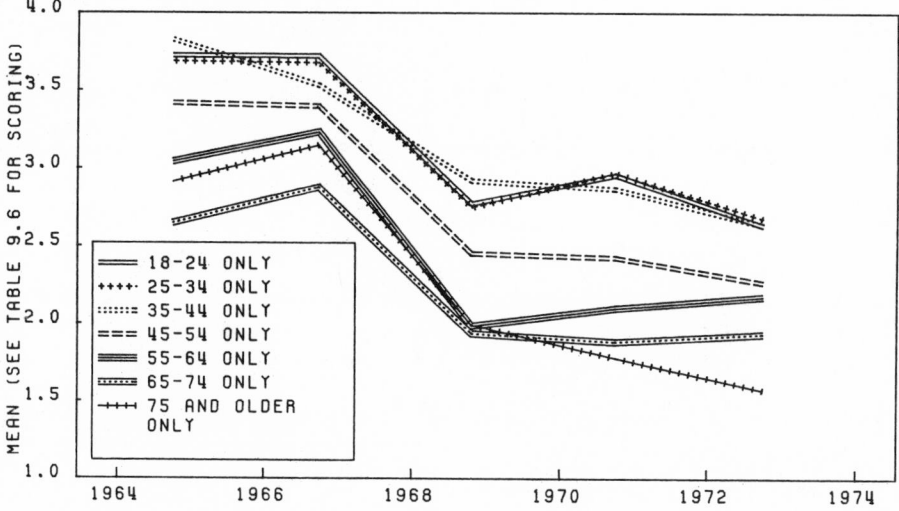

Table 9.10
Were We Right to Fight in Vietnam?
Age of Respondent

|  | Year | | | | | |
|---|---|---|---|---|---|---|
|  | 1964n | 1966n | 1968n | 1970n | 1972n | |
| 18-24 Only | 54.1% | 55.9% | 38.3% | 42.1% | 36.2% | Yes,did the right thing |
|  | 1.6 | 0.9 | 0.9 | 1.4 | 4.3 | It depends |
|  | 25.0 | 26.1 | 48.3 | 44.0 | 53.5 | No,should have stayed out |
|  | 19.3 | 17.1 | 12.6 | 12.4 | 6.0 | Don't know |
|  | (244) | (111) | (230) | (252) | (398) | Weighted N |
| 25-34 Only | 57.2 | 57.2 | 37.8 | 41.1 | 35.8 | Yes,did the right thing |
|  | 2.0 | 0.0 | 2.0 | 1.0 | 4.9 | It depends |
|  | 27.5 | 28.4 | 49.0 | 42.5 | 52.0 | No,should have stayed out |
|  | 13.3 | 14.4 | 11.2 | 15.4 | 7.3 | Don't know |
|  | (738) | (215) | (606) | (366) | (575) | Weighted N |
| 35-44 Only | 56.2 | 52.9 | 40.3 | 36.5 | 33.3 | Yes,did the right thing |
|  | 1.3 | 1.2 | 1.2 | 0.8 | 9.0 | It depends |
|  | 23.0 | 30.5 | 43.7 | 41.8 | 50.2 | No,should have stayed out |
|  | 19.5 | 15.4 | 14.7 | 20.9 | 7.5 | Don't know |
|  | (799) | (259) | (647) | (319) | (442) | Weighted N |
| 45-54 Only | 45.6 | 45.0 | 28.3 | 30.1 | 26.9 | Yes,did the right thing |
|  | 0.0 | 0.8 | 0.6 | 1.1 | 5.4 | It depends |
|  | 29.9 | 30.0 | 49.8 | 54.8 | 61.2 | No,should have stayed out |
|  | 24.6 | 24.2 | 21.2 | 13.9 | 6.5 | Don't know |
|  | (680) | (240) | (622) | (319) | (446) | Weighted N |
| 55-64 Only | 36.9 | 41.6 | 19.5 | 21.1 | 22.9 | Yes,did the right thing |
|  | 0.6 | 1.2 | 1.8 | 1.2 | 6.2 | It depends |
|  | 35.3 | 32.9 | 61.4 | 56.4 | 59.2 | No,should have stayed out |
|  | 27.2 | 24.2 | 17.3 | 21.3 | 11.7 | Don't know |
|  | (529) | (161) | (456) | (293) | (385) | Weighted N |
| 65-74 Only | 30.6 | 33.1 | 19.0 | 16.5 | 17.8 | Yes,did the right thing |
|  | 2.1 | 0.7 | 0.6 | 0.6 | 5.5 | It depends |
|  | 44.2 | 37.5 | 62.8 | 58.9 | 64.7 | No,should have stayed out |
|  | 23.1 | 28.7 | 17.6 | 24.0 | 12.0 | Don't know |
|  | (337) | (136) | (347) | (193) | (275) | Weighted N |
| 75 And Older Only | 32.6 | 38.6 | 18.8 | 14.0 | 11.5 | Yes,did the right thing |
|  | 0.0 | 0.0 | 1.3 | 0.0 | 1.9 | It depends |
|  | 35.6 | 33.3 | 58.1 | 57.5 | 73.7 | No,should have stayed out |
|  | 31.9 | 28.1 | 21.9 | 28.5 | 12.8 | Don't know |
|  | (135) | (57) | (160) | (107) | (156) | Weighted N |

Table 9.11
Chances of Staying Out of War
Total Population

QUESTION: During the last few years, do you think our chances of
staying out of war have been getting better, getting worse, or
stayed the same?

|  |  | Year | | |
|---|---|---|---|---|
|  |  | 1956n | 1960n | 1964n |
| Getting better | (1) | 42.5% | 18.9% | 31.2% |
| Stayed the same | (3) | 41.1 | 41.3 | 47.9 |
| Getting worse | (5) | 12.6 | 36.2 | 17.9 |
| Don't know |  | 3.8 | 3.5 | 3.0 |
| Total |  | 100% | 100% | 100% |
| Weighted N |  | 1755 | 1916 | 4598 |
| Unweighted N |  | 1755 | 1156 | 1811 |
| Mean |  | 2.38 | 3.36 | 2.73 |
| Standard Deviation |  | 1.38 | 1.47 | 1.40 |

1964n includes Black supplement.

Figure 9.7
Chances of Avoiding War--Total Population

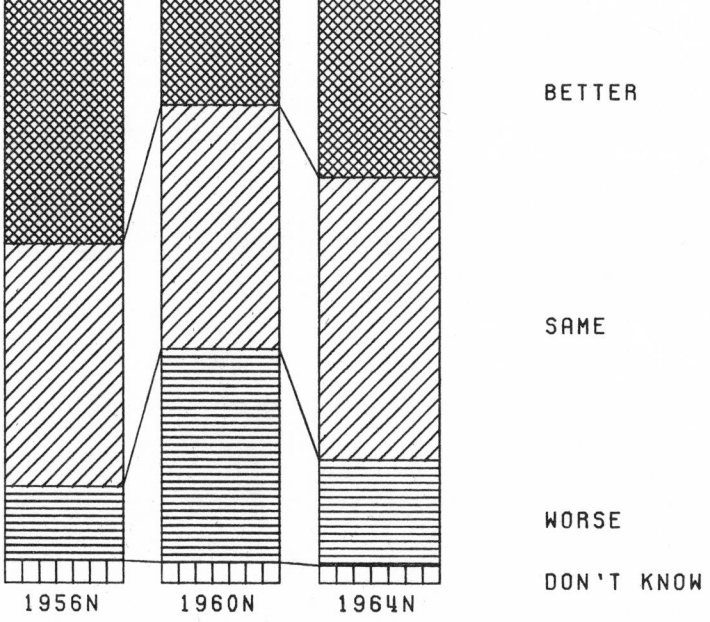

BETTER

SAME

WORSE

DON'T KNOW

1956N    1960N    1964N

Table 9.12
Chances of Staying Out of War
Sex of Respondent

|  | Year | | |
|---|---|---|---|
|  | 1956n | 1960n | 1964n |
| Males Only | 47.0% | 23.5% | 36.3% Getting better |
|  | 38.8 | 46.0 | 45.3  Stayed the same |
|  | 14.2 | 30.4 | 18.4  Getting worse |
|  | (768) | (854) | (2048) Weighted N |
|  |  |  |  |
| Females Only | 41.8 | 16.3 | 28.6  Getting better |
|  | 45.9 | 40.1 | 52.9  Stayed the same |
|  | 12.3 | 43.6 | 18.5  Getting worse |
|  | (921) | (994) | (2412) Weighted N |

Table 9.13
Race of Respondent

|  | 1956n | 1960n | 1964n |
|---|---|---|---|
| Whites Only | 45.9% | 19.7% | 31.5% Getting better |
|  | 41.3 | 42.3 | 49.6  Stayed the same |
|  | 12.7 | 37.9 | 18.9  Getting worse |
|  | (1546) | (1684) | (4026) Weighted N |
|  |  |  |  |
| Blacks Only | 24.8 | 20.5 | 38.7  Getting better |
|  | 58.4 | 47.3 | 47.4  Stayed the same |
|  | 16.8 | 32.2 | 14.0  Getting worse |
|  | (137) | (146) | (401) Weighted N |

Table 9.14
Chances of Staying Out of War
Education of Respondent

|  | Year | | | |
|---|---|---|---|---|
|  | 1956n | 1960n | 1964n | |
| Grade School Only | 40.0% | 20.1% | 33.0% | Getting better |
|  | 47.8 | 45.8 | 53.2 | Stayed the same |
|  | 12.2 | 34.1 | 13.8 | Getting worse |
|  | (500) | (546) | (1086) | Weighted N |
| High School Only | 40.8 | 15.7 | 30.9 | Getting better |
|  | 45.6 | 43.0 | 49.6 | Stayed the same |
|  | 13.5 | 41.4 | 19.5 | Getting worse |
|  | (857) | (894) | (2279) | Weighted N |
| College Only | 59.3 | 27.8 | 34.2 | Getting better |
|  | 27.5 | 38.6 | 45.5 | Stayed the same |
|  | 13.3 | 33.7 | 20.3 | Getting worse |
|  | (324) | (407) | (1068) | Weighted N |

Table 9.15
Chances of Staying Out of War
Age of Respondent

|  | Year | | | |
|---|---|---|---|---|
|  | 1956n | 1960n | 1964n | |
| 18-24 Only | 37.1% | 14.8% | 27.5% | Getting better |
|  | 47.6 | 35.2 | 39.0 | Stayed the same |
|  | 15.2 | 50.0 | 33.5 | Getting worse |
|  | (105) | (54) | (349) | Weighted N |
| 25-34 Only | 39.7 | 17.9 | 28.1 | Getting better |
|  | 45.5 | 40.7 | 53.6 | Stayed the same |
|  | 14.8 | 41.4 | 18.3 | Getting worse |
|  | (413) | (403) | (911) | Weighted N |
| 35-44 Only | 43.3 | 16.2 | 36.5 | Getting better |
|  | 44.0 | 46.4 | 46.6 | Stayed the same |
|  | 12.6 | 37.4 | 17.0 | Getting worse |
|  | (427) | (470) | (990) | Weighted N |
| 45-54 Only | 44.2 | 19.5 | 32.0 | Getting better |
|  | 41.4 | 39.6 | 47.9 | Stayed the same |
|  | 14.3 | 40.9 | 20.1 | Getting worse |
|  | (321) | (364) | (885) | Weighted N |
| 55-64 Only | 55.0 | 24.8 | 36.5 | Getting better |
|  | 35.9 | 41.6 | 48.9 | Stayed the same |
|  | 9.1 | 33.6 | 14.5 | Getting worse |
|  | (220) | (274) | (654) | Weighted N |
| 65-74 Only | 47.6 | 28.2 | 33.6 | Getting better |
|  | 41.3 | 42.1 | 51.8 | Stayed the same |
|  | 11.1 | 29.7 | 14.5 | Getting worse |
|  | (126) | (202) | (434) | Weighted N |
| 75 And Older Only | 49.2 | 14.3 | 20.3 | Getting better |
|  | 37.3 | 57.1 | 63.5 | Stayed the same |
|  | 13.6 | 28.6 | 16.2 | Getting worse |
|  | (59) | (77) | (222) | Weighted N |

Table 9.16
Chances of Getting into a Bigger War
Total Population

QUESTION: How about the chances of our country getting into a bigger
war?  Compared to a few years ago, do you think we are more likely,
less likely, or have about the same chances to get into a bigger war?

|  |  | Year | | | |
|  |  | 1966n | 1968n | 1970n | 1972n |
|---|---|---|---|---|---|
| More likely | (5) | 33.6% | 28.7% | 30.2% | 19.6% |
| About the same | (3) | 32.7 | 40.3 | 32.1 | 29.1 |
| Less likely | (1) | 21.3 | 17.6 | 25.7 | 41.3 |
| Don't know/Depends |  | 12.4 | 13.3 | 11.9 | 10.0 |
| Total |  | 100% | 100% | 100% | 100% |
| Weighted N |  | 1285 | 3089 | 952 | 1356 |
| Unweighted N |  | 1285 | 1665 | 994 | 1356 |
| Mean |  | 3.28 | 3.26 | 3.10 | 2.52 |
| Standard Deviation |  | 1.56 | 1.44 | 1.59 | 1.57 |

1968n and 1970n include Black supplement.

Figure 9.8
Chances of Bigger War--Total Population

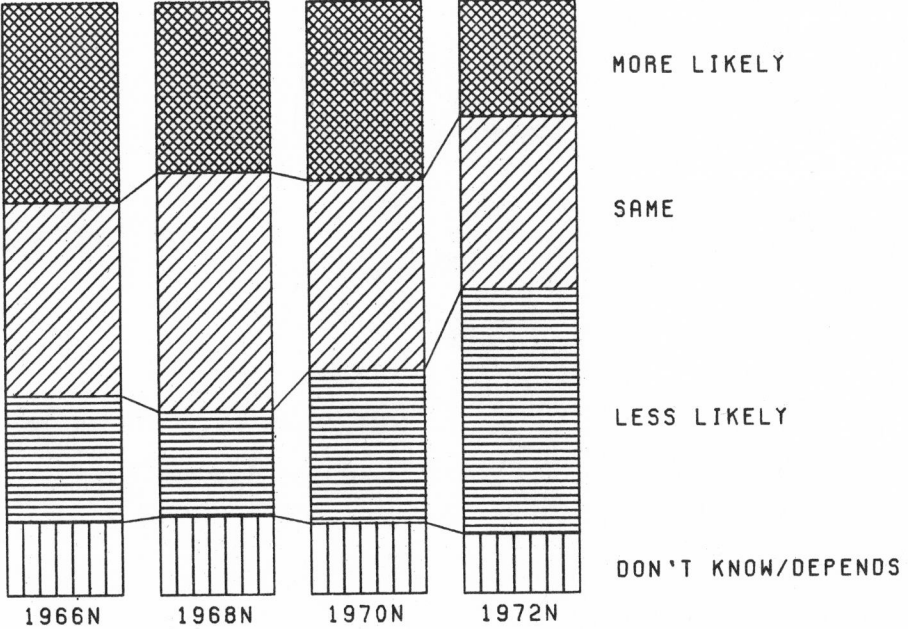

Table 9.17
Chances of Getting into a Bigger War
Sex of Respondent

|  |  | Year |  |  |  |
|  | 1966n | 1968n | 1970n | 1972n |  |
|---|---|---|---|---|---|
| Males Only | 32.2% | 26.1% | 28.6% | 16.3% | More likely |
|  | 31.5 | 40.5 | 30.0 | 28.5 | About the same |
|  | 27.1 | 23.3 | 31.5 | 49.1 | Less likely |
|  | 9.3 | 10.1 | 9.9 | 6.1 | Don't know/Depends |
|  | (569) | (1354) | (424) | (578) | Weighted N |
| Females Only | 34.8 | 30.8 | 31.5 | 22.1 | More likely |
|  | 33.7 | 40.2 | 33.8 | 29.4 | About the same |
|  | 16.8 | 13.2 | 21.1 | 35.5 | Less likely |
|  | 14.8 | 15.8 | 13.6 | 13.0 | Don't know/Depends |
|  | (716) | (1735) | (527) | (778) | Weighted N |

Table 9.18
Race of Respondent

|  | 1966n | 1968n | 1970n | 1972n |  |
|---|---|---|---|---|---|
| Whites Only | 33.2% | 28.6% | 29.3% | 18.2% | More likely |
|  | 33.0 | 41.3 | 31.9 | 28.4 | About the same |
|  | 22.3 | 18.7 | 27.8 | 43.9 | Less likely |
|  | 11.5 | 11.4 | 11.0 | 9.5 | Don't know/Depends |
|  | (1132) | (2766) | (853) | (1209) | Weighted N |
| Blacks Only | 36.8 | 31.8 | 35.9 | 32.3 | More likely |
|  | 32.4 | 30.7 | 32.7 | 36.2 | About the same |
|  | 12.5 | 8.1 | 8.9 | 18.5 | Less likely |
|  | 18.4 | 29.3 | 22.4 | 13.1 | Don't know/Depends |
|  | (136) | (283) | (84) | (130) | Weighted N |

Table 9.19
Chances of Getting into a Bigger War
Education of Respondent

|  | Year | | | | |
|---|---|---|---|---|---|
|  | 1966n | 1968n | 1970n | 1972n | |
| Grade School Only | 39.7% | 33.2% | 30.5% | 25.3% | More likely |
|  | 29.6 | 31.5 | 31.1 | 23.8 | About the same |
|  | 9.3 | 10.8 | 14.3 | 30.0 | Less likely |
|  | 21.5 | 24.4 | 24.2 | 20.9 | Don't know/Depends |
|  | (335) | (701) | (202) | (277) | Weighted N |
| High School Only | 33.2 | 29.8 | 32.8 | 19.8 | More likely |
|  | 35.7 | 41.0 | 34.7 | 31.4 | About the same |
|  | 20.9 | 17.4 | 22.7 | 40.6 | Less likely |
|  | 10.2 | 11.8 | 9.8 | 8.3 | Don't know/Depends |
|  | (645) | (1541) | (490) | (678) | Weighted N |
| College Only | 27.3 | 23.3 | 24.9 | 15.3 | More likely |
|  | 29.7 | 46.4 | 28.6 | 28.6 | About the same |
|  | 36.0 | 23.8 | 41.2 | 50.8 | Less likely |
|  | 7.0 | 6.4 | 5.3 | 5.3 | Don't know/Depends |
|  | (300) | (840) | (255) | (398) | Weighted N |

Table 9.20
Chances of Getting into a Bigger War
Age of Respondent

|  | Year | | | | |
|---|---|---|---|---|---|
|  | 1966n | 1968n | 1970n | 1972n | |
| 18-24 Only | 39.0% | 39.2% | 33.5% | 23.8% | More likely |
|  | 20.3 | 38.4 | 33.0 | 29.1 | About the same |
|  | 31.4 | 16.8 | 28.4 | 41.8 | Less likely |
|  | 9.3 | 5.6 | 5.1 | 5.3 | Don't know/Depends |
|  | (118) | (232) | (124) | (189) | Weighted N |
| 25-34 Only | 33.9 | 32.4 | 33.3 | 18.5 | More likely |
|  | 39.1 | 41.9 | 34.0 | 33.5 | About the same |
|  | 20.4 | 15.3 | 26.9 | 41.1 | Less likely |
|  | 6.5 | 10.4 | 5.9 | 6.9 | Don't know/Depends |
|  | (230) | (608) | (194) | (275) | Weighted N |
| 35-44 Only | 33.2 | 28.4 | 21.1 | 17.4 | More likely |
|  | 36.8 | 42.1 | 33.8 | 32.1 | About the same |
|  | 21.3 | 19.3 | 35.8 | 46.3 | Less likely |
|  | 8.7 | 10.3 | 9.4 | 4.1 | Don't know/Depends |
|  | (277) | (649) | (163) | (218) | Weighted N |
| 45-54 Only | 29.8 | 22.2 | 30.8 | 19.4 | More likely |
|  | 33.3 | 47.5 | 37.9 | 30.8 | About the same |
|  | 21.7 | 18.8 | 20.2 | 38.9 | Less likely |
|  | 15.1 | 11.6 | 11.1 | 10.9 | Don't know/Depends |
|  | (258) | (623) | (168) | (247) | Weighted N |
| 55-64 Only | 34.7 | 27.1 | 38.4 | 19.7 | More likely |
|  | 33.5 | 35.0 | 24.4 | 24.5 | About the same |
|  | 19.7 | 21.0 | 20.7 | 42.6 | Less likely |
|  | 12.1 | 16.8 | 16.6 | 13.3 | Don't know/Depends |
|  | (173) | (457) | (139) | (188) | Weighted N |
| 65-74 Only | 32.1 | 28.9 | 27.4 | 18.8 | More likely |
|  | 25.6 | 32.7 | 28.3 | 21.7 | About the same |
|  | 20.5 | 17.8 | 26.8 | 44.9 | Less likely |
|  | 21.8 | 20.6 | 17.5 | 14.5 | Don't know/Depends |
|  | (156) | (349) | (103) | (138) | Weighted N |
| 75 And Older Only | 40.3 | 31.9 | 23.0 | 19.8 | More likely |
|  | 25.8 | 33.8 | 28.4 | 24.4 | About the same |
|  | 12.9 | 6.9 | 15.3 | 29.1 | Less likely |
|  | 21.0 | 27.5 | 33.3 | 26.7 | Don't know/Depends |
|  | (62) | (160) | (55) | (86) | Weighted N |

Table 9.21
Strength of U.S. Position in the World
Total Population

QUESTION: Would you say that in the past year or so our position
in the world has become stronger or less strong or has it stayed
about the same?

|  |  | Year | | | |
|  |  | 1958n | 1960n | 1964n | 1968n |
|---|---|---|---|---|---|
| Stronger | (5) | 22.8% | 22.0% | 27.5% | 7.2% |
| About the same | (3) | 37.7 | 31.0 | 36.0 | 28.1 |
| Less strong | (1) | 23.2 | 31.6 | 20.6 | 47.6 |
| Don't know |  | 16.2 | 15.4 | 15.9 | 17.1 |
| Total |  | 100% | 100% | 100% | 100% |
| Weighted N |  | 1812 | 1916 | 1562 | 1553 |
| Unweighted N |  | 1442 | 1158 | 1562 | 1553 |
| Mean |  | 2.99 | 2.77 | 3.16 | 2.02 |
| Standard Deviation |  | 1.48 | 1.58 | 1.50 | 1.30 |

Figure 9.9
Strength of U.S. Position--Total Population

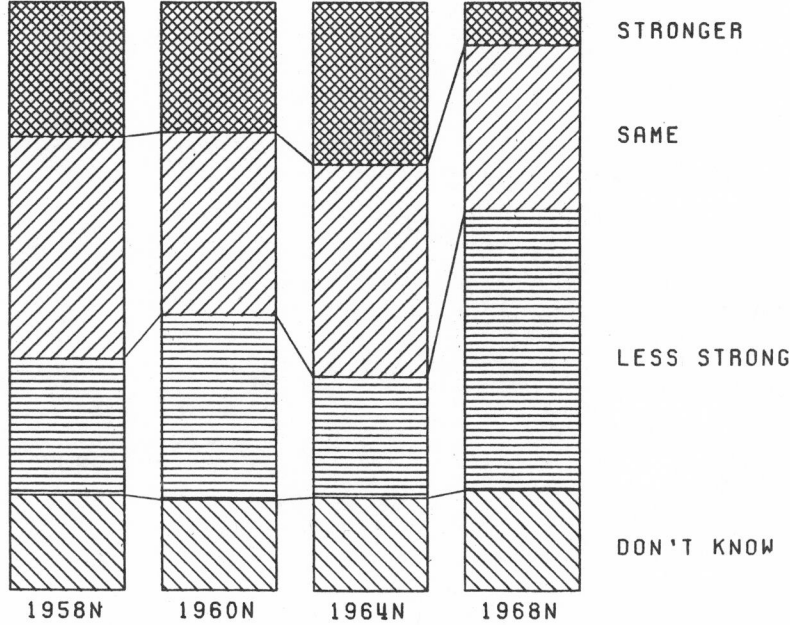

1958N    1960N    1964N    1968N

STRONGER

SAME

LESS STRONG

DON'T KNOW

Table 9.22
Strength of U.S. Position in the World
Sex of Respondent

|  |  | Year |  |  |  |
|  | 1958n | 1960n | 1964n | 1968n |  |
| Males Only | 27.9% | 26.5% | 30.6% | 7.6% | Stronger |
|  | 38.2 | 33.3 | 35.9 | 30.0 | About the same |
|  | 24.7 | 33.4 | 23.3 | 50.7 | Less strong |
|  | 9.2 | 6.8 | 10.2 | 11.7 | Don't know |
|  | (849) | (862) | (699) | (681) | Weighted N |
| Females Only | 18.3 | 18.3 | 25.0 | 6.9 | Stronger |
|  | 37.4 | 29.1 | 36.0 | 26.6 | About the same |
|  | 21.9 | 30.2 | 18.4 | 45.3 | Less strong |
|  | 22.4 | 22.4 | 20.5 | 21.2 | Don't know |
|  | (963) | (1054) | (863) | (872) | Weighted N |

Table 9.23
Race of Respondent

|  | 1958n | 1960n | 1964n | 1968n |  |
| Whites Only | 22.2% | 21.7% | 26.4% | 6.1% | Stronger |
|  | 38.9 | 31.5 | 37.6 | 29.2 | About the same |
|  | 24.1 | 33.3 | 21.9 | 50.2 | Less strong |
|  | 14.8 | 13.4 | 14.2 | 14.5 | Don't know |
|  | (1633) | (1734) | (1391) | (1384) | Weighted N |
| Blacks Only | 28.4 | 22.0 | 38.0 | 15.4 | Stronger |
|  | 27.2 | 27.4 | 20.3 | 19.5 | About the same |
|  | 16.0 | 17.1 | 11.4 | 24.8 | Less strong |
|  | 28.4 | 33.5 | 30.4 | 40.3 | Don't know |
|  | (162) | (164) | (158) | (149) | Weighted N |

Table 9.24
Strength of U.S. Position in the World
Education of Respondent

|  | Year | | | | |
|---|---|---|---|---|---|
|  | 1958n | 1960n | 1964n | 1968n | |
| Grade School Only | 24.2% | 27.6% | 30.1% | 7.0% | Stronger |
|  | 37.0 | 26.2 | 32.7 | 27.0 | About the same |
|  | 14.1 | 19.8 | 8.4 | 31.2 | Less strong |
|  | 24.7 | 26.4 | 28.8 | 34.8 | Don't know |
|  | (546) | (572) | (382) | (359) | Weighted N |
| High School Only | 24.2 | 19.2 | 30.5 | 8.6 | Stronger |
|  | 38.0 | 35.4 | 36.3 | 28.5 | About the same |
|  | 22.8 | 33.0 | 19.9 | 47.4 | Less strong |
|  | 15.0 | 12.4 | 13.4 | 15.5 | Don't know |
|  | (885) | (918) | (801) | (766) | Weighted N |
| College Only | 17.9 | 20.5 | 18.3 | 2.9 | Stronger |
|  | 38.8 | 27.8 | 39.4 | 26.5 | About the same |
|  | 38.3 | 44.7 | 34.8 | 67.6 | Less strong |
|  | 5.0 | 7.1 | 7.5 | 2.9 | Don't know |
|  | (363) | (425) | (371) | (204) | Weighted N |

War And Peace

Table 9.25
Strength of U.S. Position in the World
Age of Respondent

|  | Year | | | |  |
|---|---|---|---|---|---|
|  | 1958n | 1960n | 1964n | 1968n |  |
| 18-24 Only | 28.1% | 10.3% | 31.7% | 12.4% | Stronger |
|  | 31.5 | 34.5 | 37.5 | 32.7 | About the same |
|  | 19.1 | 25.9 | 22.5 | 45.1 | Less strong |
|  | 21.3 | 29.3 | 8.3 | 9.7 | Don't know |
|  | (89) | (58) | (120) | (113) | Weighted N |
| 25-34 Only | 25.4 | 23.1 | 30.4 | 6.5 | Stronger |
|  | 32.4 | 33.7 | 38.3 | 31.4 | About the same |
|  | 27.9 | 33.5 | 18.7 | 48.7 | Less strong |
|  | 14.2 | 9.7 | 12.6 | 13.4 | Don't know |
|  | (401) | (412) | (326) | (306) | Weighted N |
| 35-44 Only | 23.4 | 19.6 | 21.5 | 7.3 | Stronger |
|  | 39.4 | 31.9 | 39.2 | 32.0 | About the same |
|  | 21.3 | 35.4 | 23.3 | 48.5 | Less strong |
|  | 15.9 | 13.1 | 15.9 | 12.2 | Don't know |
|  | (465) | (480) | (339) | (328) | Weighted N |
| 45-54 Only | 25.0 | 21.8 | 31.6 | 8.0 | Stronger |
|  | 38.8 | 31.6 | 32.6 | 27.5 | About the same |
|  | 23.4 | 35.1 | 21.4 | 49.2 | Less strong |
|  | 12.8 | 11.4 | 14.4 | 15.3 | Don't know |
|  | (376) | (376) | (313) | (313) | Weighted N |
| 55-64 Only | 19.2 | 30.0 | 32.4 | 7.1 | Stronger |
|  | 39.7 | 25.9 | 27.6 | 21.2 | About the same |
|  | 23.4 | 24.6 | 22.2 | 51.3 | Less strong |
|  | 17.6 | 19.5 | 17.8 | 20.4 | Don't know |
|  | (239) | (297) | (225) | (226) | Weighted N |
| 65-74 Only | 16.9 | 19.8 | 21.0 | 5.6 | Stronger |
|  | 40.0 | 29.5 | 36.9 | 26.7 | About the same |
|  | 23.8 | 24.6 | 17.2 | 42.8 | Less strong |
|  | 19.4 | 26.1 | 24.8 | 25.0 | Don't know |
|  | (160) | (207) | (157) | (180) | Weighted N |
| 75 And Older Only | 12.2 | 17.1 | 18.2 | 2.4 | Stronger |
|  | 46.3 | 30.5 | 44.2 | 18.3 | About the same |
|  | 13.4 | 32.9 | 13.0 | 37.8 | Less strong |
|  | 28.0 | 19.5 | 24.7 | 41.5 | Don't know |
|  | (82) | (82) | (77) | (82) | Weighted N |

War And Peace

## Appendix A. Principal Investigators

The principal investigators of the studies included in this volume are listed alphabetically below, along with the series in which they participated. The particular studies within the series in which each was involved are not shown. Unless otherwise indicated, all were associated with the Institute for Social Research at the time of their involvement.

Jerald G. Bachman: Omnibus Studies

Nancy Baerwaldt: Productive Americans Study

Richard E. Barfield: Omnibus Studies

Jacob Benus: Panel Study of Income Dynamics

Harvey E. Brazer: Patterns of Family Change Study

Richard Brody (Stanford University): American National Election Studies

Angus Campbell: American National Election Studies; Omnibus Studies; Quality of American Life Study.

Wilbur J. Cohen: Patterns of Family Change Study

Philip E. Converse: American National Election Studies; Quality of American Life Study

Richard T. Curtin: Surveys of Consumer Attitudes and Behavior

Martin H. David: Patterns of Family Change Study

Jack Dennis (University of Wisconsin): American National Election Studies

Jonathan Dickinson: Panel Study of Income Dynamics

Katherine Dickinson: Panel Study of Income Dynamics

Elizabeth Douvan: Americans View Their Mental Health

Greg J. Duncan: Panel Study of Income Dynamics

William Dunkelberg: Surveys of Consumer Finances; Surveys of Consumer Attitudes and Behavior

Shelia C. Feld: Americans View Their Mental Health

Janet Fisher: Surveys of Consumer Finances

Robert M. Groves: Omnibus Studies

Gerald Gurin: Americans View Their Mental Health; American National Election Studies

Gary Hendricks: Surveys of Consumer Finances

Mary Jackman: Inter-group Attitudes and Group Consciousness Study

F. Thomas Juster: Surveys of Consumer Attitudes and Behavior

Robert L. Kahn: Omnibus Studies

George Katona: Surveys of Consumer Finances; Surveys of Consumer Attitudes and Behavior

Daniel Katz: Omnibus Studies

Lawrence R. Klein: Surveys of Consumer Finances

F. Gerald Kline: American National Election Studies

Richard F. Kosobud: Surveys of Consumer Finances

David Kovenock (University of North Carolina): American National Election Studies

John B. Lansing: Surveys of Consumer Finances; Surveys of Consumer Attitudes and Behavior

Charles A. Lininger: Surveys of Consumer Finances

Eleanor Maccoby: Surveys of Consumer Finances

Louis Mandell: Surveys of Consumer Finances

Arthur H. Miller: American National Election Studies

Warren E. Miller: American National Election Studies

James N. Morgan: Surveys of Consumer Finances; Surveys of Consumer Attitudes and Behavior; Patterns of Family Change; Panel Study of Income Dynamics; Productive Americans Study

Eva L. Mueller: Surveys of Consumer Finances; Surveys of
    Consumer Attitude and Behavior

Walter Murphy (Princeton University): American National
    Election Studies

Willard L. Rodgers: Quality of American Life Study

Jay Schmiedeskamp: Surveys of Consumer Finances; Omnibus
    Studies

John C. Scott: Omnibus Studies

Merrill Shanks (University of California, Berkeley):
    American National Election Studies

Ismail A. Sirageldin: Productive Americans Study

John A. Sonquist: Surveys of Consumer Finances

Frank Stafford: Surveys of Consumer Finances

Donald E. Stokes: American National Election Studies

Burkhard Strumpel: Surveys of Consumer Finances

Joseph Tanenhaus (University of Iowa): American National
    Election Studies

Joseph Veroff: Americans View Their Mental Health

Stephen B. Withey: Omnibus Studies; News Media Studies

## Appendix B. Sample Design And Study Series

The Survey Research Center (SRC) of the Institute for Social Research at the University of Michigan has been conducting national probability samples since 1947. This appendix describes the overall sampling design employed by the Survey Research Center and its application to the various studies contributing data to this volume.

### General Sample Design

The Survey Research Center's multistage area sample is designed to represent dwelling units in the conterminous United States exclusive of those on military reservations. The 74 current sample points (up from 66 before 1972) include the 12 largest major metropolitan areas, other Standard Metropolitan Statistical Areas (SMSAs), and counties or county-groups representing the nonmetropolitan or rural sections of the country. First-stage stratification of SMSAs and counties is carried out independently within each of four major geographic regions defined by the Census Bureau. Each region receives representation in the final sample in proportion to its population. Thus for any sample of 1,000 dwellings based on 1970 Census information, we would expect to find about 240 dwellings from the Northeast; 280 dwellings from the North Central region; 310 from the South; and 170 from the West.

Over all regions, the SMSAs and counties are assigned to relatively homogeneous groups or strata. Twelve of these strata contain only one primary area each; these are the two Standard Consolidated Areas and the ten largest SMSAs, outside the Consolidated Areas, which are included with certainty in each sample. The remaining strata (62 currently, 54 before 1963) may contain from two to 200 or more primary areas (SMSAs or county groups). From each stratum, one primary area is selected with probability proportionate to population. This sampling process leads to approximately equal sample sizes from these sample areas. Unless research needs dictate otherwise, a self-weighting sample of dwellings is drawn.

Instead of independent selections within each of these strata, controlled probability selection is introduced for a more efficient sample. Within each of the four geographic regions, the selections of primary areas are linked by a procedure that controls the distribution of sample areas by states and degree of urbanization beyond the controls effected through the formation of the strata. This controlled selection yields a more balanced sample and increases the precision of sample estimates.

As the multistage area sampling continues within the primary units, the area is divided and subdivided, in two to five stages, into successively smaller sampling units. By definition and procedure, each dwelling belongs uniquely to one sampling unit at each stage. Within the primary areas, cities, towns, and rural areas are the secondary selections. Blocks or clusters of addresses in cities and towns and chunks of rural areas are the third-stage units. In a fourth stage there is a selection of small segments or clusters of dwellings where interviews are taken for a study. In the last stage of sampling, one or more respondents may be randomly selected from among household members, using a Kish Selection Table. When study purposes dictate that the head of household is to be the designated respondent, the husband has always been considered to be the head among married couples, unless otherwise stated.

Probability selection is enforced at all stages of the sample selection. The interviewer has no freedom of choice either among dwelling units or among household members within designated dwelling units. The total procedure yields a sample in which each individual member of the population universe has a known probability of selection, and for the typical self-weighting cross-section design, these probabilities of selection at the level of the dwelling unit are equal.

### Major Studies Contributing Data

All of the studies contributing data to this volume involved the most general of the sample design specifications described above. Variants of this design were developed at various times within various study series to cope more efficiently with special research purposes. We shall now review these variants.

Surveys of Consumer Finances.

The Surveys of Consumer Finances were conducted annually from 1946 through 1971 by the Economic Behavior Program. These surveys were dedicated to the collection of statistics on the distribution of consumer income, assets, debts, and major transactions. The samples were drawn in general conformity with the Survey Research Center multistage area probability sampling design. In the early years, the ultimate interviewing unit was defined as the spending unit, or related people living together and pooling their incomes for major items of expenditure. In 1964, the definition was changed to the family unit, or persons in the same dwelling unit who are related by blood, marriage or adoption. The designated respondent for these studies was the head of household, with the wife or other responsible adults substituting to report for the unit only when the head was not available during the interviewing period. Before 1959, higher-income groups were oversampled to provide more efficient estimates of income, savings and assets. During this period, the data were weighted to correct for differential sampling rates among classes of respondents. Beginning with 1959, the data were weighted when necessary to provide a representative cross-section of spending or family units. Interviewing was conducted between January and March of each year.

The component studies contributing data to this volume, with specifications for each, are as follows:

1947 Survey of Consumer Finances: 3,058 respondents, weighted data.

1948 Survey of Consumer Finances: 3,562 respondents, weighted data.

1949 Survey of Consumer Finances: 3,510 respondents, weighted data.

1950 Survey of Consumer Finances: 3,512 respondents, weighted data.

1951 Survey of Consumer Finances: 3,415 respondents, weighted data.

1952 Survey of Consumer Finances: 2,820 respondents, weighted data.

1953 Survey of Consumer Finances: 3,097 respondents, weighted data.

1954 Survey of Consumer Finances: 3,000 respondents, weighted data.

1955 Survey of Consumer Finances: 3,119 respondents, weighted data.

1957 Survey of Consumer Finances: 3,041 respondents, weighted data.

1958 Survey of Consumer Finances: 3,117 respondents, weighted data.

1959 Survey of Consumer Finances: 3,100 respondents, weighted data.

1960 Survey of Consumer Finances: 2,972 respondents, self-weighting.

1961 Survey of Consumer Finances: 1,981 respondents, weighted data.

1962 Survey of Consumer Finances: 2,117 respondents, weighted data.

1964 Survey of Consumer Finances: 1,549 respondents, self-weighting.

1965 Survey of Consumer Finances: 1,349 respondents, self-weighting.

1966 Survey of Consumer Finances: 2,419 respondents, self-weighting.

1967 Survey of Consumer Finances: 3,165 respondents, weighted data.

1968 Survey of Consumer Finances: 2,677 respondents, weighted data.

1969 Survey of Consumer Finances: 2,317 respondents, weighted data.

1970 Survey of Consumer Finances: 2,576 respondents, self-weighting.

Surveys of Consumer Attitudes and Behavior.

The Surveys of Consumer Attitudes and Behavior, also known as Interim and Omnibus Studies, were initiated in 1947 and have been conducted quarterly since the early 1950s by the Economic Behavior Program. The purposes of the surveys have been to measure changes in consumer attitudes and expectations, to understand why these changes occur, and to evaluate how they relate to consumer decisions to save, borrow, or make discretionary purchases. Each quarterly survey contains forty questions probing different aspects of consumer confidence. In order to make available a summary measure of change in consumer sentiment, the answers to five questions are used to calculate the Index of Consumer Sentiment.

The SRC multistage area probability sampling design is used to select a sample of housing units representative of all families in the conterminous United States. The designated respondent has changed several times during the series. Before 1972, the most frequently used procedure was to select unmarried heads of families and, when the head was married, to make a random selection of head or wife using a predetermined designation for that househould. (The data from these studies have not been corrected for differential sampling rates.) For other studies, only the head of household was interviewed. In the earliest years of the series, respondents were chosen randomly within households. Beginning in 1972, the sampling base was permanently changed to include all adults. To maintain strict comparability with the earlier period, the Economic Behavior Program weights these data to include only heads and wives. This volume presents the data without these weights, as a representative cross-section sample of adults. The 1976 Fall study includes a telephone reinterview component and is weighted to adjust for panel mortality.

Due to the relatively short interviewing time needed to administer the consumer sentiment items, they have often been "piggy backed" onto other surveys. The winter quarter, for example, was combined with the Survey of Consumer Finances through 1971, when that series ceased. The following studies contributed data to this volume:

1951 Spring Survey of Consumer Attitudes and Behavior: 999 respondents, all adults, self-weighting.

1951 Fall Survey of Consumer Attitudes and Behavior: 958 respondents, all adults, self-weighting.

1952 Summer Survey of Consumer Attitudes and Behavior: 929 respondents, all adults, self-weighting.

1953 Fall Survey of Consumer Attitudes and Behavior: 1,023 respondents, all adults, self-weighting.

1954 Fall Survey of Consumer Attitudes and Behavior: 999 respondents, all adults, self-weighting.

1956 Fall Survey of Consumer Attitudes and Behavior: 1,448 respondents, heads and wives only, self-weighting.

1957 Spring Survey of Consumer Attitudes and Behavior: 1,356 respondents, heads and wives only, self-weighting.

1958 Spring Survey of Consumer Attitudes and Behavior: 1,456 respondents, heads and wives only, self-weighting.

1958 Fall Survey of Consumer Attitudes and Behavior: 1,343 respondents, heads and wives only, self-weighting.

1959 Spring Survey of Consumer Attitudes and Behavior: 1,313 respondents, heads and wives only, self-weighting.

1960 Spring Survey of Consumer Attitudes and Behavior: 1,407 respondents, heads and wives only, self-weighting.

1961 Spring Survey of Consumer Attitudes and Behavior: 1,363 respondents, heads and wives only, self-weighting.

1961 Fall Survey of Consumer Attitudes and Behavior: 956 respondents, heads and wives only, self-weighting.

1962 Spring Survey of Consumer Attitudes and Behavior: 1,299 respondents, heads and wives only, self-weighting.

1962 Summer Survey of Consumer Attitudes and Behavior: 1,317 respondents, heads and wives only, self-weighting.

1962 Fall Survey of Consumer Attitudes and Behavior: 1,352 respondents, heads and wives only, self-weighting.

1963 Spring Survey of Consumer Attitudes and Behavior: 1,310 respondents, heads and wives only, self-weighting.

1963 Summer Survey of Consumer Attitudes and Behavior: 1,359 respondents, heads and wives only, self-weighting.

1963 Fall Survey of Consumer Attitudes and Behavior: 1,322 respondents, heads and wives only, self-weighting.

1964 Spring Survey of Consumer Attitudes and Behavior: 1,502 respondents, heads and wives only, self-weighting.

1965 Fall Survey of Consumer Attitudes and Behavior: 1,658 respondents, heads and wives only, self-weighting.

1966 Summer Survey of Consumer Attitudes and Behavior: 1,228 respondents, heads and wives only, self-weighting.

1967 Fall Survey of Consumer Attitudes and Behavior: 1,329 respondents, heads and wives only, self-weighting.

1968 Summer Survey of Consumer Attitudes and Behavior: 1,322 respondents, heads and wives only, self-weighting.

1969 Summer Survey of Consumer Attitudes and Behavior: 1,557 respondents, heads only, self-weighting.

1969 Fall Survey of Consumer Attitudes and Behavior: 1,469 respondents, heads only, self-weighting.

1971 Fall Survey of Consumer Attitudes and Behavior: 1,303 respondents, heads only, self-weighting.

1972 Spring Survey of Consumer Attitudes and Behavior: 1,297 respondents, all adults, self-weighting.

1973 Winter Survey of Consumer Attitudes and Behavior: 1,348 respondents, all adults, self-weighting.

1976 Fall Survey of Consumer Attitudes and Behavior: 1,254 respondents, all adults, weighted data.

American National Election Studies.

The American National Election Studies, conducted by the Survey Research Center and later by the Center for Political Studies, have investigated citizen attitudes, beliefs, and behavior in connection with all but one of the biennial national presidential and off-year congressional elections since 1948. Until 1978, the samples were drawn in accordance with the SRC multistage area probability sampling design and were intended to provide cross-section samples of citizens of voting age living in households within the conterminous United States. Minimum voting age in 1952 was eighteen in Georgia and twenty-one in all other states; from 1956 through 1970, voting age was eighteen in Georgia and Kentucky and twenty-one in all other states (Alaska, with a voting age of nineteen, and Hawaii, with a voting age of twenty, are not included in the sample); since 1972, minimum voting age has been eighteen in all states. Politically ineligible persons were interviewed in 1970, when eighteen to twenty year olds were included, and in 1974 when sixteen and seventeen year olds were included. The 1974 data does not include data for the sixteen and seventeen year olds.

Supplemental respondents and weighting procedures were instituted to produce the representative cross-section sample in those years where a reinterview panel design was also being carried out (1958, 1960, 1974, and 1976), or when additional respondents in some population subgroup (such as the black supplement in 1964, 1968, and 1970) were interviewed.

The standard format for field work surrounding presidential elections involves a pre-election interview conducted during the six or eight weeks before the election, and a briefer post-election reinterview in November and December. For the off-year congressional elections, a single post-election interview has been conducted.

In 1978, research needs dictated a major change in the first stage of the SRC sampling design. The primary sampling units were recast to fit lines of congressional districts in the conterminous United States, to facilitate analysis of the dynamics of congressional elections. The 432 eligible congressional districts were divided into 108 strata. Each stratum contained four districts of roughly comparable characteristics that insofar as possible were homogeneous with respect to geographic region, state, degree of urbanization, and recent voting behavior. From each state, one district was chosen with a probability proportionate to its 1975 estimated population. The sample comprises a probability sample of both United States citizens and congressional districts, but it does not permit estimates of each district's constituency, since sampling and field costs prohibited within-district selections from being distributed across the district. As always in all districts and at each stage of sampling, strict probability sampling procedures were used.

The following studies contributed data to this volume:

1952 American National Election Study: 1,899 respondents, self-weighting.

1956 American National Election Study: 1,762 respondents, self-weighting (conducted in conjunction with the 1956 Fall Survey of Consumer Attitude and Behavior).

1958 American National Election Study: 1,450 respondents, weighted data.

1960 American National Election Study: 1,181 respondents, weighted data.

1962 American National Election Study: 1,297 respondents, self-weighting (conducted in conjunction with the 1962 Fall Survey of Consumer Attitudes and Behavior).

1964 American National Election Study: 1,834 respondents, weighted data (1,571 respondents in cross-section sample, 263 respondents in black supplement).

1966 American National Election Study: 1,291 respondents, self-weighting (conducted in conjunction with 1966 Fall Survey of Consumer Attitudes and Behavior).

1968 American National Election Study: 1,672 respondents (1,557 respondents in cross-section sample, 116 respondents in black supplement), combined sample and black sample are weighted; cross-section is self-weighting.

1970 American National Election Study: 1,694 respondents (1,580 respondents in cross-section sample, 114 respondents in black supplement), combined sample, black sample and some questions in cross-section sample are weighted.

1972 American National Election Study: 2,705 respondents, self-weighting.

1974 American National Election Study: 1,575 respondents, weighted data.

1976 American National Election Study: 2,248 respondents, weighted data.

1978 American National Election Study: 2,304 respondents, self-weighting.

Panel Study of Income Dynamics.

The Economic Behavior Program has conducted a yearly panel study since 1968 to discover the determinants of short-term changes in the economic status of families and individuals. In 1968, a national cross-section sample of 2,930 families, drawn in accordance with the SRC multistage area probability sampling design, was supplemented by a subsample of 1,872 families that had been interviewed in 1966 and 1967 by the Bureau of the Census. This latter group consisted of a sample of families living in SMSAs in all regions and in non-SMSAs in the South that had incomes in 1966 equal to or below twice the federal poverty level at that time.

Except for losses due to nonresponse, reinterviews have been conducted annually with the families in the original sample and with newly formed families containing members of original panel families. No attempt was made to interview in subsequent waves those who were lost in previous ones. By 1976, 55 percent of the families interviewed in 1968 were still in the panel. Newly formed families, added during each year of the panel, have raised the number of families in the 1976 wave to 5,862.

For the first eight waves, the designated respondent was the head of household. In 1976, both the head and wife were interviewed. Until 1973, interviews were conducted in person. Beginning in that year, telephone interviewing was conducted whenever possible to minimize costs. Respondents were paid small amounts for their interviews and for mailing a card to the Economic Behavior Program each January with their current addresses. Interviews were conducted from March through August of each year.

The sample, when weighted, is a representative cross-section sample of families in each year. Weights were constructed in 1968 to correct for disproportionate selection rates and response rates and again in 1972 for disproportionate response losses since 1968. Response rates have fallen below 96 percent only in 1968 and 1969 when they were 76 percent and 89 percent, respectively. Data from the following studies are included in this volume:

1968 Panel Study of Income Dynamics: 4,802 respondents, weighted data.

1969 Panel Study of Income Dynamics: 4,460 respondents, weighted data.

1970 Panel Study of Income Dynamics: 4,644 respondents, weighted data.

1971 Panel Study of Income Dynamics: 4,840 respondents, weighted data.

1972 Panel Study of Income Dynamics: 5,060 respondents, weighted data.

1973 Panel Study of Income Dynamics: 5,285 respondents, weighted data.

1974 Panel Study of Income Dynamics: 5,517 respondents, weighted data.

1975 Panel Study of Income Dynamics: 5,725 respondents, weighted data.

1976 Panel Study of Income Dynamics: 9,344 respondents (5,862 heads of households, 3,482 wives), weighted data.

Omnibus Studies.

The Omnibus Studies, begun in 1973, were sponsored by the Survey Research Center for researchers who wanted to collect data on national samples but required only part of an interview. The quarterly Survey of Consumer Attitudes and Behavior, for example, was included in the Omnibus Studies. A representative cross-section sample of adults in dwelling units in the conterminous United States was selected according to the SRC multistage area probability sampling design. The data are weighted by the number of adults in the household to correct for disproportionate sampling rates among households of different sizes. The following studies have contributed data to this volume:

1973 Spring Omnibus Study: 1,433 respondents, weighted data.

1973 Fall Omnibus Study: 1,436 respondents, weighted data.

1974 Fall Omnibus Study: 1,519 respondents, weighted data.

1975 Fall Omnibus Study: 1,519 respondents, weighted data.

1976 Spring Omnibus Study: 1,548 respondents, weighted data.

Other Studies.

News Media Studies. The News Media Studies, conducted by the Survey Research Center in 1957 and 1958, explored the role of the mass media in informing the public about developments in science. The surveys measured public attitudes toward science and scientists and gathered data about the use of newspapers, magazines, radio, and television. A cross-section sample of 1,919 respondents representative of the United States adult population was drawn in March and April of 1957, according to the SRC multistage area probability sampling design. Approximately 25 percent of the survey was repeated in conjunction with the 1958 Spring Survey of Consumer Attitudes and Behavior, with 1,578 respondents. The data are self-weighting.

Patterns of Family Change Study. The Patterns of Family Change Study, conducted by the Economic Behavior Program in 1960, examined the distribution and redistribution of family income in the United States, as well as family attitudes, histories, and motivations that determine income.

A cross-section sample of 2,513 families was drawn according to the SRC multistage area probability sampling design. A supplement of 296 low-income families that had been interviewed in the 1960 Survey of Consumer Finance was added to the sample so that reliable estimates would be available for all income groups. Thus, the total sample includes 2,800 families, or 2,997 spending units.

The designated respondent was the head of household, and in the 26 cases where the husband was not available, the wife answered all but the attitudinal items, which were coded as missing data. Interviews were taken in March 1960. The sample is weighted to correct for disproportionate sampling and provides a representative cross-section sample of spending units in the conterminous United States.

Quality of American Life Study. The 1971 Quality of American Life Study was designed to measure respondents' perceptions of their socio-psychological condition, their needs and expectations from life, and the degree to which these needs were satisfied. The sample of 2,164 persons, drawn in accordance with the SRC multistage area probability sampling design, is a representative cross-section of persons eighteen years of age and older living in households in the conterminous United States. The data are weighted to adjust the proportion of males to the 1970 Census proportion for the total population, and to compensate for undercoverage of households, underreporting of males, and nonresponse. Interviews were conducted during July and August, 1971.

Americans View Their Mental Health. These studies, conducted in 1957 and 1976, were designed to assess people's own evaluations of their mental health and the ways they handled problems of mental ill health. They focused on various areas of life in which problems may be felt--including marriage and parenthood, the work situation, and general social relationships.

Samples for the two surveys were selected in accordance with the SRC multistage area probability sampling design to constitute representative cross-sections of persons twenty-one years of age or older living in private households in the conterminous United States. There were 2,460 respondents in 1957 and 2,264 in 1976. In 1957, interviewing was conducted between March and August; in 1976, between June and September. The 1957 data are self-weighting; the 1976 data are weighted by the number of adults in the household to correct for disproportionate sampling rates among households of different sizes.

1965 Productive Americans Study. The 1965 Productive Americans Study examined the total economic effort of families, the outside constraints and inner desires that affected that effort, and the attitudes and views that might affect the quality and efficiency of people's work effort. Information was obtained to help explain the extent to which families work, plan ahead, accept change, avoid risk, and keep a reasonable set of goals.

A national cross-section sample of 2,214 families was drawn according to the SRC multistage area probability sampling design. The unit of analysis was the family and designated respondents were family heads. Information was obtained from the wife if the husband was unavailable for the entire interviewing period. Interviews were taken in January and February 1965. The data are self-weighting.

1975 Inter-group Attitudes and Group Consciousness Study. The 1975 Inter-group Attitudes and Group Consciousness study was designed to examine the attitudes of blacks and whites, of different socio-economic groups, and of men and women toward each other and themselves. The main objectives were to further understanding of each of these cleavages in its own right and to develop an integrated theoretical framework for the analysis of inter-group attitudes and group consciousness as a general problem extending beyond the boundaries of any one cleavage. A national cross-section sample of 1,914 respondents was drawn in accordance with the SRC multistage area probability sampling design. Interviewing was conducted between September and November 1975. The data are self-weighting.

The following studies, described above, contributed data to this volume:

1957 News Media Study: 1,919 respondents, self-weighting.

1958 News Media Study: 1,578 respondents, self-weighting.

1960 Patterns of Family Change: 2,800 families, weighted data (2,513 cross-section families, 296 supplement families).

1971 Quality of American Life Study: 2,164 respondents, weighted data.

1957 Americans View Their Mental Health: 2,460 respondents, self-weighting.

1976 Americans View Their Mental Health: 2,264 respondents, weighted data.

1965 Productive Americans Study: 2,214 respondents, self-weighting.

1975 Inter-group Attitudes and Group Consciousness Study: 1,914 respondents, self-weighting.

## Bibliography

This appendix was compiled from the following sources:

Center for Political Studies and Inter-university Consortium for Political and Social Research. A Continuity Guide to the American National Election Studies. Institute for Social Research, University of Michigan, Ann Arbor, November 1976.

Comment, Robert. "Weights for the Survey of Consumer Attitudes," unpublished manuscript. Economic Behavior Program, Institute for Social Research, University of Michigan, Ann Arbor, March 1979.

Economic Behavior Program. Patterns of Family Change, codebook and study materials, unpublished documentation. Institute for Social Research, University of Michigan, Ann Arbor, 1960.

_____. Survey of Consumer Finances, annual volumes. Institute for Social Research, University of Michigan, Ann Arbor, 1960-1970.

Institute for Social Research, Social Science Archive. The Quality of American Life, codebook. University of Michigan, Ann Arbor, 1975.

Inter-university Consortium for Political and Social Research. The American National Election Study, 1978, codebook. Institute for Social Research, University of Michigan, Ann Arbor, 1979.

_____. Guide to Resources and Services 1978-1979. Institute for Social Research, University of Michigan, Ann Arbor, 1978.

Jackman, Mary. "Inter-group Attitudes and Group Consciousness," unpublished proposal to the National Science Foundation. January 1975.

Kish, Leslie, and Irene Hess. "The SRC's National Sample of Dwellings," unpublished manuscript. Survey Research Center, Institute for Social Research, University of Michigan, Ann Arbor, 1965.

Kulko, Richard A., Joseph Veroff, and Elizabeth Douvan. "Social Class and the Use of Professional Help for Personal Problems." Journal of Health and Social Behavior, 20 (March 1979): 2-17.

Morgan, James N., Ismail A. Sirageldin, and Nancy Baerwaldt. Productive Americans, Survey Research Center Monograph 43. Institute for Social Research, University of Michigan, Ann Arbor, 1966.

Survey Research Center. A Panel Study of Income Dynamics, codebooks for Waves I-IX. Institute for Social Research, University of Michigan, Ann Arbor, 1972-1976.

_____. "Revised Sample Base for the Surveys of Consumer Sentiment," unpublished manuscript. Institute for Social Research, University of Michigan, Ann Arbor, April 1974.

Survey Research Center, Sampling Section. "A Brief Description of the Survey Research Center's National Sample of Dwellings," unpublished manuscript. Institute for Social Research, University of Michigan, Ann Arbor, January, 1973.

13

coll.
B168